European Union and its Neighbours in a Globalized World

Volume 29

The series publishes monographs and edited volumes in the field of European and international law and policy. A special focus is put on the European neighbourhood policy, current problems in European and international law and policy as well as the role of the European Union as a global actor. The series supports the publishing and distribution of research results of cross-border research consortia. Besides renowned scientists the series is also open for publication projects of young academics. The series emphasizes the interplay of the European Union and its neighbouring countries as well as the important role of the European Union as a key player in the international context of law, economics and politics.

Agnė Limantė • Rūta Vaičiūnienė
Editors

Children's Rights in Central and Eastern Europe

A Comparative Analysis with a Spotlight on Lithuania

Springer

Editors
Agnė Limantė
Law Institute of the Lithuanian Centre for Social Sciences
Vilnius, Lithuania

Rūta Vaičiūnienė
Law Institute of the Lithuanian Centre for Social Sciences
Vilnius, Lithuania

ISSN 2524-8928 ISSN 2524-8936 (electronic)
European Union and its Neighbours in a Globalized World
ISBN 978-3-032-07091-3 ISBN 978-3-032-07092-0 (eBook)
https://doi.org/10.1007/978-3-032-07092-0

This work was supported by Law Institute of the Lithuanian Centre for Social Sciences. The open access of this book was funded by the Research Council of Lithuania (LMTLT), agreement No S-LISs-25-3.

This Springer imprint is published by the registered company Springer Nature Switzerland AG
The registered company address is: Gewerbestrasse 11, 6330 Cham, Switzerland

Foreword

The book in front of you—*Children's Rights in Central and Eastern Europe: A Comparative Analysis with a Spotlight on Lithuania*—is a timely scholarly contribution that advances our understanding of children's rights in a comparatively underexplored region.

Children are universally recognised as full holders of human rights under international, European, and national legal frameworks. Yet, despite this recognition, the effective consideration and implementation of children's rights often remain insufficient. This is underlined and analysed in the volume you are reading now, which offers an in-depth, multidisciplinary examination of children's rights in a rapidly changing part of Europe.

The significance of this work lies in its comparative lens. The book brings together the perspectives of researchers from multiple Central and Eastern European states who expose diverse challenges while also highlighting common trends and shared aspirations of their home countries. The book demonstrates progress in fields such as child protection, justice, education, and healthcare, while also acknowledging persistent difficulties, such as uneven implementation of child-friendly justice. These issues remind us that children's rights are never a finished project but a continuing agenda requiring constant attention.

Another strength of the volume is its attention to social context. Legal and policy developments are not presented in isolation, but are situated within the broader transformations that have shaped the region. This approach enriches the analysis, offering a nuanced view of reform processes and the structural challenges that remain.

Equally important is the book's broad thematic scope. Covering constitutional protections, family law, child justice, inclusive education, minority rights, and digital-age challenges, it demonstrates that children's rights span multiple legal and policy fields and require holistic, interdisciplinary engagement.

I believe that the knowledge and recommendations gathered here can inform reforms and strengthen efforts to ensure that services—including, but not limited to, justice, education, social support, and healthcare—become genuinely child-friendly.

UN Committee on the Rights of the Child
Geneva, Switzerland
CFJ-EN – Child Friendly Justice European Network
Molenbeek, Belgium

Benoit Van Keirsbilck

Foreword

Children are recognised as full holders of human rights and as beneficiaries of all human rights under international, European, and national legal frameworks. Despite this formal recognition, genuine acknowledgement and implementation remain inadequate. Although the United Nations Convention on the Rights of the Child has been in force for over 35 years, and numerous legislative and institutional reforms have been undertaken to advance the protection of children's rights and prevent violations, paradoxically, criticism persists from opposing perspectives. On the one hand, international organisations, ombudspersons, and non-governmental organisations continue to voice concerns about the inadequate implementation of child rights instruments. On the other hand, certain groups opposing the expansion of children's rights challenge the very foundations of such protections. These challenges often originate from divergent societal attitudes towards respecting children and their interests. Respect for children encompasses more than merely listening to them; it requires genuinely hearing their voices, prioritising the full realisation of their rights and interests, and facilitating their meaningful participation in decisions affecting them. In Central and Eastern European countries, including Lithuania, public discourse has been largely shaped by tensions with advocates of the so-called traditional family values. These disputes typically concern issues such as non-violent parenting, inclusive education, child vaccination, sexual education, and related matters.

Regrettably, many professionals working with children on a daily basis still lack a rights-based approach. Societal structures tend to prioritise fast-paced, efficiency-driven adults, and many professionals—including those in social services, the judiciary, medicine, and law enforcement—are no exception. Violations of children's procedural rights remain prevalent and are often normalised. Effective communication with a child, including the provision of comprehensive information and the assessment of their interests, demands a high level of concentration, empathy, insight, and restraint. Any adult engaging with a child must dedicate their full attention and time to the child and to the questions they raise. Many professionals acknowledge their limited expertise in working with children and would prefer the presence of a psychologist or social worker to facilitate communication. However, such support is often unavailable in practice. It is neither feasible nor sustainable to train a sufficient number of psychologists to accompany every child across all sectors of society. Instead, professionals must be equipped with broader knowledge and enhanced competencies relevant to their interactions with children.

In parallel, public authorities bear the responsibility of initiating systemic changes by aligning legislation and administrative practices with the obligations set forth in the United Nations Convention on the Rights of the Child, thereby integrating theoretical principles with practical application. Nobel Prize winner Prof J. Heckman, together with a multidisciplinary team comprising economists, psychologists, statisticians, and neuroscientists, has demonstrated that early childhood development has a direct and lasting impact on economic, health, and social outcomes at both the individual and societal levels.[1] Following these findings, and under the encouragement of the UN Committee on the Rights of the Child and the European Commission, numerous European countries have intensified their commitment to early childhood development by investing in comprehensive social, health, and educational services. These developments underscore the critical importance of sustained and coordinated efforts by all levels of government to transform the normative framework of the Convention on the Rights of the Child into tangible policies and practices that promote the well-being and holistic development of every child from birth.

Furthermore, there is a distinct moral imperative to address the specific needs of adolescents. Adolescence is marked by profound cognitive, physical, and social transformations, during which young people face complex challenges, assimilate new experiences rapidly, and are exposed to both constructive and adverse situations. This period is also characterised by heightened risk-taking behaviours and, at times, conduct that may be inappropriate or even criminal. Despite the existence of a robust international legal framework on juvenile justice, many systems in CEE countries fail to fully safeguard the rights of adolescents. This shortfall is largely attributable to limited resources and the predominance of punitive approaches within these systems. As Martin Luther King Jr. poignantly observed, "a right delayed is a right denied".

This edited volume presents a rigorous analysis of children's rights across Europe, with particular emphasis on the CEE region and Lithuania. The publication brings together scholars from diverse academic disciplines—including law, sociology, and criminology—and various national backgrounds, to identify and critically assess key obstacles, while drawing upon their respective areas of expertise to address salient issues. Offering a comprehensive perspective, the book emphasises qualitative evaluation, examines relevant jurisprudence, and includes key international and regional legal instruments. The value of this research as a strategic reference point is indisputable. Academic inquiry is uniquely positioned to assess the effectiveness of legal and policy frameworks, identify inconsistencies and lacunae in legislation, benchmark cross-national experiences, highlight best and worst

[1] The Heckman Equation. See: https://heckmanequation.org/

practices, analyse ineffective solutions, and formulate recommendations for reform and improvement.

As the Ombudsperson for Children's Rights, I am committed to grounding all institutional activities—from the investigation of individual complaints to policy dialogue with public authorities—in empirically supported research findings. I am confident that this volume will serve as an essential resource for all stakeholders engaged with children, on behalf of children, and in partnership with children. As the Ombudsperson, I believe that this scholarly work will inform and inspire a wide audience—including professionals in the field of child rights, policymakers, non-governmental organisations, researchers, students, and parents—to enhance the protection of children's rights and to initiate reforms aimed at ensuring that all services, including healthcare, social support, justice, and penal systems, are truly child-friendly.

Ombudsperson for Child's Rights of the Republic of Lithuania
Vilnius, Lithuania
Edita Žiobienė

Contents

Exploring Children's Rights in the Realm of Criminal Law and Criminal Procedure

Emerging and Cross-Cutting Issues

Contributors

Jolanta Aleknevičienė Faculty of Philosophy, University of Vilnius, Vilnius, Lithuania

Kristina Ambrazevičiūtė Law Institute of the Lithuanian Centre for Social Sciences, Vilnius, Lithuania

Jolanta Apolewicz Law Institute of the Lithuanian Centre for Social Sciences, Vilnius, Lithuania

Lina Beliūnienė Law Institute of the Lithuanian Centre for Social Sciences, Vilnius, Lithuania

Jolita Buzaitytė-Kašalynienė Faculty of Philosophy, University of Vilnius, Vilnius, Lithuania

Dario Đerđa Faculty of Law, University of Rijeka, Rijeka, Croatia

Kristīne Dupate Faculty of Law, University of Latvia, Riga, Latvia

Ioan Durnescu Faculty of Sociology and Social Work, University of Bucharest, Bucharest, Romania

Merle Erikson School of Law, University of Tartu, Tartu, Estonia

Mindaugas Girdauskas Law Institute of the Lithuanian Centre for Social Sciences, Vilnius, Lithuania

Vaidas Kalpokas Law Institute of the Lithuanian Centre for Social Sciences, Vilnius, Lithuania

Eglė Kavoliūnaitė-Ragauskienė Law Institute of the Lithuanian Centre for Social Sciences, Vilnius, Lithuania

Elżbieta Kuzborska-Pacha Faculty of Law and Administration, University of Lodz, Poland

Mindaugas Lankauskas Law Institute of the Lithuanian Centre for Social Sciences, Vilnius, Lithuania

Gergely Ferenc Lendvai Luvodika University of Public Service, Budapest, Hungary University of Richmond, School of Arts and Sciences, Richmond, VA, USA

Agnė Limantė Law Institute of the Lithuanian Centre for Social Sciences, Vilnius, Lithuania

Milda Mačėnaitė Law Institute of the Lithuanian Centre for Social Sciences, Vilnius, Lithuania

Ingrida Mačernytė Panomariovienė Law Institute of the Lithuanian Centre for Social Sciences, Vilnius, Lithuania

Renata Mieńkowska-Norkiene Faculty of Political Science and International Studies, University of Warsaw, Warsaw, Poland

Ingrida Milkaitė Faculty of Law and Criminology, Ghent University, Ghent, Belgium

Simonas Nikartas Law Institute of the Lithuanian Centre for Social Sciences, Vilnius, Lithuania

Justyna Omeljaniuk Faculty of Law, University of Białystok, Białystok, Poland

Aušra Pocienė Faculty of Philosophy, University of Vilnius, Vilnius, Lithuania

Neža Pogorelčnik Vogrinc Faculty of Law, University of Ljubljana, Ljubljana, Slovenia

Darius Pranka Law Institute of the Lithuanian Centre for Social Sciences, Vilnius, Lithuania

Dovilė Pūraitė-Andrikienė Law Institute of the Lithuanian Centre for Social Sciences, Vilnius, Lithuania

Katarzyna Roszewska Institute of Law and Administration, Cardinal Stefan Wyszyński University, Warsaw, Poland

Gintautas Sakalauskas Faculty of Law, University of Vilnius, Vilnius, Lithuania

Birutė Švedaitė-Sakalauskė Faculty of Philosophy, University of Vilnius, Vilnius, Lithuania

Rokas Uscila Law Institute of the Lithuanian Centre for Social Sciences, Vilnius, Lithuania

Rūta Vaičiūnienė Law Institute of the Lithuanian Centre for Social Sciences, Vilnius, Lithuania

Tatjana Wrocławska Faculty of Law and Administration, University of Lodz, Poland

Anna Wysocka-Bar Private International Law Center, Law Faculty, Jagiellonian University, Kraków, Poland

Edita Žiobienė Law School, Mykolas Romeris University, Vilnius, Lithuania

Ombudsperson for Child's Rights, Vilnius, Lithuania

Bruna Žuber Faculty of Law, University of Ljubljana, Ljubljana, Slovenia

Researching Children's Rights: Focus on Central and Eastern Europe and Spotlighting Lithuania

Agnė Limantė and Rūta Vaičiūnienė

"A person's a person, no matter how small."— Dr. Seuss, Horton Hears a Who!

Abstract Since the 1990s, Central and Eastern European (CEE) countries have made considerable progress in strengthening the legal and institutional frameworks for children's rights. The last 30 years brought about fundamental changes, including the adoption of international conventions such as the United Nations Convention on the Rights of the Child and alignment with European Union (EU) standards. Significant reforms have been implemented in areas such as child protection, education, healthcare and juvenile justice. Governments across the region have established independent child rights institutions, improved children's position in various legal areas, from digital rights to child justice procedures, and worked to eradicate harmful practices such as institutionalised care for children.

1 Introduction

Since the 1990s, Central and Eastern European (CEE) countries have made considerable progress in strengthening the legal and institutional frameworks for children's rights. The last 30 years brought about fundamental changes, including the adoption of international conventions such as the United Nations Convention on the Rights of the Child and alignment with European Union (EU) standards. Significant

A. Limantė (✉) · R. Vaičiūnienė
Law Institute of the Lithuanian Centre for Social Sciences, Vilnius, Lithuania
e-mail: agne.limante@teise.org; ruta.vaiciuniene@teise.org

A. Limantė, R. Vaičiūnienė (eds.), *Children's Rights in Central and Eastern Europe*, European Union and its Neighbours in a Globalized World 29,
https://doi.org/10.1007/978-3-032-07092-0_1

reforms have been implemented in areas such as child protection, education, healthcare and juvenile justice. Governments across the region have established independent child rights institutions, improved children's position in various legal areas, from digital rights to child justice procedures, and worked to eradicate harmful practices such as institutionalised care for children.

One of the persistent challenges in the CEE region is the lingering influence of Soviet-era mentality and cultural norms regarding children and their role in society.[1] Under the communist system, children were often viewed as part of a collective rather than as individuals with distinct rights. They were considered to be under the authority of parents, teachers, or other adults, who were seen as superior and granted broad rights over them. This legacy, for a long time, continued to affect parenting practices, educational approaches, and societal attitudes toward children and their welfare. However, generational shifts and increasing exposure to Western values have begun to change these perceptions. As a result, legal frameworks and institutional practices in CEE countries are gradually converging with Western European standards, yet some areas still remain in transition.

In this introductory chapter, we will first briefly present the challenges faced by children in the CEE countries, presenting the statistics of the region. Then, we will overview the international context of the development of children's rights, and introduce to children's rights development in CEE countries with a specific focus on Lithuania. Finally, we will present the concept and structure of this book that explores the selected aspects of children's rights across the CEE region.

2 Children in CEE Countries and Challenges Faced

According to Eurostat, as of 1 January 2022, the population of the European Union was estimated at 446.7 million. Within this total, young people under the age of 18 accounted for 18.0% of the population.[2] Although the overall situation of children residing in the EU remains notably more favourable compared to global standards, certain challenges persist and warrant continued attention.

One of the concerning figures regarding the situation of children in Europe is the percentage of children at risk of poverty or social exclusion in the EU. Although between 2022 and 2023 this percentage remained relatively stable, in 2023, 24.8% of children (under 18 years) in the EU were still at risk of poverty or social exclusion, compared to 20.6% of adults (aged 18 and over). At the national level, the percentage of children at risk of poverty or social exclusion varies across CEE countries. While the most significant decreases were observed in Romania, this country still reported the highest rates at 39.0%. Meanwhile, in CEE countries, such as Slovenia and Croatia, the lowest rates were recorded.

[1] On children in Soviet occupied Lithuania see, e.g. Leinarte (2021); Grišinaitė (2017); Naudžiūnienė (2021); Balčiūnė (2022).

[2] Eurostat. (2024). Discover Eurostat's data on children. Retrieved from https://ec.europa.eu/eurostat/web/products-eurostat-news/w/wdn-20240722-1.

The data also indicate a clear link between parental educational attainment and child poverty risk: the higher the parents' educational level, the lower the proportion of children at risk.[3] The CEE countries like Lithuania, Czechia, Poland, Slovakia and Latvia (excluding Romania) have the lowest shares of people with a low level of education in the EU,[4] which can be considered an effective factor in reducing the number of children at risk of poverty or social exclusion. Additionally, the share of 'early school leavers' (18–24 year olds who had completed at most, a lower secondary education and were not in further education or training) has steadily decreased across the EU over the past decade, from 11.8% in 2013 to 9.5% in 2023, bringing the EU members closer to the target of reducing early school leaving to below 9.0% by 2030. Among EU countries, Romania reported the highest share of early school leavers in 2023 (16.6%), while other CEE countries such as Croatia (2.0%) and Poland (3.7%) recorded the lowest rates.[5] Ensuring the right to education is therefore crucial for combating child poverty in CEE countries and beyond. However, many countries still lack sufficiently trained professionals to address the needs of diverse groups of children within the educational system, including children with special educational needs and disabilities, migrant children, children with mental health issues and those experiencing poverty and exclusion.[6]

Access to healthcare is another critical indicator of the quality of life of children and is of paramount significance to both EU residents and policymakers. Although many young people in Europe perceive themselves to be in very good or good health (in 2022, 90.1% of 16–29 year-olds in the EU reported this), mental health issues are becoming an increasingly critical concern. In the 15–29 year old age group, almost 1 in 5 deaths in the EU in 2021 were registered as intentional self-harm, while for the total population, self-harm accounted for less than 1 in 100 deaths. That same year, over half of all deaths (53.0%) among young people aged 15–29 were linked to external causes, such as accidents, intentional self-harm, or assault (to compare, more than half (53.9%) the deaths in the total population were caused by circulatory diseases and cancer).[7] The highest standardised death rates for intentional self-harm in 2021 were recorded in Slovenia (19.8 per 100,000 inhabitants), followed closely by Lithuania (19.5 per 100,000 inhabitants).[8] These figures highlight that young people,

[3] Eurostat. (2024). Children at risk of poverty or social exclusion. Retrieved from https://ec.europa.eu/eurostat/statistics-explained/index.php?title=Children_at_risk_of_poverty_or_social_exclusion#Data_sources.

[4] Eurostat. (2024). Educational attainment statistics. Retrieved from https://ec.europa.eu/eurostat/statistics-explained/index.php?title=Educational_attainment_statisti.

[5] Eurostat. (2024). Early leavers from education and training. Retrieved from https://ec.europa.eu/eurostat/databrowser/view/EDAT_LFSE_14__custom_6078836/bookmark/table?lang=en&bookmarkId=41c6e587-cd58-4683-bdfb-b17263bca853.

[6] Eurochild. (2024). Children's Realities in Europe: Progress & Gaps. Eurochild 2024 Report on Children in Need Across Europe. Retrieved from https://eurochild.org/uploads/2024/11/Eurochild-Flagship-Report-Childrens-Realities-in-Europe.pdf.

[7] Eurostat. (2024). Young people—health. Retrieved from https://ec.europa.eu/eurostat/statistics-explained/index.php?title=Young_people_-_health.

[8] Eurostat. (2024). Mental health and related issues statistics. Retrieved from https://ec.europa.eu/eurostat/statistics-explained/index.php?title=Mental_health_and_related_issues_st.

in particular, face a range of developmental, emotional, and cognitive challenges, underscoring the urgent need for adequate mental health support services. Early intervention must be prioritised and significantly strengthened to better support children and young people experiencing mental health difficulties.[9]

Another critical issue in the policy agenda is the fundamental children's right to a family environment and permanent relationships with lifelong caregivers. Despite the well-documented and devastating effects of family separation and institutionalisation, 277 children per 100,000 live in residential care across Europe, nearly three times the global average.[10] According to UNICEF, CEE countries like Lithuania, Latvia, and Poland have some of the highest rates of children in residential care.[11] Despite ongoing reform efforts, challenges persist in Eastern Europe due to a historical reliance on institutional care and inconsistent resources and infrastructure to support family-based alternatives. Continued investment and comprehensive policy reforms are essential to ensure that all children in these regions have access to safe, nurturing, and family-like care environments. More investment is needed to prevent family separation, strengthen support for foster carers and community-based care, ensuring robust monitoring and evaluation of progress in implementing policies for children in alternative care.[12]

Furthermore, it is estimated that around 2.5 million children in the European Union come into contact with the justice system every year. This can be a highly stressful and even harmful experience for a child, whether they are involved as a victim, witness, accused, or suspect. Children may also be parties in civil proceedings such as divorce, custody, or adoption, as well as in administrative procedures related to nationality or migration. International organisations and policymakers should prioritise the development of child-friendly justice systems due to the particularly vulnerable position of children. The concept of child-friendly justice acknowledges the universal rights and specific needs of children, ensuring that they are treated with respect and protection, are heard, informed, and receive timely responses. It also acknowledges the particular difficulties and vulnerabilities that children may encounter, which must be carefully assessed, addressed, and individualised. Recent reports on the implementation of child-friendly justice highlight a persistent lack of specialised training among professionals working with children, especially among law enforcement officers, judicial authorities, and defence lawyers.[13] This issue is particularly pronounced in some CEE countries, where gaps

---

[9] Eurochild. (2024). Children's Realities in Europe: Progress & Gaps. Eurochild 2024 Report on Children in Need Across Europe. Retrieved from https://eurochild.org/uploads/2024/11/Eurochild-Flagship-Report-Childrens-Realities-in-Europe.pdf.

[10] UNICEF. (2023). Keeping families together in Europe. Retrieved from https://www.unicef.org/eca/reports/keeping-families-together-europe.

[11] UNICEF. (2024). Country Overviews—DataCare Project. Retrieved from https://www.unicef.org/eca/media/20271/file/Country%20Overviews%20-%20DataCare%20project.pdf.

[12] UNICEF. (2023). Keeping families together in Europe. Retrieved from https://www.unicef.org/eca/reports/keeping-families-together-europe.

[13] European Union Agency for Fundamental Rights (FRA). (2022). Children in criminal proceedings: Procedural safeguards. Retrieved from https://fra.europa.eu/sites/default/files/fra_uploads/fra-2022-children-procedural-safeguards_en.pdf.

remain in ensuring procedural safeguards.[14] While there is growing intention across CEE countries to prioritise non-custodial measures over detention, countries such as Lithuania, Slovakia, Bulgaria, and Hungary still often rely on conventional approaches like probation and custodial sentences.[15] Therefore, much opportunity exists to enhance interventions to meet the specific needs of each child and to promote an individualised, resocialization-oriented approach.

Another point to mention is emerging transnational concerns such as child labour, online safety, and digital exploitation that necessitate not only national measures but also international collaboration. In 2022, 96% of young people aged 16–29 years in the EU reported using the internet daily compared with 84% of the adult population. Some of the highest rates, at 99%, were recorded in seven EU members, including CEE countries such as Czechia, Lithuania, Slovenia and Latvia. According to the data, 84% of young people used the internet to participate in social media networks.[16] It is evident that youthful individuals are more likely to use the internet than the general population; however, these opportunities also come with substantial risks. Every time a young person logs into social media, they may be subjected to cyberbullying and other forms of peer-to-peer violence. Additionally, they may be exposed to conspiracy theories, disinformation, violent content, and hate speech. Most concerning, however, is the ongoing threat of online sexual exploitation and abuse.[17] Child sexual abuse is a growing problem, both online and offline. In 2023 alone, there were 1.3 million reports of child sexual abuse in the EU, which included more than 3.4 million images and videos. Alarmingly, the EU remains the top global host of such material, with 59% of reported child sexual abuse content located on servers within EU Member States.[18]

In this context, debates on children's privacy and protection have become increasingly prominent. According to the latest Eurobarometer data, many Europeans expect a balance between privacy and security: 92% of surveyed citizens agree that children are increasingly at risk online, and 96% believe that the ability to detect child abuse is equally or more important than the right to online privacy.[19] Another survey reveals that children show a nuanced understanding of privacy and protection. While many support strong online safety measures when facing risks, they generally call for the mutual reinforcement of protection and

[14] See chapter "Peculiarities of Criminal Liability of Children in Lithuania" of this book.

[15] See chapter "Drug Offences Committed by Minors in Lithuania and Poland: Penal Responses and the Rights of Underaged Offenders" of this book.

[16] Eurostat. (2023). 96% of young people in the EU uses the internet daily. Retrieved from https://ec.europa.eu/eurostat/web/products-eurostat-news/w/ddn-20230714-1.

[17] United Nations. (2023). Child and youth safety online. Retrieved from https://www.un.org/en/global-issues/child-and-youth-safety-online.

[18] European Commission. (2024). Protecting children from sexual abuse. Retrieved from https://home-affairs.ec.europa.eu/policies/internal-security/protecting-children-sexual-abuse_en.

[19] European Commission. (2023). The Flash Eurobarometer survey on "Protection of Children against Online Sexual Abuse". Retrieved from https://europa.eu/eurobarometer/surveys/detail/2656.

privacy mechanisms. The research also highlights that children often prefer to keep their online activities private and struggle to discuss online risks with adults. While nearly 90% of caregivers surveyed in the study believe they are somewhat aware of their children's online activities, children in the study reveal otherwise.[20] Furthermore, 80% of young people aged 13 to 17 years old from 13 EU Member States, including CEE countries such as the Czech Republic, Poland, Hungary, and Slovakia, report that they would not feel comfortable being politically active or exploring their sexuality if authorities were monitoring their digital communications to detect child sexual abuse.

Consequently, adhering to international standards and the most recent international policy agenda could enhance the protection of children's rights in the CEE region. The subsequent section will briefly discuss the international context for the development of children's rights.

3 Development of Children's Rights: International Context and CEE

Children are at the heart of every society, yet for much of history, their rights were overlooked and their needs were secondary to the priorities of adults. For centuries, children were viewed as objects of law rather than independent subjects with their own legal rights. In most societies, including Europe, they were seen as dependents under the authority of adults, primarily their fathers, with little recognition of their autonomy within legal systems.

In pre-industrial societies, European children were considered economic assets, contributing to household labour and subsistence farming.[21] In the CEE region, from an early age, most children joined their parents in agricultural labour participating in cultivating land, tending to livestock, gathering firewood, and domestic tasks.

In the Early Modern Period (roughly fifteenth to eighteenth centuries) the position of children in Europe was shaped by a combination of religious, economic, and social factors. For instance, in Lithuania, in the Grand Duchy of Lithuania during the sixteenth and seventeenth centuries, the family played a central role in shaping children's socialisation and education, though within a strict and often unequal framework. Boys and girls were raised according to distinct societal expectations, reflecting broader gender roles. While boys were prepared to become active citizens contributing to the Republic and the Church, girls were primarily trained in domestic skills, with an emphasis on morality and piety. Education for girls was limited, not necessarily as a form of discrimination, but under the belief that intellectual

[20] ECPAT International. (2023). The VOICE report: Speaking up for change—Children's and caregivers' voices for safer online experiences. Retrieved from https://ecpat.org/resource/voice-report-speaking-up-for-change-childrens-and-caregivers-voices-for-safer-online-experiences/.

[21] On pre-industrial societies see Crone (2003).

pursuits might endanger their moral integrity. Parental authority was seen as essential in instilling discipline, often reinforced through physical punishment, and excessive parental affection was discouraged as weakening proper upbringing. The family was thus not just a private unit but a structured institution that mirrored the rigid hierarchy and values of the broader society, reinforcing traditional roles and ensuring conformity from an early age (Sarcevičienė, 2003).

Later stages of industrialisation led to a shift in child labour from traditional family and community-based work to employment in factories, mines, and other industrial settings. This transition exposed children to harsh and often dangerous working conditions, including long hours and physically demanding tasks that posed serious health risks. However, this in turn sparked public awareness and advocacy for child labour laws, leading to international regulations such as the ILO Conventions on child labour and minimum age requirements (Dahlén, 2007; Honeyman, 2016; Rahikainen, 2017).

Urbanisation and the transition from extended to nuclear families changed child-rearing and education practices. The shift from agricultural to urban societies led to an emphasis on formal education as a means of preparing children for future economic participation. Compulsory schooling was introduced in many industrialised nations (Carl, 2009), reinforcing the notion that childhood should be dedicated to learning rather than labour. Additionally, emerging psychological and educational theories changed views about children and their position in society.

The idea that children deserve legal protection, autonomy, and a voice in decisions affecting their lives is a relatively modern development. It was not until the early twentieth century that the recognition and protection of children's rights began to take shape as part of broader social and legal reforms (Barnett, 2021, pp. 2–4). A key milestone at the international level was the adoption of the Geneva Declaration of the Rights of the Child by the League of Nations (1924),[22] just a bit more than a hundred years ago. This very brief document (including only five points) underlined the universal duty to prioritise the well-being of children and established the first list of children's rights.

Since then, the recognition and enforcement of children's rights have evolved significantly, influenced by shifting societal structures, changes in family dynamics, and the development of international legal instruments. The need to afford special protection for the child was recognised in the Universal Declaration of Human Rights (1948), the International Covenant on Civil and Political Rights (1966),[23] the International Covenant on Economic, Social and Cultural Rights (1966)[24] and other instruments of international organisations concerned with human rights in general or child rights and welfare in particular.

---

[22] Geneva Declaration of the Rights of the Child of 1924, adopted Sept. 26, 1924, League of Nations O.J. Spec. Supp. 21, at 43 (1924).

[23] International Covenant on Civil and Political Rights (1966), adopted by General Assembly resolution 2200A (XXI) of 16 December 1966.

[24] International Covenant on Economic, Social and Cultural Rights (1966), adopted by General Assembly resolution 2200A (XXI) of 16 December 1966.

Among the international instruments designed to protect children, the most important is the UN Convention on the Rights of the Child (1989).[25] This Convention sets the main principles of child protection, and the civil, political, economic, social, health and cultural rights of children. Of particular importance is Article 3 of this Convention, which states that in all actions concerning children, the best interests of the child shall be the primary consideration. This principle has influenced the evolution of child protection laws, education policies, child justice systems, and family law by ensuring that children's welfare and development take precedence over competing interests. The General Comments of the UN Committee on the Rights of the Child further elaborate on the content of the rights established in the UNCRC.[26]

While the UN Convention on the Rights of the Child is a general instrument, there are also a number of instruments addressing concrete child rights. For instance, the 1996 Hague Child Protection Convention[27] establishes a legal framework for international cooperation in matters of child protection and aims to ensure the recognition and enforcement of protective measures across borders, addressing issues such as parental responsibility, guardianship, and the relocation of children; the 1980 Hague Abduction Convention[28] establishes a legal framework for the prompt return of children who have been wrongfully removed or retained across international borders, aiming to prevent parental child abduction and ensure respect for custody rights.

Children's rights are further addressed in regional instruments. In Europe,[29] the Council of Europe has adopted numerous conventions that address specific aspects of child rights protection. The European Convention on Human Rights (ECHR), adopted in 1950 by the Council of Europe, does not contain a specific provision dedicated exclusively to children's rights. However, it establishes several fundamental rights that are crucial for the protection and well-being of children.[30] Provisions such as the right to life (Article 2), the right to liberty and security (Article 5), the right to

[25] UN Convention on the Rights of the Child (1989), adopted by the United Nations General Assembly on 20 November 1989. The UNCRC consists of 54 articles and establishes children's fundamental rights, including life, protection, education, family, and expression, and requires governments to uphold them. Three optional protocols strengthen the UNCRC: two from 2000 prohibit child soldier recruitment and child exploitation, while a 2011 protocol allows children to report rights violations to the UN Committee on the Rights of the Child.

[26] See, e.g. (UN Committee on the Rights of the Child 2009, 2019; UN Human Rights Committee (HRC) 2007).

[27] The Hague Convention of 19 October 1996 on Jurisdiction, Applicable Law, Recognition, Enforcement and Co-operation in Respect of Parental Responsibility and Measures for the Protection of Children.

[28] The Hague Convention of 25 October 1980 on the Civil Aspects of International Child Abduction.

[29] For a more extensive analysis see chapter "Constitutional Protection of Children's Rights in Central and Eastern European States" of Taylor (2024).

[30] While there is no consensus about the concept of well-being it has been understood as inherently multi-dimensional, taking into account the complexity of children's lives and relationships (Richardson et al. 2008).

a fair trial (Article 6), and the right to respect for private and family life (Article 8) are particularly relevant to children. The European Court of Human Rights (ECtHR) has played a vital role in interpreting these provisions in ways that recognise and address children's unique vulnerabilities, reinforcing the obligation of states to ensure their protection. The ECtHR has repeatedly emphasised children's vulnerability in various legal contexts, highlighting their need for special protections. In cases involving child neglect, abuse, unsafe environments, and legal conflicts, the Court has recognised that children's young age and physical and mental immaturity place them at a distinct disadvantage in safeguarding their rights (Limante, 2022).[31]

Besides the ECHR, there are many other relevant instruments adopted under the auspices of the Council of Europe. For instance, the European Convention on the Exercise of Children's Rights (1996) aims at protecting the best interests of children and promoting their rights, particularly as regards family proceedings before judicial authorities; the Council of Europe Guidelines to respect, protect and fulfil the rights of the child in the digital environment (2018) focussses on technology age rights. As to child-friendly justice, the most comprehensive framework is found in the Guidelines of the Committee of Ministers of the Council of Europe on Child-Friendly Justice (2011), which outline measures to ensure children's participation, protection, and access to justice in a manner suited to their age and vulnerability.

The EU also plays a significant role in shaping and strengthening children's rights across its Member States through a combination of legislation, political instruments[32], policies, strategic initiatives and funding of research and civil society projects. As for primary law, the Treaty on European Union outlines the Union's responsibility to promote the protection of children's rights (see Article 3(3) TEU). The EU Charter of Fundamental Rights dedicates a separate article (Article 24) for the rights of the child. This Article 24 incorporates key rights and principles from the UN Convention on the Rights of the Child, including the best interests of the child (Article 3) and child participation (Article 12). Additionally, several other Charter provisions relate to children's rights, such as Article 7 (respect for private and family life), Article 8 (protection of personal data), Article 14 (right to education), Article 21 (non-discrimination), Article 32 (prohibition of child labour), and Article 33 (reconciliation of family and professional life). The protection of these and other children rights are further strengthened in secondary law instruments,[33] and interpreted in the case law of the Court of Justice of the European Union (CJEU)[34].

---

[31] For the case law of the ECtHR see *Guide on the Case-Law of the European Convention on Human Rights. Rights of the Child* 2024.

[32] E.g., the EU Strategy on the Rights of the Child (2021–2024) which provides a comprehensive framework to enhance child protection, participation, and well-being. It is the fourth strategy in a series designed to promote children's rights across Europe.

[33] Examples of secondary law EU instruments are Directive (EU) 2016/800 of the European Parliament and of the Council of 11 May 2016 on procedural safeguards for children who are suspects or accused persons in criminal proceedings; and Directive 2011/93/EU of the European Parliament and of the Council of 13 December 2011 on combating the sexual abuse and sexual exploitation of children and child pornography. See further FRA (2022).

[34] See, e.g. Frasca and Carlier (2023); Lonardo (2022).

Overall, while the development and reinforcement of children's rights have been ongoing at both international and regional levels, the most significant progress has taken place since 1990. This evolving legal framework has profoundly influenced CEE countries, particularly in the wake of their political and social transformations during the 1990s. As these nations transitioned to democratic governance, they were able to integrate international standards into their legal systems at a pace comparable[35] to that of Western countries, leading to substantial advancements in children's rights across the region. Since then, child protection standards in Europe have become increasingly aligned, fostering a more cohesive European approach to children's rights.

Similar to other CEE countries, the position of children in Lithuania has undergone significant transformations over the past three decades, largely influenced by the country's regaining of independence, accession to international instruments, and membership in the EU. This period is also characterised by demographic shifts,[36] economic changes, and evolving societal attitudes toward family and child-rearing.[37] The State and societal approach towards childhood and children is also affected by an overall decline in the child population, which reflects broader trends of an ageing society, with fewer births and an increasing median age for first-time parents.[38] Changes in family structures—the rise in divorce rates and the increasing prevalence of single-parent households[39]—have also played a role in shaping public policies and the experience of children in Lithuania.[40] As for the economic perspective, economic improvements following Lithuania's accession to the European Union in 2004 have had a positive impact on child welfare and increased household incomes (Vilpišauskas, 2019). This economic progress enhanced children's living conditions and access to resources that contribute to their overall well-being. However, economic disparities persist, and continued efforts are required to ensure that vulnerable children, particularly those from low-income families, do not fall behind.

[35] See also Kabašinskaitė and Bak (2006).

[36] According to the data of the State Data Agency, in the 1990s, Lithuania's population was 3,69 million, whereas by 2024, it had decreased to 2,89 million.

[37] For instance, the practice of shared care (joint custody, in Lithuanian case law refered to as '50:50 child contact arrangement') after the separation of parents recently started to become popular in Lithuania.

[38] State Data Agency, Lietuvos Gyventojai (2022m. Leidimas). Gimstamumas (2023). This demographic shift is driven by factors such as greater individual autonomy, changing gender roles, and the prioritisation of personal and professional aspirations over early parenthood. See also Charenkova (2025).

[39] As of 2020, approximately 14% of households with children in the European Union were single-parent households, representing about 4% of total households. After Sweden, Denmark and Estonia, Lithuania (25%) ranked among the countries with the highest percentage of single-parent households in Europe (*How Many Single-Parent Households Are There in the EU?*).

[40] On changing historical approach to families see Maslauskaitė (2023).

4 About this Book

This book *Children's Rights in Central and Eastern Europe: Comparative Analysis with a Spotlight on Lithuania* is a thorough, multi-disciplinary examination of children's rights in CEE countries with a focus on Lithuania. Taking a comparative approach, it explores various aspects of children's rights, established in constitutional, civil, administrative, and criminal law in the region, also discussing emerging issues relevant to the twenty-first century. The book offers unique insights into the challenges and progress specific to CEE countries, many of which have undergone significant political, social, and legal transformations in recent decades.

The comparative analysis of practices and legal frameworks between Lithuania and other countries in the region and across various CEE countries is a key feature of the book. By comparing practices, case law and legal regulations across different CEE countries, the book highlights both the diversity and the common challenges in the region. Moreover, such a comparative perspective is invaluable for policymakers, practitioners, and academics in identifying best practices and learning from the experiences of different countries. The book's chapters seek to provide evidence-based insights and recommendations that can guide the development of more effective and rights-based approaches to child protection.

While aiming to enhance awareness and understanding of children's rights, the book also seeks to fill a gap in the literature by focusing on the CEE region, an area often underrepresented and overlooked in global discussions about children's rights. The publication brings together a wide range of theoretical and empirical research from Lithuania and other CEE countries. It features contributions from researchers across several countries, including the three Baltic States, Poland, Slovenia, Hungary, Croatia, and Romania, who co-author the majority of the chapters. The collaboration of academics from multiple countries allows for a horizontal overview of the region and offers a more holistic understanding of the challenges and advancements in children's rights in the CEE region.

This book is divided into three parts, each addressing a distinct aspect of children's rights.

4.1 Part I: Children's Rights Across Legal Frontiers

Part I: Children's Rights Across Legal Frontiers explores the legal dimensions of children's rights in constitutional, civil, administrative, and labour law across CEE countries. Chapters cover topics on constitutional court jurisprudence, family law, procedural capacities in administrative procedures, and the nuances of child labour laws.

The opening chapter, "Constitutional Protection of Children's Rights in Central and Eastern European States" by Dr. Dovilė Pūraitė-Andrikienė, explores the role of constitutional courts in safeguarding children's rights in CEE countries. The author claims that while the inclusion of children's rights provisions in constitutions is crucial, real protection depends on judicial enforcement. Through a comparative analysis of constitutional frameworks and landmark cases, the chapter identifies the contributions of constitutional courts in strengthening children's rights protection and reveals common trends in constitutional jurisprudence.

In the next Chapter, "Children in Family Law Cases: Comparative Study of Custody and Contact Arrangements in Slovenia and Lithuania," Dr. Neža Pogorelčnik Vogrinc and Dr. Agne Limante compare child custody and contact arrangements in these two jurisdictions. Despite their geographical and cultural differences, both countries share similarities in family law challenges. The authors analyse legislative frameworks and case law, illustrating how custody decisions and contact arrangements shape children's post-separation experiences and discussing how contact arrangements can approximate shared physical custody in systems where it is not explicitly recognised by law.

"Hearing of the Child in International Child Abduction Cases: A Comparative Analysis of Practices in Poland and Lithuania" by Dr. Agne Limante and Dr. Anna Wysocka-Bar, focuses on Lithuanian and Polish practices of hearing children in cross-border child abduction cases and the role given to the opinion of the child. The chapter examines the application of the Brussels IIter regulation and the 1980 Hague Child Abduction Convention in Poland and Lithuania, critically assessing domestic practices in light of international obligations.

In "The Procedural Capacity of a Child in an Administrative Procedure: The Case of Slovenia and Croatia", Dr. Bruna Žuber and Dr. Dario Đerđa analyse children's participation in administrative procedures in Slovenia and Croatia. Given their shared legal heritage from the former Yugoslav state, the chapter examines how both countries regulate children's procedural capacity and legal representation in administrative matters. The discussion extends to the right of children to express their views and be heard, assessing the effectiveness of legal provisions ensuring their participation in administrative decisions affecting them.

The chapter "The Employment of Adolescents and Children: Minimum Working Age in Lithuanian and Polish Law" by Dr. Ingrida Mačernytė Panomariovienė and Dr. Tatiana Wrocławska, starts the discussion on child labour by examining the regulation of young workers in Lithuania and Poland. Through a comparative analysis, the authors highlight differences in minimum age thresholds, permissible employment types, and exceptions, weighing the tension between preventing child labour and ensuring safe working conditions for adolescents.

The final chapter, "Child Work in the Digital XXI Century: The Experience of the Baltic States" by Dr. Kristina Ambrazevičūtė, Dr. Kristine Dupate, and Dr. Merle Erikson, continues to labour law related discussion and addresses the changing nature of child labour in the digital economy. They argue that traditional labour laws primarily designed for industrial-era work may no longer sufficiently regulate modern forms of child employment, particularly in digital environments. Focusing on Estonia, Latvia, and Lithuania, this chapter evaluates whether existing regulations adequately protect children engaged in digital work, advocating for a reassessment of legal frameworks to address new occupational realities.

4.2 Part II: Exploring Children's Rights in the Realm of Criminal Law and Criminal Procedure

Focusing on criminal law, *Part II: Exploring Children's Rights in the Realm of Criminal Law and Procedure* offers academic perspectives on the vulnerability of child victims in criminal processes, peculiarities of criminal liability of minors, juvenile delinquency, victimisation, and the implementation of individual assessments in criminal proceedings. It also examines such topics as the responses to drug offences committed by juveniles and the effectiveness of juvenile resocialisation measures.

The opening chapter, "Vulnerability of Child Victims in Criminal Process: A Comparative Analysis of Development and Vulnerability Criteria in Lithuania and Croatia" by Dr. Eglė Kavoliūnaitė-Ragauskienė explores how children as victims are protected in criminal proceedings across Europe, focusing on the concept of vulnerability and the criteria to define the vulnerability of children in EU law. It examines Directive 2012/29/EU and compares how Lithuania and Croatia apply special protections for child victims. Then, "Children's Victimisation in Lithuania: Context, Forms and Prevalence" by Dr. Aušra Pocienė, Vaidas Kalpokas and Dr. Jolanta Aleknevičienė focuses on recorded children's criminal victimisation and their latent victimisation in Lithuania. The chapter reveals that cyberbullying, theft, and parental violence are those infringements that most commonly affect children and are often underreported or unreported.

In the chapter "Understanding Juvenile Delinquency in Lithuania: From Misconceptions to Negative Attitudes", Dr. Gintautas Sakalauskas, Vaidas Kalpokas, Dr. Jolita Buzaitytė-Kašalynienė, and Dr. Birutė Švedaitė-Sakalauskė note that many young people engage in minor, temporary delinquent acts. They highlight that media portrayals often sensationalise isolated cases, fostering a distorted public perception that overlooks the widespread and typically minor nature of adolescent misbehaviour. The authors argue that more serious forms of delinquency frequently originate in deeper, systemic social problems and recognising this distinction is essential to ensure that interventions address root causes rather than superficial symptoms.

"Peculiarities of Criminal Liability of Minors and Release from It in Lithuania" by Mindaugas Girdauskas and Dr. Darius Pranka, moves to the question of criminal liability and analyses certain peculiarities in the regulation and application of criminal liability for children in Lithuania within the context of international child rights protection standards. The authors also address the question of the regulation and application of diversion concerning children. They argue that Lithuania's reforms in juvenile justice, which limit the application of criminal liability for children and promote alternative measures, have contributed to a decline in child delinquency in line with European trends. However, further improvements are needed to expand these measures, clarify legal provisions, and strengthen procedural safeguards for children's rights.

Continuing the discussion, in the chapter "Ensuring and Implementing Individual Assessments of Adolescents in Criminal Proceedings in Lithuania and Croatia", Dr. Rūta Vaičiūnienė and Dr. Anja Mirosavljevic analyse the challenges and current practices of individual assessment in accordance with Directive 2016/800 in two EU Member States, Croatia and Lithuania. Best practices from these two countries are presented in this chapter to illustrate the need for a child-friendly, multidimensional, and interdisciplinary approach in assessing children in conflict with the law.

The next chapter takes a closer look at one type of offence often committed by young people. In particular, in their research entitled "Drug Offences Committed by Minors in Lithuania and Poland: Penal Responses and the Rights of Underaged Offenders", Dr. Mindaugas Lankauskas and Dr. Justyna Omeljaniuk offer a comparative legal analysis of adolescent drug offences in Lithuania and Poland. The authors discover the similarities, differences, and possible societal factors influencing penal responses to adolescent drug offences.

In "Community Sanctions for Children in Lithuania and Romania: Diverging Paths of Juvenile Justice", Dr. Simonas Nikartas and Dr. Ioan Durnescu compare the juvenile justice systems in Lithuania and Romania, focusing on community sanctions and measures for children. The authors conclude with policy recommendations encouraging policymakers to strengthen rehabilitation measures, promote greater institutional specialisation, improve the training of specialists, and reduce regional disparities in access to juvenile justice services.

The final chapter, "Criminological Analysis of Juvenile Resocialisation Measures in Lithuanian Probation Service," by Dr. Rokas Uscila and Dr. Renata Mienkowska Norkienė, explores the current situation of juvenile offenders within the Lithuanian Probation Service. The study seeks to evaluate the existing resocialisation measures, focusing on their types, diversity, and probation officers' perceptions of their effectiveness.

4.3 Part III: Emerging and Cross-Cutting Issues

The final section, *Part III: Emerging and Cross-Cutting Issues*, addresses contemporary and complex issues like inclusive education for children with disabilities and special needs, the rights of national minorities, children's privacy and data protection rights, the regulatory challenges of 'sharenting' (sharing of children's information and images online by parents) and children's right to health.

"Advancing Children's Privacy and Data Protection Rights: Emerging Data Protection Trends and Challenges in Selected CEE Countries" by Dr. Ingrida Milkaitė and Dr. Milda Mačėnaitė, focuses on the impact of the digital environment on children's privacy. The chapter examines how the European Union's General Data Protection Regulation (GDPR) has been implemented and enforced in six CEE countries. The authors identify enforcement trends, challenges, and potential gaps, showing that while the GDPR provides a robust framework for data protection, disparities remain in national enforcement.

In the chapter "Parenting in the Digital Age: Addressing the Sharenting Phenomenon in Central and Eastern Europe," Gergely Ferenc Lendvai and Dr. Kristina Ambrazevičiūtė explore the increasingly prevalent practice of sharenting—parents sharing images and information about their children online. The researchers examine international trends in sharenting, with a focus on the Visegrad 4 and Baltic States, assessing the lack of specific legal frameworks in most European countries. The authors highlight jurisdictional conflicts, enforcement difficulties, and regulatory gaps that result from the absence of comprehensive sharenting-related legislation.

"Towards Inclusive Education for Children with Disabilities: Developments and Challenges in Lithuania and Poland" by Dr. Lina Beliūnienė and Dr. Katarzyna Roszewska, brings attention to the educational rights and critically assesses the implementation of inclusive education policies in Lithuania and Poland. They argue that despite legislative reforms aligned with the UN Convention on the Rights of Persons with Disabilities, children with disabilities and special needs continue to face significant barriers, including discrimination, lack of reasonable accommodation, and insufficient individualised support. This chapter provides a comparative analysis of legal frameworks, national reports, and academic literature to identify systemic challenges and advocate for stronger mechanisms to ensure equitable educational access for children with disabilities.

Educational rights are further discussed in the chapter "Education Rights of Children Belonging to National Minorities in the Baltic States" by Dr. Jolanta Apolewicz and Dr. Elżbieta Kuzborska-Pacha. The authors examine the historical, legal, and policy dimensions of minority education rights in Lithuania, Latvia, and Estonia. The chapter explores the balance between strengthening education in the state language and preserving minority language rights. The authors highlight key challenges, such as limited access to quality education, inadequate consultation with minority communities, and socio-economic disparities.

The final chapter in this section, "Challenges to the Protection of the Child's Right to Health" by Dr. Edita Žiobienė notes that the right to the highest attainable standard of health is recognised in international and national law, with parents generally responsible for healthcare decisions. The author claims that in Europe, states seek to uphold the child's best interests in health-related matters, allowing flexibility for parents, doctors, and, where appropriate, the child to determine the most suitable course of action. The author argues that involving children in decision-making not only supports their personal development and competence but also promotes broader health literacy, which is increasingly vital in the face of public scepticism and misinfomation.

References

Balčiūnė I (2022) Atsikratymas vaikais sovietmečio Lietuvoje: Tėvai, valstybė ir nereikalingi vaikai [PhD, Vilnius University]. https://doi.org/10.15388/vu.thesis.407

Barnett H (2021) Children's rights and the law: an introduction. Routledge. https://doi.org/10.4324/9780429452710

Carl J (2009) Industrialization and public education: social cohesion and social stratification. In: Cowen R, Kazamias AM (eds) International handbook of comparative education. Springer, Netherlands, pp 503–518. https://doi.org/10.1007/978-1-4020-6403-6_32

Charenkova J (2025) Conceptualizing 'children' across age groups in Lithuania: a preliminary account using free list tasks. Anthropol Humanistic Sci, 165–179. https://doi.org/10.15388/Anthro.2025_9

Crone P (2003) Pre-industrial societies: anatomy of the pre-modern world, 2nd edn. Oneworld

Dahlén M (2007) The negotiable child: the ILO labour campaign 1919–1973. Department of Law, Uppsala University

FRA (2022) Handbook on European law relating to the rights of the child. Koninklijke Brill NV. https://fra.europa.eu/sites/default/files/fra_uploads/fra-coe-2022-handbook-child-rights_en.pdf

Frasca E, Carlier J-Y (2023) The best interests of the child in ECJ asylum and migration case law: towards a safeguard principle for the genuine enjoyment of the substance of children's rights? Common Mark Law Rev 60(2). https://kluwerlawonline.com/api/Product/CitationPDFURL?file=Journals\COLA\COLA2023024.pdf

Grišinaitė R (2017) Vaiko ir vaikystės sampratos ir jų kūrimas viešajame vėlyvojo Sovietmečio Lietuvos pedagoginiame diskurse (1962–1984). Lietuvos istorijos studijos 39:84–104

Guide on the case-law of the European Convention on Human Rights. Rights of the child (2024). https://ks.echr.coe.int/documents/d/echr-ks/guide_rights_of_the_child_eng

Honeyman K (2016) Childhood and child labour in industrial England: diversity and agency, 1750–1914. Routledge

How many single-parent households are there in the EU? (n.d.) Retrieved 15 December 2023, from https://ec.europa.eu/eurostat/web/products-eurostat-news/-/edn-20210601-2

Kabašinskaitė D, Bak M (2006) Lithuania's children's policy in the period of transition. Int J Soc Welf 15(3):247–256. https://doi.org/10.1111/j.1468-2397.2006.00428.x

Leinarte D (2021) Family and the State in Soviet Lithuania. 1–226

Lietuvos gyventojai (2022 m. Leidimas). Gimstamumas (2023). https://osp.stat.gov.lt/lietuvos-gyventojai-2022/gimstamumas

Limante A (2022) Vulnerable groups in the case law of the European court of human rights. In: Limantė A, Pūraitė-Andrikienė D (eds) Legal protection of vulnerable groups in Lithuania, Latvia, Estonia and Poland, vol 8. Springer International Publishing, pp 29–54. https://doi.org/10.1007/978-3-031-06998-7_2

Lonardo L (2022) The best interests of the child in the case law of the court of justice of the European Union. Maastricht J Eur Comp Law 29(5):596–614. https://doi.org/10.1177/1023263X221144829

Maslauskaitė A (2023) Lithuanian families. In: Adler IMA, Lenz K (eds) The changing faces of families, 1st edn. Routledge, pp 101–121. https://doi.org/10.4324/9781003193500-6

Naudžiūnienė A (2021) "Naujasis žmogus" iki pareikalavimo: Mokinys vėlyvojo sovietmečio (1964–1988 m.) Lietuvos mokyklose. Lietuvos istorijos studijos 47:99–117

Rahikainen M (2017) Centuries of child labour: European experiences from the seventeenth to the twentieth century. Routledge. https://doi.org/10.4324/9781315260716

Richardson D, Hoelscher P, Bradshaw J (2008) Child Well-being in central and eastern European countries (CEE) and the commonwealth of independent states (CIS). Child Indic Res 1(3):211–250. https://doi.org/10.1007/s12187-008-9020-8

Sarcevičienė J (2003) Vaikas XVI-XVII a. Lietuvos Didžiosios Kunigaikštystės visuomenėje: Galimi auklėjimo ir socializacijos modeliai. Menotyra 2(31):4–10

Taylor R (2024) Fortin's children's rights and the developing law, 4th edn. Cambridge University Press

UN Committee on the Rights of the Child. (2009). General Comment No. 12 (2009): The right of the child to be heard. https://www.refworld.org/docid/4ae562c52.html

UN Committee on the Rights of the Child. (2019). General Comment No. 24, replacing General Comment No. 10 (2007). Children's rights in juvenile justice. https://www.ohchr.org/Documents/HRBodies/CRC/GC24/GeneralComment24.pdf

UN Human Rights Committee (HRC) (2007, August 23). General Comment no. 32, Article 14, Right to equality before courts and tribunals and to fair trial (CCPR/C/GC/32)

Vilpišauskas R (2019) Lithuania and the European Union. In: Vilpišauskas R (ed) Oxford research Encyclopedia of politics. Oxford University Press. https://doi.org/10.1093/acrefore/9780190228637.013.1113

Agnė Limantė is a Chief Researcher at the Law Institute of the Lithuanian Centre for Social Sciences. She has received an MA in EU law from King's College London (awarded with the Prize for Best Dissertation on the MA in EU Law) and a PhD from Vilnius University, Lithuania. In May 2023–May 2025, she served as a Member of the Humanities and Social Sciences Expert Committee at the Research Council of Lithuania.

A considerable part of Agne's research focuses on family and children's rights law, and her recent works analyse the interplay between human rights and technology. Dr. Limantė is a co-editor of several edited collections: *Cambridge Handbook of AI and Technologies in Courts* (CUP, forthcoming 2026); *Gender-Based Violence and Law: Global Perspectives and Eastern European Practices* (Routledge, 2023); *Legal Protection of Vulnerable Groups in Lithuania, Latvia, Estonia and Poland: Trends and Perspectives* (Springer, 2022); *The Regulation of Matrimonial Property and Property of Registered Partnerships* (Intersentia, 2022). Overall, Dr. Limantė has published over 40 research papers in national and international journals or as book chapters. https://orcid.org/0000-0001-7365-787X

Rūta Vaičiūnienė is a Chief Researcher and the Head of the Criminological Research Department at the Law Institute of the Lithuanian Centre for Social Sciences. Her research interests encompass the sociology of imprisonment, the sociology of gender with a focus on domestic violence, youth justice, and correctional programming. She has authored over 30 scientific papers, including research articles published in highly-ranked journals. Dr Vaičiūnienė has accrued diverse research experience, contributing to more than 10 national and international research projects. Since 2023, she serves as the president of the Lithuanian Association of Criminology. https://orcid.org/0000-0002-6342-9635

Children's Rights Across Legal Frontiers in Constitutional, Civil, Administrative, and Labour Law

Constitutional Protection of Children's Rights in Central and Eastern European States

Dovilė Pūraitė-Andrikienė

Abstract The distinction between democratic and authoritarian constitutions can hardly be drawn by referring to anything other than human rights (especially rights of the most vulnerable groups) and their real protection in the state and society. Among these vulnerable groups, children stand out, being unable to select the social and physical environments into which they are born and raised, with their voices and interests frequently overlooked or not accorded the seriousness they deserve. This vulnerability places them at risk of enduring profound injustices due to their dependent status. However, merely including a children's rights provision in a constitution is not enough; it does not guarantee a means of redress if those rights are not upheld. The most obvious way in which constitutional rights can be enforced is through their protection in constitutional courts.

Despite the critical importance of safeguarding the rights of this vulnerable group, there is little discussion about the way constitutional courts contributed to the legal situation of children in general and about the enhancement of their protection in Central and Eastern European (CEE) countries in particular. Thus, this chapter aims to shed more light on the constitutional protection of children in these countries. To achieve this, focusing on the CEE region, the following tasks will be addressed: (1) to provide a comparative analysis of the constitutional framework for the protection of children's rights; (2) to discuss the role of constitutional courts in the protection of human rights; (3) to identify the constitutional justice cases which most contributed to enhancing the protection of children, as well as to distinguish common trends in the constitutional jurisprudence in the area discussed.

D. Pūraitė-Andrikienė (✉)
Law Institute, Lithuanian Centre for Social Sciences, Vilnius, Lithuania

A. Limantė, R. Vaičiūnienė (eds.), *Children's Rights in Central and Eastern Europe*, European Union and its Neighbours in a Globalized World 29,
https://doi.org/10.1007/978-3-032-07092-0_2

1 Introduction

The adoption of the United Nations Convention on the Rights of the Child (CRC) in 1989 marked a global acknowledgement of children as holders of legal rights. Since then, this acknowledgement has spread to other international agreements and has been incorporated into national legal frameworks at different levels, including constitutions. The adoption of the CRC coincided almost exactly with the beginning of the so-called fourth phase of constitutional development in the 1990s, which began after the collapse of totalitarian regimes in Central and Eastern Europe (CEE). In this period most of the countries of this region have adopted new constitutions or substantially revised old ones. These countries, following the example of older democracies, have much more explicitly enshrined a range of human rights and mechanisms of their protection in their constitutions. All the constitutions of the CEE also introduced at least some provisions for children's rights. However, merely including a children's rights provision in a constitution is not enough; it does not guarantee a means of redress if those rights are not upheld. The most obvious way in which constitutional rights can be enforced is through their protection in constitutional courts or other constitutional justice institutions.

All new democracies in CEE set up constitutional courts, as the very existence of these courts served as a 'trademark' of the democratic character of the respective state (Sólyom 2003, pp. 133–134). Although the effectiveness of these institutions in CEE varies, their contribution to the constitutional transition process has been highly significant. The constitutional justice institutions have played an important role in ensuring respect for the rule of law, constitutionality, legality, human rights, and fundamental freedoms (Petrič 2016, p. 173). Although the original function of constitutional adjudication was to protect the constitutions against unconstitutional laws, constitutional courts have now also become important elements of the system for protecting fundamental rights (Somody and Vissy 2012, p. 1). Reflecting this trend, the constitutional courts in CEE have, from the very beginning of their activities, formulated a broad official constitutional doctrine on various issues concerning the protection of human rights and freedoms; this doctrine is also relevant in the context of protecting the rights of vulnerable groups in society (Pūraitė-Andrikienė 2022, pp. 55–77). Among these vulnerable groups, children stand out, being unable to select the social and physical environments into which they are born and raised, with their voices and interests frequently overlooked or not accorded the seriousness they deserve. This vulnerability places them at risk of enduring profound injustices due to their dependent status.

Nevertheless, there is little discussion about the way constitutional justice institutions have contributed to the legal situation of vulnerable groups in general and to the enhancement of children's rights and their protection in this region. There is a limited number of publications in the area; moreover, often they focus on the specific issues of a particular state and not on comparative research. The constitutional protection of children was analysed in the report of the European Commission for Democracy through Law (Venice Commission) (2014), however, this study mainly focused on the provisions of constitutions on this issue, but not on their implementation through constitutional jurisprudence. There are publications on the impact of the decisions of the constitutional courts of certain countries in the region on the protection of other vulnerable groups (Pūraitė-Andrikienė 2022; Pūraitė-Andrikienė 2023a), but they do not analyse the decisions in the field of protection of children's rights. Some publications are dedicated to the role of these institutions in the protection of children in a particular state of the region (Toader and Safta 2013).

Nonetheless, societies of the region continue to evolve dynamically and new threats to children's well-being emerge. We have recently experienced the life-changing epidemiological crisis of COVID-19 and the consequences of Russian aggression against Ukraine, which threaten the social solidarity and human rights protection that has been growing in Europe for more than six decades. In light of these threats, the question arises as to whether the constitutions of the region provide sufficient protection for children. These tendencies as well as the particular vulnerability of children also require a more comprehensive comparative analysis of the role of constitutional justice institutions in enhancing the protection of children. Thus, this chapter aims to shed more light on the constitutional protection of children in CEE countries.[1] To achieve this, the following tasks will be addressed: (1) to provide a comparative analysis of the constitutional framework for the protection of children's rights; (2) to discuss the role of constitutional courts in the protection of human rights; (3) to identify the constitutional cases which most contributed to enhancing the protection of children, as well as to distinguish common trends in the constitutional jurisprudence in the area discussed. It should also be noted that this chapter discusses the provisions of the region's constitutions and analyses the decisions of the constitutional courts in the context of the general principles of the CRC.

2 Comparative Analysis of the Constitutional Framework for the Protection of Children's Rights in the States of CEE

At the international level, the CRC remains the foundational standard for recognizing children as autonomous rights holders and protecting their rights. Nonetheless, the UN Committee on the Rights of the Child (the Committee) has explicitly emphasized the significance of enshrining children's rights in constitutions (UN Committee on the Rights of the Child 1998). Where states do include child-specific provisions in their national constitutions, the Committee has emphasised the importance of a rights-based approach and the general principles of the CRC. The Committee welcomes the inclusion of sections on the rights of the child in national constitutions, reflecting key principles in the CRC, which helps to underline the key message of

[1] This chapter focuses only on the constitutional provisions and decisions of the constitutional courts of those CEE states that are EU Member States.

the CRC—that children alongside adults are holders of human rights (European Commission for Democracy through Law 2014). Of course, constitutionalising children's rights does not automatically ensure respect for the rights of children. However, we should agree with the Committee that it is an important step 'towards the full implementation' of the rights in the CRC (Committee on the Rights of the Child 1998).

The adoption of the CRC coincided almost exactly with the beginning of the so-called fourth phase of constitutional development in the 1990s. This period is characterised by the collapse of the totalitarian regimes in CEE. In December 1991, the Soviet Empire ceased to exist, and in 1991–1992 Europe saw the fall of Yugoslavia. As a result, in 1992–1997, new constitutions were adopted or substantially amended in Lithuania, Estonia, Latvia, Poland, the Czech Republic, Slovakia, Hungary, Bulgaria, Romania, Croatia, and Slovenia. The new or substantially updated constitutions in the region were based on the experience of the development of democratic constitutionalism and, in those countries where there was already a tradition of constitutional regulation, on the national legal heritage. Most of the region's constitutions emphasise political, economic, social, and cultural rights and freedoms and are grounded on the universal rights and freedoms enshrined in international law.

None of the countries of the region has a separate chapter on the protection of children's rights in their constitution. At the same time, there are no countries in the region whose constitutions do not contain any provisions on children's rights, and some include articles specifically dedicated to the rights of children (e.g. Article 56 "The Rights of Children" of the Slovenian Constitution and Article 49 "Protection of children and young people" of the Romanian Constitution). However, in many states, constitutional provisions mainly focus on the family and only broadly refer to the protection of children, without specifying the details of what that protection includes. The most common formulation in this category is a subsection of a general provision on the family that guarantees special state protection to parents and children; this approach can be seen in Bulgaria, the Czech Republic, Estonia, and Lithuania (European Commission for Democracy through Law 2014). For example, Article 38(2) of the Lithuanian Constitution states that family, motherhood, fatherhood, and childhood shall be under the protection and care of the State. Some constitutions mention children's rights but fall short of explicitly enshrining them. In these instances, the constitution mandates that the law must ensure care and protection for children. This approach is exemplified by the Lithuanian Constitution which states that under-age children shall be protected by law (Art. 39 (3)).

The Committee has identified four general principles among the CRC provisions: non-discrimination (Art. 2); the best interests of the child must be a primary consideration in all actions concerning the child (Art. 3); the right of the child to life, survival and development (Art. 6) and the right of the child to be heard in all decisions that affect him/her (Art. 12) (Committee on the Rights of the Child 1991). Although the constitutional frameworks of the states in the region can be analysed from various perspectives concerning the protection of the rights of the child, the present chapter will further analyse to what extent the above-mentioned general principles are reflected in the constitutions of these states.

Probably the most frequently found provisions in the region's constitutions relate to the principle set out in Article 6 of the CRC—the child's right to survival and development. This principle, to a greater or lesser extent, features prominently in all constitutions of the region, although the importance of ensuring the adequate development of children takes many forms. Some constitutions assert that children are entitled to the maximum possible development of their personality and potential. Others emphasise development by requiring the state to safeguard children from particular threats to their growth, such as economic exploitation. Additionally, many legal systems highlight the crucial role of education in children's development.

The most widespread constitutional provision related to this principle is the right to education, which is contained in all the constitutions of the discussed region. The presence of a constitutional right to education has significant potential to advance the indivisible rights of children, and particularly their right to development since education is a pre-requisite to the enjoyment of other rights—most obviously, the child's right to development (European Commission for Democracy through Law 2014).

Almost all constitutions in the region stipulate that education shall be compulsory for persons under a certain age: until the age of 16 (Art. 53(2) of the Bulgarian Constitution) or 18 (Art.70 (1) of the Polish Constitution) or, without specifying a specific age, but by enshrining the provision that the right to education is provided by the compulsory general education (Art. 32 (1) of the Romanian Constitution). Provisions on free primary and/or secondary education are also common (Art.112 of the Latvian Constitution, Art. 37 of the Estonian Constitution, Art. 33 (2) of the Czech Charter of Fundamental Rights, Art. 11 (2) of the Hungarian Constitution, Art. 53 (3) of the Bulgarian Constitution) or similar provisions stating that State education shall be free (Art. 32 (4) of Romanian Constitution). Some constitutions in the region combine these two provisions, e.g. the Slovenian Constitution states that primary education is compulsory and shall be financed from public funds (Art. 57(2)). The Croatian Constitution states that compulsory education shall be free (Art. 66 (2)).

Another child-specific right related to the principle of a child's right to survival and development. explicitly recognised at the constitutional level, is the right to protection from harm. Hungarian Constitution states that every child shall have the right to the protection and care required for his or her proper physical, mental, and moral development (Art. 16 (1)). In Poland, the Constitution states that everyone shall have the right to demand that public authorities protect children against violence, cruelty, and exploitation (Art. 72 (1)). In some cases, this principle is also reflected by constitutional provisions on the protection of children from economic exploitation (Art. 49(3) of the Romanian Constitution; Art. 18 of the Hungarian Constitution, Art. 65(3) of the Polish Constitution).

Provisions can also be found in the region's constitutions relating to another important principle of the CRC: non-discrimination (Art. 2 of the CRC). This principle is set out in the constitutions of the region by the child-specific provision of the equal status of children irrespective of parentage. For example, the Slovak Constitution (Article 41(3)), Romanian Constitution (Article 48(3)), and Slovenian Constitution (Article 54(2)) all guarantee equal rights to children, regardless of whether they are born within or outside of wedlock.

Another provision in the constitutions of the countries of the region that, to some extent, guarantees the principle of non-discrimination is related to the protection of the rights of children with disabilities. The right of children with disabilities to special care is protected in some constitutions of the region, either in the form of a right (Slovenia) or in the form of an obligation of the state (e.g. Latvia, Romania). For instance, Article 52 (2) of the Slovenian constitution states that physically or mentally handicapped children and other severely disabled persons have the right to education and training for an active life in society. Article 110 of the Latvian Constitution states that the State shall provide special support to disabled children.

However, the principle set out in Article 12 of the CRC—the right to be heard, is not common in constitutions of the region. Only the Constitution of Poland makes a significant exception on this issue, stating that public authorities and persons responsible for children, in the course of establishing the rights of a child, shall consider and, insofar as possible, give priority to the views of the child (Art. 72 (3)). Similarly, that the principle set out in Article 3 of the CRC—requiring that the best interests of the child are a primary consideration in all matters affecting the child—is not directly set out in any constitution of the region. However, as we will see from section 4 of this chapter, this principle has been repeatedly revealed and safeguarded in the jurisprudence of the constitutional courts.

In summary, there is no uniform approach to expressing children's rights in the national constitutions of the discussed states. Each country must consider various factors when deciding which rights to enshrine constitutionally, how to articulate those rights and the state's corresponding duties, and how to ensure the enforcement of those rights. According to the Venice Commission, constitutions that express children's rights in a manner reflecting the indivisibility of rights, enshrining the general principles of the CRC, recognising the status of children as rights holders with an entitlement to have those rights vindicated against the state express the highest forms of compliance with international norms (European Commission for Democracy through Law 2014). As can be seen, some of the general principles of the CRC are quite prominent in the region's constitutions, while others are only episodic or do not appear *exspressis verbis* at all.

However, merely including a children's rights provision in a constitutional document does not guarantee a means of redress if those rights are not upheld. Therefore, a crucial measure of the constitutional protection of children's rights is the extent to which these rights can be enforced through judicial processes or alternative mechanisms like a children's ombudsman. Generally, the most obvious way in which constitutional rights can be enforced is through their protection in constitutional courts or other constitutional justice institutions.

3 The Role of Constitutional Courts in the Protection of Human Rights in CEE Region

Constitutional justice institutions in the CEE states were created or reinstated approximately 30 years ago, following the events of late 1989 that started a transition process towards democracy. All the countries in the region adopted a concentrated constitutional review model, conducted by a constitutional court composed of judges appointed by the highest state authorities for a time-limited tenure of office. As a rule, the constitutional courts of these countries carry out abstract *ex-post*[2] and final scrutiny over the constitutionality of laws (statutes) and other legal acts. However, in Estonia, the functions of a constitutional court are performed by the Constitutional Review Chamber, which is a structural part of the National Court (the equivalent of the Supreme Court). Apart from rare exceptions,[3] these states had no constitutional review tradition, and the introduction of constitutional control in the region marked the transition from the former governing principle of the unity of state powers. Although the effectiveness of constitutional justice institutions in these states varies, their contribution to the process of constitutional transition has been highly significant. It is precisely the constitutional justice institutions that have played an important role in ensuring respect for the rule of law, constitutionality and legality, and human rights and fundamental freedoms (Petrič 2016).[4]

Human rights protection system can be viewed from two perspectives: subjective and objective. Subjectively, the protection of human rights relates to the judicial or quasi-judicial process in a particular case, in other words, to the defence of human rights. Objectively, it also covers the further consequences of these procedures, which go beyond the case, as well as additional measures or activities aimed at protecting and promoting human rights, even in the absence of a specific violation of human rights, but rather with preventive objectives. Constitutional courts by examining requests from the highest state institutions on the conformity of legal acts with the constitution, remove legal acts that violate constitutional human rights

[2] Although the dominant model of constitutional review in this region is that of *ex-post* review, i.e., of legal acts that have already entered into force, there are also some exceptions. In Estonia and Poland, *ex-ante* constitutional review of parliamentary acts can be conducted upon the initiative of the President.

[3] Before the fall of communism in the CEE states, constitutional justice institutions had only been established in Yugoslavia and its separate republics after 1963 and in Poland in 1985, though their real powers were inevitably subject to restrictions by the Communist Party (Sadurski 2008, p. 1).

[4] Nevertheless, the activity of constitutional courts in CEE states is also marked by some challenges: the introduction of constitutional review lags behind in terms of time; is imbedded in an immature legal system; and is often involved in conflicts with other branches of state power, which seek to maintain their dominance during the transitional period. For example, constitutional justice institutions in Hungary and Poland used to be characterised as highly prominent and robust and played a path-breaking role in the democratic transformation of the Eastern and Central European region, serving as a model for other courts, but they have nevertheless experienced particularly drastic restrictions on their powers, and their activity has been otherwise inhibited (Pūraitė-Andrikiene 2023a).

from the legal system and formulate the official constitutional doctrine in the field of human rights, and in this way, it contributes to the strengthening of the protection of human rights from the objective aspect, and, by examining the requests from the courts, and natural and legal persons, on the conformity of legal acts with the Constitution, it examines them from both the objective and the subjective aspect, i.e. contributing both to the protection and defence of human rights (for more in this see Pūraitė-Andrikienė 2023b, p. 57).

In the context of all the powers exercised by the constitutional courts, the individual constitutional complaint procedure has a major direct effect on a person whose rights have allegedly been violated.[5] The institution of individual constitutional complaints has been established in most states of the region (except Bulgaria). However, recourse to the constitutional courts is less straightforward in the context of enforcing the constitutional rights of children, since children may often face barriers to accessing court proceedings. Minors are usually unable to use the individual constitutional complaint procedure themselves. A child's rights can usually be defended in constitutional courts on the initiative of his or her parents or other legal representatives. For example, Article 34 (2) of the Lithuanian Constitutional Court Law states that the interests of minors are represented before the Constitutional Court by their legal representatives (parents, adoptive parents, guardians, custodians) (The Law on The Constitutional Court 1993). Another possible way is the application of children's rights ombudsmen to the constitutional courts. However, not all states in CEE grant children's ombudsmen access to the constitutional courts.

As mentioned before, the constitutional courts protect human rights (including the rights of a child) not only with the help of individual constitutional complaints but also by implementing their other powers. By examining the requests of state institutions and bodies regarding the constitutionality of legal acts, constitutional justice institutions are enhancing the protection of human rights, legal acts violating constitutional human rights are being removed from the legal system, and the official constitutional doctrine in the field of human rights is being formed. Therefore, these institutions can contribute to the protection of the rights of a child in this, indirect, way.

As society changes, new issues arise that the constitutional courts must respond to, and the constitutional justice cases brought before the constitutional courts and the constitutional doctrine formulated in its acts reflect the challenges posed by the evolution of the state. The constitutional doctrine of human rights is, therefore, not static. It is constantly evolving with the state, responding to the challenges it faces, thus embodying the idea of a living constitution (Pūraitė-Andrikienė 2023b, p. 57).

The jurisprudence of the constitutional courts of the region on the protection of the rights of the child, discussed below, is a perfect example of this tendency.

---

[5] However, this procedure has a wider impact than just the protection of the applicant's rights. It includes consequences that go beyond the specific case, as decisions in individual constitutional complaint cases usually have an *erga omnes* effect, and, in resolving this type of case, official constitutional doctrine in the area of human rights is also formed.

4 Protection of the Rights of Children in the Jurisprudence of Constitutional Courts of CEE

It is often emphasised that the situation of the most vulnerable members of society effectively reflects the level of progress and democracy of the state. Therefore, this section of the chapter seeks to reveal how constitutional justice institutions in CEE have contributed to enhancing the protection of children. It discusses the most significant decisions adopted by these institutions that have changed the legal situation of children in the countries in question and seeks to distinguish common trends in the constitutional jurisprudence of these states.

It is, of course, only possible to speak in general terms about how the constitutional judiciary has contributed to the protection of children in three decades of existence and functioning. Therefore, only the most significant or the most recent jurisprudence of the constitutional justice institutions in the region will be presented in this section of the chapter. Constitutional jurisprudence on children's rights is grouped by topics representing the general principles of the CRC: non-discrimination (Art. 2); the best interests of the child must be a primary consideration in all actions concerning the child (Art. 3); the right of the child to life, survival and development (Art. 6); and the right of the child to be heard in all decisions that affect him/her (Art. 12). However, it should be noted that this classification is conditional, as some cases may be assigned to more than one category.

4.1 Constitutional Jurisprudence Related to the Principle of Non-Discrimination of Children and Their Parents

Article 2 of the CRC states, that States Parties shall respect and ensure the rights set forth in the present Convention to each child within their jurisdiction without discrimination of any kind, irrespective of the child's or his or her parent's or legal guardian's race, colour, sex, language, religion, political or other opinion, national, ethnic or social origin, property, disability, birth or other status. It is important to note that the provision of 'or other status' makes clear that this list is non-exhaustive (Lansdown 2022). The Committee elaborated on the provision 'or other status' to identify additional grounds for discrimination, including, for example, sexual orientation and transgender or intersex status (UN Committee on the Rights of the Child 2016). The CRC, uniquely, protects children from discrimination based not only on their personal traits and protected characteristics but also from discrimination based upon their parents' or guardians' association with a class of persons protected from discrimination (Lansdown 2022).

Over recent years, constitutional courts in CEE have addressed issues of discrimination concerning the rights of same-sex couples, particularly in relation to adoption, foster care and parental leave. These landmark decisions have not only contributed to the protection LGBTQI individuals, but also were important for the development of children's rights.

The first court to deal with this type of case was the Czech Constitutional Court (CCC). In 2016 this Court recognized the country's ban on gay people adopting children (though only for individuals) is unconstitutional (The Constitutional Court of Czech Republic 2016). The Czech Republic's Parliament introduced registered partnerships in 2006, passing a law that granted some limited rights to same-sex partners—including the right to inheritance and health care. However, registered partnerships were limited in the rights they grant compared to civil unions operated elsewhere, and the law also did not allow same-sex registered partnerships adopting children, either as a couple or as individuals (LGL 2016). In this decision, the CCC found that banning individuals in registered partnerships from adopting constituted discrimination, as this right was granted to single individuals regardless their sexual orientation. The CCC concluded that the regime was a violation of equality, human dignity, and the right to private life. However, the Court's ruling kept a ban on same-sex partners adopting children together—meaning that while individuals can adopt within partnerships, partners cannot gain joint parenting rights.

A few years later, the Croatian Constitutional Court (CrCC) decided on a similar case. In 2020, this Court published a ruling recognising equal rights of same-sex couples to be foster carers (The Constitutional Court of the Republic of Croatia 2020). In 2018, the Croatian Parliament passed a new foster care law, which excluded same-sex couples as possible foster parents. However, the CrCC clarified that the family status of the potential foster parent was not decisive, "but rather the willingness and ability of the foster parent and the person who lives with him/her to provide the beneficiary the fostered child … with all that is in his/her best interest". Explaining its decision, the President of CrCC stated that the Court found that the Foster Care Law "produced general discriminatory effects" on same-sex couples (BalkanInsights 2020). It is important to note that this decision of the CrCC was taken in the light of the principle of the best interests of children.

In the same year, the Latvian Constitutional Court (LCC) announced judgment on the right of a same-sex couple to parental leave (The Constitutional Court of the Republic of Latvia 2020). LCC had received an appeal from a mother whose female partner was unable to receive the ten-day leave which, according to the Labor Act, is to be granted to the child's father. The applicant argued that this was contrary to the best interests of the child since it did not allow the person to provide physical and emotional support to his or her partner and her child. According to the applicant, Article 110 of the Latvian Constitution was infringed, which stipulates that the legislator has an obligation to provide protection for all families. The Court acknowledged that the provision of the Labor Act, in so far as it did not provide protection and support for the mother's partner due to the birth of the child, did not comply with Section 110 of the Constitution. According to the Court judgment, this legal regulation was deemed null and void as of 2022. The exception was made for the family who started this constitutional case, and regarding them, it was deemed to be invalid from the time of the infringement of their fundamental rights. The Court stressed that, in the case of legal relations concerning a child, his or her interests and rights are a priority. As far as possible, the country should ensure that children grow up in a family environment that the best interests of a child are taken into account.

The latest decision of the region's constitutional courts in this area is the decision of the Slovenian Constitutional Court (SCC) adopted in 2022 (The Constitutional Court of the Republic of Slovenia 2022). The Court recognized that the ban on same-sex couples marrying and adopting children is unconstitutional and ordered the Parliament to amend the law within six months. SCC ruled that discrimination against same-sex couples "cannot be justified with the traditional meaning of marriage as a union between a man and a woman, nor with special protection of the family". After this decision, The Slovenian Parliament, at the end of 2022, passed an amendment allowing same-sex couples to marry and adopt and made it the first country in the region to do so (EuroNews 2022). In this decision the principle of the best interests of the child was mentioned several times in the court's argumentation.

4.2 *Constitutional Jurisprudence Related to the Principle of the Best Interests of the Child*

Article 3 (1) of the CRC states, that in all actions concerning children, whether undertaken by public or private social welfare institutions, courts of law, administrative authorities or legislative bodies, the best interests of the child shall be a primary consideration. Some authors state that the concept of the best interest of a child is based on the idea that the child has different rights and needs in relation to those of the parents, so his interest may be different from that of his parents or guardians. In these circumstances, the child's interests should prevail over other interests when taking action in his respect (Toader and Safta 2013).

Although this principle is not *exspressis verbis* enshrined in the constitutions of the region, it has been revealed in the constitutional jurisprudence of some constitutional courts of the region. For example, the academic literature highlights the role of the Romanian Constitutional Court (RCC) in protecting the principle of the best interests of the child (Toader and Safta 2013) The content of this principle has been elaborated in the jurisprudence of the RCC in the various cases concerning the protection of children (*inter alia* the child's right to establish filiation to the father, the right to a name, the legal status of the child in case of medically assisted human reproduction, the status of the married minor, State allowance for children) (for more on these cases see Toader and Safta 2013). As mentioned above, the region's constitutional courts have also relied on this principle in cases concerning the principle of non-discrimination against the child or his/her parents/guardians. The principle of non-discrimination underpins the determination of the best interests of the child (Lansdown 2022).

The most recent decisions focusing on the bests interests of the child were adopted by the Lithuanian Constitutional Court (LiCC).

In 2019, the Constitutional Court ruled that the provisions of the Law on Child Maintenance Benefits were unconstitutional. Specifically, the law required both the applicant and/or the child to have permanent residence in Lithuania in order to qualify for child maintenance benefits, and it also stipulated that these benefits would be terminated if the applicant or child moved abroad to establish permanent residence. The Court determined that a child's interests should not be compromised solely due to a change in their permanent residence, particularly if they move away from Lithuania. It is important to emphasize that in this ruling the constitutional imperative of the priority of the interests of a child was revealed for the first time. Then deciding on the constitutionality of legal regulation related to payment of child maintenance benefits, the LiCC held that the constitutional imperative of the priority of the interests of a child stems from the Constitution, among others, Article 38(2), which consolidates childhood as a particularly protected and fostered constitutional value, Article 39(3), according to which under-age children are protected by law and the state must, by means of a law, guarantee the sufficient and effective protection of the rights and legitimate interests of under-age children, as well as from the striving, entrenched in the Preamble to the Constitution, for an open, just, and harmonious civil society. This imperative implies the duty of the state to ensure that account is, first of all, taken of the interests of a child and no preconditions are created for violating these interests in the course of adopting laws and other legal acts, as well as in the course of applying them and deciding on other issues related to a child.

Another important case related to the principle of the best interests of the child was decided by this Court in 2024 (The Constitutional Court of the Republic of Lithuania 2024). By this ruling, the LiCC ruled unconstitutional the provision of the Civil Code, according to which people aged 65 or older (except for a close relative) could not be appointed a guardian of a child under ten years old. The petitioner submitted the individual constitutional complaint when she was refused to be appointed as a guardian of the minor daughter of her deceased niece. The LiCC noted that, when implementing its constitutional obligation to create an environment favourable to childhood, the state must pay special attention to the protection of the interests of those minor children whose relationships with their parents have ceased or have not arisen at all due to certain circumstances and where, therefore, state intervention is necessary in order to enable them to develop healthily and fully.

The Court also emphasised that the legislature must prioritise the child's best interests, and that laws should ensure decisions about guardianship are based on a full assessment of the individual's ability to care for, raise, and represent a child, especially when the child has no relationship with their parents or that relationship has ended. The abovementioned examples of constitutional jurisprudence show that constitutional courts in CEE when deciding cases concerning the rights of the child give priority to the interests of a child, and thus ensure that the child's interest must not only be one factor in deciding such cases, but a primary one.

4.3 *Constitutional Jurisprudence on the Right to Life and Development of a Child*

CRC states that States Parties recognize that every child has the inherent right to life (Art. 6(1)) and that States Parties shall ensure to the maximum extent possible the survival and development of the child (Art. 6(2)). In this area constitutional courts dealt with cases linked to abortion rights, the right to education and the right to information.

As regards the child's right to life, it is important to mention the recent controversial decision of the Polish Constitutional Tribunal (PCT), adopted in October 2020, that outlawed almost all forms of abortion. The PCT ruled that pregnancy terminations should be illegal even in cases where a fetus is diagnosed with a serious and irreversible birth defect (Constitutional Tribunal of the Republic of Poland 2020). According to the PCT, the constitutional principles of the protection of life and human dignity mean that 'human life is subject to legal protection, including at the prenatal stage, and the legal subjectivity of a child is inextricably linked with its dignity'. The PCT considered that a fetus is merely the medical/biological name for a child and, therefore, equated the meaning of the term fetus and the term child (Stambulski 2024). Such ruling allowed for further tightening of Poland's abortion laws, which were already among the strictest in Europe, and prompted the largest protests since the fall of communism.

It should be stressed that the PCT focused exclusively on the perspective of the fetus, devoting little space to the welfare of women, who were reduced to 'other persons.' The term 'woman' appears only five times in the judgment. In contrast, the words 'mother' and 'pregnant woman' appear a total of 42 times ('mother' 22 times, 'pregnant woman' 20 times) (Stambulski 2024). Moreover, the Tribunal stated that the legislator erroneously used the term 'fetus' and should replace it with the term 'child,' while with regard to women, it should use the term 'mother of the child' and not the 'pregnant woman', so as to emphasise 'the legal subjectivity of the child in the prenatal period of life.' It also stated that 'the protection of maternity cannot mean solely the protection of the interests of the pregnant woman and the mother' (Stambulski 2024).

Reacting to the situation, the European Parliament adopted a resolution affirming that the ruling to make abortion illegal in cases involving severe and irreversible fetal defects "puts women's health and lives at risk". Banning that option, would lead to an increase in "unsafe, clandestine and life-threatening abortions". The European Parliament underscored that in line with ECtHR case law, restrictive abortion laws violate women's human rights (European Parliament News 2020).

Other recent constitutional cases decided by the constitutional courts of CEE and related to the principle of development of a child concerned mostly the issues of the right to education. In 2021, the SCC decided on a case regarding the education of children during the COVID-19 pandemic (The Constitutional Court of the Republic of Slovenia 2020). The petitioners in this case were the parents of two children with special educational needs. They argued that the prohibition of in-person assembly in educational institutions, which offered only online education, violated their children's right to education and active participation in society. The parents claimed that their children were denied access to special assistance, individualized approach, physiotherapy, working therapy, therapies in the pool, logo pediatric and psychological treatment, which they as parents could not provide themselves.

Even though the contested acts were not anymore in force at the time of the procedure before the Court, the case was considered since children with special educational needs could be subjected to and affected by similar measures in the future.

The SCC noted that the small number of children with special needs and the professional expertise of scientists showed that the prohibition of reunion of these children in schools cannot substantially contribute to preventing the spread of the virus. In the opinion of the SCC, the government's arguments regarding the lack of human resources and restrictions on public transport during the pandemic could not justify the interference with the rights of children with special educational needs. The SCC also made a comparison with a governmental decision that kindergartens could stay open for those parents who otherwise could not work.

Another important case related to the right to education and COVID-19 restrictions was decided by the LCC in 2022 (The Constitutional Court of the Republic of Latvia 2022). However, this Court took a different approach. The case was initiated on the basis of an application filed by several school students of different ages (pupils of lower/upper secondary school). The applicants stated that at the end of the COVID-19 emergency situation across the entire territory of Latvia, they continued to study remotely. They challenged compliance of several COVID-19 related regulations with the Latvian Constitution and argued that the provisions in question restricted their possibilities and accessibility to education and violated Art. 112 of the Constitution. The Applicants stated that the quality of education had declined and their education was impeded in certain other ways.

The Court did not find any violation of the Constitution. Reviewing the provisions of Art. 112 (right to education) of the Constitution and assessing the conditions of the spread of COVID-19 and the role of the state during the pandemic, the Court emphasized that (1) the education system needed to be flexible enough to respond to the challenges of the COVID -19 pandemic; (2) the Cabinet of Ministers observed the granted powers by the legislator; (3) the Regulation determined the principles when distance learning could be introduced and the cases when face to face learning could be continued; it did not provide new educational methods or standards that changed the education system as a whole; (4) with regard to the quality of education, the Court stated that the possible deterioration of the quality for a certain period of education did not mean that the State did not take appropriate action to ensure the admissibility aspect of the right to education. The Court also did not find any significant violation of the legislative procedure while adopting the contested norms and concluded that the measures taken by the legislator to ensured the possibility, accessibility, acceptability, and adaptation of the right to education were appropriate.

Another recent decision on the right to inclusive education was made by the Czech Constitutional Court. In 2023, the CCC found that a child with disabilities had been unconstitutionally denied access to education and a fair trial due to the failure of the lower courts to adequately address the discrimination claims of a child with autism (The Constitutional Court of the Czech Republic 2023).

The case started in 2015, and concerned an obligation imposed on the child's mother to pay a teaching assistant's salary. The child could only go to school if his mother paid for the assistant. Despite reports confirming the school's misconduct, the courts dismissed the family's legal actions on multiple occasions. Even more, they ordered the mother to reimburse the school's legal costs which placed a heavy burden on her. The CCC has overruled the lower courts and accepted that the child's rights had been breached. The CCC found that the lower courts had wrongly imposed an obligation on the mother to pay excessive court fees. The decision set a significant precedent for promoting inclusion and equal opportunities within the Czech education system for children with disabilities, with the CCC explicitly acknowledging that each child is entitled to inclusive education (Validity 2023).

The most recent case related to the right to development of the child was decided by the Lithuanian Constitutional Court. At the end of 2024, the LiCC ruled that certain provisions of the Law on the Protection of Minors Against the Detrimental Effect of Public Information violated the Constitution (The Constitutional Court of the Republic of Lithuania 2024b). The contested provisions classified information about family models other than those based on marriage between a man and a woman as inconsistent with constitutional family values. Such information was restricted and could only be shared with minors in exceptional cases The LiCC found that these restrictions narrowed the constitutional concept of family, unreasonably limited freedom of information, and failed to provide minors with objective information reflecting real societal relationships. According to LiCC, this failure undermined the state's obligation to help minors form a worldview based on constitutional values, including respect for others' rights and dignity.

The LiCC concluded that restricting information about diverse family models and relationships obstructs children's development into well-rounded individuals. Such restrictions contradict the state's constitutional duty to ensure the child's comprehensive development, which must align with democratic values like equality, pluralism, and tolerance.

However, another court in the region adopted an opposite decision on similar issues. In 2021, the Hungarian Constitutional Court upheld the Parliament's decision to hold a referendum on four questions related to child protection and LGBTQ+ issues (The Constitutional Court of Hungary 2021). These questions addressed topics such as sexual orientation education for minors, promotion of sex reassignment therapy for children, exposure of children to sexually explicit media, and showing sex-change media content to minors. This decision has been considered controversial as part of the government's broader legislative agenda aimed at restricting LGBTQ+ rights under the guise of protecting children

4.4 Constitutional Jurisprudence on the Right of the Child to be Heard in All Decisions That Affect Him/Her

The CRC states that States Parties shall assure to the child who is capable of forming his or her own views the right to express those views freely in all matters affecting the child, the views of the child being given due weight in accordance with the age and maturity of the child (Art. 12(1)). For this purpose, the child shall should be provided the opportunity to be heard in any judicial and administrative proceedings affecting the child, either directly, or through a representative or an appropriate body, in a manner consistent with the procedural rules of national law (Article 12(2)).

It should be noted that the jurisprudence of the constitutional courts of the region on the right of the child to be heard is not extensive, as this right is already well established in the countries of the region. However, one important decision of the CCC can be mentioned (The Constitutional Court of Czech Republic 2009). In 2009, the CCC adopted a decision that completely granted the constitutional complaint, since the ordinary court, by not hearing the petitioner-son, violated his fundamental right to judicial protection under Art. 36(1) of the Charter of Fundamental Rights, in connection with Art. 12 (2) of the CRC.

The Court stated that it is essential to have the fundamental right to be heard before a court whenever a decision is made regarding the limitation of personal freedom. This right must apply at all times during such decision-making. In principle, considered the Court, there is no reason for a child not to have the fundamental right to be heard directly before a court when a decision on restricting their personal freedom is being taken whilst an adult has such a right in the same circumstances. A relevant reason for denying the right of a child to be heard only occurs when the child is not capable, with respect to the level of their development, of forming an opinion and evaluating the bearing of the measures relating to them. The Court considered that a person mentally matures between 11 and 12 years old, and peak performance is seen when they reach 16. Therefore, in the case of decision-making on imposing institutional upbringing on a child older than 12 years of age, there is, in principle, no reason for denying the right of a child to be heard directly by a court. Thus, alternatives provided by law were always to be considered as exceptions which must be properly substantiated by the court in its decision. In the case under consideration, the ordinary court was thus obliged to allow the petitioner-son, with respect to his intellectual development, to exercise his right to be heard directly before the court, and should not have settled for merely a statement that the petitioner-son's opinion was known to the court, which is what actually took place.

5 Concluding Remarks

All the constitutions of CEE states include at least some provisions on the rights of a child. Some of the general principles of the CRC are quite prominent in the constitutions of CEE, while others are only episodic or do not appear in the constitutions *exspressis verbis* at all. However, including children's rights in a constitution is not enough; what matters is how constitutional courts interpret and enforce these rights, as well as their recognition in national laws. Constitutional courts in CEE by deciding different cases related to the rights of a child elaborated on the general principles of CRC even though they were not *expressis verbis* enshrined in the national constitutions.

Although some separate decisions reflect the opposite trend, in general, the constitutional jurisprudence of CEE states demonstrates a broader commitment of these courts to uphold and enhance the rights of children, aligning with international standards set by treaties like the CRC. Constitutional courts in CEE, when deciding cases concerning the rights of the child, give priority to the interests of a child. Recent cases heard by the region's constitutional courts have also shown that these courts have had the difficult task of interpreting and protecting the constitutional rights of the child in the context of changing social circumstances and contemporary challenges, such as changing the concept of the family or COVID-19 restrictions.

However, the protection of children's rights in constitutional courts remains limited, as it often emerges in the context of disputes centred on the rights of other persons. As a result, safeguarding children's interests is frequently not the primary focus of these cases. Nevertheless, as society increasingly recognises children as individuals with distinct personalities, the future will likely see a rise in cases addressing children's digital rights, the right to a healthy environment, and other emerging human rights relevant to the new generation.

Legal Acts

United Nations. (1989). *Convention on the Rights of the Child*. Retrieved from https://www.ohchr.org/en/instruments-mechanisms/instruments/convention-rights-child.

The Constitution of the Republic of Bulgaria 1991 CONSTITUTION OF THE REPUBLIC OF BULGARIA - National Assembly of the Republic of Bulgaria (parliament.bg)

The Constitution of the Republic of Croatia 1990 Croatia 1991 (rev. 2013) Constitution - Constitute (constituteproject.org)

The Constitution of the Czech Republic 1992 Constitution of the Czech Republic (psp.cz)

The Constitution of the Republic of Lithuania, Official Gazette Valstybės žinios, 1992, No. 33-1014;

The Constitution of the Republic of Latvia 1922 (reinstated in 1991). https://www.satv.tiesa.gov.lv/en/2016/02/04/the-constitution-of-the-republic-of-latvia/

The Constitution of the Republic of Estonia 1992. https://www.riigiteataja.ee/en/eli/ee/530102013003/consolide

The Constitution of the Republic of Poland 1997. http://www.sejm.gov.pl/prawo/konst/angielski/kon1.htm>

The Constitution of the Republic of Romania 1991The Constitution of Romania (presidency.ro)
The Constitution of the Slovak Republic 1992 CONSTITUTION (prezident.sk)
The Constitution of the Republic of Slovenia 1991 venice.coe.int/webforms/documents/?pdf=CDL(2000)059-e
The Fundamental Law of Hungary 2011 The Fundamental Law of Hungary (parlament.hu)
The Law on The Constitutional Court of the Republic of Lithuania 1993 The Law on the Constitutional Court - Constitutional Court of The Republic of Lithuania (lrkt.lt)

Jurisprudence of Constitutional Courts of CEE

The Constitutional Court of the Republic of Croatia (2020). Decision of 7 February 2020, case No. U-II-7019/2021
The Constitutional Court of Czech Republic (2009). Decision of 2 April 2009, case No. II. ÚS 1945/08:
The Constitutional Court of Czech Republic (2016). Decision of 28 June 2016, case No. Pl. ÚS 7/15.
The Constitutional Court of the Czech Republic (2023). Decision of 4 December 2023, case No. Pl. ÚS 39/22.
The Constitutional Court of Hungary (2021). Decision of 7 December 2021, case No. IV/03330/2021.
Th The Constitutional Court of the Republic of Latvia (2020). Judgement of 12 November 2020, case No. 2019-33-01.
The Constitutional Court of the Republic of Latvia (2022). The decision of 26 May 2022, case No. 2021-33-0103
The Constitutional Court of the Republic of Lithuania. Ruling of 8 November 2019. Register of Legal Acts 2019, No. 17963
The Constitutional Court of the Republic of Lithuania(2024). Ruling of 20 May 2024, case No. 10-A/2023.
The Constitutional Court of the Republic of Lithuania (2024 b). Ruling of 18 December 2024, case No. 3/2024.
The Constitutional Tribunal of the Republic of Poland. Ruling of 22 October 2020, ref. (K 1/20).
The Constitutional Court of the Republic of Slovenia (2020). Decision of 21 December 2020, case No. U-I-473/20-14
The Constitutional Court of the Republic of Slovenia (2022). Decision of 9 July 2022, case No. U-I-486/20.

References

Books and Articles

Lansdown G (2022) Article 2: the right to non-discrimination. In: Vaghri Z, Zermatten J, Lansdown G, Ruggiero R (eds) Monitoring State Compliance with the UN Convention on the Rights of the Child. Children's Well-Being: Indicators and Research, vol 25. Springer, Cham

Pūraitė-Andrikienė D (2022) the role of constitutional justice institutions in the protection of Vulnerable Groups. In: Limantė A, Pūraitė-Andrikienė D (eds) Legal Protection of Vulnerable Groups in Lithuania, Latvia, Estonia and Poland. Springer, Cham, pp 55–77

Pūraitė-Andrikienė D (2023a) The Istanbul Convention in the constitutional jurisprudence of Central and Eastern European states. In: Limantė A, Tereškinas A, Vaičiūnienė R (eds) Gender-based violence and the law global perspectives and Eastern European practices. Routledge, London

Pūraitė-Andrikienė, D. (2023b) Protection and defence of human rights in the Constitutional Court of the Republic of Lithuania. Law Institute of the Lithuanian Centre for Social Sciences. Microsoft Word - Zmogaus teisiu apsauga-maketas.docx (teise.org)

Sadurski W (2008) Rights before courts. A study of constitutional courts in Postcommunist States of Central and Eastern Europe. Springer, Nederlands

Sólyom L (2003) The role of constitutional courts in the transition to democracy: with special reference to Hungary. Int Sociol 18

Somody B, Vissy B (2012) Citizen's Role in constitutional adjudication in Hungary: From the *actio popularis* to the constitutional complaint. Acta Juridica Hungarica 53(4)

Stambulski M (2024) Populist jurisprudence? Examining selected case law of the Polish Constitutional Court After 2016. Hague J Rule Law

Toader T, Safta M (2013) Best Interests of the Child Achieved Through Constitutional Case-Law. Available at SSRN: https://ssrn.com/abstract=2340922 or https://doi.org/10.2139/ssrn.2340922

Other Sources

BalkanInsight (2020) Croatia's Top Court Rules Same-sex Couples Can Foster. https://balkaninsight.com/2020/02/07/croatias-top-court-rules-same-sex-couples-can-foster/

EuroNews (2022) Slovenia's top court strikes out bans on same-sex couples marrying and adopting children. https://www.euronews.com/2022/07/09/slovenias-top-court-strikes-out-bans-on-same-sex-couples-marrying-and-adopting-children

European Commission for Democracy Through Law (2014) Report on the Protection of Children's Rights: International Standards and Domestic Constitutions, Venice, default.aspx (coe.int)

European Parliament News (2020) Polish de facto ban on abortion puts women's lives at risk, says Parliament. https://www.europarl.europa.eu/news/en/press-room/20201120IPR92132/polish-de-facto-ban-on-abortion-puts-women-s-lives-at-risk-says-parliament

LGL (2016) Czech court strikes down ban on gay people adopting children. Czech court strikes down ban on gay people adopting children - LGL

Petrič E (2016) The Role of Constitutional Courts in the Implementation of the Rule of Law in States in Transition, the report delivered at the international conference dedicated to the 25th anniversary of the Constitutional Court of the Republic of Slovenia, http://www.us-rs.si/media/zbornik.25.let.pdf

UN Committee on the Rights of the Child (1991) Treaty-specific guidelines regarding the form and content of periodic reports to be submitted by States parties under article 44, paragraph 1 (b), of the Convention on the Rights of the Child (30th October 1991) UN Doc. CRC/C/5

UN Committee on the Rights of the Child. Concluding Observations of the (1998): Ireland CRC/C/15/Add. 85 February 4, 1998
UN Committee on the Rights of the Child (2016) General comment no. 20 (2016) on the implementation of the rights of the child during adolescence, CRC/C/GC/20
Validity (2023) Czech Constitutional Court Rules in Landmark Decision on Inclusive Education and Access to Justice. https://validity.ngo/2023/12/08/czech-constitutional-court-rules-in-landmark-decision-on-inclusive-education-and-access-to-justice/

Dovilė Pūraitė-Andrikienė is a senior researcher at the Law Institute of the Lithuanian Centre for Social Sciences. Dr Pūraitė-Andrikienė is an expert on Lithuanian and comparative constitutional law, constitutional justice institutions, human rights, and legal protection of vulnerable groups. Dr Pūraitė-Andrikienė has published over 35 papers (articles, studies, monographs, parts of monographs). Her most recent publications include “Legal Protection of Vulnerable Groups in Lithuania, Latvia, Estonia, and Poland” (Springer, 2022, co-editor and co-author); “The Istanbul Convention in the constitutional jurisprudence of Central and Eastern European States”, in Limantė, A., Tereškinas, A., Vaičiūnienė, R. (eds.), Gender-Based Violence and the Law Global Perspectives and Eastern European Practices (Routledge, 2023); “The Lithuanian Constitutional Court: The Gradual Emergence of a Strong Guardian”, In Kálmán Pócza (ed.), Constitutional Review in Central and Eastern Europe (Routledge, 2024). She has also experience working on international projects in the area of human rights and conducting comparative research.

Dr Pūraitė-Andrikienė is also an associate professor at the Faculty of Law of Vilnius University, where she teaches constitutional law and European Union law, she is also a member of the Young Academy of Lithuanian Academy of Sciences. https://orcid.org/0000-0001-6964-1568,

Children in Family Law Cases: Comparative Study of Custody and Contact Arrangements in Slovenia and Lithuania

Neža Pogorelčnik Vogrinc and Agnė Limantė

Abstract Focusing on child custody and contact arrangements, this chapter explores the legal aspects related to children in family law cases in Slovenia and Lithuania. It compares the approaches of the two countries, which, on the one hand, are similar in a number of factors (e.g. population size, time of independence), but on the other hand are located in different parts of Europe, which brings with it different history, culture, traditions, as well as (family) legal rules. The chapter examines the national legislation of the countries concerned and the case law of their courts. The authors claim that physical custody, which determines the child's primary residence, and contact arrangements, which regulate the interaction between the child and the non-resident parent, are intricately connected as they jointly shape the child's experience of parental care after separation. Moreover, child contact arrangements can be structured to closely resemble shared physical custody in countries where this possibility is not foreseen in law.

1 Introduction

In family law, few issues are as delicate and complex as those involving children. In the case of parents living separately, the intersection of parental rights and duties, custody, contact arrangements, and financial support of the child presents both legal challenges and profound emotional stakes. The legal system is tasked with

N. Pogorelčnik Vogrinc (✉)
Faculty of Law, University of Ljubljana, Ljubljana, Slovenia
e-mail: neza.pogorelcnik@pf.uni.lj.si

A. Limantė
Law Institute of the Lithuanian Centre for Social Sciences, Vilnius, Lithuania
e-mail: agne.limante@teise.org

A. Limantė, R. Vaičiūnienė (eds.), *Children's Rights in Central and Eastern Europe*, European Union and its Neighbours in a Globalized World 29,
https://doi.org/10.1007/978-3-032-07092-0_3

balancing several interests: first and foremost, the welfare and needs of children, then the rights and duties of parents, and, finally, the broader societal interest in preserving family relationships. At the heart of these family cases lies a fundamental question: how can law and, in case of a dispute, judges applying the law best ensure the protection and promotion of a child's welfare, while respecting the autonomy and responsibilities of parents?

Court cases on parental responsibilities[1] are often complex. Custody arrangements necessitates judge's careful consideration of the child's best interests and, in the case of shared custody, finding the model that would work for both parents. Contact arrangements, or how much time the child spends with each parent, are equally complex, often requiring a balance between maintaining a stable environment for the child and ensuring that the child maintains strong relationships with both parents. Child maintenance adds another layer of complexity as it is not simply a matter of calculating payments, but of ensuring that the child's needs are met fairly and consistently, while also considering the financial capacities of both parents.

This chapter will focus on two aspects of family law following divorce and separation: children's living arrangements (child physical custody), and child contact with both parents. The chapter will compare the legal regime and relevant case law in this area in Slovenia and Lithuania—two small European countries with different languages, histories, traditions, and legal systems. The divorce rates between these two countries reveal that Lithuanians tend to divorce more (49.3 divorces per 100 marriages) than Slovenians (34 divorces per 100 marriages) (*Divorce Rates in European Countries 2020*). However, even more differs the statistics on single-parent households in these two countries. In 2023, single parents accounted for 12.4% of households with children in the EU as a whole. Among households with children in the EU, the highest proportions of single parents were recorded in Lithuania, Estonia, and Latvia (all above 25%). By contrast, Slovenia, Slovakia, Greece, and Croatia had the lowest shares, all below 5% (*Household Composition Statistics*).

First, the authors will explore how child custody is determined in both countries and what are the current trends in judicial practices. Second, the child's right to maintain regular and meaningful contact with both parents, even when living apart, and the mechanisms used to facilitate this, will be analysed. The authors view child custody and contact arrangements as closely related, as both concern child-parent relation after parental separation and are typically decided together, shaping the post-divorce parent-child relationship.

[1] The Commission on European Family Law (CEFL) define 'parental responsibilities' as 'a collection of rights and duties aimed at promoting and safeguarding the welfare of the child. They encompass in particular: (a) care, protection and education; (b) maintenance of personal relationships; (c) determination of residence; (d) administration of property, and (e) legal representation." (Boele-Woelki, 2007, p. 281) For an earlier definition see Council of Europe Committee of Ministers Recommendation No R (84) 4, 1984. For a detailed definition of what falls under the concept of parental responsibility in 23 different countries, see Boele-Woelki 2005, pp. 1–17.

2 Child (Physical) Custody

As an increasing number of children worldwide are seeing their parents' relationships dissolve, the living arrangements of these children, referred to in this chapter as physical custody,[2] become an important issue to be addressed. While until the IX century children were generally considered the property of their fathers (e.g. in England (Kruhar-Winter 2018, p. 15.), Austria, Belgium, France, Germany (Boele-Woelki 2005, p. 77–86)) and thus always assigned to them in the (rare) case of parental separation, this has gradually changed with industrialisation in the ninth century. Fathers went to work, and mothers stayed at home, slowly leading to the development of the tender years doctrine, according to which it was considered more appropriate for young children to live with their mothers (Kruhar-Winter 2018, p. 15). Only in XXI century, awareness of the role of both parents began to grow, ultimately leading to the development of the institution of joint custody.

Nowadays, when resolving the issue of custody, the national law of each country plays the primary role. EU law cannot be of any help as it does not contain provisions addressing the substantive content of the right to parental care and child custody. Instead, its legal instruments focus on cross-border matters, such as the recognition and enforcement of judgments between Member States.[3] Despite that, in the field of parental responsibilities, the differences among the European systems are considerably less strong than in other fields of family law (Boele-Woelki 2021, p. 54), which can also be noted with regard to child custody.

When determining physical child custody, courts are largely guided by the best interests of the child, which is a principle enshrined in national laws and international conventions, such as the UN Convention on the Rights of the Child (UN 1989), the European Convention on Human Rights (Council of Europe 1950) and the EU Charter of Fundamental Rights (EU, 2000). However, as noted in the doctrine, the principle's broad formulation leads to a demand for more specific meaning in court practice (Forslund et al. 2022, p. 4). Although specific laws and procedures in family law vary between Western tradition's countries, some common factors that courts typically consider when deciding on custody include parental capability to provide for the emotional and physical well-being of the child (parental fitness); stability and continuity; the parent-child relationship (child attachment and emotional ties with parents[4]); and the child's wishes. These factors, as discussed below, are also evident in the practice of Slovenian and Lithuanian courts.

[2] Child custody refers to the legal relationship between the parents and their child. This concept encompasses various aspects, including the right to make significant decisions about the child's life, such as education, healthcare (legal custody) and the right to have the child live with the parent (physical custody). This subchapter focuses on the latter, and the legal custody is not discussed in more detail.

[3] (Council Regulation (EU) 2019/1111 of 25 June 2019 on Jurisdiction, the Recognition and Enforcement of Decisions in Matrimonial Matters and the Matters of Parental Responsibility, and on International Child Abduction (Recast) 2019).

[4] For a psychological perspective, see Forslund et al. (2022).

In recent decades, in Slovenia and Lithuania, as well as Europe-wide, a certain trend can be noted in the approach towards child custody models. In particular, joint child custody has become increasingly common in EU Member States,[5] promoting shared parental responsibilities after separation or divorce and ensuring the child has access to both parents' social, emotional, and not just financial resources.[6] Joint physical custody is commonly defined as a parental care arrangement in which a child lives with each parent for at least 25–50% of the time after separation or divorce (Steinbach 2019, p. 353; Smyth 2017, p. 494). This phenomenon has been studied from various (legal, sociological, psychological) perspectives.[7] In general, it is based on the understanding that when assessing the best interests of the child, the principle is that it is in the child's best interests to have care and upbringing as if the parents' living community were still in place, and therefore joint care and upbringing should be the basic, primary solution (Jager 2023, p. 29).

2.1 General Principles of Awarding Physical Child Custody to a Parent in the Researched Countries

Deciding who will care for a child after parental separation is one of the most sensitive issues in family law. Both Slovenia and Lithuania place great emphasis on cooperative decision-making between parents, but they also provide legal safeguards to ensure that, when agreement is out of reach, the child's best interests remain protected.

In Slovenia, the Family Code (SLFC)[8] in Article 138 provides for the option for parents to agree that (1) (in the first place) both parents will share custody of their children, that (2) all the children will be in the custody of one of them, or that (3) some children will be in the custody of one while the others in the custody of the other parent. If the parents cannot reach an agreement, the matter is resolved by

[5] In 2021, in Europe, 12.5% of children in separated families lived in equal joint physical custody arrangements, 8.2% lived in unequal joint custody arrangements, and 79.3% lived in the more traditional sole physical custody arrangement (Hakovirta et al. 2023, p. 481).

[6] The emergence of joined physical custody can be attributed to the growing aspirations for gender equality among parents. Mothers are increasingly active in the labor market, pursuing demanding professional careers, and seeking an equal distribution of household responsibilities. Simultaneously, fathers are expressing a stronger desire to engage in childcare. The adoption of more gender-neutral family policies, including longer parental and paternal leave, has been instrumental in promoting active fatherhood and driving this change. See further (Bernardi and Mortelmans 2021a), p. 2. The researches also show that the practice of joint physical custody also has a lower risk of stress and feelings of time pressure compared to residential mothers with non-joint physical custody (Augustijn 2023, p. 2374).

[7] See, for instance, research papers in Bernardi and Mortelmans (2021b).

[8] Slovenian Family Code (SLFC), Official Gazette RS, no. 15/17 with subsequent amendments.

court, which can decide based on the same custody options.[9] In Lithuania, similarly, all matters relating to the upbringing of children are decided by both parents by mutual agreement, but if the parents do not agree, the matter is decided by the court (Article 3.169(2) of the Civil Code of Lithuania (LTCC)[10]). Mutual agreement between parents regarding the residence of their child is always encouraged (Article 3.53(3) LTCC), as judicial resolution of such disputes is seen as going against the child's interests and can be liable to cause emotional distress (Kudinavičiūtė-Michailovienė and Uusen-Nacke 2022, p. 84). The Supreme Court of Lithuania has also emphasized that for a decision regarding with whom the child should live to be successfully implemented, it is best when all interested parties, especially the child, agree with it.[11] To achieve this, the parties may seek assistance from intermediaries, mediators, psychologists, and others, as only a solution found through mutual agreement will be implemented in good faith and will best serve the child's interests.[12]

In both countries, the child is heard in custody cases and support of social services is foreseen. The legislation of Lithuania obliges the court hearing cases concerning a child to include the child protection authority as an opinion-giving body (Article 3.80 CC). In addition to a representative of the child's rights protection authority, a teacher and/or a psychologist may be invited to hear the views and wishes of the child at the hearing. During the hearing of the child's views and wishes, at the discretion of the court, any person(s) involved in the proceedings may be excluded from the courtroom, and upon his/her return to the courtroom, the child's expressed wishes shall be announced.

In Slovenia, the court is not obliged to appoint an expert (e.g. psychologist) in proceedings concerning children, but it usually uses such evidence to help it decide what is in the best interests of the child. In deciding on custody and upbringing (as well as maintenance of a child, contacts, exercise of parental responsibility and attribution of parental responsibility to a relative), a court shall also take into account the child's opinion if it has been expressed by the child or by a person the child trusts and was chosen by the child, provided that the child is capable of understanding its meaning and consequences (Article 143/I of SLFC). The child can express his or her opinion at the social work centre or in an interview with the child's advocate, or, with regard to the age and other circumstances, in an informal interview with a judge, which can also take place in cooperation with professionally qualified persons, but always in the absence of parents (Article 96/II of Non-Contentious

[9] A court settlement or decision on joint custody shall also define the child's permanent residence, which of the parents shall be delivered mail addressed to the child, and maintenance of the child (Article 139 of the SLFC).

[10] Civil Code of the Republic of Lithuania, *Official Gazette,* 2000, No. 74 with subsequent amendments.

[11] LT Supreme Court, ruling of 1 June 2018, No. 3K-3-241-687/2018.

[12] LT Supreme Court, ruling of 3 February 2016, No. 3K-3-16-706/2016; LT Supreme Court, ruling of 3 August 2023, No. e3K-3-256-781/2023.

Civil Procedure Act[13] (NCCPA)). Additionally, in such proceedings, the court shall also consider the opinion of a social work centre (Article 143/II of SLFC). The public shall be excluded from all proceedings regulating family relations (Article 43 of NCCPA). For the best interests of the child, the court may also decide not to allow the child's parents to view the record or to listen to the audio record or watch the audio-video record of the interview of a child conducted at the social work centre or with the judge, if recorded (Article 96/IV of NCCPA). This is to protect the child from pressure from the parent(s) about the content of the statement the child would make.

When determining physical child custody, courts in Slovenia and Lithuania consider various factors to ensure that the child's best interests are prioritised. As discussed in the next section, the primary form of physical custody in Slovenia is joint custody. However, in situations when the joint custody is not in the best interests of a child, custody is awarded to the parent with better parental capacity. The principles of promoting the child's development (i.e. with which parent the child will have the most support in building his or her personality) and of continuity of care and upbringing (i.e. with which parent the child will have a better chance of maintaining his or her existing relationships with the outside world) must be taken into account.[14] This should always be done in the best interests of the individual child, rather than on general factors such as the child's gender or age (e.g., assuming that a preschool-aged girl is better off with her mother) (Novak 2022, p. 244). The court must not base custody decisions on the personal characteristics of the parents, such as their religion, race, nationality, disability, etc., however, the child's will, if declared, is an important[15] (but not decisive) circumstance (Novak 2022, pp. 246–247).[16]

Lithuanian law does not set out specific criteria for deciding the child's residence. One could assert that the best interests of the child are perhaps the only unquestionable criterion to be considered in resolving disputes concerning the child (Kudinavičiūtė-Michailovienė and Uusen-Nacke 2022, p. 82). Guidance on how to apply this overarching criterion was given by the Supreme Court of Lithuania. In particular, the Senate of the Supreme Court[17] explained that, when resolving disputes between separated parents regarding the determination of a child's place of

[13] Slovenian Non-Contentious Civil Procedure Act, Official Gazette RS, no. 16/19.

[14] Novak et al. (2019), p. 421. For more on both principles see Novak (2022), pp. 242–243.

[15] It is important to check first whether the child is able to understand the meaning of the procedure and the consequences of the decision, because only then can his or her opinion be taken into account. Končina Peternel (2019), pp. 100–101.

[16] In the Ljubljana Higher Court, ruling of 8 December 2021, No. IV Cp 1907/2021, the 15-year-old child expressed a strong wish to live with his father and to have no contact with his mother, but the court concluded that it could not take such a wish into account, as it was very likely to have been expressed under the influence of the child's father. The child's expressed wishes cannot, therefore, always be equated with the child's best interests, although the child's expressed opinion always carries significant weight and thus probative value.

[17] Resolution No. 35 of the Senate of the Lithuanian Supreme Court on the overview of case law concerning the determination of residence for minors whose parents live separately, approved on 21 June 2002. Teismų praktika, Issue No. 17, 2002.

residence, courts must establish the following legally significant facts: (i) each parent's ability and efforts to ensure the child's fundamental rights (such as, inter alia, the right to live and develop healthily, the right to education, and the right to a safe social environment); (ii) family environment conditions of each parent, specifically the conditions in which the child will live if placed with one parent; (iii) the child's wishes and views.[18] The Supreme Court suggested that courts must also assess the degree of the child's attachment to each parent, siblings, and other relatives, as well as the character and values of the parents, their approach to the child's upbringing, and their involvement prior to the dispute. Furthermore, the court should evaluate whether each parent can provide a suitable living and developmental environment for the child, considering the parent's work and lifestyle; the child's living environment with each parent, and their ability to maintain the child's connections with the other parent and relatives; whether the parent, in exercising parental authority, does not abuse their rights or violate the child's dignity, personal integrity, or privacy, and similar factors.[19] As stated in the doctrine, this resolution of the Senate of the Supreme Court plays a significant role, even if it does not provide a definite answer to an exhaustive list of the problems encountered by the courts when tackling disputes concerning child residence (Kudinavičiūtė-Michailovienė and Uusen-Nacke 2022, p. 85).

It should be noted that both, in Lithuania and Slovenia, a court cannot focus on a single factor from the ones listed above but must consider the child's interests comprehensively. This presents the court with the complicated task of balancing and finding the right model for each case.

2.2 *Joined Physical Custody Possibilities in Slovenia and Lithuania*

Joint custody has become the primary norm in several European countries, e.g. Sweden, Finland, France, England, Belgium, Spain, Germany, Denmark, Italy (Kruhar-Winter 2018, p 15, Hakovirta et al. 2023, p. 479, Novak 2019, p. 79; Ložina 2004, pp. 58–59). Similarly, in Slovenia, over 20% of children of separated couples lived under the joint custody model in 2021 (Hakovirta et al. 2023, p 479) and the numbers are likely growing further. In Lithuania, however, only sole parental custody is a rule and, after a divorce or separation child's place of residence is determined with one of the parents, and a non-resident parent receives visitation rights (Maslauskaitė and Tereškinas 2020, p. 292). However, these visitation rights, as discussed below, are sometimes designed to resemble shared custody.

[18] In the practice of Lithuanian courts, it is recognised that the child's opinion is not binding on the court; it must be evaluated alongside other evidence in the case (Limantė and Račkauskaitė-Burneikienė 2018).

[19] Ibid.

In Slovenia, before the adoption of the SLFC in 2017, when the Marriage and Family Relations Act[20] was still in force, a form of joint custody existed, but only if the parents mutually agreed to it.[21] It was believed that forced joint custody could not work (Novak 2009, p. 81). The SLFC has changed the approach. Since parents' principal and equal responsibility for the care and upbringing of children (Article 135 SLFC) remains the same even when the parents are separated, and since it is in the child's best interests to be brought up and cared for as if the parents were still living together (Čujovič n.d., p. 84), joint custody is considered to be the primary form of parental care (Novak 2019, p. 130). The SLFC therefore allows courts to establish joint custody even without the consent of one or both parents.[22] When establishing custody arrangements, the court must thus first examine whether both parents are suitable for custody or, even if they are not equally suitable, whether joint custody would be in the child's best interests.[23]

There are different forms of joint custody,[24] but it does not necessarily mean that the child must spend 1 week with one parent and the next week with the other (Jager 2023, p. 29), nor does it require that the child has to spend exactly the same amount of time with each parent.[25] For example, in one case the court granted joint custody even when the child's father mostly lived in Australia, and returned to Slovenia only for 4 months per year. The court decided that despite ongoing conflict, the parents had reached an agreement, both demonstrated comparable parenting skills, and maintained close relationships with their son. The court determined that significant distance alone could not prevent joint custody. However, since the child lives primarily with his mother, the court ordered that the father and son make up this gap during holidays and when the father stays in Slovenia, and that the boy shall thus spend 70% of all holidays with the father.[26]

---

[20] Official Gazette SRS, No. 15-644/1976.

[21] The possibility of a joint custody agreement has existed in the Slovenian legal system since 2004 as a result of the Constitutional Court's decision No U-I-312/00-40. In its decision, the Constitutional Court stated that where parents, even if they do not live together, wish to have joint custody of the child and the parents' agreement on that does not conflict with the child's best interests, there is no need to restrict the parents' rights by law. For more see Novak (2017), pp. 198–199, Novak (2009), p. 80, and Ložina (2004), pp. 56–62.

[22] Ljubljana Higher Court, ruling of 8 November 2023, No. IV Cp 1618/2023. See also (Jager 2023), pp. 30–31. Some people are sceptical about this, arguing that joint custody is not in the child's best interests if the relationship between his or her parents is in conflict. See (Ložina 2004), p. 71.

[23] See Novak et al. (2019), p. 420. See also (Weber et al. 2024), pp. 392–395.

[24] E.g. the nest form, in which the child lives in a flat where the parents take turns, the pendulum form, in which the child moves e.g. from one parent to the other on a weekly basis, and the residence form, in which the child stays with one parent most of the time, although often with the other parent as well. For more see (Novak 2017), pp. 200–202, Novak (2009), pp. 83–84, and Novak (2022), pp. 239–241.

[25] SL Supreme Court, ruling of 22 February 2023, No. II Ips 8/2023, Maribor Higher Court, ruling of 28 November 2023, No. III Cp 815/2023, Ljubljana Higher Court, ruling of 8 November 2023, No. IV Cp 1618/2023. See also (Weber et al. 2024), p. 393.

[26] Ljubljana Higher Court, ruling of 8 November 2023, No. IV Cp 1618/2023.

Only if, in the light of the circumstances of the particular case, it is established that joint custody would not be in the best interests of the child, should the child be entrusted to the care and upbringing of one parent only.[27] The court interprets the concept of the best interests of the child in each specific case. However, case law has identified some circumstances where joint custody is not possible: if one of the parents lacks adequate parental capacity, neglects or abuses the child, or if other obstacles to the implementation of parental care exist.[28] For example, the court granted sole custody to the mother, despite the child's emotional attachment to both parents, as the mother demonstrated better parental capacity and was better able to act in child's best interests. The father, however, had limited insight into his daughter's needs and prioritized his own interests. Furthermore, he developed a destructive, symbiotic and possessive relationship with the daughter, endangering her healthy psychosocial development in the long term.[29]

Another reason to refuse joint custody is a high degree of conflict between the parents, which endangers the child.[30] In a case like this, where both parents have comparable parental skills, the court will take into account which parent is better able to give the child healthy development, which environment is better for the child, and will also ensure contact with the other parent (Weber et al. 2024, pp. 388–389).

Case law frequently emphasises that, however, (only) poor communication between ex-partners is a normal situation, and this alone is not a sufficient reason to deny joint custody.[31] However, the conflicting relationship between the parents impacts how joint custody is organised. When the court establishes joint custody despite parents' poor communication, it defines the exchange of the child between the parents in as exact manner as possible, preferably with the parents having minimum contact. For example, the court might order the exchange of a child at (nursery) school (one parent brings the child there, the other picks him or her up, and *vice versa*), enabling the parents to share custody without having direct daily contact with each other.[32]

In Lithuania, physical custody was traditionally awarded solely to the mother, with fathers often receiving only scheduled and relatively short visitation rights.

---

[27] SL Supreme Court, ruling of 22 February 2023, No. II Ips 8/2023, Ljubljana Higher Court, ruling of 15 February 2024, No. IV Cp 2113/2023, Ljubljana Higher Court, ruling of 28 November 2023, No. IV Cp 1394/2023.

[28] See for example, Maribor Higher Court, ruling of 16 February 2023, No. III Cp 34/2023, Maribor Higher Court, ruling of 28 November 2023, No. III Cp 815/2023.

[29] Ljubljana Higher Court, ruling of 30 March 2023, No. IV Cp 2022/2022.

[30] Maribor Higher Court, ruling of 16 February 2023, No. III Cp 34/2023, Maribor Higher Court, ruling of 28 November 2023, No. III Cp 815/2023. Also (Čujovič n.d.), p. 85, and (Weber et al. 2024), p. 388. In a case of Maribor Higher Court, ruling of 25 October 2022, No. III Cp 699/2022, the court awarded custody of the child to one parent, finding that although both parents were capable of that, there was a conflict between them, with a complete lack of communication, which would make joint custody unconstructive.

[31] Maribor Higher Court, ruling of 25 January 2023, No. III Cp 9/2023.

[32] See for example Ljubljana Higher Court, ruling of 28 November 2023, No. IV Cp 1394/2023.

However, recently the nurturing role of the father has gained significance and has been reinforced by social policies (often implementing EU laws) aimed at promoting more gender-equal parenting within families (Maslauskaitė and Tereškinas 2017).

As noted above, in Lithuania, joint custody is not foreseen in the law, therefore, one parent is always set as a residential parent, and another one is granted visitation rights. However, in recent years, the option of '50:50 child contact arrangement' (the term used by courts), very similar to that of joint physical custody, has become a viable possibility for both parents due to changing court practice. In particular, when applying and interpreting Article 3.169 LTCC, courts tend to conclude that a child's residence, even by mutual agreement of the parents, cannot be established with both parents living separately (Vilkelytė 2024). Therefore, if parents, after separation, wish to continue sharing the child's care equally, the child's residence is determined with one parent, while a '50:50 contact arrangement' is established with the other parent.

One of the first cases considering the possibility '50:50 child contact arrangement' at the Supreme Court level was decided in 2016.[33] Similarly to Slovenian case law, initially, the court saw it as a model that is subject to both parents' consent; later, however, this requirement was abandoned.[34] The analysis of court cases decided in 2024 reveals, that a '50:50 child contact arrangement' can be established even in case of a conflictual relationship between the parents.[35]

Child age is also not a barrier for such a model, though it is taken into consideration. Lithuanian courts establish a '50:50 child contact arrangement' even for relatively young children (e.g. 3 or 5 years old).[36] However, if the child is very young and has a very close attachment to the mother, courts might consider the potential difficulties the child may face when separated from her. In such cases, a transitional arrangement for communication with the father may be established, gradually increasing the number of days spent with the father.[37]

Naturally, a '50:50 child contact arrangement' can only be established if it is determined that this arrangement best serves the child's interests. In addition to psychological welfare of the child, Lithuanian courts also evaluate practical details, such as the residence of each parent, the location of the child's educational institutions, the child's social connections in the parents' respective places of residence or nearby, each parent's work schedule, and their ability to transport the child to and from educational institutions. Moreover, when establishing a '50:50 child contact arrangement', the child's previous relationship with both parents and the extent to

[33] LT Supreme Court, ruling of 19 February 2016, No. 3K-3-99-969/2016.

[34] LT Supreme Court, ruling of 19 September 2019, No. 3K-3-279-969/2019. Debate of whether joint physical custody should be mandated by judges even against the will of one of the parents was also active in other European countries. See Steinbach (2019), p. 354.

[35] E.g. Vilnius regional court, ruling of 21 March 2024, No. Civil case e2S-702-340/2024.

[36] Vilnius Regional Court, ruling of 29 February 2024, No. Civil case e2S-498-643/2024; Vilnius Regional Court, ruling of 7 March 2024, No. Civil case e2S-582-643/2024; Vilnius Regional Court, ruling of 21 March 2024, No. Civil case e2S-702-340/2024.

[37] Vilnius Regional Court, ruling of January 9, 2024, No. Civil Case e2A-109-855/2024.

which each parent has been involved in the child's life are seen as important factors—the parent who had previously spent little time with the child has less chances to have such model approved.[38]

3 Contact Arrangements

Communication between the child and their parents is vital to family life and cannot be restricted by changes in the relationship between the parents. This is due to the fact that, from the child's point of view, their family concept continues to include their relationship with both parents (Kairienė et al. 2022), moreover, family links play an important role in a child's self-identity and healthy development. As noted by the Supreme Court of Lithuania, establishing the contact arrangements between a child and a non-residential parent is not an end in itself; rather, it primarily aims to maintain or restore, if it has been disrupted or weakened, the child's relationship with the non-residential parent. This relationship is essential for the child's development as a complete individual, requiring the support and care of both parents. The child needs to know that they are equally important to both parents and that both parents are equally accessible, meaning they are present for the child when needed.[39]

The child's right to maintain contact with both parents[40] is firmly rooted in international human rights law and is always interpreted via the best interests of the child prism. Under the EU Charter of Fundamental Rights, unless that is contrary to his or her interests, every child has the right to maintain on a regular basis a personal relationship and direct contact with both his or her parents.[41] Similarly, under Council of Europe law, the right of every child to maintain contact with both parents is implied in Article 8 of the ECHR. The European Court of Human Rights (ECtHR) has held that the mutual enjoyment by parent and child of each other's company is a fundamental aspect of family life.[42] This right is also reiterated in the Convention on the Rights of the Child (Article 9(3))[43] and the Convention on Contact Concerning Children.[44]

[38] Vilnius Regional Court, ruling of 12 December 2023, No. Civil case e2A-2723-855/2023.

[39] LT Supreme Court, ruling of 3 August 2023, No. e3K-3-256-781/2023; LT Supreme Court, ruling of 11 April 2014, No. 3K-3-202/2014.

[40] See also CJEU, Judgment of 31 May 2018, *Neli Valcheva v Georgios Babanarakis*, C-335/17, EU:C:2018:359, on the rights of access of other persons with whom it is important for the child to maintain a personal relationship, among others, that child's grandparents, whether or not they are holders of parental responsibility.

[41] See (Charter of Fundamental Rights of the European Union 2000) Article 24(3).

[42] ECtHR, *K. and T. v. Finland*, Application No. 25702/94, 12 July 2001; *A. V. v. Slovenia*, Application No. 878/13, 9 April 2019.

[43] See Articles 7(1), 8(1), 9(3) and 10(3).

[44] Council of Europe, No. 192, 15 May 2003.

In Slovenia, the right of contact is enshrined in the Constitution (Articles 53 and 54) and is specified and defined in detail in the SLFC. As a general rule, parents who do not live together or do not intend to do so shall agree on their contact with a child. If they fail to agree, the matter shall be decided by a court. The SLFC provides that a child shall have the right to have contact with both parents, and both parents[45] shall have the right to have contact with their child (Article 141 of the SLFC). The right is, therefore, reciprocal, but it is primarily a right of the child.[46] A very similar approach is taken in Lithuania. Under Article 3.170 LTCC, a father or a mother who does not live with the child has the right and the duty to communicate with the child and to participate in its upbringing. Likewise, a child has the right to regular, direct contact with both parents, regardless of their residence.[47] In case of dispute, the matter is resolved via mediation[48] and, if this fails, by court.

When joint custody (or, in case of Lithuania, a '50:50 child contact arrangement') is established, the child spends with each parent for a part of the time, and as a consequence, the arrangements for contact with each of the parents are not usually determined.[49] The situation is different when the child is entrusted to the custody of one parent. In this case, it is necessary to determine the manner and amount of contact with the other parent. The details of the contact arrangements depend, in particular, on the (non-) conflict nature of the relationship between the parents and the ability of the parents to communicate with each other.

In Lithuania, once it is determined which parent will provide the most stable and secure living environment for the child, a visitation schedule is set for the other

[45] The SLFC further provides for child's right to contacts with other persons with whom they are related by family and to whom they are personally attached, but due to its limited scope, this chapter does not deal with this issue.

[46] Novak (2022), p. 261. See also Ljubljana Higher Court, ruling of 19 October 2022, No. Cst 314/2022. The Constitutional Court of the Republic of Slovenia has also indirectly ruled on whether the right of access is a right of children and/or a right of parents in its decision U-I-53/93 of 9 March 1995. On that see also (Trefalt and Jager Agius 2014), pp. 31–32.

[47] If this child's right is not ensured, state and municipal institutions and agencies shall take action, in accordance with laws and other legal acts, to guarantee this child's right. Article 12(1) of the Law on the Fundamentals of Protection of the Rights of the Child of the Republic of Lithuania. *Official Gazette*, 1996-04-12, No. 33-807.

[48] As of January 1, 2020, following amendments to the Law on Mediation of the Republic of Lithuania (*Official Gazette*, 2008-07-31, Nr. 87-3462), mandatory mediation has been introduced for family cases, including those related to contact arrangements with children. In Slovenia mediation is not mandatory. Parents can agree to use mediation before the commencement, during or after the end of court proceeding (Article 205 of Family Code). When parents do decide to go to the mediation during the court proceeding, the mediation is carried out as a court annexed mediation. Mediation in family disputes has traditionally higher rates of success compared to mediation in civil or commercial matters. Beside mediation, the SLFC provides also for prior counselling at the social work centre. The parents shall attend such prior counselling before asking a court to decide on the child's custody, maintenance and contacts with parents and other persons or on issues concerning the exercise of parental responsibility which significantly affect the child's development (Article 200 of the SLFC). The purpose of such counselling is to try to find common interests and possible solutions to outstanding issues between the divorcing spouses.

[49] For more see (Novak et al. 2019), pp. 428–429, and (Jager 2023), p. 30.

parent. Typically, courts set precise schedules for contact between a non-residential parent and the child. This schedule specifies the exact days and times for visits, as well as the procedures for pick-up and drop-off. It also includes arrangements for holidays and birthdays, covering both the child's and the parents' special occasions. Usually, if the child and the parent live in Lithuania, non-residential parent will have a right to take the child for weekends (often with concrete hours listed in the court ruling), part of child's holidays, while spending Christmas/Easter is established between both parents on rotating order. In cases where in-person visits are not possible (e.g. the parent of the child lives abroad), alternative arrangements, like virtual meetings or mechanisms to make up for missed time, are established. In such a case spending time on child's holidays is often foreseen and communication via internet/telephone is set (again, often stating days and hours when such communication should be organized). Overall, Lithuanian case law prioritises maximum communication with the child (Kudinavičiūtė-Michailovienė and Uusen-Nacke 2022, p. 88). Only if frequent contact is found to cause psychological harm to the child, conflict with their best interests, or hinder their development, minimal visitation may be arranged.[50] If there is a risk of child abduction, improper behaviour of non-residential parent, the meetings might be supervised.

In Slovenia, besides the best interests of the child, further criteria regarding for establishing contact arrangements are not provided by law. Courts thus often rely on criteria determined in the Marriage and Family Relations Act, which stated that contacts are not in child's best interests if they put the child under psychological stress for the child or if they otherwise endanger child's physical or mental development (Article 106(5)).[51] In one of the cases, father's serious alcohol problem led the first instance court to abolish direct physical contact, replacing it with telephone contact.[52] On appeal, the Ljubljana Higher Court ruled that the facts did not justify such a restrictive measure, emphasizing that only contacts causing psychological stress or endangering child's development warrants this level of restriction. Instead, the Higher Court suggested supervised contact[53] as a less severe alternative, however noting that such contacts can be established only temporarily and by interim injunction.[54] In another case,[55] the court limited contact to written communication

[50] LT Supreme Court, ruling of 6 April 2005, No. 3K-3-242/2005; LT Supreme Court, ruling of 3 August 2023, No. e3K-3-256-781/2023.

[51] See Ljubljana Higher Court, ruling of 9 May 2023, No. IV Cp 702/2023, Ljubljana Higher Court, ruling of 8 December 2022, No. IV Cp 1962/2022, Ljubljana Higher Court, ruling of 9 November 2023, No. IV Cp 1077/2023.

[52] Ljubljana Higher Court, ruling of 9 May 2023, No. IV Cp 702/2023.

[53] In Slovenia, supervised contacts (Article 173 of the SLFC) are carried out in the presence of a professional of the social work centre or institution where the child is placed (Article 163 of the SLFC).

[54] In the final decision, though, the court may decide that contact should not take place in person or through social contacts, but in some other form, if this is the only way to protect the child's best interests.

[55] Ljubljana Higher Court, ruling of May 3, 2023, No. IV Cp 313/2023.

due to the father's violence towards the child, while allowing the father to maintain a connection with the child until his behaviour improved.

In Slovenia, depending on the level of conflict between the parents, contact should be defined in less (if parents are able to communicate and reach an agreement) or more (if there is a high level of conflict between the parents) detail. In the latter case, the court decision on contacts should specify the days and times of contact, as well as which parent brings the child to and from contact, which parent the child stays with if he or she falls ill before or during contact, which things the custodial parent must bring to the meeting (e.g., child's ID card), the distribution of holidays and public holidays, and similar. The parent with whom the child lives in custody shall refrain from anything that might hinder or prevent such contacts. They shall strive to maintain the appropriate attitude of the child concerning contact with the other parent (Article 141(2) of the SLFC).[56] If a custodial parent prevents the other from having contact with the child, this may be a reason to withdraw custody and entrust the child to the custody to the other parent,[57] if the latter will allow contact and the child's best interests can thus be protected.[58]

Balancing the best interests of the child and parents' rights, in both countries, the position is taken that even if the child is unwilling to keep contact with the non-residential parent,[59] this should be encouraged. As noted by the Supreme Court of Lithuania, ongoing parental conflicts often lead to a child's desire to withdraw or disappear from the conflict zone, meaning they may choose not to communicate. However, such withdrawal does not ensure the child's interests, thus the unwillingness of the child to communicate with non-residential parent in itself cannot lead to the establishment of a minimal communication procedure.[60] In such a case, means to encourage communication between the child and the parent must be sought. In general, this should be done by the residential parent, though often this is not the case because of conflicting relationships. In such a situation, a psychologist should be involved in the process of communicating with the non-residential parent and the child, and if the court determines that it is possible for the child to communicate with the parent without intermediaries, such a child's right should be ensured.[61] At the same time, though the child's wishes (if the child can express them) is a

[56] See also Ljubljana Higher Court, ruling of 19 October 2022, No. Cst 314/2022.

[57] Novak et al. (2019), p. 573. If a child is estranged from one parent because of contact restrictions, experts suggest removing custody from the parent who has previously had it and giving it to the other parent as a measure to reduce signs of estrangement, but such a measure is mostly only suggested for cases of moderate or severe estrangement. Exceptionally, such a measure is also suggested for a more mildly estranged child, if the expert assesses that the parent with a custody wants to alienate the child from the target parent. See Zaplotnik (2017), p. 42. Research shows that none of the children later regretted being forced as a child to make contact with an estranged parent (Zaplotnik 2017, p. 44).

[58] See Novak (2022), p. 263, Kraljić (2019), pp. 460–461, and Strobelj (2020), p. 67.

[59] In the case of a child refusing contact, it is necessary to find out whether the refusal is genuine or the result of manipulation by the other parent or a third party. For more see (Kraljić 2019), p. 458.

[60] LT Supreme Court, ruling of 11 April 2014, No. 3 K-3-202/2014.

[61] See also Kudinavičiūtė-Michailovienė and Uusen-Nacke (2022), p. 90.

significant circumstance when deciding on the establishment of a communication procedure, however they cannot be determinative on the court. Wishes of the child cannot be a condition to parent-child contact: i.e. that the child will keep contact with non-residential parent only if he/she wishes so.[62]

4 Concluding Remarks

While family law remains within the sovereign domain of Member States under the EU Treaties, some areas such as child custody and contact are loosely covered by international and regional treaties and conventions, leading to a certain level of approximation. As seen from a comparison above, Slovenia and Lithuania, both countries illustrate a broader trend towards convergence in this area. This convergence is not the result of direct EU intervention, but rather a reflection of shared values and principles that are increasingly shaping national laws. These principles of the developed societies—grounded in the protection of the best interests of the child, equality in parental responsibilities, and the right of the child to maintain relationships with both parents—demonstrate the growing influence of European human rights norms and jurisprudence. This allows to argue that despite the national competence over family law, the legal systems of European countries will continue to draw closer, guided by common principles and shared judicial interpretations.

References

Augustijn L (2023) Joint physical custody and mothers' Well-being. An analysis of life satisfaction, depressiveness, and stress. Appl Res Qual Life 18(5):2371–2395. https://doi.org/10.1007/s11482-023-10190-z

Bernardi L, Mortelmans D (2021a) Introduction: advances in research on shared physical custody by interdisciplinary approaches. In: Bernardi L, Mortelmans D (eds) Shared physical custody, vol 25. Springer International Publishing, pp 1–18. https://doi.org/10.1007/978-3-030-68479-2_1

Bernardi L, Mortelmans D (eds) (2021b) Shared physical custody: interdisciplinary insights in child custody arrangements, vol 25. Springer International Publishing. https://doi.org/10.1007/978-3-030-68479-2

Boele-Woelki K (ed) (2005) European family law in action. 3: parental responsibilities. Intersentia

Boele-Woelki K (2021) A European model for harmonizing the law on parental responsibilities: the family law perspective. In: Bernardi L, Mortelmans D (eds) Shared physical custody, vol 25. Springer International Publishing, pp 51–72. https://doi.org/10.1007/978-3-030-68479-2_4

Charter of Fundamental Rights of the European Union, OJ C 326, 26.10.2012, pp. 391–407 (2000)

Council of Europe (1950) European Convention on Human Rights. https://www.echr.coe.int/documents/convention_eng.pdf

Council Regulation (EU) 2019/1111 of 25 June 2019 on Jurisdiction, the Recognition and Enforcement of Decisions in Matrimonial Matters and the Matters of Parental Responsibility,

[62] Similar ECtHR, *A. V. v. Slovenia*, Application No. 878/13, 9 April 2019, point 72.

and on International Child Abduction (Recast), 178 OJ L (2019). http://data.europa.eu/eli/reg/2019/1111/oj/eng

Čujovič M (n.d.) Odvzem in namestitev otroka v postopku odločanja o varstvu in vzgoji. Pravni Letopis 2019:79–92

Divorce rates in European countries 2020 (n.d.) Statista. Retrieved 16 December 2024, from https://www.statista.com/statistics/612207/divorce-rates-in-european-countries-per-100-marriages/

Forslund T, Granqvist P, Van IJzendoorn MH, Sagi-Schwartz A, Glaser D, Steele M, Hammarlund M, Schuengel C, Bakermans-Kranenburg MJ, Steele H, Shaver PR, Lux U, Simmonds J, Jacobvitz D, Groh AM, Bernard K, Cyr C, Hazen NL, Foster S et al (2022) Attachment goes to court: child protection and custody issues. Attach Hum Dev 24(1):1–52. https://doi.org/10.1080/14616734.2020.1840762

Hakovirta M, Meyer DR, Salin M, Lindroos E, Haapanen M (2023) Joint physical custody of children in Europe: a growing phenomenon. Demogr Res 49:479–492. https://doi.org/10.4054/DemRes.2023.49.18

Household Composition Statistics (n.d.) Retrieved 16 December 2024, from https://ec.europa.eu/eurostat/statistics-explained/index.php?title=Household_composition_statistics

Jager P (2023) Zaupanje v varstvo in vzgojo skozi prizmo otrokove koristi. Odvetnik 109–110(1–2):27–31

Kairienė B, Valackienė A, Blauzdžiūnaitė-Pavlovič J (2022) Ensuring the child's right to communication with both parents in the context of parental divorce: a Lithuanian case study. J Teacher Educ Sustainab 24(2):67–82. https://doi.org/10.2478/jtes-2022-0017

Končina Peternel M (2019) Postopki za varstvo koristi otroka in vloga otroka v teh postopkih. Pravosodni Bilten. chrome-extension://efaidnbmnnnibpcajpcglclefindmkaj/https://cip.gov.si/media/1785/pravosodni_bilten_-2019-1.pdf

Kraljić S (with Slovenia) (2019) Družinski zakonik (I. izdaja). Poslovna založba MB, založništvo d.o.o

Kruhar-Winter A (2018) Skupno varstvo in vzgoja. Pravna Praksa 22:15–17

Kudinavičiūtė-Michailovienė I, Uusen-Nacke T (2022) Protection of child rights in family cases in Lithuania and Estonia. In: Limantė A, Pūraitė-Andrikienė D (eds) Legal protection of vulnerable groups in Lithuania, Latvia, Estonia and Poland, vol 8. Springer International Publishing, pp 81–105. https://doi.org/10.1007/978-3-031-06998-7_4

Limantė A, Račkauskaitė-Burneikienė A (2018) Vaiko išklausymo reikalavimas šeimos bylose. Teisė 106:99–113. https://doi.org/10.15388/Teise.2018.106.11655

Ložina N (2004) Skupno varstvo in vzgoja otrok, pravni vidik—Ob noveli ZZZDR-C. Pravosodni Bilten 25(2):53–72

Maslauskaitė A, Tereškinas A (2017) Involving nonresident Lithuanian fathers in child-rearing: the negative impact of income inequalities and sociolegal policies. Men Masculinities 20(5):609–629. https://doi.org/10.1177/1097184X17727798

Maslauskaitė A, Tereškinas A (2020) Quality of non-resident father-child relationships: between "caring for" and "caring about". In: Mortelmans D (ed) Divorce in Europe, vol 21. Springer International Publishing, pp 291–311. https://doi.org/10.1007/978-3-030-25838-2_14

Novak B (2009) Skupno varstvo in vzgoja otroka, ko starši živijo ločeno. Pravosodni Bilten 30(1):79–97

Novak B (2017) *Družinsko pravo* (2. spremenjena in dopolnjena izdaja). Uradni list Republijke Slovenije

Novak B (2019) Družinski zakonik: Z uvodnimi pojasnili (2. ponatis). Uradni list Republike Slovenije

Novak B (2022) Družinsko pravo: Po družinskem zakoniku in zakonu o nepravdnem postopku

Novak B, Čujovič M, Del Fabro A, Dolčič T, Dugar G, Erjavec N, Klemenčič A, Kralj S, Murgel S, Pirc Musar N, Podgoršek B, Pogorelčnik Vogrinc N, Rijavec V, Vrtačnik U, Weber N, Žnidaršič Skubic V (2019) Komentar družinskega zakonika. Uradni list Republike Slovenije

Smyth BM (2017) Special issue on shared-time parenting after separation. Fam Court Rev 55(4):494–499. https://doi.org/10.1111/fcre.12299

Steinbach A (2019) Children's and parents' Well-being in joint physical custody: a literature review. Fam Process 58(2):353–369. https://doi.org/10.1111/famp.12372

Strobelj T (2020) Odvetnik, 94(1). chrome-extension://efaidnbmnnnibpcajpcglclefindmkaj/https://www.odv-zb.si/upload/revija/Revija%20Odvetnik%202020/ODVETNIK%20st-94.pdf

Trefalt J, Jager Agius I (2014). Pregled ustavnosodne presoje otrokovih pravic. In Otrokove pravice v Sloveniji—Od normativnih standardov do učinkovitega varstva (p. 274). Fakulteta za družbene vede, Založba FDV and Ministrstvo za zunanje zadeve Republike Slovenije. chrome-extension://efaidnbmnnnibpcajpcglclefindmkaj/https://www.gov.si/assets/ministrstva/MZZ/Dokumenti/multilaterala/mednarodno-pravo/6e21ab8014/Otrokove_pravice_v_Sloveniji.pdf

UN (1989) United Nations Convention on the Rights of the Child, adopted by General Assembly resolution 44/25, on 20 November 1989. https://www.ohchr.org/EN/professionalinterest/pages/crc.aspx

Vilkelytė S (2024) Tėti, tėti, kaip gera į tave žiūrėti—Teisė profesionaliai. Teise.Pro. https://www.teise.pro/index.php/2024/06/10/s-vilkelyte-teti-teti-kaip-gera-i-tave-ziureti/

Weber N, Ahlin Doljak S, Betetto N, Caharijaz Ferme N, Drnovšek K, Felc B, Jambrek P, Jambrek Lampret E, Jančar M, Jelen Kosi V, Juhart M, Križnik A, Lemut-Strle R, Murgel J, Nussdorfer V, Plevnik P, Ratnik A, Smrkolj N, Švigelj J (2024) Družinski zakoniki s komentarjem. Lexpera, GV založba

Zaplotnik M (2017) Starševsko odtujevanje. Pravosodni Bilten 3:35–49

Neža Pogorelčnik Vogrinc is an Associate Professor of civil and commercial law at the Faculty of Law, University of Ljubljana, and a researcher at the Institute for Comparative Law at the Faculty of Law in Ljubljana, Slovenia. Her main fields of interest are civil procedural law, European civil procedural law and mediation. After an internship at the Ljubljana Court of Appeals, she passed the Slovenian Bar Exam in 2012. She defended her doctoral thesis with the title "Provisional measures in civil court procedures" in 2014 at the University of Ljubljana (cum laude). She has been a member of several national and European projects. Dr Pogorelčnik Vogrinc has published papers in several national and foreign journals, is an author of the individual chapters of ten books and a sole author of the book Začasne odredbe v civilnih sodnih postopkih (Provisional measures in civil court procedures). https://orcid.org/0000-0002-1706-1729

Agnė Limantė is a Chief Researcher at the Law Institute of the Lithuanian Centre for Social Sciences. She has received an MA in EU law from King's College London (awarded with the Prize for Best Dissertation on the MA in EU Law) and a PhD from Vilnius University, Lithuania. In May 2023–May 2025, she served as a Member of the Humanities and Social Sciences Expert Committee at the Research Council of Lithuania.

A considerable part of Agne's research focuses on family and children's rights law, and her recent works analyse the interplay between human rights and technology. Dr. Limantė is a co-editor of several edited collections: *Cambridge Handbook of AI and Technologies in Courts* (CUP, forthcoming 2026); *Gender-Based Violence and Law: Global Perspectives and Eastern European Practices* (Routledge, 2023); *Legal Protection of Vulnerable Groups in Lithuania, Latvia, Estonia and Poland: Trends and Perspectives* (Springer, 2022); *The Regulation of Matrimonial Property and Property of Registered Partnerships* (Intersentia, 2022). Overall, Dr. Limantė has published over 40 research papers in national and international journals or as book chapters. https://orcid.org/0000-0001-7365-787X

Hearing of the Child in International Child Abduction Cases: A Comparative Analysis of Practices in Poland and Lithuania

Agnė Limantė and Anna Wysocka-Bar

Abstract Parental child abductions, where a parent unlawfully takes or retains a child in another country, are a global negative phenomenon. It is also common in Europe and is highly relevant to CEE countries. In Europe, the legal framework for such type of cases is provided by the Brussels IIb Regulation and the 1980 Hague Child Abduction Convention. This chapter discusses cross-border child abductions from a child rights perspective. In particular, it sketches the overall situation of international parental child abduction cases in Poland and Lithuania, and focuses on the duty of hearing the child, in this way exploring the evolving role of the child's perspective in judicial considerations.

1 Introduction

In family law, cross-border child abduction refers to the wrongful removal or retention of a child across international borders, typically by one parent or guardian, in violation of custody rights granted by law or court order in the country of the child's habitual residence. A common example of parental child abduction is a situation when a parent takes the child to live abroad without the required consent of the other parent or does not return the child to the country of his or her habitual residence in agreed terms. In such a situation, private international law foresees the possibility of starting child return proceedings, which are designed to ensure that, upon application by an interested party, typically the left-behind parent, the child is returned to the country of their habitual residence unless some exceptions for return exist.

Parental child abduction is often (but not always) a side effect of the breakdown of the relationship between the parents of the child. It often (but—again—not always) happens in 'international' families, where parents originate from different

A. Limantė (✉) · A. Wysocka-Bar
Law Institute of the Lithuanian Centre for Social Sciences, Vilnius, Lithuania

Private International Law Center, Law Faculty, Jagiellonian University, Kraków, Poland
e-mail: agne.limante@teise.org; anna.wysocka@uj.edu.pl

A. Limantė, R. Vaičiūnienė (eds.), *Children's Rights in Central and Eastern Europe*, European Union and its Neighbours in a Globalized World 29,
https://doi.org/10.1007/978-3-032-07092-0_4

countries or simply have stronger or weaker links to more than one single country (e.g. both being same country nationals but living in another country).[1] Child abduction is a worldwide phenomenon,[2] and the European Union, including Poland and Lithuania, is obviously not an exception.

In Poland, statistics published by the Central Authority[3] show a steady growth in child abduction cases, from 70 applications for return of the allegedly abducted child filed in 2008 to 105 in 2016.[4] The countries from which children were abducted to Poland in this period in Poland include other EU Member States, mainly Germany, Sweden, Italy, the Netherlands and Ireland (with the UK taking the lead and covering almost half of all cases). The countries to which children from Poland were abducted in this period include mainly Germany, Ireland, Denmark, and again the UK is taking the lead. The statistics for the period from 2019 to 2024 are published on the general website of the Government.[5] These statistics only include applications filed with the courts of the first instance and then proceedings in front of the court of the second instance. They do not contain any information on states involved and no information on outgoing applications, and therefore, cannot be compared with the ones previously published by the Central Authority. Still, one may draw a very general conclusion on the steady growth in child abduction cases to Poland, as there were 116 applications filed with the court of the first instance in 2019, 152 in 2020, 141 in 2021, 148 in 2022, 148 in 2023 and 138 in 2024.

In Lithuania, the statistics on cross-border child abduction cases are handled by the State Child Rights Protection and Adoption Service. It reveals notable trends in Lithuania between 2019 and 2024 in the movement of abducted children to and from the country.[6] While the total number of applications fluctuates yearly, the data

---

[1] On the reasons behind the child abduction see (Schuz 2024).

[2] See Part I—A statistical analysis of applications made in 2015 under the Hague Convention of 25 October 1980 on the Civil Aspects of International Child Abduction—Global report by Nigel Lowe and Victoria Stephens accessible at the website of the Hague Conference on Private International Law at: https://www.hcch.net/en/publications-and-studies/details4/?pid=6598&dtid=32 On the phenomenon from different perspectives, including the one of the child see Kruger (2011).

[3] The statistics on child abduction cases in Poland pose some challenges if one wants to analyse them and draw some general conclusions. The statistics concerning applications filed in Poland based on the 1980 Hague Convention for the period between 2008 and 2016, disaggregated by incoming and outgoing applications and states involved used to be published at the official website of the Ministry of Justice (being the Central Authority). Since 2017, such statistics have no longer been published. It is not clearly stated in the documents presenting these data, but it seems that these statistics include applications filed with the Central Authority.

[4] Available at: https://arch-bip.ms.gov.pl/pl/ministerstwo/wspolpraca-miedzynarodowa/konwencja-haska-dot-uprowadzenia-dziecka/.

[5] Available at: https://dane.gov.pl/pl/dataset/3757,ewidencja-spraw-cywilnych-prowadzonych-na-podstawi.

[6] Annual Reports of State Child Rights Protection and Adoption Service under the Ministry of Social Security and Labour. Available at: https://vaikoteises.lrv.lt/lt/administracine-informacija/ataskaitos/metines-veiklos-ataskaitos/.

consistently show that more cases involve children being abducted from Lithuania than being brought into the country. This suggests that Lithuania may be more frequently a country of departure in international child abduction cases rather than a destination. The highest number of applications concerning children taken from Lithuania was recorded in 2021 (29 cases), while the lowest was in 2020 (20 cases). The number of applications regarding children being brought to Lithuania also fluctuated. The lowest number of cases was in 2022 (13 cases), while the highest was in 2024 (21 cases). Similar to Poland, many cross-border child abductions are linked to EU Member States and the UK (Limante and Wysocka-Bar 2025), where the Lithuanian and Polish expat communities are larger.

Many of the cross-border child abductions end up before courts and a judge has to decide whether the child has to be returned to his or her country of habitual residence. Hearing the child in such child abduction cases is essential to ensuring that their rights and best interests are respected. International legal instruments, first and foremost Article 12 of the 1989 UN Convention on the Rights of the Child (UNCRC)[7] emphasise the child's right to express their views in matters affecting them. The obligation to hear the child in judicial proceedings is also addressed in the 1996 European Convention on the Exercise of Children's Rights,[8] and the 2010 Council of Europe Guidelines on Child-Friendly Justice.[9] In the EU, the right to be heard is enshrined in Article 24(1) of the Charter of Fundamental Rights of the European Union[10] and reiterated in various legal acts. However, the practice of hearing the child varies across jurisdictions, and there is no clear common standard.

This chapter is devoted to the right of the child to be heard and the practical aspects of hearing the child in a specific type of proceeding related to parental child abduction in two Central and Eastern European (CEE) Member States of the European Union (EU), namely Poland and Lithuania. First, we will briefly discuss the legal framework governing cross-border child abductions in the EU and the child's right to participate in such proceedings. We will then focus on the practices of hearing the child in the analysed countries.

[7] UN Convention on the Rights of the Child (1989), adopted by the United Nations General Assembly on 20 November 1989.

[8] Available at: https://rm.coe.int/european-convention-on-the-exercise-of-children-s-rights/1680a40f72#:~:text=The%20object%20of%20the%20present,to%20participate%20in%20proceedings%20affecting.

[9] Guidelines of the Committee of Ministers of the Council of Europe on child-friendly justice adopted by the Committee of Ministers of the Council of Europe on 17 November 2010 and explanatory memorandum. Available at: https://rm.coe.int/CoERMPublicCommonSearchServices/DisplayDCTMContent?documentId=090000168045f5a9.

[10] OJ C 326, 26.10.2012, pp. 391–407.

2 Legal Framework for Child Abductions in the EU

On the international level, child abduction is addressed in the Convention of 25 October 1980 on the Civil Aspects of International Child Abduction, adopted under the auspices of the Hague Conference on Private International Law[11] (1980 Hague Convention) to which all EU Member States are parties.[12] Poland is a party to this Convention since 1 November 1992, and Lithuania since 1 September 2002. The Convention is designed to protect children from the harmful effects of parental child abductions in cross-border cases by providing a rapid procedure for the return of the child to the state of the child's habitual residence. According to Article 12 of the 1980 Hague Convention, if a child has been wrongfully removed or retained in a Contracting State, in general, the competent authority in that state should order the return. However, certain limited exceptions are foreseen, in which the return of the child might be refused. Pursuant to Article 13(1)(b), return might be refused if there is a grave risk that the return would expose the child to physical or psychological harm or otherwise place the child in an intolerable situation. Another exception to the prompt return of the child is to be found in Article 13(2) allowing the competent authority to refuse to order the return of the child if it finds that the child objects to being returned and has attained an age and degree of maturity at which it is appropriate to take account of their views.[13] Return can also be refused under Article 12(2) if more than 1 year has passed between the wrongful removal or retention of the child and the commencement of return proceedings, and it is established that the child is settled in their new environment.[14] In all these cases, a child's testimony and opinion are of particular importance.

In addition to this international instrument, within the EU Member States (with the exception of Denmark), the Brussels IIb Regulation,[15] regulating jurisdiction in matrimonial and parental responsibility matters also applies to cross-border child abductions. The rules of the Brussels IIb Regulation complement the 1980 Hague

[11] Available, together with status table, at: https://www.hcch.net/en/instruments/conventions/full-text/?cid=24.

[12] In general, the 1980 HCCH Convention is very successful in terms of ratifications, as currently it has more than 100 contracting parties. On the 1980 Hague Convention and its main concepts see Baruffi and Halliday (2022).

[13] See Schuz (2013), pp. 317–253.

[14] See further, e.g. Limante and Honorati (2018).

[15] Council Regulation (EU) 2019/1111 of 25 June 2019 on jurisdiction, the recognition and enforcement of decisions in matrimonial matters and the matters of parental responsibility, and on international child abduction (recast), OJ L 178, 02/07/2019, pp. 1—115. Pursuant to its Article 96: 'Where a child has been wrongfully removed to, or is being wrongfully retained in, a Member State other than the Member State where the child was habitually resident immediately before the wrongful removal or retention, the provisions of the 1980 Hague Convention shall continue to apply as complemented by the provisions of Chapters III and VI of this Regulation. Where a decision ordering the return of the child pursuant to the 1980 Hague Convention which was given in a Member State has to be recognised and enforced in another Member State following a further wrongful removal or retention of the child, Chapter IV shall apply'.

Convention in relations between the Member States (Articles 22, 96 Brussels IIb) and the Regulation refers directly to the 1980 Hague Convention in several cases.[16]

One of the most prominent features of the Brussels IIb Regulation rules related to child return is the so-called 'overriding mechanism' (Biagioni 2023). It allows the authorities of an EU Member State from which the child was abducted to order the return, even if the authorities of the Member State to which the child was abducted refused the return on the basis of the abovementioned Article 13(1)(b) or Article 13(2) of the 1980 Hague Convention. Such a decision as 'privileged' is subject to almost automatic enforcement in another EU Member State (González Beilfuss 2023).

Both the 1980 Hague Convention and the Brussels IIb Regulation place an important role on the central authorities[17] of the Contracting/Member States. In Poland, the Ministry of Justice is a central authority under the 1980 Hague Convention and Brussels IIb Regulation. In Lithuania, the State Child Rights Protection and Adoption Service performs the functions of a central authority for the fulfilment of the obligations laid down in the 1980 Hague Convention and the Regulation Brussels IIb.

In both countries, jurisdiction in child abduction cases is concentrated. In Poland, currently, 11 specialised Regional Courts are competent to hear applications for child return in abduction proceedings. Their decisions can be appealed to the Court of Appeal in Warsaw. Additionally, second instance decisions can be subject to cassation appeal and extraordinary appeal to the Supreme Court.[18] In Lithuania, in international child abduction cases, jurisdiction lies with the Vilnius Regional Court, and its ruling can be appealed to the Court of Appeal (*Apeliacinis teismas*).

3 Hearing of the Child in Abduction Proceedings

In the 1970s, when the 1980 Hague Convention was being drafted, the participation of the child in proceedings was considered primarily in relation to older children who objected to being returned. As noted in the Explanatory Report, 'the fact must be acknowledged that it would be very difficult to accept that a child of, for

[16] For detailed commentary of the provisions of the Brussels IIb regulation, see Chapter 7 in (Wilderspin 2023) and Chapter 7 in (Lowe et al. 2024).

[17] Such central authorities are responsible for the fulfilment of the duties of the states under the 1980 Hague Convention/ Brussels IIb Regulation, for example discovering the whereabouts of a child who has been abducted.

[18] Some peculiarities of the proceeding under 1980 HCCH Convention in Poland are explained in Pawliczak (2021), pp. 560–586; see also Schulz (2023), pp. 481–505. Case law of the Supreme Court was presented in Kubicka-Grupa (2021), pp. 641–666 and Bobrzyńska and Pilich (2024), pp. 154–183. For case law concerning child abduction from the UK to Poland see: Limante and Wysocka-Bar (2025).

example, fifteen years of age, should be returned against its will'.[19] The drafters agreed that, in certain circumstances, the views of the child should be considered. At the same time, they could not agree on a minimum age of a child for the purpose of taking their views into account, as any such indication would be artificial and arbitrary. It was therefore left to the discretion of the states and their competent authorities.

When it comes to procedures for hearing the child, and determining whether the child objects to return, the HCCH Guide to Good Practice notes considerable differences in approach to the question of interviewing the child, and indicates that some states have strong reservations about the appropriateness of interviewing young children in connection with return applications.[20] The HCCH Guide to Good Practice underlines that where it is appropriate and necessary to hear the child, it is desirable that the person interviewing the child should be properly trained or experienced and should shield the child from the burden of decision-making.[21]

The Brussels IIb Regulation, drafted nearly half a century after the 1980 Hague Convention and after years of testing in practice of its predecessor Brussels IIa Regulation,[22] puts a strong emphasis on the child's right to be heard.[23] It states that, in accordance with national law and procedure, the child should be afforded a genuine and effective opportunity to express his or her views (either directly, or through a representative or an appropriate body), provided that the child is capable of forming his or her own views. If the child were given this opportunity, the court should then give due weight to the expressed views, having in mind the age and maturity of the child (Articles 21 and 26).

It should be however noted that in the above provision, the Regulation refers to 'national law and procedure'. Thus, the question of who will hear the child and how the child will be heard is left to be determined by national law and procedure of the

---

[19] *Explanatory Report* (by Elisa Pérez-Vera) in *Acts and Documents of the Fourteenth Session (1980), tome III, Child abduction*, p. 433.

[20] Appendix I 'Conclusions and Recommendations of the Fourth Meeting of the Special Commission to Review the Operation of the Hague Convention of 25 October 1980 on the Civil Aspects of International Child Abduction (22–28 March 2001) drawn up by the Permanent Bureau' to Guide to Good Practice under the Hague Convention of 25 October 1980 on the Civil Aspects of International Child Abduction. Part I—Central Authority Practice, p. 103.

[21] Ibid.

[22] On child abductions within EU and Brussels IIa Regulation see Trimmings (2013). For the overall account of the participation of the child in child abduction proceedings see: Report requested by the JURI Committee: Marilyn Freeman, *The child perspective in the context of the 1980 Hague Convention* (European Parliament 2020).

[23] Biagioni and Carpaneto (2020/2021), pp. 146–150.

EU Member States.[24] The Brussels IIb Regulation purposefully does not provide 'whether the child should be heard by the judge in person or by a specially trained expert reporting to the court afterwards, or whether the child should be heard in the courtroom or in another place or through other means.'[25]

Referring to the case law of the Court of Justice of the European Union (CJEU) and the Charter of Fundamental Rights, the preamble of the Brussels IIb Regulation explains that it is not always required that the court obtain the views of the child by means of a hearing. The court retains 'a degree of discretion' in that respect. Thus, the hearing of the child does not constitute an absolute obligation. Whether the child will be heard is assessed by the competent authority in an EU Member State in a particular case, considering the best interests of the child (Recital 39).

However, once the court 'decides to provide the opportunity for the child to be heard, the court is required to take all measures which are appropriate to the arrangement of such a hearing, having regard to the best interests of the child and the circumstances of each individual case, in order to ensure the effectiveness of those provisions, and to offer to the child a genuine and effective opportunity to express his or her views' (Recital 39). For this purpose, the court should 'use all means available', be it national law or international instruments. It is also for the authority of an EU Member State to decide about the appropriate method for hearing a child (Recital 57). In cases where it is not possible to hear a child in person, and where the technical tools are available, the Brussels IIb Regulation suggests that the court might consider, for instance, the use of videoconference (Recital 53).

4 Hearing of the Child and the Child's Objection to Return

Given the above legal framework, the child's right to be heard must be implemented and guaranteed at the national level in EU Member States. The 'lacunas' left by the 1980 Hague Convention and Brussels IIb Regulation—particularly regarding the modalities of hearing the child in the context of child abduction cases—are to be addressed through national legal provisions and judicial practice. As these instruments do not prescribe uniform standards on how the hearing should be conducted, Member States retain discretion in determining the appropriate procedures. The approach taken in Poland and Lithuania with respect to hearing the child—both in general family law proceedings and specifically in cross-border child abduction cases—will be examined below.

[24] Recital 39 Brussels IIb Regulation.

[25] Ibid.

4.1 *Hearing of the Child in Poland*

In Poland, the hearing of the child is regulated in the Code of Civil Procedure.[26] These rules were subject to an important amendment in 2024.[27] As the amendment is still relatively new, there is no case law which could reveal how the new rules operate, in particular in child abduction cases in practice. Yet the comparison between old provisions and new ones already shows a visible shift towards a more child-friendly justice system.

Before the 2024 amendment, the general rule (Articles 576 and 216[1] Code of Civil Procedure) only provided that in cases involving the person or property of a child, the court heard the child if the child's mental development, health and maturity permitted so, if possible, considering the child's reasonable wishes. This rule remains unchanged. Previously, it was also specified that the hearing should occur outside the courtroom; this requirement has now been removed. Beyond these provisions, the Code of Civil Procedure was silent on other aspects of the hearing of the child. As a result, different approaches existed in courts, including in child abduction cases as to how the hearing was conducted in practice.[28]

The 2024 amendment to the Code of Civil Procedure, together with its implementing regulation[29] brings some changes to the previous rules but most importantly provides for additional clarifications as to how the court should assess whether the hearing of the child should be conducted, describes in detail the manner of preparation and conduct of the actual hearing, as well as the requirements for premises at the court where the child might be heard. The Code of Civil Procedure still provides that the court hears the child if the child's mental development, health and

[26] Ustawa z 17 listopada 1964 r Kodeks postępowania cywilnego [Act of 17 November 1964—Code of Civil Procedure] Dz. U. z 2024 r., poz 1568. All Polish legislation may be located in the official journal (*Dziennik Ustaw*, in short *Dz. U.*) by year, number (*nr*) and position (*poz*), or - starting from 2012—year and position (*poz*) only. *Dziennik Ustaw* is avalable (in Polish language) online at www.isap.sejm.gov.pl.

[27] Ustawa z dnia 28 lipca 2023 r. o zmianie ustawy - Kodeks rodzinny i opiekuńczy oraz niektórych innych ustaw [Act of 28 July 2023 on amendment of the Family and Guardianship Code and certain other acts], Dz.U. z 2023, poz. 1606.

[28] The following practice, observed in one of the courts, was described in the literature and assessed as an adequate one: 'The judge conducts the hearing of the child in person. The judge talks with the child in the presence of an expert psychologist. The hearing takes place in the so-called 'blue room'. The child's parents and their attorneys remain outside the hearing room. The attorneys are allowed to observe the hearing from an adjacent room separated by a Venetian mirror. They may communicate with the judge using an audio system. The judge listens to what parents have to say through headphones, so that the child cannot hear it. The hearing is included in the minutes and recorded.' See Wierciński (2021), p. 66.

[29] Rozporządzenie Ministra Sprawiedliwości z dnia 21 października 2024 r. w sprawie sposobu przygotowania i przeprowadzenia wysłuchania dziecka oraz warunków, jakim mają odpowiadać pomieszczenia przeznaczone do przeprowadzania takich wysłuchań [Regulation of the he Minister of Justice of 21 October 2024 on the manner of preparation and conduct of a child's hearing and the conditions to be met by the premises intended for holding such hearings], Dz.U. 2024, poz. 1579.

maturity permits so, if possible, considering the child's reasonable wishes. If the court decides against hearing the child, it must now state the reasons for such decision in the minutes of the proceedings.

As to practicalities of hearing of the child, under current rules, in general the hearing of the child must be held in a court, in an adapted room. The hearing must be held in a closed session, and in addition to the judge, only an expert psychologist may participate. The participation of the expert psychologist is required if, due to the child's health, mental development or age, it is necessary to provide psychological assistance to the child during the hearing, or the judge requires support in identifying the needs of the child. The hearing is evidenced only in an official note. The hearing shall not be recorded (neither video nor audio).

One might note that the 2024 amendment does not consider the specificity of cross-border cases, including cross-border child abduction cases. This becomes evident when one realises that the 2024 amendment is silent as to the possibility of hearing through videoconferencing. The question remains open as to how the court should proceed if the child is not present in Poland, and therefore, cannot participate in the hearing in person.

The Code of Civil Procedure currently also clearly states that the child will not be heard if the child refuses. Additionally, the child may be heard only once during the proceedings, unless the best interest of the child requires the subsequent hearing or the child themselves requests to be heard again. The re-hearing of the child should be conducted by the same court, unless this is impossible or contrary to the best interest of the child.

As to the preparatory stage, the court prepares a hearing of the child on the basis of the information gathered in the case file and after hearing of the child's parent (or, depending on the circumstances of the case, the guardian, the custodian, the curator or an expert witness). The court assesses whether the child might be heard considering the child's mental development, state of health and degree of maturity. It also assesses the manner in which the child communicates and the manner in which the child functions as to be able to establish contact with the child and being able to conduct the hearing. The date of the hearing of the child must be set for a day other than the date of the court hearing in the given case. The implementing regulation provides for a very detailed guidelines for the court while planning the time and duration of the hearing.[30]

The Court also assesses whether there are special circumstances justifying the presence of an expert psychologist at the hearing. In the case of children who do not speak Polish—a situation likely to arise more frequently in child abduction cases than other family law matters—the court should consider providing the interpretation services.

The implementing regulation requires that, together with the summon indicating the place and time of the hearing, the person bringing the child to the hearing is

[30] For instance, in scheduling the time and duration of the hearing, the court should consider among others, the age of the child or a need for a break. The court should consider also the timing of the optimal cognitive activity of the child.

served also with a leaflet designed for the child. It must be drawn up in a manner understandable to the child and explain the purpose, manner and place of the hearing and contain an information that after arriving at the court and seeing the place of the hearing, the child is allowed to decide not to participate in the hearing.

Before the hearing begins, the judge explains to the child the right to refuse to participate in the hearing, and informs about the purpose of the hearing, explaining also that the child is not responsible for the content of the decision that will be made by the court. The judge also explains to the child the role of another person (the expert psychologist) participating in the hearing. The judge should talk in a manner understandable to the child and adapted to child's needs. Official attire is not used during the hearing. The judge instructs the child that if the child does not understand a question, does not know the answers to a question, needs clarification or further explanations, believes that he or she has been misunderstood, or has any other needs, the child can communicate it. The judge agrees with the child on how the child will signal such situations.

During the hearing, the judge must communicate with the child in simple, neutral language, using open-ended, non-suggestive questions and avoiding figurative expressions. The judge should refrain from commenting on the child's relatives, carefully observe the child's emotional state, and respond appropriately. At the conclusion of the hearing, the judge should engage the child in a neutral conversation and invite any questions from the child. The implementing regulation explains also the duties of an expert psychologist assisting in the hearing.[31] The second part of the implementing regulation focuses in detail on the place in which the child will be heard.[32]

Despite the new detailed rules, the case law might still serve as guidance as to assessing whether the child should be heard and which weight should be given to their views. Following the case law, the court would not hear the child if it would be inappropriate in terms of the age and maturity of the child. As explained in one of the judgements handed down in the context of a child abduction case, hearing is not appropriate if the child is unable to comprehend the long-term consequences of his or her possible wishes to stay in the new country or to return to the country where he or she previously lived.[33] The decision on the hearing of a child is therefore never automatic. While assessing the child's degree of maturity, the court may (but is not obliged to) make recourse to the opinion of the expert, most frequently a psychologist.[34]

[31] For instance, the expert psychologist should provide the judge with assistance in formulating questions to the child or responding to situations that impede the course of the hearing.

[32] For instance, the regulation makes clear that children under 13, should be heard in premises which are suitably adapted (meaning that the walls should be kept in light colours, the floor covered with soft carpet and adjustable lighting). If justified by the needs of the child, materials to facilitate the conversation, in particular crayons, paper, drawings or other visual aids should be provided.

[33] Decision of the Supreme Court (Sąd Najwyższy) of 14 January 2021, signature: II Ca 217/16.

[34] Białecki (2021), p. 54.

There is no standard age at which a child is perceived as fit to be heard. In the literature, it is argued that children below 12 years of age should not, in general, be heard.[35] In practice, the decision as to whether children younger than 12 years old can be heard is taken by the courts on a case-by-case basis. In a case concerning the child abduction of two minors below 5 years of age from Ireland to Poland,[36] the first instance court took evidence from an expert psychologist. In the expert's opinion, the minor, after examination, was found—primarily due to their age—to lack understanding of the family situation and the capacity to assess it, displaying significant dependence on others and adopting their views. The minors were unable to clearly articulate their views, including on the possibility of returning to Ireland; consequently, their views could not be taken into account.

In another case concerning an application for the return of an abducted child, the second instance court decided not to hear two children abducted to Poland by their mother. Such an approach was accepted by the Supreme Court.[37] It explained that the minors, due to their age and stage of development, were unable to foresee the consequences of their decisions concerning key aspects of their life (e.g., their place of residence). Additionally, as evidence showed in this case, the minors were under the strong influence of their mother, with whom they were emotionally connected. They did not separate their own will from the will of their mother. The mother had a decisive influence on their attitudes. This caused, for example, that under her influence, they refused to disclose the origin of the injuries on their bodies. The children signalled that they were forbidden to speak on the subject. As a result, the assessment of the age and maturity of the minors justified the decision to abstain from their hearing.

On the contrary, in a case concerning a 7-year-old child abducted from the UK by her mother and taken care of in Poland by the maternal grandmother, the Supreme Court stated that the hearing of the child should have been considered.[38] As follows from the case, in the event of a return to the UK, the court found that the child's parents would be unable to provide proper care. The Court suggested that it would be advisable for the courts of lower instances to consult experts about determining the minor's state of development in terms of her ability to oppose to a change of her residence, as well as concerning the nature of the changes that a return to the UK would bring about in her life (e.g. the need to make up curriculum differences at school, building new friendships and the absence of persons from Poland currently playing a significant role in her life and possibly remaining in the UK under the care of persons other than her parents and grandmother).

[35] Wierciński (2023), p. 367.

[36] Decision of the Supreme Court (Sąd Najwyższy) of 14 April 2021, signature: I NSNc 36/21.

[37] Decision of the Supreme Court (Sąd Najwyższy) of 28 June 2023, signature: II CSKP 47/23.

[38] Decision of the Supreme Court (Sąd Najwyższy) of 13 September 2022, signature: II CSKP 1553/22.

In one of the cases,[39] the Polish Supreme Court explained the meaning of the 'objection' exception by stating that the 1980 Hague Convention does not simply grant the child the right to decide where he or she will live. Hence, a non-return order cannot be issued solely based on the child's preference to reside in one country rather than another. The Court further observed that the existence of a close relationship between the minor and the abducting mother does not, in itself, amount to the child's objection to returning to their former country of residence. Similarly, in another case,[40] the Supreme Court held that a child's strong attachment to the parent responsible for the wrongful removal, and the potential separation from this parent resulting from a change in environment, does not, in itself, constitute a ground for refusing return. Based on the psychological opinion prepared in the proceedings before the foreign court in Norway, the minor's opposition to return was not an autonomous decision, but rather reflected the mother's influence. Although the child expressed a wish to remain in Poland, she/he was unable to justify this position.

The analysed case law indicates that Polish courts recognise the importance of giving the child a voice in child abduction proceedings. However, this voice often appears not to have a decisive impact, likely due to the young age of the children involved. The amended rules of the Code of Civil Procedure and those of the implementing regulation should further enhance the trend towards more child-centred justice. The rules are relatively new, and, therefore, no case law discussing their application in practice is available. The time will show how these rules operate and, most importantly, how they are adapted to be applied in cross-border family matters involving children, including in child abduction cases.

4.2 Hearing of the Child in Lithuania

In Lithuania, the hearing of the child is regulated by the Civil Code of the Republic of Lithuania and the Code of Civil Procedure of the Republic of Lithuania. These legal acts establish the obligation to hear the child in any matter concerning them and to take their views into account.

Article 3.164 of the Civil Code (Participation of a minor in the protection of their rights) provides that when any issue concerning the child is being decided, a child capable of forming their own views must be heard directly, or, if that is not possible, through a representative. The child's views must be taken into consideration when making a decision, provided this does not conflict with the child's own best interests. In matters concerning the appointment of a guardian (curator) or adoption, the child's views must be given particular consideration. Article 380 of the Code of Civil Procedure (Participation of children in court proceedings) similarly states that

[39] Decision of the Supreme Court (Sąd Najwyższy) of 19 October 2023, signature: II CSKP 457/23.
[40] Decision of the Supreme Court (Sąd Najwyższy) of 13 October 2022, signature: I CSKP 1697/22.

when any issue relating to a child is being considered, a child capable of forming their own views must be heard directly, or, if this is not possible, through a representative. The child's opinion must be taken into account in the decision-making process, provided it does not conflict with the child's best interests. The child's views may be expressed orally, in writing, or by any other means chosen by the child.

In Lithuania, the law does not set an age limit for children to be heard, so it is left to the court to assess whether the child is able to formulate and express his or her thoughts. The law only refers to maturity and the ability to formulate views. Reiterating such provisions of law, the Supreme Court of Lithuania underlines that a child's opinion must be assessed not on the basis of the child's age, but on the basis of the child's maturity.[41] If the court finds that the child is capable of forming an independent opinion, it is obliged to hear the child.

In child abduction cases, children of school age seem to be always heard, however, when children are younger, their objection to being returned is less likely to be taken into account. For instance, in one case, the court cited the report of social services which, after hearing the children who were aged 6 and 10, concluded that they were not of the age and maturity to make a personal and independent decision on their own as to whether to reside permanently in one or another country, and to be able to understand the consequences of that decision in the long term.[42] On the other hand, in another case, a 7-year-old child was heard (in fact, he was heard three times by social services and was constantly objecting to the return), and his refusal was the basis to apply Article 13(2) of the Hague Convention. In the view of the court, although the child was only 7 years old at the time of the interviews, his maturity and ability to express his opinion made it reasonable for the court to take the child's opinion into account. Such a conclusion was based on the reports of social services which stated that the child was able to use simple sentences to express his/her wishes, needs, and ideas; that the child's comprehension skills were good for his/her age; that although the child was of a young age, the child's opinion should be taken into account; the child had a good memory for facts, and was able to express his or her own opinion; that he justified his wish to stay in Lithuania not only by making general statements, but also by giving reasons (he stated that he felt happy in Lithuania, that his family was in Lithuania, that Lithuania was his home).[43]

It should be noted that when children are heard by social services, the social services often provide their opinion as to the maturity of the child. When children are heard directly in court, or when there are doubts as to their maturity, their opinion might be evaluated by a psychologist. For instance, in the case cited above, the psychologist issued a written report on the children's statements. In the report, the psychologist stated that the children's testimony raised doubts as to its objectivity in

---

41 Supreme Court of Lithuania (Lietuvos Aukščiausiasis Teismas), 29 May 2014, civil case No. 3K-3-308/2014.

42 Court of Appeal of Lithuania (Lietuvos apeliacinis teismas), 26 July 2022 Civil case No. e2-816-407/2022.

43 Court of Appeal of Lithuania (Lietuvos apeliacinis teismas), 22 April 2022 Civil case No. e2-474-790/2022.

the light of the fact that they were young (6 and 10 y.o) and have been living with their mother for almost 2 years since the separation of their parents, from whom they may have picked up negative attitudes towards their father and a bias in relation to the dispute that had arisen between the two of them.[44]

In practice, there are two ways of hearing the child's opinion: (i) directly at the court hearing; (ii) indirectly in court (by obliging the social services to hear the child's opinion, or by appointing a forensic expert). In general, in family cases the Supreme Court of Lithuania considers that the court should seek to hear the child directly if his age and maturity allow him to express his thoughts and formulate his answers.[45]

In child abduction cases, when the case reaches the court, social services visit the family to draw a report on the situation and living conditions of the child in Lithuania; they also always hear the children (except very young ones who do not talk). If parents do not allow their children to be heard, the social services note that in their report, and a court may oblige the parent to bring the child to court to be heard. Overall, children are typically first heard by social services, and then (less commonly for smaller children) they also may be heard in court if the court considers this necessary.

As a result, in Lithuania children are not always heard directly by judges in child abduction cases. In a recent Appeal Court case,[46] the children were heard by social services, which drafted the report (there is no information in the case on how old the children were, but reading the file, one of them seemed to be under 5 years old while the other was school age). However, they were not heard directly by the first instance court; moreover, there was also no request from the mother to hear the children, and the mother did not challenge the social services report itself. On appeal, however, she claimed that it was the duty of the first instance court to hear the children. The Appeal Court noted that the mother, considering that the social services did not conduct a full hearing of the children, was entitled to request the first instance court to order the social services to conduct a re-hearing or to initiate a hearing of the children at a hearing. In appeal proceedings, in the view of the court, it was already unreasonable to hear the children, and it would unreasonably delay the proceedings and would be inconsistent with one of the fundamental objectives of the 1980 Hague Convention, namely that the courts should deal expeditiously with the issue of the return of the children to their country of origin and to ensure their prompt return (Articles 1 and 2 of the Hague Convention). The Court of Appeal also referred to the case law of the European Court of Human Rights (ECtHR) that recognises that the court should not be obliged to hear the child at all times at the hearing and should have the discretion to assess the need for a hearing in the light of the particular

[44] Court of Appeal of Lithuania (Lietuvos apeliacinis teismas), 26 July 2022 Civil case No. e2-816-407/2022.

[45] Supreme Court of Lithuania (Lietuvos Aukščiausiasis Teismas), 8 December 2016, civil case No. 3K-3-502-916/2016.

[46] Court of Appeal of Lithuania (Lietuvos apeliacinis teismas), 31 March 2022 Civil case No. e2-369-1120/2022.

circumstances of the case and the age and maturity of the child concerned.[47] The Court of Appeal noted that the case law of the Court of Justice of the European Union (CJEU) also takes the view that the court, which has to decide on the return of the child, has the discretion to hear the child. The child's right to express his or her views does not create an absolute obligation for the court to hear him or her in every abduction case.[48]

The court is not required to give decisive weight to the child's views solely because they have been heard. In a recent child abduction case,[49] the Court of Appeal repeatedly noted that Article 13(2) of the Hague Convention establishes the right, but not the obligation, of the court to take into account the views of the children when deciding on the return of the children to the State of origin. Article 13(2) of the Hague Convention provides that the court may refuse to order the return of the child if it finds that the child opposes the return and has reached an age and maturity at which it is appropriate to take his or her views into account, but this is for the court to decide.

5 Concluding Remarks

The overall approach to children's participation in legal proceedings in both Poland and Lithuania is gradually evolving, reflecting a broader shift towards recognising children as active rights-holders. This development can also be noted in the context of child abduction cases, where the legal acts and courts are increasingly attentive to the procedural guarantees related to the hearing of the child. While differences remain in practice and implementation, both jurisdictions demonstrate a growing awareness of the importance of ensuring that the child's voice is heard and taken into account in a manner consistent with their age, maturity, and best interests. These changes align with the evolving standards set by European and international legal frameworks and mark a continued progression towards more child-sensitive justice systems.

References

Baruffi MC, Halliday J (2022) Child abduction. In: Beaumont P, Halliday J (eds) A guide to global private international law. Hart Publishing, Oxford

Biagioni G (2023) The interplay of EU regulation 2019/1111 with the 1980 Hague convention in matters of child abduction. Cuadernos de Derecho Transnacional 1:1077–1089

---

[47] Judgment of the European Court of Human Rights (Grand Chamber) of 8 July 2003 in the case of Sahin v. Germany (Application No 30943/9)).

[48] CJEU, Joseba Andoni Aguirre Zarraga v Simone Pelz (Case C-491/10).

[49] Court of Appeal of Lithuania (Lietuvos apeliacinis teismas), 31 March 2022 Civil case No. e2-369-1120/2022.

Biagioni G, Carpaneto L (2020/2021) Children under Brussels IIter Regulation. Yearb Priv Int Law 2020/2021:139–154
Białecki M (2021) Orzekanie w sprawach o wydanie dziecka w trybie Konwencji dotyczącej cywilnych aspektów uprowadzenia dziecka za granicę sporządzonej w Hadze w dniu 25 października 1980 r. Instytut Wymiaru Sprawiedliwości, Warszawa
Bobrzyńska O, Pilich M (2024) Cases of cross-border child abduction in times of populism: Polish perspective. J Priv Int Law 1:154–183. González Beilfuss, Cristina. What's new in Regulation (EU) No 2019/1111? Yearbook of Private International Law 2020/2021, pp. 95–116
Kruger T (2011) International child abduction. The inadequacies of the law. Hart Publishing, London
Kubicka-Grupa Z (2021) A review of the Polish Supreme Court case law in international family law matters (from January 2015 to April 2021). Polski Proces Cywilny 4:641–666
Limante A, Honorati C (2018) Chapter 4 "Jurisdiction in cases of child abduction. Proceedings for the return of the child". In: Honorati C (ed) Jurisdiction in matrimonial matters, parental responsibility and international abduction. Peter Lang
Limante A, Wysocka-Bar A (2025) Cross-border child abduction from the UK: comparative analysis of polish and Lithuanian court cases. Int J Law Policy Fam 39(1):ebae027. https://doi.org/10.1093/lawfam/ebae027
Lowe N, Honorati C, Hellner M (2024) Brussels II-Ter: cross-border marriage dissolution, parental responsibility disputes and child abduction in the EU. Intersentia, Cambridge
Pawliczak J (2021) Reformed polish court proceedings for the return of a child under the 1980 Hague convention in the light of the Brussels IIb regulation. J Priv Int Law 3:560–586
Schulz AN (2023) The principle of the best interests of the child and the principle of mutual trust in the justice systems of EU Member States - Return of a child in cross-border cases within the EU in the light of EU Council Regulation 2019/1111 and the situation in Poland. J Priv Int Law:481–505
Schuz R (2013) The Hague child abduction convention. A critical analysis. Hart Publishing, London
Schuz R (2024) International child relocation after relationship breakdown. In: Carruthers JM, Lindsay BWM (eds) Research handbook on international family law. Edward Elgar Publishing, pp 130–152
Trimmings K (2013) Child abduction with the European Union. Hart Publishing, London
Wierciński J (2021) 'Cywilne aspekty uprowadzenia dziecka za granicę w Unii Europejskiej', *Zeszyty Prawnicze*. Uniwersytet Kardynała Stefana Wyszyńskiego 3:51–79
Wierciński J (2023) Uprowadzenie dziecka za granicę. In: Mostowik P (ed) Międzynarodowe prawo rodzinne. Filiacja. Piecza nad dzieckiem. Alimentacja. Wolters Kluwer, Warszawa, pp 329–373
Wilderspin M (2023) European private international family law: the Brussels IIb regulation. Oxford University Press, Oxford

Agnė Limantė is a Chief Researcher at the Law Institute of the Lithuanian Centre for Social Sciences. She has received an MA in EU law from King's College London (awarded with the Prize for Best Dissertation on the MA in EU Law) and a PhD from Vilnius University, Lithuania. In May 2023–May 2025, she served as a Member of the Humanities and Social Sciences Expert Committee at the Research Council of Lithuania.

A considerable part of Agne's research focuses on family and children's rights law, and her recent works analyse the interplay between human rights and technology. Dr. Limantė is a co-editor of several edited collections: *Cambridge Handbook of AI and Technologies in Courts* (CUP, forthcoming 2026); *Gender-Based Violence and Law: Global Perspectives and Eastern European Practices* (Routledge, 2023); *Legal Protection of Vulnerable Groups in Lithuania, Latvia, Estonia and Poland: Trends and Perspectives* (Springer, 2022); *The Regulation of Matrimonial Property and Property of Registered Partnerships* (Intersentia, 2022). Overall, Dr. Limantė has published over 40 research papers in national and international journals or as book chapters. https://orcid.org/0000-0001-7365-787X

Anna Wysocka-Bar is an Assistant Professor at the Private International Law Center at the Law Faculty of the Jagiellonian University (Poland). She is the coordinator of the EU co-funded EU Success Project. Dr Wysocka-Bar is an author or co-author of many publications, including a monograph "Private International Law in Poland" (Wolters Kluwer). She is an ordinary member of the European Association of Private International Law (EAPIL), a member of its working groups and one of the editors of the EAPIL blog. She has given guest lectures on judicial cooperation in civil and commercial matters at different universities in Italy, the Netherlands, China, Jordan, Turkey and Egypt. She was a speaker at conferences organised by the European Law Academy in Trier. Dr Wysocka-Bar is also a licensed attorney at law. https://orcid.org/0000-0001-8893-9845

The Procedural Capacity of a Child in an Administrative Procedure: The Case of Slovenia and Croatia

Bruna Žuber and Dario Đerđa

Abstract This chapter discusses the procedural capacity of a child in administrative procedures in Slovenia and Croatia. Both countries were formerly part of a Yugoslav state and have a common tradition of administrative procedure. Since independence, each country has addressed the challenges of administrative procedure in its own way. The chapter begins by examining international legal instruments that ensure children's active participation in an administrative procedure through the right to be heard and to express their opinions. It then presents the regulation of the procedural capacity of a child and the child's legal representation in an administrative procedure in Slovenia and Croatia. The possibility of consulting and expressing the child's views in administrative procedures in Slovenia and Croatia is also analysed.

1 Introduction

Administrative procedure is the most common legal procedure in national practices due to its legal nature and purpose. Because of its importance in everyday life, both adults and children are involved as parties in these procedures. In EU countries, the procedural rights of children in administrative procedures are generally well protected. This protection also includes, under certain conditions, the child's right to express an opinion on matters relevant to the resolution of the administrative matter at hand.

In Slovenia, administrative procedure is used to decide on a party's rights, obligations, or legal benefits in administrative law. The decision-making of an authority

B. Žuber (✉)
Faculty of Law, University of Ljubljana, Ljubljana, Slovenia
e-mail: bruna.zuber@pf.uni-lj.si

D. Đerđa
Faculty of Law, University of Rijeka, Rijeka, Croatia
e-mail: dario.derda@pravri.uniri.hr

A. Limantė, R. Vaičiūnienė (eds.), *Children's Rights in Central and Eastern Europe*, European Union and its Neighbours in a Globalized World 29,
https://doi.org/10.1007/978-3-032-07092-0_5

in an administrative procedure is unilateral and authoritative; it relates to an individual and concrete case, resulting in the issuance of an administrative decision with direct legal effect. In addition to decision-making in an administrative procedure, administrative authorities also carry out 'substantive acts' as part of their administrative function. These are organisational, analytical, or technical tasks, such as maintaining the population register, keeping the civil register, issuing certificates, and issuing consents or opinions (Kerševan and Androjna 2017, p. 53). Unlike administrative decisions, substantive acts have no direct legal effect. However, they constitute a significant part of administrative actions and play a vital role in the functioning of society. Children are frequently subjects of administrative procedures, and administrative authorities perform various substantive acts that directly affect their legal status. For example, a child must be given a name immediately after birth and registered with the administrative unit to be entered into the civil register. A child must be registered for compulsory health insurance to access and receive reimbursement for healthcare services covered under the scheme. A newborn is also assigned a tax identification number. For identification and international travel, a child must obtain an identity card and a passport. These examples illustrate that administrative action follows everyone from birth onwards.

In Croatia, as in Slovenia, the administrative procedure is a unilateral and authoritative decision-making process by an administrative authority concerning individuals' rights, obligations, or legal benefits within the scope of administrative law. This procedure results in a legally binding decision that extends or limits the rights or obligations of the parties involved. Due to its legal nature, it is essential to safeguard the rights of the parties involved in the administrative procedure. This objective is supported by various legal safeguards, including the right to be heard, the right to access and review case files, the right to present evidence, the right to receive a reasoned explanation for administrative decisions, and the right to appeal such decisions. Under Croatian law, any natural or legal person may participate as a party to an administrative procedure. Consequently, a child may also be a party to administrative procedure. Common examples of administrative procedures that may involve potential risks to children's rights include matters concerning the appointment of guardians, changes to a child's name, the granting or revocation of citizenship, and the allocation of specific social, healthcare, or educational rights.

This chapter presents key international legal instruments that ensure children's active participation in an administrative procedure, allowing them to express their opinions. It then explores legal regulations governing children's participation in administrative procedures in Slovenia and Croatia. In addition, the chapter analyses specific aspects related to the legal position and representation of children in these procedures. The chapter also identifies special administrative procedures in which children can act independently without special legal representation. Finally, the chapter considers how administrative authorities should proceed when parents, as the child's representatives, cannot agree on a particular action.

2 International Standards for the Active Participation of Children in Administrative Procedure

Protecting children's rights represents a civilisational achievement protected at national and international levels (Hrabar 2013, p. 69; Bruning and Doek 2021, pp. 231–232). The procedural protection of children's rights places particular emphasis on the child's right to express their opinion when decisions are made regarding their rights or obligations.

The child's right to express opinion is established by the United Nations Convention on the Rights of the Child of 1989 (CRC), which sets universal standards for protecting children from all forms of discrimination or punishment and promotes the respect and affirmation of children's rights. The CRC has been ratified by Slovenia and Croatia, and it obliges contracting states to prioritise the best interests of the child in all decisions that may affect them. When making any decisions or taking actions that affect a child or children as a group, the child's welfare must be the most important consideration. This applies to decisions made by governmental, administrative, or legislative bodies and those made by families (UNICEF Croatia 2025, p. 1).

Art. 12 of the CRC mandates contracting states guaranteeing a child's right to express their opinion. Consequently, through its legislation, each state must ensure that any child capable of forming an opinion can express views on all matters affecting him, with due consideration given to the child's views based on their age and maturity. To achieve the objectives of the CRC, it is imperative that in any judicial or administrative procedure concerning a child, the child is allowed to make statements, either directly or through a representative, in line with the procedural rules of national legislation (Bruning and Doek 2021, p. 249).

The procedural rights of children in legal proceedings are further protected by the European Convention on the Exercise of Children's Rights of 1996 (CECR). Slovenia ratified the CECR as the third country in 1999, while it has been in force in Croatia since 2010. The purpose of the CECR is to promote children's rights in their best interests, grant them specific procedural rights, and facilitate the exercise of these rights by ensuring that children, either on their own or through other persons or bodies, are informed and allowed to participate in procedures before judicial or administrative bodies that concern them (CERC, Art. 1). The CECR establishes the child's right to be informed and to express their views in proceedings. In Art. 3, the CECR provides that a child who, according to the national law of the contracting state, has sufficient maturity should be allowed to receive all relevant information in procedures concerning them, be consulted, express their views, and be informed of the possible consequences that may arise from their expressed opinion, as well as the consequences of any decision that may be made in such procedures. Therefore, by the CECR, the court or administrative body involved in procedures concerning a child is required, before making a decision, to consider whether the child has sufficient information to decide on their best interest and, if necessary, to obtain further information, particularly from the holders of parental responsibility.[1] If, under the law of the contracting state, the child is deemed to have sufficient maturity, it is essential for the body conducting the procedures to ensure that the child has received all relevant information. If necessary, the administrative body should advise the child, either directly or through other persons or bodies, in a manner appropriate to the child's level of understanding. Finally, under the CECR, the court or administrative body is obliged to give due weight to the opinions expressed by the child during the procedures (CERC, Arts. 3, 6).

European Union law further strengthens the child's right to express their opinion. The Charter of Fundamental Rights of the European Union in Art. 24 establishes that children have the right to the protection and care necessary for their well-being and that they may freely express their opinions. Their views must be taken into account, in accordance with their age and maturity, in matters concerning them. This applies to parents, guardians of children, third parties, courts and administrative bodies in procedures concerning children's rights and obligations.

The aforementioned international instruments significantly influence the national legislation of each contracting state and provide for direct applicability, allowing individuals to invoke their provisions if the state fails to implement them into national legislation. The provisions of international treaties in Croatia are directly applicable. Although Croatia ratified the CECR in 2010, it was among the first member states of the Council of Europe to sign it and has since revised its family legislation to meet the CECR's standards (Hrabar 2013, p. 70). Also, in Slovenia, laws and other regulations must comply with generally accepted principles of international law and treaties binding on Slovenia. Ratified and published treaties shall be applied directly. In Slovenia, the provisions of the CECR were considered when adopting relevant family legislation even before the CECR came into force, reflecting the high commitment of the Republic of Slovenia to the protection of children's rights.

[1]Although the CECR uses the term "judicial bodies", in accordance with art 2 of this Convention, the term "judicial body" is understood to mean any court or administrative body that possesses equivalent authority.

3 The Procedural Capacity of a Child in Administrative Procedure in Slovenia

3.1 General Rules on the Legal Position of a Child in an Administrative Procedure

3.1.1 The Child as a Party to Administrative Procedure

According to the Slovenian General Administrative Procedure Act (GAPA), a party to an administrative procedure may be any natural and legal person under private or public law on whose request the procedure has been initiated or against whom the procedure is conducted. A natural person acquires legal capacity, and therefore the capacity to be a party to an administrative procedure, at birth and loses it at death. This means a child can also be a party to an administrative procedure. It should be noted that, according to the GAPA, throughout the procedure, the authority must *ex officio* ensure that all those whose rights or legal benefits may be affected by the administrative decision participate in the procedure. Throughout the procedure, the authority must, *ex officio*, ensure that a person acting as a party can be a party to the procedure and that a party without procedural capacity is represented by its legal representative. In this respect, it is considered a substantial violation of administrative procedure if a legal representative does not represent a party. The extraordinary legal remedy of reopening the procedure may also be used for this procedural violation.

Depending on the position in the administrative procedure, a distinction is made between active and passive parties to the procedure. Active parties are those at whose request the procedure is initiated to enforce a right or to release or reduce an obligation. Passive parties are parties against whom an administrative procedure is in progress in which an obligation is to be imposed or a right is to be reduced (Kerševan and Androjna 2017, p. 133). The child will mainly be an active party to the administrative procedure. Still, it may also act as a passive party (e.g., in an inspection procedure concerning a property owned by a child).

A party may actively participate in an administrative procedure if it has the capacity to be a party to an administrative procedure, procedural capacity, and the capacity to bring proceedings. Procedural capacity implies the existence of legal capacity and represents the ability to act independently in the procedure. The capacity to bring proceedings is the ability to demonstrate an adequate entitlement to participate in the procedure to protect a personal interest. It is acquired by asserting substantive standing, e.g., claiming that the child fulfils the conditions for recognising the right in the specific administrative procedure. The capacity to bring proceedings requires the capacity to be a party to an administrative procedure but does not depend on procedural capacity (Kerševan and Androjna 2017, p. 141–144). It follows from the above that most issues relating to the child's position in an administrative procedure are related to the child's procedural capacity, which will be discussed in more detail below.

3.1.2 Procedural Capacity and Representation of the Child in an Administrative Procedure

Art. 46 of the GAPA provides that only parties with full capacity to contract may perform procedural actions by themselves, thus defining procedural capacity in administrative procedure. In Slovenia, a child usually acquires full procedural capacity at the age of majority, i.e. when a child reaches the age of 18. In exceptional circumstances, a child may attain full procedural capacity even before the age of 18. This capacity is granted through marriage. Additionally, a court may recognise a child's full procedural capacity if they have become a parent and have reached adequate physical and mental maturity to be capable of independent life (Family Act, Art. 152).

The GAPA further provides that a minor who has not obtained the full capacity to contract shall have the procedural capacity within the limits in which their capacity to contract has been recognised. In this regard, it should be noted that in Slovenia, children under the age of 15 do not have the capacity to contract. Children over the age of 15 may conclude legal transactions independently, provided that the transactions do not significantly impact the child's life before or after they reach majority and that the law does not provide otherwise (Family Act, Art. 150). In practice, this means that if a child is between 15 and 18 years old, the administrative authority will not recognise the child's procedural capacity in administrative procedures, which could significantly impact a child's life. An example is the administrative procedure for granting scholarships, which are intended to promote the education of secondary school and university students. However, if the legal requirements provided in the Scholarship Act are not met, the scholarship recipient is obliged to repay the scholarship. The situation is different regarding administrative procedures involving children over the age of 15 who are employed. According to the Slovenian Family Act, a child who is 15 years old may freely dispose of their wages. This means, for example, that a child who has reached the age of 15, has an employment contract and receives a wage has full procedural capacity in the administrative procedure of personal income tax assessment (Kmecl 2020, p. 349).

A child who is a party to an administrative procedure and does not have procedural capacity shall be represented by their representative. A representative may perform all procedural actions on behalf of the child, except where a regulation provides that special permission must be obtained for individual procedural actions. The child's representative may appoint an authorised person to represent a child in an administrative procedure, whereas any person with full capacity to contract may act as an authorised person. In this case, the authorised person acts in place of the child's representative in an administrative procedure to which the child is a party.

According to Slovenian legislation, children are generally represented by their parents. Parents acquire the right to represent their child *ex-lege* from the moment the child is born. The representation of children is part of the concept of parental responsibility. This means that, in principle, each parent can represent a child in an administrative procedure without the need to obtain the formal consent of the other parent unless the law specifically provides otherwise. This is the case, for example, with the registration of a child's permanent residence, where the Residence Registration Act requires the formal consent of both parents to register the child's permanent residence. Exceptions where the formal consent of the other parent is not needed are expressly provided for in the Residence Registration Act (e.g. registration of the child at the address in the Republic of Slovenia, which is the same as the address of both parents). Since, in most cases, each parent can represent a child in an administrative procedure, this also means that a child may be represented first by one parent and then by the other parent in the same procedure (Kmecl 2020, pp. 352–353). The parents will jointly represent the child by mutual agreement, even if they do not live together. In such cases, only delivery or communication is made to the parent with whom the child lives or to the parent indicated in the court settlement or court decision on joint custody of the child. If parents disagree on issues critical for the child's development, the matter is decided by a civil court. The court's decision in such a case may also significantly impact the scope of a child's representation in an administrative procedure related to such issues.

In some situations, the parents cannot represent a child. This is the case when a child has no parents, if a child is not taken care of by their parents, when a court prohibits one or both parents from exercising certain rights relating to parental responsibility or when a court withdraws parental responsibility from one or both parents. In these cases, a child is placed under guardianship and appointed a guardian by a court. A guardian acts as a child's representative but is not fully equal to parents in representing a child. Parents are authorised to undertake all procedural actions on behalf of the child without special consent. On the contrary, the guardian is not allowed to do anything that would exceed the framework of regular operations and management of the child's property without the authorisation of the social work centre (Family Act, Art. 247 and 248). The guardian also needs the authorisation of the social work centre to do the following: enrol a child at a school, withdraw a child from school, change the type of the child's education, decide on the selection of a child's profession or the carrying out of a child's profession; implement other necessary measures concerning a child, if so provided by another act (Family Act, Art. 260). The scope of the child's representation in an administrative procedure relating to such issues is also significantly affected by all the above limitations. Suppose the authority conducting the administrative procedure establishes that the representative of a person under guardianship does not demonstrate due diligence regarding representation. In that case, it reports this to the authority in charge of guardianship (GAPA, Art. 47).

There are also some particularities in representing children placed in foster care. When a child is placed in foster care, the parents retain those rights and obligations which are compatible with the purpose of the foster care unless they have been deprived of them to protect the best interests of the child (Provision of Foster Care Act, Art. 26). However, the Provision of Foster Care Act expressly delegates to the foster carer the representation of the child in the administrative procedure for issuing identity card. It also empowers the foster carer to make decisions concerning the child's daily life. This is not reasonably possible without the representation of the child in some administrative procedures, particularly those relating to education.

In an administrative procedure, the interests of the child and the child's representative may also conflict. In this case, the authority may appoint a temporary representative for the child. A temporary representative is appointed by the authority conducting the procedure if a child does not have a legal representative, and if this is required by the urgency of the case or interest of the party, a procedure needs to be carried out. In the procedure and for the actions for which they have been appointed, a temporary representative shall have all the rights and obligations of a child's legal representative. Suppose the concrete administrative procedure is not urgent. In that case, a social work centre or a court should appoint a collision guardian to a child instead of appointing a temporary representative in an administrative procedure (Žuber 2020, p. 369).

3.2 *Children's Right to Express Their Opinion in an Administrative Procedure*

As explained above, children generally lack procedural capacity and, therefore, need a legal representative to act on their behalf in an administrative procedure. This also means that the right to be heard, as one of the fundamental procedural guarantees of a fair procedure, which gives the party the status of an active subject of the administrative procedure and not merely an object to be decided upon, is in most cases primarily exercised through the child's legal representative.

In Slovenia, the right to be heard in an administrative procedure consists of the party's right to participate in a fact-finding procedure, right to give the necessary data and defend their rights and legally protected benefits, right to state facts which might contribute to resolving the case and challenge the correctness of assertions which do not match their assertions. More specifically, the party should be given the right to be heard on all circumstances and facts indicated in the fact-finding procedure, the right to be heard on the proposals and evidence offered, the right to participate in evidence taking, the right to ask questions to other parties, witnesses and expert witnesses, and the right to be informed of the successfulness of the presenting of evidence and be heard thereon. The administrative authority may not issue a decision before the party is given the opportunity to be heard on the facts and circumstances relevant to the issuing of a decision (GAPA, Art. 9 and Art. 146).

The right to be heard also includes the right of the child considered by national law to have sufficient understanding to be consulted and to express their views in the procedure, as provided for in the CRC and CECR. The child's right to be heard is directly linked to the right of the child to be adequately represented in proceedings (Končina Peternel 2015, p. 73). As a rule, a child who is a party to an administrative procedure has the right to be heard, and, in most cases, it exercises this right through a legal representative. However, the child may also exercise this right directly and thus express their views, as stipulated in the CRC and CECR. The child's right to express their views does not diminish the legal representative's right to be heard in the same administrative matter, as both aim to safeguard the child's best interests.

In Slovenia, children's right to express their views is commonly exercised in civil court proceedings since matrimonial and parent-child disputes are predominantly resolved within the civil court proceedings (Končina Peternel 2015, p. 72–73). However, the child's right to express their views is also exercised through administrative procedures. The high level of protection of the child's right to express their views in Slovenia is proven by some sectoral laws that explicitly provide for the child's active participation in the procedure. Some examples are shown below.

A personal name is a personal right. An adult citizen or a minor's legal representative or guardian may apply for a personal name change to the competent authority. A decision on the change of a personal name is made through administrative procedure. Suppose a change of the personal name of a minor child has been requested. In that case, the consent of the child is required if the child has reached the age of nine and is capable of expressing their will in light of their personal development (Personal Name Act, Art. 12). Case law shows that this legal requirement is duly respected in practice (in the Decision of the Ljubljana High Court IV Cp 72/2020 of 26 February 2020 the child's opinion on the change of personal name was decisive for the court's final decision; in the Decision of the High Court in Maribor III Cp 1189/2007 of 10. August 2007, the court annulled the decision to change the child's name and referred the case back for a new decision, since the decision was taken without the child's opinion, although the child had already reached the age of 11 at the time of the decision).

A child's active participation is also required in some administrative procedures concerning citizenship of the Republic of Slovenia. In administrative procedures concerning the acquisition of citizenship by origin, acquisition of citizenship by naturalisation and termination of citizenship by release, the consent of the child is required to acquire or terminate citizenship of the Republic of Slovenia if the child is older than 14 years of age (Citizenship of the Republic of Slovenia Act, Art. 8, Art. 14, Art. 24). The application of this provision does not seem to be a problem in practice, since there is no case law on this issue.

A special position in terms of the child's active participation is also ensured in administrative procedures for international protection. Children's rights in migration and international protection are given special attention at the international level and in European Union law (Samobor 2024, pp. 54–58). In addition to the general procedural guarantees that must be guaranteed to all applicants for international protection, Slovenian law provides additional procedural guarantees for vulnerable persons needing special procedural guarantees and for unaccompanied minors (International Protection Act, Art. 14 and 16). Procedural guarantees for minors applying for international protection include, in particular, the appointment of a legal representative for the unaccompanied minor, informing the unaccompanied minor of their rights and obligations in the procedure in a manner appropriate to their age and level of mental development, and adapting the personal interview to the age of the applicant. The legal representative of the unaccompanied minor must perform all their duties following the principle of the best interests of the child and must have special knowledge in this respect. The legal representative must consult the minor on all important decisions and take their opinion into account with regard to their age, maturity and developmental capacity. The case law explicitly requires an active role of the legal representative in the procedure (in this regard, the Supreme Court of the Republic of Slovenia, in its decision I Up 177/2015 of 23 September 2015, stated that the authority must protect the rights of the minor applicant throughout the procedure, but that at the same time, the legal representative is also obliged to point out possible violations of the minor's rights and, if necessary, request their remedy). Personal interviews in international protection procedures are fundamental to the right to be heard and are intended to establish the grounds relevant to the decision. Slovenian case law guarantees a high level of protection of this right and has already taken a position on omitting a personal interview. In doing so, it has been considered that the principle of the best interests of the child requires that in a procedure for granting international protection, an applicant who is a minor and who is unaccompanied must be ensured all procedural rights that enable him or her to present the elements necessary to substantiate his or her application as completely as possible (on this point, see Constitutional Court decision No. Up-748/16 of 25 April 2018, Supreme Court decision No. I Up 104/2018 of 19 May 2021).

To ensure the most effective exercise of the right under Article 12 of the CRC, the institution of Children's Advocacy was established in Slovenia in 2017. Initially, a pilot project named 'A Child's Voice' was set up in 2007 to test how children's advocacy could function in specific proceedings. On this basis, amendments to the Slovenian Human Rights Ombudsman Act were adopted, and today, Children's advocacy is defined as one of the regular tasks of the Ombudsman. The purpose of Children's advocacy is to provide professional assistance enabling a child to express an opinion in all procedures and cases the child is involved in and to communicate the child's opinion to the competent authorities and institutions that decide on the child's rights and best interests. Professional assistance consists of psychosocial support provided to the child, conversations about their wishes, feelings and opinions, providing information to the child as to procedures and activities in a child-appropriate manner, seeking the best solution together with the child, and accompanying the child before authorities and institutions deciding on the child's rights and best interests (Human Rights Ombudsman Act, Art. 25.a).

The appointment of an advocate may be proposed by anyone who believes a child cannot exercise the right to express an opinion. Suppose the Ombudsman considers the proposal to be justified. In that case, the Ombudsman shall obtain the consent of both parents or legal representatives and shall appoint an advocate from the list of advocates. It shall not be required to obtain the consent of a parent who has been deprived of parental responsibility or is permanently incapable of expressing will. The consent of parents or legal representatives is not required if a child who has reached the age of 15 consents to the appointment of an advocate. If parents or legal representatives refuse to give their consent to the appointment of an advocate or if they subsequently withdraw it, the Ombudsman shall send a proposal for the appointment of an advocate to the competent social work centre or court, which shall then appoint one from the list of advocates if it considers that this is in the child's best interest in the procedure before the social work centre or court (Human Rights Ombudsman Act, Art. 25.a).

The Ombudsman's annual reports show that children's advocacy is well accepted in practice. In 2023, the Ombudsman received 101 petitions to appoint an advocate, and 85 children were assigned an advocate. The most frequent initiatives for the appointment of an advocate came from parents, social work centres or courts (Summary of the Work of the Ombudsman of the Republic of Slovenia for 2023).

4 The Procedural Capacity of a Child in Administrative Proceedings in Croatia

The significance of children as integral members of the community is particularly emphasised in the Republic of Croatia. As a nation with a relatively small population and a high average age, Croatia recognises the critical importance of demographic reinforcement, wherein natality policies hold a central position (Malnar and Malnar 2019, p. 51; Ivanda 2017, p. 11).[2] The state's focus on children is visible in numerous legal and strategic documents. Croatia has ratified the CRC (1989) and the CERC (1996). By ratifying these conventions, Croatia has committed to upholding all the standards prescribed therein. Additionally, as a member state of the European Union, Croatia is bound by the Charter of Fundamental Rights of the European Union and its provisions aimed at protecting children. The importance and protection of children are also enshrined in the Constitution of the Republic of Croatia. The Constitution stipulates that the family is under special protection by the state, that the state safeguards children and youth, and that parents have a duty to raise, support, and educate their children. Parents are further responsible for ensuring the child's right to complete and harmonious personality development. Moreover, the Constitution guarantees that children with physical or mental impairments or those who are socially neglected have the right to special care, education, and protection. The state holds particular responsibility for minors without parental care and those whose parents fail to provide for them. A significant constitutional provision mandates that everyone must protect children (Constitution of the Republic of Croatia, Arts. 61–64). This obligation extends beyond parents, guardians, relatives, and teachers to include administrative bodies and courts responsible for deciding children's rights in legal proceedings (Čop and Svalina 2015, p. 140). The constitutional provisions are further elaborated through numerous laws within Croatia's legal framework. For example, children's rights are protected under the Family Act, the Social Welfare Act, the Personal Name Act, and some procedural laws such as the Civil Procedure Act. Croatia's commitment to children is further

[2] In 2024, the Croatian Parliament adopted the Strategy for the Demographic Revitalization of the Republic of Croatia until 2033, published in the Official Gazette of the Republic of Croatia, no. 36/24.

demonstrated by adopting the National Plan for Children's Rights in the Republic of Croatia for 2022–2026 and the National Action Plan for the Implementation of the Council Recommendation establishing a European Child Guarantee. The importance of children within a state reflects a collective awareness of the child as a distinct community member, requiring productive coexistence within a given social milieu (Pintar 2018, p. 8).

However, scientific literature underscores that children's rights, as guaranteed by international conventions and the constitution, hold little practical value if children cannot realise them effectively. Accordingly, it is emphasised that comprehensive legislative provisions must ensure children's procedural rights, empowering them to safeguard their endangered or infringed subjective rights in judicial proceedings. It is argued that children, as holders of specific subjective rights, should be able to independently initiate legal proceedings to assert or protect these rights. Regrettably, in practice in Croatia, it is more common for children to become involved in proceedings initiated by their parents regarding specific aspects of parental care or by the social welfare centre acting in a guardianship capacity rather than being authorised to initiate proceedings independently (Aras 2014, p. 35).

The position of children in legal proceedings in Croatia has been the focus of continuous improvement. A notable milestone in this area is the Family Act (2015), which prescribes that a child is a party in all court proceedings concerning their rights and interests (Family Act, Art. 358). This represents a significant advancement in the protection of children, who, under previously applicable legislation, were not consistently granted party status in proceedings affecting their rights. For instance, children were not recognised as parties in cases related to their parents' divorce, decisions on visitation and custody, or the imposition of protective measures (Šantek and Parać Garma 2016, p. 35; Uzelac and Rešetar 2009, p. 176). Regrettably, this provision of the Family Act is limited to protecting children in court proceedings and does not extend to administrative proceedings. Considerable efforts have also been made to enhance the protection of children within the realm of criminal law.[3] However, the situation within administrative law is significantly less developed. The position of children in administrative proceedings and the decision-making in administrative matters remains insufficiently addressed.

Although numerous children's rights in administrative matters are decided in administrative proceedings in Croatia, the General Administrative Procedure Act, as the fundamental law governing decision-making in all administrative matters, does not include specific provisions regarding the protection of children or, in particular, the representation of children in administrative proceedings. A child is considered a party in administrative procedures, guaranteeing all procedural rights. As a person granted legal and subsequently capacity to be a party (Borković 2002, p. 420), a child is a party in administrative procedures whenever a decision made by the administrative body may affect the child's rights or obligations in any way (General Administrative Procedure Act, Art. 4). A child's right to participate as a party in the

[3] For this purpose, see more Vuletić (2019), pp. 209–228, Herceg Pakšić (2024), pp. 9–26.

procedure is based on its capacity to bring proceedings—the legal interest of an individual in participating in a specific procedure, which must always be grounded in the legal connection between the individual and the subject of the administrative procedure (Đerđa 2010, p. 90). Thus, in administrative procedures, a child is a party only if the adjudication concerns their personal or property rights and obligations. The party's status in administrative procedures is significant, as it is associated with the person's right to be heard in the proceeding. This right empowers the party to comment on the facts, circumstances, and legal issues relevant to resolving the administrative matter. An administrative procedure can only proceed without giving the party the right to be heard if the party's request is entirely accepted if the decision in the procedure does not negatively affect the legal interests of the party, or if it is prescribed by law (General Administrative Procedure Act, Art. 30). The right to be heard also aids the administrative body in determining the facts, as the factual situation in the specific case, which serves as the basis for granting rights or imposing obligations to individual, is generally well known to the party. On the other hand, the right to be heard enables the party to protect its interests, as it can contest the statements of other parties, witnesses, and experts and highlight potential factual inaccuracies, errors in logical reasoning, or misinterpretations of legal provisions to the body conducting the procedure (Turčić 2012, pp. 80–81; Krijan 2004, pp. 33–34).

However, for a party in administrative procedures to exercise the right to be heard, they must possess procedural capacity. The ability to undertake any legal action requires procedural capacity. In Croatia, procedural capacity is generally closely linked to the full capacity to contract, which refers to a person's ability to create legal effects through their declarations of will, i.e., to acquire rights and obligations (Borković 2002, p. 420; Krijan 2004, p. 72). For a party in administrative procedures to be authorised to undertake procedural actions, they must have full capacity to contract, or at least limited capacity to contract, in the administrative matter at hand (General Administrative Procedure Act, Art. 31).[4] A person acquires full capacity to contract upon reaching the age of 18. The only exception to this rule applies to individuals over 16 who have entered into marriage, as marriage grants them full capacity to contract (Family Act, Art. 117). Scientific literature indicates

[4] In accordance with Article 234 of the Family Act (Official Gazette of the Republic of Croatia, no. 103/15, 98/19, 47/20, 49/23, 156/23), the court, in non-contentious proceedings, may partially deprive an adult of the capacity to contract if the individual, due to mental health issues or other reasons, is unable to manage certain rights, needs, or interests, or if their actions threat to the rights and interests of others. Exceptionally, the court may fully deprive an adult of the capacity to contract when it is deemed essential for protecting the individual's rights and interests, particularly if the person is incapable of establishing meaningful contact with others or expressing their will. The court's decision regarding the deprivation of the capacity to contract will specify the actions and transactions the individual is deemed incapable of undertaking independently, whether related to their personal affairs or property. However, actions not explicitly restricted in such decision may still be undertaken independently by a person who has been partially deprived of the capacity to contract. Pursuant to Article 85 of the Family Act, a child over the age of 15 who earns income acquires limited legal capacity. Such a child may independently perform legal actions within the scope of their earnings, provided these actions do not jeopardize their financial support.

that, in practice, there is often no distinction made in Croatia between a child's capacity to be a party and their procedural capacity. While a child acquires the capacity to be a party at birth and loses it upon death, they acquire the full capacity to contract either upon reaching the age of 18 or through marriage before reaching that age (Šantek and Parać Garma 2016, p. 36). Therefore, in Croatia, children do not possess procedural capacity unless they have entered into marriage after the age of 16, thus acquiring the full capacity to contract. As a result, they are not authorised to undertake procedural actions in administrative procedures, as it is considered that they are insufficiently capable of assessing the significance of their statements and actions.

For this reason, a child's rights and legal interests in administrative procedures must be mandatorily protected by a person authorised to represent the child. The individuals authorised to represent a child in administrative procedures include the legal representative, a temporary representative, or an authorised person.[5] When an authorised representative represents a child, the administrative body must communicate with this individual throughout the procedure. In exceptional cases, and only when necessary to establish facts of the case, the administrative body may request the child's direct involvement in the procedure, primarily to hear the child regarding facts and circumstances pertinent to resolving the administrative matter (General Administrative Procedure Act, Art. 32).

In administrative procedures, the child is generally represented by their parents, who exercise parental care.[6] Parents have both the right and the obligation to represent their child in matters concerning personal and property rights by mutual agreement in relation to third parties, including in administrative procedures (Lucić 2021, p. 817; Guštin 2024, p. 33; Turčić 2012, p. 85; Krijan 2004, p. 72). A legal presumption exists that one parent has given consent for the other to represent the child without explicit consent, except in procedures concerning changing the child's name or selecting their residence or domicile. In these cases, the parent representing the child must have written consent from the other parent with the right to represent the child. A parent is authorised to independently represent the child only in areas of parental care where the other parent is legally restricted or limited by a court decision (Family Act, Arts. 99–100). A parent, on behalf of and for the child's

[5] In Croatia, a joint representative may also serve as an authorized representative. However, as this role is not pertinent to the subject matter of this study, it will not be discussed in further detail.

[6] In Croatia, pursuant to Articles 91 and 92 of the Family Act, parental care encompasses the responsibilities, duties, and rights of parents, exercised to protect and promote the child's personal and property rights, as well as their overall well-being. Parental care includes the right and duty to safeguard the child's personal rights, such as health, development, care, protection, upbringing, and education, as well as to maintain personal relationships and determine the child's place of residence. These provisions also carry significant implications for representing the child in administrative proceedings, as parental care extends to the right and duty to represent the child's personal and property rights and interests. Parents are required to exercise parental care in alignment with the developmental needs and abilities of the child. Moreover, a parent cannot waive their right to parental care.

benefit, is authorised to undertake all procedural actions in administrative procedures, from submitting a request to initiate the procedure to filing legal remedies.

A child's legal representative also includes the child's guardian. A guardian is appointed for a child without parental care whose parents are deceased, missing, unknown, deprived of parental rights, or lack legal capacity, or who is otherwise unable to care for the child. The Croatian Centre for Social Welfare appoints a guardian for the child in the administrative procedure (Family Act, Arts. 218, 224). Unlike parents, a guardian does not have absolute freedom to represent the child but must obtain prior approval from the Croatian Centre for Social Welfare in proceedings relating to the child's personal status and property management (Guštin 2024, p. 33).

In addition to parents and guardians, a child may also be represented in administrative procedure by a special guardian. A special guardian is appointed to protect the child's rights and interests or when there is a conflict of interest between the child and their legal representatives. The Croatian Centre for Social Welfare or a court may appoint a special guardian to represent the child in all administrative procedures where it is necessary to safeguard the child's rights and interests.[7] Unlike a guardian, a special guardian represents the child only in the specific proceedings for which they are appointed. At the same time, the parents continue to exercise parental care over the child but do not represent them in that particular procedure. The decision appointing the special guardian specifies their duties in relation to the child (Family Act, Arts. 99, 240, 242; Guštin 2024, p. 34).

Exceptionally, a child may be represented by a temporary representative or an authorised person. A temporary representative is appointed for a child who does not have a legal representative because the parents or guardian are deceased or because the guardian or special guardian has been relieved of their duties. A temporary representative for a child without parental care is appointed by the administrative body conducting the procedure until a special guardian is appointed or if the actions of the parents or guardian, by the opinion of the administrative body conducting the procedure, are deemed to harm the child's interests (Guštin 2024, pp. 34–35). The temporary representative participates in the administrative procedure and performs actions for which they were appointed until a new guardian is appointed or until the actions for which they were appointed are completed (General Administrative Procedure Act, Art. 34). Finally, in administrative procedures, a child is represented by an authorised person when decided by the child's parents or guardian, as a child without procedural capacity is not authorised to appoint an authorised person independently.[8] Actions taken by the authorised person within the scope of the given power have legal effect as if the party had taken them (General Administrative Procedure Act, Art. 36).

---

[7] A special guardian may be an employee of the Centre for Special Guardianship who has passed the bar exam.

[8] An authorised person may be an attorney, a law firm, or another legal entity authorized by law to represent a party. Additionally, any individual with full capacity to contract, except one engaged in unauthorized legal practice, may also serve as a authorised person.

All of these individuals, as persons authorised to represent a child without procedural capacity, are empowered to undertake procedural actions in administrative procedures on behalf of and for the child's benefit, thereby safeguarding its rights and legal interests. A specific feature of Croatian administrative procedure is the obligation of the administrative body to prioritise the protection of the rights and legal interests of all parties involved, regardless of whether they are children. The administrative body is also obliged to assist a party whenever, during the procedure, it becomes aware of or believes that the party has grounds to exercise a specific right. This obligation is one of the key principles of administrative procedure. Consequently, the administrative body must inform the party of the legal consequences of their actions or omissions and ensure that any lack of knowledge or inexperience does not harm the rights to which the party is legally entitled (General Administrative Procedure Act, Art. 7). This principle obliges the administrative body not only about the party itself but also to its authorised representative, ensuring that the rights of all parties, particularly those of a child, are adequately protected. Nevertheless, despite this institute, the procedural mechanisms designed to protect a party's rights are not specifically tailored to children.

The representation of children in administrative procedure in Croatia is governed by the General Administrative Procedure Act, as for any other party without procedural capacity. However, the influence of the CRC and the CECR is reflected in certain laws governing specific administrative areas that pertain to cases in which a child is a party. As previously emphasised, these conventions impose an obligation on contracting states to ensure that children have the right to express their opinions in legal proceedings. Accordingly, the Croatian Family Act stipulates that parents and other persons responsible for the child's care must respect the child's opinion following the child's age and maturity. This right is particularly highlighted in procedures where decisions regarding the child's rights or interests are made. In such cases, the child is entitled to know more about the relevant case circumstances, receive advice, and, importantly, express their opinion and be informed of the potential outcomes of considering their opinion. However, since children do not have full capacity to contract, the weight of their statements remains limited by their age and maturity (Family Act, Art. 86).[9]

Similar provisions are found in particular laws that govern specific administrative procedures. For example, in procedures concerning the rights and interests of a child within the social welfare system, the child has the right to be appropriately informed about the key circumstances of the case, to receive advice, to express their opinion, and to be notified of the potential consequences of their opinion being considered. In this context, the administrative body is also obliged to take the child's opinion into account in accordance with their age and maturity (Social Welfare Act, Art. 10). In procedures related to the appointment of a guardian; the administrative body must seek the opinion of the child who is capable of understanding the

[9] The right of a child to express their views was introduced into Croatian legislation in 1998, with the purpose of directly implementing Article 12 of the Convention on the Rights of the Child. For further details, see Rešetar et al. (2021), pp. 143–144.

significance of guardianship and the role of the guardian. The child's wishes regarding the selected guardian must be considered unless such wishes are contrary to the child's best interests (Family Act, Art. 225). In certain administrative procedures, a child is not only entitled to express their opinion but also to give their consent to the decision of the administrative body. For instance, the child's consent is required for adoption if the child is 12 years old or older. If the child is younger than 12, they have the right to express their opinion on the adoption, which must be considered in accordance with their age and maturity. However, the validity of the decision is not contingent upon the child's consent (Family Act, Art. 191). Similarly, a child older than 10 must consent to change their name (Personal Name Act, Arts. 4, 7).[10] In this regard, when obtaining a statement from a child, the administrative body is bound by a specific procedure in the Regulation on the Method of Obtaining the Child's Opinion. However, in areas where special laws do not establish the child's right to express their opinion in administrative procedure, all statements made on behalf of the child must be provided exclusively by the person authorised to represent the child and not by the child.[11]

Although the laws mentioned above establish the child's right to be heard before judicial or administrative bodies whenever decisions are made regarding their rights and interests, the child's right to express an opinion in the administrative procedure is not unconditional. It is limited by their age and maturity and their ability to understand the meaning of their statements and actions, which must be taken into account by the body conducting the administrative procedure. In other words, the administrative body must continually assess whether the child is capable of expressing an opinion, thereby ensuring the protection of their rights and legal interests (Hrabar 2021, p. 33; Rešetar 2022, p. 350; Guštin 2024, pp. 28, 41). The child's right to express an opinion in administrative procedure implies their active participation in the adjudication process concerning the administrative matter. This raises the question of whether the provisions of the laws mentioned above extend the procedural capacity of the child in these proceedings, i.e., whether they exclude the requirement for the child to be represented by an authorised representative. We believe that the child's right to express opinion should serve as a source of information for the

[10] In Croatia, certain laws completely disregard a child's opinion regarding their personal rights, even when these rights are the subject of administrative proceedings. For example, in proceedings related to the naturalization of their parents, a minor child automatically follows the legal status of their parents and acquires Croatian citizenship irrespective of their own will. Likewise, a child loses Croatian citizenship, again regardless of their will, if their parents cease to be Croatian citizens. Articles 13 and 20 of the Croatian Citizenship Act, Official Gazette of the Republic of Croatia, No. 53/91, 70/91, 28/92, 113/93, 4/94, 130/11, 110/15, 102/19, 138/21.

[11] See more in: Administrative Court in Zagreb, Case no. UsI-2342/21-5, March 1, 2022, Administrative Court in Rijeka, Case no. 3 Us I-1248/2021-11, December 23, 2021, Administrative Court in Rijeka, Case no. 2 Us I-1100/2020-8, February 10, 2021, Administrative Court in Rijeka, Case no. 3 Us I-281/2023-9, April 25, 2023, Administrative Court in Rijeka, Case no. 3 Us I-763/2021-8, October 14, 2021, Administrative Court in Rijeka, Case no. 3 Us I-113/2022-8, March 31, 2021, Administrative Court in Rijeka, Case no. 2 Us I-450/2022-11, September 21, 2022 etc.

administrative body regarding the facts relevant to resolving the administrative matter. The child's opinion of the guardian or adoptive parent, along with any prior experiences with these individuals, assists the body in conducting the procedure of determining whether the potential guardian or adoptive parents will act in the child's best interests. A similar approach applies to considering the child's opinion regarding a personal name change. It is important to remember that children's rights and legal interests are more strongly protected in administrative procedures due to their vulnerability and inability to fully comprehend the meaning and consequences of their statements and actions. This protection is reinforced by the requirement for authorised representatives to represent it. The apparent expansion of their rights, allowing them the right to be heard, could result in significant harm—particularly when children are not adequately represented by responsible individuals authorised to do so. This would be due to the child's inability to recognise and understand the importance of the statements made in the administrative procedures. Under international conventions and laws governing specific administrative areas, children in some administrative procedures in Croatia have the right to express their opinions. However, they still lack procedural capacity, which is necessary for undertaking all procedural actions, including filing legal remedies. Therefore, when a child is requested to give a statement, the administrative body must also inform the authorised representative simultaneously (General Administrative Procedure Act, Art. 32).

In administrative procedures in Croatia, the rights of children are further strengthened. In addition to procedural actions being taken on behalf of and for the child's benefit by authorised representatives, children also have the right to express their opinions, thereby voicing their views in the procedures (Guštin 2024, p. 37). When considering the child's opinion, particular attention must be paid to the maturity of each child, as this is a fundamental assumption for determining the relevance of the expressed opinion. A child's maturity and ability to understand the situation are essential in Croatia when deciding whether and to what extent a child should be actively involved in the administrative procedures, all to protect their welfare (Hrabar 2013, p. 71). This approach to child representation in administrative procedures is consistent with the convention-based guarantees that authorise the child to express their opinion in resolving an administrative matter.

Croatia has established a dedicated ombudsman for children to further protect their rights, especially in administrative procedures. This special ombudsman has been operational since 2003. Its core responsibilities include monitoring the compliance of laws and regulations in the Republic of Croatia relating to the protection of children's rights and interests with the Constitution, conventions, and other international instruments; overseeing the implementation of Croatia's obligations arising from conventions and other international instruments; monitoring the application of regulations related to the protection of children's rights; warning on violations of individual children's rights; advocating for the protection and promotion of the rights of children with difficulties; proposing measures to build a comprehensive system for the protection and promotion of children's rights; preventing harmful actions that threaten children's rights; and informing the public about the state of children's rights (Children's Ombudsman Act, Art. 7).

5 Concluding Remarks

In conclusion, the Slovenian and Croatian legal systems are comparable in their provisions for protecting children's rights in administrative procedures. Both frameworks recognise children as parties in such procedures, requiring them to be represented by a legal representative until they reach the age of majority. Both countries also have detailed regulations ensuring that representation conforms with the principle of the child's best interests. Additionally, both countries effectively incorporate commitments from international documents, allowing children deemed sufficiently mature under national law to be consulted and express their views during administrative procedures. Slovenia and Croatia demonstrate a proactive approach to protecting children's rights through the work of their respective Ombudsman offices. Slovenia has established a specialised institution called Children's Advocacy, which provides professional support to help children voice their opinions in proceedings and matters that affect them. Similarly, Croatia has created the Ombudsman for Children, a dedicated institution for protecting and promoting the rights and interests of children. This high level of protection reflects a shared dedication to upholding the rights and voices of children in administrative matters.

Legislation

Act on Croatian Citizenship, Official Gazette of the Republic of Croatia, Nos. 53/91, 70/91, 28/92, 113/93, 4/94, 130/11, 110/15, 102/19, 138/21.
Act on Identity Cards, Official Gazette of the Republic of Croatia, no. 62/15, 42/20, 144/20, 114/22, 18/24.
Act on Mandatory Health Insurance of the Republic of Croatia, Official Gazette, no. 80/13, 137/13, 98/19, 33/23.
Act on Personal Identification Number of the Republic of Croatia, Official Gazette, no. 60/08.
Charter of Fundamental Rights of the European Union, Official Journal of the European Union, C 202/2016.
Children's Ombudsman Act, Official Gazette of the Republic of Croatia, no. 73/17.
Citizenship of the Republic of Slovenia Act, Official Gazette of the Republic of Slovenia no. 1/91 as amended.
Civil Procedure Act, Official Gazette of the Republic of Croatia, no. 148/11, 25/13, 89/14, 70/19, 80/22, 114/22, 155/23.
Constitution of the Republic of Croatia, Official Gazette of the Republic of Croatia, no. 56/90, 135/97, 113/00, 28/01, 76/10, 5/14, 85/10.
Constitution of the Republic of Slovenia, Official Gazette of the Republic of Slovenia no. 33/91-I, 42/97, 66/2000, 24/03, 69/04, 68/06, 47/13, 75/16 and 92/21.

Croatian Citizenship Act, Official Gazette of the Republic of Croatia, No. 53/91, 70/91, 28/92, 113/93, 4/94, 130/11, 110/15, 102/19, 138/21.
Employment Relations Act, Official Gazette of the Republic of Slovenia no. 21/13 as amended.
European Convention on the Exercise of Children's Rights, Official Gazette - International Agreements, No. 1/10.
Family Act, Official Gazette of the Republic of Croatia, no. 103/15, 98/19, 47/20, 49/23, 156/23.
Family Act, Official Gazette of the Republic of Slovenia no. 15/17, 21/18, 22/19, 67/19, 200/20, 94/22, 94/22, 5/23, 34/24.
Financial Administration Act, Official Gazette of the Republic of Slovenia no. 25/14, 39/22, 14/23 in 47/24.
General Administrative Procedure Act, Official Gazette of the Republic of Croatia, no. 47/09, 110/21.
General Administrative Procedure Act, Official Gazette of the Republic of Slovenia, no. 24/06, 105/06, 126/07, 65/08, 8/10, 82/13, 175/20-ZIUOPDVE in 3/22 – Zdeb.
Health Care and Health Insurance Act, Official Gazette of the Republic of Slovenia no. 72/06 as amended.
Human Rights Ombudsman Act, Official Gazette of the Republic of Slovenia no. 71/93 as amended.
Identity Card Act, Official Gazette of the Republic of Slovenia no. 35/11, 41/21 and 199/21.
International Protection Act, Official Gazette of the Republic of Slovenia no. 22/16 as amended.
Personal Name Act, Official Gazette of the Republic of Croatia, no. 118/12, 70/17, 98/19.
Personal Name Act, Official Gazette of the Republic of Slovenia, no. 20/06 and 43/19.
Provision of Foster Care Act, Official Gazette of the Republic of Slovenia, no. 110/02 as amended.
Regulation on the Method of Obtaining the Child's Opinion, Official Gazette of the Republic of Croatia, no. 103/15)
Social Welfare Act, Official Gazette of the Republic of Croatia, no. 18/22, 46/22, 119/22, 71/23, 156/23.
Travel Documents Act, Official Gazette of the Republic of Slovenia no. 29/11.
United Nations. (1989). *Convention on the Rights of the Child*. Retrieved from https://www.ohchr.org/en/instruments-mechanisms/instruments/convention-rights-child.

References

Aras S (2014) Položaj djeteta u postupku prema novom Obiteljskom zakonu. In: Barbić J (ed) Novo uređenje obiteljskih sudskih postupaka. Hrvatska akademija znanosti i umjetnosti, Zagreb
Borković I (2002) Upravno pravo. Narodne novine, Zagreb
Bruning M, Doek J (2021) Characteristics of an effective child protection system in the European and international contexts. Int J Child Maltreat Res Policy Pract:4
Čop M, Svalina I (2015) Obiteljskopravni aspekt izdvajanja djeteta iz obitelji. Pravnik 48(98)
Đerđa D (2010) Opći upravni postupak u Republici Hrvatskoj. Inženjerski biro, Zagreb
Guštin M (2024) Zaštita procesnih prava djeteta u upravnim postupcima s posebnim osvrtom na postupanja u vezi s osobnim stanjima građana. Dijete i obitelj u suvremenom društvu 1(1)
Herceg Pakšić B (2024) (Kazneno)pravni položaj djeteta u sukobu sa zakonom u Republici Hrvatskoj: temeljni obrisi. Dijete i obitelj u suvremenom društvu 1(1)
Hrabar D (2013) Nova procesna prava djeteta—europski pregled. Godišnjak Akademije pravnih znanosti Hrvatske 4(1)
Hrabar D (2021) Uvod u prava djece, Prava djece—multidisciplinarni pristup. Pravni fakultet u Zagrebu, Zagreb
Ivanda K (2017) Demografija Hrvatske: stanje, zablude i perspektive. Polit Anal 7(31)
Kerševan E, Androjna V (2017) Upravno procesno pravo. IUS Software, GV Založba, Ljubljana
Kmecl A (2020) In: Kovač P, Kerševan E (eds) Komentar Zakona o splošnem upravnem postopku (ZUP), Uradni list. Pravna fakulteta Univerze v Ljubljani, Ljubljana
Krijan P (2004) Komentar Zakona o općem upravnom postupku. Novi informator
Lucić N (2021) Zastupanje u vezi s bitnim osobnim pravima djeteta, Zbornik radova Pravnog fakulteta u Splitu, god 58, br. 3
Malnar A, Malnar D (2019) Demografska problematika u strateškim političkim dokumentima Republike Hrvatske. Forum za sigurnosne studije 3(3)
Končina Peternel, Mateja (2015) Pravice otrok v družinskem pravu – razvoj v RS od uveljavitve KOP dalje. In: Šelih A, Filipčič K (eds) Otrokove pravice v Sloveniji: Sedanje stanje in izzivi za prihodnost, Slovenska akademija znanosti in umetnosti, Ljubljana
Pintar Ž (2018) Dijete kao vrijednost suvremenoga društva. Acta Iadertina 15(2)
Rešetar B, Lucić N Croatia S (2021) International handbook on child participation in family law. Intersentia, Cambridge
Rešetar B (2022) Komentar Obiteljskog zakona (Knjiga I.). Organizator, Zagreb
Samobor A (2024) Pravice otrok in Skupni evropski azilni sistem; Kaj prinaša reforma evropske azilne zakonodaje. In: Šelih A, Filipčič K, Briški L (eds) Otrok kot žrtev kaznivih dejanj, Slovenska akademija znanosti in umetnosti. Inštitut za kriminologijo pri Pravni fakulteti, Ljubljana
Šantek R, Parać Garma M (2016) Sudjelovanje djeteta u sudskim postupcima te zaštita prava i dobrobiti djeteta u tim postupcima. Pravosudna akademija, Zagreb
Turčić Z (2012) Komentar Zakona o općem upravnom postupku. Organizator
UNICEF Croatia (2025) Convention on the Rights of the Child, url: https://www.unicef.hr/wp-content/uploads/2017/05/Konvencija_20o_20pravima_20djeteta_full.pdf (23.1.2025)
Uzelac A, Rešetar B (2009) Procesni položaj i zastupanje djeteta u sudskom postupku. In: Rešetar B (ed) Dijete i pravo. Pravni fakultet u Osijeku, Osijek
Vuletić I (2019) Položaj djeteta u hrvatskom kaznenom materijalnom pravu. In: Župan M (ed) Prekogranično kretanje djece u Europskoj uniji. Pravni fakultet u Osijeku, Osijek
Žuber B (2020) In: Kovač P, Kerševan E (eds) Komentar Zakona o splošnem upravnem postopku (ZUP), Uradni list. Pravna fakulteta Univerze v Ljubljani, Ljubljana

Bruna Žuber is an Associate Professor at the Faculty of Law, University of Ljubljana, Department of Administrative Law. She holds the position of Vice Dean of the Faculty of Law. Previously, she was the Head of the Department of Administrative Law. She defended her doctoral thesis at the University of Ljubljana in 2017 (cum laude) and successfully passed the national bar exam in 2014. She is the author of numerous scientific publications in the field of administrative and constitutional procedural law, which have been published by esteemed national and international academic publishers and journals. She is the project leader of several national research projects focused on administrative procedural law and is also involved in international research projects. In addition to her academic work, she has been a member of national expert groups for the reform of national legislation and has acted as a legal expert for the preparation of national legislation in recent years. Her professional excellence and academic contributions have recently been recognised with four prestigious awards. https://orcid.org/0000-0003-1137-4561

Dario Đerđa Ph.D., a Full Professor of Administrative Law, is the Dean at the University of Rijeka, Faculty of Law, and the Head of the Department of Administrative Law. He is the author of over 100 scientific and professional articles and papers, as well as monographs on the General Administrative Procedure in the Republic of Croatia, Fundamentals of Administrative law of the European Union, Administrative Procedure, and Administrative Dispute. In 2013, he was awarded the state legal award Jadranko Crnić for his book, which made a significant contribution to the legal profession in 2012. He has been an active presenter and moderator at numerous international and domestic scientific and professional conferences. As a member of various working groups, he has contributed to drafting numerous laws in the field of administrative law, including the General Administrative Procedure Act and the Law on Administrative Disputes. https://orcid.org/0000-0002-1095-1155

Employment of Adolescents and Children: Minimum Working Age in Lithuanian and Polish Law

Ingrida Mačernytė Panomariovienė and Tatiana Wrocławska

Abstract This chapter examines the employment of individuals under the age of 18 within the framework of Lithuanian and Polish labour laws, highlighting the requirements set by ILO Convention No 138 to establish and progressively raise the minimum age for work or employment. This approach aims to ensure alignment with the fullest physical and mental development of young individuals. The analysis is grounded in international standards that define age limits and provide guidelines for acceptable working conditions for young workers. Given the regulatory flexibility permitted by these standards, national statutory regulations display notable variations, particularly in terms of minimum age requirements and permissible employment based on psychophysical characteristics and contractual frameworks. The chapter offers a comparative analysis by identifying the differences in labour regulations between the examined countries, with a particular focus on the extent of prohibitions on work and employment. Additionally, it addresses two critical challenges in contemporary labour policies: on the one hand, the effective abolition of child labour, and on the other, ensuring the safety and proper development of working children.

1 Introduction

Child labour has long been recognised as a significant social and economic human rights issue. The protection of children in the workplace is enshrined in several international human rights instruments. The International Covenant on Economic,

I. Mačernytė Panomariovienė (✉)
Lithuanian Centre for Social Sciences, Law Institute, Vilnius, Lithuania
e-mail: ingrida.macernyte@teise.org

T. Wrocławska
University of Lodz, Faculty of Law and Administration, Lodz, Poland
e-mail: twroclawska@wpia.uni.lodz.pl

A. Limantė, R. Vaičiūnienė (eds.), *Children's Rights in Central and Eastern Europe*, European Union and its Neighbours in a Globalized World 29,
https://doi.org/10.1007/978-3-032-07092-0_6

Social and Cultural Rights (1966)[1] and the UN Convention on the Rights of the Child (1989)[2] (UNCRC) explicitly affirm the necessity of protecting children and young individuals from economic exploitation and forced labour.[3] This framework raises critical discussions regarding the hierarchy of children's rights, emphasising fundamental protections such as the right to childhood, the right to education, and freedom from exploitation. These rights are upheld through the prohibition of all forms of labour that could interfere with a child's development or physical and mental well-being.

Globally, approximately 250 million children are engaged in work, many of whom are deprived of access to education, healthcare, and basic freedoms. According to the latest estimates, 160 million children—comprising 63 million girls and 97 million boys—were engaged in child labour at the beginning of 2020, representing nearly one in ten children worldwide. About half of these children were involved in hazardous work that poses serious risks to their health, safety, and moral development (ILO and UNICEF 2021, p. 8). The effective abolition of child labour is one of the four fundamental pillars (rights at work)[4] of the ILO Decent Work Agenda and constitutes an integral part of Goal 8 of the UN 2030[5] Agenda for Sustainable Development. It is also central to the ILO's flagship initiative, the Framework for Action on Child Labour 2023–2025.[6] The presented data suggests a concerning outlook regarding Target 8.7 of the Sustainable Development Goals, which calls for the prohibition and elimination of the worst forms of child labour and aims to eradicate child labour in all its forms by 2025 (UN Agenda 2030).

Efforts to prohibit child labour face challenges in all countries worldwide, both developing and developed. These challenges arise from factors such as large-scale migration, global business structures based on supply chains, and the expanding digital economy.[7] It is important to recognise that the primary goal of sustainable social development is to ensure that its progress and implementation do not harm future generations. Within this framework, the concept of sustainable life-cycle work warrants special attention.This approach necessitates viewing every worker through the lens of the working life cycle, adapting their labour activity to the conditions characteristic of different life stages.[8] Moreover, this perspective raises the question of how to assess the widely adopted policy of extending labour force participation—driven by demographic ageing—in relation to child labour concerns.

[1] Adopted and opened for signature, ratification and accession by General Assembly resolution 2200A (XXI) of 16 December 1966 entry into force 3 January 1976, in accordance with Art. 27.

[2] UN Convention on the Rights of the Child. 1989. OHCHR. Retrieved 28 October 2024.

[3] See: General Comment of CESCR No 18 of 2005 (Right to Work), para 18.

[4] Rights at work, social dialog, social protection and employment creation.

[5] Transforming our world: the 2030 Agenda for Sustainable Development, Resolution adopted by the General Assembly on 25 September 2015, A/RES/70/1: https://sdgs.un.org/2030agenda.

[6] Framework for action on child labour 2023–2025. https://www.ilo.org/publications/framework-action-child-labour-2023-2025.

[7] For more see Siewert (2024).

[8] For more see Mačernytė Panomariovienė and Wrocławska (2023) and Wrocławska (2024).

These considerations highlight the issue of job security for young people, who will face increasing demands for prolonged working periods in the future. Consequently, the minimum age for admission to work or employment remains a highly relevant topic.

Half of the eight fundamental International Labour Organisation (ILO) conventions, which are of an imperative nature and must be implemented by states without reservations (Mačernytė Panomariovienė 2010, p. 101) pertain to the abolition of forced labour. These include the Forced Labour Convention of 1930 (No 29), Abolition of Forced Labour Convention of 1957 (No 105), Convention on Minimum Age of 1973 (No 138) (Convention No 138), Convention on the Worst Forms of Child Labour of 1999 (No 182 (Convention No 182)). Two of these conventions—Convention No 138 and Convention No 182—specifically focus on the prohibition of child labour. It is also essential to note that the Charter of Fundamental Rights of the European Union (2000)[9] (EU Charter) mandates the prohibition of child labour, albeit allowing their employment under specific conditions. Similarly, Directive 94/33/EC,[10] in its preamble, calls for the prohibition of child labour while permitting derogations only in exceptional cases and under strict conditions that do not hinder children's full access to education.[11]

International[12] and European legal instruments do not provide a universal definition of child labour, leaving its interpretation to national regulations.[13] However, guidelines exist: according to international standards, child labour is understood as work that is hazardous to a child's health, physical and mental development, or moral well-being, as well as work that interferes with a child's right to education or deprives them of their childhood.[14] Consequently, not all forms of work undertaken by children fall under the category of child labour that must be abolished.[15] Convention No 138 allows for certain exceptions and derogations (flexibility clauses) for work classified as *'light work.'* Such work must not pose a danger to young people and should contribute to their development by equipping them with skills and experience, considering the economic and educational differences across countries. The aim of preparing young individuals to become productive members

[9] Charter of Fundamental Rights of the European Union of 2000. Official Journal of the European Communities 2000/C 364/01.

[10] Council Directive 94/33/EC Protection of Young People at Work, OJ L 216 (1994).

[11] The Directive 94/33/EC in its Preambule calls to the prohibition of child labour, while in Articles state the prohibition of work by children (Art. 4).

[12] The ILO has provided a comprehensive legal definition of 'child labour' (van Daalen and Hanson 2019, point 8).

[13] Though this definition has been met with critical remarks in academic literature. (Mavunga 2014, p. 126).

[14] Child labour. https://www.ilo.org/topics-and-sectors/child-labour.

[15] For further insights, see discussions on the shift from the objective of abolishing 'all child labour' to the abolition of 'harmful work,' thereby redefining child labour in operational terms (van Daalen and Hanson 2019, point 19).

of society in adulthood, thereby contributing to sustainable social development, should not be underestimated.

This chapter analyses the employment of young persons under Lithuanian and Polish legal frameworks and evaluates the quality of employment regulations. It examines minimum age requirements and permissible types of work in line with the obligation to ensure the effective abolition of child labour and the progressive increase of the minimum age for employment. These considerations take into account global demographic trends, particularly ageing workforces, and the necessity of extending the working lives of adults. In Lithuania, the procedure for child employment, health inspections, and the determination of young persons' suitability for specific jobs are regulated by the Labour Code of the Republic of Lithuania of 14 September 2016[16] (LLC), the Republic of Lithuania Law on Safety and Health at Work of 16 July 2003[17] (SHW), other laws (as Republic of Lithuania Law on Child Rights Protection of 12 April 1996)[18] and legal acts,[19] while in Poland, the employment and working conditions of young persons are primarily governed by the Polish Labour Code (PLC) of 26 June 1974,[20] along with additional relevant regulations[21] that constitute the main bases for the legal regulations on adolescent employment before reaching the age of 18.

2 Data on Youth Employment

At the beginning of 2024, Lithuania's population included approximately 503,510 children under the age of 18, representing 17.44% of the country's total permanent population.[22] According to the 2024 Polish National Census of Population, Poland had 5,229,726 children aged 0–17, constituting around 13.29[23] % of the total population. Despite a declining trend in recent years, this remains a significant

[16] *Official Gazette*, 2016, No 23709.

[17] *Official Gazette*, 2003, No 70-3170.

[18] *Official Gazette*, 1996, No 33-807 (1996).

[19] Resolution of 28 June, 2017 of the Government of Lithuania No 518 On the approval of the Procedure for the Organization of Employment, Work and Vocational Training of Persons Under the Age of Eighteen, and the Description of the Conditions for the Employment of Children. *Official Gazette*, 2017, No 11078 (Resolution No 518).

[20] *Official Gazette*, 1974, No 24 item 141 with amendements.

[21] The Regulation of the Council of Ministers of 26 May 1996 on the vocational training of adolescents and their remuneration (*Official Gazette*, 2018, No 2010), along with the Regulation of the Council of Ministers of 19 June 2023 concerning the list of work prohibited for adolescents and the conditions under which they may be employed in certain occupations (hereinafter referred to as Regulation 2023) (*Official Gazette*, 2023, No 1240), establish the legal framework governing youth employment.

[22] Lithuanian Department of Statistics. https://osp.stat.gov.lt/.

[23] GUS. Polish Central Statistical Office, https://dbw.stat.gov.pl/en/baza-danych.

demographic group that will shape the future labour force. A key question arises: how many children within the aforementioned age range are engaged in employment?

According to Eurostat (Fig. 1), in 2023, Poland had a significantly higher share of young people aged 15–19 engaged in temporary and seasonal employment (80.7%) compared to Lithuania (29.2%).

However, Eurostat data (Fig. 2) indicate that Lithuania had a slightly higher percentage of 15–19-year-olds employed on a permanent basis compared to Poland. In 2023, 5.8% (7900 individuals) of this age group were in stable employment in Lithuania, whereas in Poland, the figure was 5% (33,500 individuals[24]).

A more detailed analysis of statistical data presents certain challenges. Eurostat's labour statistics classify employment by broad age groups (15–19, 15–24, and 15–25), but do not include data on younger children. While the available data provide valuable insights, they do not offer a comprehensive picture of employment among 15–18-year-olds, nor do they reflect the extent of work among children under 15. Notably, employment of the youngest age group is permitted under specific conditions and only for certain activities. Another limitation in the statistical data arises from its focus on formally registered employment relationships. Consequently, it is difficult to determine the real number of working children and adolescents in each country.

National data provide additional insights into youth employment. According to the Social Insurance Fund Board, in Lithuania in 2024, approximately 1500 individuals aged 15–17 were employed, representing 0.11% of the total workforce. In Poland, according to the Polish Central Statistical Office,[25] 18,200 individuals aged

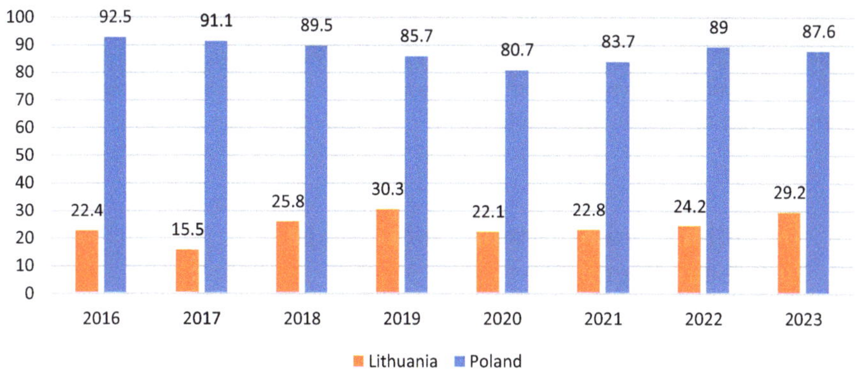

Fig. 1 Temporary and seasonal employment among 15–19-year-olds in Poland and Lithuania (2016–2023, %). *Source*: Eurostat

[24] National Population and Housing Census 2021, op.cit., Table 8.

[25] GUS. (2022). Raport zawierający wstępne wyniki Narodowego Spisu Powszechnego 2021. Główny Urząd Statystyczny. National Population and Housing Census 2021.Population. Size and demographic-social structure in the light of the 2021 Census results, Statistics Poland, Warszaw 2023. https://stat.gov.pl/en/.

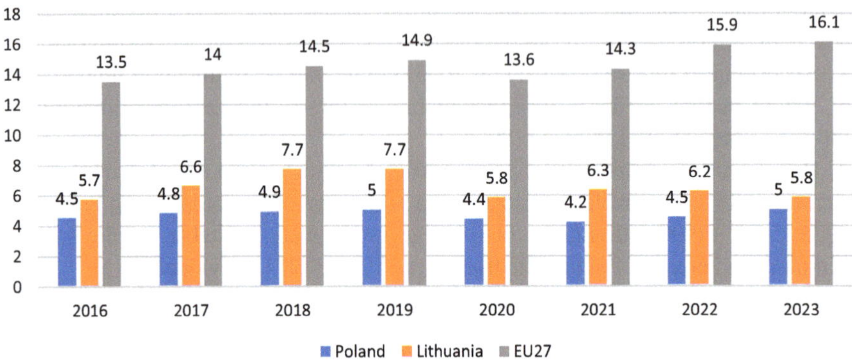

Fig. 2 Youth employment (ages 15–19) in Poland, Lithuania, and the EU27 (2016–2023, %). *Source*: Eurostat

15–17 (referred to as those 'at pre-working age') were employed, accounting for about 0.13% of the workforce. Data from national institutions responsible for issuing employment permits provide only an approximate estimate of the number of children under 16 engaged in work. According to the Polish Chief Labour Inspectorate,[26] in 2023, regional labour inspectorates received 2689 applications for permits allowing children under 16 to undertake work or other gainful activities. The number of applications has risen in 2023, with 2568 applications in 2022 and 1773 in 2021. The figures have fluctuated over the years: 2041 in 2020, 3155 in 2019, 2659 in 2018, 2477 in 2017, and 1729 in 2016. However, as noted earlier, these statistics represent only a fraction of reality, as they account solely for officially registered employment. A significant proportion of children work informally, outside formal employment relationships. Unlike Poland, Lithuania does not require official permits or approvals from public authorities for child employment, making it impossible to obtain comparable data.

3 Definitions and Minimum Working Age in Labour Regulations

First and foremost, it is important to highlight that not all legal sources provide explicit definitions of young persons, children, or adolescents. However, differentiation in labour law based on the calendar age at which individuals enter the workforce serves a specific purpose and constitutes a key issue in labour law, particularly in relation to its protective function.[27] Distinctions based on age groups in terms of

[26] The Polish Chief Labour Inspectorate. GIP-GBI.0701.142.2024.3.

[27] As Weerman and Beijerse point out: "*In various legal areas, there are rules and procedures that apply only to certain ages, as they are related to varying responsibilities, levels of cognition, or socio-emotional capacities to make and understand decisions*" (Weerman et al. 2020).

admission to work and employment are fundamental for the proper protection of young people, as different types of work are permitted for adolescents and children within the statutory framework.

Article 1 of the United Nations Convention on the Rights of the Child (UNCRC) defines a child as anyone under the age of 18 unless legal adulthood is attained earlier. Similarly, Convention No. 182 defines a child as *'all persons under the age of 18'*. However, this general principle is not uniformly applicable across all labour law regulations. For comparison, the Night Work of Young Persons Convention of 1946 (No 79) differentiates between children "under 14" and those "14 and older," while the Night Work of Young Persons Convention of 1948 (No 90) distinguishes between young persons 'under 16' and those aged 16 and above. Within this protected category of childhood, Convention No. 138 establishes minimum age thresholds for different types of employment: 15 years for ordinary work, 18 years for hazardous work, and 13 years for light work (ILO 2011).[28] Regarding European Union (EU) legal frameworks, the EU Charter distinguishes between children and young people but does not provide explicit definitions for these categories. However, under Directive 94/33/EC, the term 'young person' refers to any individual under the age of 18. Additionally, the directive applies the terms "child" and "adolescent," with the criteria for distinction based on calendar age and the requirement to comply with compulsory schooling as defined by national law. A "child" is any young person under the age of 15 or still in compulsory education, while an "adolescent" is any young person aged at least 15 but under 18 who is no longer subject to compulsory education (Art. 3(a)). Similar terminology is used in Article 7 of the European Social Charter (1961)[29] (ESC) and in the Revised European Social Charter (1996)[30] (Revised ESC).

In the national labour laws of the analysed countries, we observe alignment with Directive 94/33/EC, albeit with minor differences regarding the minimum working age for adolescents and the definition of a child. In Lithuania, Article 2 of the SHW defines an adolescent as a person aged between 16 and 18, while a child is a person under 16. Similarly, the Polish Labour Code (PLC) distinguishes between adolescents and children. However, under Article 190(1) of the PLC, adolescents are defined as individuals aged 15–18, while Article 304^5(1) defines children as those under 16. Within these definitions, Polish labour law introduces an intermediate category of "young persons" aged between 15 and 16, who may simultaneously hold the status of both child and adolescent. Notably, in both countries, reaching the age of legal adulthood (i.e., full legal capacity) before 18 does not affect an individual's status as a worker. The determining factor in labour law remains calendar age, rather than the attainment of full legal capacity. It is generally acknowledged

[28] Different minimum working ages apply to "developed" countries. See Art. 2, 3 and 7 of Convention No 138. For more see van Daalen and Hanson 2019, point 8).

[29] European Social Charter (1961). CETS No 035. Turin 18/10/1961.

[30] European Social Charter (revised) (1996). ETS No 163. Strasbourg 03/05/1996.

that individuals under 18 not only lack work-related skills and experience but also have limited general education, are physically and morally vulnerable, and are therefore unable to perform certain types of work or compete on equal terms with experienced adult workers (Mačernytė Panomariovienė 2008, p. 8).

The age criterion, as a reflection of an individual's physical and psychological development, is often linked to the attainment of legal subjectivity. However, in the context of employment, age categories may depend on multiple parameters, including the type of work performed, the basis of employment relationships, and the age at which compulsory education ends.

It is important to distinguish between the legal working age and the minimum working age, as they constitute two separate legal categories, despite being frequently used interchangeably. The term 'legal working age' refers to the age at which an individual is legally permitted to enter into an employment contract. This often includes the general age at which a person can be employed without restrictions regarding specific types of work. By contrast, the 'minimum working age' denotes the lowest age at which an individual may undertake work or enter into employment relationships under conditions governed by labour regulations. The minimum working age varies depending on factors such as the nature of the work, the industry, and the level of risk associated with the employment. In many countries, including Lithuania and Poland, distinct minimum age thresholds exist, differentiated by the type of work performed and the purpose of the work—whether as a gainful activity or as part of professional education.

Notably, Article 3 of International Labour Organization (ILO) Convention No 138 states that the minimum age for admission to any employment or work that, by its nature or due to the circumstances in which it is carried out, is likely to jeopardise the health, safety, or morals of young persons shall not be less than 18 years. The Convention also provides for a number of exceptions and derogations based on justified grounds. For this reason, Convention No. 138 emphasises the progressive raising of the minimum age for admission to employment or work to ensure the optimal physical and mental development of individuals (Art. 1). This raises the question of whether this requirement applies to all age categories or only to those subject to specific exceptions, such as substituting the ages of 12 and 14 with 13 and 15, and replacing 14 with 15 (Art. 7 (4)). The wording of this provision suggests that this remains a general requirement, despite the specific regulations outlined in Article 7 of the Convention.

Within the European Union (EU), the EU Charter does not specify a minimum working age but establishes general restrictions on admission to employment and work. According to Article 32, the minimum age for admission to employment may not be lower than the minimum school-leaving age, subject to more favourable provisions for young people and certain limited derogations. Furthermore, young people admitted to employment must have working conditions appropriate to their age and be protected from economic exploitation or any work likely to harm their safety, health, physical, mental, moral, or social development, or interfere with their education (Art. 32). Directive 94/33/EC introduces different age categories, distinguishing between individuals aged 15, 13, and 14. Additionally, Article 6(1) of Directive

2000/78/EC states that the requirement of a minimum age for admission to employment does not constitute discrimination on the grounds of age (Petrylaite et al. 2008, p. 122). The age thresholds established in these regulations correlate with the types of work permitted and the prohibition of work that may pose risks to the physical and psychological development, health, and safety of young workers. A different approach is observed in the European Social Charter (ESC), which focuses on work restrictions based on the chronological age of young persons. It establishes a minimum age for admission to work at 15 years, with additional restrictions for children under 16. The Revised ESC maintains this minimum age criterion but introduces exceptions for the employment of children in certain types of light work.

In both Lithuania and Poland, the minimum working age is set in relation to the category of adolescents. The general age threshold for their employment is 15 in Poland, while in Lithuania, it is 16. In Lithuania, this threshold is also linked to the attainment of legal subjectivity in employment relations, although additional requirements exist, which will be discussed in the subsequent sections of this chapter. These age thresholds allow individuals to enter into employment relationships without the consent of authorities or parents (legal representatives).[31] However, employment below these ages requires parental or legal representative consent. For instance, such consent is necessary for entering into an employment contract for professional education from the age of 14, as well as for the employment of children under 16. A concerning issue is that the labour law regulations of both countries do not establish a specific minimum age for children's employment or their admission to work. Some academics criticise this omission, arguing that it creates conflicts with the right to education (Dambrauskienė 2001) and poses additional risks due to the absence of a lower age criterion for child employment (Szuba 2018).

There is a strong correlation between the minimum working age and the age at which compulsory education ends. All international legal instruments acknowledge this interdependence. According to Article 1 of Directive 94/33/EC, Member States must ensure, under the conditions laid down in the Directive that the minimum age for employment is not lower than the minimum age at which compulsory full-time schooling ends under national law, or 15 years in any event. Differences in compulsory education requirements are evident in the analysed countries. The Polish Constitution of 2 April 1997[32] stipulates that education is compulsory until the age of 18, although the specific manner in which full-time compulsory education is implemented is determined by law (Art. 70). Under the Polish Law on Education,[33] compulsory education lasts until the completion of eight-year primary school, but no longer than until the age of 18 (Art. 35). In principle, schoolchildren complete this level of education at approximately 15 years of age. By contrast, the Lithuanian Constitution of 30 November 1992[34] provides that education is compulsory for

[31] Art. 190 (1) of PLC and Art. 21 of LLC.

[32] Constitution of the Republic of Poland. *Official Gazette*, 1997 No 78, item 483, as amended.

[33] The Law on School Education. *Official Gazette*, 2024, item 737.

[34] *Official Gazette*, 1992, No 33-1014.

individuals under the age of 16. Furthermore, the Lithuanian Education Law[35] obliges children under 16 to continue their education.

As demonstrated, the right to education is a fundamental right, guaranteed and protected by the constitutions of both countries. However, fulfilling this right does not necessarily prohibit employment for those who have not yet completed their compulsory education. In both Lithuania and Poland, the age of compulsory education generally coincides with the acquisition of legal capacity in employment—meaning the ability to acquire labour rights and assume labour obligations (including the conclusion of employment contracts) through one's own actions. This legal capacity in labour relations is attained at the age of 16 in Lithuania (Art. 21 of the Labour Code) and at the age of 15 in Poland (Art. 22(3) of the PLC). If compulsory education has not been completed, additional restrictions apply to employment. In such cases, adolescents may only be employed for the purpose of professional education and must obtain consent from their parents (or legal representatives) as well as consent from the school's director. Consequently, young persons who are subject to compulsory schooling and/or do not yet meet the minimum age for legal capacity in employment require primarily parental (or legal representative) consent to work.

4 Scope of Restrictions on the Employment of Young Persons

The scope of restrictions on the employment of young persons depends on legal regulations concerning children and adolescents. These restrictions specify both prohibited types of work and the limited categories of employment permitted for young workers. As previously discussed, the prohibition of child labour primarily targets its worst forms. According to Article 3 of ILO Convention No. 182, the term '*worst forms of child labour*' encompasses all forms of slavery or practices similar to slavery. The terms *'slavery,' 'exploitation,' 'serfdom,' 'child trafficking,' 'drug trafficking/production,' 'armed conflict,' 'prostitution,'* and *'pornography'* refer to illegal criminal activities that fall outside the scope of labour law regulation (Guobaitė-Kirslienė 2016, pp. 357–359). Meanwhile, work that, by its nature or circumstances, is likely to harm the health, safety, or morals of children—as defined in Article 3 of the Convention—should be considered a central issue in the field of labour law. ILO Recommendation No 190 defines 'hazardous work'as any activity that exposes children to abuse, dangerous conditions, toxic substances, excessive working hours, or unreasonable confinement.

When determining the conditions for the admission of individuals under 18 to employment or work, states must identify the economic sectors or types of enterprises involved and assess whether such employment poses risks to the health, safety, or morals of young persons. Without exception, the provisions of Convention No. 138 apply to at least the following sectors: mining and quarrying,

[35] Republic of Lithuania Law on Education. *Official Gazette*, 1991, No 153-0.

manufacturing, construction, electricity, gas and water supply, sanitation, transport, storage and communications, crop production and other agricultural enterprises, production for commercial purposes, excluding family and small-scale farming, production for local consumption and irregular employment of hired workers (Art. 5(3)). However, these provisions exclude family-based businesses, such as family farms and enterprises that do not regularly employ outside workers (Edmonds 2014). National laws or regulations may permit the employment of individuals aged 13 to 15 in "light work" (Art. 7), but no one below this age may be admitted to employment or work in any occupation (Art. 2(1)). Although a distinction is made between employment and "light work," the term itself is not explicitly defined (Edmonds and Shrestha 2012). Accordingly, states must determine the specific sectors in which employment or work is permitted and establish the hours and conditions under which such work may be carried out (Art. 7(3)).

Similarly, Directive 94/33/EC grants the right to make exceptions to the prohibition of child labour for occasional or short-term work (Art. 2), as well as for employment in cultural, artistic, sports, and advertising activities, professional education, and certain forms of light work (Art. 4). All of the aforementioned derogations,[36] with the exclusion of the first, include an age criterion that generally aligns with the minimum working age of 13. Directive 94/33/EC also outlines protective measures, requiring consideration of children's physical and mental development, emotional immaturity, and lack of experience. These principles govern the classification of prohibited and conditional work, emphasising supervised "light work" and establishing specific criteria for permissible activities. Additionally, the Directive mandates restrictions such as prohibitions on night and overtime work, limitations on working hours, and requirements for more frequent breaks and extended rest periods.

The provisions of the European Social Charter (ESC) are also crucial for understanding the nature and extent of the restrictions on child employment. Article 7 of the ESC sets the minimum working age at 15, except for light work (Art. 7.1). It also introduces restrictions on working hours, such as prohibitions on night work, additional holiday entitlements, and increased age thresholds for hazardous work. Further protections include requirements for fair remuneration, additional medical examinations, and safeguards against physical and moral hazards for individuals under 18 (Arts. 7–10). According to the European Committee of Social Rights, Article 7(1) applies to all forms of work, including agricultural and domestic labour, as such employment cannot automatically be classified as "light work" under this provision (Conclusions I, 1969).[37]

Key conclusions from international legal instruments are as follows. In the context of remunerated work, young persons under 18 are permitted to engage in

[36] According to Art. 5(1) and 5(4), the employment of children for cultural, artistic, sports, or advertising performances must receive prior authorisation from the competent authority on a case-by-case basis. However, for children aged at least 13, derogations from this procedure may be authorised through legislative or regulatory provisions, subject to specific conditions.

[37] Conclusions I (1969)—Statement of interpretation—Article 7-1, 01/01/1965—31/12/1967.

certain types of employment, depending on their age and the nature of the work. Therefore, the right of young people to work remains conditional and must be assessed within the framework of the right to light work. The most hazardous and dangerous forms of work are classified as child labour and are strictly prohibited.

The prohibition of permanent employment for children under 16 is explicitly stated in the Polish Constitution (Art. 65(3)).[38] Furthermore, the Polish Labour Code (PLC) prohibits the employment[39] – but not the engagement in work—of individuals under the age of 15, setting the number of exceptions. In Lithuania, there is no explicit constitutional prohibition on child employment. However, Article 36 of the Lithuanian Labour Code, which regulates the employment of individuals under 18, explicitly prohibits the employment of children under 16.[40] Despite these prohibitions, neither country enforces an absolute ban, as numerous exceptions are provided within their legal frameworks.

5 Right to Work of Young Persons Under Lithuanian and Polish Regulations

In both Lithuania and Poland, the Labour Codes stipulate that individuals under 18 may be employed under specific conditions.[41] These conditions vary depending on whether the young person is legally classified as a child or an adolescent.

With regard to the employment of children (individuals under 16), both countries restrict such employment to *'light work.'* However, the Polish Labour Code use this term explicitly for employment of persons under 16 (in chapter that regulates employment of adolescents (Art. 200^2(3) of the PLC) but instead in relation to work of children refers to *'work performed for the purposes of cultural, artistic, sports, or advertising activities.'* In Lithuania, the State Health and Work (SHW) regulations contain a separate section on the employment of children aged 14–16,[42] whereas the Polish Labour Code does not differentiate employment regulations based on age of children as defined in PLC.[43] In Lithuania, the employment of children may be based on either employment contracts (for individuals aged 14 and above, granting them employee status) or civil contracts (voluntary activities or training contracts), while in Poland the lack of explicit regulations in PLC that specify the basis for the employment of children leads to varying interpretations. Some scholars argue that only civil law contracts may be concluded (Prusinowski 2022),

[38] Similarly, the PLC specifies that individuals under 16 may not be employed (Art. 190), reinforcing the general restrictions while allowing for regulated exceptions.

[39] Art. 190 (2) of PLC.

[40] Art. 36 (1).

[41] Art. 21(2) of LLC and Art. 22(2) of PLC.

[42] Art. 36.

[43] Which work is regulated in Art. 304^5 of PLC.

whereas others contend that both employment and civil contracts are permissible (Goździewicz and Hajn 2017). Notably, in Poland, unlike in Lithuania, the employment of children requires a Labour Inspector's permit specifying the working conditions for each individual case.

The Lithuanian SHW regulations explicitly associate the concept of "light work" with the employment of children, whereas in the Polish Labour Code, the term is expressly addressed to the employment of[44] adolescents (individuals aged 15–18). Both countries apply similar criteria for determining whether a job qualifies as light work.[45] Therefore, under national law, the employment of children is generally prohibited, except in cases where the work corresponds to their physical capabilities and does not negatively affect their safety, health, physical, mental, moral, or social development, while also ensuring compliance with school attendance requirements. It is noteworthy that in both Lithuania and Poland, separate regulations govern the employment of adolescents for professional education, distinct from the rules applicable to light work.

The employment of individuals under 18 in both countries requires a medical certificate confirming that the specific type of work is not harmful to their health.[46] In addition, employment for professional education purposes entails a legal obligation to inform the statutory representative about any occupational risks associated with the work. Legal regulations in both Lithuania and Poland define specific types of work that are prohibited for young persons. In Lithuania, prohibited occupations for individuals under 18 are listed in Resolution No 518. In Poland, similar restrictions apply to adolescents but not to all individuals under 18, as outlined in the 2023 Regulation.[47] The employment of young workers is also subject to specific working conditions, including prohibitions on night shifts and overtime work, restrictions on working hours, extended break and rest periods,[48]and longer annual leave entitlements.[49]

---

[44] In such cases, employment is formalised through contracts specifically designed for professional education.

[45] Examples of permitted light work include tasks such as caring for animals, washing dishes, and cleaning cars.

[46] The Polish Regulation of the Minister of Health and Social Welfare on Medical Examinations of Employees (*Official Gazette*, 2023, item 607) and Lithuanian SHW regulations (Art. 36(2) and Resolution No. 518) provide further details on these requirements.

[47] Prohibited types of work include jobs that expose employees to dust, fumes, or toxic sprays, as well as activities related to the production and handling of explosive devices, fireworks, or other hazardous products. Polish regulations additionally restrict work that involves excessive physical effort, forced body positions, or risks to proper mental development, as well as exposure to harmful chemical, physical, or biological factors.

[48] Art. 36(6.8) of SHW; Art. 202-203 of PLC.

[49] Employees under the age of 18 are entitled to extended leave periods. According to Article 126(3) of the LLC, young workers in Lithuania receive 25 or 30 working days of leave. In Poland, Article 205(1)–(2) of the PLC stipulates that an adolescent in their first year of employment is entitled to 12 working days of statutory leave after 6 months and, after 1 year, to an additional 26 calendar days of leave.

In summary, the right to work for young persons (both adolescents and children) is restricted to light forms of work. Since it is not feasible to define all possible types of light work, the legal regulations in both Lithuania and Poland provide general guidelines for understanding this concept, making employers (part to employment relationships) responsible for ensuring safe working conditions for adolescents and children. However, labour laws in both countries do not regulate short-term or occasional activities undertaken by young persons outside formal employment relationships, such as seasonal harvesting, household work, family business activities, or online work. In such cases, legal responsibility for ensuring the health and safety of young persons falls on their legal representatives. The issue of effectively abolishing child labour and determining the minimum age for employment remains particularly relevant in such circumstances.

6 Violations of Labour Rights of Young Persons in Lithuania and Poland

Judicial cases highlight the most frequent violations of labour laws concerning young workers, which are discussed below.

In Lithuania, case law reveals that young persons are employed in various sectors, including cafes, markets, bars, car washes, agriculture, and factories. Some are engaged in high-risk industries such as construction, operating machinery, handling pyrotechnics, or performing prohibited tasks such as selling alcohol. Additionally, minors are sometimes assigned roles involving material responsibility, such as night-time property security. Many of these young workers are employed illegally, with employers misrepresenting their work as informal assistance or training without formal contracts. Employers and legal guardians often tolerate such practices, contributing to workplace accidents and injuries.[50]

Both legally and illegally employed young workers frequently encounter unsafe working conditions, excessive working hours, inadequate remuneration, and insufficient training. Many are required to work shifts of up to 15–16 hours per day, including nights and weekends, in violation of labour laws. In some cases, they are paid informally in cash, leaving them vulnerable to underpayment, tax evasion, and the absence of employment benefits such as unemployment protection or paid leave. Minors are sometimes assigned hazardous tasks, such as operating metalworking machines or handling alcohol, without adequate safety instructions. Due to their inexperience and limited awareness of their rights, young workers are more

[50] Administrative case No ATP-17-134/2014; Administrative case No ATP-326-116/2015; Administrative case No ATP-61-175/2015;Administrative case No AN2-470-458/2017; Criminal case No ATP-200-290/2017; Administrative case No A2.1.-1488-540/2017;Criminal case No 1-19-606/2017;Administrative case No ATP-2-530/2018;Criminal case No 1A-95-491/2021; Administrative case No AN2-285-988/2021;Administrative case No 12-1293-979/2023.

susceptible to workplace injuries and often sign employment contracts without fully understanding their implications, further increasing their vulnerability.[51]

Similar issues are prevalent in Poland, where violations of youth employment regulations primarily involve breaches of health and safety requirements, including the failure to prevent work-related accidents.Case law analysis indicates that the primary causes of work-related accidents among adolescents stem from the absence of mandatory medical examinations, inadequate health and safety training, and insufficient job coaching. Additionally, minors are often assigned hazardous tasks without appropriate supervision by personnel responsible for vocational training. A further issue is the[52]absence of a comprehensive list of prohibited work activities within some entities.[53] The most frequent violations of labour laws involve breaches of regulations concerning working hours, night work,[54]and overtime restrictions. Other common infractions include the failure to provide young workers with the necessary protective measures and withholding crucial safety information from both the adolescent and their legal representative.[55] Another significant issue is the misclassification of employment contracts, where civil law contracts are used in place of employment[56] contracts governed by the Polish Labour Code (PLC). Additionally, non-payment of wages remains a recurring problem.[57] Case law also highlights the negative consequences of adolescents seeking employment independently without adhering to statutory regulations on professional training.[58]Further violations involve the assignment of unsafe or prohibited tasks to adolescents, such as working on live electrical lines or engaging[59] in construction activities.[60]

Cases of employment abuses involving young people, as analysed by courts and labour regulation authorities, represent only a fraction of the most commonly detected violations in the countries analysed. However, these cases do not fully capture the extent of hidden, informal, and often illegal employment, which includes breaches of existing regulations and engagement in prohibited forms of work.

---

[51] Administrative case No A2.1.-1488-540/2017; Criminal case No 1-340-926/2021;Criminal case No 1-138-1083/2021.

[52] Judgement of Supreme Court of 26.01.1982, VPZP 8/81, Lex 12,736, judgment of the Regional Court in Płock of 27.08.2021, I C 2359/20, LEX No 3283133, judgment of the District Court in Poznań of 2.03.2018, XVII Ka 965/17, LEX No 2474577.

[53] Judgment of the District Court in Poznań of 2.03.2018, XVII Ka 965/17.

[54] Judgments of the: Olsztyn District Court of 17.02.2017, IX W 2892/16, LEX No 2250712, Olsztyn District Court of 12.04.2017, IX W 4166/16, LEX No 2285100, Białystok Regional Court of 16.01.2014, XV K 391/13, LEX no. 1912478.

[55] Ibid. and judgment of the District Court in Siedlce of 25.11.2014, IV P 6/12, LEX No 1868635.

[56] Ibid.

[57] Judgment of SR in Gorlice of 13.02.2018, II K 265/17, LEX no. 2512775, judgment of the Białystok Regional Court of 16.01.2014, XV K 391/13, LEX No 1912478.

[58] Judgment of the Regional Court in Płock of 27.08.2021, I C 2359/20.

[59] Judgment of the District Court in Poznań of 2.03.2018, XVII Ka 965/17.

[60] Judgment of the Regional Court in Płock of 27.08.2021, I C 2359/20.

The effective abolition of child labour and the enforcement of restrictions on youth employment cannot be achieved without appropriate and proportionate sanctions. The key question remains: Are the sanctions imposed in the analysed countries adequate to prevent infringements and ensure compliance with labour laws? While violations of young people's labour rights in some cases result in criminal or administrative liability, it is necessary to examine the extent to which labour law sanctions effectively deter such breaches.

In Lithuania, there are no separate or differentiated fines for employers based on the age of the employees they hire. Article 56 of the Lithuanian Law on Employment stipulates general fines for employers who engage in illegal employment (where administrative liability does not apply), ranging from three minimum wages (EUR 3,114 in 2025) to twelve minimum wages (EUR 12,456 in 2025). According to the Code of Administrative Offences (10 July 2015), illegal work incurs fines ranging from EUR 1,000 to EUR 5,000 (Art. 95), violations of labour laws, occupational safety, and health regulations result in fines ranging from EUR 240 to EUR 880 (Art. 56), failure to ensure workplace measures preventing violence and harassment is penalised with fines ranging from EUR 500 to EUR 1,400 (Art. 96).

In contrast, the Polish Labour Code imposes distinct sanctions for violations related to adolescent and child employment. Article 281(1.5) of the PLC states that any individual or legal entity violating employment regulations concerning adolescents is subject to a fine ranging from 1,000 PLN (EUR 240) to 30,000 PLN (EUR 7,200). Article 283(2.9) of the PLC classifies the employment of a child under the age of 16 without the authorisation of the competent labour inspector as a breach of occupational health and safety obligations, leading to the highest level of liability. Since higher or maximum fines in Poland can only be imposed by a court (rather than by the labour inspection authorities), and because child and adolescent employment is often informal and/or undeclared,[61] these penalties do not serve as an effective deterrent. As a result, young workers' rights remain inadequately protected.

Building on previous observations, the most significant regulatory gap lies not only in the absence of age-based differentiation in employer liability for youth employment (as observed in Lithuania) but also in the failure at the statutory level to acknowledge that violations of working conditions in permitted employment and acceptable types of work can result in consequences akin to those of prohibited work. The social consequences of violating the rights of young workers are profound and constitute one of the major barriers to achieving sustainable social development.

[61] Numerous surveys conducted by foundations reveal that the actual number of individuals under 18 engaged in employment is significantly higher than official statistics indicate. *WEI. (2024). [REPORT] Child labor in Poland. How do the young acquire their first work experience?* https://wei.org.pl/wp-content/uploads/2024/05/Praca-dzieci-w-Polsce.-Raport-WEI.pdf.

7 Concluding Remarks

In the countries analysed, the definitions of *'child'* and *'adolescent'* are not consistently aligned with the minimum working age that permits one to engage in employment. Consequently, the issue under Lithuanian and Polish labour laws is not merely the broad objective of raising the age for specific work activities for children but, more importantly, the need to clearly define a minimum age at which children may start working or be employed. Therefore, the definition of a child in labour law should be accompanied by the establishment of minimum age thresholds for employment, which should vary according to the type of work involved. This should also be supplemented by official statistics on the number of children engaged in employment or certain types of work.

The general prohibition on the employment and work of children, given the numerous legally permitted exceptions, is questionable. Similar observations can be made in the context of Agenda 2030's goal for the complete abolition of child labour in all its forms. For this reason, both international and national regulations should focus not on a general prohibition but on the restriction of specific, clearly defined types of work.

Furthermore, improving the working conditions of young workers should be considered a fundamental goal, regardless of the form or basis of their employment (such as employment contracts, civil agreements, or other arrangements). In both Lithuania and Poland, young workers also face significant risks in permitted types of work, yet the existing sanctions for violations of labour laws are inadequate and insufficient. Sanctions should be imposed for violations across all forms of employment, both formal and informal, holding accountable those who permit or tolerate prohibited work or hazardous working conditions. The establishment of young workers' right to decent working conditions cannot be realised without proportionate sanctions for violations. Accordingly, while not all types of work are subject to the same restrictions, every kind of work activity—whether short-term, occasional, training-based, or voluntary—requires appropriate supervision and awareness of the consequences of violations. In this context, it is reasonable to propose a definition of *'illegal child labour'* that would replace the term *'abolition of child labour*,'shifting the focus toward safeguarding workers' rights.

The legal framework regarding employment below the legal working age in both countries tends to focus on imposing numerous obligations on employers. It does not prioritize the subjectivity of children and adolescents in the labor process, nor does it emphasize their rights in employment—in particular, their right to work with dignity. Although the topic of a child's right to decent work warrants separate study, it is evident that, within the scope of this chapter, it should be examined solely through the lens of the right to light work. Such work must comply with the minimum age requirement and occur under conditions that do not undermine the child's right to education and childhood.[62] A child's right to work is conditioned by a

[62] Compare: van Daalen and Hanson (2019), point 31.

hierarchy of superior rights, as outlined above. Existing regulatory deficiencies should be addressed by emphasising the obligation to respect the rights of adolescents and children in employment through clear and transparent regulations. Prohibited forms of work for individuals under 18 should be widely recognised, and a definition of illegal child labour (or work performed below the legal working age) would be beneficial. These issues are crucial for the contribution of young people to sustainable social development and should form an integral part of school education.

Considerations in the designated areas confirm that the national regulations, established many years ago under the influence of the previously dominant narrative, require re-evaluation and the adoption of a new approach centred on the protection of the labour rights of young persons.[63] Employment and work for individuals under 18 should be incorporated into national policy as a contribution to sustainable social development, with the young age period considered from the perspective of the working life cycle, while still addressing the challenges posed by sustainable social security schemes. The issue of sustainable work across the life cycle must be adequately addressed when designing legal regulations concerning the employment and work of children and adolescents. It is therefore time for reforms that align with the new social and economic realities and the challenges they present.

References

Dambrauskienė G (2001) Vaikų ir paauglių užimtumo teisinio reguliavimo problemos. Jurisprudencia 20(12):50–58

Edmonds EV (2014) Does minimum age of employment regulation reduce child labor? IZA World Labor 2014:73. https://doi.org/10.15185/izawol.73

Edmonds EV, Shrestha M (2012) The impact of minimum age of employment regulation on child labor and schooling. IZA J Labor Policy 1(14) https://izajolp.springeropen.com/articles/10.1186/2193-9004-1-14

Goździewicz G, Hajn Z (2017) 5.1.4. Podmiotowość pracownicza dzieci. In: System Prawa Pracy. Indywidualne prawo pracy. Wolters Kluwer Polska, pp 138–139

Guobaitė-Kirslienė R (2016) Visų formų priverstinio ir privalomo darbo draudimas. In: *Darbo teisės principai ir jų taikymas Lietuvos teismų praktikoje* [kolektyvinė monografija, mokslinis redaktorius I.Mačernytė Panomariovienė]. MRU, Vilnius. 551 p

ILO (2011) Children in hazardous work: what we know, what we need to do. International Labour Office Brookings Institution Press. http://site.ebrary.com/id/10512167

Internationales Arbeitsamt & UNICEF (ed) (2021) Child labour: global estimates 2020, trends and the road forward. International Labour Office. https://www.ilo.org/sites/default/files/wcmsp5/groups/public/%40ed_norm/%40ipec/documents/publication/wcms_797515.pdf

Mačernytė Panomariovienė I (2008) Įsidarbinimo amžiaus cenzo nustatymas ir jo pagrįstumas. Teisės problemos 1(59):5–23

Mačernytė Panomariovienė I (2010) TDO įtaka Lietuvos darbo teisės raidai. In: Lietuvos darbo teisės raida ir perspektyvos Liber Amicorum et Collegarum Profesorei Genovaitei Dambrauskienei. MRU, Vilnius, p 379. ISBN 978-9955-19-193-3

[63] Ibidem.

Mačernytė Panomariovienė I, Wrocławska T (2023) Sustainable work over the course of life: a new paradigm for decent work. In: Law and sustainability: perspectives for Lithuania and beyond. Księgarnia akademicka publishing, Kraków, pp 107–134. https://doi.org/10.12797/9788381388405
Mavunga R (2014) A critical assessment of the Minimum Age Convention 138 of 1973 and the Worst Forms of Child Labour Convention 182 of 1999. Potchefstroom Elec LJ 16(5):121–168. https://doi.org/10.4314/pelj.v16i5.3
Petrylaite D, Davulis T, Petrylaitė V (2008) Europos Sąjungos teisės aktų įgyvendinimas Lietuvos darbo teisėje. Registų centras, Vilnius, p 499. ISBN 978-9955-30-043-4
Prusinowski P [w:] Kodeks pracy. Komentarz. Tom II. Art. 94–304(5), wyd. VI, red. K. W. Baran, Warszawa 2022, art. 304(5). OpenLEX. https://sip.lex.pl/komentarze-i-publikacje/komentarze/undefined
Siewert F (2024) New forms of child labour. A study on Kidfluencing from a human rights perspective. UMEA University. https://www.diva-portal.org/smash/get/diva2:1879389/FULLTEXT01.pdf
Szuba M (2018) The definition of the chlid under art. 3045 of polish labor code—in comaparative. Roczniki Administracji i Prawa 1(XVIII):379–390. https://doi.org/10.5604/01.3001.0012.6010
Transforming our World: The 2030 Agenda for Sustainable Development | Department of Economic and Social Affairs. Retrieved 19 October 2022, from https://sdgs.un.org/publications/transforming-our-world-2030-agenda-sustainable-development-17981
van Daalen E, Hanson K (2019) The ILO'S shifts in child labour policy: regulation and abolition. Int Dev Policy Revue internationale de politique de développement:133–150. https://doi.org/10.4000/poldev.3056
Weerman F, Beijerse J, uit. (2020) Age limits in law: between Behavioural science and human rights. Erasmus Law Rev 13(1):1–3. https://doi.org/10.5553/ELR.000164
Wrocławska T (2024) Decent and Sustainable Work: Around the Discussion on the Importance of International Law in the Regulation of Employment Relations. Acta Universitatis Lodziensis Folia Iuridica 107. https://doi.org/10.18778/0208-6069.107.01

Dr. Ingrida Mačernytė Panomariovienė has been the Head of the Law Institute of the Lithuanian Centre for Social Sciences since 2019. Ingrida Mačernytė Panomariovienė is also a professor at Mykolas Romeris University, Lithuania. Her areas of interest include non-discrimination, employee and representative guarantees, working conditions and remuneration, European Union labour law, and international labour law. Specialising in labour law since 1998, she has over 20 years of teaching experience. Dr. Mačernytė Panomariovienė has conducted extensive research in labour law for more than two decades and is the author or co-author of approximately 60 research papers.

Dr. Tatiana Wrocławska is Assistant Professor at the Department of Labour Law, Social Security Law and Social Policy at the Faculty of Law and Administration of the University of Lodz. Author or co-author of approximately 80 scientific works in the field of labour law, including various types of publications (chapters, commentaries, articles, expert opinions). She conducts research in different areas of broadly understood labour law (individual and collective labour law, labour market regulations) and participates in scientific events and projects of a transnational and national scope. Her current research interests focus on the legal aspects of extending professional activity of older people and their right to work.

Child Work in the Digital Twenty-First Century: The Experience of the Baltic States

Kristina Ambrazevičiūtė, Kristine Dupate, and Merle Erikson

Abstract Traditionally, children are considered to be a particularly protected group in the labour market, necessitating special protection due to their physical and mental immaturity, as well as their mandatory education. As a result, numerous restrictions have been imposed on their employment. However, labour laws designed for the industrial era may no longer fully address the realities of the twenty-first century. Beyond conventional roles like sales assistants, waitstaff, and leaflet distributors, children are increasingly working in digital environments. This evolving landscape demands a reassessment of existing legal frameworks to ensure adequate protection for young workers. This chapter examines whether the current legal regulations in Estonia, Latvia, and Lithuania sufficiently safeguard children engaged in employment in light of today's conditions.

1 Introduction

Child employment is not common in the Baltic countries. Based on Eurostat data from 2023, 5.8% of young people aged 15–19 were employed in Lithuania, 5.9% in Latvia, and slightly more, at 10.2%, in Estonia. In contrast, the average employment rate for this age group across the European Union was 16.2% (Eurostat 2024). The low level of child employment in the Baltic countries can be attributed to several key factors. First, national and international legal norms have long established strict

K. Ambrazevičiūtė (✉)
Law Institute, Lithuanian Centre for Social Sciences, Vilnius, Lithuania
e-mail: kristina.ambrazeviciute@teise.org

K. Dupate
Faculty of Law, University of Latvia, Riga, Latvia
e-mail: kristine.dupate@lu.lv

M. Erikson
School of Law, University of Tartu, Tartu, Estonia
e-mail: merle.erikson@ut.ee

A. Limantė, R. Vaičiūnienė (eds.), *Children's Rights in Central and Eastern Europe*, European Union and its Neighbours in a Globalized World 29,
https://doi.org/10.1007/978-3-032-07092-0_7

regulations regarding child employment, including setting a minimum working age, limiting working hours, and prohibiting dangerous or exploitative work. Second, the developed social security systems and family support in these countries reduce the need for children to work, as families can often secure adequate living conditions without involving their children in the labour market. Third, compulsory education laws require children to attend school until 16 in Lithuania, Latvia and until 17 in Estonia. This significantly decreases the likelihood of children taking on jobs, as any work interfering with their education is highly restricted. Finally, cultural and social norms in the Baltic countries prioritise childhood as a period meant for learning and development. Together, these factors contribute to the rarity of child employment in the Baltic.

The digital revolution of the twenty-first century has introduced new challenges. The digital space, particularly social networks and platforms like YouTube, TikTok, and Instagram, allows children to communicate, play games, and create video content. While these activities may initially seem like simple entertainment, for some children, this recreational time evolves into a pursuit that demands constant creativity and a sense of responsibility. They start producing digital content to maintain their followers and attract new ones. This trend often draws the attention of brands and advertising agencies, which hire young influencers, or "kidfluencers," to promote their products. As a result, initially playful engagement evolves into a job for these children. At first glance, it is not easy to identify this activity with work because what the child does on the computer, tablet or phone screen seems to be a private matter of his or her family. Parents are held responsible for their children's use of social networks, including the time spent on them and how the money the child earns is spent. However, on the other hand, this activity often exceeds the boundaries of family autonomy and becomes publicly visible, commercially essential and socially significant. Children operate in the public space, and their content generates profit. This raises the risk of child exploitation, pressure and possible rights violations. Therefore, the issue of the child rights protection mechanism is no longer just a private family matter and must be regulated at the state level.

This chapter seeks to answer the question of whether the existing legal regulations of Lithuania, Latvia, and Estonia adequately respond to modern forms of child work, with special emphasis on the digital space. To answer this question, the child employment sectors, the regulation of child work globally, regionally, and in the Baltic states, and changes related to the emergence of new digital forms of work will be discussed.

2 Work Performed by Children and Its Regulation

2.1 Children's Employment Sectors

Traditionally, the work performed by children is divided into several sectors. Most children work in agriculture, including family and commercial farm tasks, accounting for approximately 70% of all child labour globally. In the industrial sector, 10.3% of children are employed, primarily in production roles. Meanwhile, the service sector employs 19.7% of children, typically in trade, catering, and newspaper distribution. In Europe and North America, the distribution of child labour across these sectors differs, with a higher proportion of children working in industry and services compared to other parts of the world (International Labour Office and United Nations Children's Fund 2021).

In the twenty-first century, a new sector of child work can be identified. This sector can be partly attributed to the third, the service sector. Still, it has peculiarities and nuances and can be singled out into a separate group. It is clear that with the change in technology, the peculiarities of human work are also changing (Thévenon and Edmonds 2019, p. 9). In the twenty-first century, computers, tablets, mobile phones and the Internet became universal everyday means of working and entertaining. Accordingly, adults and children are increasingly beginning to work in the digital space. Often, they express themselves as influencers, or, in the case of children, kidfluencers, on social networking platforms such as Facebook, Instagram, YouTube, TikTok, or e-sports. Kidfluencers create content, attracting many followers and, accordingly, advertisers to include them as a marketing communication tool. For the goods, services or brands advertised, many kidfluencers receive free products, and some are paid. To become and maintain his or her status and followers, a kidfluencer must constantly work on social networks—continuously create quality content or train for an e-sports tournament (Van der Hof et al. 2020, p. 847). Parents often participate in the activities of kidfluencers, helping to create an account, prepare scripts, and create and edit videos (Van der Hof et al. 2020, p. 843).

In the case of success, kidfluencers bring notable economic and financial impacts, whether for their families, who frequently earn significant income or for the brands that successfully sell products through advertising. Kidfluencers have emerged as some of the most successful social media influencers and have become among the most successful influencers overall (Shomai et al. 2024). The world's most famous kidfluencer, Ryan Kaji, behind the "Ryan's World" YouTube channel, brought in over $30 million in 2020 (Ambrose 2023) and currently has 37.8 million viewers on the YouTube platform. Regarding e-sports, during the first Fortnite World Cup, organised in the summer of 2019, a 16-year-old gamer won three million dollars in prize money (Van der Hof et al. 2020, p. 847).

In other words, in the era of digital technology, it is not uncommon for the line between a child's entertainment in the online space and a child's work to be blurred. Kidfluencers endure significant physical and psychological stress to earn material rewards. Results of a study that used semi-structured interviews to capture the retrospective experiences of ten young people as "kidfluencers" on social media show that being a kidfluencer led to various negative experiences for participants. Survey participants indicated that the time required to create a week's content varied between 40 and 60 h. Children noted that their activities required a sheer level of tenacity and dedication and indicated they experienced sleep deprivation. Work affected their mental health and well-being: the children experienced a vast social media pressure to share content constantly, to increase Instagram followers and YouTube views, and to recruit subscribers. Participants shared the tendency to feel isolated despite having thousands of followers. They also shared the struggles of coping with the negative and hurtful comments. Moreover, the study showed that the work of the kidfluencers was difficult to reconcile with their education and school attendance, which resulted in their education suffering. Moreover, even on several occasions, children's parents had permitted them to skip school (Shomai et al. 2024). In addition, kidfluencers are often at risk of financial exploitation by their parents. Parents have the legal right to use the income generated from their child's influencer activities for their own benefit, but they may not save any money for the child's future (LePage 2023, p. 774; Reardon 2022, p. 181).

Can kidfluencers activity be considered an employment relationship? Although customers do not exert significant control over the work performed by children, the advertising created by kidfluencers must align with customer requirements. In contemporary forms of work, employer control is often less significant than before, as seen in remote work and platform-based jobs. Additionally, some legal scholars argue that platforms like YouTube could be viewed as joint employers of these children since they control the distribution of revenue (Morris 2023, p. 123). Kidfluencers generate economic value, perform substantial amounts of work, and receive payment; thus, these relationships are classified as employment relationships in legal doctrine (Employment Relationship Recommendation No.198 2006; Siewert 2024, p. 11; Van der Hof et al. 2020, p. 848).

2.2 Regulation of Employment of Children

The fundamental principles and norms for regulating child labour were established in the 19th and 20th centuries in response to the harsh realities of child labour. The main principle of regulating work for children is that it should be light, non-harmful, and not interfere with their development. Regulating a child's work typically involves several measures: establishing a minimum working age, limiting working hours, and identifying and prohibiting jobs that are harmful to them. Legal requirements and restrictions on children's work have been established by most countries, as well as by international and regional organisations.

International regulations on child labour, led by the International Labour Organisation, include Conventions No. 138 (Minimum Age Convention 1973) and No. 182 (Worst Forms of Child Labour Convention 1999), which establish minimum working ages (15 years, in some countries for light jobs - from 13 or 12 years) and prohibit hazardous forms of child labour. The United Nations Convention on the Rights of the Child (1989) further asserts children's rights to protection from economic exploitation and work that could hinder their development. The European Social Charter by the Council of Europe (1961) also sets a minimum employment age of 15, with specific protections for young workers to prevent harm to their health, morals, and education. The European Union Directive on the Protection of Young People at Work (Council Directive 94/33/EC 1994) establishes a minimum employment age of 15 and differentiates protections for 'children' (under 15) and 'adolescents' (15–17). It restricts working hours for minors, prohibits night work, and forbids employment in hazardous conditions, such as work with dangerous substances or heavy machinery, that could harm their health, safety, or development. The Directive ensures that work does not interfere with minors' education and prioritises protective measures to support their well-being.

Thus, under international and regional regulations, people under 18 can perform light and non-hazardous jobs. Their working hours are limited, and employers must ensure safe working conditions. Such regulation protects young workers from exploitation and harmful working conditions. In addition, it universally enshrines the priority of children's education and ensures that their right to education is not restricted.

As already mentioned, the digitalisation of the world has brought new forms of work and new challenges to classical labour law. The emergence of new forms of work often slips through the established framework of perception. As a result, they remain unrecognised as work (Siewert 2024, p. 7) and are not sufficiently protected by the mechanisms created by classical labour law (LePage 2023, p. 44). Of course, the fundamental principles of labour law can be applied to children's digital work, emphasising the importance of prioritising the child's best interests, protecting them from harmful or hazardous work, and ensuring their right to education. However, they do not fully address the changes in society's way of life. Traditional child labour regulations primarily focus on safeguarding children from physical exploitation, often overlooking the psychological and emotional strains associated with digital child labour. Kidfluencer activities are frequently undertaken by children below the minimum age set by legal standards. In the absence of specific legal frameworks, the protection of kidfluencers' interests relies largely on parental discretion.

In recent years, the challenges posed by children's online activities, particularly digitalised child labour, have become increasingly acknowledged (Council of Europe 2018; Shomai et al. 2024; United Nations Committee on the Rights of the Child 2014). In 2021, France became the first country to regulate digital child labour by establishing a legal framework for child influencers. The regulatory model for kidfluencers developed by France has set a pioneering example for other countries and will be further discussed below.

In France, the Labour Code (FLC 1973) sets the minimum working age at 16, except for apprenticeships or light work during school holidays starting at 14. Strict regulations govern rest periods, working hours, and health checks for minors. Employment in hazardous jobs or jobs exceeding minors' physical capabilities is prohibited (Articles L4153-8, L3162-1). Child entertainers are another exception from the minimum working age requirement. Articles L7124-1-L7124-35 of the FLC regulate the work of minors in the entertainment, film, advertising and modelling sectors. Following the expansion of the scope of article L7124-1 in 2020 (Loi visant à encadrer l'exploitation Commerciale de l'image d'enfants de moins de Seize Ans Sur Les Plateformes En Ligne (1) 2020) (the 2020 law), this category of working children assigns minor influencers. Thus, France gives kidfluencers the same protection as they give to child models or child actors.

It should also be noted that such regulation of kidfluencers' activities indicates that, in France, influencers are governed by labour law. Although kidfluencers may not be fully controlled regarding working time or location, they are obliged to publish content at a specified time, follow predetermined guidelines and receive remuneration for these services. Therefore, kidfluencers are classified as employees under French labour law (Reardon 2022, p. 179; Siewert 2024, p. 14) and are protected even if they are employed without a formal employment contract (Reardon 2022; Weiss 2021, p. 179).

Article L7124-1 of the FLC stipulates that when a kidfluencer is the main focus of audiovisual recordings and participates in activities seeking profit on a video-sharing platform, their legal representatives must seek authorisation from the administrative authority.[1] A separate permit is issued only when the activities intended for the child are in their best interests. This assessment considers the child's ability to perform the job, taking into account their age and health condition, as well as the suitability of the activity. The working conditions are also evaluated, including working hours, rest periods, salary, hygiene, safety measures, and access to health care. It is also required that the child attends school regularly. Effective child care is entrusted to the child's family or those responsible (Assemblée Nationale 2020). If authorisation is granted, the administrative authority shall provide the legal representatives with information about protecting the child's rights in producing these videos, including the consequences on the child's private life and the financial obligations incumbent upon them (Article L7124-1 of the FLC). The individual's prior authorisation for the employment of a child may be withdrawn at any time (Article L7124-4 of the FLC). Also, recruiting a minor over thirteen is requested to be provided with his favourable written opinion (Article L7124-2 of the FLC). Finally, working time may not exceed the maximum daily and weekly duration established by the resolution of the Council of State (L7124-6 of the FLC).

French law regulates the financial side of the work of kidfluencers and other children working in the entertainment sector, ensuring that most of the income

[1] France also has implemented legal protections for children whose activities cannot be classified as employment, but their images are frequently used in the audiovisual recordings. When the duration, frequency, or income generated from these records exceeds the limits set by the Council of State, the child's parents are required to submit a declaration to the relevant authorities. After submitting this declaration, parents will receive information about their child's rights and the potential consequences of sharing their child's image online (Assemblée Nationale 2020; the 2020 law).

ultimately goes to the child—and not to his legal representatives. Article L7124-9 of the FLC provides that only a portion of the remuneration received by the child may be left at the disposal of their legal representatives. Another portion of remuneration is paid into the deposit in a special state-handled fund (Caisse des Dépôts et Consignations) and managed by this fund until the child reaches the age of majority or is emancipated. Withdrawals may be authorised in cases of emergency and exceptionally and must be carried out exclusively in the child's best interests (Assemblée Nationale 2020). Such legal regulation ensures that the child is not financially exploited by his parents or other legal guardians.

Finally, the law entitles child influencers to request the removal of their content from online platforms, even without parental consent (Article 6 of the 2020 law). This provision seeks to strengthen privacy and provide greater control over personal data.

Thus, the legal mechanism developed by France seeks to solve the main problems raised by the new digital forms of child work. It is ensured that the work of children on social platforms does not interfere with their development and education, and the possible financial exploitation of the child by the parents is prevented. These developments concerning kidfluencers in France highlight growing awareness and action in this field. Legislation protecting kidfluencers' rights is being debated or passed in several countries (California Assembly Bill No.1880 2024; California Senate Bill No. 764 2024; Illinois Public Act 103-0556 2024; Digital, Culture, Media and Sport Committee of UK Parliament 2022). The problem was also raised at the EU level (European Parliament 2023). In 2024, the EU Council emphasised the need for better protection and support for influencers under 18. This includes creating guidelines for parents of kidfluencers and ensuring that young content creators know their legal obligations. Member States are encouraged to adopt policies to regulate influencers' activities, and there are discussions about harmonising these rules across the EU to avoid a fragmented legal framework (Council Conclusions 2024).

3 Regulation of Employment of Children in Baltic States

There is no doubt that in the Baltic States, children's participation in social media aligns with global trends, and the number and influence of kidfluencers are on the rise. For instance, in Lithuania, adult influencers play a significant role on social networks, often involving their children in content creation to promote products.[2] Although there are fewer child influencers in Lithuania, their presence is still significant.[3] In 2024, the information portal surveyed Lithuanian influencers who

[2] For example see patricija_gadzijeva, veronikamontvydiene, ieva.macke, ingazuolyte on Instagram; BabyBlog on Facebook etc.

[3] For example see ROKONUOTYKIAI on Youtube, knyguolis, estela_stumbraite, pjuksas on Instagram etc.

involve their children in content creation regarding their earned income, work regime, and rest periods. However, the absolute part refused to respond to the request (Jablonskaitė 2024). It can be argued that such a reaction identifies the fear and insecurity of parents, which is also caused by undefined legal regulations. This further highlighted the need to regulate the participation of minors in social media activities, which is what journalists, lawyers and the Ombudsman for the Protection of the Rights of the Child pay attention to (Adverum 2020; Sakalauskienė 2021; Jablonskaitė 2024; Vilkelytė 2023). In contrast to Lithuania, there has not been extensive public debate in Latvia and Estonia regarding the protection of children's rights as influencers. This lack of awareness about the issue may be attributed to the absence of high-profile cases drawing attention to the problem.

Next, it will be assessed whether the norms established in Lithuanian, Latvian and Estonian legal acts regulating child work are sufficient and can be adapted to address the employment relationships of kidfluencers.

3.1 Regulation of Child Employment in Lithuania

3.1.1 Child Work Under Employment Contracts

In the Lithuanian legal system, children under the age of 18 are assigned to the group of vulnerable workers and deserve additional protection. Legal regulation is aimed at ensuring that a person under the age of 18 does not suffer any economic exploitation and that the work he performs does not harm his physical and psychological development. Therefore, the conditions of employment of young people in Lithuania are strict (Davulis 2018, p. 81). It is important to note that Lithuanian employment legislation does not recognize child performers as a distinct category and lacks specific provisions to regulate their work.

According to Lithuanian labour law, two categories of young people under 18 are distinguished (Article 2(25), 2(32) of the Law on Safety and Health at Work 2003, LSHW). The first category is defined as 'children' (persons under the age of 16). The work of children in this category is prohibited· except for an exclusive group of children between the ages of 14 and 16 who can do light work. The second group is 'adolescents' (persons between the ages of 16 and 18). These two groups are provided for different regulating modes.

Stricter employment requirements are provided for children aged 14–16 (Articles 13–15 of the Resolution of the Government on the Approval of the Procedure for the Organisation of Recruitment, Work and Vocational Training of Persons under the Age of 18, 2017, Resolution of the Government). In particular, the employer may employ such a child or change the conditions of employment only if the employer has obtained the written consent of one of the parents or the representative of the other child regarding the work of the child; secondly, the employer must have received a conclusion from the personal health care institution that the child is suitable for a specific job; and thirdly, if the child is working during the school year, the child must provide the written consent of the school. In addition, the employer must inform the child's parents or another representative of the child about the occupational risks that may arise for the child and measures to protect the child's safety and health.

The nature of the allowed works is also differentiated according to the young person's age. Children between the ages of fourteen and sixteen can only perform light work that corresponds to their physical capabilities, which does not adversely affect their safety, health, physical, mental, moral or social development. Such work can not interfere with the child's attendance at school and study (Article 36(1), 36 (2) of the LSHW). However, there is no list of these works or more precise limits of possibilities. Meanwhile, individuals belonging to the adolescent group can work a more comprehensive range of jobs than children. Still, some restrictions remain to protect against risks to their safety, health or development. They are prohibited from performing work involving hazardous chemicals, dangerous environmental conditions, mechanical hazards, biological hazards, or heavy physical activity.[4]

Young people have special working and rest time rules. Children can work up to 6 h a day and 30 h a week outside school hours, with a maximum of 2 h per day and 12 h per week during school time. Work between 8:00 PM and 6:00 AM is prohibited for children, with a required 14-hour daily rest period. Adolescents may work up to 8 h a day and 40 h a week, with no work allowed between 10:00 PM and 6:00 AM and a required 12-hour daily rest period. Both age groups must have two weekly rest days, preferably consecutive, with one being Sunday. Additionally, they receive extended leave: 25 working days per year (for a five-day work week) or 30 days (for a six-day work week). Young workers cannot be assigned passive on-call duty (LSHW, Article 36; Labour Code 2016, Articles 126(3) and 118(5)).

Thus, in Lithuania, the regulation of child work complies with international and regional standards and is quite strict. It is undoubtedly positive that the legal framework aims to prevent economic exploitation and protect the development of children. However, these laws mainly cover traditional and physical work, leaving digital activities like kidfluencing outside their scope. The current legal framework does not address the specific challenges of kidfluencers, such as long working hours, unpredictable schedules, public exposure, and financial management. These factors, coupled with the lack of specific legal protections, leave young content creators particularly vulnerable to exploitation, overwork, and financial mismanagement.

3.1.2 Child Work Under Civil Service Contracts

The Lithuanian legal system allows minors to work under contracts regulated by civil law, most often contracts for providing services, which are also signed by children working as performers. There is no specific legal act directly regulating the work of children under service contracts or the work of children's performers. The practice is based on the Civil Code (2000), the Law on Fundamentals of Protection

[4] For details see the fifth chapter of the Government Resolution "On the approval (…)."

of the Rights of the Child (1996), the Law on Copyright and Related Rights (1999), the Law on the Provision of Information to the Public (2006) and other legal acts.

In Lithuania, the ability of children to act independently depends on their age and civil capacity. The legal capacity of children under the age of 14 is minimal. Therefore, any significant transactions on their behalf are concluded by parents or guardians, who are obliged to act exclusively in the child's best interests. Minors can independently conclude only small household transactions and transactions related to using funds earned by themselves if a notarial or other form is not required to conclude these transactions (Article 2.7 of the Civil Code). This means children of this age can independently participate in civil relations, and their earned income is limited.

At the age of 14, children acquire partial civil capacity and can enter into transactions with the consent of their parents or guardians. In addition, they have the right to independently dispose of their income and property acquired for this income, to exercise copyright in their works, and to conclude small household transactions (Article 2.8 of the Civil Code). In this way, the ability of children over 14 to work under service or other civil contracts, including the activities of performers or work in the digital space, is less limited and controlled. In addition, in the case of continuous activity, such children should register individual activities—this is allowed for a minor who has reached the age of 14 and has the consent of one of the parents (State Tax Inspectorate 2023).

Unlike employment relationships, children working under civil contracts are not controlled in terms of working time and rest time. These issues are left to the children's or their parents' discretion. However, they are subject to Article 16 of the Law on Fundamentals of Protection of the Rights of the Child, according to which the child has the right to rest and leisure time corresponding to his age, health and needs. As for child performers, in practice, filming limits vary by age: from 4 h per day for toddlers to 12 h for those aged 16 (Jurkonytė 2020). Such a determination of time is out of step with the regulation of labour law, the regulation of working and rest stricter time.

In cases where children work in a public space, regulating the use of their image becomes essential. According to the laws of the Republic of Lithuania, a picture of a child cannot be filmed, photographed or used without the consent of one of the parents, guardians or the child himself (Article 2.22 of the Civil Code, Article 13(1)(5) of the Law on the Provision of Information to the Public). Thus, the child has the right to decide on the appropriateness of using his image and may require that it not be used, even if the parents consent or already use it. This ensures that the child can protect his personal life and privacy, even if he is involved in public activities or a public space.

Child work under civil contracts in Lithuania is significantly less regulated than employment relationships, making it particularly attractive to kidfluencers creating digital content. However, this lack of regulation also reveals critical gaps in legal protections, leaving children vulnerable to exploitation and excessive demands. Digital work often requires not only prolonged hours but also continuous creative effort, which is difficult to balance with education and leisure. Another pressing issue is the management of kidfluencers' income, as the absence of robust safeguards creates risks of financial mismanagement and loss of future financial security. These shortcomings raise concerns about the potential for educational neglect, overwork, and exploitation.

3.2 Regulation of Child Employment in Latvia

3.2.1 Child Work Under Employment Contracts

Similarly to Lithuania, children are considered as vulnerable group of employees, thus they enjoy specific protection. First, the Labour Law (LL 2001) provides that employment of a child in permanent work is prohibited. Second, a 'child' means a person who is below the age of 15 or who is below the age 18 and continues acquiring basic education (Article 37(1)).

Latvian LL distinguish two groups of children with regard to employment conditions. First group are children who are at least 13 years old and up to the age of 15. Their employment is allowed under strict conditions: (1) they may be employed in light work, i.e., which is not harmful to the child's security, health, morals and development of the child (light works as defined by the Regulations of the Cabinet of Ministers (Latvian Regulations regarding Work in which Employment of Children from the Age of 13 is permitted 2002)); (2) the work shall not interfere with the education of a child; (3) there must be a permit given by one of the parents (guardian) (Article 37(2)); and (4) prior entering into employment contract a child must undergo medical examination, which up to age of 18 must be provided at least once a year (Article 37(6)); (5) prior entering employment contract an employer is under obligation to assess risks of working environment and inform of the result the parents (Article 37(5)).

The second group are adolescents. Those are children between the age of 15 to 18. Similarly to the younger children, adolescents are also prohibited from being employed in jobs associated with increased risk to their safety, health, morals and development (Article 37(4). Respective jobs are defined by the Regulations of the Cabinet of Ministers, which also covers jobs related to occupational training (Latvian Regulations regarding Work in which Employment of Adolescents is prohibited and Exceptions when Employment in such Work is Permitted in Connection with Vocational Training of the Adolescent, 2002).

According to legal regulation also the third group may be distinguished. Those are children who are performers in cultural, artistic, sporting and advertising activities. In the event of employment in listed activities, children of any age may be employed; however, in this case specific permit from the State Labour Inspectorate must be received. The Cabinet of Ministers Regulation No.205 defines in more detail permitted employment conditions and work environment (Latvian Procedures for Issuing Permits for Employment of Children as Performers in Cultural, Artistic, Sporting and Advertising Activities, and Restrictions to be included in Permits 2002).

As it follows from above, works permitted for children and adolescents must be assessed not only according to their substantial nature, but also from the perspective of employment environment and impact on the ability to obtain education. Children under the age of 13 may be employed only in cultural, artistic, sporting and advertising activities if they are performers and under the condition that a permit is provided by the State Labour Inspectorate. Children between ages of 13 to 15 may be employed in light work. While adolescents—children between the age of 15 to 18 may be employed in works not entailing a dangerous employment environment, subject to exceptions in case of occupational training. Concerning, all groups the work may not be such as to pose an increased risk to their safety, health, morals and development, as well as employment must no interfere with education of a child (adolescent).

There is a specific—shorter maximum working time for children and adolescents. First, all persons who are younger than the age of 18 may not be employed for more than 5 days per week. Second, children starting from age 13 may not be employed (1) for more than 2 h per day and 10 h per week during the active education period; (2) for more than 4 h per day and 20 h per week during school holidays. Meanwhile, adolescents (children starting from the age of 15) may be employed for no longer than 7 h per day and 35 h per week. If, however, an adolescent continues obtaining education then overall time spent studying and working may not exceed 7 h per day and 35 h per week.

3.2.2 Child Work Under Civil Contracts

The Civil Law (1937) provides, as a general rule, that a person acquires the capacity to act only starting from age 18 (Articles 219 and 1408). Until then a minor in civil transaction is to be represented by the parents (guardians) (Article 1411). Although a minor lacks capacity to act, in case he/she has concluded an agreement without the permission of the parents (guardians) it is in force such a contract is favourable to a minor (Article 261). Latvian Civil Law was adopted in 1937 and has not been amended significantly since then in relation to the rights of the minors, thus more detailed legal regulation is missing. At the same time according to the Law on the Protection of the Rights of the Children (1998) in all transactions the best interests of the child must be observed.

Children's employment in Latvia is subject to strict regulations, covering job nature, work environment, and education impact. However, the legal framework for civil transactions remains too simplistic to address the complexities of work in the digital economy. As a result, the current system lacks the flexibility and safeguards needed for children's digital work. Still, the regulation of performers in cultural, artistic, sporting, and advertising activities could serve as a foundation for future kidfluencer regulation, following France's example in ensuring proper working conditions and income protection.

3.3 Regulation of Child Employment in Estonia

3.3.1 Child Work Under Employment Contracts

In Estonia, the rules for the employment of children are established mainly by the Employment Contracts Act (TLS 2009)[5] and they depend on the child's age and compulsory schooling.[6] The general rule is that an employer must not conclude an employment contract with a child under 15 years of age or subject to the obligation to attend school or allow such a child to work.

However, as an exception, an employer may enter into an employment contract with a child of 13–14 years of age or a child of 15–16 years of age subject to the obligation to attend school and allow them to work if the duties are simple and do not require any significant physical or mental effort (light work). Moreover, children of 7–12 years of age are allowed to do light work in the field of culture, art, sports or advertising. A child subject to the obligation to attend school can work during the school holiday for no more than half of the school holiday.

All children must have the consent of a legal representative (parent) to start working. A child of 7–12 years of age must also have the consent of the labour inspector.

As mentioned above, children of 13–14 years of age and children of 15–16 years of age subject to the obligation to attend school can do light work; and children of 7–12 years of age can do light work in the field of culture, art, sports or advertising. In addition, the TLS specifies that a child of 13 years of age can do agricultural work, ancillary work performed in trade or service establishments, ancillary work performed in catering or accommodation establishments and other suitable light work.

In Estonia, an employer is prohibited from concluding an employment contract with a child or allowing a child to work if the work: (1) is beyond the child's physical or psychological capacity; (2) is likely to harm the moral development of the child; (3) involves risks which the child cannot recognise or avoid owing to lack of experience or training; (4) is likely to hinder the child's social development or the acquisition of their education; (5) is likely to harm the child's health due to the nature of the work or the working environment.[7] Thus, the law protects children from inappropriate work by allowing them to do work that is developmentally suitable for them.

In Estonian law, special attention is paid to the occupational safety and health protection of employees under the age of 18 and the acquisition of education. Therefore, the working time of a minor is generally shorter, and the rest time is

[5] See Section 6 and 7 for details on the conclusion of the employment contract.

[6] A minor is required to attend school until they acquire basic education (until passing the ninth grade) or attain the age of 17 years.

[7] The corresponding list of the work and hazards is established by the Government regulation.

longer than that of an adult (Sections 43, 47, 49 and 51 of the TLS regulate minors' work and rest time).

Just like the employment of a child, the duration of his maximum working time and minimum rest period also depends on his or her age, compulsory schooling, the content of the work and whether the job is done during the academic term or the school holidays.

For example, a child who is 7–12 years of age may work up to 2 h a day and 12 h over a period of 7 days during academic term outside of school hours and 3 h a day and 15 h over a period of 7 days during school holidays. A child who is 13–14 years of age or an older child who is subject to the obligation to attend school may work up to 2 h a day and 12 h over a period of 7 days during academic term outside of school hours and 7 h a day and 35 h over a period of 7 days during school holidays. A child may not work overtime. Generally, it is forbidden for a child to work at night (from 10:00 p.m. to 6:00 a.m.).

Regarding rest time, for example, a child who is 7–12 years of age must have over a period of 24 h during academic term at least 22 h of consecutive rest time and during school holidays at least 20 h of consecutive rest time. A child who is 13–14 years of age or an older minor who is subject to the obligation to attend school must have over a period of 24 h during academic term at least 21 h of consecutive rest time and during school holidays at least 15 h of consecutive rest time.

Thus, the work of a child is also very limited in terms of time, and he must have enough time to rest. The regulation of child work and rest time is very detailed, considering the different needs and obligations of the child.

In summary, it can be concluded that Estonian law guarantees children extensive protection that aligns with ILO and EU acts. As stated above,[8] kidfluencers can also work in a subordinate relationship and, therefore, based on an employment contract. However, since the work of kidfluencers can be responsible and require significant mental effort, a child of compulsory schooling may not do such work based on an employment contract, although they work in a subordinate relationship. Thus, they have no labour law protection and are vulnerable in their activities. It is questionable whether such an approach can be considered justified and the regulation of child labour protection in this regard needs to be reviewed. On the other hand, if the work of kidfluencers can be considered light work that children of 7–12 years of age or children of compulsory schooling can do, this situation also requires more precise regulation.

3.3.2 Children Work Under Civil Contracts

In addition to employment contracts, minors in Estonia also work based on civil law contracts (contracts for providing services under the law of obligations). This field is regulated by the Law of Obligations Act (2001), which, unlike the TLS, does not

[8] See Sect. 2.1.

provide any guarantees for minor workers. A minor must generally have the consent of a legal representative to enter into a civil law contract.

Concerning civil law contracts, the biggest problem in Estonia is that employers want to sign these contracts even if a person (including a minor) actually works in a subordinate relationship, and an employment contract should be concluded with him. Choosing the correct type of contract is especially important for a minor because he is generally not as knowledgeable a service provider as an adult and can harm himself by working. Although a minor can also dispute the nature of a contract in court, it is not known that there are such disputes. Neither the minor nor his legal representative may know the legal consequences that the conclusion of various contracts entails.

Kidfluencers may also face problems because they are incorrectly classified as entrepreneurs, or a civil law contract is concluded because they are not allowed to do such non-light work under an employment contract. However, there may also be independent kidfluencers who do not work in a subordinate relationship. They, in turn, may face the issue of income protection, which requires special regulation.

4 Concluding Remarks

The regulation of child employment in the Baltic States demonstrates a strong commitment to protecting children, who are recognised as a vulnerable group with ongoing physical and mental development needs. In Lithuania, Latvia, and Estonia, labour laws based on EU standards establish strict regulations that set clear minimum age limits, define permissible types of work, regulate working conditions, and limit working hours. These regulations are designed to ensure that children's work does not endanger their health, safety, or education.

Child work under civil contracts is not predominant but is relatively common in Lithuania, Latvia, and Estonia. However, there is a lack of specific protections for children employed under civil contracts across the Baltic countries. The situation in Estonia highlights this legal gap, which creates an incentive for employers to enter civil contracts with child, even when their working relationships resemble traditional employment. Such arrangements increase the risk of abuse and exploitation, as civil contracts do not offer the same protections as employment contracts. To ensure equal protection of children's rights, comprehensive legal regulations are needed to establish consistent safeguards for all working children, regardless of whether they are engaged under employment or civil law contracts.

Baltic child labour laws primarily focus on physical well-being and traditional forms of employment. However, they do not adequately address the psychological, emotional, and privacy-related risks associated with digital work, particularly kidfluencers. Introducing aspects of the French model, which regulates child influencers under performer laws and provides a comprehensive framework for managing working hours, income, and digital privacy, could be beneficial. In Latvia and Estonia, existing labour regulations offer some protections for child performers by covering their cultural, artistic, sporting, and advertising activities. In contrast, Lithuania lacks formal protections for child performers under either labour or civil contracts, leaving children's rights in creative and digital fields largely unprotected.

References

Adverum (15 May 2020) Vaikai influenceriai—vis dar naujiena Lietuvai? Adverum. https://adverum.lt/lt/vaikai-influenceriai-vis-dar-naujiena-lietuvai/

Ambrose A (2023) Kidfluencers Recast Spotlight on Children's Rights in Digital Entertainment. https://itif.org/publications/2023/09/05/kidfluencers-recast-spotlight-on-children-s-rights-in-digital-entertainment/

Assemblée Nationale (2020) Rapport sur la proposition de loi visant à renforcer la protection des enfants influençeurs sur les plateformes en ligne (No. 2651). https://www.assemblee-nationale.fr/dyn/15/rapports/cion-cedu/l15b2651_rapport-fond

California Assembly Bill No.1880, California Legislature (2024). https://leginfo.legislature.ca.gov/faces/billTextClient.xhtml?bill_id=202320240AB1880#99INT

California Senate Bill No. 764, California Legislature (2024). https://leginfo.legislature.ca.gov/faces/billTextClient.xhtml?bill_id=202320240SB764#99INT

Code Du Travail, Legifrance (1973). https://www.legifrance.gouv.fr/codes/texte_lc/LEGITEXT000006072050/

Convention on the Rights of the Child (1989). https://www.ohchr.org/en/instruments-mechanisms/instruments/convention-rights-child

Council Conclusions on Support for Influencers as Online Content Creators, OJ C, C/2024/3807 (2024). https://eur-lex.europa.eu/eli/C/2024/3807/oj

Council Directive 94/33/EC on the Protection of Young People at Work, OJ L 216 (1994). http://data.europa.eu/eli/dir/1994/33/oj/eng

Council of Europe (2018) Guidelines to respect, protect and fulfil the rights of the child in the digital environment. https://rm.coe.int/guidelines-to-respect-protect-and-fulfil-the-rights-of-the-child-in-th/16808d881a

Davulis T (with Lithuania) (2018) Lietuvos Respublikos darbo kodekso komentaras. Registrų centras

Digital, Culture, Media and Sport Committee of UK Parliament (2022) Influencer culture: MPs call for action on advertising and employment rules to protect children and online performers - Committees - UK Parliament. https://committees.parliament.uk/committee/378/digital-culture-media-and-sport-committee/news/170678/influencer-culture-mps-call-for-action-on-advertising-and-employment-rules-to-protect-children-and-online-performers/

Employment Relationship Recommendation No.198, R198 (2006). https://normlex.ilo.org/dyn/normlex/en/f?p=NORMLEXPUB:12100:0::NO::P12100_INSTRUMENT_ID:312535

Estonian Employment Contracts Act, Official Gazette RT I 5, 35 (2009). https://www.riigiteataja.ee/en/eli/529052024001/consolide/current

European Parliament (16 May 2023) Answer to parliamentary question E-000496/2023. https://www.europarl.europa.eu/doceo/document/E-9-2023-000496-ASW_EN.html

European Social Charter (1961). https://rm.coe.int/168006b642

Eurostat SE (13 September 2024) Youth employment by sex, age and educational attainment level. https://ec.europa.eu/eurostat/databrowser/view/yth_empl_010__custom_12899916/default/table?lang=en

Illinois Public Act 103-0556, Illinois General Assembly (2024). https://www.ilga.gov/legislation/publicacts/fulltext.asp?Name=103-0556

International Labour Office and United Nations Children's Fund (2021) Child Labour: Global estimates 2020, trends and the road forward | International Labour Organization. https://www.ilo.org/publications/major-publications/child-labour-global-estimates-2020-trends-and-road-forward

Jablonskaitė D (18 May 2024) Nusprendė uždėti apynasrį influenceriams: Ieško būdų neleisti dėl turinio išnaudoti vaikus. Delfi. https://www.delfi.lt/seima/idomu/nusprende-uzdeti-apynasri-influenceriams-iesko-budu-neleisti-del-turinio-isnaudoti-vaikus-96501665

Jurkonytė D (4 April 2020) Vaikų filmavimas. Media Law. https://medialaw.lt/vaiku-filmavimas/

Latvian Civil law, Official Gazette, No.41 (1937). https://likumi.lv/doc.php?id=90223

Latvian Labour Law, Official Gazette, No.105 (2001). https://likumi.lv/doc.php?id=26019

Latvian Law on the Protection of the Children's Rights, Official Gazette, No.199/200 (1998). https://likumi.lv/doc.php?id=49096

Latvian Procedures for Issuing Permits for Employment of Children as Performers in Cultural, Artistic, Sporting and Advertising Activities, and Restrictions to be included in Permits, Pub. L. No. 205, Official Gazette, No.81 (2002). https://likumi.lv/doc.php?id=62588

Latvian Regulations regarding Work in which Employment of Adolescents is prohibited and Exceptions when Employment in such Work is Permitted in Connection with Vocational Training of the Adolescent, Pub. L. No. 206, Official Gazette, No.82 (2002). https://likumi.lv/doc.php?id=62644

Latvian Regulations regarding Work in which Employment of Children from the Age of 13 is permitted, Pub. L. No. 10, Official Gazette, No.6 (2002). https://likumi.lv/doc.php?id=57347

Law of Obligations Act, RT I 81, 487 (2001). https://www.riigiteataja.ee/en/eli/ee/524032023004/consolide/current

LePage K (2023) From playtime to paychecks: how parents of child influencers continue to evade child labor Laws. J High Technol Law XXIV(1):741–785

Loi Visant à Encadrer l'exploitation Commerciale de l'image d'enfants de Moins de Seize Ans Sur Les Plateformes En Ligne (1), Pub. L. No. n° 2020-1266, Légifrance (2020). https://www.legifrance.gouv.fr/jorf/id/JORFTEXT000042439054

Minimum Age Convention, No. 138 (1973). https://normlex.ilo.org/dyn/normlex/en/f?p=NORMLEXPUB:12100:0::NO::P12100_ILO_CODE:C138

Morris M (2023) Kidfluencers and conundrums: The rising need for Internet policy that addresses child labour and safety. The Motley Undergraduate Journal, 1(1). https://doi.org/10.55016/ojs/muj.v1i1.76422

Reardon J (2022) New Kidfluencers on the block: the need to update California's Coogan law to ensure adequate protection for child influencers. Case West Reserv Law Rev 73(1):190

Republic of Lithuania Civil Code, Official Gazette, Nr. 74–2262 (2000). https://www.e-tar.lt/portal/lt/legalAct/TAR.8A39C83848CB/asr

Republic of Lithuania Labour Code, Pub. L. No. XII–2603, Official Gazette, Nr. 23709 (2016). https://www.e-tar.lt/portal/lt/legalAct/f6d686707e7011e6b969d7ae07280e89

Republic of Lithuania Law on Copyright and Related Rights, Pub. L. No. VIII–1185, Official Gazette, Nr. 50-1598 (1999). https://www.e-tar.lt/portal/lt/legalAct/TAR.551F0CDE5B64

Republic of Lithuania Law on Fundamentals of Protection of the Rights of the Child, Official Gazette, Nr. 33-807 (1996). https://e-seimas.lrs.lt/portal/legalAct/lt/TAD/TAIS.26397/asr

Republic of Lithuania Law on Provision of Information to the Public, Official Gazette, Nr. 82-3254 (2006). https://e-seimas.lrs.lt/portal/legalAct/lt/TAD/TAIS.286382?jfwid=oikisy64s

Republic of Lithuania Law on Safety and Health at Work, Pub. L. No. IX–1672, Official Gazette, Nr. 70-3170 (2003). https://www.e-tar.lt/portal/lt/legalAct/TAR.95C79D036AA4

Resolution of the Government of the Republic of Lithuania On the Approval of the Procedure for the Organisation of Recruitment, Work and Vocational Training of Persons under the Age of 18, and the Description of the Conditions of Employment of Children, Pub. L. No. 518, Official Gazette, Nr. 11078 (2017). https://www.e-tar.lt/portal/lt/legalAct/46a43c005cd411e79198ffdb108a3753

Sakalauskienė G (1 June 2021) Influencinate išnaudodami savo vaiką?! Delfi. https://www.delfi.lt/m360/naujausi-straipsniai/guoda-sakalauskiene-influencinate-isnaudodami-savo-vaika-87348815

Shomai S, Unwin P, Sealey C (2024) Kidfluencers' lived experiences of influencer culture: a time for regulation? Int J Sociol Soc Policy 44(11/12):1109–1122. https://doi.org/10.1108/IJSSP-03-2024-0109

Siewert F (2024) New forms of child labour—a study on Kidfluencing from a human rights perspective. Umeå University. https://urn.kb.se/resolve?urn=urn:nbn:se:umu:diva-227477

State Tax Inspectorate (2023) Peculiarities of Individual Activities Conducted Under a Certificate. https://www.vmi.lt/evmi/documents/20142/391098/KD-0001778+leidinys+individualios+veiklos+pagal+pa%C5%BEym%C4%85+ypatumai.pdf/968b944a-689a-ff44-bec0-625574837d52?t=1726128237775

Thévenon O, Edmonds E (2019) Child labour: causes, consequences and policies to tackle it (OECD social, employment and migration working papers no. 235). OECD Publishing. https://read.oecd-ilibrary.org/social-issues-migration-health/child-labour_f6883e26-en

United Nations Committee on the Rights of the Child (2014) Digital media and children's rights. https://www.ohchr.org/en/events/days-general-discussion-dgd/2014/2014-day-general-discussion-digital-media-and-childrens

Van der Hof S, Lievens E, Milkaite I, Verdoodt V, Hannema T, Liefaard T (2020) The child's right to protection against economic exploitation in the digital world. Int J Child Rights 28(4):833–859. https://doi.org/10.1163/15718182-28040003

Vilkelytė S (5 October 2023) Kai žaidimai tampa darbu: Kas uždirba iš „kidfluencerio" veiklos? eTeismai. https://eteismai.lt/straipsniai/kita/kai-zaidimai-tampa-darbu-kas-uzdirba-is-kidfluencerio-veiklos

Weiss MA (1 Feb 2021) Pour les Enfants: A New French Law Regulates Influencers Who Are Under the Age of 16. MAW-LAW Web Site. https://www.maw-law.com/uncategorized/pour-les-enfants-a-new-french-law-regulates-influencers-who-are-under-the-age-of-16/

Worst Forms of Child Labour Convention, No. 182 (1999). https://normlex.ilo.org/dyn/normlex/en/f?p=NORMLEXPUB:12100:0::NO::P12100_ILO_CODE:C182

Dr. Kristina Ambrazevičiūtė is a research fellow and Head of the Legal System Research Department at the Law Institute of the Lithuanian Centre for Social Sciences. She holds academic degrees in both philosophy and law. Her work focuses on private and labour law, with particular attention to the legal protection of socially vulnerable groups. Dr. Ambrazevičiūtė has published extensively on issues such as the effects of demographic change on the labour market, age discrimination, gender inequality in employment, women's rights in the workplace, and the position of older individuals in the labour market. She has also explored the concept of family, as well as legal challenges related to minors' right to privacy.

Dr. Ambrazevičiūtė has also carried out numerous legal reviews and expert evaluations of legislation and draft laws. She has authored over 20 scientific publications and book chapters in both national and international outlets, regularly presents at academic conferences, and participates in national and international research projects.

Kristīne Dupate is an associate professor at the University of Latvia, Faculty of Law, Department of International and European Law Sciences. Her main field of expertise and scientific research is international and national human rights, especially labour, gender equality and non-discrimination law. In 2007 Kristīne Dupate was awarded a doctoral degree in international law by the University of Latvia (under a cooperation programme with the universities of Denmark). Since 2008 she has been a member (national expert) of the European Networks for the EU Commission in the fields of gender equality, labour law, free movement of workers and social security coordination. She has participated in various projects for the international (UN, CoE) and the EU institutions as an expert in international human rights, especially gender equality and non-discrimination law, labour and social rights. Since January 2017, she has been a member of the Committee of Social Rights of the Council of Europe, re-elected in 2022 with a term of office until 2028. Overall, she possesses 20 years of professional experience in the field of human rights, including gender equality, non-discrimination, labour and social security law.

Prof. Merle Erikson (dr. iur.) graduated from the University of Tartu in 1994, and the doctor iuris degree was conferred to her in 2001. From 1994 to 2011, Merle Erikson was a lecturer and associate professor of labour and social security law at the School of Law of the University of Tartu. Since 2011, she has been a labour law professor at the University of Tartu. Her main areas of research and teaching are international labour law, the European Union social policy and labour law, comparative labour law, and Estonian labour and social security law. Prof. Erikson is competent in both individual and collective labour law issues and occupational health and safety. Prof. Erikson has carried out research at various universities in Europe and Asia. In 2024, she was a visiting researcher at Meiji University. Prof. Erikson has published over 110 publications and participated in dozens of international and Estonian research projects. Recently, she has focused on studying the impact of technological developments on employment relationships. Prof. Erikson has been involved in drafting the Estonian labour law Acts.

Exploring Children's Rights in the Realm of Criminal Law and Criminal Procedure

Vulnerability of Child Victims in Criminal Procedure in EU: Cases of Lithuania and Croatia

Eglė Kavoliūnaitė-Ragauskienė

Abstract Historically, children as victims in criminal procedure had a specific status in European countries. Several Council of Europe and European Union documents invite countries to grant particular rights to children in criminal procedure. The current main document the countries need to adhere to is Directive 2012/29/EU, establishing minimum standards on the rights, support, and protection of victims of crime. Although the European countries follow the same direction, the development, rationale, and steps taken in the Member States differ due to various factors. For example, in Lithuanian criminal procedure, there is no separate notion of "vulnerable persons". However, children have always received a higher standard of protection, which at some point is different from the current European standards, to which the country is gradually striving to comply. A similar normative approach can be found in Croatian criminal procedure, which grants children special protection without specifying their vulnerability. However, Art. 43a Para 2 of the Code of Criminal Procedure obliges the criminal prosecution authorities to pay special attention, inter alia, to victims who are particularly vulnerable due to their relationship with the perpetrator. While the concept of vulnerability is subtly revealed in the most important procedural normative act, the special vulnerability of children due to their age is explicitly acknowledged in the Criminal Code.

The chapter describes the concept of vulnerability and vulnerability of children, assesses the criteria to define the vulnerability of children in EU laws governing criminal procedure, as well as provides a case analysis of the national legal systems of Croatia and Lithuanian with an aim to understand the context which explains national peculiarities and the particular provisions governing the establishment and assessment of child victims' vulnerability.

E. Kavoliūnaitė-Ragauskienė (✉)
Law Institute, Lithuanian Centre for Social Sciences, Vilnius, Lithuania

A. Limantė, R. Vaičiūnienė (eds.), *Children's Rights in Central and Eastern Europe*, European Union and its Neighbours in a Globalized World 29,
https://doi.org/10.1007/978-3-032-07092-0_8

1 Introduction

Child vulnerability has become a cornerstone in developing European Union (EU) legal frameworks, particularly in protecting children's rights in criminal proceedings. Rooted in international obligations, such as the United Nations Convention on the Rights of the Child (UN CRC 1989), the EU has progressively established specialised criteria to protect child victims within its Member States. These criteria are essential in ensuring that the legal system acknowledges and responds to the unique vulnerabilities of children, recognizing both inherent vulnerabilities (e.g., age, developmental stage, prior experiences of a child) and situational vulnerabilities (e.g., nature of the crime, suffered damages, injuries, etc.). Understanding the significance of these criteria is crucial, as they serve not only to protect children's rights but also to ensure their full participation in judicial processes, preventing re-traumatization and safeguarding their well-being.

Directive 2012/29/EU, known as the Victims' Rights Directive, marked a significant step in formalising these protections by requiring that children be automatically considered vulnerable victims who require special measures throughout criminal proceedings. However, as will be seen from the legislative examples of Lithuania and Croatia, the implementation and the significance of child vulnerability criteria vary across EU Member States, reflecting different interpretations and adaptations within national legal systems. Nonetheless, it is crucial to consider how the establishment of the vulnerability and its extent affects the child victim during the criminal procedure. It is also important how the establishment of criteria, as provided in the laws, is implemented in practice. However, the aim of this chapter is limited to reviewing the legislative prerequisites that open the possibilities to apply proper protection of child victims. The chapter is based on the presumption that an appropriate legislative background is the first step towards ensuring the implementation of the principle of the best interests of the child in the criminal procedure, as the actions of courts, pre-trial institutions, and other participants of the criminal procedure are strictly regulated by the laws and, as a general rule, there can be no laisser-faire attitude in this process.

The topic of child vulnerability in Lithuania and Croatia has been explored in various contexts. In Balkan countries, various relevant issues have been analysed. For example, researchers have proposed a victimological landscape of the Balkans, including child victims (Meško et al. 2020). Additionally, the trafficking of minors and the risks faced by migrant children have been examined (Ritossa 2009; Miloshevska and Fritzhand 2018). Furthermore, in Croatia, reforms in social services have been discussed in relation to the needs of the most vulnerable populations (Bošnjak and Stubbs 2007).

In Lithuania, studies have examined the vulnerability of victims, including child victims, in human rights reviews and legal analyses of vulnerable groups in the Baltic region (Žmogaus teisių stebėjimo institutas 2024; Limantė and Pūraitė-Andrikienė 2022). Other research has focused on the assessment of vulnerability in criminal proceedings and the right to legal defence for individuals with disabilities

(Ažubalytė and Zajančkauskienė 2014; Zajančkauskienė 2012). However, despite these contributions, existing research lacks an extensive analysis of the criteria defining child victims' vulnerability.

This chapter consists of four main parts. Section 2 discusses the concept of "vulnerability" in EU criminal procedure law in general. It analyses its aim, origin, and development in EU strategic documents and laws, as well as the types of vulnerability criteria that appear in legal acts. Section 3 is particularly devoted to the vulnerability of children, as provided for in EU legal acts, also providing an overview of how the vulnerability of children is defined in other legal acts of the EU beyond criminal procedure—i.e. migration, asylum, trafficking, sexual exploitation, and sexual abuse, as well as domestic violence. Section 4 analyses the national legal systems of Croatia and Lithuania with a view to understanding the context, which explains national peculiarities and the particular provisions governing the establishment and assessment of child victims' vulnerability. Section 5 summarises the current status of the establishment of the child victims' vulnerability, its effect on the protection of children in criminal procedure, its shortcomings, and the further steps initiated by the European Commission in this field.

2 The Concept of "Vulnerability" in EU Criminal Procedure Law

The concept of vulnerability to children implies those who are more exposed to risks than their peers. Vulnerability refers to an individual's predisposition to develop or the susceptibility to negative developmental outcomes that can occur under high-risk conditions (Zimmerman and Arunkumar 1994, p. 2). It is a relative state that may range from resilience to total helplessness. One of the widely used definitions defines vulnerable children as "the ones not having certain of their basic rights fulfilled" (Skinner et al. 2006, p. 620). Apart of orphanhood being a major determinant of vulnerability, the definition is usually centred around the three fundamental aspects of dependence: (1) material aspects — money, food, clothing, shelter, health care and education; (2) emotional aspects — care, love, support, space to grieve and containment of emotions; (3) social aspects — absence of a supportive peer group, of role models to follow, or of guidance in difficult situations, and risks in the immediate environment. Many vulnerable children fall into multiple categories (Arora et al. 2015, p. 193). Other authors, for example, Weithorn classify child vulnerability into harm-based vulnerability, influence-based vulnerability, capacity-based vulnerability, status-based vulnerability and dependency-based vulnerability (Weithorn 2018, pp. 203–215). According to Grans, vulnerability refers to the state of being exposed to physical, emotional, or psychological harm, but in a broader sense, it also encompasses the risk of human rights violations (Grans 2023, p. 1). Legally, vulnerable groups refer to individuals or communities that face a higher likelihood of human rights abuses compared to others in similar situations

(Nifosi-Sutton 2017, p. 270). This heightened risk can stem from various factors, including discrimination, marginalisation, or socioeconomic disadvantages. These groups may include individuals subject to prejudice based on their race, gender, age, disability, sexual orientation, or other personal characteristics, leading them to be disproportionately affected by rights violations.

From a legal perspective, recognizing vulnerability is crucial for ensuring targeted protection. For example, international human rights frameworks often place a special focus on protecting the rights of children, people with disabilities, ethnic minorities, and other groups identified as more susceptible to systemic injustice. Legal frameworks and policies aimed at safeguarding these groups are designed to reduce their exposure to harm and address the factors contributing to their vulnerability. Thus, vulnerability in the context of human rights law encompasses not only physical or emotional risk but also the structural and systemic challenges that increase the likelihood of certain groups experiencing injustice.

Vulnerability can manifest in two distinct forms: inherent vulnerability and situational vulnerability. The inherent vulnerability arises from innate or physical characteristics, such as age, disability, or biological conditions, which naturally place individuals in a more susceptible position. For example, children are inherently vulnerable due to their dependency, physical immaturity, and lack of experience (Ippolito 2015, p. 25). In such cases, the vulnerability exists even without discrimination or external maltreatment. Children, by virtue of their age, require specific protections under human rights law, regardless of whether they are subjected to discriminatory practices.

On the other hand, situational vulnerability stems from external conditions or circumstances, often brought about by human actions or social structures. This type of vulnerability occurs when an individual's situation is shaped or worsened by deliberate actions, such as exploitation, abuse, or neglect. For instance, refugees, victims of human trafficking, or individuals caught in violent conflicts may find themselves in vulnerable positions due to circumstances beyond their control. In these cases, the vulnerability is not inherent but imposed by the environment or actions of others, transforming individuals into victims (Ippolito and Sánchez 2015, p. 6).

While inherent vulnerability calls for ongoing, systemic protections, situational vulnerability often requires targeted interventions to address the specific harm or risks created by particular circumstances. Both forms highlight the necessity of understanding vulnerability in a nuanced way to ensure legal and social frameworks can effectively address the needs of different at-risk populations.

The concept of vulnerability in the European law tradition has evolved significantly over time, reflecting broader changes in European legal and human rights frameworks. Initially, the vulnerability element was important to define the proper compensation of losses caused by criminal activities, and only later was the concept of vulnerability in criminal procedure broadened to include the aspects of proper implementation of the right to be heard before the court and to ensure other procedural rights.

One of the first documents which recognised the special needs of victims (thus recognising the vulnerability of victims) was the Council of Europe's adopted Resolution (77) 27 on the compensation of victims of crime (Council of Europe 1977).

Although this Resolution does not contain any definition of "vulnerability", it clearly states that victims need to be adequately compensated for crime, and emphasises the importance of taking into account cases of bodily injury and the need to take care of dependents of those who are killed by crime. Also, at the Council of Europe level, this Resolution was followed by the first legally binding European instrument that specifically addressed the compensation of victims of violent crimes, highlighting the importance of providing support to vulnerable victims. Similar to the abovementioned Resolution (77) 27, the 1983 European Convention on Compensation of Victims of Violent Crimes (Council of Europe 1983) requires to compensate for the victims of crime and mentions two particularly important groups of victims—those who have sustained serious bodily injury or impairment of health directly attributable to an intentional crime of violence, and the dependants of persons who have died as a result of such crime.

Need to mention that there is also no uniform and universally accepted definition of a crime victim, leading to inconsistencies in how victims are defined at both international and national legislative levels (Vaško and Klátik 2023, p. 3). The first international document to define the concept of a victim is the EU Council Framework Decision of 15 March 2001 on the standing of victims in criminal proceedings (2001/220/JHA).[1] This Decision characterises a victim as a natural person who has experienced harm, including psychological and physical harm, emotional suffering, or economic loss, directly resulting from an act or omission that violates the law of the Member States. Additionally, Article 2 of this Decision mandates that Member States provide victims with appropriate status within their criminal law systems. Following this Decision, the Council Directive 2004/80/EC[2] was developed, which neither provides a definition of a victim nor a link to a definition thereof in any other legal act.

At the European Union level, the protection of vulnerable persons was initiated by the Stockholm Programme (European Council 2010), which placed significant emphasis on enhancing individual rights in criminal proceedings. Its 2.3.4 Point is specifically intended for the protection of victims of crime and, as will be described below, provides particular guidance on the criteria of victims' vulnerability.

Based on the fundamental principles provided by the Stockholm Programme, the Council's Resolution of 10 June 2011 on a Roadmap for strengthening the rights and protection of victims, in particular in criminal proceedings (Council of Europe 2011), called for action to protect victims' rights in several directions. In particular, it called to establish adequate procedures and structures to respect the dignity, personal and psychological integrity as well as the privacy of the victim in criminal

[1] EU Council Framework Decision of 15 March 2001 on the standing of victims in criminal proceedings (2001/220/JHA) OJ L 82, 2001, p. 1–4.

[2] Council Directive 2004/80/EC of 29 April 2004 relating to compensation to crime victims. OJ L 261, 2004, p. 15–18.

proceedings, enhance the access to justice by victims of crime, also by fostering the role of victim support services; to design adequate procedures and structures aimed at preventing secondary and repeat victimisation; to encourage the provision of interpretation and translation for the victim within criminal proceedings; where appropriate, to encourage victims to participate actively in criminal proceedings; to strengthen the right of victims and of their legal counsel to receive timely information about the proceedings and their outcomes; to encourage the recourse to restorative justice and alternative dispute resolution methods taking into account the interest of the victim; to pay special attention to children, as part of the most vulnerable group of victims, and always keep in mind the best interest of the child; to ensure that Member States provide training, or encourage the provision of training, to all relevant professionals; and to ensure that the victim may be awarded compensation as appropriate.

Directive 2012/29/EU, establishing minimum standards on the rights, support, and protection of victims of crime, also known as the Victims' Rights Directive, sets out minimum standards for the rights, support, and protection of victims of crime within the European Union. Its primary objective is to ensure that all victims, regardless of where a crime occurs within the EU, receive appropriate care, information, and protection. This directive provided several requirements for the Member States to be adopted in the field of protection of victims of crime, including the requirement that victims are recognized, treated with respect, and their dignity is preserved throughout the criminal justice process; that victims have access to free and confidential support services, which include emotional, psychological, and practical assistance, that victims are protected from further harm, intimidation, or retaliation, particularly for those deemed particularly vulnerable, such as children or victims of gender-based violence, that victims have the right to participate in criminal proceedings, including providing evidence, making statements, and receiving reimbursement for expenses, and that each victim's specific needs are assessed to determine whether they require special protection measures during the proceedings, particularly for vulnerable groups.

The concept of vulnerability continues to evolve and has its path not only in criminal procedure, but also in other contexts, and first of all, asylum and migration. For example, the Common European Asylum System (CEAS) has incorporated the concept of vulnerability to ensure that asylum seekers with special needs receive appropriate support and protection.

As might be implied from the documents discussed above, neither international legal instruments nor practice demonstrates a clear trend toward establishing a definitive list of vulnerable groups (Morawa 2003, p. 139). Despite this, the choices made by international lawmakers in adopting specialized human rights conventions aimed at protecting the rights of certain groups suggest an implicit recognition of their vulnerability. These legal measures, although not constituting a formal catalogue, indicate that certain groups are recognized as deserving of special consideration and protection due to their particular vulnerability to harm, discrimination, or marginalization in specific contexts. This approach reflects an evolving understanding of vulnerability that adapts to different social, cultural, and political circumstances rather than adhering to a clearly established set of criteria. Besides, EU law also reveals evidence of a universal approach to vulnerability, which should be tailored to individual needs and abilities. These requirements, found in the Victims' Rights Directive (Recital 21 and art.3(2)), are based on the understanding that all individuals may have difficulty understanding and appreciating information in certain circumstances, and indicate a need for a personalised approach (Waddington 2020, p. 801).

According to Ažubalytė and Zajančkauskienė, the examination of EU documents focused on improving the rights of vulnerable individuals in criminal proceedings reveals various methods for identifying vulnerability. In certain cases, vulnerability is automatically presumed, meaning that specific groups are recognized as needing special protections without requiring a detailed assessment. This presumption acknowledges that some individuals consistently face challenges within the legal system (Ažubalytė, Zajančkauskienė, p. 160).

In other instances, vulnerability is determined through a personal evaluation, which involves assessing the unique circumstances and characteristics of each individual involved in the proceedings. This approach enables a more tailored response, ensuring that specific needs are addressed based on each individual's unique situation.

Thus, the criteria for identifying "vulnerability" can be classified into two main categories. The first category encompasses the inherent characteristics of the participant, including age, mental health, and physical health. These factors can significantly impact a person's ability to navigate the complexities of the legal system, rendering them more susceptible to harm or misunderstanding.

The second category encompasses situational factors—objective circumstances that may elevate an individual's vulnerability during the proceedings. These can include aspects such as the courtroom environment, the presence of legal representation, or the overall dynamics within the courtroom.

3 Vulnerability of Children According to EU Legal Acts

The need to take into account the vulnerability factors of children stem from different global and European legal acts, including the Convention on the Rights of the Child and the European Convention on Human Rights. Preliminarily, the concept of vulnerability in criminal procedure is related to the proper use of the right to a fair trial. In the Stockholm programme, as already mentioned, there is a separate Point on the victims of crime, but with this document, the European Council calls upon the Commission also to identify measures to which the Union can bring added value in order to protect and promote the rights of the child. Further, it explains that children in particularly vulnerable situations should receive special attention, notably children who are victims of sexual exploitation and abuse as well as children who are victims of trafficking and unaccompanied minors in the context of the Union migration policy.

Directive 2012/29/EU places significant emphasis on the protection of vulnerable victims, with special provisions for children. It emphasises the need to ensure a child's safety, privacy, and emotional well-being during legal proceedings. First, the Directive ensures that children are able to express their views and participate in the proceedings in a manner appropriate to their age, maturity, and level of understanding. The child should be heard without causing additional harm. Second, the Directive provides safeguards to protect children from further trauma. For instance, measures include avoiding unnecessary questioning, allowing testimony via video link, or ensuring that they are not in direct contact with the offender. The Directive also requires ensuring special interview conditions and protection of children from public exposure. Additionally, it is essential to avoid direct contact with the offender and to ensure that information and support are tailored to meet the needs of children. Finally, according to the Directive, children should have access to specialized support services that can provide psychological, emotional, and practical assistance. These services should be sensitive to the child's developmental needs and trauma.

The Directive establishes a three-layer framework for assessing the vulnerability of children.

First, the Directive stipulates that children, defined as individuals under the age of 18, are automatically considered vulnerable under the Directive. Article 22(4) of the Directive states that child victims shall be presumed to have specific protection needs due to their vulnerability to secondary and repeat victimisation, intimidation, and retaliation. This notion comes from the Convention on the Rights of the Child, which emphasises the principle of the best interests of the child. Accordingly, this overarching principle guiding all decisions and actions taken under the Directive with regard to child victims ensures that any measures adopted prioritize the child's welfare, safety, and developmental needs, ensuring they are treated with dignity and respect throughout the process. The notion that children are regarded as vulnerable per se means that their vulnerability does not need to be proven or assessed; it is presumed due to their age.

Second, the Directive mentions certain attributes which indicate the "increased" vulnerability of children. For example, Recital 17 of the Directive explicitly states that "women victims of gender-based violence and their children often require special support and protection because of the high risk of secondary and repeat victimisation, of intimidation and of retaliation connected with such violence". Furthermore, Article 2(1) stipulates that a child-sensitive approach, taking into account the child's age, maturity, views, needs, and concerns, shall prevail. This would mean that the child's age, maturity, views, needs, and concerns should be considered important factors in determining the vulnerability of a particular child.

Finally, although all children are considered vulnerable, the Directive requires an individual assessment of each child to determine whether they require specific protection measures during the criminal proceedings. This assessment takes into account several factors, including their age and maturity, the nature and circumstances of the crime (e.g., whether the crime involved violence or sexual abuse), the potential for re-traumatization or harm during the proceedings, and any physical or mental disabilities the child might have. The aim of the assessment is to identify the most appropriate measures that should be taken to protect the child's interests and minimize further distress.

It should be noted that according to Recital 69, the Directive does not affect more far-reaching provisions contained in other Union acts that address the specific needs of particular categories of victims, such as victims of human trafficking and victims of child sexual abuse, sexual exploitation, and child pornography, in a more targeted manner. To this end, the Anti-Trafficking Directive (Directive 2011/36/EU)[3] is the cornerstone of EU legislation aimed at tackling human trafficking, including specific provisions for child victims. It takes a victim-centred approach and mandates that child victims receive particular attention and care. This Directive acknowledges that children are particularly vulnerable to trafficking and exploitation. As a result, it mandates that Member States implement measures to provide special protection for children throughout the criminal proceedings and beyond, to observe the best interest of the child, required to implement individual assessments and provide tailored support, and apply other measures as provided in the Directive 2012/29/EU, however, in a more tailored manner to situations of child sexual abuse, sexual exploitation, and child pornography. Besides, this Directive also provides that child victims of trafficking cannot be prosecuted for any criminal activities they were forced to engage in as a direct result of their trafficking. This is essential in ensuring that children are treated as victims, not offenders, regardless of their involvement in illegal activities.

Child victims of trafficking who are asylum seekers or unaccompanied minors benefit from additional protections under EU asylum law, particularly Directive 2013/33/EU (Reception Conditions Directive),[4] which ensures that unaccompanied minors have access to guardianship and specialised care; child trafficking victims can be placed in appropriate reception facilities that are equipped to meet their needs, and family reunification is facilitated when it is needed in the child's best interests.

The support to child victims was even more extended by Directive (EU) 2024/1712,[5] which amends the EU's anti-trafficking framework and brings several new provisions to enhance protections for child victims of human trafficking. One of the key updates is the recognition of additional forms of trafficking, such as illegal adoption, forced marriage, and exploitation in surrogacy, all of which often involve children. This recognition is crucial as it expands the scope of protection for children who may be trafficked under these circumstances. The Directive also

[3] Directive 2011/36/EU of the European Parliament and of the Council of 5 April 2011 on preventing and combating trafficking in human beings and protecting its victims, and replacing Council Framework Decision 2002/629/JHA. OJ L 101, 2011, p. 1–11.

[4] Directive 2013/33/EU of the European Parliament and of the Council of 26 June 2013 laying down standards for the reception of applicants for international protection (recast). OJ L 180.,2013, p. 96–116.

[5] Directive (EU) 2024/1712 of the European Parliament and of the Council of 13 June 2024 amending Directive 2011/36/EU on preventing and combating trafficking in human beings and protecting its victims. OJ L, 2024/1712, 2024.

mandates stricter penalties for those involved in child trafficking, especially where new forms of exploitation are present. Another significant advancement is the Directive's emphasis on tailored support for child victims. It obliges Member States to provide child-specific assistance, including appropriate accommodation, medical care, education, and psychological support. Special attention is given to the appointment of guardians for unaccompanied children, ensuring that their best interests are represented throughout legal processes.

As regards child victims of domestic violence, the Council of Europe Convention on the Protection of Children against Sexual Exploitation and Sexual Abuse (Council of Europe 2007) obliges its parties to take the necessary legislative or other measures to prevent all forms of sexual exploitation and sexual abuse of children and to criminalise certain intentional conduct and provides special measures for children.

To summarise, despite the fact that in the EU, all children should already be regarded as vulnerable persons in criminal procedure, their vulnerability is further assessed on additional criteria. First, Directive 2012/29/EU explicitly states that proper attention should be paid to child victims of domestic violence. Other special directives provide special rules for particular cases—child victims of trafficking who are asylum seekers, child victims of human trafficking, and victims of child sexual abuse, sexual exploitation, and child pornography. Finally, an "individual assessment" of each child needs to be carried out to determine whether they need specific protection measures during the criminal proceedings.

4 Vulnerability of Children in Criminal Procedure in Lithuania and Croatia

The Croatian Constitution[6] upholds the protection of children's best interests as a key principle. It emphasizes that parents are responsible for their children's upbringing, well-being, and education, ensuring their right to a comprehensive and balanced personal development. The state is required to provide special care for orphans and minors who are neglected by their parents, while everyone has a duty to safeguard children and report any potential harm to the relevant authorities. Furthermore, the Constitution guarantees special protection for youth, mothers, and disabled individuals in the workplace. Equal access to education is a fundamental right, with compulsory education provided free of charge as per legal provisions. The National Strategy for the Rights of Children in the Republic of Croatia for the period 2014 to 2020 (Ministarstvo socijalne politike i mladih 2014) was adopted in September 2014 by the Croatian Government. It establishes four main aims in the field of child protection: ensuring that services in various areas are adapted to children (such as justice, health care, social welfare, education, sport, and culture),

[6] Constitution of the Republic of Croatia (1990) https://www.ombudsman.hr/wp-content/uploads/2020/06/Constitution-of-the-Republic-of-Croatia.pdf.

eliminating all forms of violence against children, ensuring that the rights of children in vulnerable situations are respected and ensuring the active participation of children.

The national legal acts governing criminal procedure in Croatia establish a wide range of provisions enabling courts and law enforcement institutions to properly individualise and address child victims' needs. Although a child, according to the Criminal Code of Croatia,[7] is held as a person of 18 years of age, the Criminal Procedure Code[8] states that in case the age of the victim is not known, it shall be presumed to be a child if there is a probability that the victim has not reached the age of eighteen.[9] It should be noted that according to the Criminal Procedure Code of Croatia the child's age is a factor in deciding whether she/he himself may apply to a court—as children above 16 years of age might refer to courts without their representatives, and in case of criminal proceedings, they may submit a private charge without representation.

In Croatia, the court, the State Attorney's office, the investigator, and the police are obliged to treat the child victim of the crime with special care, bearing in mind age, personality, and other circumstances in order to avoid harmful consequences for the upbringing and development of the child. In dealing with the child victim, the competent authorities will first and foremost be guided by the best interests of the child (Courts of the Republic of Croatia 2024).

According to Article 43a of the Criminal Procedure Code of Croatia, prior to questioning the victim, the body conducting the examination shall, in cooperation with bodies, organizations, or institutions for assistance and support to victims of crime, conduct an individual assessment of the victim. An individual victim assessment includes determining whether there is a need to apply special protection measures in relation to the victim and, if so, what special protection measures should be applied (measures to protect the victim's safety, a special way of interrogating the victim, the use of communication technologies to avoid visual contact with the offender and other measures prescribed by law). When the victim of a crime is a child, it will be assumed that there is a need to apply special protection measures and determine which special protection measures should be applied.

The Criminal Procedure Code also states that undertaking an individual assessment of the victim, the personal characteristics of the victim, the type or nature of the criminal offence and the circumstances of the commission of the criminal offence shall be taken into account. In doing so, special attention is paid to victims who have suffered significant damage due to the gravity of the crime, victims of a crime committed due to a personal characteristic of the victim, and victims who are particularly vulnerable by their relationship with the perpetrator. When conducting an individual assessment relating to victims of violence against women, domestic

[7] Criminal Code of the Republic of Croatia. The Official Gazette of the Republic of Croatia "Narodne novine" No. 110/1997.

[8] Criminal Procedure Code of the Republic of Croatia. Official Gazette of the Republic of Croatia "Narodne novine" No. 62/2003.

[9] Article 44(3) of the Criminal Procedure Code of Croatia.

violence, and violence against close persons, additionally, special consideration shall be given to risk factors for the recurrence of violence, as well as the results of the previous assessment of the victim's needs. It is also stated that an individual assessment of the victim shall be carried out with the participation of the victim and taking into account his/her wishes, including the desire not to use special protection measures prescribed by law.[10]

The Criminal Procedure Code provides a special regime for children who are victims of a criminal offence against sexual freedom, and a victim of a criminal offence of trafficking. In this case, the victims are entitled to additional public funds for services (e.g. consulting and advisor before the examination), as additional procedural rights (e.g. to be questioned by a person of the same sex by the police and the public prosecutor's office and, if possible, to be questioned by the same person in the event of re-interrogation).

Besides the Criminal Procedure Code, additional safeguards for child victims are provided for in other pieces of legislation in Croatia. For example, the Ministry of Family, Homeland War Veterans and Intergenerational Solidarity in 2008 issued The Protocol on Procedures in Domestic Violence Cases (Ministarstvo za demografiju, obitelj, mlade i socijalnu politiku 2019) which provides additional measures in case of domestic violence, such as that the victim must be granted legal aid, interviewed in separate premises without the alleged perpetrator being present, and also that in case of child victims, specially trained officers must carry out all tasks, etc.

The Protocol on Conduct in Cases of Sexual Violence (Vlada Republike Hrvatske 2023) adopted by the Croatian Government in 2023 provides that all actions by the police, save for urgent measures, are to be carried out by officers specially trained in sexual violence cases and that the police must inform the victim of the possibility of obtaining expert help for the protection of his or her physical and psychological well-being. According to this document, victims of sexual violence, including children, are entitled to receive legal aid, as well as counselling and psychosocial support.

Finally, in 2014, the Croatian Government adopted the Protocol on Conduct in Cases of Ill-treatment and Neglect of Children (Vlada Republike Hrvatske 2014). It provides that the best interests of a child have primary importance in all matters covered by it. The procedures followed should be efficient in order to ensure that the child is given prompt and coordinated protection from further ill-treatment, including sexual abuse or neglect, as well as provided appropriate support. All procedures conducted by State bodies are to be carried out by experts in the relevant fields. A social welfare centre should appoint a special guardian for the child if its experts assess that the child's interests are in conflict with those of the parent. It should also instruct the parent to seek counselling or involve the child in appropriate forms of psychosocial help, rehabilitation programmes, and other forms of expert help and support. Additionally, medical institutions are obligated to ensure cooperation

[10] Article 43a of the Criminal Code of the Republic of Croatia.

through a multidisciplinary team approach in order to prevent the recurrence of traumatic experiences.

However, in Croatia, the concept of child victimization lacks a unified and comprehensive legal or institutional framework. Instead, it is primarily addressed through provisions in the Criminal Code and other related laws, which define various forms of abuse, neglect, and exploitation of children. However, the response to child victimisation is fragmented across multiple institutions, including the police, judiciary, social welfare centres, health institutions, and the education system. Each of these entities plays a role in addressing different aspects of child victimization, but coordination between them is often inconsistent.

Key challenges include variations in procedures, differences in professional competencies, and a lack of an integrated approach to protecting and supporting child victims. For instance, social welfare centres handle cases of neglect and abuse within families, while the police and judiciary deal with criminal cases of violence, exploitation, or trafficking. This division can sometimes lead to inefficiencies in providing timely and effective support for child victims (Meško et al. 2020, pp. 225–230).

In addition to state institutions, several non-governmental organisations (NGOs) actively support child victims by offering psychological counselling, legal assistance, shelter, and advocacy. NGOs such as Brave Phone (Hrabri telefon) provide helpline services for children, while others focus on specific issues like child trafficking, domestic violence, or online safety.

Whereas the Lithuanian legal regulation of the vulnerability of children in the criminal process is not as elaborated as in Croatia. Similarly, the special status of a child stems from the Constitution of the Republic of Lithuania,[11] which provides that childhood is under the protection and care of the State (Article 38 of the Constitution of Lithuania) and that children are protected by law (Article 39 of the Constitution of Lithuania), as well as there are provisions on the State support to families and parent's duty to raise their children properly (Article 38 of the Constitution of Lithuania).

One of the basic documents on the protection of children in Lithuania is the Law on the Fundamentals of Protection of the Rights of the Child,[12] which aims at ensuring the implementation, defence, and protection of children's rights and freedoms, strengthening the responsibility and ability of parents and other legal representatives of the child to care for the child, safeguarding the child's interests, establishing the foundations for organising assistance to the child, family, or other legal representatives, taking into account the provisions of the Constitution of the Republic of Lithuania, the United Nations Convention on the Rights of the Child and its optional protocols, defining the mechanisms for ensuring and protecting children's rights, the institutions of the child protection system, the legal foundations of their

[11] Constitution of the Republic of Lithuania. Official Gazette, 1992, No 33-1014.

[12] Law of the Republic of Lithuania on the Fundamentals of Protection of the Rights of the Child. Official Gazette 1996, No. 33-807.

activities, and general provisions of responsibility for violations of children's rights. This law provides the basic principles that need to be considered throughout Lithuania's legal system.

Similarly, as in Croatia, a child is a person under 18 years of age unless it is not possible to determine her/his age—in such case she/he is also considered a child (Article 27(1) of the Criminal Procedure Code of Lithuania[13]).

Interestingly, but Lithuanian Code of Criminal Procedure establishes a requirement to perform an individual assessment only in respect of underage suspects and accused persons (in this case, an individual assessment is a summary of information about the personality, environment, and needs of a juvenile suspect or accused in the areas of protection, education, and social integration. This assessment is carried out by the state child protection authority or the detention facility where the juvenile is held) (Articles 27(2) and 189(1) of the Criminal Procedure Code of Lithuania). As regards child victims, there are special procedural requirements related to the interviews of child victims and witnesses. For example, they need to be interviewed in specially adapted premises, and preferably not more than once; interviews must be carried out without the participation of the perpetrator, etc.(Article 186 of the Criminal Procedure Code of Lithuania). Additional measures (participation of certain childcare specialists and psychologist, etc.) are provided in case of very serious crimes. Thus, one of the criteria of child vulnerability in the Lithuanian criminal process is the nature of criminal activity.

Furthermore, the Criminal Procedure Code establishes an "assessment of the victim's special protection needs" (Article 186-1 of the Criminal Procedure Code of Lithuania), which does not specifically speak about children. It is stated that the pre-trial investigation officer or prosecutor assesses the victim's special protection needs. If necessary, a psychologist or other persons with specific knowledge or skills may be involved. The data collected during the assessment of the victim's special protection needs are considered when organising the criminal process, and when determining whether one or more of the safeguards provided in this Code should be applied to the victim due to their special protection needs. This indicates that in Lithuania, the vulnerability of the child in criminal procedure is first of all intended for the protection of the child during the criminal process (and is not extended, for example, to speaking about the proper compensation for losses due to criminal activity). The Recommendations of the Prosecutor General[14] state describe the special protection needs as the needs of the victim arising from personal characteristics, the nature of the criminal offense, or the circumstances under which it was committed, which require the victim to utilize the guarantees established by the Criminal Procedure Code in order to be protected from psychological trauma, criminal influence, or other negative consequences. Although the Criminal Procedure Code does not explicitly state that children are always regarded as vulnerable

[13] Criminal Procedure Code of the Republic of Lithuania. Official Gazette 2002, No. 37-1341.

[14] Recommendations of the Prosecutor General of the Republic of Lithuania on the performance of the assessment of the victim's specific needs. TAR, 2016, No. 4051.

victims, the abovementioned Recommendations of the Prosecutor General clearly state that in case a victim is a child, the assessment process needs to be carried out in all cases. Interestingly again, although the Criminal Procedure Code provides that „the process of the assessment of the victim's specific needs"shall be established by the Prosecutor General (Article 186-1(4) of the Criminal Procedure Code of Lithuania), as mentioned above, this process is established in the form of Recommendations, not a fully binding document.

The Recommendations of the Prosecutor General on the performance of the assessment of the victim's specific needs provide a form that needs to be filled in by the pre-trial investigator or the prosecutor. The form contains criteria in order to establish whether the vulnerability of a child is high, medium or low. The criteria are divided into two parts: a description of the activity and a description of the victim. Description of the activity includes criteria on the nature of the criminal activity (the biggest score is attributed to the criminal offenses against human health, freedom, sexual self-determination, inviolability, children and family, or morality; the lower score is given to other very grave and grave crimes, and the least important are other criminal activities); the subject to which the activity was directed at (the child, her/his relatives or property); the nature of the act (physical violence, psychological violence or none of these); the damage incurred (physical, moral, damage to property); external injuries (significant injuries, insignificant injuries, absence of injuries). Description of the child victim includes the age group (0–10, 11–14, 15–18 years of age), social environment (negative, no data, positive (when it is evident that the child was properly cared of), behaviour during the assessment (evident post-traumatic behaviour, evident fear or anxiety, no specific signs); the previous suffers from criminal activity (the child suffered from family members; suffered from others than family members; no previous harmful activities against her/him); representation (the representative by law cannot properly ensure child's interests (e.g. has violated against her/him or has a conflicting interest); the representative is granted by the state, the representative can properly defend the child).

Although there are differences between the countries on the establishment of the vulnerability criteria for child victims, it may be noted that both in Croatia and Lithuania, the vulnerability criteria includes inherent characteristics (i.e., features describing the victim) and situational factors (features describing the criminal activity and criminal proceedings related environment). However, the assessment, the significance, and the outcomes of the establishment of vulnerabilities are of greater differences—these include the enactment level (e.g. in Lithuania, the individual assessment is regulated by recommendations of the Prosecutor general rather than law), the level to take individualised measures (in Lithuania particular measures are prescribed, in Croatia a budget allocation is allowed with a possibility to take individual decisions), etc.

5 Further Development of Legislation and Implications of the Use of Child Vulnerability Criteria

As illustrated in the previous section, EU countries employ diverse approaches to implement the child vulnerability criteria outlined in Directive 2012/29/EU, which provides minimum standards for the rights, support, and protection of victims, including children. This Directive mandates that vulnerable victims, particularly children, receive special protection based on an assessment of their individual needs. However, the methods of translating these provisions into national law vary considerably in different countries.

First, the differences stem from the flexibility to select instruments to achieve the goals as provided for in the Directive. This applies as well to the application of vulnerability criteria for child victims, and as well for the establishment of such criteria without mentioning the potential outcome of the result when the vulnerability level of a particular child is established. The different practices of countries are determined by different legal systems, institutional childcare infrastructure, embedded principles of the criminal procedure, the budget allocations for this purpose, etc. However, it may be noticed that even more peculiar aspects are different—for example, in the Croatian Criminal Procedure Code, it is clearly stated that the child ex officio needs the application of special protection measures and describes in detail the individual assessment conditions and process whereas Lithuanian Criminal Procedure code only mentions the possibility to assess whether the victim has "special protection needs", which, in its essence, is similar to individual assessment of vulnerability. However, in contrast, this is not a legal requirement but only a recommendation of the Prosecutor General. Not surprisingly, the leverage of certain factors in determining the vulnerability are also varying among countries.

In 2022 the European Commission assessed the Directive 2012/29/EU. Although the evaluation shows that over the past ten years, the Directive has greatly contributed to improving the lives of victims across the EU, it still identified the need for a targeted revision to ensure victims would fully benefit from their rights. This leads to the adoption of the Commission's proposals for a revised Directive (Proposal for a Directive of the European Parliament and of the Council amending Directive 2012/29/EU establishing minimum standards on the rights, support and protection of victims of crime, and replacing Council Framework Decision 2001/220/JHA). One of the causes for the initiation of the review of the Directive 2012/29/EU is that as stated, vulnerable victims (such as children, older people, persons with disabilities, victims of hate crimes, and victims in detention) do not always benefit from a timely assessment of their needs for protection and are deprived of effective protection measures, such as protection orders. This means that despite the establishment of vulnerability of a person, the individual assessment is not always performed as required thus leading to failure to make use of individually tailored support to victims. As EuroChild points out (EuroChild 2024), in improving the vulnerable child victims' rights, it is necessary to improve statistical data disaggregated by intersectional indicators, including gender, disability, age, citizenship, or statelessness. As often child victims are not aware of their victim status, it is crucial that the Directive calls for information to be provided to children in an age-appropriate and culturally sensitive manner.

To summarise, while the Directive 2012/29/EU sets a common baseline for protecting child victims across the EU, the implementation of its provisions varies depending on the legal systems, social services infrastructure, and specific vulnerabilities identified in each Member State. This diversity in implementation reflects the flexibility allowed by the Directive to adapt to different national contexts while still meeting the overarching goal of providing special protections for vulnerable children.

6 Concluding Remarks

The child vulnerability criteria are of major importance in legal and social frameworks for several key reasons, primarily because of the need to protect children's rights and well-being in contexts where they are especially susceptible to harm. Recognising child vulnerability is fundamental for ensuring that children receive the necessary support, protection, and accommodations during legal, social, and institutional processes. Historically, the victim vulnerability significance emerged in the need to properly identify victims and to provide reasonable compensation for suffered criminal activities. Later this notion was developed to primarily reflect the need to properly make use of the right to a fair trial and to receive necessary support, protection, and accommodations during legal, social, and institutional processes related to undergone criminal activities.

According to EU legal documents and countries' national laws, child victims are automatically recognized as vulnerable, in accordance with the principles of the UNCRC. This recognition reflects the special attention and protection that children require due to their vulnerability as a result of their age, cognitive development, and dependence on adults. EU laws and national frameworks aim at ensuring that child victims receive enhanced protection and support, aligning with the UNCRC's core idea that the best interests of the child should be a primary consideration in all actions affecting them.

In addition to recognizing the general vulnerability of all victims, including children, certain EU laws give special emphasis to the heightened vulnerability of specific groups, such as victims of domestic violence, sexual abuse, and trafficking. These groups face unique and often more severe risks of harm due to the nature of the crimes committed against them, which are often deeply personal, exploitative, and can lead to long-term trauma. For this reason, EU legislation provides extra protections and support mechanisms tailored to these groups, ensuring they receive specialized assistance throughout criminal proceedings.

Finally, Directive 2012/29/EU calls the Member States to perform individual assessment of vulnerable persons to be able to individualise the support measures applicable to a particular person. The criteria for identifying vulnerability in legal settings can indeed be classified into two key categories: inherent characteristics and situational factors. Inherent characteristics refer to the personal attributes of the individual that make them naturally more vulnerable within the legal system. Such factors are intrinsic to the person and can significantly impair their ability to understand and engage with legal proceedings, making them more prone to harm or exploitation. As a general rule, these include age, mental health, physical health, previous experiences, etc. Situational factors are external circumstances or conditions related to criminal activity or the legal process that can exacerbate an individual's vulnerability, even if they do not possess inherent vulnerabilities. Such factors are often temporary and are based on the specific context and include the nature of criminal activity, impact, damage, bodily injuries, also courtroom environment, presence of legal representation, etc.

The implementation of vulnerability assessments and protection measures for victims of crime varies across EU Member States, as seen in the presented examples of Croatia and Lithuania. These differences arise from each country's interpretation and application of Directive 2012/29/EU, which leaves some flexibility in implementation. In 2023 the European Commission evaluated the implementation of Directive 2012/29/EU and concluded that while the Directive provides a robust framework for victim protection, the different national practices often result in unequal treatment of vulnerable victims across the EU. In conclusion, the variability in how vulnerability assessments and protection measures are applied in countries like Croatia and Lithuania underscores the importance of the EU's efforts to standardize victim protection and close the gaps between different national legal systems. The proposed revisions to the Victims' Rights Directive represent a step forward in ensuring equal access to justice and support for all vulnerable victims across the EU.

References

Arora SK, Shah D, Chaturvedi S, Gupta P (2015) Defining and measuring vulnerability in young people. Indian J Community Med 40(3):193–197

Ažubalytė R, Zajančkauskienė J (2014) Vulnerability assessment of participants in Lithuanian criminal proceedings in the context of EU regulations. Baltic J Law Politics 7(2):152–178. https://doi.org/10.1515/bjlp-2015-0006

Bošnjak V, Stubbs P (2007) Towards a new welfare mix for the Most vulnerable: reforming social Services in Bosnia-Herzegovina, Croatia and Serbia. In: Social policy and regional development proceedings. The Institute of Economics, Zagreb Friedrich Ebert Stiftung, Zagreb

Constitution of the Republic of Croatia (1990). https://www.ombudsman.hr/wp-content/uploads/2020/06/Constitution-of-the-Republic-of-Croatia.pdf

Constitution of the Republic of Lithuania. Official Gazette, 1992, No 33-1014. Council Directive 2004/80/EC of 29 April 2004 relating to compensation to crime victims. OJ L 261, 2004

Council of Europe (1977) Resolution (77) 27 on the compensation of victims of crime. https://rm.coe.int/16804f3e59

Council of Europe (1983) European Convention on Compensation of Victims of Violent Crimes. https://rm.coe.int/1680079751

Council of Europe (2007) Council of Europe Convention on the Protection of Children against Sexual Exploitation and Sexual Abuse. https://www.coe.int/en/web/conventions/full-list?module=treaty-detail&treatynum=201
Council of Europe (2011) Roadmap for strengthening the rights and protection of victims, in particular in criminal proceedings. eur-lex.europa.eu/legal-content/EN/TXT/PDF/?uri=CELEX:32011G0628(01)
Courts of the Republic of Croatia. Retrieved on 25 September 2024. https://sudovi.hr/en/citizens/victims-rights
Criminal Code of the Republic of Croatia. The Official Gazette of the Republic of Croatia "Narodne novine" No. 110/1997
Criminal Procedure Code of the Republic of Croatia. Official Gazette of the Republic of Croatia "Narodne novine" No. 62/2003.Criminal Procedure Code of the Republic of Lithuania. Official Gazette 2002, No. 37-1341.Directive 2011/36/EU of the European Parliament and of the Council of 5 April 2011 on preventing and combating trafficking in human beings and protecting its victims, and replacing Council Framework Decision 2002/629/JHA. OJ L 101, 2011
Directive (EU) 2024/1712 of the European Parliament and of the Council of 13 June 2024 amending Directive 2011/36/EU on preventing and combating trafficking in human beings and protecting its victims. OJ L, 2024/1712, 2024
Directive 2012/29/EU of the European Parliament and of the Council of 25 October 2012 establishing minimum standards on the rights, support and protection of victims of crime, and replacing Council Framework Decision 2001/220/JHA. OL L 315, 2012
Directive 2013/33/EU of the European Parliament and of the Council of 26 June 2013 laying down standards for the reception of applicants for international protection (recast). OJ L 180, 2013
EU Council Framework Decision of 15 March 2001 on the standing of victims in criminal proceedings (2001/220/JHA) OJ L 82, 2001
Eurochild (2024) The revision of the EU Victims' Rights Directive: an opportunity to strengthen the rights of child victims. Retrieved on 12 October 2024. https://eurochild.org/news/the-revision-of-the-eu-victims-rights-directive-an-opportunity-to-strengthen-the-rights-of-child-victims/
European Commission (2022) Commission staff working document: Evaluation of Directive 2012/29/EU of the European Parliament and of the Council of 25 October 2012 establishing minimum standards on the rights, support and protection of victims of crime, and replacing Council Framework Decision 2001/220/JHA. https://eur-lex.europa.eu/legal-content/FR/TXT/?uri=SWD:2022:179:FIN
European Council (2010) The Stockholm Programme — An Open and Secure Europe Serving and Protecting Citizens. OJ C 115, 4.5.2010
Grans L (2023) The impact of vulnerability on state obligations in criminal proceedings on domestic violence: interpreting the Istanbul convention and the European convention on human rights. Women Crim Just:1–16. https://doi.org/10.1080/08974454.2023.2296624
Hrabri telefon. https://udruga.hrabritelefon.hr/en/about/who-we-are/
Ippolito F (2015) (De)constructing children's vulnerability under European law. In: Ippolito F, Sánchez SI (eds) Protecting vulnerable groups, the European human rights framework. Hart Publishing, pp 23–47
Ippolito F, Sánchez SI (2015) Introduction. In: Ippolito F, Sánchez SI (eds) Protecting vulnerable groups, the European human rights framework. Hart Publishing, pp 1–20
Law of the Republic of Lithuania on the Fundamentals of Protection of the Rights of the Child. Official Gazette 1996, No. 33-807
Limantė A, Pūraitė-Andrikienė D (2022) Legal protection of vulnerable groups in Lithuania, Latvia, Estonia and Poland. Trends and perspectives. Springer, Cham
Meško G, Sárik E, Getoš Kalac AM (eds) (2020) Mapping the Victimological landscape of the Balkans. Duncker & Humblot, Berlin
Miloshevska T, Fritzhand A (2018) Risk factors increasing vulnerability of migrant children. Bezbednosni dijalozi 9(2):47–58

Ministarstvo socijalne politike i mladih (2014) Nacionalna strategija za prava djece u Republici Hrvatskoj. https://vlada.gov.hr/UserDocsImages/ZPPI/Strategije%20-%20OGP/socijalna%20 politika/NACIONALNA%20STRATEGIJA%20ZA%20PRAVA%20DJECE%20U%20 RHZA%20RAZDOBLJE%20OD%202014.%20DO%202020.%20GODINE%5B1%5D.pdf

Ministarstvo za demografiju, obitelj, mlade i socijalnu politiku (2019) Protokol o postupanju u slučaju nasilja u obitelji. https://mup.gov.hr/UserDocsImages/dokumenti/Protokol_o_postupanju_u_slucaju_nasilja_u_obitelji-usvojila_Vlada_19_6_2019.pdf

Morawa AHE (2003) Vulnerability as a concept of international human rights law. J Int Relat Dev 6(2):139–155

Nifosi-Sutton I (2017) The protection of vulnerable groups under international human rights law. Routledge

Proposal for a Directive of the European Parliament and of the Council amending Directive 2012/29/EU establishing minimum standards on the rights, support and protection of victims of crime, and replacing Council Framework Decision 2001/220/JHA. https://eur-lex.europa.eu/legal-content/EN/TXT/?uri=CELEX%3A52023PC0424

Recommendations of the Prosecutor General of the Republic of Lithuania on the performance of the assessment of the victim's specific needs. TAR, 2016, No. 4051

Ritossa D (2009) Traficking of minors in Croatia: present situation. Eur J Crime Crim Law Crim Just 17:137

Skinner D, Tsheko N, Mtero-Munyati S, Segwabe M, Chibatamoto P, Mfecane S, Chandiwana B, Nkomo N, Tlou S, Chitiyo G (2006) Towards a definition of orphaned and vulnerable children. AIDS Behav 10:619–626

UN (1989) United Nations Convention on the Rights of the Child. https://www.ohchr.org/en/instruments-mechanisms/instruments/convention-rights-child

Vaško A, Klátik J (2023) Criminal law protection of a child by means of Slovak criminal law and European Union law. Access Justice Eastern Europe 3(20):1–12. https://doi.org/10.33327/AJEE-18-6.3-a000301

Vlada Republike Hrvatske (2014) Protokol o postupanju u slučaju zlostavljanja i zanemarivanja djece. https://zdravlje.gov.hr/UserDocsImages/dokumenti/Programi,%20projekti%20i%20 strategije/Protokol%20o%20postupanju%20u%20slu%C4%8Daju%20zlostavljanja%20i%20 zanemarivanja%20djece.pdf

Vlada Republike Hrvatske (2023) Protokol o postupanju u slučaju seksualnog nasilja https://mrosp.gov.hr/UserDocsImages/dokumenti/Socijalna%20politika/Protokol%20o%20postupanju%20u%20slu%C4%8Daju%20seksualnog%20nasilja.pdf

Waddington L (2020) Exploring vulnerability in EU law: an analysis of 'vulnerability' in EU criminal law and consumer protection law. Eur Law Rev 45(6):779–801

Weithorn LA (2018) A constitutional jurisprudence of children's vulnerability. US Hastings College of the Law. Hastings Law.J 69. 179, 293:179–274

Zajančkauskienė J (2012) Asmens, turinčio negalią, teisė gintis padedant gynėjui ["The right to defence of a disabled person with the help of a defence lawyer"]. Soc Innov Global Growth Res Papers 1(1):105–122

Zimmerman MA, Arunkumar R (1994) Resiliency research: implications for schools and policy. Social policy report / Society for Research. Child Dev 8(4):1–20

Žmogaus teisių stebėjimo institutas (2024) *Žmogaus teisės Lietuvoje 2022–2023*. https://hrmi.lt/wp-content/uploads/2024/12/2022-2023-Zmogaus-teises-Lietuvoje-apzvalga.pdf

Dr. Eglė Kavoliūnaitė-Ragauskienė is an experienced researcher and trainer. She works as a researcher at the Law Institute of the Lithuanian Centre for Social Sciences. She has also worked on a wide range of issues on legal regulation, public administration, and policy making, including IJJO EU project "Alternatives to custody and fostering programmes"; Project "EU Judiciary Training on Brussels IIa Regulation: From South to East" (co-financed by EU Justice Program) (2015–2017); Public Accountability Mechanisms (PAM) Initiative (2010, World Bank); Global

Integrity Report 2008 (2008, Global Integrity); EU Profiler (2009, Roman Schuman Centre for Advanced Studies (European University Institute); EUandI (2014, European University Institute); EU Member States' Consultations with Civil Society on European Policy Matters (2010, European University Institute), etc.

Dr Kavoliūnaitė-Ragauskienė authored over 35 research papers published in national and international journals. Dr Kavoliūnaitė-Ragauskienė lectured at Mykolas Romeris University (Vilnius, Lithuania, 2007–2011); Vytautas Magnus University (Kaunas, Lithuania, 2013), and provided training to law enforcement officials in the Second, the Third and the Fourth International Training Conference within the Rising of the Anticorruption System project (Warsaw, Poland, 2013–2014); and trainings to lawyers and advocates in the ERA (Academy of European Law) workshop on Cross-border divorce and maintenance: Jurisdiction and applicable law.

Children's Victimisation in Lithuania: Context, Forms and Prevalence

Aušra Pocienė, Vaidas Kalpokas, and Jolanta Aleknevičienė

Abstract Children's victimisation is one of the indicators of the child's rights situation in a country. This chapter focuses on recorded children's criminal victimisation and their latent victimisation in Lithuania. The authors first briefly look at the changing social context since the 1990s. On the one hand, growing economic welfare and decreasing overall crime rates seem to be laying the foundations for a safer and better life for all residents and children, too. On the other hand, an ageing society, growing divorce rates, and accelerating adolescents' involvement in cyberspace open new potential sources of insecurity. Secondly, the chapter focuses on registered criminal victimisation of Lithuanian children, noting that though general registered numbers of victimised children are decreasing, the forms of crime children are exposed to are of a dangerous nature. Most children experience physical or sexual violence, and adults from their close environment are the perpetrators in the majority of cases. Thirdly, the authors present the quantitative data from youth delinquency and victimisation surveys that revealed the high latency of children's victimisation. Victimisation survey data showed that cyberbullying, theft, and parental violence are those infringements that most commonly affect children and are often underreported or unreported.

A. Pocienė (✉) · J. Aleknevičienė
Faculty of Philosophy, University of Vilnius, Vilnius, Lithuania
e-mail: ausra.pociene@fsf.vu.lt; jolanta.alekneviciene@fsf.vu.lt

V. Kalpokas
Law Institute, Lithuanian Centre for Social Sciences, Vilnius, Lithuania

A. Limantė, R. Vaičiūnienė (eds.), *Children's Rights in Central and Eastern Europe*, European Union and its Neighbours in a Globalized World 29,
https://doi.org/10.1007/978-3-032-07092-0_9

1 Introduction

Although in public discourse, adolescent delinquency drags much attention, children's victimisation is no less important for at least two reasons. First, children are one of the most vulnerable and fragile groups in society due to their physical and social immaturity, and the physical or sexual violence they experience in the early years of their lives can not only hurt their present but also very badly affect their future. It can lead to further physical and psychological problems or push towards delinquency and social exclusion. Secondly, children's victimisation, in comparison with adults', is a phenomenon with even higher latency. Therefore, officially registered trends can sometimes be deceiving, and this phenomenon should be scrutinised more precisely. This chapter aims to pay attention to children's victimisation in Lithuania during the last three decades. Taking into account a significantly changed social context that presumably should guarantee a safer environment for children, we note that even decreasing trends in registered victimisation give no grounds for relaxing. Much victimisation remains latent: children do not recognise or are in a powerless or subordinated position, and do not dare to report their victimisation. They are being victimised not only by their peers but by their close adults as well. The chapter also glances at two "risky" environments: family—where cases of domestic violence tend to be hidden from public eyes—and cyberspace, which is still lacking control and protection. We also analyse Lithuanian adolescents' victimisation differences among age and gender groups.

2 Contextualising and Theorising Children Victimisation in Lithuania

In evaluating the situation of children in the country, first of all, it is important to outline the context in which they are born, grow up, and socialise. This leads to a better understanding of the situation of a child's well-being, one of the indicators of which is child victimisation. In 1990, when Lithuania regained its independence from the Soviet Union, fundamental political, economic, cultural, and demographic changes began. In the long run, Lithuania followed the scenario of Western countries—the ageing processes in society started. Ageing was determined by the declining birth rate and increasing life expectancy. In the 1990s, Lithuania had 3,693,708 residents, so in 2024, this number is 2885891 inhabitants.[1] The number of children and minors under 18 decreased, as well as the share of this age group in the general population. In 2001, minors comprised 24.4% of the total population, so in 2024, this part was 17.4%. In other words, if at the beginning of the century, almost every

[1] Data presented in this and the next section is based on the data of the State Data Agency and the Official Lithuanian Criminal Register. Not all data have been collected since 1990. Some of the statistical studies were performed only once or twice.

fourth Lithuanian resident was a child or teenager, currently less than every fifth is under the age of 18. One of the reasons for the decreasing birth rate is postponed marriage to a later time: in 2000, women first married at 23.6, and men at 25.7, so in 2022, these ages were 28.3 and 30,0, respectively. Sociologists associate the lower birth rate and the decline in the number of children in the family with secularization and emancipation, equal opportunities, individual freedom of choice, and self-expression (Ariès 1980). Children are now treated not as a tribute to society but as a matter of individual choice, clearly realizing that a child requires significant emotional, financial, and other investments. In other words, in more than a quarter of a century, the situation has changed in such a way that now we are facing society ageing.

We will not say anything new, noting that the child's well-being depends greatly on the situation in the family. The last three decades in Lithuania have been characterised by a delay or decrease in marriages and a growing number of divorces. In the 1990s, Lithuania was one of Europe's leaders in divorces: 3.4 divorces per 100,000 population. After divorces, children stayed in single-parent families. For example, in 1990–45% of households raising children were single-parent families (Kanopienė et al. 2015). During the last three decades, new forms of family appeared. For example—transnational families—that emerged as a result of emigration.[2] Scholars (Juozeliūnienė et al. 2008) have noticed that such families face many challenges, including emotional consequences for children and their stigmatization.

The welfare of children is very dependent on the general economic situation in the country. A noticeable economic improvement began after 2004 when Lithuania became a member of the European Union. In 2005, 68% of the population had income less than the amount needed to meet basic needs, so in 2013, this part was less –48%, and in 2020, even less –34%. The growth of the household's average monthly disposable monetary income also shows improvement: if in 2005 it was 355 euros, in 2013–731 euros, so in 2022 it is 1491 euros. Statistical research performed in 2014 and 2021 also revealed an increase in children's well-being:

- if in 2014, there were 6.5% of households in which at least one child younger than 16 years old could not participate in paid trips and events organised by the school due to lack of funds, so in 2021, there were only 1% of such households;
- in 2014, there were 16.5% of households in which at least one younger than 16 years old child could not leave home for at least 1 week a year on vacation, including staying in a non-main residence or with friends or relatives due to lack of funds, so in 2021 m. this part was much less—4.7%;
- in 2014, there were 10.1% of households in which at least one younger than a 16-year-old child could not replace at least part of the worn-out clothes with new ones due to lack of funds, so in 2021, there were 3.2% of them.

[2] The peaks of emigration in Lithuania were recorded in 2005 (57,885 emigrants), in 2010 (83,157 emigrants), and in 2016 (50,333 emigrants).

Hirschi's (1969) Social Control Theory of Crime emphasises the importance of social relations. It also states that a controlled environment leads to a lower probability of youth delinquency. It is difficult to assess how much control there is in Lithuanian children's environment, but we can presume that more involvement in formal education assures some level of control. Young people up to the age of 18 spend time in families, educational institutions, and extracurricular activities, as well as with friends or on the Internet. Statistical data show that from 2007 to 2022, the bigger part (from 71% to 85%) of teenagers continued their education in secondary schools after having already acquired compulsory general education. Also, more than every fourth child (27% in 2018 and 25.9% in 2020) had some activity after school. So, they remained in a more or less controlled environment until adulthood. Unfortunately, there is little or no control in cyberspace. Therefore, online delinquency, as well as victimisation, has a higher probability of occurring. Over the last two decades, the involvement of adults and young people in the virtual space has grown. In 2004, 59% of the population used the internet at least once in the last 3 months, and 15% used it daily, so in 2022, these shares increased to 100% and 98%, respectively. Also, internet use has increased significantly from 2004 to 2022 among 16–24-year-olds. Participation in chat sites increased from 43% to 87%; gameplay from 50% to 79%; communication in social networks from 82% to 92%; chatting in real-time (in 2019–86%, in 2022–94%).[3]

Last but not least, the contextual point that needs attention is the registered crime rate in Lithuania. The general trends can be described as follows: from 1990 to 2004, there was a steady growth in the total number of crimes: in 1990–37,056 crimes, in 2004–93,419. Since 2004 until now a steady decrease in numbers has been observed. In 2023–45,181 criminal acts were registered, more than twice less as in 2004. The same trends are observed in registered criminal acts committed by minors. In 2004, there were 4232 criminal acts, the commission of which were suspected (accused of) minors, so in 2023, this number was much less—677. A similar downward trend can be seen in the dynamics of another indicator—identified minors suspected (accused) of committing criminal acts. The highest value of this indicator—4232 minors—was reached in 2003, and in 2022 this number decreased to 631 minors (almost seven times less). Relative indicators show that the changes in registered adolescent delinquency during the analysed period are not as pronounced as the absolute numbers, but trends of decrease are also visible. In 2004, there were 2386 criminal acts per 100,000 population, the commission of which were suspected (accused) of minors, so in 2022, much less—861. The structure of criminal acts committed by minors has not changed much in the last year. Almost two-thirds of these acts consisted of various thefts, causing physical pain, minor

[3] Source: Digital Ethics Center. Statistics: Computer and Internet use at home https://e-etika.lt/statistika-kompiuteriai-ir-internetas-namuose/.

It is assumed that the greater involvement of the public and youth in the Internet in 2020–2022 was determined by the restrictions caused by the global COVID-19 pandemic when most of social life moved to virtual space.

health disorders, and violations of public order (Sakalauskas et al. 2022). It should also be noted that throughout the analysed period, the vast majority (about 90% or more) of minors suspected (accused) of committing criminal acts were boys. The highest proportion of girls (10.9%) was recorded in 2012.

Why is it important to take into account crime and delinquency when talking about child victimisation? There are two reasons for this. The first: children become the victims of crimes committed by adults. Therefore, a high number of crimes is likely to lead to a higher level of children's victimisation. Second, researchers have found that adolescent delinquency is closely correlated with their victimisation. For example, it has been found that boys who have delinquent friends, skip classes, and live in a disorganised environment are more likely to be victims of theft, extortion, and assault (Posick 2018). Children can be victimised by friends, parents, neighbours, or strangers. However, this victimisation often remains unknown because young people do not report it to the institutions. Particularly latent is the part of delinquency and victimisation that takes place online (Livingstone et al. 2018).

It is also important to emphasise that the relationship between delinquency and victimisation is mutual: not only do young people with delinquent behaviour become victims of crimes more often, but the victimisation they experience may lead to their delinquent behaviour (Posick 2013). There is research data (Steketee et al. 2021) proving that if children experience physical violence from their parents, they are much more likely to engage in delinquent behaviour. The General Strain Theory (GST) could partially explain this phenomenon. One of its authors and developers, the American criminologist Robert Agnew (2001), examined those types of strains that lead to crime. The theory distinguishes two types of strains: objective and subjective. Objective strains are events or conditions that are disliked by most members of a given group. Such events and conditions can range from physical violence to a lack of food or housing etc. Subjective strains are events or conditions that are disliked by the people who have experienced them. In other words, subjective strain is when a person experiences something that he/ she does not like. Research shows that people accept their experiences differently-subjectively. For example, acceptance of the death of a family member can differ among different people and vary according to circumstances. The acceptance depends on individual factors (e.g. irritability), personal and social resources (self-confidence, autonomy, social support from others), goals/values/ identities, and a series of life circumstances. There are many types of stressors, but the stressors that lead to crime, according to Agnew (2001) must: *(1) be seen as unjust, (2) be seen as high in magnitude, (3) be associated with low social control, and (4) create some pressure or incentive to engage in criminal coping.* Reframing the General Strain Theory, it can be presumed that victimisation of children is a problem of particular importance as the victimised child, if his strain experiences meet the four conditions mentioned above, can react to it in a delinquent or even criminal way.

3 Registered Children's Victimisation

Presuming that adolescent victimisation and delinquency are phenomena that often go hand in hand, it is worth looking at Fig. 1. It shows the number of children under the age of 18 who have been victimised by criminal acts and minors suspected (accused) of committing criminal acts. Although it is not possible to talk about the exact correlations between crime and victimisation, the graph shows that adolescent delinquency is steadily decreasing, as well as children's victimisation. However, the victimisation trend has not been so steady, with a sharp rise from 2017 to 2019. From the year 2005 to 2023, the number of child victims of criminal acts decreased from 4955 to 1693. It is also clear that during the period from 2005 to 2023 (with the exceptions in 2009 and 2014), the number of victims was higher than that of those who committed a crime.

The extraordinary increase in child victimisation in 2017–2019 (respectively: 3635, 3337, and 2522 victimised children) can be explained by the reform of the child rights protection system. This reform is also known as "Matas reform".[4] The result of this was a centralisation of the child rights protection system and the setting of stricter childcare requirements for parents. Any violence against minors was prohibited, and children under the age of six could not be left alone without parental care anymore. This reform made it possible to bring out of latency several cases where children experienced domestic violence, and this is reflected in the statistics in 2017–2019. Later, the trend of decrease has settled down.

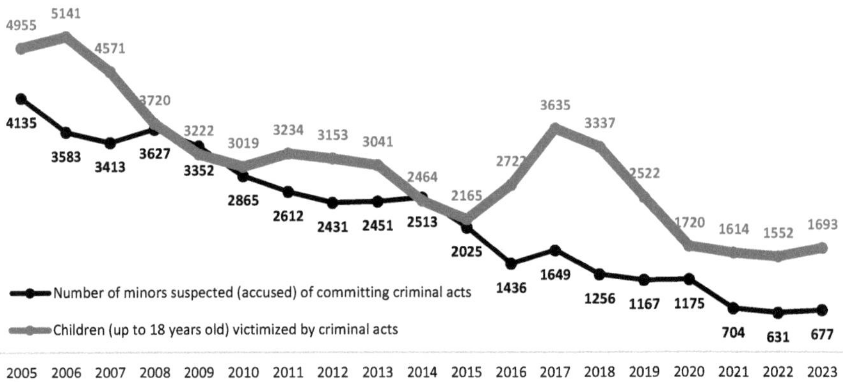

Fig. 1 Adolescents delinquency and victimisation (persons)

[4]Five-year-old Matas died in January 2017 after being brutally beaten by his parents. The child was admitted to the hospital with multiple bruises on his body. It was determined that he had been hit at least 135 times. Crime has received a great response from society and politicians. With the "Matas reform," the Lithuanian Parliament banned all forms of violence against children and the use of physical punishments.

Another important issue is children's victimisation by gender. As shown in Fig. 2, boys were victims of criminal acts more often than girls. However, if the gender gap was larger at the beginning of the period in 2005, boys were victimised twice as many times as girls (3329 and 1626, respectively); later, this difference disappeared, especially at the end of the period. In 2023, gender victimisation was almost the same: 874 boys and 819 girls. It can also be observed that the number of victimised girls throughout the period was small and constantly fluctuated within the limits: from a maximum of 1817 in 2006 to the aforementioned 819 cases in 2023. So, it can be concluded that a general decrease in children's victimisation was due to boys' victimisation drop.

Looking at age groups, it makes sense to single out two: children up to 13 years old age and 14–17 years old teenagers. The data show (Fig. 3) that from 2005–2016

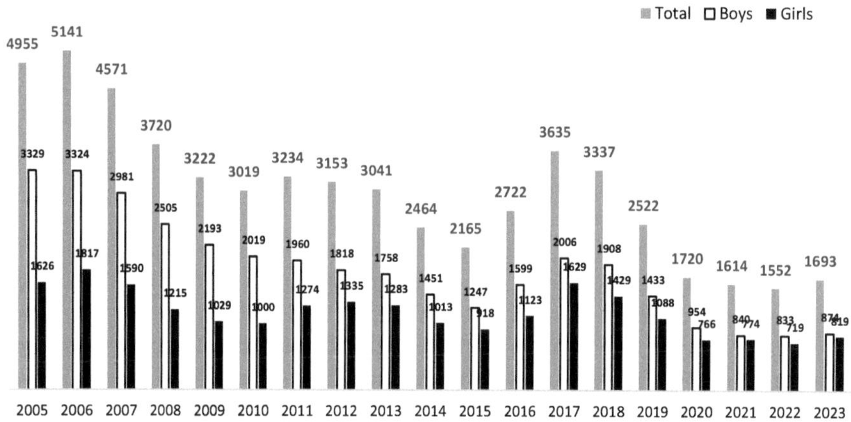

Fig. 2 Number of children victims of criminal acts by gender (persons)

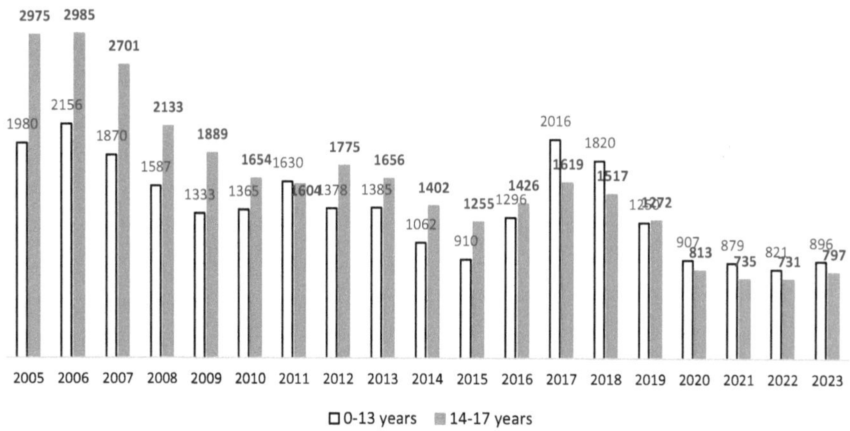

Fig. 3 Number of children victims of criminal acts by age group (persons)

(except 2011), older teenagers were more often victimised than younger children. Since 2017, the situation has changed. Children up to 13 years were victimised more often or almost as often as older teenagers. Again, this can be explained in light of the aforementioned reform of the child rights protection system. Presumably, more public and institutional attention to violence against children in a close environment increased registered numbers. The positive news is that for the last four years, the number of victims of both: children up to 13 years old and 14–17 years old teenagers has not increased and is less than a thousand per year.

When examining by place of residence, cities, and rural areas, the situation is no doubt determined by the territorial distribution of the population: more crime victims are from cities and towns than from rural areas (Fig. 4).

Analysing what crimes Lithuanian children suffer from and what damage they experience, it is worth focusing on the present situation: the year 2022–2023. Table 1 shows that children suffer from physical and sexual violence mostly. Causing physical pain, traffic violations (resulting in children victimisation), molestation, minor health impairment, sexual assault, and rape are the main crimes against children that are counted in hundreds or tens.

The above-mentioned trends are supported and replicated by the data in Table 2. It clearly shows that in 2022–2023 children experience physical violence most often, sexual abuse in second place, and property damage in third place. Neglect was rarely experienced, with a sharp decrease in 2023.

As noted, the well-being of the child is strongly determined by the situation in the family. Analysing the family composition of victimised children, one can see that victimised children mostly lived in families with both or one parent. Many fewer of them lived with relatives or were under the custody of another person or legal entity (Table 3). This consistently explains the data in Table 4, which shows who the perpetrators were. Children were mostly victimised by people from their close environment: parents, step-parents, or adoptive parents. Also, they became victims of close relatives or guardians. Only some suffered from teachers. Every third child was victimised by a stranger. In other words, two out of three victimised children in Lithuania are victimised by adults from a close or familiar environment.

There is also data showing that in 2022–2023, from 21 to 22 children were victimised while being in a helpless state, from 21 to 17 were intoxicated by alcohol, and

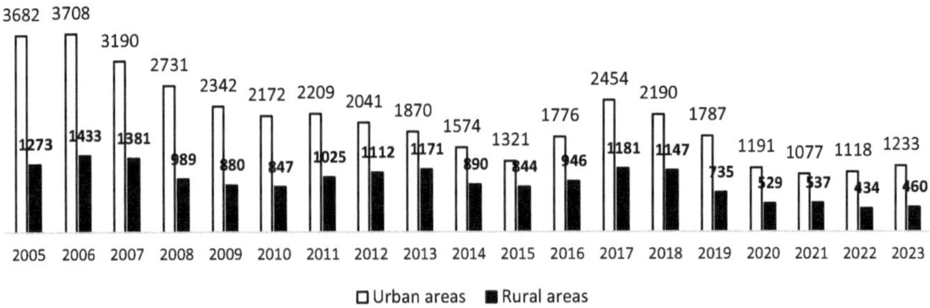

Fig. 4 Number of children victims of criminal acts by area of residence (persons)

Table 1 The number of children victimised by different criminal acts

	Criminal act	Year	
		2022	2023
1	Causing physical pain	796	842
2	Violation of traffic safety rules	178	159
3	Molestation of a minor	108	157
4	Minor health impairment	61	49
5	Sexual assault	27	43
6	Rape	33	40
7	Avoiding child support	14	33
8	Abuse of the rights and duties of a parent or guardian	25	10
9	Extortion of property	6	10
10	Exploitation of a child for pornography	4	7
11	Severe health impairment	2	5
12	Involvement of a child in drinking	4	5
13	The murder	2	4
14	Unlawful deprivation of liberty	3	2
15	Involvement of a child in a criminal act	0	2
16	Human trafficking	0	1
17	Coercion to have sex	0	1
18	Child abduction or exchange	0	1
19	Inclination to use narcotic or psychotropic substances	1	1
20	Buying or selling a child	1	0

Table 2 Harm suffered by the victimised child

	Year	
	2022	2023
Physical violence	509	524
Sexual abuse	73	102
Property damage	50	73
Psychological abuse	37	31
Neglect	29	4

in 2023, there were two children who were intoxicated by narcotics or psychotropic drugs during victimisation. Some victimisations had very serious outcomes. In 2023 83 children experienced a minor health disorder, ten children's health was seriously impaired, and 15 children died.

So, these registered numbers partially reveal the situation of children's victimisation in Lithuania. Thus, the victimisation of children is of high latency. The inability to recognise the situation, the inability or fear to report to the responsible authorities, especially when harm is experienced in the close environment—all these factors taken together lead to the fact that we do not know everything about the victimisation of children and adolescents. Therefore, criminological studies of victimisation are used to help.

Table 3 Family status of the victimised child

	Year	
	2022	2023
Lives with both parents	701	728
Lives with one of the parents	655	727
Lives with a relative when the child has not been assigned custody	20	22
In a custody of a person	56	68
In a custody of a legal entity	57	78

Table 4 Perpetrators children have been victimised by

	Year	
	2022	2023
Parents	440	478
Strangers	279	358
Stepparents or adoptive parents	132	145
Close relatives	56	69
Guardians	18	13
Teachers	11	6

4 Latent Children Victimisation

One of the most significant scientific studies providing data on child victimisation is the International Self-Report Delinquency Study (ISRD). This study, which is currently being conducted in numerous countries across Europe and the world, was initiated and implemented in the 1990s. Lithuanian researchers have been participating in this study since 2006. The ISRD is an ongoing international, collaborative effort designed as a standardised school-based survey to describe and explain adolescents' experiences with crime and victimisation, test criminological theories, and develop recommendations for prevention and interventions.[5]

In Lithuania, three waves of this study have been carried out: in 2006 (ISRD2), 2013 (ISRD3), and 2022 (ISRD4). Due to the comparative nature of the study, city-based sampling was preferred over national samples, as this approach facilitates the expectation that the sample structure would be similar across different countries. The primary sampling unit for the study was school classes. Due to differences in

[5] More information about the ISRD study, its methodology, and participating countries, as well as datasets from previous waves of the study, can be found on the project's website https://isrd-study.org/.

the questionnaire structure used in various waves of the ISRD studies, changes in some question formulations, and differences in the composition of the study sample, direct comparison becomes challenging. Therefore, the analysis will primarily rely on the data from the most recent survey conducted in 2022.

In the selected cities (Vilnius, the capital of Lithuania, and Šiauliai in the northern part of the country), 1914 students from grades 7 to 11 were surveyed using a standardised questionnaire. The questionnaire was divided into thematic sections, covering adolescents' experiences with delinquency and victimisation, as well as various theoretical correlates of these experiences. ISRD4 includes six types of victimisation from the previous wave: robbery, assault, personal theft, cyberbullying, hate crime, and two items assessing parental physical violence. To address the increasing concerns about online victimisation, two additional items—posting intimate images and online hate speech—have been incorporated into this section of the questionnaire. The prevalence of these victimisations was measured over the respondents' lifetime and within the past twelve months. The phrasing for the types of victimisation used in the survey is presented in Table 5 (Marshall et al. 2022).

Figure 5 illustrates the prevalence of victimisation experiences, both over the respondents' lifetimes and within the last year, highlighting nine distinct types of victimisation.

The findings indicate that the three most prevalent forms of victimisation can be identified (Pocienė et al. 2023). The most commonly reported type of victimisation, based on lifetime prevalence, is minor parental violence, with a lifetime prevalence of 28.5% and a last-year prevalence of 9.9%. This is followed closely by personal theft, which has a lifetime prevalence of 28% and a reported prevalence of 9.3% last

Table 5 The wording for the types of victimisation

Robbery	Has anyone ever used a weapon, force, or threat of force to get money or things from you?
Assault	Has anyone ever beaten you up or hurt you with a stick, knife, or gun so badly that you were injured?
Personal theft	Has something ever been stolen from you (such as a book, money, mobile phone, sports gear, bicycle)
Hate crime	Has anyone ever threatened you with violence or committed physical violence against you because of your race, ethnicity or nationality, religion, gender identity, sexual orientation, or for similar reasons?
Cyberbullying	Has anyone ever threatened you on social media?
Intimate posting	Has anyone ever posted, re-posted, or texted an intimate photo or video of you that you did not want others to see?
Online hate speech	Has anyone ever sent you hurtful messages or comments on social media about your race, ethnicity, nationality, religion, gender identity, sexual orientation, or for similar reasons?
Parental violence—minor	Has your mother or father (or your stepmother or stepfather) ever hit, slapped, or shoved you (including as a punishment)?
Parental violence—serious	Has your mother or father (or your stepmother or stepfather) ever hit you with an object, punched or kicked you forcefully, or beaten you up (including as a punishment)?

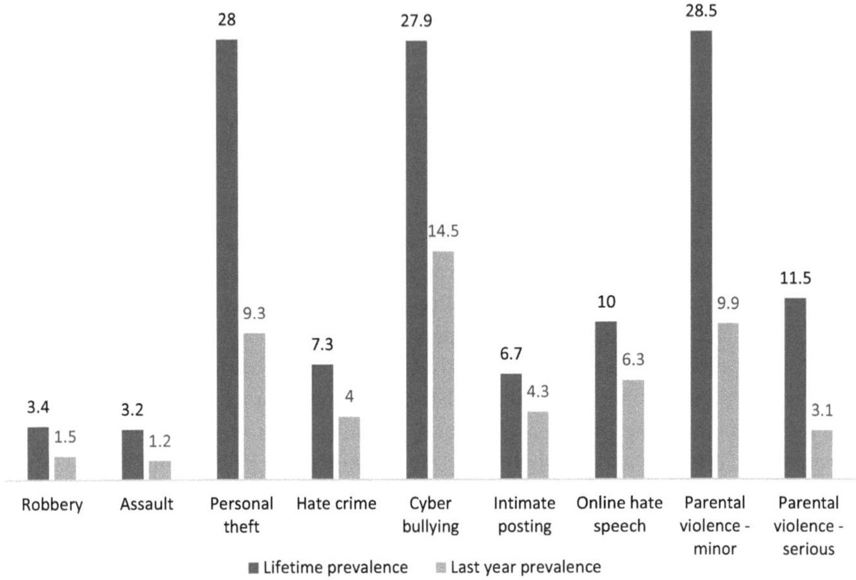

Fig. 5 Lifetime and last year's prevalence of various victimisation types (percent)

year. Cyberbullying is the third most reported type, with 27.9% of respondents indicating they had experienced it at some point in their lives and 14.5% reporting incidents within the last year.

Next, 11.5% of respondents reported victimisation from serious parental violence in their lifetime and 3.1% within the last 12 months. The fifth most frequent category is online hate speech victimisation, which includes various forms of emotional abuse mediated by online platforms, showing a lifetime prevalence of 10% and a last year prevalence of 6.3%.

The sixth category reveals that 7.3% of respondents reported having been victims of hate crime offline in their lifetime, and 4% reported experiencing this type of crime within the last year. This is followed by victimisation of intimate posting, also known as the non-consensual dissemination of intimate images, with a lifetime prevalence of 6.7% and 4.3% indicating occurrences within the last year.

The eighth category addresses victimisation from robbery that occurred offline, with 3.4% of respondents reporting lifetime experiences and 1.5% indicating such incidents within the last year. Finally, victimisation from assault is the least frequently reported type, with a lifetime prevalence of 3.2% and a last-year prevalence of 1.2%.

Thus, the data indicate that a significant part of Lithuanian adolescents participating in the study have experienced some form of victimisation. Aggregating the available data, we find that as many as 56.5% of children have been victimised at least once in their lifetime by at least one of the mentioned victimisation types, while 29.8% have experienced victimisation in the last 12 months. These are substantial figures, considering that official statistics indicate that only about 1600 children in Lithuania become victims of crime annually. It is also important to note that the three most frequently mentioned types of victimisation in the ISRD study reflect three different spheres of children's lives: thefts occurring in everyday life, cyberbullying in the online environment, and parental violent behaviour in the close environment or at home.

The analysis of victimisation distribution by gender, as presented in Table 6, reveals some noteworthy differences between boys and girls, both over their lifetime and in the past year.

In terms of offline crimes, the data highlights distinct gender disparities in personal theft and hate crime victimisation. Girls exhibit a higher lifetime prevalence of theft victimisation at 30.9%, compared to boys, who report a prevalence of 25.6%. This substantial difference is indicated by a significant Chi-Square value ($p < 0.05$). However, the difference disappears when looking at the victimisation of personal theft in the last year. Moreover, girls report higher victimisation rates in hate crime, with a lifetime prevalence of 9.3%, significantly surpassing the 5.5% reported by boys ($p < 0.01$). This difference is also evident when examining the data for the past 12 months.

Regarding online crimes, the gender disparities are equally pronounced. For intimate posting victimisation, girls are more affected, with a reported lifetime prevalence of 8%, compared to boys at 5.3%. The Chi-Square analysis confirms the significance of this difference ($p < 0.05$). Online hate speech victimisation follows a similar pattern, with 13.9% of girls experiencing such incidents in their lifetime and 8.6% within the last year, compared to 6.3% of boys in their lifetime and 4.5 within the last year ($p < 0.01$). This indicates a gendered trend in online victimisation, where both intimate posting and online hate speech more frequently target girls.

Differences in the victimisation of boys and girls are also evident in cases of parental violence. Serious parental violence has been reported by 7.6% of boys and 15.8% of girls over their lifetime, with the difference being statistically significant

Table 6 Lifetime and last year victimisation prevalence by gender (percent)

	Lifetime		Last year	
	Boys	Girls	Boys	Girls
Robbery	3.8	3.1	1.5	1.5
Assault	3.3 mn,	3.2	1.5	1
Personal theft	*25.6*	*30.9**	9.5	9.9
Hate crime	*5.5*	*9.3***	*2.7*	*5.4***
Cyberbullying	27	29.3	15.7	14.9
Intimate posting	*5.3*	*8**	3.5	5
Online hate speech	*6.3*	*13.9***	*4.5*	*8.6***
Parental violence -minor	*23.2*	*34.1***	*7.5*	*13.4***
Parental violence -serious	*7.6*	*15.8***	*2*	*4.4***

Note: *Chi-Square, $p < 0.05$; **Chi-Square, $p < 0.01$

($p < 0.01$). In the last year, these figures were 2% for boys and 4.4% for girls. Minor parental violence also shows a higher lifetime prevalence among girls (34.1%) compared to boys (23.2%), and in the past year, 13.4% of girls reported experiencing it compared to 7.5% of boys. In both cases, the difference was statistically significant ($p < 0.01$). These findings highlight a concerning trend of higher exposure to both serious and minor parental violence among girls.

It can be observed that these survey findings differ from the official statistics, which indicate that boys are more frequently victims of crimes compared to girls, although this disparity has significantly decreased in recent years (Fig. 2). In contrast, the ISRD4 study consistently shows that girls are more often victims in all cases where there is a significant gender difference in victimisation.

It is also noteworthy that in the previous ISRD3 study conducted in 2013, the gender differences in the prevalence of victimisation were different (Justickaja et al. 2015). At that time, girls reported experiencing more cyberbullying, with a 22.3% lifetime prevalence compared to 12.9% for boys. However, in cases of robbery, assault, and hate crime, boys were more frequently the victims.

Of course, it is impossible to compare official crime statistics directly with data from victimology studies for numerous reasons. One of the most evident points is that official crime statistics encompass all registered offences under criminal law where children are the victims. In contrast, the study provides data only on a few specific crimes included in the survey questionnaire and reported by the children of selected age groups to the researchers. It is also reasonable to assume that even if all these incidents were reported to the police, some would not be recognised as crimes and thus would not be included in crime statistics. However, previous ISRD studies have revealed that even in cases of serious crimes such as robbery or assault, only a small proportion of these incidents are reported to the police (Enzmann et al. 2017).

In the ISRD4 survey, respondents were also asked whether they had reported the crimes they experienced to the police (excluding two items of parental violence). Based on the children's responses, the prevalence of police reports was calculated, indicating the proportion of respondents who had reported at least one of their incidents to the police, regardless of how many incidents of the same type they had experienced. The distribution of responses is presented in Fig. 6.

As indicated by prior studies, the findings suggest that only a small fraction of experienced incidents are reported to law enforcement authorities. Survey participants who encountered crimes were more likely to report serious offences occurring in physical settings (offline) to the police. For example, 16.1% of respondents who had experienced assault reported the incident to the police at least once, 11% reported personal theft, and 9.7% reported robbery. These crimes, often referred to as "hard crimes," generally imply that victims recognise these incidents as criminal offences warranting police notification.

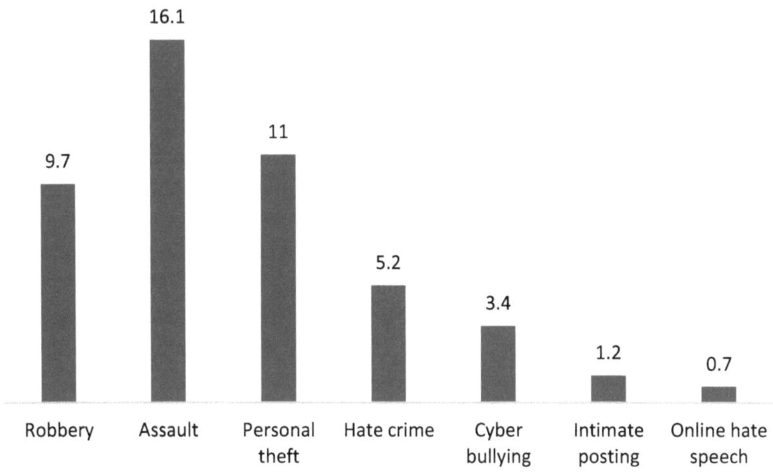

Fig. 6 Prevalence of incidents reported to the police (percent)

Conversely, less apparent incidents, particularly those occurring online, were reported to the police far less frequently: 5.2% of respondents who experienced hate crime reported it, intimate posting was reported by only 1.2%, and online hate speech was reported by merely 0.7% of affected children. This discrepancy suggests that children might not fully comprehend whether these actions constitute crimes or if they should be reported.

However, 31% of children who experienced intimate posting and 21.6% who experienced online hate speech disclosed these incidents to another adult. This suggests several important points that require further examination. Firstly, the low reporting rates to law enforcement may indicate a lack of awareness and education about what constitutes a crime, particularly in the digital domain. Children may not fully comprehend the seriousness of online victimisation or know the appropriate channels for reporting such incidents. Secondly, the higher rates of disclosure to other adults suggest a reliance on immediate social support systems rather than formal authorities. This trend implies that children might feel more at ease or find it more convenient to confide in trusted adults rather than deal with the bureaucratic complexities associated with police reporting. This behavioural pattern underscores the importance of educating both children and their guardians about the necessity of reporting all forms of victimisation and understanding the resources available to assist them through these processes.

Finally, it could be speculated that differences in reporting incidents to the police might vary based on the gender of the children. However, the study's data do not support this hypothesis. In all cases, irrespective of the type of victimisation experienced, no significant gender differences were found in the likelihood of reporting to the police.

5 Concluding Remarks

Children's victimisation is a significant indicator of children's rights and protection, highlighting the challenges and threats faced by children. While Lithuania's overall economic and social conditions are improving, children's quality of life remains affected by structural shifts, such as an ageing population, rising divorce rates, and changing family dynamics. In recent years, both the nature of child victimisation and the demographic profile of victimised children have shifted. For instance, victimisation has become more evenly distributed across genders, with younger children (under 13 years) now experiencing victimisation as frequently as older adolescents. These trends illustrate the scope of the issue and indicate heightened insecurity among children across age groups and genders.

Official statistics show that Lithuanian children most often experience physical and sexual abuse, with two-thirds of children suffering harm from adults within their close environment. This raises significant concern, as children may struggle to identify or report abuse due to fear or close ties with the abuser. With the growing engagement of children in virtual reality, new sources of insecurity have emerged, particularly involving cyberbullying and other forms of online violence, which often remain unreported.

Although the number of recorded cases of child victimisation is declining, the extent of latent victimisation remains substantial. The ISRD4 study results reveal that three forms of victimisation are most prevalent among Lithuanian adolescents: minor parental violence, personal property theft, and cyberbullying. In the second place are severe, serious parental violence and online hate speech. Data indicate that more than half of Lithuanian children have experienced some form of victimisation at least once in their lifetime, with nearly a third affected in the last year. While official statistics report lower numbers of child victims, this ISRD4 study reveals a broad scope of unreported or unrecognised violence. The analysis also highlighted significant gender differences. Girls are more likely to experience parental violence, personal property theft, and online hate speech. Furthermore, girls are more affected by emotional abuse online, emphasizing the impact of gender on the prevalence of various forms of victimisation. The low rate of crime reporting to police indicates a pronounced lack of awareness about reportable crimes, particularly on the internet. Children are more likely to disclose experiences of violence to trusted adults rather than to law enforcement.

What does the Lithuanian case of children's victimisation look like in an international context? Unfortunately, statistical data is very limited or almost non-existent for international comparisons. At best, we can rely on the data of the Eurobarometer for children's victims of intentional homicide and sexual exploitation.[6] Data is inconsistent: not all countries and years are included.

---

[6] Statistics | Eurostat (n.d). *Victims of intentional homicide and sexual exploitation by age and sex*. Retrieved February 12, 2025, from https://ec.europa.eu/eurostat/databrowser/view/crim_hom_vage$dv_2603/default/table?lang=en&category=chldyth.chld.chld_viol

However, some relative comparisons could be made. Let us take data for intentional homicide. The period 2016–2022 and the number of intentionally murdered children (under 18 years old) per 100,000 population. Numbers fluctuate. If in 2016 Lithuania had an indicator of 1.19, and neighbouring Latvia 0.28, so in 2022, the situation will be the opposite: Latvia is on the top with 1.68, and Lithuania somewhere in the middle among such countries as (the Netherlands, Hungary, and Switzerland) with 0.40. In this context, the extreme indicator was registered for Montenegro in 2018–2.92 murdered children under 18 per 100,000 population. In comparison, Iceland, Slovenia, and Malta always had indicators that were zero throughout the entire period.

Another characteristic indicator is the sexual exploitation of children under 18 years old—victim cases per 100,000 population. There is no clear trend for each country, but the numbers are not decreasing: they are either fluctuating or increasing (Croatia, Germany, Norway). Lithuanian numbers fluctuate: 2016–18,33, increase in 2018 to 55,66, then drop in 2019 to 34,83, and a slight increase in 2021 up to 41,14. We should note that in 2018, Lithuania was in first place (55,66) for victimisation, even slightly exceeding France (55, 50). In 2021, the top countries for children's sexual victimisation were Croatia −82,24, France—65,93, Norway—43,72, and Lithuania—41,14. Neighbouring Latvia also demonstrates a slight increase in this indicator. Though it is not as high as in our country: in 2021–23,43 cases of victimisation were registered per 100,000 population of Latvia. Slovakia, Denmark, and Austria are countries where indicators of children's sexual victimisation are the lowest during the whole period.

Thus, recorded statistics show only a small part of young people's reality. In scientific studies, the problem of children's victimisation is usually analysed in association with delinquency (Posick 2012; Marshall et al. 2019). Though not so many, there are some papers focused precisely on victimisation or poly-victimisation as a specific issue. The risk of victimisation is analysed through sociodemographic factors (Aho et al. 2016). Other scholars (Bills 2017) explore the association between the level of self-control and lifestyles and victimisation. We can also find studies analysing how parental abuse may lead to further victimisation (Jiang and Shi 2024). So, all this shows that children's victimisation is becoming no less important issue than delinquency in an international context.

So, summarising, we can conclude that children's victimisation in Lithuania reflects the deeper changes occurring within society. It is evident that latent victimisation is significantly more prevalent than reported cases and that threats in online environments are on the rise. Domestic violence remains notably high. The low rate of crime reporting to law enforcement underscores a lack of information among children regarding the need and means to report violence. Children's reliance on trusted adults instead of law enforcement highlights the importance of involving communities in ensuring children's safety. The study's findings underscore the need to enhance preventive measures that meet children's needs and address various forms of victimisation, including cyber violence. Finally, integrating official statistics with criminological research data is important to understand child victimisation comprehensively and to develop evidence-based recommendations to address these challenges.

References

Agnew R (2001) Building on the Foundation of General Strain Theory: specifying the types of strain Most likely to Lead to crime and delinquency. J Res Crime Delinq 38(4):319–361. https://doi.org/10.1177/0022427801038004001

Aho N, Gren-Landell M, Svedin CG (2016) The prevalence of potentially victimizing events, poly-victimisation, and its association to sociodemographic factors: a Swedish youth survey. J Interpers Violence 31(4):620–651. https://doi.org/10.1177/0886260514556105

Ariès P (1980) Two successive motivations for the declining birth rate in the west. Popul Dev Rev 6(4):645–650

Bills M (2017) *The impact of low self-control and risky lifestyles on juvenile victimisation.* (M.A.). Sam Houston State University, Ann Arbor. Retrieved from http://hdl.handle.net/20.500.11875/2238

Enzmann D, Kivivuori J, Marshall I, Steketee M, Hough M, Killias M (2017) A Global Perspective on Young People as Offenders and Victims: First Results from the ISRD3 Study. https://doi.org/10.1007/978-3-319-63233-9

Hirschi T (1969) The causes of delinquency. University of California Press, Berkeley

Jiang C, Shi J (2024) Why are adolescents harshly punished by parents more vulnerable to bullying victimisation? Evidence across nine countries. Appl Res Qual Life. https://doi.org/10.1007/s11482-024-10413-x

Juozeliūnienė I, Kanapienienė L, Kazlauskaitė A (2008) Atotolio šeima: nauja užduotis šeimos sociologijai. Sociologija Mintis ir veiksmas 21:119–133. https://doi.org/10.15388/SocMintVei.2008.1.6051

Justickaja S, Aleknevičienė J, Kalpokas V, Giedraitytė-Mačiulienė R, Mickevič A, Žilinskienė L, Žėkas T (2015) Jaunimo delinkvencinis elgesys ir nepilnamečių justicijos politika lietuvoje: tendencijos ir lyginamieji aspektai. Justitia, Vilnius

Kanopienė V, Mikulionienė S, Česnuitytė V (2015) Lietuvos šeima Europos kontekste. Mykolo Romerio universitetas, Vilnius

Livingstone S, Mascheroni G, Staksrud E (2018) European research on children's internet use: assessing the past and anticipating the future. New Media Soc 20(3):1103–1122. https://doi.org/10.1177/1461444816685930

Marshall IH, Neissl K, Markina A (2019) A global view on youth crime and victimisation: results from the international self-report delinquency study (ISRD3). J Contemp Crim Justice 35(4):380–385. https://doi.org/10.1177/1043986219884814

Marshall IH, Birkbeck C, Enzmann D, Kivivuori J, Markina A, Steketee M (2022) International self-report delinquency (ISRD4) study protocol: background, methodology and mandatory items for the 2021/2022 survey. Northeastern University

Pocienė A, Aleknevičienė J, Kalpokas V (2023) Jaunuolių delinkventinis elgesys Lietuvoje: Ką atskleidžia naujas delinkvencijos ir viktimizacijos tyrimas? Filos Sociol 34. https://doi.org/10.6001/fil-soc.2023.34.4Priedas.Special-Issue.4

Posick C (2012) Untangling offending and victimisation: A comparative study of the victim-offender overlap. (Ph.D.). Northeastern University, Ann Arbor. Retrieved from http://hdl.handle.net/2047/d20003232

Posick C (2013) The overlap between offending and victimisation among adolescents: results from the second international self-report delinquency study. J Contemp Crim Justice 29(1):106–124. https://doi.org/10.1177/1043986212471250

Posick C (2018) Reappraising the impact of offending on victimisation: a propensity score matching approach. Int J Offender Ther Comp Criminol 62(8):2374–2390. https://doi.org/10.1177/0306624X17708179

Sakalauskas G, Kalpokas V, Buzaitytė-Kašalynienė J, Švedaitė-Sakalauskė B (2022) Latentinės nepilnamečių delinkvencijos apraiškų ir tendencijų Lietuvoje tarptautinis palyginimas. Socialinė teorija, empirija, politika ir praktika 24:101–117. https://doi.org/10.15388/STEPP.2022.40

Steketee M, Aussems C, Marshall IH (2021) Exploring the impact of child maltreatment and Interparental violence on violent delinquency in an international sample. J Interpers Violence 36(13–14):NP7319–NP7349. https://doi.org/10.1177/0886260518823291

Dr. Aušra Pocienė is a social science doctor specialising in criminology and sociology. Since 2024, she has been the director of the Institute of Sociology and Social Work at the Faculty of Philosophy. She is an associate professor in the Criminology Department at Vilnius University. She has previously worked as a researcher at the Law Institute of Lithuania, where she was involved in national and international scientific research projects. Aušra Pocienė is also one of the editors of the scientific journal "Criminological studies". She was Lithuanian representative at the International Self Report Delinquency Study for the fourth wave - ISRD4. Her scientific interests include social research methodology, sociology of punishment, criminal policy, youth delinquency and victimisation, and urban safety. In recent years, her scientific research has primarily focused on youth delinquency and victimisation, and youth drug-related issues. She is a member of the Lithuanian Association of Criminologists and the European Society of Criminology.

Vaidas Kalpokas obtained his master's degree in Sociology at Vilnius University in 1998. He works at the Law Institute of the Lithuanian Centre for Social Sciences. Since 2019, he has been a PhD student in criminology at the Institute of Sociology and Social Work at Vilnius University. Mr. Kalpokas has participated in more than 20 national and international scientific research projects in the field of criminology and is a co-author of about 15 scientific publications. His research interest is in juvenile delinquency and comparative criminology.

Dr. Jolanta Aleknevičienė is a doctor of social science who specialises in criminology at Vilnius University. From 2018 onward, she has been the vice-dean for studies at the Faculty of Philosophy. She is also an associate professor at the Department of Criminology at the Institute of Sociology and Social Work. Her research interests include youth delinquency and victimization, imprisonment, corruption, the field of professional criminology, and social research methodology. In addition to her research activities, Dr. Aleknevičienė teaches criminology at Vilnius University. She is a member of the Lithuanian Association of Criminologists and the European Society of Criminology, and one of the representatives of Vilnius University in the Common Study Programme in Critical Criminology.

Understanding Juvenile Delinquency in Lithuania: From Misconceptions to Negative Attitudes

Gintautas Sakalauskas, Vaidas Kalpokas, Jolita Buzaitytė-Kašalynienė, and Birutė Švedaitė-Sakalauskė

Abstract Criminological research indicates that the majority of individuals engage in illicit activities on an episodic or regular basis, at a young age. The majority of these individuals are not subject to formal control mechanisms, and this behaviour typically ceases upon reaching adulthood. The majority of these offences are minor in nature. It is almost universally the case that young people with a history of serious criminal behaviour have experienced multiple violations of their rights during infancy and early childhood, which have had a deleterious impact on their biological and social development. While there is a general consensus that minor delinquency is a pervasive phenomenon and that the social and psychological factors contributing to more serious forms of criminal behaviour are complex, there is nevertheless a tendency to condemn, intimidate and impose harsh penalties on those who engage in such behaviour. The media plays a significant role in shaping these attitudes, with public opinion often influenced by emotional responses. Furthermore, a segment of the public that is less aware of the context of young people's lives and the factors that contribute to delinquency also has a more negative view of the importance of protecting the rights of the child in all circumstances.

G. Sakalauskas (✉)
Faculty of Law, University of Vilnius, Vilnius, Lithuania
e-mail: gintautas.sakalauskas@tf.vu.lt

V. Kalpokas
Law Institute, Lithuanian Centre for Social Sciences, Vilnius, Lithuania
e-mail: vaidas.kalpokas@fsf.vu.lt

J. Buzaitytė-Kašalynienė · B. Švedaitė-Sakalauskė
Faculty of Philosophy, University of Vilnius, Vilnius, Lithuania
e-mail: jolita.kasalyniene@fsf.vu.lt; birute.svedaite-sakalauske@fsf.vu.lt

A. Limantė, R. Vaičiūnienė (eds.), *Children's Rights in Central and Eastern Europe*, European Union and its Neighbours in a Globalized World 29,
https://doi.org/10.1007/978-3-032-07092-0_10

1 Introduction

In the public sphere, juvenile delinquency is typically regarded as a significant societal issue, often evoking concern and apprehension. This perception has contributed to the view that juvenile delinquency poses a potential threat to the future of society or the state, necessitating specialised measures and enhanced interventions across various levels and forms. This particularly critical perspective is disproportionately directed at the entire juvenile age group, a phenomenon not observed in attitudes towards other age groups. For the state, communities, and professionals to respond effectively to juvenile delinquency, it is essential to analyse the underlying factors contributing to such behaviours. Furthermore, it is crucial to critically evaluate the narrative perpetuated by the media and the societal attitudes shaped by it. Media representation significantly influences public perceptions and can exacerbate misconceptions about juvenile delinquency. This chapter presents findings from a study conducted by the authors on the factors influencing juvenile delinquency, its portrayal in the media, and the opinions of the Lithuanian population.[1]

2 The Phenomenon of Juvenile Delinquency and Its Perception in the Context of Children's Rights

Juvenile delinquency is a ubiquitous and pervasive phenomenon that emerges during the developmental and maturational phases of an individual's life. It is a transient issue, often challenging to control (Dollinger and Schmidt-Semisch 2011; Reinecke et al. 2013; Dollinger and Schadbach 2013) and is intrinsically linked to the processes of personality, identity, and autonomy formation (Riesner 2014). Behaviours associated with juvenile delinquency often stem from a natural desire to take risks, test boundaries, explore and understand new experiences, provoke, resist established authority, seek individuality, and maintain social connections with peers. These behaviours may also reflect the fulfilment of personal inclinations, fantasies, or social expectations. Furthermore, analogous characteristics associated with biological and social maturation frequently result in contraventions of legal norms (Jusienė 2007; Sakalauskas 2007, 2013; Schumann 2011). Such characteristics are closely linked to neurobiological processes occurring in the brain during adolescence (Dünkel et al. 2020). Research on juvenile delinquency suggests that the majority of young people have, at some point, engaged in unlawful behaviour, underscoring the transient and developmental nature of this phenomenon (Dollinger and Schadbach 2013). However, the majority of these crimes are minor, with only a

[1] Most of the data used in this chapter were collected during the research project Reactions to Juvenile Delinquency and Their Consequences in Lithuania: From Scandalising in the Media to Professional Performance, implemented from 2020 to 2024 at Vilnius University and funded by the Council of Sciences of the Republic of Lithuania (Grant No. S-MIP-20-367).

very small proportion of young people demonstrating persistent or intense delinquent behaviour. Such behaviour is often impulsive, reckless, and episodic in nature, and it typically resolves itself without intervention (United Nations 1990; Icenogle et al. 2019). Therefore, it is not a reliable indicator of poor parenting (Heinz 2017).

More severe cases are almost invariably associated with a combination of structural, social, and psychological problems, both past and present, that serve as risk factors for delinquency (Laurinavičius 2020). Conversely, certain protective factors have been identified, including a favourable social environment (Tillmann 2010), timely and competent support (Enke 2003; Riesner 2014; Švedaitė-Sakalauskė and Eidukevičiūtė 2015), and the opportunity to take on new roles and achieve successful integration into the labour market (Gečienė et al. 2007). These factors have been shown to protect against or prevent offending. The opportunity to assume new roles and achieve successful integration into the labour market (Gečienė et al. 2007) can therefore serve as a protective factor against or a means of preventing offending. The primary—and perhaps most challenging—task in professional responses to juvenile delinquency lies in distinguishing between typical, transient acts of delinquency that do not significantly increase the risk of a criminal career and those behaviours that do. Inappropriate or disproportionate responses to juvenile offences may inadvertently heighten the risk of recidivism (Dollinger and Schmidt-Semisch 2011), reinforce negative self-perceptions, or create self-fulfilling prophecies (Heinz 2017). Such outcomes further entrench the stigmatisation associated with criminal behaviour (Markina 2019).

It is critical to note that this conceptualisation of juvenile delinquency as a universal and transient phenomenon contrasts sharply with the theoretical and practical approaches of former Soviet criminology and pedagogy. Soviet ideology did not prioritise understanding the tensions inherent in the biological and social maturation of young people, nor did it acknowledge the structural and systemic factors contributing to juvenile delinquency. Instead, the Soviet approach was characterised by an emphasis on identifying distinctive personality traits of juvenile delinquents. The focus was on categorising, registering, and segregating these individuals into institutions, modifying their behaviour and thinking, disciplining them, and imposing external values upon them. The use of coercive language and practices towards children displaying delinquent behaviour, rooted in these outdated approaches, remains evident today. This persists despite the Law on the Protection of the Rights of the Child, which is based on the UN Convention on the Rights of the Child (ratified by Lithuania in 1995). This legislation guarantees every child the right to normal development and full integration into society. Furthermore, the law explicitly prohibits any action that would degrade a child's honour or dignity.

Public indignation towards juvenile delinquency, often fuelled by concentrated media coverage (Ruigrok et al. 2017), is a phenomenon observed across various geographical contexts. However, the ramifications of this indignation differ depending on the specific political, cultural, and legal frameworks in place (Sakalauskas 2008, 2018; Reuband 2011). In this context, public reactions to juvenile delinquency in Lithuania frequently give rise to the assumption that the country's juvenile delinquency problems are unique. This assumption, however, necessitates further investigation to determine its validity.

3 Prevalence and Trends in Juvenile Delinquency in Lithuania

Comparative analysis reveals that both registered and latent juvenile delinquency have demonstrated a decline or remained relatively stable in numerous Western countries, including Lithuania, over recent decades.

3.1 Registered Juvenile Delinquency and Trends

Registered criminal offences committed by juveniles represent the most severe manifestations of juvenile delinquency, for which data are systematically collected in every country. In Lithuania, the collection of such data is relatively comprehensive (Sakalauskas 2011). Over the past two decades, the absolute numbers of registered juvenile criminal offences in Lithuania have consistently declined. In particular, the relative indicators of registered juvenile criminal behaviour have shown a marked decrease in the last 5 years.

As illustrated in Fig. 1, the primary indicators of juvenile delinquency among 14–17-year-olds in Lithuania displayed relatively consistent trends from 1993 to 2014, with a significant decline in the past decade. The number of recorded criminal offences suspected or attributed to juveniles per 100,000 inhabitants of the same age group dropped substantially, from 2625 in 2014 to 857 in 2024. Similarly, the number of juveniles suspected or accused of offences decreased from 1948 to 593 during the same period. Notably, a significant discrepancy emerged in 2004 between the number of juveniles suspected or accused of criminal offences and those ultimately convicted. This discrepancy can be attributed to the enactment of the revised Criminal Code of the Republic of Lithuania on 1 May 2003. The revised Criminal

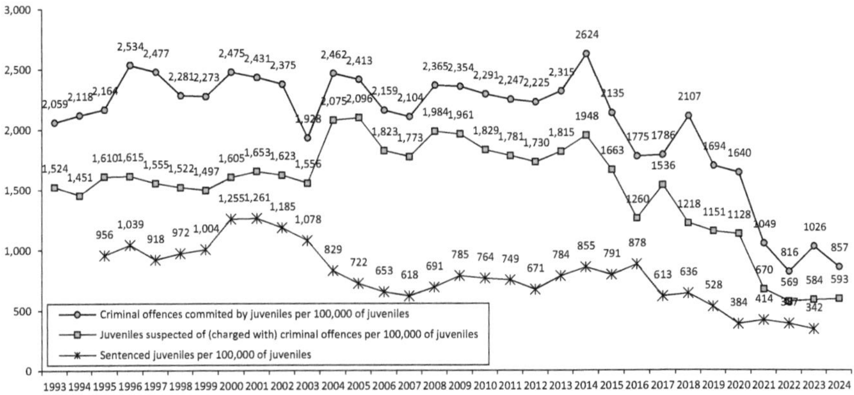

Fig. 1 Main indicators of registered juvenile delinquent behaviour in Lithuania from 1993 to 2024 in relative terms (per 100,000 population of the same age at the end of the year)

Code introduced more lenient provisions, allowing for the imposition of educational measures as an alternative to criminal penalties for juveniles. Conversely, the observed disparity in the proportion of juveniles convicted and subjected to penalties has been on a declining trajectory over the past two decades, with an increasing share of juveniles facing convictions.

The majority of minors are suspected or accused of theft, which remains the most common offence for which juveniles are convicted. Over the past few years, the average proportion of such cases has been approximately 30%, with slightly higher proportions observed in earlier years. Following theft, the infliction of physical pain or minor bodily harm and violations of public order rank second and third, respectively, in prevalence. These offences have demonstrated similar patterns of occurrence over the past few years. Collectively, theft, minor bodily harm, and public order violations account for approximately two-thirds of all offences for which minors are suspected or accused.

The most serious violent crimes, including homicides and serious bodily injuries, constitute only a small proportion of all offences involving juveniles. Nevertheless, these crimes often receive disproportionate media attention and are frequently misrepresented as typical examples of juvenile delinquency, despite a lack of empirical evidence to substantiate this narrative. Since 2006–2008, the number of homicides (e.g., 28 (!) registered in 2006) and serious bodily injuries (31 in 2008) attributed to juveniles has been steadily decreasing, even when assessed in relative terms per 100,000 juveniles. This decline reflects the unique characteristics of juvenile delinquency and the significant repercussions of these crimes. In 2024, only one homicide and six instances of serious bodily injury were recorded as suspected or accused offences committed by juveniles, marking the lowest figures observed during the entire period of analysis. These isolated instances of juvenile homicide, which have attracted considerable media coverage in recent years, thus represent exceptions rather than normative examples of juvenile criminal behaviour. The number of such cases has continued to decline consistently, reaching its lowest point in 2023.

Since 2017, when Lithuania transitioned from administrative to exclusively criminal liability for possession of small amounts of drugs, an average of 130 drug-related offences involving minors have been registered annually. This figure has not increased in recent years, although the high latency of such criminal behaviour should be acknowledged.

It is a well-established principle in criminology that recorded criminal behaviour represents only a small fraction of the actual criminal activity committed (Conklin 1989; Barlow 1990; Sakalauskas 2011). Furthermore, the practice of recording or failing to record criminal behaviour can vary significantly across countries (Christie 1970; Jehle and Harrendorf 2010; Harrendorf 2018; Aebi et al. 2021). The recorded aspect of criminal activity is often regarded as an indicator of law enforcement performance (Neubacher 2014), whereas the unrecorded element depends on several factors. Some offences are characterised by lower latency, meaning they are more likely to be detected and recorded, while others exhibit higher latency. The latter category encompasses the majority of offences committed by juveniles (Dollinger and Schadbach 2013). On the one hand, juvenile offences are frequently committed impulsively, recklessly, and in groups, which increases the likelihood of detection and investigation. On the other hand, juvenile offenders typically engage in minor offences, often directed at their peers, in which cases formal measures of social control are less likely to be applied. In such cases, formal social control measures are less likely to be applied.

The existing literature suggests that serious, victim-specific crimes, such as bodily harm, committed by juveniles are recorded at a substantially higher rate than minor offences (Raithel and Mansel 2003; Heinz 2016). Despite the episodic and widespread nature of juvenile delinquency—an almost universal phenomenon among young people during periods of intense biological and social maturity (Dollinger and Schadbach 2013; Dollinger and Schmidt-Semisch 2011)—the probability of being apprehended for non-serious behaviour remains statistically very low. The probability of being apprehended for non-serious behaviour remains statistically very low (Sakalauskas 2007; Reinecke et al. 2013). Nevertheless, statistics on recorded juvenile criminal behaviour are often presented in the media and even in academic articles as though they accurately reflect actual trends and the structure of juvenile criminal activity. A more comprehensive and nuanced understanding of juvenile delinquent behaviour requires not only an investigation into its underlying factors but also a re-evaluation of the legal categorisation of such behaviour. This is especially important to facilitate meaningful cross-national comparisons.

Differences between countries regarding the minimum age of legal responsibility (Decker and Martaeche 2017), the composition of offences, and the classification of offences under various types of legal responsibility (e.g., administrative or criminal liability) further complicate such comparisons. Moreover, disparities in the broader domain of social protection (Dünkel 2014), the rules governing the registration of offences, and other related areas highlight the limitations of confining the scope of legal responsibility solely to offences registered under criminal responsibility.

3.2 Latent Juvenile Delinquency: Structure and Trends

When evaluating the patterns and structure of juvenile delinquency, there is a prevailing tendency to rely primarily on official recorded indicators. However, criminological research has long established that these indicators represent only a small part of the overall phenomenon which is often hidden or underreported (Sakalauskas 2011). In addition to traditional factors that influence the latency of criminal behaviour, such as distrust in law enforcement, preference for informal criminal conflict resolution, differences between informal and formal social control, the subjective minimisation of the damage caused, of moral panic, the influence of the media, the latency of juvenile delinquency is also shaped by the models of juvenile legal responsibility adopted in different countries. These models define formal delinquency in varied ways across different countries and set different age thresholds for its occurrence (Sakalauskas 2009; Dünkel 2014; Decker and Martaeche 2017).

Furthermore, the registration of juvenile delinquency is typically influenced by those responsible for the child or young person involved. These may be parents, guardians, or individuals in positions of authority in educational establishments, childcare facilities, sports clubs, or other organisations. The decisions and willingness of these individuals to pursue formal control measures play a significant role in determining whether the delinquency is officially recorded and whether formal processes are initiated. It can be reasonably deduced that the attitudes of individuals or groups, whether social, cultural or legal, and the discrepancies between these attitudes across different social classes, regions or countries, influence practices regarding the registration of juvenile delinquency. It is also noteworthy that in cases of juvenile delinquency involving specific victims, these victims are often minors themselves (Justickaja and Giedrytė-Mačiulienė 2017). Consequently, the individuals or groups responsible for the juvenile's actions also influence the decision-making process regarding the use of formal social control measures for the victims.

Assessing the true extent of juvenile delinquency presents challenges common to empirical research, which are further compounded by the young age of the respondents. The various questionnaires commonly used to measure juvenile delinquency (both for perpetrators and victims) must be adapted to suit the cognitive and attentional capacities of young respondents, while minimising the influence of their generally greater tendency for imagination compared to adults.

Numerous international studies on youth behaviour include Lithuania as a participant, and their results facilitate comparisons of delinquent behaviour across different countries. The Health Behaviour in School-aged Children (HBSC) study, launched in 1982, is conducted every 4 years as part of a cross-national initiative, with nearly all European countries participating. The International Self-Report Delinquency Study (ISRD), initiated in 1992, has been regularly conducted (depending on the organisers) with almost 60 countries participating in recent years. The European School Survey Project on Alcohol and Other Drugs (ESPAD), launched in 1995 is conducted every four years, with 35 European countries participating in recent surveys.

The ISRD survey utilises the self-report methodology, a widely accepted approach in empirical criminological research. This method involves questioning respondents about their experiences and asking them to recall the frequency of such experiences over a specified period. The structure of offences committed by minors in Lithuania is similar to that observed in other countries, as demonstrated by data from the ISRD Study. In both Lithuania and other participating countries, the most prevalent offence among minors is the illegal downloading of content from the Internet. The prevalence of this offence in Lithuania aligns with the average response from pupils in all countries included in the study, though notable differences exist between countries. These differences may be attributed to variations in the legal regulation of such activities across the countries surveyed. Furthermore, the prevalence of offences committed by students, while exhibiting some variation between countries, generally follows a ranking similar to that observed in Lithuania. In most countries, shoplifting is the second most common offence, followed by gang fights, vandalism and damage to property, and theft from the person. It is noteworthy that other offences are relatively uncommon among schoolchildren in Lithuania, as is the case in many other countries. However, the prevalence of such offences is slightly higher in Lithuania compared to other nations. The same trend applies to other listed offences (excluding the illegal downloading of content from the Internet). While the prevalence of some offences may be marginally higher among Lithuanian students compared to specific countries, it remains slightly or even significantly lower than the overall average prevalence for the countries included in the study.

The most recent ESPAD survey, conducted in 2019, revealed that 19% of Lithuanian students aged 15–16 had experimented with illicit drugs at least once in their lifetime. This represents a slight increase compared to the 2015 survey findings. Among these students, the highest proportion of first-time illicit drug use involved cannabis, with 18% of respondents reporting cannabis as their initial drug experience (Rupšienė et al. 2020). With regard to the use of illicit drugs by minors, Lithuania shows no significant distinction, with prevalence rates of 18% and 17%, respectively.

While cases of serious violence and substance abuse among minors attract considerable public attention, latent delinquency among minors in Lithuania is particularly characterised by the high prevalence of bullying. Despite its significance, the issue of bullying in Lithuania has received disproportionately low attention, especially when considering findings from the HBSC survey. This survey identifies bullying as the most prevalent form of violence among students across all three age groups and highlights a significant disparity between Lithuania and the majority of other European countries. The first systematic publication addressing this issue was issued by Povilaitis and Valiukevičiūtė (2006). Even at that time, it was noted that the bullying behaviours of Lithuanian pupils were exceptionally high (Povilaitis and Valiukevičiūtė 2006). Although subsequent studies have consistently demonstrated the substantial short- and long-term harm caused by bullying—both to individuals and society—the situation in Lithuania has only partially improved. While there has been some decline in bullying rates, the gap between Lithuania and other countries remains significant.

Lithuania consistently ranks among the top five countries with the highest bullying prevalence across six age groups, specifically for 11-year-olds (with an average of 13% and 12% in 2014 and 2018, respectively), 13-year-olds (12% and 11%), and 15-year-olds (9% and 8%). Furthermore, Lithuania holds the second position in the 11-year-old group (7% and 6%), following Moldova, and ranks first in the 13-year-old group (9% and 7%) and the 15-year-old group (9% and 7%) for instances of bullying. No other country ranks as highly in all categories as Lithuania (Inchley et al. 2020). By contrast, countries like Finland, Sweden, and Germany exhibit bullying prevalence rates that are three to four times lower across all age groups, and significantly lower—by several times—among those who engage in bullying. In contrast, Lithuanian students across all age categories exhibit bullying rates that are approximately three times higher than the overall average for all countries (Inchley et al. 2020).

An analysis of the national HBSC study in Lithuania correctly identifies that both being a victim of bullying and engaging in bullying behaviours are associated with numerous adverse outcomes. These include physical health issues, impaired emotional well-being, difficulties in interpersonal relationships, and the development of problematic behaviours such as aggression, violence, and alcohol misuse. Substance use is associated with a range of detrimental effects, many of which are interconnected with aggressive behaviour. Notably, there is a direct correlation between aggressive conduct and diminished social support. Young individuals who perceive insufficient support from family, friends, and educators are more likely to engage in aggressive behaviours (Šmigelskas et al. 2019). It is evident that school bullying, across various age groups, serves as a significant differentiating factor between Lithuania and other European countries. The prevention of this phenomenon is achievable if it is grounded in scientific insights (Povilaitis and Valiukevičiūtė 2006; Ttofi and Farrington 2011). However, it is regrettable that neither the national nor international HBSC reports offer any conclusions—or even hypotheses—regarding the reasons behind the substantial variation in bullying prevalence among pupils across countries, or why Lithuania exhibits the highest prevalence. It is evident that the underlying causes of these discrepancies can largely be attributed to the social structures and educational systems prevalent in the respective countries, which are likely influenced by the legacy of totalitarianism. Bullying, in particular, is a distinct form of juvenile delinquency that reflects a need to belittle and stigmatise others, demonstrating a lack of respect and an inability to accept differences. This behaviour often stems from personal experiences of feeling undervalued and disapproved.

Despite the absence of a significant rise in juvenile delinquency, the non-severe nature of most offences, and the increasing involvement of younger perpetrators, media narratives have nonetheless constructed a perception of an escalating problem. This narrative influences public perceptions of juvenile delinquency and its underlying causes. We have analysed one such case in more detail below.

4 Depicting Juvenile Delinquency in Lithuanian Media: "The Jurbarkas Case"

The "Jurbarkas case" of 2019–2023 was selected for the case analysis, in which a minor was accused and ultimately convicted of sexual assault causing harm to a minor. A total of 310 media messages, including articles and video reports, published across online media portals over 37 months (from May 2019 to June 2022) were collected for analysis. Both quantitative and qualitative content analysis were performed.

A seventeen-year-old teenager sexually harassed a sixteen-year-old girl. When the girl resisted, the young man physically assaulted her. The minor was charged with attempted rape, sexual assault and causing harm to another minor. The crime was committed during the victim's class party, which the accused attended with a friend invited by the victim's classmate. The accused was an active participant in sports, attended a martial arts club, and had won prizes in the championships. The accused's parents were members of a political party in the region and were well-known figures in the community. The victim was raised by her father after her mother passed away when she was 3 years old.

The investigation and trial lasted almost 4 years, with two appeals, multiple court hearings and four final decisions.

The first media coverage of the crime was published the day after the incident. In the 37 months following the crime, 310 publications related to the case appeared on eight online media portals: six national and two regional. In the first 18 days, 42 articles were published, with some portals posting more than 10 articles per day. Media coverage was intense for the first five months, then subsided. However, public interest spiked with each court hearing.

The uproar in the mass media was fuelled by public outcry on social media, where relatives of the victim called for donations, while concerned citizens threatened the suspect and called for action. Representatives of professional organisations, including the police, municipal politicians, and other experts, responded to the media uproar. The newly elected president visited the victim in the hospital, journalists interviewed various field experts, and quoted politicians and ministers in the media. Influencers defended the victim, publishing messages on social media, participating in TV shows, and having their statements widely quoted.

Fifty percent of publications were featured in the country's leading daily newspapers such as *Lithuania*, and *Actuality*. Publications also appeared in columns dedicated to crime (40.3%), celebrities (6.2%), and sports (3.2%). The suspect was a martial arts champion. The martial arts club publicly condemned the accused's actions disassociated itself from him.

The headlines of the publications sensationalised the crime, attempting to capture readers' attention with dramatic phrases like: "The question that haunts all of Lithuania", "The story that shocked Lithuania", "The case that shocked the public", "Bloody drama", "Jurbarkas in shock", "Jurbarkas' county rape case". The crime was depicted with emotional and graphic language: "severely beaten", "brutally assaulted", "horrible attack", "violent assault", "tragic event", and "the nightmare continues." The severe and long-term consequences of the injuries were highlighted with phrases like "tormenting nightmares", "the victim still fears for her safety"; "in intensive care", "the consequences will last for years", "unable to speak", "needed more medicine", "psychological state is concerning", "the surgeons worked for three hours"; "disabled child"; "injuries continue to heal even after two and a half years", "cries at night" and others.

Both the perpetrator and the victim were minors at the time of the crime. Despite the protection of their rights and privacy, the photos of both were published and circulated on social media. The boy's photo was shared with a call for people to harass him, while the girl's photo was posted by a relative, requesting donations for her treatment and legal expenses. The victim's name and photos were never published in the mass media, whereas the perpetrator's images were widely circulated.

During the pre-trial process, the most common photo of him showed him in sweatpants, his muscular build clearly visible, with his face obscured by a black square. After turning 18, the media used photos of him taken in the courtroom. In headlines, the suspect was labelled a sadist, rapist, violent person, abuser, thug, and juvenile executioner. Neither the young man nor the victim gave interviews to the media.

The perpetrator's situation was significantly aggravated by two factors, both of which were exploited by the media. Firstly, he was an athlete with a well-trained body who, despite his physical capabilities, could not control his impulses and used his strength against a helpless girl. Secondly, his parents were politicians, and although they left the party after the incident, this connection was heavily exploited by the media, with references to it appearing in 20% of publications. In Lithuania, there is a general public perception that politics is often associated with corruption and self-serving interests.

The media rarely used only factual information and often cited multiple individuals in a single publication. The victim's advocate was the most frequently quoted source (41%), followed by prosecutors (27.4%). In contrast, the perpetrator's lawyer (6.1%) and parents (0.6%) were quoted the least. Politicians, including Members of the Seimas, the President, municipal council members, the Minister of Social Security and Labour, the Minister of the Interior, and the Minister of Justice, were cited in 7.4% of publications.

The case was used to portray a worsening problem of juvenile delinquency, with several key themes emerging in media coverage. First, media outlets disseminated messages suggesting that unruly minors were "rampaging" in Jurbarkas, intimidating residents, and that professional systems were failing to provide children and young people with adequate education and support. Second, events in Jurbarkas were linked with incidents involving juveniles in other Lithuanian cities, attempting to convince readers that juvenile delinquency was on the rise across the country. News stories emphasising the prevalence or perceived increase in juvenile delinquency appeared in 5.8% of analysed publications.

Furthermore, the same information was frequently recycled across different outlets. Identical factual details or quotes from interviewees were repeated in multiple publications, often with minor variations in presentation or emphasis, and published on the same day or within a few days. Second, even when new information regarding the case was published, previously disseminated details about the circumstances of the crime, the progression of the trial, court verdicts, the victim's physical and psychological suffering, and information about the young offender were repeatedly included.

This repetitive approach inflated the volume of publications, ostensibly to sustain public interest and engagement. The frequency of publication was artificially increased by re-releasing the same articles multiple times a day or republishing identical content under different headlines.

Content analysis of these publications reveals clear media bias. Such bias is reflected in the headlines and the specific manner in which the content was constructed. Journalists selectively chose which individuals and excerpts from interviews to quote, determined how to organise the narrative, decided on the starting and concluding points, and often presented either a single perspective or limited contrasting opinions on the issue.

Quantitative analysis of the articles revealed prevailing trends in the media discourse, particularly concerning how society should address juvenile delinquents—whether to punish them or focus on education and rehabilitation—and whose perspectives were amplified. Approximately 45.2% of the articles advocated for stricter pretrial detention or prison sentences for the young offender, while 42.3% presented neutral reports on the case's developments. Notably, no publication unequivocally supported or defended educational and rehabilitative measures for the juvenile. In 10.3% of the articles, differing opinions were provided. For example, alongside calls for harsher sentencing, there were mentions that the pretrial measures and sentences considered the offender's age and adhered to legal provisions for minors, including features specific to the juvenile criminal process.

Nearly one-fifth of the publications reflected on juvenile crimes and minors' criminal liability more broadly. During the trial, another crime involving juveniles occurred in Jurbarkas. Approximately 20% of the articles juxtaposed these two incidents, reinforcing narratives about "rampant" juvenile delinquency in Jurbarkas and suggesting an increase in juvenile crime across Lithuania. Only 8.1% of the analysed articles echoed the idea that minors should be educated and rehabilitated rather than punished. Moreover, a mere 1.3% of the publications unequivocally supported the view that juvenile offenders should not face punitive measures but should instead receive education and assistance. An additional 6.8% presented differing viewpoints, featuring individuals who advocated for stricter penalties for minors alongside those calling for their education and rehabilitation. Representatives from helping professions, including lawyers commenting on the criminal liability of minors, as well as psychologists and criminologists discussing the underlying causes of juvenile delinquent behaviour, predominantly advocated for educational measures rather than punitive actions for minors. However, none of the publications suggested that this particular individual required support or assistance.

In 17.7% of the publications, representatives of professional systems, including the police, education, social services, and courts, were cited. Of these, 40% did not express either a defensive or an offensive stance toward the accused. In another 40% of the articles, supportive positions for the defendant were juxtaposed with punitive statements from the victim's family, lawyers, or prosecutors. However, the viewpoints defending the juvenile were not highlighted in the titles or summaries of these articles. For the reader to be exposed to the defence of the accused, they had to engage with the full content of the article or video. In this way, the dominant narrative in the media largely accused, condemned, and called for stricter punishments for juveniles.

This illustrates the partial and distorted representation of juvenile delinquency in the media, which serves as the primary source of information for the public. To better understand the public's perception of this issue, we conducted a quantitative survey of the Lithuanian population, the findings of which are presented in the subsequent section of this chapter.

5 Public Attitudes and Reactions to Juvenile Delinquency: Results of the Representative Survey of Lithuanian Residents

Studying public attitudes and reactions to manifestations of juvenile delinquency is crucial, as societal perspectives often influence the formulation of general criminal policies (Baker et al. 2016; Canton 2015; Dzur 2010) and specific decisions regarding the implementation of juvenile justice policies (Steinberg and Piquero 2010). Populist political parties, keen to garner voter support, are particularly sensitive to public opinions and sentiments, often shaping their political agendas around public concerns about juvenile justice. They monitor societal emotions, such as fears regarding increasing juvenile delinquency and anxieties about public safety, especially in relation to rising juvenile crime rates (Gutiérrez 2018). In turn, these parties respond to public demands for stricter punishments for young offenders (Rogowski 2014). Minkes (2007) and Rogowski (2014) argue that broader political contexts and prevailing public sentiments exert a more significant influence on national youth justice trends than scientific research on the effectiveness of various crime reduction measures.

The following presents some key findings from a representative survey conducted in Lithuania. The primary aim of the study was to explore public attitudes toward juvenile delinquency by investigating:

a) the emotional responses of residents towards minors who commit offenses and crimes;
b) how residents perceive the causes of juvenile delinquency;
c) the punitive or supportive, educational measures that residents endorse for minors who engage in criminal behaviour.

A representative survey of Lithuanian residents aged 18 and older was conducted between July and September 2021. The study employed a multi-stage probability sampling method, incorporating geographic stratification based on the size and administrative classification of the respondents' place of residence. In total, 1508 individuals participated in the survey.

The investigation into attitudes toward juvenile delinquency was rooted in the social psychology tradition and the tripartite model of attitudes (Fabrigar et al. 2005; Van de Ven et al. 1996). According to this model, the internal structure of an attitude comprises three components: affect, or emotions, which refer to the positive and negative feelings an individual experiences towards the attitude object; cognition, which encompasses the beliefs an individual holds about the attitude object; and behaviour, which involves direct actions or behavioural responses towards the attitude object. The formation and manifestation of an attitude occur through the interaction of these three components (Fabrigar et al. 2005; Van de Ven et al. 1996). To measure public attitudes towards juvenile delinquency, the study employed a strategy based on assessing various indicators within the affective, cognitive, and behavioural domains. Participants were presented with a set of statements and asked to indicate their level of agreement or disagreement on a 4-point scale, ranging from "strongly disagree" to "strongly agree," with an additional option of "don't know/can't evaluate."

In order to capture the emotional reactions of Lithuanian residents toward minors committing offenses and crimes, respondents were presented with statements designed to reflect both positive and negative emotional responses for evaluation. Figure 2 illustrates how study participants assessed statements related to the emotions they experience towards juveniles who commit offenses and crimes.

Just over one-fifth (21.7%) of respondents indicated that they were indifferent to juveniles committing offenses or crimes, while another 3.9% chose not to evaluate this statement. However, the majority—74.4%—either completely or somewhat disagreed with the notion of indifference. This suggests that the issue of juvenile delinquency does not leave individuals unaffected; rather, it provokes strong and possibly conflicting emotions in most people. Approximately half of the respondents (50.4%) agreed with the statement that juveniles committing offenses or crimes disgust them, and a slightly larger proportion (53.7%) reported feeling hopeless and helpless about the issue. An even greater proportion of participants agreed with the statements that juveniles committing offenses or crimes evoke feelings of fear (68.6%) and annoyance (76.9%). Additionally, 70.5% of respondents stated that they condemn such juveniles. However, it is noteworthy that a similar proportion of respondents (71.2%) believed that every juvenile, regardless of their behaviour, deserves understanding and respect. A substantial majority (86.7%) tended to agree with the statement that they are concerned about the future of juveniles committing offenses or crimes.

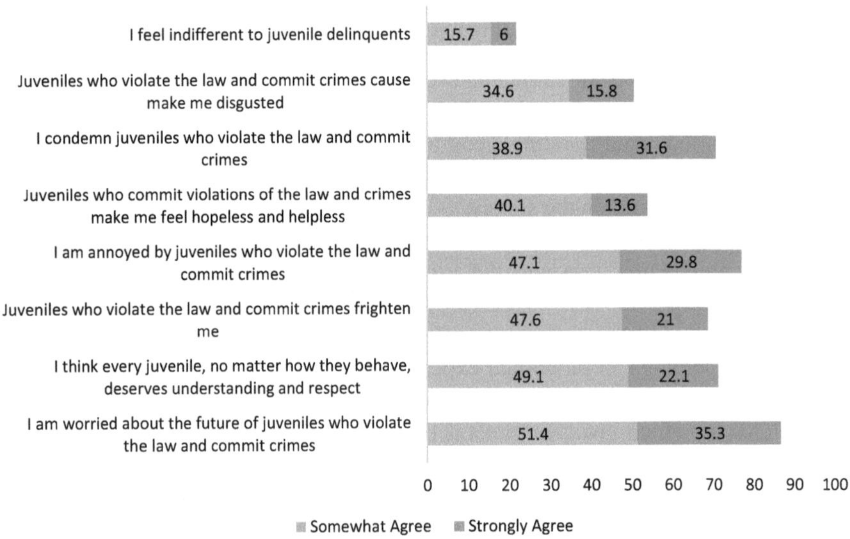

Fig. 2 Evaluation of Statements Reflecting the Emotions Caused by Juvenile Delinquents (Percentage)

In order to understand how Lithuanian residents explain juvenile delinquent behaviour, respondents were asked to evaluate 15 statements about the various causes of juvenile delinquency. These statements were crafted using both theoretical insights from criminology and various societal clichés and stereotypes related to the causes of juvenile delinquency. A larger portion of these statements (nine in total) was based on scientific knowledge, meaning they were derived from criminological and other social science research, as well as theoretical insights. These statements can be conditionally labelled as "correct" explanations. The remaining six statements, on the other hand, reflected "incorrect" explanations, which were based not on scientific evidence but on common stereotypes regarding the causes of juvenile delinquency. It is important to note that, when evaluating the statements, study participants were unaware of which explanations the authors of the questionnaire considered to be "correct" and which were deemed "incorrect," as all statements were mixed and randomly arranged in the questionnaire.

A larger proportion of survey respondents tended to agree with all of the "correct" explanations for the causes of juvenile delinquency (Fig. 3). The percentage of respondents who agreed with these statements ranged from 57.5% to 92.3%. The lowest level of agreement (57.5%) was with the statement that juveniles commit legal violations and crimes because they lack opportunities to acquire things that are important to them. Additionally, 63.4% of respondents agreed that juveniles who are labelled as "bad" from a young age and discarded by society are more likely to engage in criminal behaviour. A similar proportion (65.3%) agreed that it is natural for juveniles to take risks, experiment, and test boundaries at this stage of life.

Moreover, three other causes received similar levels of agreement: 73.9% believed that juveniles commit crimes spontaneously, without planning; 74.6% thought it was due to a need to rebel against adults; and 74.8% attributed it to a lack of positive role models and proper examples. Furthermore, 79.9% agreed that

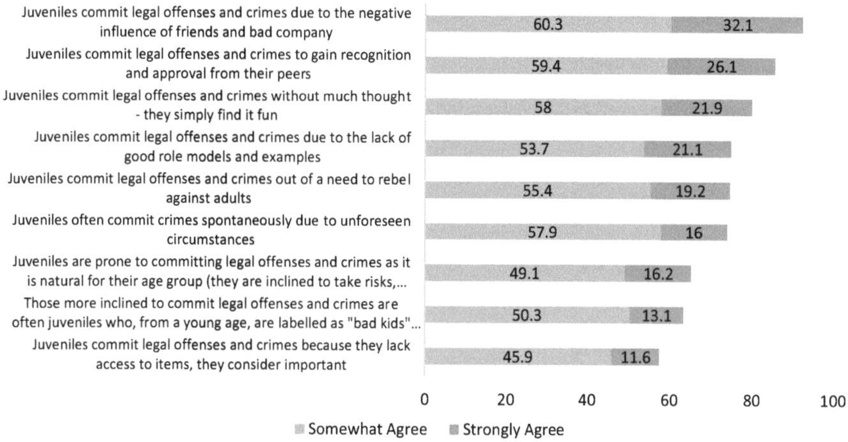

Fig. 3 Evaluation of statements reflecting "correct" explanations of juvenile delinquency (percentage)

juveniles commit offenses simply for fun, without much forethought. The highest levels of agreement were with the final two statements: 85.5% believed that juveniles commit crimes to gain peer recognition and approval, and 92.4% thought it was due to the bad influence of friends or bad company.

When analysing responses to the "incorrect" explanations for juvenile delinquency, it is evident that a smaller proportion of respondents agreed with these explanations compared to the "correct" ones. Nevertheless, more than half of the study participants completely or somewhat agreed with three of the statements (Fig. 4).

The statement that juveniles commit crimes because corporal punishment is now banned and they fear nothing received the most agreement. This explanation was supported by 62.3% of respondents, nearly two-thirds. Similarly, 61.9% of respondents somewhat or strongly agreed that juveniles are spoiled and, therefore, commit crimes because they do not know what else they want. Moreover, more than half (57.9%) of respondents somewhat or strongly agreed with the statement that only juveniles who lack willpower and a sense of responsibility engage in criminal behaviour. The statement that juvenile delinquency in Lithuania is increasing due to the negative influence of Western countries was supported by 45.8% of respondents, while 39.2% believed that children's actions are determined by their family environment, with bad parents raising bad children. The least agreement (31.3%) was with the statement that criminal behaviour is inherent in one's nature and genes, suggesting that such juveniles cannot be reformed.

To ascertain the opinions of Lithuanian residents on potential responses to juvenile delinquency, respondents were asked to evaluate various societal actions or methods aimed at reducing juvenile delinquency. Some of these statements focused

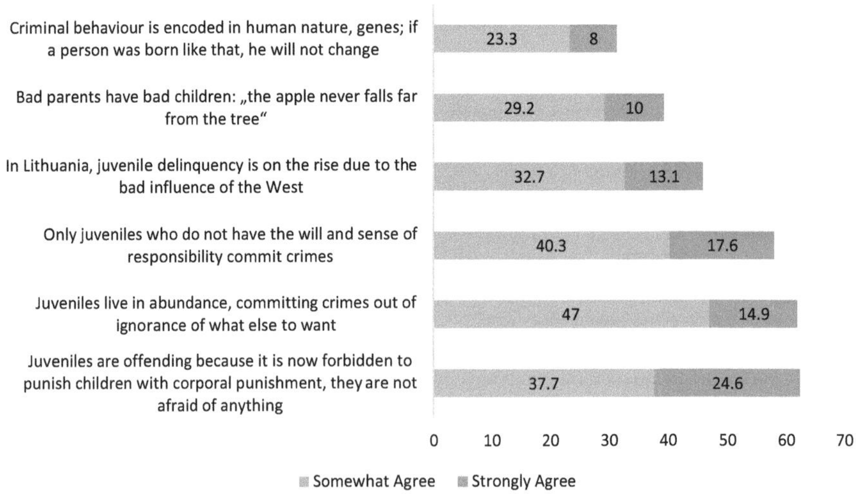

Fig. 4 Evaluation of Statements Reflecting "Incorrect" Explanations of Juvenile Delinquency (Percentage)

on providing support to juveniles who commit offences and to their families, while others emphasised the imposition of punishments or the tightening of existing penalties (Fig. 5).

Statements advocating for support and education garnered almost unanimous agreement from respondents. A significant 88.2% tended to agree that it is more important to educate and assist juveniles who commit offences and crimes, rather than punish them. Moreover, these respondents also believed that support should be extended to the parents of such juveniles. A slightly smaller, yet still substantial majority (71.2%), agreed that juveniles committing offences should only be incarcerated in exceptional or extreme cases.

While the majority favoured responses based on education and support, a significant portion also supported stricter punishments. Just over one-third of the study participants (35.3%) tended to agree that criminal responsibility should be applied to younger juveniles than it currently is. Slightly less than one-third (31.6%) believed that juveniles committing offences should be punished in the same way as adults. Notably, 41.3% tended to agree that parents should be allowed to use physical punishment.

As previously mentioned, the study measured the following aspects of attitudes towards juvenile delinquents: (1) the emotional or affective aspect, i.e., the feelings experienced by the study participants towards offending juveniles; (2) the cognitive or knowledge aspect, expressed as agreement or disagreement with "correct" and "incorrect" explanations for the causes of juvenile delinquency; and (3) the reaction aspect refers to the measures or actions that study participants would support in addressing the problem of juvenile delinquency.

In the further analysis of the study data, the aim was to determine how these three aspects of attitudes interact with one another. To this end, four scales were developed based on the groups of statements discussed: the emotional domain, the cognitive domain (comprising both "correct" and "incorrect" explanations for the causes

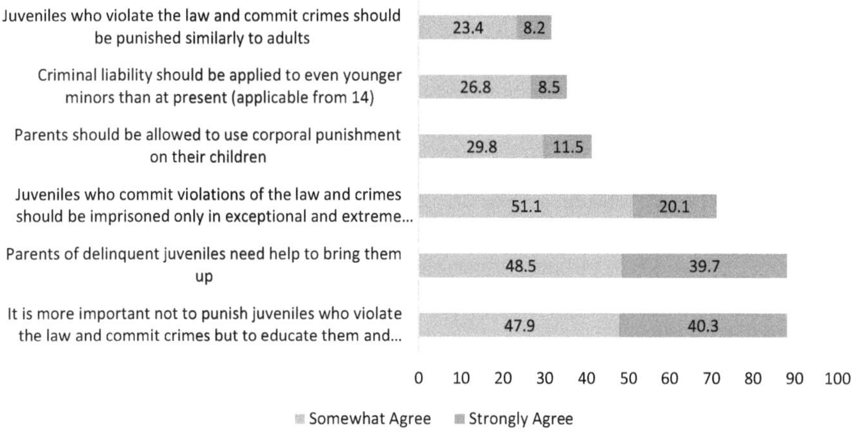

Fig. 5 Evaluation of Statements Reflecting Juvenile Delinquency Reduction Methods (Percentage)

of delinquency), and the reaction domain. All these scales were constructed in a similar manner:

- Higher values on the emotional scale indicate that respondents experience more negative feelings.
- Higher values on the "correct" explanation scale reflect greater agreement with "correct" explanations for the causes of delinquency.
- Higher values on the "incorrect" explanation scale reflect greater agreement with "incorrect" explanations for the causes of delinquency.
- Higher values on the reaction scale indicate more support for punitive measures and less support for measures related to assistance and education.

Table 1 shows the correlations between these four scales.

Correlation analysis revealed that nearly all of the examined aspects of attitudes were statistically significantly related. A noticeable correlation was found between the emotions felt by respondents and their explanations for delinquency: respondents who experienced more negative feelings toward juvenile offenders were more likely to agree with "incorrect" explanations for the causes of delinquency and less likely to agree with "correct" explanations, and vice versa. Emotions were also linked to reactions—those with more negative feelings were more likely to support harsher punitive measures. Harsher measures were also more strongly supported by those respondents who agreed more with "incorrect" explanations for the causes of juvenile delinquency, whereas agreement with "correct" explanations did not correlate with such reactions. The strongest negative correlation was observed between agreement with "correct" and "incorrect" explanations for the causes of juvenile delinquency. The more respondents agreed with "correct" explanations, the less they agreed with "incorrect" ones, and vice versa.

When evaluating which aspect—emotional or cognitive—had a greater impact on respondents' reactions, it can be stated that reactions were more strongly correlated with the cognitive aspect. It is important to emphasise that the greatest influence on the severity of reactions was exerted by agreement with "incorrect" explanations for the causes of juvenile delinquency, as agreement with "correct" explanations did not statistically significantly correlate with the severity of the reaction.[2]

Table 1 Correlations between aspects of attitudes towards juvenile delinquents (Pearson correlation coefficient)

	"Incorrect" explanations	"Correct" explanations	Punitive reactions
Negative feelings	0.453[a]	−0.256[a]	0.292[a]
"Incorrect" explanations	–	−0.526[a]	0.389[a]
"Correct" explanations		–	−0.037

[a] $p = 0.01$

[2] See also Buzaitytė-Kašalynienė et al. (2024).

In conclusion, this study highlights the complex and multifaceted nature of public attitudes towards juvenile delinquency in Lithuania. The findings reveal that emotions, beliefs, and reactions towards juvenile offenders are deeply interconnected. Most respondents experience strong emotions such as fear, annoyance, and concern for the future of these juveniles. The study also demonstrates that while there is significant support for educational and supportive measures, a notable portion of the population still favours stricter punitive actions. These insights underscore the importance of understanding public sentiment when addressing juvenile delinquency, as it can significantly influence the effectiveness of interventions and policies.

6 Concluding Remarks

The way society approaches juvenile delinquency and evaluates the effectiveness of responses depends on the knowledge we have about its prevalence and the underlying circumstances. The media often sensationalise and scandalise individual cases of juvenile delinquency to attract public attention and generate readers' interest. This tendency can result in a distorted perception of the issue, obscuring the fact that minor forms of delinquency are significantly more prevalent and frequently constitute a characteristic aspect of adolescent behaviour. However, the origin of more severe acts of delinquency is often traced back to more profound, systemic social issues. It is imperative to acknowledge this distinction to ensure that interventions target the fundamental causes rather than merely addressing the symptoms.

Developing an effective policy to reduce adolescent misbehaviour necessitates moving beyond emotionally charged responses to prominent cases. Hence, it would be erroneous to assume that emotional appeals for a harsh response should dictate a policy focused solely on the prevention of adolescent delinquency.

References

Aebi MF et al (2021) Original data of the European Sourcebook of Crime and Criminal Justice Statistics 2021 (6th ed.). Series UNILCRIM, (2) 2021

Baker T, Cleary HMD, Pickett JT, Gertz MG (2016) Crime salience and public willingness to pay for child saving and juvenile punishment. Crime Delinq 62(5):645–668

Barlow HD (1990) Introduction to criminology, 5th edn. Harper Collins Publishers

Buzaitytė-Kašalynienė J, Švedaitė-Sakalauskė B, Kalpokas V, Sakalauskas G (2024) Is juvenile delinquency in Lithuania increasing because of the bad influence of the west? Punitive attitudes of the Lithuanian population towards juvenile offenders. East Eur Politics Soc 38(2):411–431

Canton R (2015) Crime, punishment and the moral emotions: righteous minds and their attitudes towards punishment. Punishment Soc 17(1):54–72

Christie N (1970) Comparative criminology. Can J Corrections 12(1):40–46

Conklin JE (1989) Criminology, 3rd edn. Maximilian Publishing Company

Decker SH, Martaeche N (eds) (2017) International handbook of juvenile justice, 2nd edn. Springer

Dollinger B, Schadbach M (2013) Jugendkriminalität. Springer VS

Dollinger B, Schmidt-Semisch H (2011) Sozialpädagogik und Kriminologie im Dialog. Einführende Perspektiven zum Ereignis "Jugendkriminalität". In: Dollinger B, Schmidt-Semisch H (eds) Handbuch Jugendkriminalität. Kriminologie und Sozialpädagogik im Dialog. 2., durchgesehene Auflage. VS Verlag, pp 11–22

Dünkel F (2014) Juvenile justice systems in Europe—reforms developments between justice, welfare and "new punitiveness". Kriminologijos studijos 1:31–76

Dünkel F, Geng B, Passow D, Sakalauskas G (2020) Neuromokslų išvados apie smegenų brendimą—argumentai išskirtinei jaunimo baudžiamajai atsakomybei. Kriminologijos studijos 8:84–106

Dzur AW (2010) The myth of penal populism: democracy, citizen participation, and American hyperincarceration. J Specul Philos 24(4):354–379

Enke T (2003) Sozialpädagogische Krisenintervention bei delinquenten Jugendlichen. Eine Längsschnittstudie zuVerlaufstrukturen von Jugenddelinquenz. Juventa Verlag

Fabrigar LR et al (2005) The handbook of attitudes. Routledge, pp 79–124

Gečienė I, Buzaitytė-Kašalynienė J, Švedaitė-Sakalauskė B, Stakėnaitė D, Čiupailaitė D (2007) Socialiai pažeidžiamo jaunimo integracijos į darbo rinką prielaidos Lietuvoje. Viešosios politikos ir vadybos institutas

Gutiérrez DR (2018) The media and intervention in youth offending: a narrative review. Artículo/Castalia 31:48–61

Harrendorf S (2018) Prospects, problems, and pitfalls in comparative analyses of criminal justice data. Crime Justice A Rev Res 47:159–207

Heinz W (2016) Jugendkriminalität—Zahlen und Fakten. Bundeszentrale für politische Bildung

Heinz W (2017) Alternatyvos įkalinimui: bausmių taikymo teorija ir praktika Vokietijoje, bausmių veiksmingumo ir recidyvo tyrimų rezultatai. Iš Sakalauskas G (moksl. red.). In: Bausmių taikymo ir vykdymo tarptautinis palyginimas, tendencijos ir perspektyvos Lietuvoje. Lietuvos teisės institutas

Icenogle G et al (2019) Adolescents' cognitive capacity reaches adult levels prior to their psychosocial maturity: evidence for a "maturity gap" in a multinational, cross-sectional sample. Law Hum Behav 43(1):69–85

Inchley J et al (2020) Spotlight on adolescent health and Well-being. Findings from the 2017/2018 health behaviour in school-aged children (HBSC) survey in Europe and Canada. International report. Volume 2. Key data. World Health Organization

Jehle J-M, Harrendorf S (eds) (2010) Defining and registering criminal offences and measures. Standards for a European comparison. Universitätsverlag Göttingen

Jusienė R (2007) Sunkūs paaugliai arba kodėl paaugliai elgiasi agresyviai? Iš Nepilnamečių justicija Lietuvoje: teorija ir praktika. Metodinis leidinys. NPLC, 113–124

Justickaja S, Giedrytė-Mačiulienė R (2017) Viktimizaciją patyrusių ir delinkvencinio elgesio patirties turinčių 7–9 klasių moksleivių ypatumai. Teisės problemos 2(94):44–61

Laurinavičius A (2020) Nepilnamečių teisės pažeidėjų rizikos ir apsauginių veiksnių analizė. Vilniaus universiteto leidykla, Vilnius

Markina A (2019) Problems related to reintegration of young ex-offenders in Estonia. Kriminologijos studijos 7:56–74

Minkes J (2007) Change, continuity, and public opinion in youth justice. Int Criminal Justice Rev 17(4):340–349

Neubacher F (2014) Kriminologie. 2. Auflage. Nomos Verlag

Povilaitis R, Valiukevičiūtė J (2006) Patyčių prevencija mokyklose. UAB Multiplex

Raithel J, Mansel J (eds) (2003) Kriminalität und Gewalt im Jugendalter. Hell- und Dunkelfeldbefunde im Vergleich. Juventa Verlag

Reinecke J et al (2013) Entstehung und Entwicklung von Kinder- und Jugenddelinquenz: Erste Ergebnisse einer Längsschnittstudie. Neue Kriminalpolitik 25(3):207–226

Reuband KH (2011) Einstellungen der Bevölkerung gegenüber jugendlichen Straftätern. Eine empirische Analyseihrer Erscheinungsformen und Determinanten. In: Dollinger B and

Schmidt-Semisch H (eds) HandbuchJugendkriminalität. Kriminologie und Sozialpädagogik im Dialog 2., durchgesehene Auflage. VS Verlag, pp 507–531

Riesner L (2014) Die Möglichkeiten und Grenzen der Vorhersage delinquenten Verhaltens von jungen Menschen anhand ihrer Jugendhilfeunterlagen. Dissertation zur Erlangung des Doktorgrades der Philosophischen Fakultät der Christian-Albrechts-Universität zu Kiel

Rogowski S (2014) Radical/critical social work with young offenders: challenges and possibilities. J Soc Work Pract 28(1):7–21

Ruigrok N, van Atteveldt W, Gagestein S, Jacobi C (2017) Media and juvenile delinquency: a study into the relationship between journalists, politics, and public. Journalism 18(7):907–925. https://doi.org/10.1177/1464884916636143

Rupšienė L, Saveljeva R, Šutinienė I (2020) ESPAD—2019. Alkoholio ir kitų psichotropinių medžiagų vartojimas Lietuvoje. Tyrimo ataskaita

Sakalauskas G (2007) Socialinė vaikų ir jaunimo nusikalstamo elgesio kontrolė. Iš Aleknevičienė J (sud.). In: Socialinės deviacijų problemos. Eugrimas, Vilnius, pp 158–190

Sakalauskas G (2008) Tarpdalykinės kriminologijos studijos: patirtis ir perspektyvos. Teisės problemos 1(59):77–91

Sakalauskas G (2009) Minimalaus baudžiamosios atsakomybės amžiaus problema: lyginamieji teisiniai ir kriminologiniai aspektai. Teisės problemos 2(64):81–103

Sakalauskas G (moksl. red.) (2011) Registruotas ir latentinis nusikalstamumas Lietuvoje: tendencijos, lyginamieji aspektai ir aplinkos veiksniai. Lietuvos teisės institutas, Vilnius

Sakalauskas G (2013) Nepilnamečių baudžiamosios atsakomybės ypatumų prasmė. Teisės problemos 3(81):5–55

Sakalauskas G (2018) Nepilnamečių nusikalstamumo baimę kursto išgalvoti mitai. Spectrum 2(28):46–51

Schumann KF (2011) Jugenddelinquenz im Lebensverlauf. In: Dollinger B, Schmidt-Semisch H (eds) Handbuch Jugendkriminalität. Kriminologie und Sozialpädagogik im Dialog 2., durchgesehene Auflage. VS Verlag, pp 243–257

Šmigelskas K, Lukoševičiūtė J, Slapšinskaitė A, Vaičiūnas T, Bulotaitė J, Žemaitaitytė M, Šalčiūnaitė L, ZaborskisA (2019) Lietuvos moksleivių gyvensena ir sveikata: 2018 m. situacija ir tendencijos. HBSC tyrimas, LSMU

Steinberg L, Piquero AR (2010) Manipulating public opinion about trying juveniles as adults: an experimental study. Crime Delinq 56(4):487–506

Švedaitė-Sakalauskė B, Eidukevičiūtė D (2015) Socialinis darbas su jaunimu gatvėje—pirmoji patirtis Lietuvoje. STEPP 11:37–53

Tillmann K-J (2010) Sozialisationstheorien. Eine Einführung in den Zusammenhang von Gesellschaft, Institution und Subjektwerdung. Rowohlt Verlag GmbH

Ttofi MM, Farrington DP (2011) Effectiveness of school-based programs to reduce bulling: a systematic and meta-analytic review. J Exp Criminol 7:27–56

United Nations (1990) Guidelines for the Prevention of Juvenile Delinquency (The Riyadh Guidelines)

Van de Ven P, Bornholt L, Bailey M (1996) Measuring cognitive, affective, and behavioral components of homophobic reaction. Arch Sex Behav 25:155–179

Dr. Gintautas Sakalauskas is an associate professor in the Faculty of Law at Vilnius University. He graduated from the same institution with a law degree in 1998. He obtained a Master of Laws (LL.M.) degree in 2003 and defended his doctoral dissertation in social sciences (law) at the University of Greifswald (Germany) in 2005. He is a founder member of the Lithuanian Criminologists' Association and served as its chairman from 2010 to 2012 and again from 2018 to 2021. From 1997 to 2018, he worked at the Lithuanian Law Institute. From 2007 to 2010, he was editor-in-chief of the journal Teisės problemos (Legal Issues). He is a member of the editorial team of the journal Criminological Studies. He is also a member of the European Society of Criminology and the International Penal and Penitentiary Foundation (IPPF). He is a member of the Clemency

Commission, the Council of Social Work and the Parole Commission. He is also one of the founders of, and a member of the board of, two non-governmental organisations working with children and their families, founded in 2000 and 2015 respectively. He is a research fellow of the Alexander von Humboldt Foundation, the Research Council of Lithuania and the University of Greifswald. He has published over 120 peer-reviewed scientific papers on criminology, criminal policy, the enforcement of sentences, juvenile delinquency, and juvenile justice.

Vaidas Kalpokas obtained his master's degree in Sociology at Vilnius University in 1998. He works at the Law Institute of the Lithuanian Centre for Social Sciences. Since 2019, he has been a PhD student in criminology at the Institute of Sociology and Social Work at Vilnius University. Mr. Kalpokas has participated in more than 20 national and international scientific research projects in the field of criminology and is a co-author of about 15 scientific publications. His research interest is in juvenile delinquency and comparative criminology.

Dr. Jolita Buzaitytė-Kašalynienė is an associate professor at the Institute of Sociology and Social Work at Vilnius University. She pursued studies in sociology, social work, and education. As a member of the first cohort of the Master's program in Social Work at Vilnius University, she was subsequently invited to join the newly established Department of Social Work at the same university. In 2003, she successfully defended her doctoral dissertation in educational sciences, focusing on "Preconditions of the Need for Social Services in Secondary Schools." In 2009–2015, she headed the Department of Social Work. Jolita has engaged in national and international scientific projects as an expert, researcher, and project manager within the frameworks of EUQUAL, ERASMUS, and various National Research Programs. Her research endeavors have focused on risk and protective factors in youth development, the challenges youth face and the conditions necessary for their integration into the labor market, youth participation, societal responses to juvenile delinquency, threats and possibilities of distant learning, effects of social support and school social capital on the academic success of 11–19-year-old students. Since 2011, she has been an active National Youth Researchers Network member. In 2021, she also became a member of the Youth Work Council under the Department of Youth Affairs within the Ministry of Social Security and Labour. A member of the Scout movement since 1991, she possesses extensive experience in non-formal education for children and youth. Additionally, she is the founder and president of the Group Relations Society, which seeks to promote intensive experiential learning in groups, organisations, and communities by applying the experiential learning method and a psychodynamic-systemic approach.

Dr. Birutė Švedaitė-Sakalauskė is an associate professor at the Institute of Sociology and Social Work at Vilnius University. She has studied social work in Dresden and Cologne, Germany. She is a supervisor and group psychotherapist. In 2006, she completed her doctoral thesis in Sociology. From 2015 to 2020, she held the role of vice-rector at Vilnius University. She is a member of the editorial board of three scientific journals in Lithuania. She is the founder and board member of two non-governmental social welfare organisations. She is a member of the Lithuanian Association of Supervision and the Lithuanian Youth Research Network, and an expert at the Research Council of Lithuania. Since 2024, she has been a member of the Council of Vilnius University. She is the author and co-author of more than 40 scientific publications. Her research interests: development of social work, power dynamics within social work, social work methodology, juvenile delinquency.

Peculiarities of Criminal Liability of Children in Lithuania

Mindaugas Girdauskas and Darius Pranka

Abstract This chapter provides an analysis of certain peculiarities in the regulation and application of criminal liability for children in Lithuania, examined within the context of international child rights protection standards. It briefly reviews the evolution of national regulation and highlights recent trends. A concise overview of juvenile delinquency statistics and tendencies is provided. The analysis includes court decisions addressing issues related to the suspension of the execution of custodial sentences imposed on minors. Specific features of the release of children from criminal liability and trends in judicial practice are also discussed. Additionally, the regulation and application of diversion concerning children are examined. The conclusions suggest that children's criminal justice could be further improved by expanding the use of these measures, clearly delineating provisions that establish the peculiarities of criminal liability of minors in legislation, elaborating on diversion procedures, and ensuring the protection of child rights.

1 Introduction

The application of criminal liability to individuals who have committed law violations can result in severe consequences. In many countries, including across Europe, contemporary legal principles emphasise that such liability must be individualised, considering the offender's personality and that sanctions should not exceed what is strictly necessary. One of the harshest sanctions—imprisonment—should be reserved as a measure of last resort. For child offenders, due to their lower (social) maturity and reduced ability to comprehend the danger of their actions or control them, special additional conditions of criminal liability, alternative measures to

The original version of the chapter has been revised. A correction to this chapter can be found at https://doi.org/10.1007/978-3-032-07092-0_21

M. Girdauskas (✉) · D. Pranka
Law Institute, Lithuanian Centre for Social Sciences, Vilnius, Lithuania
e-mail: m.girdauskas@lat.lt; darius.pranka@teise.org

A. Limantė, R. Vaičiūnienė (eds.), *Children's Rights in Central and Eastern Europe*, European Union and its Neighbours in a Globalized World 29,
https://doi.org/10.1007/978-3-032-07092-0_11

such liability, and more lenient sanctions should be applied (e.g., Dünkel 2022). The principle of applying special, more lenient criminal liability to children is enshrined in various provisions of international legal instruments and recommendations, for instance, in the United Nations Convention on the Rights of the Child ([UN CRC] 1989), the Committee of Ministers of the Council of Europe Recommendation to member states on the European Rules for juvenile offenders subject to sanctions or measures (2008), and the Guidelines on child-friendly justice (2010). However, countries implement these provisions to varying extents and in diverse ways (See, for instance, Decker and Marteache 2017; Liefaard 2020).

After restoring its independence, Lithuania acceded to the UN CRC in 1992. In the same year, the Constitution of the Republic of Lithuania, adopted by referendum (Constitution),[1] established the principles of criminal liability and the rights of suspects and accused persons applicable to both adults and minors,[2] as well as an important provision stipulating that underage children shall be protected by law.[3] On May 1, 2003, the new Criminal Code[4] (CC) and Code of Criminal Procedure[5] (CCP) came into force. Various authors have analysed the peculiarities and reforms of children's criminal liability in Lithuania that are related to the implementation of these constitutional and international acts (e.g., Dapšys 1994a; Drakšienė 1998; Sakalauskas and Jatkevičius 2000; Michailovič 2001; Jatkevičius 2003; Drakšienė 2005; Pakštaitis 2007; Dapšys et al. 2008, pp. 70–85, 122; Drakšienė and Drakšas 2008; Sakalauskas 2013; Švedas et al. 2020, pp. 297–335; Žiobienė 2024). A smaller proportion of works has briefly presented this subject to an international audience in English (e.g., Dapšys 1994b, pp. 20–22; Dapšys et al. 1998, pp. 61–74; Jurka et al. 2007; Vileikienė 2007, pp. 36–38; Sakalauskas 2011, pp. 872–875; Dünkel 2015, pp. 12, 14, 19, 22, 24; Dünkel 2022, pp. 32, 37–38; Kavoliūnaitė-Ragauskienė 2022, pp. 234–235; Švedas 2022, pp. 102–103, 152, 168–170, 174). Among these, only one study analysed judicial practice (Pakštaitis 2009), while more detailed comparative research on regulation was conducted over a decade ago (Dünkel et al. 2011a, b).

Procedural aspects related to the non-application of criminal liability to children, particularly diversion mechanisms, have been briefly analysed in earlier works (some of the referenced above and, for instance, Goda 2003, pp. 569, 577; Ažubalytė et al. 2011, pp. 280–285; Gensing 2011, pp. 1621, 1623). This book chapter synthesises and provides a more comprehensive analysis of specific aspects of regulating and applying children's criminal liability in Lithuania within the context of international child rights protection standards. It evaluates recent legal amendments, trends in registered crime, and procedural decisions alongside newer judicial practices. The discussion begins with an overview of general trends, followed by an examination of the suspension of the execution of a sentence, release from criminal liability, and the regulation and application of diversion to children. The analysis is grounded in the provisions of international legal treaties and recommendations, the

[1] *Official Gazette*, 1992, No. 33-1014 with subsequent amendments.

[2] For example, Constitution, Articles 20, 31.

[3] Constitution, Article 39(3).

[4] *Official Gazette,* 2000, No. 89-2741 with subsequent amendments.

[5] *Official Gazette,* 2002, No. 37-1341 with subsequent amendments.

Constitution of Lithuania, criminal law, and related legislation. Separate comparative insights with the laws of other European countries are provided, accompanied by an evaluation of statistical data on registered crime and procedural decisions, as well as the jurisprudence of the Supreme Court of Lithuania and other courts. The analysis is further enriched by the scholarship of Lithuanian criminal and procedural law and comparative academic literature. The insights from this chapter may prove valuable for other countries seeking to regulate the criminal liability of children, helping them to apply the same effective measures, avoid similar challenges and ensure better protection of children's rights.

2 General Trends in the Regulation and Application of Children's Criminal Liability

Under the UN CRC, states must recognise the right of every child alleged as, accused of, or recognised as having infringed the penal law to be treated in a manner consistent with the promotion of the child's sense of dignity and worth, which reinforces the child's respect for the human rights and fundamental freedoms of others and which takes into account the child's age and the desirability of promoting the child's reintegration and the child's assuming a constructive role in society. For this purpose, states are required to seek to promote the establishment of laws and procedures specifically applicable to such children (UN CRC, Article 40(1) and (3)). At the time of Lithuania's accession to this Convention, the Criminal Code in force[6] already provided for certain peculiarities of criminal liability of children, such as age limitations (the liability applied since 16 years of age, and for some crimes—from 14 years of age), restrictions on the length of imprisonment (not exceeding 10 years), prohibition of the death penalty, more lenient conditions for the release from criminal liability, applying in such cases only reformative sanctions of educational nature, and recognition of the commission of a crime by a child as a mitigating circumstance when imposing a sentence.[7] Subsequently, efforts were made to reform the regulation of children's criminal liability, ensuring, as far as possible, the implementation of international standards (e.g., Dapšys 1994b, p. 20). More favourable conditions for the suspension of the execution of a sentence and the imposition of penalties less severe than those provided by law were established, along with restrictions on the size of fines and the length of combined imprisonment sentences, a reduction by half of the minimum of the custodial sentence, and the possibility of not applying confiscation of property and non-application of life imprisonment for minors.[8] Only stricter conditions for the release from criminal liability were

[6] *Official Gazette*, 1961, No. 18-147 with subsequent amendments.

[7] Articles 11, 24, 25, 32, 40, 52[1], 61.

[8] Article 25, wording effective from July 29, 1998; Articles 35, 42, 45, 47[1].

stipulated than before.[9] Simultaneously, the new Criminal Code was drafted. It was adopted in 2000, incorporating most of the provisions mentioned above alleviating children's criminal liability, except for the previously noted mitigating circumstance.

The Criminal Code (CC) establishes a special Chapter IX, regulating the main peculiarities of children's criminal liability,[10] and specifies its purpose, which is significant for guiding courts in applying these provisions: (1) to ensure correspondence of liability to the age and social maturity of these persons; (2) to restrict the possibilities of imposition of a custodial sentence and broaden the possibilities of imposition of reformative sanctions against these persons; (3) to help a minor to alter his manner of living and conduct by co-ordinating a penalty for the committed criminal act with the development and education of his or her personality and elimination of reasons for the unlawful conduct; and (4) to prevent a minor from committing new criminal acts.[11] Furthermore, the Code provides a more detailed regulation of reformative sanctions, including warnings, compensation for or elimination of property damage, unpaid reformative work, placement for upbringing and care with parents or other natural or legal persons taking care of children, restriction on conduct, and placement in a special reformative facility.[12] While applying the restriction of conduct, the court is also granted the right to impose other obligations or prohibitions not provided for in the criminal law, which, in the court's opinion, could positively influence the child's behaviour.[13] The legal consequences of non-compliance with the reformative sanctions are also clearly defined.[14] Additional circumstances to be considered when imposing a sentence on a child have been established (e.g., the living and upbringing conditions of the child, the state of health and social maturity of him or her, previously imposed sanctions on the child, and the effectiveness thereof, and the child's conduct following the commission of a criminal act).[15] The opportunities for the suspension of the execution of the sentence and the release of children from criminal liability have also been expanded.[16] The possibilities of the suspension of the execution of the sentence have been broadened several times since the Code's enactment, the last time in recent years. CC generally established more lenient criminal liability for individuals who committed offences, reduced the scope of criminalisation of acts, and mitigated prescribed punishments. This has also resulted in more lenient liability for child offenders and may have influenced the extent of its application.

---

[9] Article 52^1, wording effective from January 1, 1995.

[10] Inconsistently, some of such peculiarities are also addressed in specific paragraphs of articles outlined in other chapters of this Code (CC, Articles 13, 46, 48, 67, 71, 97).

[11] CC, Article 80.

[12] CC, Articles 82–88.

[13] CC, Article 87(4).

[14] CC, Article 89.

[15] CC, Article 91.

[16] CC, Articles 92 and 93.

According to registered crime statistics, the number of child offenders and offences committed by them consistently increased during the last decade of the previous century, reaching a peak around the year 2000. However, since then, these numbers have steadily declined and, in recent years, have reached their lowest levels.[17] The decrease is significant,[18] with a similarly notable reduction in the number of children suspected (or accused) of crimes[19] (Sakalauskas et al. 2021, p. 178; Information Technology and Communications Department under the Ministry of the Interior of the Republic of Lithuania [ITCD] 2025a, b).

The dynamics of offences committed by children are not exceptional, as they essentially reflect general crime trends (ITCD 2025c). However, it is even more significant that the share of offences committed by minors as a proportion of all offences has decreased more than threefold[20] (ITCD 2025a).

By the beginning of this decade, the number of convicted children had significantly decreased[21] and has since remained relatively stable[22] (Sakalauskas et al. 2021, p. 178; State Data Agency 2025a). There has been a notable decrease in the number of children sentenced to actual imprisonment.[23] An analysis of sentencing statistics reveals that arrest penalties are not imposed on children or applied minimally.[24] The most frequently applied penalty is the restriction of liberty[25] (Lithuanian Probation Service 2025).

There has also been a significant decrease in the application of reformative sanctions.[26] The most frequently imposed reformative sanction remains restriction on conduct, which is applied in the vast majority of cases. In fact, its proportion in application even increased.[27] The warnings and unpaid reformative work are second in frequency, and each type is applied approximately in one-fifth of cases. The proportion of unpaid work has augmented.[28] The other types of reformative sanctions

---

[17] In 2000–5559 cases; in 2024–1025 cases; counting per 100.000 inhabitants of the same age at the end of the year: 2475 cases in 2000; 1053 cases in 2021.

[18] More than five times.

[19] In 2004, there were 4232 cases; in 2024, there were 428 cases, in the first eight months of 2025—563 cases.

[20] In 2005–12.7%; in 2024–3.5%.

[21] In 2000–2799 cases; in 2020–400 cases, a decrease of 7 times.

[22] In 2024–393.

[23] Between 1995 and 2002, the proportion of such children ranged from 22.2% to 46.9% (Children's Justice Program for 2004–2008, approved by the Government of the Republic of Lithuania on May 19, 2004, Resolution No. 600. *Official Gazette*, 2004, No. 83–3008). At the end of 2024, only 7 children were serving sentences of imprisonment (State Data Agency 2025c).

[24] In 2020–1 case; in 2021–2 cases; in 2022–0 cases (ITCD 2025d).

[25] In 2022—68 cases; in 2024—73 cases.

[26] In 2004, there were 984 cases (Sakalauskas 2013, p. 29); in 2024, there were 120 cases (State Data Agency 2025b, a decrease of more than 8 times.

[27] From sixty-eight percent in 2005 to eighty-seven percent in 2024.

[28] Increased by ten percent from 2005 to 2024.

were and remain applied very rarely.[29] Though notably, when the reformative sanctions are applied, in almost half of cases a few such sanctions are imposed (State Data Agency 2025b).

In summary, the presented registered statistical data indicate a decrease in the number of delinquent children, a rare application of particularly severe penalties, and a declining use of various reformative sanctions. Similar trends of declining child delinquency since the 2000s can be observed across European countries (Sakalauskas et al. 2021, p. 192). Moreover, in Eastern and Central European countries, as well as in Germany, a significant reduction in the application of custodial sentences has also been noted (Dünkel 2022, pp. 34, 44). Thus, it can be concluded that the situation in Lithuania aligns with these European trends.

3 Suspension of the Execution of Custodial Sentences for Children

One of the dispositions that should be possible to apply under the UN CRC to ensure that children are dealt with in a manner appropriate to their well-being and proportionate both to their circumstances and the offence is probation (UN CRC, Article 40(4)). The child justice system should provide ample opportunities to apply social and educational measures, to strictly limit the use of deprivation of liberty, and maximise the effective application of alternative measures such as probation, for example, via suspended sentences (United Nations Committee on the Rights of the Child [UN CRC Committee] 2019, § 19; United Nations 1985, Rule 17.1(b) and commentary, 18.1(b)). The conditions for the suspension of sentences for children should be more favourable than those for adults (Council of Europe 1987, Rule 16). In its latest concluding observations on Lithuania's report regarding the implementation of the UN CRC, the UN CRC Committee recommended that Lithuania promote, whenever possible, the use of non-custodial sentences for children, such as probation (UN CRC Committee 2024, § 45(a)).

In Lithuania, a court may suspend the execution of a custodial sentence for a period ranging from one to three years for a child convicted of one or more negligent offences or a child convicted with a sentence of up to five years for one or more intentional offences. The execution of the sentence may be suspended where the court rules that there is a reasonable ground for believing that the purpose of the penalty will be achieved without the sentence actually being served.[30] These conditions are more favourable than those for adults, for whom the suspension of sentence execution generally applies only if convicted of negligent offences with a sentence for a term of up to six years or intentional offences classified as minor or

[29] In sum up to six percent in 2024.

[30] CC, Article 92(2) and (4).

less serious,[31] with a sentence for a term of up to four years.[32] When suspending the execution of a sentence, the court imposes upon a minor one or several mutually compatible reformative sanctions, except placement in a special reformative facility. The court also sets a time limit for the minor to comply with the reformative sanctions.[33] The criminal law further provides for the possibility of imposing the following penal sanctions on a child when suspending the execution of a sentence: payment of a contribution to the fund of crime victims, confiscation of property, and extended confiscation of property.[34]

At the request of a probation service, a court may decide to revoke the suspension of the execution of the sentence and enforce the punishment imposed by the judgment if, during the suspension period, the probation service identifies an increased risk of criminal behaviour or harm to others by the convicted child. There is sufficient reason to believe that the purpose of the sentence suspension will not be achieved. If the suspension is not revoked by the end of the suspension period, the child is considered to have served the sentence.[35] As noted, in judicial practice, the sentence is most often suspended when a child is sentenced to custodial penalty.[36]

In light of the aforementioned provisions of the CC, which establish the purpose of features of children's criminal liability and the peculiarities of the imposition of a penalty on them,[37] the application of the suspension of the execution of a sentence for children requires an assessment of both the circumstances related to the committed offence and those pertaining to the child's personality (Levon and Švedas 2022, p. 180).

An analysis of criminal cases over the past 10 years in which children were convicted and appeals on questions of fact or law to a higher court[38] or the cassation appeals to the Supreme Court of Lithuania (Supreme Court) were submitted, reveals that in the vast majority of these cases, issues related to the suspension of the execution of the sentence are often among the arguments presented in the appeals, and courts devote significant attention to this matter. In some cases, the court of first instance did not apply the suspension, while the higher court held a different

[31] According to Article 11 of CC, intentional crimes are classified based on the maximum imprisonment penalty stipulated by law as follows: minor (up to 3 years), less serious (up to 6 years), serious (up to 10 years), and grave (over 10 years).

[32] CC, Article 75(2).

[33] CC, Article 92(5).

[34] CC, Article 67(2).

[35] Law of the Republic of Lithuania on Probation. *Official Gazette*, 2012, No. 4–108, with subsequent amendments (Article 30).

[36] For example, at the end of 2024, there were 7 children sentenced with custodial sentences (State Data Agency 2025c), while in the same year, 196 children had their sentence execution suspended (State Data Agency 2025d).

[37] CC, Articles 80 and 91.

[38] Regional courts hear such appeals against judgments of district courts, and the Court of Appeal of Lithuania hears such appeals against judgments of regional courts.

opinion upon reviewing the appeal. In such cases, the decision to suspend the execution of a custodial sentence was influenced by the following circumstances:

1. the child had no prior convictions, no administrative sanctions,[39] was attending school, and more than five years had passed since the commission of the crime. There is no evidence to suggest that, apart from one other earlier offence, the child committed additional offences during their minority that would characterise them negatively.[40]
2. the child committed a single offence for the first time, is of young age, attended school before the crime, and is deeply remorseful about the offence. Prior to the offence, the child had no criminal convictions, and though convicted once later, there is no evidence in the case file to indicate the child committed new offences after that. The child has no administrative sanctions, and the offence did not cause serious harm.[41]
3. the child was convicted for the first time, committed the crime as a minor, is of young age, attends school, participates in sports, and there is no evidence in the case file that negatively characterises the child. The offence committed did not cause serious harm. In both cases of criminal activity, the narcotics intended for inmates of a penitentiary did not reach their intended recipients. The child's role in the offences was limited to that of an executor, with no evidence that the child organised these criminal acts.[42]

These typical examples, where the decision was made to apply a suspension of the execution of a sentence, demonstrate the similarity of the arguments used by courts. The suspension is typically applied to children with no prior convictions before the commission of the offence under the trial, even if they were subsequently convicted of another offence. Such children are generally positively characterised, engaged in education or other activities, and less emphasis is placed on the severity or nature of the offence committed.

However, in most cases where disputes arose regarding the suspension of the execution of a sentence, the courts concluded that there was no basis to apply the suspension. An analysis of the reasons for such decisions reveals that the suspension is typically not applied due to factors related to the child offender's characteristics: having multiple prior convictions and having already benefited from the suspension several times, yet committing a new offence during the suspension period for which the child is convicted in the current case[43]; being convicted four times and committing the new offence not only during the suspension period but also while under a court-ordered medium-level supervision measure—placement in a child socialisation

[39] Since 2017 such sanctions are imposed under the Code of Administrative Offences. *Register of Legal Acts* (TAR), 2015, 11216, with subsequent amendments.

[40] Panevėžys Regional Court, March 9, 2015, Decision No. 1A-82-719/2015.

[41] Šiauliai Regional Court, May 11, 2016, Decision No. 1A-173-167/2016.

[42] Kaunas Regional Court, October 22, 2014, Decision No. 1A-400-327-2014.

[43] Supreme Court, March 24, 2015, Decision No. 2K-194-895/2015. Here and elsewhere, the referenced decisions of this court were adopted by three-judge panels unless otherwise specified.

centre, committing administrative offences during this period[44]; having prior convictions and committing the offence during the execution of a penalty of restriction of liberty and being prosecuted in the current case for four intentional less serious offences (three thefts and one robbery)[45]; committing eight intentional crimes, several of which were violent in nature.[46]

In some decisions, significant attention was devoted to the offender's personality: the court considered the convicted child's living and upbringing conditions, evaluating their characterisation from the educational institution. This assessment revealed that the child rarely attended school, was conflicting, unresponsive to feedback, used offensive language, created disturbances, behaved poorly with classmates, and bullied smaller and more defenceless peers, thus demonstrating a contemptuous attitude toward socially accepted norms of behaviour. Furthermore, all three criminal offences were committed while serving a previously imposed penalty of restriction of liberty.[47]

In other cases, in addition to the child's characteristics, the nature and severity of the offences committed are also mentioned, for example, the frequency of criminal and administrative offences, active violent behaviour in mocking a victim in a helpless state.[48]

In summary, the examples from the cases indicate that decisions regarding the suspension of the execution of a sentence most often focus on the child's personality and characteristics—these factors become the key arguments that enable the court to decide on the possibility of not enforcing the imposed custodial sentence. Less frequently, and seemingly as an additional argument, the severity of the offence or the number of offences committed is mentioned. Such reasoning by the courts aligns with the provisions of CC regarding the purpose of the features of children's criminal liability and the peculiarities of imposing penalties on them, which place significant emphasis on the personality of a child who has committed a criminal act.

The latest amendments to CC introduced the possibility of suspending the execution of arrest sentences and applying a partial suspension of the execution of a sentence. This partial suspension may be applied after the child has served a portion of the sentence, ranging from half to one year, in cases where the child has committed a more serious offence and received a stricter sentence that precludes the possibility of full suspension of the execution of a sentence. However, partial suspension is not allowed for grave offences or other serious crimes specified by the legislator, such as severe health impairment. Additionally, a new provision allows for the full or partial suspension of the execution of a sentence for a child if the imposed imprisonment sentence's enforcement would contradict the principle of justice, except in

[44] Supreme Court, January 27, 2015, Decision No. 2K-3-489/2015.

[45] Supreme Court, September 26, 2017, Decision No. 2K-201-222/2017.

[46] Supreme Court, February 14, 2019, Decision No. 2K-48-628/2019.

[47] Supreme Court, May 9, 2017, Decision No. 2K-111-788/2017.

[48] Supreme Court, February 3, 2022, Decision No. 2K-29-976/2022.

cases involving grave crimes.[49] Furthermore, the amendments establish the possibility, when suspending sentence execution, to impose the following penal sanctions in addition to those already mentioned: the obligation to reside separately from the victim and/or prohibition to approach the victim closer than a prescribed distance; participation in programs correcting violent behaviour; and participation in alcoholism and drug addiction prevention, early intervention, resocialisation, or other programs and courses.[50] These provisions expand the opportunities of the courts to suspend the execution of a sentence for a child offender.

4 Release of Children from Criminal Liability

International child protection standards encourage the granting of authority to the institution handling the case to discontinue the proceedings against a child, taking into account the circumstances of the case, while avoiding the stigmatisation associated with the conviction and punishment of a child (e.g., United Nations 1985, Rule 17.4 and commentary, Rule 11 commentary). At the same time, the child justice system should provide ample opportunities to apply social and educational measures (UN CRC Committee 2019, § 19). This is facilitated by provisions in the criminal and criminal procedure laws that allow courts, upon hearing a case, to release a child who has committed a criminal offence from criminal liability by applying coercive educational sanctions. Such a court-applied mechanism, which also ensures the procedural rights of the child, is rare in other countries (Dünkel et al. 2011b, p. 1660), but it contributes to achieving the aforementioned objectives, too.

According to Article 93 of the CC, a child who has committed a misdemeanour, a negligent crime, or a minor or less serious intentional crime for the first time may be released from criminal liability by the court through the application of reformative sanctions where the child:

1. has offered an apology to the victim and has compensated for or eliminated by his work or in monetary terms, entirely or in part, the pecuniary and/or non-pecuniary damage incurred; or
2. is found to be of diminished capacity or
3. pleads guilty and regrets having committed a criminal act, or there are other grounds for believing that the minor will abide by the law and will not commit new criminal acts in the future.

Release from criminal liability means that, despite establishing that the child committed a criminal offence, no conviction is rendered, and the act does not result in a criminal record. In such instances, the case is closed not by a decision but by a

[49] *Register of Legal Acts* (TAR), 2019, 11177, effective from July 1, 2020.

[50] *Register of Legal Acts* (TAR), 2024, 08214 and 18357, effective from February 1, 2025.

judgment, as the case is examined on its merits, and the reasoning of this procedural document confirms that the child committed the criminal offence.[51] The release of children from criminal liability, unlike the suspension of the execution of the sentence, is unconditional. If a child unjustifiably fails to comply with the imposed reformative sanctions, these sanctions may only be replaced with other reformative sanctions, the strictest of which is placement in a special reformative facility.[52] In such cases, the criminal proceedings against the child cannot be reopened, nor can a conviction be rendered or a sentence imposed.

In recent years, approximately one-tenth of cases involving children who committed criminal offences have been resolved by a judgment discontinuing the case and imposing reformative sanctions rather than issuing a conviction. While the trend has decreased in the past three years, this approach still represents a significant portion.[53] The court has the authority to discontinue a criminal case during its preparatory stage for trial if the grounds specified in Article 93 of the CC for releasing the child from criminal liability are met. However, in practice, this option is rarely applied.[54]

Disputes regarding the release of children from criminal liability also arise in judicial practice. The Supreme Court encourages the application of such release. This court has emphasised that any state intervention can have a long-term stigmatising effect, potentially pushing a young person who has committed an offence further to the margins of society in a very short time. To positively influence a young person's behaviour, measures appropriate to their maturity are effective, whereas inappropriate or overly harsh measures can encourage recidivism. Even when it is established that some of the other alternative conditions for the release from criminal liability under Article 93 of the Criminal Code are not met, for example, the child does not plead guilty and does not regret having committed a criminal act, does not seek to compensate the victim for the damage caused by the criminal act, release from criminal liability can still be applied if one of the alternative conditions is met, such as there are other grounds for believing that in the future the minor will abide by the law and will not commit new criminal acts. Such grounds may be established by considering the child's personality, living and upbringing conditions, and behaviour before, during, and after the commission of the offence. Considering these circumstances, the Supreme Court discontinued a criminal case against a child sentenced to arrest by lower courts, instead imposing the reformative sanction of restriction on conduct.[55] This court has similarly resolved other cases.[56]

---

[51] CCP, Articles 303(4), 305(1)(1) and (4); CC, Article 97.

[52] CC, Article 89.

[53] In 2018, 74 cases; in 2023, 24 cases, amounting to 6% (National Court Administration, personal communication, November 26, 2024).

[54] From 2018 to 2023, there was only one such case (National Court Administration, personal communication, November 7, 2024).

[55] Supreme Court, December 22, 2015, Decision No. 2K-599-976/2015.

[56] For example, Supreme Court, June 16, 2015, Decision No. 2K-362-942/2015.

Under Article 93 of CC, a child may be released from criminal liability only if the child committed a criminal offence for the first time. A question regarding this condition has arisen in judicial practice. The Plenary Session of the Criminal Cases Division of the Supreme Court interpreted that, under this article, a person is considered to have committed a criminal offence for the first time if it is recognised that, without having committed any prior offences, the person has committed only one or several offences that are not repetitive in relation to each other and constitute a full concurrence. The fact of committing a previous offence loses its legal significance when the criminal legal relationship arising from it has completely ended. For example, this occurs when the statute of limitations for the offence expired, or the previous conviction expired or was expunged, the individual has been released from criminal liability for that offence (also under the same Article 93), and there is no legal basis to revoke it or for it to become invalid. In such instances, it is concluded that a person who later commits another offence is considered to have committed a criminal offence for the first time.[57]

In legal scholarship, it was noted that when a child is released from criminal liability and reformative sanctions are imposed, implementing these measures may take time, during which the criminal-legal relationship can be considered ongoing. If, during this period, the child commits another criminal offence and can still be released from criminal liability, the situation is contradictory in terms of interpretation. Furthermore, the consequences of such an interpretation have been criticised. A situation resulting from this interpretation is considered contrary to the principle of justice when one child who commits two criminal offences without being convicted for either cannot be released from criminal liability under Article 93. In contrast, another child who commits the same offences but is first released from criminal liability for the first offence can be released again in a subsequent proceeding for the second offence. Therefore, it has been suggested that the legislature amend this article to include a provision clearly defining when a child can be considered to have committed a criminal offence for the first time (Drakšienė 2011, pp. 142–146, 149).

Thus, the Supreme Court's narrow interpretation of the condition in CC that limits the release of children from criminal liability to offences committed for the first time has resulted in inequality among child offenders. In later practice, this court criticised the provisions of Article 93 as overly restrictive, particularly regarding their applicability only to first-time offenders. According to the court, such a system distorts the very essence of the peculiarities of children's criminal liability, as established by international standards—the application of educational measures should be the foundation, not an exception to the rule, and the core of children's criminal liability, not a consequence of release from criminal liability.[58]

CC includes a separate Chapter VI that regulates the release from criminal liability. Article 38 of this chapter provides for the release when the offender and the victim reconcile. This release differs from the child-specific provision in Article

[57] Supreme Court, May 20, 2008, Decision No. 2K-P-85/2008.

[58] Supreme Court, June 16, 2015, Decision No. 2K-362-942/2015.

93 in that it imposes additional conditions, such as the requirement for a confession. It specifies circumstances under which such release may be revoked or invalid, for example, due to committing other criminal offences within 1 year after the release. However, Article 38 does not require the released person to be a first-time offender. This raises the question of whether this general basis for the release from criminal liability can also be applied to children.

Legal scholars expressed differing opinions on this issue. Some authors believe that children can only be released from criminal liability under the special provisions established in Article 93 (Pakštaitis 2009, p. 57). Others partially question this interpretation, arguing that it could prevent the application of other general grounds for the release from criminal liability, enshrined in Chapter VI, such as the release of those who actively assisted in disclosing offences committed by an organised group[59] (Ažubalytė et al. 2011, p. 284). Another perspective suggests that to achieve a more substantial educational effect, children could also be released from criminal liability under the partially stricter conditions in Article 38 (S. Bikelis, in Michailovič et al. 2014, p. 217). These scholarly works highlight the differing practice of courts, including the Supreme Court, on this issue.

Article 40, in the same Chapter VI of CC, also establishes a general ground for the release from criminal liability under suretyship with or without bail. Such release may also be revoked or become invalid if the conditions established by law are not met. In a recent ruling, the Supreme Court clarified that, when considering the release of children from criminal liability, the application of Article 93 must first be assessed. However, acknowledging that the lower court had failed to apply the criminal law correctly, the Supreme Court upheld the child's release from criminal liability under the suretyship, reasoning that the principle of justice had still been upheld.[60] Such contradictory practice also fails to provide a clear answer as to whether a non-first-time offender child could be eventually released from criminal liability under the provisions of Article 38. This demonstrates the importance of clearly delineating, within the Criminal Code itself, the application of provisions establishing the peculiarities of children's criminal liability and the application of other provisions of the Criminal Code.

Based on the favourable results of surveys conducted among judges, prosecutors, and scholars, legal scholarship has already proposed removing the condition in Article 93 that limits release from criminal liability to children who have committed a criminal offence for the first time (Švedas et al. 2017, pp. 212–213). The removal of this condition would ensure equality before the law for children who have committed multiple offences and further implement the general principle that children should be subject to more lenient criminal liability. This principle aligns with another proposal in legal scholarship to provide courts with the discretion to release a child who has committed a serious crime from criminal liability (Levon and Švedas 2022, p. 174). However, additional conditions should apply to such release.

---

[59] CC, Article 39^1.

[60] Supreme Court, March 5, 2024, Decision No. 2K-22-648/2024.

For example, in Germany, there are no restrictions on the severity of the crime when discontinuing proceedings against a child, but the termination occurs only if specific conditions are met, such as reparation of damages for the victim (Dünkel and Heinz 2017, p. 319). International standards similarly encourage the application of discontinuation, even for more serious offences, under certain conditions, such as when the child has committed a first offence or acted under peer pressure (United Nations 1985, Rule 11.4 commentary).

Under CC, at least one reformative sanction must be imposed when children are released from criminal liability.[61] In such cases, penal sanctions may not necessarily be imposed for adults.[62] This distinction can be justified by the peculiarities of children's criminal liability, which focuses on educational influence. To achieve this objective, it may suffice to impose the most lenient reformative sanction—a warning.[63]

The latest amendments provide for the possibility of imposing a penal sanction when releasing children from criminal liability.[64] The applicable penal sanctions are the same as those available when suspending the execution of a sentence.

5 Application of Diversion to Children

Preserving public safety is a legitimate aim of the justice system, including the child justice system. However, the experience of criminal justice interventions can harm children and negatively affect their personal development (e.g., UN CRC Committee 2019, §§ 2 and 3). UN CRC establishes the obligation of states to seek to establish, whenever appropriate and desirable, such procedures that children alleged as, accused of, or recognised as having infringed the penal law do not have to resort to judicial proceedings, provided that their human rights and legal safeguards are fully respected (UN CRC, Article 40(3)(b)). This is referred to as diversion, whereby children are referred away from the judicial system at any time, prior to or during relevant proceedings. Diversion typically involves participation in programs or activities, such as community service, mediation, or compensating victims, after which the child's case is considered fully resolved without being classified as a conviction. The application of diversion avoids the stigmatisation of children associated with criminal proceedings and criminal records of conviction, prioritises education instead of punishment, ensures the principle of proportionality in interventions, and takes into account that children's offences are typically episodic, of petty nature, and a passing phenomenon linked closely to age. Diversion grants children a social credit of trust, increasing the likelihood that they will adhere to social norms in the

[61] CC, Article 93(2).

[62] CC, Article 67(2).

[63] CC, Article 83.

[64] *Register of Legal Acts* (TAR), 2024, 08214 and 18357, effective from February 1, 2025.

future while also reducing the burden on courts. Diversion is applied to children in many countries worldwide, including European states, where opportunities for its application are being expanded (UN CRC Committee 2019, §§ 8, 13(a), 15, 18; Dünkel et al. 2011b, p. 1653; Dünkel 2022, pp. 33–34).

The application of diversion to children has long been encouraged in recommendations by the United Nations and the Council of Europe (e.g., United Nations 1985, Rule 14; 1990, Rule 5; United Nations Economic and Social Council 1997, Rule 15; Council of Europe 1987, Section II; 2003, Rule 7; 2008, Rule 12; 2010, Guidelines 24–26).

In its latest concluding observations on Lithuania's report regarding the implementation of UN CRC, the UN CRC Committee recommended that Lithuania promote non-judicial measures, such as diversion, for children suspected or accused of crimes to ensure the compliance of Lithuania's child justice system with the Convention and related standards in the light of the Committee's General Comment No. 24 (2019) on children's rights in the child justice system (UN CRC Committee 2024, § 45(a)).

In a broad sense, the discontinuing of criminal proceedings in court can also be considered a form of diversion (e.g., Dünkel and Heinz 2017, pp. 319–320). The previous section discussed this possibility and its potential expansion in Lithuania. The current section focuses on the application of diversion during the pre-trial investigation phase, where its benefits are most significant.

Under Lithuanian criminal procedure law, a pre-trial investigation may also be discontinued when the grounds for the release from criminal liability provided in Article 93 of CC are met.[65] As noted, this article governs the release of children from criminal liability, with the mandatory imposition of reformative sanctions prescribed by CC in such cases. These sanctions are also imposed when discontinuing a pre-trial investigation under this article (Goda 2003, p. 569).[66] Thus, diversion for suspected children is established and applied at the pre-trial investigation stage. Legal scholars in Lithuania advocate for the application of diversion as frequently as possible (e.g., Ažubalytė et al. 2011, p. 282).

International standards recommend that diversion be applied as early as possible after a child's contact with the justice system and at various process stages (UN CRC Committee 2019, § 16). In Lithuania, diversion at the pre-trial investigation stage is applied by a decision of the pre-trial investigation judge, who approves the prosecutor's decision to discontinue the pre-trial investigation.[67]

The primary pre-trial investigation authority, typically the police, who is usually the initial point of contact for a child suspect, does not have the authority to

[65] CCP, Article 212(8).

[66] For example: Klaipėda Regional Court, January 17, 2008, Decision No. 1S-16-417/2008; Kaunas Regional Court, March 9, 2015, Decision No. 1S-382-319/2015; Šiauliai Regional Court, July 23, 2015, Decision No. 1S-469-116/2015; Panevėžys Regional Court, December 7, 2015, Decision No. 1S-577-531/2015; Vilnius City District Court, June 16, 2017, Decision No. 1.1-406512-988/2017.

[67] CCP, Article 214(2).

discontinue a pre-trial investigation, including through the application of diversion. This limitation can primarily be linked to the provision in the Constitution that stipulates that the prosecutor organises and directs pre-trial investigations and upholds charges on behalf of the State in criminal cases.[68] Similarly, in some other countries, such as Germany, the police do not have the authority to discontinue pre-trial investigations via diversion, a practice stemming from historical reasons and past abuses. Only prosecutors or judges in Germany can perform this function (Dünkel and Heinz 2017, p. 319).

A comparative study highlighted that in Lithuania, along with Italy and Poland, unlike in many other European countries, prosecutors cannot independently apply diversion; a judge's decision is required. In Italy, this limitation is explained by the constitutional provision mandating that prosecutors ensure the principle of equality before the law by pursuing criminal prosecution, leaving no discretionary power for prosecutors to withhold prosecution (Gensing 2011, pp. 1621–1623). Similarly, the Lithuanian Constitution, like the Italian Constitution, establishes the principle of prosecutorial independence. This principle also applies to the Prosecutor General, who cannot be removed from office solely on the grounds of political mistrust.[69] From a comparative perspective, this can explain why, under the Lithuanian Constitution, prosecutors also lack discretion in deciding whether or not to pursue criminal prosecution (Girdauskas 2014a, b). Consequently, Article 93 of CC stipulates that the court, not the prosecutor, may release a child offender from criminal liability. CCP, linking the termination of pre-trial investigations with this specific article of CC, requires a judge to approve the prosecutor's decision to apply diversion. In this respect, it can be argued that the judge ensures the principle of equality for children, enshrined in Article 2 of the UN CRC, and protects against potential prosecutorial abuse. Such regulation is also consistent with international standards, which indirectly suggest that decisions on the application of diversion under conditions established by law can be made by the police, prosecutors, or other authorities, including courts as an example (UN CRC Committee 2019, § 18(c); UN, 1985, Rule 11.2 and commentary).

The question of ensuring the presumption of innocence in the application of diversion is a more complex issue. International standards indicate that diversion may only be applied when there is convincing evidence that the child committed the alleged offence and freely and voluntarily admits responsibility (UN CRC Committee 2019, § 18(a)). Therefore, these circumstances must be established in the decision to apply diversion. However, the UN CRC conditions the application of diversion to protection of human rights entirely. One such right is the child's right to be presumed innocent until proven guilty according to the law (UN CRC, Art. 40(2)(b)(i), (3)(b)). In interpreting this Convention, attention has been drawn to the greater risk of children wrongfully incriminating themselves due to their age and developmental stage (UN CRC Committee 2019, § 59). This raises the question of

[68] Constitution, Article 118(1).

[69] Constitution, Articles 75, 84(11) and 118(3) and (5).

whether procedural documents applying diversion may and should state that the child committed an offence. In Lithuanian judicial practice, there are cases where court decisions applying diversion in the pre-trial stage explicitly identify a child as having committed a criminal act.[70]

The presumption of innocence is also enshrined in Article 6(2) of the European Convention on Human Rights (Council of Europe 1950/2021). In interpreting this provision, the European Court of Human Rights (ECHR) has clarified that the presumption of innocence will be violated if, without the accused having previously been proven guilty according to law and, notably, without his having had the opportunity of exercising his rights of defence, a judicial decision concerning him reflects an opinion that he is guilty. This may be so even in the absence of any formal finding; it suffices that there is some reasoning suggesting that the court regards the accused as guilty. The decision of the court to discontinue criminal proceedings may include statements that the accused committed the offence if such decision is rendered after examining the charge on the merits, questions of fact and law, granting the opportunities of exercising rights of defence. In other instances, in the decision to discontinue criminal proceedings, only suspicion regarding the accused's guilt may be expressed (Girdauskas 2020, p. 35).[71]

It is significant that these provisions also apply in cases where criminal proceedings are discontinued, for instance, due to the statute of limitations, during pre-trial investigations.[72] Diversion may bear similarities to a case where, following negotiations, the accused admits the charges, thereby waiving the right to a fair trial, which includes the presumption of innocence, and the requirements arising from this presumption are not applicable. However, a significant distinction can be observed. ECHR linked the waiver of the right to a fair trial to the resolution of the question of guilt through negotiation.[73] However, it can be argued that when diversion is applied during the pre-trial investigation stage, the question of the individual's guilt is not addressed (Dölling 1989, as cited in Voss 1995, p. 354), and since the criminal proceedings are discontinued, the presumption of innocence and the requirements arising from it remain valid. This understanding is applied, for instance, in Austria (Mitgutsch 2006, pp. 79, 82; Schwaighofer 2024, p. 401). The Council of Europe recommendations emphasise that elements of due process, such as the presumption of innocence, should be guaranteed for children just as they are for adults and should not be minimised or denied under the pretext of serving the child's best interests. This applies to all judicial and non-judicial proceedings (Council of Europe 2010, Guideline E.2).

---

[70] E. g., Panevėžys Regional Court, January 13, 2009, Decision No. 1S-86-2009; Kaunas Regional Court, March 9, 2015, Decision No. 1S-382-319/2015.

[71] For example: ECHR, *Allen v. United Kingdom* [GC], no. 25424/09, §§ 120–122, 5 July 2013; *Constantin Florea v. Romania*, no. 21534/05, 19 June 2012; *G.I.E.M. S.R.L. and others v. Italy* [GC], nos. 1828/06 and 2 others, §§ 315–318, 28 June 2018.

[72] E. g., ECHR, *Farzaliyev v. Azerbaijan*, no. 29620/07, § 61, 28 May 2020.

[73] *Natsvlishvili and Togonidze v. Georgia*, no. 9043/05, § 91, 29 April 2014.

The violation of the presumption of innocence in the application of diversion may also be linked to the specific features of the presumption of innocence established in national law and the nature of the measures applied when discontinuing criminal proceedings. The Constitution of Lithuania stipulates that a person is presumed innocent until proven guilty according to the procedure established by law and declared guilty by an effective court judgment.[74] Thus, it can be argued that in the absence of a court judgment rendered after examination of the charge on the merits, a person cannot be identified as guilty of committing a crime, for instance, in another form of decision of a first-instance court. Since diversion in the pre-trial investigation stage is applied not through the judgment but other court decisions, this provides grounds to argue that statements in the prosecutor's decision to discontinue the pre-trial investigation and the approving court decision that declares the child committed a crime violate the constitutional presumption of innocence.

Moreover, according to the Constitution, penalties may only be imposed based on law, and justice in the Republic of Lithuania is administered solely by the courts.[75] Therefore, the Constitutional Court has concluded that a person may be sentenced only by an effective court judgment.[76] The discussed reformative sanctions, especially penal ones, given that they are established in CC and considering their nature, can be recognised as penalties in the constitutional term. Consequently, the imposition of such sanctions without an examination of the case on the merits by judgment, but rather by discontinuing a pre-trial investigation through a court decision approving a prosecutor's decision, may be deemed contrary to the aforementioned constitutional provisions. The principle of the presumption of innocence in the application of diversion to children would be better ensured by regulations under which the measures imposed in such cases are educational in nature, established in CCP or a special child justice law, and are not characterised as criminal by their nature or by legislative designation. Similar regulatory examples can be found in countries such as Germany.[77]

According to international standards, when applying diversion, the child must freely and voluntarily consent to the diversion and the measures being applied based on adequate and specific information about the nature, content, and duration of the measures, as well as an understanding of the consequences of failure to cooperate or complete the measures (Council of Europe 1987, Rule 3; UN CRC Committee 2019, § 18(b)). These matters are not regulated in CCP. It is only stated that the pre-trial investigation is discontinued under Article 93 of CC by the decision of the pre-trial investigation judge of the district court that approves the relevant decision of

[74] Constitution, Article 31(1).

[75] Constitution, Articles 31(4) and 109(1).

[76] Constitutional Court, March 24, 2003, Ruling. *Official Gazette*, 2003, No. 29-1196. See also on the similarity of a penal sanction with a penalty according to the Court, February 6, 2025, Ruling. *Register of Legal Acts* (TAR). 2025, 1892.

[77] Youth Court Act (JGG), Sections 10 and 45; German Code of Criminal Procedure (StPO), Section 153a. See references in the available translations section.

the prosecutor.[78] One of the drafters of this Code, the current President of the Constitutional Court of Lithuania Gintaras Goda, commented that when discontinuing a pre-trial investigation regarding a child under Article 93 of CC, the prosecutor's decision must include a proposal for the reformative sanction to be imposed. When deciding on the approval of the prosecutor's decision, the pre-trial investigation judge must hold a hearing during which the participants should be heard regarding this sanction (Goda 2003, p. 214). However, judicial practice regarding the holding of hearings varies. Some courts require[79] and conduct such hearings,[80] while others do not hold hearings and make decisions through a written procedure.[81]

The position of suspected children is safeguarded by the fact that a district court's decision concerning the discontinuation of the pre-trial investigation and applied sanctions can be appealed to the regional court.[82] However, to ensure effective protection of the child's rights, proper information regarding the prosecutor's proposed diversion and sanctions should already be guaranteed in the district court's procedure. In light of the aforementioned international standards, criminal procedure law should explicitly include a provision stating that diversion may only be applied with the child's consent.

6 Concluding Remarks

Lithuania has made significant progress in implementing international standards by mitigating children's criminal liability and its application. Its example confirms that such measures are compatible with a substantial decline in child delinquency and align with general European trends. The suspension of the execution of a sentence, release from criminal liability, and the application of diversion may be considered among the effective measures. However, child criminal justice can be improved, for example, by expanding the use of these measures, clearly delineating the application of provisions that establish the peculiarities of children's criminal liability from other provisions of the Criminal Code, more thoroughly regulating the procedures for rendering decisions on the application of diversion and ensuring the presumption of innocence and other child rights.

---

[78] CCP, Articles 19, 212(8), and 214(2).

[79] E. g., Šiauliai Regional Court, December 19, 2007, Decision No. I-43-210/2007.

[80] For example, Pasvalys District Court, October 27, 2015, Court Hearing Record No. 01-1-51604-15.

[81] E. g., Vilnius City District Court, April 30, 2015, Decision No. NP-4295-929/2015.

[82] CCP, Article 214(4).

References

Ažubalytė R, Jurgaitis R, Zajančkauskienė J (2011) Specifinės baudžiamojo proceso rūšys. Mykolo Romerio universitetas, Vilnius.

Dapšys A (1994a) Nepilnamečių nusikalstamumo prevencijos sistemos esmė ir jos kūrimo kryptys. Teisės problemos 3:34–38

Dapšys A (1994b) Lithuania. In: International Catholic Child Bureau (ed) Children and youth in conflict with the law: report of the regional seminar for the Baltic States. International Catholic Child Bureau (ICCB), Geneva, pp 19–22

Dapšys A, Piliavecas A, Sakalauskas G (1998) The system of children's rights and thier protection in Lithuania: general situation, problems, solutions and perspectives. In: Bikauskienė MN (ed) Children's rights in the legislations of the Baltic States. Lithuanian Human Rights Association, Vilnius, pp 55-74

Dapšys A, Misiūnas J, Čaplinskas A (2008) Bausmės individualizavimo teisinės problemos. Teisės institutas, Vilnius

Decker S, Marteache N (eds) (2017) International handbook of juvenile justice, 2nd edn. Springer, Cham. https://doi.org/10.1007/978-3-319-45090-2

Drakšienė A (1998) Nepilnamečių baudžiamoji atsakomybė Lietuvos Respublikos baudžiamojo kodekso projekte. Teisė 32:32–53

Drakšienė A (2005) Vaiko teisių konvencijos nuostatų įgyvendinimas nacionalinėje baudžiamojoje teisėje. Teisė 54:59–69

Drakšienė A (2011) Kai kurie nepilnamečių atleidimo nuo baudžiamosios atsakomybės aspektai. In: Švedas G (ed) Lietuvos Respublikos baudžiamajam kodeksui—10 metų. Vilniaus universiteto Teisės fakultetas; Registrų centras, Vilnius, pp 131–150

Drakšienė A, Drakšas R (2008) Nepilnamečių baudžiamoji atsakomybė: vadovėlis, 2-oji pataisyta ir papildyta laida. Eugrimas, Vilnius

Dünkel F (2015) Juvenile justice and crime policy in Europe. In: Zimring FE, Langer M, Tanenhaus DS (eds) Juvenile justice in global perspective. New York University Press, New York, pp 9–62. https://doi.org/10.18574/nyu/9781479826537.003.0001

Dünkel F (2022) Youth justice: European and international developments and (good) practices. In: Nelken D, Hamilton C (eds) Research handbook of comparative criminal justice. Edward Elgar, Cheltenham, pp 30–48. https://doi.org/10.4337/9781839106385.00011

Dünkel F, Heinz W (2017) Germany. In: Decker S, Marteache N (eds) International handbook of juvenile justice, 2nd edn. Springer, Cham, pp 305–325. https://doi.org/10.1007/978-3-319-45090-2_15

Dünkel F, Grzywa J, Pruin I, Šelih A (2011a) Juvenile justice in Europe—legal aspects, policy trends and perspectives in the light of human rights standards. In: Dünkel F, Grzywa J, Horsfield P, Pruin I (eds) Juvenile justice Systems in Europe: current situation and reform developments, vol 4, 2nd edn. Forum Verlag Godesberg, Mönchengladbach, pp 1839–1898

Dünkel F, Pruin I, Grzywa J (2011b) Sanctions systems and trends in the development of sentencing practices. In: Dünkel F, Grzywa J, Horsfield P, Pruin I (eds) Juvenile justice Systems in Europe: current situation and reform developments, vol 4, 2nd edn. Forum Verlag Godesberg, Mönchengladbach, pp 1649–1716

Gensing A (2011) Jurisdiction and characteristics of juvenile criminal procedure in Europe. In: Dünkel F, Grzywa J, Horsfield P, Pruin I (eds) Juvenile justice Systems in Europe: current situation and reform developments, vol 4, 2nd edn. Forum Verlag Godesberg, Mönchengladbach, pp 1649–1716

Girdauskas M (2014a) Teismo įgaliojimai keisti inkriminuojamos veikos kvalifikavimą: Konstitucijos reinterpretavimo prielaidų paieška. Teisė 90:126–141. https://doi.org/10.15388/Teise.2014.0.2875

Girdauskas M (2014b) Teismo galios keisti inkriminuojamos veikos kvalifikavimą: Konstitucijos reinterpretavimo prielaidos. Teisė 91:154–171. https://doi.org/10.15388/Teise.2014.0.3367

Girdauskas M (2020) Bylos nutraukimas nuosprendžiu ir nekaltumo prezumpcija: probleminiai aspektai tarptautinės ir konstitucinės teisės kontekste. Teisės problemos 1:26–56. Available via https://teise.org/wp-content/uploads/2023/11/Girdauskas_2020_1.pdf. Accessed 7 Dec 2025
Goda G (ed) (2003) Lietuvos Respublikos baudžiamojo proceso kodekso komentaras, I knyga. Teisinės informacijos centras, Vilnius
Jatkevičius A (2003) Nepilnamečių smurtinio nusikalstamumo prevencija. Daktaro disertacija, Vilniaus universitetas
Jurka R, Juzukonis S, Matijaškaitė A, Uselė L (2007) The juvenile justice system in Lithuania. In: Giostra G, Pairè V (eds) European juvenile justice systems, vol 1. Giuffrè Editore, Milano, pp 273–297
Kavoliūnaitė-Ragauskienė E (2022) Developing a child-friendly juvenile justice system in Lithuania. In: Limantė A, Pūraitė-Andrikienė D (eds) Legal protection of vulnerable groups in Lithuania, Latvia, Estonia and Poland. Springer, Cham, pp 225–246. https://doi.org/10.1007/978-3-031-06998-7_10
Levon J, Švedas G (2022) Bausmės vykdymo atidėjimo nepilnamečiams naujovės ir probleminiai aspektai. In: Sudavičius B (ed) Kelyje su Konstitucija: recenzuotų mokslinių straipsnių rinkinys. Vilniaus universiteto leidykla, Vilnius, pp 167–191.
Liefaard T (2020) Juvenile justice. In: Todres J, King S (eds) The Oxford handbook of children's rights law. Oxford University Press, Oxford, pp 282–306. https://doi.org/10.1093/oxfordhb/9780190097608.013.15
Michailovič I (2001) Baudžiamajame įstatyme numatytų nepilnamečių resocializacijos priemonių taikymas. Vilniaus universiteto leidykla, Vilnius
Michailovič I, Bikelis S, Čepas A, Dobrynina M, Simaitis R, Šneideris D, Ūselė L, Venckevičienė J (2014) Atkuriamojo teisingumo perspektyvos Lietuvoje. Lietuvos teisės institutas, Vilnius
Mitgutsch I (2006) A brief survey of the Austrian diversification concept. Jurisprudencija 7:77–85
Pakštaitis L (2007) Nepilnamečių baudžiamosios atsakomybės reglamentavimo bei taikymo problemos. Jurisprudencija 8:13–19
Pakštaitis L (2009) Trends in the practical implementation of criminal responsibility of juveniles according to the criminal law of Lithuania. Socialinių mokslų studijos/Soc Sci Stud 4:49–62
Sakalauskas G (2011) Lithuania. In: Dünkel F, Grzywa J, Horsfield P, Pruin I (eds) Juvenile justice Systems in Europe: current situation and reform developments, vol 2, 2nd edn. Forum Verlag Godesberg, Mönchengladbach, pp 871–909
Sakalauskas G (2013) Nepilnamečių baudžiamosios atsakomybės ypatumų prasmė. Teisės problemos 3:5–55
Sakalauskas G, Jatkevičius A (2000) Nepilnamečių baudžiamoji atsakomybė Lietuvoje: reglamentavimo problemos ir galimi jų sprendimai. Teisės problemos 3–4:7–11
Sakalauskas G, Kalpokas V, Buzaitytė-Kašalynienė J, Švedaitė-Sakalauskė B (2021) Registruotos nepilnamečių delinkvencijos apraiškų ir tendencijų Lietuvoje tarptautinis palyginimas. Kriminologijos studijos 9:173–198. https://doi.org/10.15388/CrimLithuan.2021.9.7
Schwaighofer K (2024) The public prosecutor in Austria. DPCE Online 1:387–405. Available via https://www.dpceonline.it/index.php/dpceonline/article/view/2085
Švedas G (2022) Criminal law in Lithuania. Kluwer Law International, Alphen aan den Rijn
Švedas G, Veršekys P, Levon J, Prapiestis D (2017) Lietuvos Respublikos baudžiamojo kodekso bendrosios dalies vientisumo ir naujovių (su)derinimo iššūkiai. Vilniaus universiteto leidykla, Vilnius
Švedas G, Abramavičius A, Prapiestis J (2020) Lietuvos baudžiamoji teisė: bendroji dalis, 2 knyga. Vilniaus universiteto leidykla, Vilnius
Vileikienė E (2007) Problems in juvenile justice in Lithuania: a sociological analysis. United Nations Development Programme; Nusikalstamumo prevencijos Lietuvoje centras, Vilnius
Voss M (1995) Efficiency interests and the "rule of law" in informal proceedings. In: Albrecht G, Ludwig-Mayerhofer W (eds) Diversion and informal social control. Walter de Gruyter, Berlin, pp 353–367. https://doi.org/10.1515/9783110815757.353

Žiobienė E (2024) Nepilnamečių baudžiamosios atsakomybės aspektai. In: Prapiestis J (ed) Lietuvos baudžiamosios justicijos teisė: patirtis ir ateitis. *Liber amicorum* profesoriui Gintarui Švedui. Vilniaus universiteto leidykla, Vilnius, pp 291–309. https://doi.org/10.15388/LBJT.2024.11

Legal Acts and Recommendations

Council of Europe (1950/2021). European Convention on Human Rights, as amended by Protocols Nos. 11, 14 and 15

Council of Europe (1987). Recommendation No. R (87) 20 of the Committee of Ministers to member states on social reaction to juvenile delinquency

Council of Europe (2003). Recommendation Rec(2003)20 of the Committee of Ministers to member states concerning new ways of dealing with juvenile delinquency and the role of juvenile justice

Council of Europe (2008). Recommendation CM/Rec(2008)11 of the Committee of Ministers to member states on the European Rules for juvenile offenders subject to sanctions or measures

Council of Europe (2010). Guidelines of the Committee of Ministers of the Council of Europe on child-friendly justice

United Nations (1985). United Nations Standard Minimum Rules for the Administration of Juvenile Justice ("The Beijing Rules"), adopted by General Assembly resolution 40/33 of 29 November 1985

United Nations (1989). United Nations Convention on the Rights of the Child, adopted by General Assembly resolution 44/25 of 20 November 1989

United Nations (1990). United Nations Standard Minimum Rules for Non-custodial Measures (The Tokyo Rules), adopted by General Assembly resolution 45/110 of 14 December 1990

United Nations Committee on the Rights of the Child (2019). General comment No. 24 (2019) on children's rights in the child justice system, UN Doc. CRC/C/GC/24

United Nations Committee on the Rights of the Child (2024). Concluding observations on the combined fifth and sixth periodic reports of Lithuania, adopted by the Committee at its ninety-fifth session (15 January–2 February 2024). UN Doc. CCR/C/LTU/CO/5-6

United Nations Economic and Social Council (1997). Guidelines for Action on Children in the Criminal Justice System, recommended by Economic and Social Council resolution 1997/30 of 21 July 1997

Statistics

Information Technology and Communications Department under the Ministry of the Interior of the Republic of Lithuania [ITCD] (2025a) Nusikalstamos veikos, kurias padarė nepilnamečiai. Available via https://www.ird.lt/lt/tvarkomu-valdomu-registru-ir-informaciniu-sistemu-paslaugos-3/nusikalstamu-veiku-zinybinio-registro-nvzr-atviri-duomenys-paslaugos-2/nusikalstamos-veikos-lietuvoje-2006-2024-metais-2/oid.1040. Accessed 7 Dec 2025

ITCD (2025b) Duomenys apie įtariamus (kaltinamus) ir nukentėjusius nepilnamečius Lietuvos Respublikoje (Forma_VSDN). Available via https://www.ird.lt/lt/reports/view_item_datasource?id=11781&datasource=110353. Accessed 7 Dec 2025

ITCD (2025c) Nusikalstamos veikos Lietuvoje 2006-2024 metais. Available via https://www.ird.lt/lt/tvarkomu-valdomu-registru-ir-informaciniu-sistemu-paslaugos-3/nusikalstamu-veiku-zinybinio-registro-nvzr-atviri-duomenys-paslaugos-2/nusikalstamos-veikos-lietuvoje-2006-2024-metais-2. Accessed 7 Dec 2025

ITCD (2025d) Bausmių vykdymo statistika. Available via https://www.ird.lt/lt/tvarkomu-valdomu-registru-ir-informaciniu-sistemu-paslaugos-3/nusikalstamu-veiku-zinybinio-registro-nvzr-atviri-duomenys-paslaugos-2/ataskaitos-3/bausmiu-vykdymo-statistika-2. Accessed 7 Dec 2025
Lithuanian probation service (2025) Metų ataskaitos. Available via https://probacija.lrv.lt/lt/apie-lietuvos-probacijos-tarnyba/statistika/metines-ataskaitos/. Accessed 7 Dec 2025
State Data Agency (2025a) Teismų nuteistų nepilnamečių skaičius. Available via https://osp.stat.gov.lt/lt/statistiniu-rodikliu-analize?hash=af4ee30e-9571-4a7c-a813-f1645b80aed8. Accessed 7 Dec 2025
State Data Agency (2025b) Nepilnamečiai, kuriems paskirtos auklėjimo poveikio priemonės. Available via https://osp.stat.gov.lt/lt/statistiniu-rodikliu-analize?hash=19032429-48ed-45c2-83ed-c671281460aa. Accessed 7 Dec 2025
State Data Agency (2025c) Nuteistų nepilnamečių laisvės atėmimo įstaigose skaičius metų pabaigoje. Available via https://osp.stat.gov.lt/lt/statistiniu-rodikliu-analize?hash=4ee9467a-4b49-4f46-8837-19c086788831. Accessed 7 Dec 2025
State Data Agency (2025d) Nepilnamečiai, kuriems atidėtas bausmės vykdymas. Available via https://osp.stat.gov.lt/lt/statistiniu-rodikliu-analize?hash=179f390a-94f5-413a-accb-6426af5ed87b. Accessed 7 Dec 2025

Available Translations of References

Constitution of the Republic of Lithuania. Consolidated version in force. Available via https://e-seimas.lrs.lt/portal/legalAct/lt/TAD/079fcad0cf8711ecb69ea7b9ba9d787b?jfwid=b454lz9dz. Accessed 7 Dec 2025
German Code of Criminal Procedure (StPO). The translation includes the amendment(s) to the Act by Article 2 of the Act of 17 July 2025. Available via https://www.gesetze-im-internet.de/englisch_stpo/englisch_stpo.pdf. Accessed 7 Dec 2025
German Youth Court Act (JGG). The translation includes the amendment(s) to the Act by Article 21 of the Act of 25 June 2021. Available via https://www.gesetze-im-internet.de/englisch_jgg/englisch_jgg.pdf. Accessed 7 Dec 2025
Lithuanian Criminal Code. Consolidated version valid until 30 September 2018. Available via https://e-seimas.lrs.lt/portal/legalAct/lt/TAD/28b18041843311e89188e16a6495e98c?jfwid=9pfnh2ul8. Accessed 7 Dec 2025

Mindaugas Girdauskas holds a Master's Degree in Law from Vilnius University, Lithuania. In 1999 he joined the Law Institute (currently the part of the Lithuanian Centre for Social Sciences), where he worked in the Problems of Prevention of Children and Youth Delinquency Sector. In 2001, he became a senior advisor in the Legal Department of the Seimas (the Parliament). There, he conducted examinations of draft criminal laws and other legal acts and represented the Parliament at the Constitutional Court. Since 2007, he has been working at the Supreme Court of Lithuania, currently as the chief advisor to the Criminal Division. In 2010, Mr. Girdauskas again joined the Law Institute as a researcher in the Criminal Justice Research Department. His recent research focuses on the presumption of innocence, allocation of criminal costs, and the powers of the criminal court to reclassify the incriminated criminal act. He has authored over 20 scientific journal articles and book chapters. Mr. Girdauskas has been a member of the Criminal Procedure Code Review Committee, appointed by the Minister of Justice, since 2017, and a member of the Prosecutor Performance Evaluation Commission, appointed by the Prosecutor General upon the proposal of the Prime Minister, since 2021.

Dr Darius Pranka holds a doctoral degree in criminal law from Mykolas Romeris University, Lithuania. In 2017, he joined the Law Institute of the Lithuanian Centre for Social Sciences as a research fellow. He served as a lecturer at Mykolas Romeris University from 2007 to 2012 and has been a lecturer at the University of Applied Social Sciences since 2012. From 2007 to 2015, he worked in the prosecutor's office, and since 2015, he has been a judge, first at Vilnius City District Court until 2019, and currently at Vilnius Regional Court, specialising in criminal cases. His main research interests lie in criminal law and criminal procedural law. Dr. Pranka is the author of over 10 scientific journal articles and book chapters, most of which he authored independently.

Ensuring and Implementing Individual Assessments of Adolescents in Criminal Proceedings in Lithuania and Croatia

Rūta Vaičiūnienė and Anja Mirosavljević

Abstract Developing a criminal justice model that includes a comprehensive assessment of juveniles in conflict with the law is crucial to making appropriate, swift and efficient decisions at the different levels of the criminal proceedings. Several legal instruments have focused on ensuring rights in juvenile criminal proceedings, but Directive 2016/800 is the most recent and important document at the European level. The Directive is an unprecedented, legally binding instrument focusing exclusively on suspected and accused minors. It addresses various legal issues and objectives related to the specific needs of minors by providing for an individualised assessment. On the one hand, an individual assessment can be considered a prerequisite for evidence-based decision-making. On the other hand, it provides an opportunity to listen to, advocate for and engage with the young person, take into account their particular circumstances and create a favourable environment for subsequent behavioural improvement. By setting out general principles, Directive 2016/800 gives Member States considerable flexibility in the implementation and application of individual assessment of children within their respective national systems. The aim of this chapter is to analyse the challenges and current practices of individual assessment in two EU Member States, Croatia and Lithuania. Best practices from these two countries are presented in this chapter to illustrate the need for a child-first, multidimensional, interdisciplinary and multi-professional approach in the investigation of children in conflict with the law.

R. Vaičiūnienė (✉)
Law Institute, Lithuanian Centre for Social Sciences, Vilnius, Lithuania
e-mail: ruta.vaiciuniene@teise.org

A. Mirosavljević
Faculty of Education and Rehabilitation Sciences, University of Zagreb, Zagreb, Croatia

A. Limantė, R. Vaičiūnienė (eds.), *Children's Rights in Central and Eastern Europe*, European Union and its Neighbours in a Globalized World 29,
https://doi.org/10.1007/978-3-032-07092-0_12

1 Introduction

Despite global legislative frameworks advocating or mandating criteria for the timely individual assessment of children in conflict with the law, debates continue regarding the implementation of these assessments, the tools to be employed, and their objectives. Directive 2016/800, the first legally binding document focused on the rights and assessments of accused and suspected children in criminal proceedings, still grants significant discretion to Member States in determining how to comply with and fulfil its requirements. This chapter seeks to compare two EU countries, Lithuania and Croatia, that have adopted particular approaches to meeting the requirements established in Directive 2016/800 and have developed their own strategies for ensuring child-friendly individual assessment in response to the needs and vulnerabilities of children.

Furthermore, youth justice has evolved significantly in recent decades due to both rapid developments in international legal instruments and paradigmatic shifts. While the current legal framework and its application in criminal proceedings unequivocally advocate for a child-friendly approach to those in conflict with the law, acknowledging their immaturity, vulnerability, and needs, the consistent implementation of child-friendly and, indeed, child-first justice remains an unresolved issue. Risk-based assessments, which frame children primarily as „risky", continue to dominate in many countries (Case et al. 2024). In this context, individual assessments can be viewed as tools for promoting children's empowerment and greater inclusion of their voices in justice decisions.

In this chapter, the authors not only analyse the EU children's rights in the criminal proceeding framework by comparing these two countries but also ruminate on the ongoing debates surrounding risk-based assessments and other assessment strategies. Additionally, they examine the challenges and highlight examples of good practices in implementing individual assessments for children in conflict with the law.

2 Assessment Goals, Criteria, and Instruments: Legal Obligations and Theoretical Considerations

2.1 Shaping the International Legal Framework for Assessing Children in Conflict with the Law

Several international agreements and standards should be referenced while unpacking fundamental concepts in youth justice, such as immaturity, vulnerability, and special needs, which are critical in making decisions and assessing the individual situation of each child in minors' criminal proceedings. The United Nations Convention on the Rights of the Child, the first legally binding instrument recognising children as full-fledged rights holders and emphasising that the child's best interests are fundamental (UN 1989), represents a critical advancement in developing international principles on children's rights. Subsequent UN recommendations articulated in comments of the Committee on the Rights of the Child more precisely guide the procedural safeguards of children in conflict with the law (See UN Committee on the Rights of the Child 2009, 2019). General Comment No. 24 (2019) offers comprehensive guidance on selecting diversionary or alternative measures, introducing the concept of evidence-based intervention programs. It underscores that these programs and interventions must be preceded by a thorough and interdisciplinary assessment of the child's needs. At the same time, the Comment emphasises the capabilities of professionals dealing with children involved in criminal justice procedures, as well as the requirement to use multidisciplinary techniques and complete knowledge, including acknowledgement of the special needs of the most marginalised children (UN Committee on the Rights of the Child 2019).

In Europe, many achievements in establishing the framework for safeguarding minors' rights are worth noting. At a broader European level, the Guidelines on Child-Friendly Justice, established by the Committee of Ministers of the Council of Europe, concentrate exclusively on children's rights and protection, taking into account not only the nature and severity of the offense but also the child's age, level of culpability, and individual needs. The guidelines underscore the necessity of a multidisciplinary approach since it is essential to evaluate and comprehend the children's needs, behaviour, and development (Committee of Ministers of the Council of Europe 2011). Although not legally binding, they likely offer one of the most comprehensive frameworks for defining and substantiating child-friendly justice within national systems.

Moving to the EU level, the first binding document that exclusively addresses a single group of individuals, suspected and accused minors, is Directive 2016/800. It enshrines key rights for suspected and accused minors, which include the right to be informed, the right to adequate legal assistance and legal aid, the right to an individual assessment and medical examination, the right to privacy, the right to be accompanied by a holder of parental responsibility, and the right to be physically present at trial. By safeguarding the aforementioned rights, the Directive aims to ensure that the child is able to understand and follow criminal proceedings, as well as to exercise his/her right to a fair trial. It also seeks to prevent reoffending and to promote the child's social reintegration (Directive (EU) 2016, p. 1). Accordingly, the Directive sets multiple ambitious goals: to ensure procedural safeguards for children in conflict with the law and promote individualised measures best suited to preventing reoffending and fostering social inclusion. Achieving these objectives underscores the necessity of recognising children's unique needs and vulnerabilities across various domains while also stipulating the requirement for a detailed and comprehensive assessment of minors. Article 7 of the Directive states: *"the individual assessment shall, in particular, take into account the child's personality and maturity, the child's economic, social and family background, and any specific vulnerabilities that the child may have. Member States shall ensure that the specific needs of children concerning protection, education, training and social integration are taken into account"*. It further specifies *that "the individual assessment shall be carried out at the earliest appropriate stage of the proceedings, shall be carried out with the close involvement of the child, as well as shall be carried out by qualified personnel, following, as far as possible, a multidisciplinary approach and involving, where appropriate, the holder of parental responsibility, or another appropriate adult"* (Directive (EU) 2016, pp. 13–14).

By establishing requirements for individual assessment, the Directive seeks to achieve a multifaceted objective. The individual assessment functions as a hybrid instrument. Firstly, it serves as a tool for identifying the child's specific needs and ensuring that those needs are appropriately addressed. In this context, psychosocial tools and the involvement of qualified, primarily non-legal, professionals play a crucial role. Secondly, by summarising the assessment data and presenting it as a legal document, it is intended to inform legal decisions. These decisions may occur at two distinct stages: during the criminal proceedings (procedural decisions) and when determining the child's sentence. As a result, the assessment is expected to serve both procedural and sanction-related decision-making purposes (Vaičiūnienė et al. 2020). This dual application may give rise to confusion among Member States, as perceived ambiguities could lead not only to inconsistent and inadequate implementation of their obligations, but also to a tendency to prioritise only one of the objectives, namely, focusing on decisions related to sentencing (De Vocht et al. 2014, p. 501; Rap and Zlotnik 2018, p. 115).

The Directive mandates a thorough evaluation of minors' mental states and related social constructions, although it does not delineate the assessment technique or identify the instruments to be employed in this evaluation. Notwithstanding the Directive's formulation of exceedingly lofty objectives, national jurisdictions retain considerable discretion in interpreting the methods and specifics of achieving these goals. Furthermore, as noted in Article 7, Member States may derogate from the obligation to carry out an individual assessment where such a derogation is warranted in the circumstances of the case, provided that it is compatible with the child's best interests. Hence, although the multiple and ambitious goals of the Directive are very welcome, there is still too much room for different interpretations of these goals, procedures, and assessment instruments.

2.2 The Evolving Theoretical Approaches and Practice of Child Assessment in Criminal Proceedings

Initially, assessments in criminal proceedings were developed in conjunction with the concepts of evidence-based practice and more informed legal decisions. Assessments designed to aid legal judgments are termed forensic assessments or risk assessments and are integral to informed, evidence-based legal decision-making in modern judicial systems. Originally focused on competency to stand trial, it has expanded to cover sentence, treatment, and recidivism. Contemporary forensic assessments inform decisions on diversion, detention, court referrals, sentencing, and post-sentence outcomes while assessing mental health, behaviour, and potential for rehabilitation and integration (Heilbrun 2014). Furthermore, forensic psychology now advocates for a more therapeutic use of the law to improve justice system outcomes (Jackson and Roesch 2016).

Assessments may vary depending on the legal inquiries they are intended to address, and the objective of the assessment pertains to professionals with specific knowledge and skills, as well as assessment procedures and methodologies (Heilbrun 2014). It occurs at various stages from the initial legal encounter to post-sentencing and can be categorised by task, legal phase, or decision point. Grisso outlines key decision points that begin with intake, ensuring procedural safeguards and pre-adjudication detention and extend through disposition, sentencing decisions, correctional placement, and community re-entry. Each stage involves specific legal and forensic questions. For instance, during pre-trial detention, decisions may focus on the risk of flight or harm, while at the disposition stage, courts assess the causes of delinquent behaviour and the best interventions to reduce reoffending (Grisso 2019). The same stages can also be classified based on their temporal focus: retrospective (e.g., criminal responsibility), present-focused (e.g., competence to stand trial), and predictive (e.g., risk of reoffending or suitability for release). These categories highlight the need for assessors to understand legal procedures, select appropriate tools, and link assessment results to the legal context. The specific stage and legal question being addressed determine the selection of assessment tools and guide the choice of the most appropriate model for data collection, interpretation, and communication, with input from professionals skilled in instrument selection and outcome formulation.

However, general knowledge alone is insufficient to ensure a high-quality assessment, especially regarding its validity and reliability. An effective assessment process depends on the use of proven, valid, and reliable instruments and procedures (Hoge 2012). The evaluation techniques in criminal justice have developed over the past 50 years, demonstrating increasing endeavours to enhance the accuracy, fairness, and individualisation of criminal behaviour prediction and management. First-generation instruments depended on unstructured clinical judgment, wherein experts evaluated dangerousness and intervention requirements purely based on their experience. Although adaptable, this approach frequently exhibited bias and lacked reliability (Van Voorhis and Salisbury 2014). The second generation introduced actuarial tools, which were statistically motivated and utilised empirical data to determine the probability of reoffending. These instruments provided a higher degree of consistency, particularly in controlled environments; however, they encountered difficulties with individualisation and frequently depended on static, unchanging risk factors (Edens et al. 2016). The third generation implemented the Structured Specialist Solution, integrating statistical methodologies with clinical expertise. It encompasses both static and dynamic risk variables, enabling specialists to evaluate individual case particulars, such as trauma history or suicide intent, prior to rendering a final decision (Hart and Logan 2011). In the present day, fourth-generation tools have advanced by incorporating case management strategies and emphasising factors that are amenable to change (Bonta and Andrews 2023). The most effective approach is to employ statistical or Structured Specialist Solution-based tools that are accompanied by professional training and clear guidelines to guarantee individualised and reliable assessments (Douglas and Otto 2021).

As already mentioned, the selection of a specific assessment instrument depends on the stage of criminal proceedings and the legal question being addressed. In the initial stage of criminal proceedings, the assessment may focus on the capacity to understand and participate in the proceedings, including the competence to stand trial. During this stage, professionals consider questions such as whether a person understands the charges, can follow the trial and its procedures, and is able to communicate effectively with their legal representative. In such cases, mental health professionals, such as psychologists or psychiatrists, typically play the primary role. These professionals also conduct assessments when it is necessary to evaluate maturity, learning disabilities, or other mental health-related issues (Vincent et al. 2012).

During the sentencing, intervention planning, and re-entry phase, risk-based assessments are most commonly used across many countries. These assessments are conducted not only by mental health professionals but also by various other practitioners, including probation officials and social workers. One of the most influential frameworks for risk-based assessments is the Risk-Need-Responsivity (RNR) model, which guides the assessment and treatment of individuals at risk of reoffending. Canadian scholars Andrews and Bonta made a significant contribution to this paradigm by systematically identifying criminogenic risk factors and proposing structured methodologies to address them. Three fundamental principles serve as the foundation of the RNR model. The initial risk principle entails the prediction of an individual's likelihood of reoffending and the alignment of intervention intensity with the assessed level of risk. Risk factors are generally classified as either individual (e.g., impulsivity, attention-deficit) or environmental (e.g., dysfunctional family dynamics, delinquent peer associations). Additionally, these factors are categorised as static risk factors, which are historical and unalterable characteristics, such as age at first offence or prior criminal history, and dynamic risk factors, which are subject to change and can be influenced through targeted interventions, such as substance abuse or poor academic performance. The second principle includes needs and highlights the importance of addressing criminogenic needs, i.e., the dynamic factors that are causally related to criminal behaviour. Interventions should prioritise these needs in order to effectively reduce future reoffending. The third principle pertains to responsiveness and emphasises the importance of delivering interventions in a manner that is tailored to the individual's cognitive abilities, learning style, motivation, and other personal characteristics. Recently, there has been an increasing emphasis on protective factors, which are attributes and conditions that reduce the probability of reoffending, in addition to risk and need factors. These may include strong family support, academic engagement, or positive peer relationships. Consequently, protective factors should be assessed comprehensively and integrated into intervention planning as potential assets to support behavioural change. The Risk-Need-Responsivity (RNR) model has been refined over the years since its original formulation, with a focus on protective factors and adaptations of RNR for specific populations (Bonta and Andrews 2023). It continues to be the most influential framework for customising interventions based on individual risk profiles.

Although most general theoretical and conceptual principles of forensic and risk assessment are relevant to the evaluation of children in conflict with the law, adolescent assessment instruments should include developmentally appropriate factors. There is an increasing acknowledgement that it is crucial to evaluate a minor's maturity in legal decision-making. However, a unified definition of maturity remains absent in both psychology and law. In practice, maturity is often evaluated based on a minor's cognitive and emotional capacities and their relevance to the specific legal issue. This is especially important when assessing trial competence, transfers to adult court, or mental state at the time of the offence. Grisso and Kavanaugh observe that in evaluating adolescents, it is important to consider not only individual maturity but also contextual, environmental, and social factors, as young people have a limited ability to avoid harmful circumstances.

The same child-centred approach should be applied to risk-based assessments of minors. While many adult risk factors are applicable in risk assessments, their relevance and manifestation often differ in adolescents. For instance, school functioning is more significant than employment, and family resources are more critical than personal ones. Given the rapid developmental changes that occur during adolescence, assessments should concentrate on dynamic, changeable factors and incorporate regular short-term reassessments. These dynamic factors, such as antisocial attitudes, interpersonal influence, and school performance, are more precise predictors of reoffending than static ones. Additionally, strengths like positive adult relationships and school motivation are essential for both risk assessment and management, alongside risk factors (De Beuf et al. 2023). Furthermore, risk-based approaches are increasingly criticised, particularly in the assessment of youth. It is facing growing criticism for its emphasis on quantified risk assessments, scaled interventions, and placing responsibility on children for their offences. This deficit-focused, adult-centric model often excludes the child's perspective, using rigid rating scales and yes/no assessments based solely on practitioners' views. As a result, young people may feel disconnected from the process, silencing their voices, limiting their engagement and reducing the effectiveness of interventions (Case and Heines 2020). Recent efforts, responding to risk-focused models that labelled children as "risky" rather than "at risk," aim to empower children to express their needs and advocate for greater inclusion of their voices in justice decisions. (Case et al. 2024) Hence, to achieve high-quality evaluations in child-friendly justice contexts, it is imperative to implement developmentally appropriate assessments and child-friendly, collaborative communication, recognising children as active participants.

3 The Puzzle of Individual Assessments of Children in Conflict with the Law in Lithuania

The provision for individual assessment (IA) of accused and suspected children in Lithuania is articulated in two distinct phases of criminal proceedings, each with its respective legal objectives. First, it is crucial to undertake IA during the initial stage of criminal proceedings to ensure the child's right to a fair trial and to the protection of their procedural safeguards. The second IA is designed to inform decisions regarding sentencing and post-sentencing, with the objective of tailoring appropriate interventions. Each approach requires a comprehensive explanation as they serve distinct legal and rehabilitation objectives.

3.1 Legal Framework and the Process for Conducting IA in Lithuania: IA During the Criminal Proceedings

Although the requirement to conduct a comprehensive assessment post-sentencing has already been implemented in Lithuania, the requirement to conduct an assessment in the first stage of criminal proceedings in accordance with Directive 2016/800 was only adopted in January 2020, and it has since been incorporated into Article 189 (1) of the Code of Criminal Procedure.[1] CCP Art. 189 (1) part 2 establishes the objectives of IA, emphasising that IA must be considered when choosing pre-trial detention and other procedural coercion measures for the minor, deciding whether to terminate the pre-trial investigation or refer the case to a court, organising proceedings with a suspected or accused juvenile, and deciding on the imposition of penalty, punitive, or educational measures on a minor.

The pre-trial investigation officer is expected to submit a request to the Child Rights Protection and Adoption Service (later SCRPA Service) for IA upon the suspect's initial questioning, following the procedures established by the Minister of Social Security and Labour. The SCRPA Service can submit a request to the municipal pedagogical psychological service to obtain data regarding the juvenile's maturation, personality assessment, and special educational requirements. The data must be provided within ten working days of the request being received.

If a minor is under arrest, the custodial institution where the minor is confined must be contacted to request that IA be conducted. A summary of the information must be submitted to the pre-trial investigation officer or prosecutor in the prescribed written form no later than twenty-five working days from receipt of the request, upon completion of the IA of the juvenile. In these cases, the

[1] *Official Gazette,* 2002, No. 37-1341 with subsequent amendments.

representatives of institutions that operate under the Ministry of Justice are responsible for administering the IA.[2]

Article 189 (1) part 3 provides that IA of a minor is not required in cases where the minor is involved in negligent offenses or misdemeanours, when a criminal injunction is issued, or when the minor is being investigated under the accelerated procedure, provided that it is not in conflict with the minor's interests. This means that in practice, IA will apply only to juveniles who have committed severe or very severe crimes. This is not contrary to the Directive, but it means that IA will apply to only a very small proportion of suspected or accused juveniles.

The form of IA depends on which institution is conducting it. Article 183 (1) states that the SCRPA Service, accountable to the Ministry of Social Security and Labour, is responsible for conducting IA for children not remanded in detention. In that case, specialists of a territorial unit of the SCRPA Service are entitled to perform IA under the order of the Minister of Social Security and Labour of the Lithuanian Republic.[3] This order establishes the form of IA (Table 1).

The form includes various information regarding the infant and his environment; however, it does not specify how this information should be interpreted and analysed. The interpretation of the information that has been collected is at the discretion of the SCRPA Service specialists, who are primarily lacking in knowledge regarding social worker or psychology competencies. It implies that the SCRPA Service is responsible for conducting IA, but there is a paucity of qualified professional involvement in the summarisation and interpretation of the data collected about children. An institution that necessitates IA, such as a pre-trial investigator or prosecutor, is also responsible for interpreting the collected information.

As previously mentioned, the SCRPA Service's specialists may also request information from the Pedagogical-Psychological Service to conclude specific aspects of the child's personal development and involvement in the educational system. Nevertheless, the Pedagogical-Psychological Service is only able to furnish other institutions with information regarding a child's assessment and special educational requirements if the child has already been assessed. A subsequent evaluation is not conducted if the Pedagogical-Psychological Service lacks information regarding the minor.

In summary, the legislation favours a hybrid institutional paradigm. The SCRPA Service, accountable to the Ministry of Social Security and Labour, conducts IA for children not remanded in detention. Meanwhile, the Ministry of Justice is responsible for conducting IA for adolescents under arrest or probation. The subsequent chapter delves into IA's process and requirements when delegated to institutions under the Ministry of Justice.

---

[2] See next section of this chapter: "Risk-based IA of Minors in Detention and During Sentencing Stages"

[3] Ministry of Social Security and Labour of the Lithuanian Republic. The order on the approval of the description of the procedure for individual assessment of a minor. (Order No. 14331, September 09, 2019).

Table 1 The form of IA ordered by the Minister of Social Security and Labour

Information about the child	• Name, date of birth, place of residence (with address), and information about with whom the child lives; • information about the child's physical/mental health relevant to the pre-trial investigation (for example, physical and/or mental disability; diagnosed behavioural and/or emotional disorders, etc.). This should be completed if such information is known to the territorial unit; • the measures of assistance provided to the child (psychologist, social services, integrated services, etc.);
Data on the child's parents and family	• data on the parents (information to be provided, which is known to the authorised territorial unit or which can be obtained by visiting the family: place of employment, occupation, relationships, upbringing of the children and ability to take care of them); • whether the child's biological family has been or is known to have violated the child's rights (if so, a concise explanation of the nature of the violation should be provided); has the necessity for assistance to the child and/or family or child protection been identified? If so, what are the reasons for this, and what assistance has been/is being provided to the family? • whether and when preventive measures have been taken against the family (warnings from the territorial unit authorised by the SCRPA Service, penalties under the Code of Administrative Offences of the Republic of Lithuania, etc.); • the child's living conditions and the people emotionally connected to the child: home environment, living conditions, economic, social and family circumstances, meeting the child's needs, the child's hobbies, relationships with parents, other relatives, friends, classmates and teachers. The information obtained during the visit to the family by the representative of the territorial unit authorised by the SCRPA Service (the information provided by the child and the parents must be marked separately);

(continued)

Table 1 (continued)

Information about the guardianship (care) of the child (to be completed if the child is placed under guardianship)	• information on the guardianship of the child: date, type and form of guardianship, grounds for guardianship; • information on the guardian (carer) if the child is in guardianship: – in the foster family: the name of the guardian, relationship to the child in guardianship, experience of the guardianship (since when has the guardian been in guardianship); – family-type care home: name of the family-type care home, number of members, number of children, experience of fostering (care) (since when fostered); – in a child care institution or a community-based children's home: name of the institution, number of children in foster care, experience of fostering (care) (since when fostered); – in a foster care centre: name of the on-call caregiver, experience in care (since when he/she has been caring for the child(ren)), number of children; • the relationship of the foster carer with the child in care, and the ability to ensure that the child's needs are met. The relationship of the child in care with other children growing up in the family, foster family or child care institution and with professionals working in the family, foster family or child care institution; • the ability of the foster parent/guardian to cooperate with the territorial unit of the SCRPA Service, the child's educational institution, social workers, etc.;
Other relevant information	• Obtained during the visit to the child's actual place of residence or contained in the child's file, as well as additional documents.

3.2 Legal Framework and the Process for Conducting IA in Lithuania: Risk-Based IA of Minors in Detention and During Sentencing Stages

The IA conducted by institutions under the Ministry of Justice is presented as a social inquiry report and conducted by prison or probation staff. These institutions have a long history of generating social inquiry reports, also called pre-sentence reports. The purpose of these reports is to customise a sentence and/or probationary conditions by utilising validated risk-based assessments. The Short-Term Assessment of Risk and Treatability: Adolescent Version (START: AV) is the current risk assessment methodology for minors, and it was approved by the Lithuanian Prison Department in 2019.[4] START: AV is a fourth-generation criminal risk assessment instrument that encompasses risk management and, in addition, planning for interventional work with adolescents. Fourth-generation risk assessment instruments are distinguished by their risk and case management plan and their particular approach to problematic cases. Even though the START: AV is a relatively new

[4] Prison Department under the Ministry of Justice of the Republic of Lithuania. (2019). Order on the Approval of the START:AV – Adolescent Version of the Short-Term Assessment of Risk and Treatability (Order No. V-235, June 14, 2019).

instrument, having been completed and made available for use in 2014, it has been extensively validated and used in countries such as the United States, the United Kingdom, the Netherlands, and Lithuania. START: AV consists of 25 statements that can be divided into three groups, covering key areas of adolescent functioning: personality, relationships with the environment, and response to interventions. The personality domain of the adolescent is described through (a) their behaviour in various situations (e.g., school, leisure time, adherence to social rules, substance use, tendency toward risky behaviour), (b) emotions and thinking (e.g., impulse control, stress coping, specific cognitive traits, attitudes, emotional state), and (c) interpersonal functioning (e.g., behaviour toward others, social skills). The relationships and environment statements cover the adolescent's relationships with (a) peers, (b) caregivers and other significant adults (e.g., parenting skills, emotional closeness, presence of abuse, social support, material resources), and (c) community members (e.g., the adolescent's neighbourhood, school environment, environmental changes, or other significant life events). The response to interventions domain analyses the adolescent's attitudes related to applied interventions and their view of the future (e.g., self-perception, having realistic plans, motivation to change) (Laurinavičius et al. 2020).

This instrument is used by trained professionals from both probation services and prison staff who specialise in working with juvenile cases. The START: AV-based IA in criminal proceedings may be conducted when an adolescent is arrested; in such cases, IA is carried out by the juvenile detention facility where the minor is being held. Given their daily opportunities to observe the adolescents, specialists in juvenile detention facilities are able to gather more detailed information about the incarcerated youths' everyday psychosocial functioning and thus provide a more comprehensive assessment.

Article 253(1) of the Code of Criminal Procedure also includes a provision allowing the court to request a social inquiry report from the probation service. The probation service must prepare this report within 20 working days. Although judges have the discretion to request a social inquiry report, in practice, it is applied in only a limited number of criminal proceedings. As previously mentioned, it is more commonly used to individualise probation conditions.

In summary, the institutions under the Ministry of Justice have an evidence-based, validated instrument, experienced and trained professionals, and the capacity to conduct comprehensive IA; however, such assessments are foreseen only in limited cases within criminal proceedings.

4 Aligning Diverse Goals, Scopes, and Tools: Croatia's Practice of Individual Assessments of Accused and Suspected Children

4.1 Legal Framework and the Process for Conducting IA of Children in Conflict with Law in Croatia

In the Republic of Croatia, the juvenile justice system is grounded in several fundamental principles outlined in key legal acts: the Criminal Code (CC),[5] the Criminal Procedure Act (CPA),[6] the Youth Courts Act (YCA),[7] and the Act on the Execution of Sanctions Imposed on Juveniles for Criminal Offences and Misdemeanours (AESIJCOM).[8] The legal framework emphasises the necessity for conducting assessments of juveniles at various stages of criminal proceedings.[9] Croatian legislation aligns with international guidelines and recommendations regarding procedures for youth offenders, and these principles are embedded within the national legal framework. In addition to general laws, there are numerous specialised documents pertaining to juveniles in conflict with the law that underscore the need for IA to determine appropriate treatment. Both past and present Croatian legislation, as well as Directive 2016/800, convey a strong message on the need for comprehensive, multi-dimensional, and interdisciplinary assessments.

The legal framework highlights the critical role of IA in decision-making processes regarding juveniles in conflict with the law. IA serves as a prerequisite for decisions made by state attorneys and youth court judges concerning the imposition of sanctions or measures. Given the wide range of possible sanctions and measures, which vary from dismissing criminal complaints to imposing educational reform measures or juvenile detention, the necessity for a thorough assessment of a juvenile's needs is evident.

The obligation to conduct IA is embedded in the principles and is mandated either directly or indirectly in Croatian laws, specifically within the Youth Court Act (YCA/11) and the AESIJCOM/12, as well as relevant ordinances. The legal provisions for IA can be broadly classified into two categories: (1) IA conducted during criminal proceedings and the execution of sanctions; (2) IA conducted for the purpose of creating an individual treatment plan when a juvenile offender is sanctioned.

During criminal proceedings, the key actors involved in IA are the State Attorney's Office, the Youth Courts, and the Centres for Social Welfare. The IA may

---

[5] Criminal Code *Official Gazette* OG 125/11, 144/12, 56/15, 61/15, 101/17, 118/18, 126/19.

[6] Criminal Procedure Act *Official Gazette* OG 152/08, 76/09, 80/11, 121/11, 91/12, 143/12, 56/13, 145/13, 152/14, 70/17, 126/19, 126/19.

[7] Youth Courts Act Act, *Official Gazette* OG 84/11, 143/12, 148/13, 56/15, 126/19.

[8] Act on Execution of Sanctions Imposed on Juveniles for Criminal Offences and Misdemeanours, *Official Gazette* OG 133/12.

[9] For detailed information on the legal framework and juvenile justice system in Croatia, refer to Mirosavljević et al. (2020).

be conducted directly by the court, utilising non-legal experts such as social pedagogues or social workers, or more frequently, it is delegated to the Centres for Social Welfare to organise or execute the juvenile's assessment for judicial purposes. When a juvenile offender is sanctioned, the Social Welfare System or the Justice System is responsible for conducting IA required for the individual treatment plan.

The principle of appropriateness or opportunity, as outlined in Article 6 of the YCA/11, serves as the foundation for IA during criminal proceedings. Alongside establishing reasonable suspicion regarding the alleged offence and its severity, the state attorney must consider the juvenile's personal characteristics, social environment, attitude toward the offence, and other relevant factors. Before opting for diversion measures, the state attorney must assess whether continuing with criminal proceedings is warranted, focusing on the juvenile's personal and social attributes.

To gather the necessary information, the state attorney may consult the juvenile's parents, guardians, or other relevant individuals and institutions, or may request data collection by a non-legal expert assistant (e.g., a social pedagogue or social worker) at the State Attorney's Office, or through the assessment team at the Centre for Social Welfare. This underscores the vital role played by non-legal professionals in the assessment process. The state attorney is also required to inform the Centre for Social Welfare about the final decision based on the IA, allowing for the application of the principles of appropriateness and the potential imposition of diversion measures.

The Youth Court conducts its own assessment to determine whether criminal proceedings against the juvenile should be initiated or dismissed. Throughout the court proceedings, the youth judge is supported by psychosocial assessments provided by non-legal professionals, including social pedagogues or social workers employed at the court. In some cases, additional assessment elements may be requested from the Centre for Social Welfare or other institutions. This demonstrates the clear intent to incorporate expert knowledge of developmental and behavioural characteristics of young offenders into the daily operations of the State Attorney's Office and Youth Courts.

When proposing interventions or sanctions fočą'r juvenile offenders, it is essential to recommend measures that are suited to the specific characteristics of the juvenile, the nature of the offence, and other significant factors. The imposition of sanctions depends heavily on IA results and takes into account various factors, including risks, strengths, needs, and the responsiveness of the juvenile and their environment. Since a "one size fits all" approach is not applied, interventions must be tailored to the level of criminogenic risk. For instance, alternative community-based measures are typically appropriate for juveniles assessed as low to moderate risk, whereas institutional sanctions are primarily reserved for high or very high-risk juveniles, as stated in Article 71, paragraph 3 of the YCA/11.

4.2 Practice of Conducting IA in Croatia: Institutional Cooperation, Integrated and Multilevel Approach

The conceptual and practical framework of IA in Croatia is well-established, particularly within the justice system for juvenile offenders. The legal structure is focused on rehabilitation and restorative justice, recognising that juvenile offenders are still developing both cognitively and emotionally. As a result, sanctions and measures imposed on youth are designed not merely to punish, but to rehabilitate, taking into account their reasoning abilities, emotional regulation, and social functioning. The importance of balancing rehabilitative, retributive, and restorative approaches is emphasised in decision-making processes for juvenile offenders. The Croatian system of IA functions across multiple stages of criminal proceedings and sanctions execution, particularly focusing on treatment and rehabilitation rather than punishment. Juvenile offenders often face interventions aimed at correcting their behaviour and reintegrating them into society. The role of IA in these interventions is crucial, as it informs the most appropriate decisions based on a youth's unique circumstances.

As it was already stipulated, in Croatia, IA for juveniles is conducted primarily within the justice and social welfare systems. Within the justice system, courts or the State Attorney's Office perform assessments for legal decision-making, often carried out by non-legal professionals such as social pedagogues or social workers. On the other hand, the social welfare system conducts assessments ordered by the courts or the State Attorney's Office to guide interventions, treatment planning, and sanctions when necessary. In certain cases, assessments also involve the health care system, depending on the juvenile's needs, the crime, and other specific factors.

Broadly, the assessments in Croatia are categorised into two types:

- Screening/Detection/Triage/Selection: This is a preliminary stage aimed at gathering initial information about a juvenile's functioning. It helps identify those who need deeper assessment and determines the urgency of proceedings or the level of criminogenic risk.
- Comprehensive Assessment: Unlike screening, comprehensive assessments delve deeper into the juvenile's behaviour, circumstances, and environment. This type of assessment helps understand the underlying "causes" of behavioural problems and criminal behaviour, and plan more targeted interventions (Mirosavljević et al. 2020).

Additionally, forensic evaluations are sometimes necessary, usually involving psychological or psychiatric assessments to assist with legal decisions. These evaluations can also include other professionals and provide insights into how a juvenile's emotional and cognitive state relates to the legal issues at hand.

In Croatia, assessments are also conducted on two levels:

- Macro-level Assessment: This level focuses on broader decision-making within the justice system. It determines the course of legal proceedings or suggests appropriate interventions for a juvenile.

- Micro-level Assessment: Once a macro-level assessment is completed, a micro-level assessment follows, providing specific treatment or sanction guidelines tailored to the individual juvenile's needs.

Both macro and micro-level assessments are integral to ensuring that the interventions are suitable and individualised (von Aster et al., 1994). These assessments focus on collecting, analysing, and interpreting data related to the juvenile's risks and strengths and the capabilities of their environment to support intervention efforts. Comprehensive assessments go beyond basic screenings, examining a juvenile's criminogenic risks, protective factors, strengths, and needs.

There are two primary paradigmatic approaches to IA in Croatian practice (Koller-Trbović et al. 2013; White and Walsh 2006):

- Actuarial or Statistical Approach. This method relies on objective, science-based tools and standardised instruments to assess personality, emotions, behaviour, and criminogenic risk. It involves mathematical risk calculations and offers a data-driven perspective on the juvenile's likelihood of reoffending.
- Clinical and Constructivist Approach. This qualitative approach employs diagnostic interviews and more participatory methods, focusing on the juvenile's positive aspects and strengths. While it is more subjective than the actuarial approach, it emphasises empowerment and the young person's involvement in the process.

These two approaches complement each other in Croatian practice. The actuarial approach helps assess the risk of reoffending and the urgency of intervention, while the clinical approach helps in planning individualised interventions (Shlonsky and Wagner 2005). Experts are expected to integrate both perspectives to provide a holistic view of the juvenile's situation. Combining and integrating the actuarial and clinical approaches ensures a well-rounded assessment process. The actuarial approach offers insights into risk management, while the clinical approach aids in understanding the contextual factors influencing a juvenile's behaviour. By integrating these methods, assessments can identify problems at the individual, family, community, and societal levels, enabling professionals to design effective interventions.

Involving the juvenile in the assessment process is also critical, especially in risk management. Juveniles are encouraged to self-assess and participate in joint decision-making regarding their behaviour and its risks. This collaborative approach fosters a sense of responsibility and empowerment, making interventions more effective.

Assessments are conducted in various settings depending on the circumstances of each case. In Croatia, the level of institutionalisation of juvenile is an important factor in determining the type of assessment (Koller-Trbović et al. 2017):

- Occasional/Discontinued Assessment. This type is most common and does not require separating the juvenile from their family. It is conducted by teams of experts (in institutions like Centres for Social Welfare, State Attorney's Offices,

Courts, health care centres, clinics and hospitals), such as social workers, psychologists, and social pedagogues, who assess the juvenile over several meetings. This short-term assessment focuses on the individual juvenile and their immediate environment and is the most commonly used in practice at this time.
- Residential Assessment. A more intensive form of assessment is conducted in a residential/correctional institution setting for high-risk juveniles. This process involves separating the juvenile from their home environment and placing them in an institution where a team of experts can assess them over an extended period (30 days). It is conducted in a group context- in a maximum group of 12 children or young people who are at high risk, have a history of criminal offences and complex needs. This type of assessment is usually reserved for juveniles with a history of criminal behaviour or those who need structured, institutional intervention.

In the Croatian system, assessments use various tools and methods, as no single tool can fully capture the complexities of human behaviour. Professional judgment is essential in interpreting the results of these tools, and the methods used depend on the goals of the assessment.

Key methods include:

- Observation: Observing the juvenile in various situations to gather behavioural data.
- Interviews: Conducting structured or semi-structured interviews with the juvenile, their family, and other key figures in their life.
- Testing: Using standardized tests to measure personality, emotional functioning, and risk.
- Self-Assessment: Involving the juvenile in evaluating their behaviour and risk factors.
- Document Gathering: Collecting relevant documentation related to the juvenile's criminal history, education, and family environment.

These methods are applied across various areas of assessment, such as the juvenile's criminal history, family dynamics, educational background, peer relationships, substance use, and overall personality and behaviour. A comprehensive assessment requires drawing data from multiple sources, including the juveniles themselves, parents, teachers, and other relevant figures.

The final step of the assessment process is creating a report, which summarises the collected data, interpretations, and recommendations for intervention. A well-written report is clear, accurate, and comprehensive, providing a strong foundation for legal and social welfare decision-making.

In conclusion, IA in Croatia is a multi-faceted process that plays a critical role in juvenile justice and rehabilitation. By combining actuarial and clinical approaches, assessments provide a thorough understanding of the juvenile's needs, risks, and strengths. This allows for tailored interventions that focus not only on managing risk but also on fostering positive change and rehabilitation, ultimately contributing to the juvenile's reintegration into society.

5 Comparing the Implementation of the IA in Lithuania and Croatia: Challenges and Good Practices

This section compares the challenges and best practices for implementing IA in Croatia and Lithuania.[10] In both countries, the IA of children in conflict with the law is established within the legal framework and aligns with the objectives set out in Directive 2016/800. The IA process is designed to ensure procedural safeguards for children involved in criminal proceedings and to promote its application in sentencing and post-sentencing decisions, with the goal of tailoring measures that are most effective in preventing reoffending and fostering social inclusion.

In both Croatia and Lithuania, IA is implemented with the intention to align with recent theoretical approaches and debates, which emphasise that fourth-generation risk assessment instruments should be prioritised. These tools focus not only on identifying risk factors but, more importantly, on those amenable to change. In Lithuania, the fourth-generation instrument START:AV has been adopted and validated for use during the sentencing stage. In Croatia, a more multidimensional approach involves comprehensive assessments at various stages and levels, supported by conclusions drawn by highly skilled professionals. The Actuarial (Statistical) Approach and the Clinical/Constructivist Approach are combined in Croatian practice. These approaches complement each other: the actuarial approach supports the assessment of reoffending risk and intervention urgency, while the clinical approach guides the planning of individualised interventions. Experts are expected to integrate both perspectives to provide a holistic understanding of the juvenile's situation.

In Croatia, all juvenile suspects or accused individuals undergo some form of IA, with different types of assessments tailored to specific objectives. However, in Lithuania, there is no such requirement; in practice, IA are conducted only for juveniles who have committed severe or very severe crimes or as requested by judges or prosecutors at their discretion. The detailed comparison of the implementation of IA is provided in Table 2.

The juvenile justice system faces several key challenges related to the implementation and use of IA in both countries (Limantė et al. 2021; Mirosavljević et al. 2020; Vaičiūnienė et al. 2020). In Croatia, these challenges include the insufficient education and training of professionals responsible for conducting and applying IA, as well as the inadequate preparation of defence attorneys for youth court proceedings. Recommendations include mandating specialised training for defence attorneys, state attorneys, and youth judges who work with juveniles. Additionally, lengthy court proceedings and delays between assessment, decision-making, and the implementation of sanctions hinder the system's effectiveness; procedural

[10] The comparison is made under implementation of EU co-funded Justice Programme project "Procedural safeguards of accused or suspected children: improving the implementation of the right to individual assessment" (IA-CHILD; JUST-AG-2017/JUST-JACC-AG-2017-802,059). See more Vaičiūnienė et al. (2020).

Table 2 Comparison of the implementation of IA in Lithuania and Croatia

	Lithuania	Croatia
IA in different stages following Directive 2016/800	Two types of IA are foreseen: (1) in criminal proceedings administered by a territorial unit of SCRPA; (2) risk-based IA of minors in detention and during sentencing stages administered by institutions under the Ministry of Justice.	IA is recognised as essential and implemented across multiple phases of criminal proceedings and sentencing stages. It has long been integrated into Croatia's justice and social welfare systems, with close collaboration between these sectors in juvenile cases. The administration of IA depends on its objectives.
Applying the latest theoretical approaches to risk-based assessment	In Lithuania, in the sentencing stages, the fourth-generation instrument START: AV is adopted and validated.	Both approaches, the Actuarial or Statistical approach and the Clinical/Constructivist approach, are combined. These approaches complement each other in Croatian practice. The actuarial approach helps assess the risk of reoffending and the urgency of intervention, while the clinical approach helps plan individualised interventions. Experts must integrate both perspectives to provide a holistic view of the juvenile's situation.
Requirements to conduct IA	In criminal proceedings, IA of a minor is not required in cases where the minor is involved in negligent offences or misdemeanours, when a criminal injunction is issued, or when the minor is being investigated under the accelerated procedure, provided that it is not in conflict with the minor's interests. In practice, IA will apply only to juveniles who have committed severe or very severe crimes. There is also the possibility for judges to request a social inquiry report at their discretion.	All juvenile suspects or accused individuals undergo some form of IA, with different types of assessments tailored to specific levels and objectives.

(continued)

Table 2 (continued)

	Lithuania	Croatia
Qualified professionals are entitled to carry out IA	Highly trained and experienced professionals conduct risk-based assessments in detention and probation, having completed the necessary training on validated instruments. However, IA reports prepared by the territorial units of the SCRPA Service are not interpreted or linked to specific legal issues and cannot be considered expert conclusions. Specialists in the territorial units of the SCRPA Service lack the knowledge, training, and competencies necessary to formulate conclusions related to legal decisions in criminal proceedings.	Highly educated professionals, with significant experience in juvenile assessments, play a key role in the process. However, there is a recognised shortage of specialised non-legal experts within the justice system and the Centres for Social Welfare.
Collaboration across sectors and conducting assessments within multidisciplinary teams	Although collaboration between the social welfare and justice sectors is ensured in Lithuania, a proper multidisciplinary teamwork approach is still lacking.	Centres for Social Welfare and Social Welfare Educational Institutions play a crucial role in juvenile assessment, with expert multidisciplinary teams available. Strong interdisciplinary cooperation, with non-legal professionals available in courts and state attorney's offices, ensures a holistic approach to juvenile assessment.

reforms are needed to expedite these processes. There is also a lack of uniformity in case law and inconsistencies among youth judges at the national level, highlighting the need for standardised assessment methods, instruments, and procedures, as well as harmonised criteria for selecting sanctions and measures aligned with juveniles' needs and risk levels. Moreover, the poor quality and inefficiency of treatments in juvenile institutions and concerns over the quality of some IA reports submitted to youth courts call for improvements in institutional sanctions and the assessment process, emphasising a strengths-based approach. Finally, financial constraints often prevent referrals for institutional or comprehensive IA, underscoring the importance of increased funding to support broader and more in-depth assessments.

In Lithuania, the challenges revolve around the need to strengthen requirements ensuring that the IA are conducted in all cases. Currently, the legal framework allows for derogation, meaning IA is typically carried out only for juveniles who have committed severe or very severe crimes. The IA in criminal proceedings, administered by the territorial units of the SCRPA Service, generally provide information about the children and their environment. However, these reports are neither interpreted nor linked to specific legal issues, and thus cannot be considered expert conclusions. Specialists in the SCRPA's territorial units often lack the knowledge, training, and competencies needed to formulate conclusions relevant to legal decisions in criminal proceedings. It is essential to rethink the structure of these reports, including sections dedicated to clear conclusions, and to promote appropriate training for these specialists. This is crucial because, at present, there is a notable quality gap between the assessments conducted by SCRPA territorial units and the risk-based assessments administered by juvenile prison and probation professionals. Therefore, sufficient education and training for all professionals involved in conducting and applying IA, as well as for defence attorneys and judges handling juvenile cases, is pivotal. Additionally, it is important to incorporate a stronger multidisciplinary teamwork approach to ensure more comprehensive and effective assessments.

6 Concluding Remarks

It is evident that the information collected about juveniles within the justice system, whether through screening or assessment, is crucial to juvenile justice and criminal proceedings in both countries. It is imperative to integrate IA into the criminal process at various stages and to prevent arbitrary and unjust decisions in order to guarantee that the process is fair, timely, and effective. Additionally, IA is crucial not only for decision-making within the juvenile justice system but also for the long-term well-being of the juveniles themselves. The application of a transdisciplinary approach by well-trained professionals is essential for the assurance of high-quality assessment and decision-making. Ultimately, the goal of the juvenile justice system must extend beyond legal outcomes to promoting the development of youth into responsible and mature adults, capable of leading fulfilling lives.

The insufficient quality of IA reports prepared by SCRPA Service territorial units, which lack legal interpretation and expert-level conclusions, and the limited legal requirement for IA, which is presently conducted only for juveniles involved in severe crimes, are key challenges in Lithuania. To resolve these concerns, it is necessary to revise report structures, enhance specialist training, and eliminate the quality disparity between territorial units of the SCRPA Service and prison/probation assessments. It is imperative to fortify multidisciplinary collaboration and improve the training of all professionals, including defence attorneys and judges, to guarantee comprehensive and effective assessments.

The analysis of the implementation of IA in Croatia indicates that it is necessary to more effectively harmonise sanctions and measures with the needs and risk levels of juveniles, as well as to standardise assessment methods, techniques, instruments, and procedures to achieve greater uniformity. Additionally, procedural reforms are needed to address lengthy court proceedings and delays between assessment, decision-making, and the implementation of sanctions. Increasing financial support could improve the quality of institutional sanctions and treatments and enable more comprehensive institutional assessments. It is also crucial to propose targeted training for defence attorneys, state attorneys, and youth judges working with juveniles, along with sustained investment in the lifelong education of professionals responsible for conducting and utilising IA.

In conclusion, IA is a vital tool in ensuring fair, informed, effective, and child-friendly juvenile justice processes in both Lithuania and Croatia. Although both systems demonstrate a commitment to enhancing IA practices, they each encounter unique obstacles: from Lithuania's limited legal scope and inconsistent report quality to Croatia's need for greater standardisation and procedural efficiency. Targeted reforms in both countries are necessary to address these disparities, particularly emphasising the continued investment in professional training. Ultimately, the juvenile justice systems in both nations must not only maintain legal fairness but also facilitate the long-term development and reintegration of young people into society.

References

Bonta J, Andrews DA (2023) The psychology of criminal conduct, 7th edn. Routledge. https://doi.org/10.4324/9781003292128

Case S, Heines K (2020) Abolishing youth justice systems: children first, offenders nowhere. Youth Justice 21(1):3–17. https://journals.sagepub.com/doi/10.1177/1473225419898754

Case S, Browning A, Hampson K (2024) The child first strategy implementation project – translating strategy into practice. Youth Justice 24(2):204–230. https://doi.org/10.1177/14732254231191978

Committee of Ministers of the Council of Europe (2011) Guidelines on child-friendly justice. Council of Europe Publ

De Beuf TLF, De Vogel V, Broers NJ, De Ruiter C (2023) Prospective field validation of the START: AV in a Dutch secure youth care sample. Assessment 30(3):633–650. https://doi.org/10.1177/10731911211063228

De Vocht D, Panzavolta M, Vanderhallen M, Van Oosterhout M (2014) Procedural safeguards for juvenile suspects in interrogations: a look at the commission's proposal in light of an EU comparative study. New J Eur Crim Law 5(4):480–506. https://doi.org/10.1177/203228441400500405

Directive (EU) (2016) Directive (EU) 2016/800 of the European Parliament and of the Council of 11 May 2016 on procedural safeguards for children who are suspects or accused persons in criminal proceedings. OL L 132, 2016 5 21, pp 1–20. https://eur-lex.europa.eu/legal-content/EN/TXT/?uri=CELEX%3A32016L0800

Douglas KS, Otto RK (eds) (2021) Handbook of violence risk assessment, 2nd edn. Routledge, Taylor & Francis Group. https://doi.org/10.4324/9781315518374

Edens JF, Penson BN, Ruchensky JR, Cox J, Smith ST (2016) Interrater reliability of violence risk appraisal guide scores provided in Canadian criminal proceedings. Psychol Assess 28(12):1543–1549. https://doi.org/10.1037/pas0000278

Grisso T (2019) Three opportunities for the future of juvenile forensic assessment. Crim Justice Behav 46(12):1671–1677. https://doi.org/10.1177/0093854819883671

Hart SD, Logan C (2011) Formulation of violence risk using evidence-based assessments: the structured professional judgment approach. In: Sturmey P, McMurran M (eds) Forensic case formulation, 1st edn. Wiley, pp 81–106. https://doi.org/10.1002/9781119977018.ch4

Heilbrun K (with Holliday SB, DeMatteo D, LaDuke C) (2014) Forensic mental health assessment: a casebook (2nd edn.). Oxford University Press, Incorporated

Hoge RD (2012) Forensic assessments of juveniles: practice and legal considerations. Crim Justice Behav 39(9):1255–1270. https://doi.org/10.1177/0093854812444024

Jackson R, Roesch R (eds) (2016) Learning forensic assessment: Research and practice, 2nd edn. Routledge, Taylor & Francis Group
Koller-Trbović N, Mirosavljević A, Jeđud Borić I (2013) Intervention needs assessment of children and youth with behaviour problems. In: Risks and strengths assessment aimed for treatment planning (results of scientific project: matching interventions with needs of children at risk-creating a model). University of Zagreb, pp 23–67
Koller-Trbović N, Mirosavljević A, Jeđud Borić I (2017) Needs assessment of children and youth with behavior disorders—conceptual and methodical guidelines. UNICEF Office for Croatia
Laurinavičius A, Klimukienė V, Laurinaitytė I, Ustinavičiūtė-Klenauskė L (2020) Nepilnamečių teisės pažeidėjų rizikos ir apsauginių veiksnių analizė. Vilniaus Universiteto leidykla
Limantė A, Vaičiūnienė R, Apolevič J (2021) Child-friendly legal aid and individual assessment of children in conflict with the law: building the basis for effective participation. Int J Environ Res Public Health 19(1):17. https://doi.org/10.3390/ijerph19010017
Mirosavljević A, Mandić S, Ricijaš N, Dodig Hundrić D (2020) Implementation of Individual Assessment in Croatia. In: Individual assessment of suspected or accused children: insights into good practice in the light of the Directive (EU) 2016/800. Žara
Rap S, Zlotnik D (2018) The right to legal and other appropriate assistance for child suspects and accused. reflections on the directive on procedural safeguards for children who are suspects or accused persons in criminal proceedings. Eur J Crime Crim Law Crim Justice 26:110–131
Shlonsky A, Wagner D (2005) The next step: integrating actuarial risk assessment and clinical judgment into an evidence-based practice framework in CPS case management. Child Youth Serv Rev 27(4):409–427. https://doi.org/10.1016/j.childyouth.2004.11.007
UN (1989) United Nations Convention on the Rights of the Child, adopted by General Assembly resolution 44/25, on 20 November 1989. https://www.ohchr.org/EN/professionalinterest/pages/crc.aspx
UN Committee on the Rights of the Child (2009) General Comment No. 12 (2009): the right of the child to be heard. https://www.refworld.org/docid/4ae562c52.html
UN Committee on the Rights of the Child (2019) General Comment No. 24, replacing General Comment No. 10 (2007). Children's rights in juvenile justice. https://www.ohchr.org/Documents/HRBodies/CRC/GC24/GeneralComment24.pdf
Vaičiūnienė R, Nikartas S, Apolevič J, Povilaitytė V, Dodig Hundrić D, Ricijaš N, Mirosavljević A, Mandić S, Pitsela A, Nouskalis G, Karagiannidis C, Giagkou A, Mavrou C, Vaičiūnienė R (2020) Individual assessment of suspected or accused children: insights into good practice in the light of the Directive (EU) 2016/800. Žara. https://teise.org/wp-content/uploads/2021/06/Handbook-Layout-WEB.pdf
Van Voorhis P, Salisbury EJ (2014) Correctional counseling and rehabilitation. Taylor and Francis
Vincent GM, Guy LS, Grisso T (2012) Risk assessment in juvenile justice: a guidebook for implementation. MacArthur Foundation
White A, Walsh P (2006) Risk assessment in child welfare. Centre for Parenting and Research

Rūta Vaičiūnienė is a Chief Researcher and the Head of the Criminological Research Department at the Law Institute of the Lithuanian Centre for Social Sciences. Her research interests encompass the sociology of imprisonment, the sociology of gender with a focus on domestic violence, youth justice, and correctional programming. She has authored over 30 scientific papers, including research articles published in highly-ranked journals. Dr. Vaičiūnienė has accrued diverse research experience, contributing to more than 10 national and international research projects. Since 2023, she serves as the president of the Lithuanian Association of Criminology.

Anja Mirosavljević PhD, is an Associate Professor at the University of Zagreb, Faculty of Education and Rehabilitation Sciences, Croatia. Her teaching, professional, and scientific interests include the assessment of children and youth with emotional and/or behavioural problems, care leavers, interventions with high-risk families, and restorative justice.

Drug Offences Committed by Minors in Lithuania and Poland: Penal Responses and the Rights of Underaged Offenders

Mindaugas Lankauskas and Justyna Omeljaniuk

Abstract Adolescent drug use is a significant concern in contemporary societies. In Central and Eastern Europe, this issue may not be as prominent as in Western Europe, but it is steadily increasing. Central and Eastern European countries often adopt stricter penal measures in addressing this social problem than their Western counterparts. This approach raises concerns about potential penal overreaction towards young offenders, risking labelling them as criminals at a very young age.

This chapter offers a comparative legal analysis of adolescent drug offences in Lithuania and Poland. The authors examine the legal provisions and relevant case law to discover the similarities, differences, and possible societal factors influencing penal responses. By methodically examining each country's legal frameworks and drug crime statistics, the authors highlight both divergences and convergences in legal responses. This analysis provides insights into how drug offences by adolescents are approached in these jurisdictions. The chapter discusses how the legal frameworks and the case law differ in addressing drug offences committed by minors in Lithuania and Poland and what repercussions these differences bring for adolescent drug offenders and their rights in both countries.

1 Introduction

Lithuania and Poland, located in Eastern Europe, share a common history marked by periods of union and conflict. Both countries were part of the Polish-Lithuanian Commonwealth from the sixteenth to the end of the eighteenth century, when they shared political and cultural ties. After World War II, both countries fell under

M. Lankauskas (✉)
Law Institute, Lithuanian Centre for Social Sciences, Vilnius, Lithuania
e-mail: mindaugas.lankauskas@teise.org

J. Omeljaniuk
Faculty of Law, University of Białystok, Białystok, Poland
e-mail: j.omeljaniuk@uwb.edu.pl

A. Limantė, R. Vaičiūnienė (eds.), *Children's Rights in Central and Eastern Europe*, European Union and its Neighbours in a Globalized World 29,
https://doi.org/10.1007/978-3-032-07092-0_13

Soviet influence, which impacted their legal and social systems. Culturally, both nations are predominantly Roman Catholic, which influences their societal values and norms. Despite these similarities, there are notable differences. Lithuania is smaller in terms of population and geographical size compared to Poland. The languages spoken are different; Lithuanian is a Baltic language, whereas Polish is a Slavic language. Economically, Poland has a more extensive, diversified economy than Lithuania, affecting the resources available for social and legal services, including those addressing adolescent delinquency.

Adolescent drug offending is a significant issue in both Lithuania and Poland, reflecting broader social, economic, and legal challenges that align with trends observed across the European Union (EU). The phenomenon involves various dynamics, including the types of drugs involved, the socio-economic backgrounds of offenders, and the effectiveness of legal responses. In a broader EU context, challenges include disparities in drug policy implementation, varying levels of resource allocation for prevention and rehabilitation, and the growing influence of cross-border drug trafficking networks. Recent empirical studies highlight an increase in the use of New Psychoactive Substances (NPS) among European youth, raising concerns about the adequacy of current legal and social responses (Orsolini et al. 2019). Theoretical insights, such as the normalisation thesis, argue that drug use among youth is increasingly embedded within mainstream culture, necessitating a shift from punitive approaches to those emphasising harm reduction and social reintegration (Parker et al. 1998).

According to Dünkel, "juvenile justice systems in Europe have developed in various forms and with different orientations. Looking at sanctions and measures, the general trend reveals the expansion of diversion, combined in some countries with educational or other measures that aim to improve compliance with the norm violated by the juvenile offender. Mediation, victim-offender reconciliation or family group conferences are good examples of such diversionary strategies"(Dünkel 2014, p. 68). However, attitudes to youth drug crime across Europe vary significantly, with some countries maintaining strict punitive approaches, while others have adopted harm reduction and diversionary strategies.

Both analysed countries face unique and shared challenges in addressing drug offences committed by young people. The purpose of this comparative analysis is to explore how Lithuania and Poland address drug offences committed by minors within their legal systems. By examining the legal frameworks and statistical data from both countries, the analysis aims to identify key differences and similarities in the penal responses and the rights of adolescent offenders. This comparative approach will help highlight best practices and areas needing reform to improve the handling of adolescent drug offences.

2 Methodology

The main research question guiding this study is: how do the legal frameworks differ in addressing drug offences committed by adolescents in Lithuania and Poland, and what are the implications of these differences on the underaged drug offenders and their rights in both countries? To answer this question, the comparative legal research method was applied to comprehensively analyse the penal responses to the phenomenon of adolescent drug offences in Lithuania and Poland. The methodology included two main components: comparative legal analysis and analysis of available statistical data regarding drug crimes, committed by underaged persons. The comparative legal analysis involved the legal frameworks governing adolescent drug offences in Lithuania and Poland, specifically the Lithuanian Penal Code[1] and two specific Polish laws: the Act on Support and Resocialization of Minors[2] and the Act on Counteracting Drug Addiction.[3] This included examining the specific provisions related to drug offences and the penalties prescribed for adolescents. Statistical data on all drug offences and adolescent drug offences were analysed to identify trends and patterns. This included data from the respective Ministry of Interior in Lithuania and the Ministry of Justice in Poland.[4] Statistics on illicit drug use and prevalence among the general population and underaged population were reviewed to provide context to the legal and social challenges faced by both countries. The availability and comparability of data from both countries limit the analysis. Moreover, the differences in legal terminology and data collection methods may have affected the findings.

3 Penal Responses to Adolescent Drug Crime in Lithuania and Poland

3.1 Criminal Liability and Sanctions for Drug Offences

First, it is important to consider the general criminal law provisions relating to drug offences. In general, the drug control policy in Lithuania is based on strict control measures. Contrary to the trends prevailing in the West, Lithuania abolished administrative liability for acquiring and possessing drugs in 2017 and criminalised this conduct, thus tightening legislative regulation (Lankauskas and Gutauskas 2022). Severe sanctions are prominent in Lithuanian criminal law regarding drug offences. For even minor drug supply offences, imprisonment is the sole possible

[1] Penal Code of the Republic of Lithuania (2000).

[2] Act of 9 June 2022 on the support and social rehabilitation of minors (2022).

[3] The Act on Counteracting Drug Addiction (2005).

[4] Data for the years 2021–2023 aren't available on the website of the Ministry of Justice and weren't made available after submitting the application.

sanction. Table 1 provides an overview of specific provisions of the Penal Code of the Republic of Lithuania.[5]

As observed, in Lithuania, the distribution of illicit drugs carries harsh penalties, with custodial sentences starting from 2 years for small amounts being the only option. Distribution of larger amounts can result in sentences ranging from 8 to 10 years, while very large amounts may lead to sentences from 10 to 15 years. In Lithuania, the severe state response to less serious drug distribution offences primarily stems from the inflexible categorisation of drug offences. The law that automatically classifies any drug distribution offence (including less serious illicit drug supply) as a serious crime and thus limits the courts' discretion should be reconsidered (Bikelis and Lankauskas 2024).

Table 1 Specific provisions of the Penal Code of the Republic of Lithuania

Possession of illicit drugs	Distribution of illicit drugs
Article 259 Paragraph 1	**Article 260 Paragraph 1**
A person who unlawfully produces, processes, acquires, stores, transports or forwards narcotic or psychotropic substances for the purpose other than selling or otherwise distributing them shall be punished by a fine or by arrest or by a custodial sentence for a term of up to 2 years.	A person who unlawfully produces, processes, acquires, stores, transports or forwards narcotic or psychotropic substances for the purpose of selling or otherwise distributing them or sells or otherwise distributes narcotic or psychotropic substances shall be punished by a custodial sentence for a term of two up to 8 years.
Article 259 Paragraph 2	**Article 260 Paragraph 2**
A person who unlawfully produces, processes, acquires, stores, transports or forwards a small quantity of narcotic or psychotropic substances for the purpose other than selling or otherwise distributing them shall be considered to have committed a misdemeanour and shall be punished by community service or by restriction of liberty or by a fine or by arrest.	A person who unlawfully produces, processes, acquires, stores, transports or forwards a large quantity of narcotic or psychotropic substances for the purpose of selling or otherwise distributing them or sells or otherwise distributes a large quantity of narcotic or psychotropic substances shall be punished by a custodial sentence for a term of eight up to 10 years.
	Article 261
	A person who distributes narcotic or psychotropic substances among minors shall be punished by a custodial sentence for a term of three up to 12 years.
Article 260 Paragraph 3	
A person who unlawfully produces, processes, acquires, stores, transports, forwards, sells or otherwise distributes a very large quantity of narcotic or psychotropic substances shall be punished by a custodial sentence for a term of ten up to 15 years.	

[5] In Lithuania, Articles 259 and 260 of the Penal Code of the Republic of Lithuania (2000) are the most frequently applied provisions specifically addressing drug offences. Article 261 is included in this table as it regulates drug offences against minors

Moreover, the research conducted in Lithuanian prisons revealed that drug use is a significant social and medical problem, closely linked to prison conditions and the atmosphere within prison facilities. Forbidden substances play a substantial role in the prison economy and contribute to the power dynamics within the informal prison hierarchy. The resulting drug debts often lead to crime and violence, undermining the stability and safety of prisons. To address these issues effectively, it is essential to reconsider the punitive approach towards drug-using offenders and transition towards a more health-oriented strategy. This could involve the introduction of a diversion institute within the Lithuanian legal system for drug-related crimes or the implementation of depenalisation, such as lowering the bottom and/or upper limits of custodial sanctions for drug possession offences where appropriate (Lankauskas 2022, pp. 121–122). This is especially relevant in cases involving underage offenders, who are particularly vulnerable. According to Dünkel, juvenile offending is different from that of adults. Its episodic nature allows for more tolerance and moderate reactions (Dünkel 2014, p. 70).

In Polish legislation, drug offences are not included in the Penal Code. They are included in the Act on Counteracting Drug Addiction (2005). Chapter 7, Art. 53–74—Punishable drug offences, e.g., production or processing of new psychotropic substances, possession, storage, sale or purchase of certain products, placing narcotic drugs on the market and facilitating their use, illegal possession of narcotic drugs, theft of narcotic drugs, advertising or promotion these measures in violation of the Act (Skibicka 2019, pp. 405–406). In this study, attention will be devoted to crimes under Art. 56, 59 and 62 (Table 2).

Drug dealing in Art. 56, in its basic form, covers the illegal introduction of narcotic drugs, psychotropic substances, poppy straw or new psychoactive substances, as well as participation in such trade. The legislator provided for fines and imprisonment from 6 months to 8 years. It is a "common crime" because its elements can be faced by any person capable of incurring criminal liability (Karnat 2024).

"Placing on the market" is the act of making narcotic drugs available to third parties, whether for a fee or free of charge. The statement that the initial transaction of the manufacturer or importer, which initiates trade in a given psychoactive substance and involves its first transfer to a third party, is considered to be placing on the market is unconvincing. Giving medicines to another person, supplying those medicines and selling those medicines are all forms of placing on the market. The person who places a substance on the market can obtain it in a variety of ways, including production, importation, theft, purchase, discovery or donation. It does not matter whether the medicine is provided free of charge or in exchange for a material benefit (e.g. money, other thing) (Karnat 2024).

Participating in trade can be divided into two categories. Firstly, all situations that are tantamount to placing on the market, but on the passive side of such a transaction. Participating in trade includes taking medicines, whether from a seller, supplier, importer, manufacturer or wholesaler. To engage in trafficking, a person must not be a consumer of the drugs in question; rather, they must have the intention to pass it on to another person (consumer or wholesaler). Secondly, any other behaviour that has any connection with the illegal drug trade. This applies, for example,

Table 2 Comparison of individual types of crimes in Poland

Art. 56	Art. 59	Art. 62
Who, contrary to the provisions of Art. 33–35, 37, 40 and 40a, places narcotic drugs, psychotropic substances, poppy straw or new psychoactive substances on the market or participates in such trade, shall be subject to a fine and imprisonment from 6 months to 8 years.	Whoever, in order to obtain financial or personal gain, gives another person a narcotic drug, a psychotropic substance or a new psychoactive substance, facilitates the use or encourages the use of such a drug or substance, is punishable by imprisonment from 1 to 10 years.	Anyone who, contrary to the provisions of the Act, possesses narcotic drugs or psychotropic substances shall be subject to the penalty of imprisonment for up to 3 years.
In a minor case, the perpetrator is subject to a fine, restriction of liberty or imprisonment for up to 1 year.	In a minor accident, the perpetrator is subject to a fine, restriction of liberty or imprisonment for up to 2 years.	In a minor case, the perpetrator is subject to a fine, restriction of liberty or imprisonment for up to 1 year.
If the subject of the act is a significant amount of narcotic drugs, psychotropic substances, new psychoactive substances or poppy straw, the perpetrator is subject to a fine and imprisonment from 2 to 12 years.	If the perpetrator of the act referred to in section 1, provides a narcotic drug, a psychotropic substance or a new psychoactive substance to a minor, facilitates the use or encourages him to use such a drug or substance, is punishable by imprisonment from 3 to 20 years.	If the subject of the act is a significant amount of narcotic drugs or psychotropic substances, the perpetrator is subject to the penalty of imprisonment from 1 to 10 years.

to storing medicines or providing premises for the purpose of placing medicines on the market, e.g. for the purpose of conducting a transaction (Karnat 2024).

The legislator established a privileged category, encompassing minor cases that could result in a fine, restriction of liberty or imprisonment for up to 2 years. In the qualified type, the perpetrator may be sentenced to imprisonment for a period of between 3 and 20 years. In a crime under Art. 56 section 2, determining whether a minor accident occurred in a given case must be based on an analysis of the type of drug (whether it was a soft drug, e.g. marijuana or hashish, or a hard drug, e.g. heroin or cocaine), its quantity, value and role commission in entering or participating in trade (Karnat 2024).

In par. 3, the legislator established that the possession of a substantial quantity of narcotic drugs, psychotropic substances, new psychoactive substances, or poppy straw is subject to a more severe penalty. “Significant quantity” has not been legally defined by the legislature, but in the case law indicates that it can be „an amount sufficient to intoxicate several tens of thousands of people at the same time”(Case II KK 47/05, 2006; Case III KK 257/06, 2007; Case III KK 30/08, 2008; Case I KZP 10/09, 2009) or “…at least several hundred people at one time”(Case II AKa 10/08, 2008).

The basic type of crime from Art. 59 involves the provision of another individual with a narcotic drug, a psychotropic substance or a new psychoactive substance, with the intention of facilitating their use or persuading them to use such a drug or substance in order to obtain financial or personal benefits. Such acts are punishable by imprisonment for a period of between 1 and 10 years.

"Possessor" is not only the individual who uses the drug or substance for their own purposes but also the individual who retains it for another person (Kulik 2017, p. 661; Raglewski 2013, pp. 1100–1101). "Possession" encompasses any physical contact with a narcotic drug or psychotropic substance, including even momentary possession (Case I KZP 24/10, 2011). The legislation provides for a special category of cases in which the accused may be subject to a sentence of restriction of liberty or imprisonment for up to 1 year. The qualified type pertains to a considerable quantity of narcotic drugs or psychotropic substances.

3.2 Age of Criminal Liability

According to Article 13 of the Penal Code of the Republic of Lithuania (2000), the age of criminal liability for most drug offences under criminal law is 16 years.[6] Recently, there were discussions about lowering this limit to 14 years, but no action was taken. The authors believe this could be dangerous, as young people are particularly vulnerable. Therefore, criminal liability should be applied to them as late as possible. The harsh nature of Lithuanian criminal law regarding drug offences supports this perspective.

In contrast, Polish law sets lower age limits for criminal liability concerning drug offences. In Polish law, the concept of "minor" (in Polish, „nieletni") is defined in Article 1 of the Act on Support and Resocialization of Minors (2022). The legislation distinguishes three age groups of young people, with the age of criminal responsibility being a key factor in determining which group a young person falls into. These are individuals:

- over the age of 10 who have not reached adulthood—in cases of demoralisation;
- who have committed an act after the age of 13 but before 17—in cases of criminal acts; a adolescent offender who was 17 years old at the time of the commission of the crime is criminally liable under the Polish Penal Code (1997) and may be subject to a fine, restriction of liberty or imprisonment.
- who have been subjected to educational measures, therapeutic or corrective measures—these measures may be imposed for a period of up to 21 years unless otherwise specified in law.

As regards drug offences, criminal liability in Poland is possible from 13 years old, which is a significant difference compared to the Lithuanian legal framework, where the lower limit is 16 years old. Moreover, Poland has a different upper age limit,

[6] Except for the theft, racketeering or other illicit seizure of narcotic or psychotropic substances (Article 263).

meaning that individuals are treated as adults under penal law from 17 years old, whereas in Lithuania, this limit is 18 years old. Therefore, in this context, Polish penal law is stricter than Lithuanian law.

3.3 Special Provisions of Criminal Law Concerning Adolescent Offenders

Special provisions of criminal law regarding adolescent offenders outline specific measures aimed at addressing the unique needs and circumstances of young individuals involved in criminal activities, including drug offences. In both Lithuania and Poland, these provisions focus on rehabilitation and reintegration rather than purely punitive measures. For instance, despite the strict provisions of criminal law regarding drug offences in Lithuania, several legal instruments can be beneficial when addressing adolescent drug offences.

Chapter XI (Articles 80–94) of the Lithuanian Penal Code addresses the criminal liability of adolescents, defined as persons under the age of 18 at the time of committing a criminal act. The purposes of this chapter, as stipulated in Article 80, are to ensure that liability corresponds to the age and social maturity of adolescents; to restrict the imposition of custodial sentences and expand the use of reformative sanctions; and to facilitate the alteration of a minor's manner of living and conduct by aligning penalties with their personality development, education, and the elimination of reasons for unlawful behaviour. While sanctions for drug supply are typically harsh, often leading to imprisonment, there are legal options available for underaged perpetrators that courts can consider. Paragraph 5 of Article 90 specifies that the period of a custodial sentence for a minor may not exceed 10 years. This means that while the sanction for the supply of a very large amount of drugs ranges from 10 to 15 years, in the case of an underaged offender, the custodial sentence cannot exceed 10 years. According to Paragraph 3 of Article 91, the court may impose a fixed-term custodial sentence on a minor if it is believed that other types of penalties are insufficient to address the minor's criminal tendencies or if the minor has committed a serious or grave crime. In such cases, the minimum penalty must equal one-half of the minimum penalty provided for by the relevant article of the Penal Code. These legal safeguards allow courts to use imprisonment less frequently or impose shorter imprisonment sentences for underaged offenders.

In addition, it is important to note that, according to Article 87 of the Penal Code, courts may impose restrictions on conduct for a term ranging from 30 days to 12 months. Subparagraph 4 of paragraph 2 of this article allows the court to order an adolescent to undergo a complete course of treatment for alcohol addiction, drug addiction, addiction to toxic substances, or a sexually transmitted disease. This mandatory injunction can be imposed at the request of parents or guardians, subject to the minor's consent.

Moreover, the Code of Penal Procedure of the Republic of Lithuania (2002) includes specific provisions regarding minors. These provisions encompass closed hearings (Article 9, paragraph 3) and privacy protection when the suspect or accused person is a minor (Articles 21–22). Additionally, Article 272 mandates the individual assessment of a minor, which involves a comprehensive evaluation of their personality, environment, and needs in the areas of protection, education, and social integration. This assessment is conducted by a state institution for the protection of the rights of the child or a custodial facility where the minor is held. According to Article 44, paragraph 11, a pre-trial investigation officer or prosecutor must take measures to prevent the application of procedural coercive measures in the presence of a minor, except when the minor is suspected of committing a criminal act. If such measures are applied in the presence of a minor, the officer or prosecutor must promptly inform a state child rights protection institution.

Additionally, Article 127 stipulates that detention of a minor may initially be imposed for a period not exceeding 2 months, with the possibility of extension for up to 4 months. In contrast, detention can be extended for up to 6 months for adults. Furthermore, Article 138 allows placing a minor suspect under the supervision of their parents, curators, or other natural or legal persons responsible for children. Additionally, Article 186 imposes special provisions for questioning a minor witness and a minor victim.

The Lithuanian Supreme Court has undertaken some initiatives to address the challenges associated with overly harsh sanctions for less serious drug distribution offences. However, these efforts remain limited in scope and consistency, often constituting exceptional cases rather than a systematic approach (Bikelis and Lankauskas 2024). On the other hand, Lithuanian courts take a different approach to cases where adolescents commit drug offences. While it is theoretically possible to incarcerate such offenders, especially for drug supply offences, in practice, courts often choose other sanctions or suspend enforcement of imposed imprisonment. A typical example is a recent judgment by the regional court. The court decided to impose a 2-year imprisonment sentence for drug distribution to an underaged person committed by a adolescent. However, the court suspended the execution of the sentence for 1 year and imposed several conduct restrictions for the same period of time (Case N1-68-557/2024).

In conclusion, the Lithuanian Penal Code and Penal Procedure Code contain special provisions tailored for adolescent offenders. It also includes special provisions for underage victims of crime. The imprisonment rate for minors, especially for drug offences, is exceedingly low, bordering on non-existent. However, there is a concern that this situation may worsen in the future due to the increased popularity of penal populism, leading to harsher sentences being applied more frequently to young people for drug offences. On the other hand, young adults aged 18–20 who commit drug-related offences are treated in the same way as all adults, indicating a need for improvement in this area.

In Poland, the Act on Support and Resocialization of Minors (2022) also includes specific criminal law provisions concerning adolescent offenders. Art. 7 contains a catalogue of educational measures, art. 8—contains medicinal products, and Art.

9—contains corrective agents. In the catalogue included in Art. 7 include measures: non-isolating (e.g. the obligation to compensate for the damage, apologising to the injured party), those related to the supervision of a minor (e.g. a professional probation officer) and isolating measures (e.g. placement in a professional foster family or care centre). A therapeutic measure means placing a minor in a treatment facility where he or she is provided with health services in the field of psychiatric care or addiction treatment.

The corrective measure is placement in a correctional centre. These are specially established facilities where adolescent offenders who have been sentenced to serve their sentences are placed by the courts. The reformatory aims to raise and rehabilitate a minor who has committed a crime in his/her young life. Correctional facilities are divided into open, semi-open, and closed, with increased educational supervision for minors over 21. As of May 2, 2024, there are 30 adolescent facilities within the structure of the Ministry of Justice. They have a total of 1629 places, including 1369 for boys and 260 for girls (Ministry of Justice in Poland, n.d.-b). In Article 107 of the Act on the Support and Resocialization of Adolescents, paragraph 1 specifies in as many as 22 points what rights a minor placed in a correctional facility has. They concern, among others: respect for personal dignity and respect for privacy, with limitations resulting from the type of centre, facility or shelter; exercising religious freedom; access to health services; science; contact with family members and other people through visits, correspondence and the use of other means of distance communication, including electronic means of communication; receiving cash and parcels; obtaining psychological, pedagogical and therapeutic help; participation in activities organised in the centre, facility or shelter, and with the consent of the director, also outside the centre, facility or shelter; food adapted to developmental needs; clothing, underwear, footwear, school materials and textbooks, equipment and cleaning products if they do not have their own.

4 Prevalence of Illicit Drug Use and Drug Crime Statistics in Lithuania and Poland

4.1 Prevalence of Illicit Drug use in Lithuania and Poland

To fully grasp the scope of the issue, it is crucial to evaluate the prevalence in both countries and to compare this data with European statistics. The most recent general population survey (conducted in 2021) in Lithuania found that the lifetime prevalence of use of any illicit drug among all adults (15–64 years) was 14.1%. Among young adults (15–34 years), the lifetime prevalence was 23.8%. The prevalence of illicit drug use among the youngest adults (aged 15–24 years) in Lithuania is significant, with a lifetime use prevalence of 22% in 2021. 10.6% of these individuals reported using drugs in the last year, while 3.5% reported drug use in the last month (EMCDDA 2023). According to the European School Survey conducted in 2019, the lifetime prevalence of the use of any illicit drug (cannabis, ecstasy, amphetamine and methamphetamine) among Lithuanian pupils (15–16 years) was 19%, and it was higher than the European average (17%) (ESPAD group 2020, p. 49). This statistic underscores the importance of addressing drug-related issues among the youth population and implementing effective prevention and intervention strategies to mitigate potential harm.

Furthermore, over the past 10 years, a large number of New Psychoactive Substances (NPS) have entered the recreational drug scenario. NPS intake has been associated with health-related risks, and especially so for vulnerable populations such as the youngsters (Orsolini et al. 2019). According to the European School Survey, the main illicit drug in Lithuania was cannabis. However, the popularity of NPS in Lithuania was higher than the European average (5.6% and 3.4%, respectively) (ESPAD group 2020, p. 51).

The situation is quite similar in Poland. The study conducted by the National Office for Counteracting Drug Addiction, presented in the Report on the State of Drug Addiction in Poland (National Office for Counteracting Drug Addiction 2021, pp. 7–8), indicates that in 2018, 5.4% of individuals aged 15–64 had contact with drugs. Among those aged 15–34, the percentage of drug users was 10.4%. The most recent survey from 2018 revealed that marijuana was the most commonly used drug among the general population, with 12.1% of respondents admitting to using it. Among those aged 15–34, 7.8% of respondents admitted using it. In the entire study population (15–64 years), a higher percentage was recorded among men (16.4%) than among women (7.7%) in the case of the rate of ever use. The largest percentage of individuals who initiated addiction treatment reported marijuana as the substance responsible for their addiction (40%). The second most prevalent substance is amphetamine, which is used at a much lower rate in the general population. Only 1.4% of respondents (aged 15–34) admitted to using amphetamines. The rate of use is higher among men than women.

According to the latest data (2018 from Poland and 2021 from Lithuania, respectively, see Fig. 1), Poland has a slightly lower prevalence of illicit drug use than Lithuania (among both the general population and youth). On the other hand, there are more young people in Poland (aged 15–24) who used drugs in the last year or last month. The main illicit drug of choice in both countries is cannabis.

The data point to the need for a well-designed approach to the prevention of drug use, harm reduction and criminal justice responses in relation to the drug problem among young people. While criminal law serves as a vital tool in combating drug use and supply, it often carries significant side effects. Therefore, caution should be exercised when applying it to young offenders.

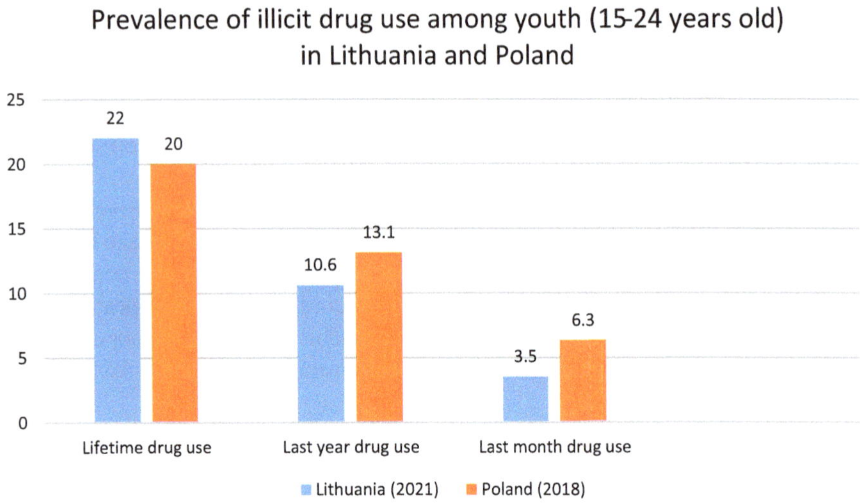

Fig. 1 Prevalence of illicit drug use (in per cent)

4.2 *Statistical data regarding drug offences and adolescent offenders in Lithuania and Poland*

In recent years, there has been an increasing number of registered drug law offences in Lithuania (Fig. 2). For example, in 2023, there was a 27.3% increase from the previous year (Information Technology and Communications Department under the Ministry of the Interior of the Republic of Lithuania n.d.). On the other hand, according to research, drug crime has a very high latency rate. When comparing self-reported drug use with registered drug offences in Lithuania, it is found that only 2–4% of illegal drug use is represented in official drug offence statistics (Lankauskas 2022, pp. 24–25). Therefore, it is not possible to draw very strict conclusions based only on registered drug crime statistics.

In the past 8 years, the number of drug offences per 100,000 inhabitants has risen from 79.3 to 136.7, indicating a more active involvement of law enforcement in addressing drug-related crime (Fig. 3). The number of drug law offences committed by minors is relatively stable, with roughly 200 offences recorded each year (Fig. 4). It is important to emphasise that individuals under 16 years old are not subject to criminal law, and their actions related to drug possession are not considered crimes or misdemeanours.

It is worth mentioning that a notable increase in drug offending can be seen among young adults (18–20 years old)—from 344 drug offences committed in 2022 to 447 in 2023. They are not subject to specific penal law provisions regarding adolescents; therefore, strict Lithuanian penalties for drug offences are applied to them in full force.

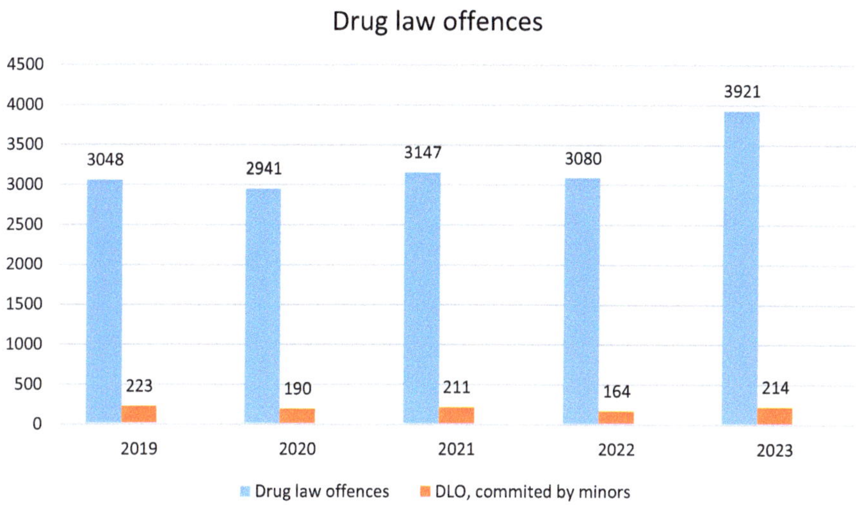

Fig. 2 Drug law offences in Lithuania (in total numbers)

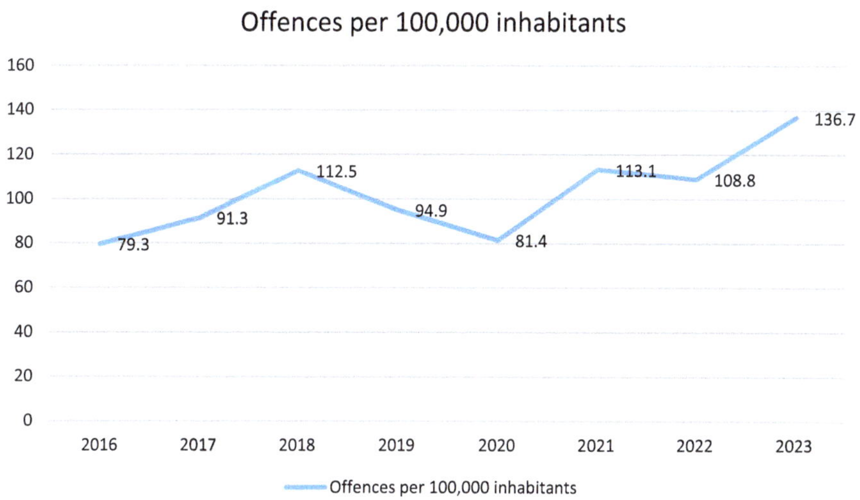

Fig. 3 Drug law offences (per capita)

Article 261 imposes sanctions for the distribution of narcotic or psychotropic substances to minors. There was a substantial increase in such offences last year, with 58 cases reported in 2023 compared to 25 in 2022. This marks a significant rise from 12 cases in 2021, 22 in 2020, and 34 in 2019.

It is noteworthy that initially, the adolescent justice process had a limited impact on sentencing practice. About 30% of convicted adolescents were still given custodial sentences. However, this proportion was much lower than in Soviet times. In contrast, in Poland, since 1990, the proportion of custodial sanctions has been

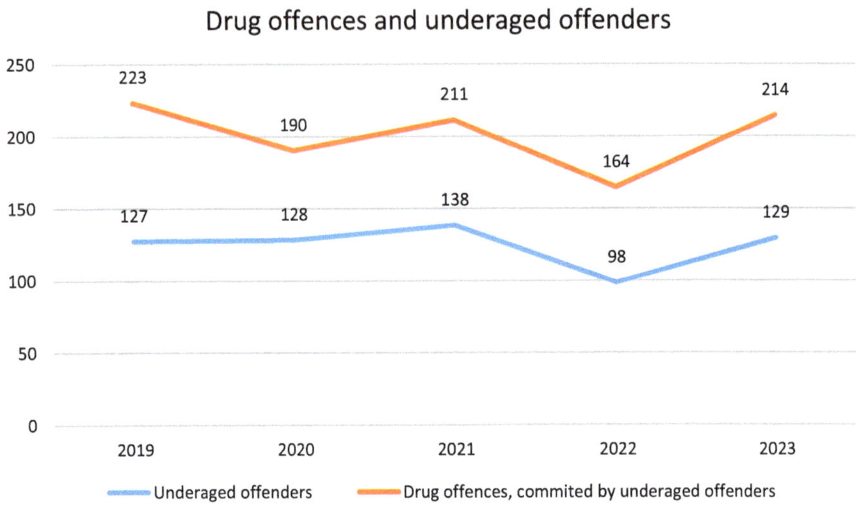

Fig. 4 Adolescents and drug offences in Lithuania (in total numbers)

reduced to a very low level of about 2 per cent of all measures issued by the family court (Dünkel 2014, p. 66). Nevertheless, the situation in Lithuania has undergone significant changes in recent years. By the end of 2023, out of a total prison population of 3829, there were only 4 underage prisoners and 73 prisoners aged 18–21 (Lithuanian Prison Service n.d.). A total of 772 prisoners were incarcerated for drug offences, accounting for slightly more than 20% of the entire prison population. According to official statistics, 129 individuals aged 16–17 committed drug offences in 2023, compared to 98 in 2022 (Information Technology and Communications Department under the Ministry of the Interior of the Republic of Lithuania n.d.). While it is difficult to determine the exact number of minors or young adults sentenced for drug offences, there are likely no adolescents imprisoned for such offences.

The analysis of data on the total number of convictions for drug offenses in Poland indicates that the majority of those convicted of drug offenses are adults (Fig. 5). Minors make up a small percentage of the total number of convictions. It is worth emphasizing, however, that these are not individual situations but amount to approximately or just over 1000 minors per year. The greatest number of minors were convicted of drug offenses in 2016 and the least in 2020. A downward trend can also be observed in the annual convictions of minors (since 2018). However, it seems more accurate to say that these numbers were at a relatively similar level in individual years.

Then, we should refer to the analysis of selected drug crimes committed by minors—i.e. those specified in Art. 56, 59 and 62 of the 2005 Act.

In Poland, it's important to note that convictions of minors for offences of the Art. 56 of the Act on Counteracting Drug Addiction (2005) into circulation by minors in 2016–2020 were recorded almost incidentally. In 2016, one conviction

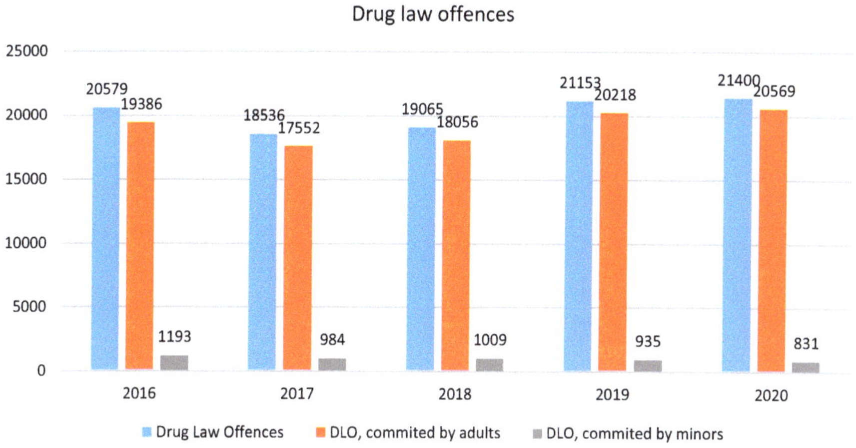

Fig. 5 Drug law offences in Poland (in total numbers). Source: Own study based on data from the Ministry of Justice (Ministry of Justice in Poland, n.d.-a)

was recorded of an underage girl in accordance with Article 56 par. 2 for an educational measure in the form of a warning. A comparable situation occurred the following year. The distinction between the two cases was that the convicted was a male. In 2018, no minor was convicted. In 2019, the highest number of such convictions was recorded—three individuals. That individuals committed an offence under par. 1 (boy and girl) and par. 3 (boy). Two of them were placed under the supervision of a probation officer, and one was placed under the responsible supervision of her parents. In 2020, one minor male was convicted under par. 1 and 3. The court imposed two educational measures: the obligation to refrain from the use of intoxicants and to participate in appropriate therapeutic activities.

In cases of criminal liability for facilitating, enabling or inducing the use of a drug or substance in order to obtain benefits, minors were convicted at a significantly higher rate than for the acts penalised in Article 56. Figure 6 shows the number of convictions of minors in Art. 59.

The total number of adolescent convictions is the type from par. 1 was in the range of 19–31 individuals per year. The lowest number was recorded in 2017. The highest—in 2016 and 2018. In this instance, the majority of perpetrators were underage boys. In the category of crimes under par. 2, the number of minors convicted between 2016 and 2020 ranged from 40 to 67 per year. The lowest number was recorded in 2018—the highest in 2016. Most of these individuals were underage males, 34–58 per year. In both types of this crime, the proportion of underage girls was significantly lower.

The category of individuals from par. 3, in terms of criminal convictions, pertained exclusively to adolescent males. These figures represented a relatively modest annual total. The largest number of individuals was recorded in 2016. In years other than 2016, the number of minor boys involved was one per year.

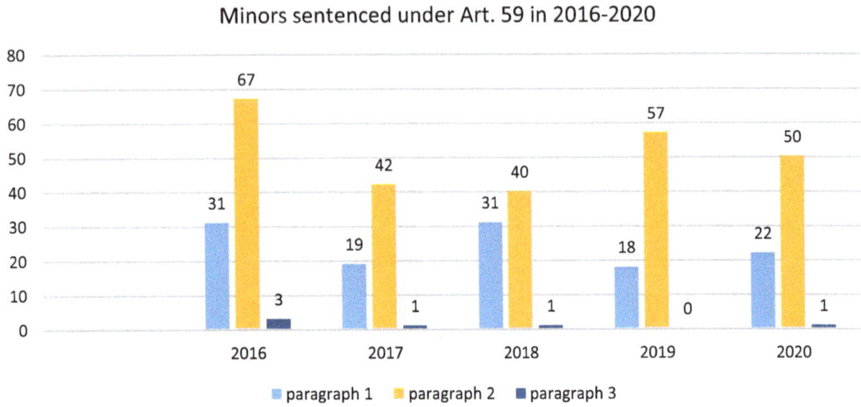

Fig. 6 Number of convictions of minors Art. 59. Source: Own study based on data from the Ministry of Justice (Ministry of Justice in Poland, n.d.-a)

Table 3 shows the number of measures courts use against adolescent perpetrators of acts under Art. 59.

The most common approach was to place a minor under the supervision of a professional probation officer. In a minority of cases, courts opted to put the responsibility for supervising minors exclusively with their parents. This is not a particularly surprising conclusion, given that parents are more likely to attempt to conceal their children's issues and inappropriate conduct. Probation officers are more objective in their approach to minors under their supervision. It will be easier for a specialist to identify cases where a minor may be trying to hide illegal activity. In cases where it was deemed necessary to separate a minor from his surroundings, the court often placed the minor in a youth educational centre or probation office.

In cases where a minor abuses narcotic substances, the courts have either imposed an obligation to refrain from using these substances or even to participate in appropriate activities, e.g. of a therapeutic nature. Activity does not have to be limited to stimulants. Programs may include learning how to deal with aggression. Statistics indicate isolated cases of minors being placed in psychiatric hospitals or other treatment facilities.

Courts often issue rebukes to minor perpetrators. The decision to apply such a measure is made through an oral warning to the minor (Article 147). If an oral warning is not possible, it may be given in writing. Considering the characteristics of the analysed crime and the data, it appears that this measure was not used as a one-off measure but in combination with other educational activities. There were also cases of minors being placed in correctional facilities (up to 5 per year).

Most convictions of minors for possession of narcotic drugs concerned the basic type of crime. The number of verdicts was not counted in dozens but in hundreds. Their total number ranged from 594 to 789 per year (Fig. 7). The lowest number of convictions was in 2020, the highest in 2016. Most of the convicted were underage boys. The number of convicts exceeded 500 per year. There were fewer girls than

Table 3 Educational measures for minors convicted from Art. 59

Educational measure/year		2016	2017	2018	2019	2020
Inspection by a	probation officer	47	32	33	44	42
	parents	8	7	3	6	5
Placement in	probation centre for youth work	4	–	2	4	1
	youth educational centre	10	3	4	4	2
Obligation	the disbursement of benefits	–	–	1	–	1
	apology injured party	–	–	–	–	2
	repair the damage	1	1	–	1	–
	continuing education	4	2	2	5	3
Obligation to refrain from	staying in certain places	3	–	–	2	1
	using of alcohol/ narcotic	7	7	–	6	3
Obligation to participate in appropriate activities	therapeutic	10	8	9	5	10
	educational/training	5	–	3	–	1
Working for the local community		3	4	4	2	11
Rebuke		10	9	18	10	13
Forfeiture of goods		1	1	5	2	2
Placement in psychiatric hospital or another medical facility		2	–	–	1	–
Correctional facility—suspending the execution of the measure	without	2	1	1	–	2
	with	1	4	4	–	–
Other measure		9	2	3	1	7

The number of measures doesn't add up to the number of convictions—the court may order several measures against a minor

Source: Own study based on data from the Ministry of Justice (Ministry of Justice in Poland, n.d.-a)

boys, although they constituted a significant percentage of the total number. Except for 2020, the number of individuals per year exceeded 100. Number of convictions under section 2 and 3 was much lower. The total number of sentenced minors under par. 3 ranged from 33 to 51 people, with most convictions involving underage boys (from 28 to 45 per year). In par. 2, there were 9–13 individuals per year (boys and girls). Table 4 shows the number of measures courts use against adolescent perpetrators of acts under Art. 62.

Courts most often imposed probation supervision on adolescent offenders—from 250 to 289 per year. The number of cases in which parents were ordered to supervise their children was less than halved yearly—from 65 to 94 per year. The courts often used rebukes—from 186 to 268 per year.

Courts also imposed obligations to refrain from using intoxicants or participating in appropriate therapeutic activities. If it is deemed necessary to separate a minor from the family or peer environment because it may lead to the demoralisation of the child, which in turn may result in the minor committing prohibited acts, the

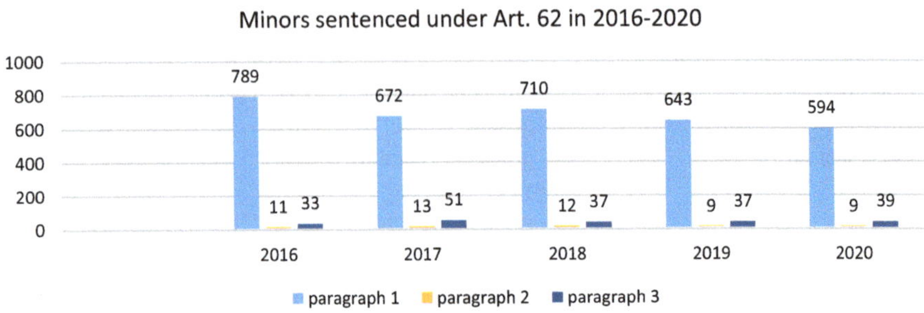

Fig. 7 Number of convictions of minors—Art. 62. Source: Own study based on data from the Ministry of Justice (Ministry of Justice in Poland, n.d.-a).

courts issued a ruling on placing the minor perpetrator in a youth educational centre or probation office.

The courts also used measures such as placing the minor in a professional foster family, the obligation to apologise to the injured party, compensation for the damage caused, and even placement in a psychiatric facility.

5 Concluding Remarks

In general, Lithuanian penal law regarding drug offences is stricter and imposes harsher penalties than Polish penal law. Additionally, Polish courts have greater discretion in deciding the appropriate penal sanction in specific cases. For example, in Lithuania, the penalty for the possession or distribution of a "large amount" of illicit drugs ranges from 10 to 15 years, while in Poland, it ranges from 2 to 12 years for a "significant amount." Furthermore, drug distribution in Lithuania is subject to imprisonment for 2–8 years (if the amount is not significant), while in Poland, it is subject to imprisonment from 1 to 10 years (in minor cases, penal sanctions include imprisonment for up to 1 year, and fines or restrictions of liberty are also possible). In Lithuania, there are no alternative sanctions for drug distribution, even in minor cases. However, the distribution of drugs to minors is subject to stricter penalties in Poland (from 3 to 20 years of incarceration) than in Lithuania (from 3 to 12 years of incarceration). In the authors' opinion, Polish penal sanctions for drug offences provide more room for courts to decide which penalty is most appropriate in specific cases. At the same time, the Lithuanian penal law in question is too rigid.

In Lithuania and Poland, adolescents are treated more leniently than adults, and incarceration is applied in rare cases. Both countries also have specific provisions concerning adolescent drug offenders. In Lithuania, it is a separate chapter in the Penal Code, while in Poland, it is a separate law. However, there is an important

Table 4 Educational measures for minors convicted from Art. 62

Educational measure/year		2016	2017	2018	2019	2020
Inspection by a	probation officer	289	261	267	250	259
	parents	94	76	74	88	65
Placement in	probation centre for youth work	11	5	3	6	8
	youth educational centre	25	27	31	23	14
	professional foster family	–	–	1	–	–
Obligation	apology to the injured party	1	1	–	2	1
	repair the damage	1	–	1	–	1
	starting/continuing education	41	35	46	35	19
Obligation to refrain from	staying in certain places	5	7	5	1	9
	using of alcohol	14	5	9	12	8
	using of narcotic	67	71	88	66	53
Obligation to participate in appropriate activities	therapeutic	80	87	107	80	103
	educational/training	7	7	4	4	7
Working for the	local community	47	41	40	33	22
	injured party	2	–	–	1	–
Rebuke		268	213	227	188	186
Forfeiture of goods		39	39	38	35	28
Placement in	psychiatric hospital	1	2	–	–	–
	another medical facility	10	9	10	4	8
Correctional facility—suspending the execution of the measure	without	7	1	1	5	2
	with	2	3	4	3	1
Other measure		32	33	30	45	41

The number of measures doesn't add up to the number of convictions
Source: Own study based on data from the Ministry of Justice (Ministry of Justice in Poland, n.d.-a)

distinction regarding age. In Lithuania, a person can be held liable for most drug offences only from 16 years old, whereas in Poland, it is possible from 13 years old. In addition, according to the criminal provisions of Polish law, persons are treated as adults from 17 years old (18 years old in Lithuania). This means that, according to Polish criminal law, minors aged 13–16 are liable for drug offences, whereas in Lithuania, only those aged 16–17 are liable. From a human rights perspective, it is worth discussing raising the age limits for criminal liability in Poland and expanding the application of less strict measures for young adults (aged 18–20) in both countries.

References

Act of July 29 2005 on counteracting drug addiction, Pub. Journal of Laws 2023, pos. 1939

Act of June 6 1997 – Penal Code, Pub. Journal of Laws discussion, Pub. Journal of Laws 2023, pos. 1939

Act of June 9, 2022 on the support and social rehabilitation of minors, Pub. Journal of Laws 2023, pos. 289, 1860

Bikelis S, Lankauskas M (2024) Penal response to *less serious* drug distribution offenses: the case of Lithuania in the regional context. Balt J Law Polit 17(1):163–180. https://doi.org/10.2478/bjlp-2024-0008

Case I KZP 10/09 (Supreme Court in Poland 2009)

Case I KZP 24/10 (Supreme Court in Poland 2011)

Case II AKa 10/08 (Court of Appeal in Wrocław 2008)

Case II KK 47/05 (Supreme Court in Poland 2006)

Case III KK 257/06 (Supreme Court in Poland 2007)

Case III KK 30/08 (Supreme Court in Poland 2008)

Case N1-68-557/2024 (Klaipėda Regional Court 2024)

Code of Penal Procedure of the Republic of Lithuania, Pub. L. No. No. 37–1341 (2002)

Dünkel F (2014) Juvenile Justice Systems in Europe – reform developments between justice, welfare and 'new punitiveness'. Kriminol Stud 1:31–76. https://doi.org/10.15388/CrimLithuan.2014.1.3676

EMCDDA (2023) Statistical Bulletin 2023—prevalence of drug use. https://www.emcdda.europa.eu/data/stats2023/gps_en

ESAPD group (2020) ESPAD Report 2019: Results from the European School Survey Project on Alcohol and Other Drugs. EMCDDA Joint Publications

Information Technology and Communications Department under the Ministry of the Interior of the Republic of Lithuania (n.d.) Open data [Open data]. https://ird.lt/lt/paslaugos/tvarkomu-valdomu-registru-ir-informaciniu-sistemu-paslaugos/nusikalstamu-veiku-zinybinio-registro-nvzr-atviri-duomenys-paslaugos/nusikalstamos-veikos-lietuvoje-2006-2023-metais/oid.1005

Karnat J (2024) Komentarz do Art. 56. In: Gadecki B, Karnat J (eds) Przepisy Karne ustawy o przeciwdziałaniu narkomanii. C. H. Beck, Warszawa

Kulik M (2017) Ustawa o przeciwdziałaniu narkomanii in Marek Mozgawa. Pozakodeksowe przestępstwa przeciwko zdrowiu. Komentarz. Wolters Kluwer Polska, Warszawa

Lankauskas M (2022) Narkotikai ir įkalinimas: Kriminologiniai baudimo už disponavimą narkotinėmis ar psichotropinėmis medžiagomis aspektai ir jų vartojimo kalinimo įstaigose ypatumai. Lietuvos socialinių mokslų centro Teisės institutas. https://teise.org/wp-content/uploads/2023/01/Narkotikai-ir-ikalinimas.pdf

Lankauskas M, Gutauskas A (2022) Chasing the high: drug users as a vulnerable group in Lithuania. In: Limantė A, Pūraitė-Andrikienė D (eds) Legal protection of vulnerable groups in Lithuania, Latvia, Estonia and Poland, vol 8. Springer International Publishing, pp 309–325. https://doi.org/10.1007/978-3-031-06998-7_14

Lithuanian Prison Service (n.d.) Open data [Open data]. https://kalejimai.lrv.lt/lt/administracine-informacija/ataskaitos/metu/

Ministry of Justice in Poland (n.d.-a) Multiannual studies. Statistic data. files: Nieletni - prawomocne orzeczenia w latach 2000–2020; Nieletni wg orzeczonych środków prawomocne orzeczenia w latach 2003–2020 and Nieletni wg wieku i płci - prawomocne orzeczenia w latach 2004–2020. https://isws.ms.gov.pl/pl/baza-statystyczna/opracowania-wieloletnie/

Ministry of Justice in Poland (n.d.-b) Zakłady dla Nieletnich: okręgowe ośrodki wychowawcze, zakłady poprawcze i schroniska dla nieletnich. https://www.gov.pl/web/sprawiedliwosc/zaklady-poprawcze-i-schroniska-dla-nieletnich

National Office for Counteracting Drug Addiction (2021) Report on the state of drug addiction in Poland from 2020. https://www.cinn.gov.pl/portal?id=105923

Orsolini L, Chiappini S, Corkery JM, Guirguis A, Papanti D, Schifano F (2019) The use of new psychoactive substances (NPS) in young people and their role in mental health care: a systematic review. Expert Rev Neurother 19(12):1253–1264. https://doi.org/10.1080/14737175.2019.1666712

Parker H, Aldridge J, Measham F (1998) Illegal leisure: the normalization of adolescent recreational drug use, 1st edn. Routledge

Penal Code of the Republic of Lithuania, Pub. L. No. No. 89–2741 (2000)

Raglewski J (2013) Kilka uwag de lege lata i de lege ferenda w kwestii karania za posiadanie narkotyku w związku z przeznaczeniem go na własne potrzeby. In: Błachnio-Parzych A, Jakubowska-Hara J, Kosonoga J, Kuczyńska H (eds) Problemy wymiaru sprawiedliwości karnej. Księga jubileuszowa Profesora Jana Skupińskiego. Wolters Kluwer Polska, Warszawa

Skibicka S (2019) Drug addiction as a criminogenic factor. Rocz Pedagog 11(47):401–418. https://doi.org/10.18290/rped.2019.11s-24

Dr Mindaugas Lankauskas is a lawyer, criminologist, and an expert in drug policy and drug-related crime. He earned an MA in International Human Rights Law from Mykolas Romeris University and was awarded a PhD in Sociology from Vilnius University in 2018. Currently, he works as a researcher at the Law Institute of the Lithuanian Centre for Social Sciences.

Dr. Lankauskas has contributed to more than 20 scientific publications, including two monographs. In addition to his research activities, Dr. Lankauskas teaches criminology at Vilnius University. He is a member of the Lithuanian Society of Criminology, the European Society of Criminology, and the European Society for Social Drug Research.

Dr Justyna Omeljaniuk is a graduate of the Faculty of Law of the University of Białystok. In 2023, she completed doctoral studies at the same university and is working as an assistant at the Department of Criminal Law and Criminology at the Faculty of Law of the University of Białystok. Her scientific interests include not only Polish criminal law but also criminology (especially aspects related to car crime and juvenile delinquency) and criminalistics (particularly forensic techniques such as dactyloscopy, osmology and traceology). She is the author of 3 scientific articles and 18 chapters in peer-reviewed monographs.

Community Sanctions for Children in Lithuania and Romania: Diverging Paths of Juvenile Justice

Simonas Nikartas and Ioan Durnescu

Abstract This chapter examines and compares the juvenile justice systems in Lithuania and Romania, focusing on community sanctions and measures for children. The authors review the juvenile justice systems of both countries, the types of community sanctions, the institutional structures, and practical challenges, emphasising compliance with international standards for the protection of children's rights in criminal justice. Although both countries share similar political experiences shaped by communist regimes, they have chosen different paths in reforming their juvenile justice systems. The authors conclude that Lithuania follows a neo-correctional approach, characterised by control-oriented sanctions, limited diversion mechanisms, and the formal involvement of children in criminal cases. Romania chose a different path—a welfare model that emphasises education, rehabilitation, and social integration, along with minimal intervention supported by diversion programmes. The chapter concludes with policy recommendations encouraging policy-makers to strengthen rehabilitation measures, promote greater institutional specialisation, improve the training of specialists working with children, and reduce regional disparities in access to juvenile justice services.

S. Nikartas (✉)
Law Institute, Lithuanian Centre for Social Sciences, Vilnius, Lithuania
e-mail: simonas.nikartas@teise.org

I. Durnescu
University of Bucharest, Bucharest, Romania

A. Limantė, R. Vaičiūnienė (eds.), *Children's Rights in Central and Eastern Europe*, European Union and its Neighbours in a Globalized World 29,
https://doi.org/10.1007/978-3-032-07092-0_14

1 Introduction

Juvenile justice systems in Eastern European countries have encountered substantial challenges in transitioning from the ideological framework of the communist era, in which children were regarded as subjects of state control and "re-education" (see Henkes 2000; Robila 2004). Juveniles were institutionalised, disciplined, and used as a means to enforce state ideology. The focus was on correction and obedience. Little attention was paid to children's individual rights or developmental needs. The post-communist shift towards democratic values, with an emphasis on children's rights, best interests, and social reintegration, required long-lasting and complex reforms. Most Eastern European states have formally committed to democratic principles and have ratified key international instruments for the protection of children. However, more than three decades after the fall of the Berlin Wall, the reform process remains uneven across countries and in many respects incomplete. For example, a number of Eastern European democracies continue to pursue stringent criminal justice policies, which scholars often attribute to the enduring legacy of communism, characterised by punitive orientations and a limited emphasis on rehabilitation (see Slade and Light 2015).

Although nearly all democratic European nations profess adherence to international norms on juvenile justice and aspire to implement more lenient policies towards minors (see Dünkel 2024), the rate and depth of reform vary considerably across the region. Juvenile justice systems in democratic Eastern Europe, based on the typologies proposed by Cavadino and Dignan (2006), can be broadly divided into two categories. The first category includes states whose systems are designed to prioritise children's rights in institutional responses to juvenile delinquency, with an emphasis on minimising the use of punitive sanctions. These jurisdictions promote non-punitive strategies such as restorative justice programmes, diversionary mechanisms, and educational interventions, in line with international standards and scholarly recommendations (e.g. Romania, Croatia, Slovenia, Latvia) (see Dünkel and Pruin 2009; Dünkel 2014, 2024).

The second category comprises states where juvenile justice policies continue to reflect a punitive ethos rooted in communist-era practices. Such jurisdictions have adopted frameworks akin to the neo-correctionalist model (Cavadino and Dignan 2006), which foregrounds juvenile culpability and retains a preference for criminal sanctions, albeit less severe than those imposed on adults. Lithuania, Hungary, Slovakia, and Bulgaria illustrate this pattern, where conventional measures—such as probation and custodial sentences—remain predominant (see Dünkel and Pruin 2009; Dünkel 2014, 2024).

This chapter examines the application of community sanctions and measures in two EU Member States that exemplify contrasting trajectories in juvenile justice reform: Romania and Lithuania. Despite their shared experience of communist governance, the two countries have developed markedly different responses to juvenile offending. Romania has embraced educational and rehabilitative approaches, whereas Lithuania continues to rely primarily on traditional punitive sanctions for minors. This chapter undertakes a comparative analysis of these two systems, with particular emphasis on the use of community sanctions and measures, to identify their convergences and divergences and to assess the extent to which they conform to international standards for child-friendly justice.

2 Community Sanctions for Children: Definition and Principles

According to the Council of Europe's Recommendations on Community Sanctions and Measures (2017), the term 'community sanctions and measures' refers to sanctions and measures that allow suspects or offenders to remain in the community, subject to certain restrictions on their liberty through the imposition of conditions and/or obligations. The concept encompasses any sanction imposed by a judicial or administrative authority. Any measure applied either prior to or in place of a formal sanction, including methods for enforcing custodial sentences outside prison facilities. Pruin & Dünkel (2011a) offer a broader interpretation, defining community sanctions as encompassing "all sanctions and measures which do not result in any form of deprivation of liberty."

The design and objectives of sanctions imposed on minors must be tailored to the unique characteristics of the child, including age, cognitive and social maturity, and individual developmental needs. Criminological research identifies three defining features of juvenile delinquency: its prevalence, its typically minor nature, and its spontaneous character. Offending behaviour is statistically more frequent during childhood and adolescence than at any other life stage. In most cases, juvenile offences are minor, involving petty theft, status offences such as truancy, or low-level property damage. Such behaviour often reflects adolescent impulsivity and a developmental stage characterised by experimentation and boundary testing, although in some cases it may also indicate underlying social or psychological difficulties requiring targeted intervention.

The labelling theory further enriches our understanding of the impact of punitive responses on juvenile behaviour. Empirical studies suggest that treating minors as offenders may lead to stigmatisation, with the imposition of a 'criminal label' increasing the likelihood of future delinquency (see Becker 1963; Bernburg et al. 2006; Liberman et al. 2014).

These criminological insights have influenced the formation of international juvenile justice norms and standards.[1] Foremost among these is the United Nations

[1] Noteworthy international documents include the United Nations Convention on the Rights of the Child (*Official Gazette*, 1995, No. 60-1501); the United Nations Standard Minimum Rules for the Administration of Juvenile Justice (Beijing Rules), adopted by General Assembly Resolution No. 40/33 on November 29, 1985; the United Nations Guidelines for the Prevention of Juvenile Delinquency (Riyadh Guidelines); the United Nations Rules for the Protection of Juveniles Deprived of Their Liberty (Havana Rules); and the Council of Europe Committee of Ministers

Convention on the Rights of the Child (CRC). Article 3 of the CRC obliges states parties to ensure that the best interests of the child are a primary consideration in all actions affecting them, whether undertaken by public or private welfare institutions, courts of law, administrative authorities, or legislative bodies.

Particularly relevant in the context of juvenile delinquency is Article 40 of the CRC, which requires states to recognise the right of every child accused of infringing criminal law to be treated in a manner that upholds their dignity and worth, respects their fundamental rights and freedoms, considers their age, and promotes their reintegration into society and their constructive engagement therein (Article 40(1) of the CRC).

The Convention also imposes specific obligations on states, including,

- Establishing a minimum age below which children are presumed not to have the capacity to infringe criminal law.
- States are also required, where appropriate, to ensure that children below this age are not subjected to judicial proceedings, while guaranteeing that their rights and procedural safeguards are fully respected (Article 40(3) of the Convention).

In addition, responses to juvenile offending should be proportionate to the nature and context of the offence, the child's age and personal circumstances, and guided by the overarching principle of the child's best interests. The Convention advocates for a range of non-institutional measures, including supervision, care, guidance, counselling, probation, educational programmes, vocational training, and other appropriate community-based responses (Article 40(4) of the Convention). When applying community sanctions to minors, international standards prioritise rehabilitative strategies that promote social inclusion, familial engagement, and community support. The United Nations Standard Minimum Rules for the Administration of Juvenile Justice (the Beijing Rules, 1985) underscore the importance of positive measures that leverage family, educational, and community resources. The Convention also establishes the principle of minimum intervention, according to which Member States should avoid involving children in criminal proceedings, especially in cases of minor offences. The penalties and measures imposed must comply with the principle of proportionality, considering the offence's gravity and the child's personal characteristics.

The concept of child-friendly justice has been developed since the adoption of the CRC. It represents a paradigmatic shift in recognising children as independent rights-holders in legal processes. This concept was further developed in the Council of Europe Guidelines on Child-Friendly Justice (2010), which provide recommendations on how to adapt legal systems to the child's needs. Child-friendly justice emphasises accessibility, age-appropriate procedures, meaningful participation, and protecting the child's dignity and privacy.

Recommendation No. (87) 20 to Member States on Social Reactions to Juvenile Delinquency, adopted by the Committee of Ministers on September 17, 1987.

Child-friendly standards are most prominently invoked during the procedural stages of criminal proceedings, such as pre-trial and trial, with particular attention to the child's right to participate, the assessment and accommodation of individual needs, and the provision of specialised legal assistance. However, these standards receive comparatively limited attention in the enforcement phase of sanctions, both within international legal frameworks and in academic discourse. In the context of community sanctions, the following aspects of child-friendly justice can be outlined:

- Sanctions and measures must be proportionate, individualized and adapted to the child's needs, characteristics and developmental stages. To this end, international legal instruments encourage the use of a wide range of measures. In implementing these measures, the best interests of the child should be safeguarded, family and community involvement promoted, and the child's connection to the education system maintained. For example, Article 1.3 of the United Nations Standard Minimum Rules for the Administration of Juvenile Justice (the Beijing Rules) underscores the importance of positive measures that mobilise all available resources—including families, volunteers, schools, and community organisations—to support the juvenile's welfare. In this regard, the Beijing Rules also recommend that children should be treated differently from adults in the justice system.
- Criminal justice interventions risk negatively affecting a child's personality development and may increase the likelihood of recidivism. Accordingly, international standards strongly support the principle of minimal intervention. In cases involving minor offences, state responses should be limited or entirely avoided, particularly by excluding formal judicial processes and the criminal justice system where possible. Criminal sanctions should not be imposed on children, especially those of a younger age, if such measures do not serve their best interests. Instead, responses to delinquent behaviour should aim to promote the social integration, development, education and general well-being of the child. Paragraph 5 of the United Nations Guidelines for the Prevention of Juvenile Delinquency (Riyadh Guidelines) emphasises the importance of advanced crime prevention strategies, systematic research and the implementation of comprehensive and well-designed preventive measures. These guidelines explicitly discourage the criminalisation of children for behaviours that do not result in serious harm to their development or to others. Furthermore, international legal instruments call for the expansion of diversionary measures, advocating the removal of law-breaking children from the criminal justice system and the redirection of their cases to social welfare and educational institutions.
- Children must be regarded as active participants in the enforcement process of any sanction or measure. This entails affording children the opportunity to express their views on both the enforcement and substance of the sanction, and ensuring that those views are taken into account. International child-friendly standards stress that the enforcement of sanctions should not be overly formalistic. Children should receive clear and constructive feedback regarding the implementation of the sanction and their personal progress. Meaningful participation

fosters a greater sense of responsibility and helps the child to comprehend the significance and purpose of the sanction imposed.

In conclusion, international legal standards articulate several key principles with regard to addressing delinquent behaviour in young children.

- Criminal sanctions should not be imposed on young children. Instead, the focus must be on promoting socialisation, providing support, facilitating education, and similar rehabilitative efforts.
- All measures must be proportionate, taking into account the severity of the offence, the surrounding circumstances, and the child's individual characteristics and best interests. In cases involving minor offences, intervention should either be avoided or applied with minimal intensity—for instance, by refraining from engaging formal institutional mechanisms, particularly those of the criminal justice system.
- International legal instruments advocate the implementation of a diverse array of measures, with a particular emphasis on the child's best interests, the involvement of family and community actors, and the preservation of the child's relationships with their family and community, without disrupting their access to the education system. For example, Article 1.3 of the United Nations Standard Minimum Rules for the Administration of Juvenile Justice (the Beijing Rules) underscores the importance of mobilising all available resources—including families, volunteers, educational institutions, and community organisations—to promote the well-being of the child, minimise legal intervention, and ensure that juveniles in conflict with the law are treated in a manner that is effective, fair, and humane.

The following sections examine the application of community sanctions for juveniles in Lithuania and Romania and offer a comparative analysis of these respective practices.

3 Legal Framework and Regulation of Community Sanctions for Children in Lithuania

Lithuania is frequently cited for its stringent criminal policy. For several decades, the country has ranked among the European nations with the highest incarceration rates, as well as the highest number of individuals under probation supervision within the European Union.[2] An analysis of the legal framework and prevailing

[2] For example, in 2024, the imprisonment rate was 156 per 100,000 inhabitants (World Prison Brief 2024). Although this figure has declined from 323.91 in 2012 (Eurostat), it remains among the highest in Europe. This is primarily due to the long average imprisonment duration—approximately 3 years (Sakalauskas et al. 2020). In 2022, more than half of all prisoners (2041 out of 3730) were serving custodial sentences longer than 5 years (Lithuanian Prison Service 2024).

practices suggests that the Lithuanian juvenile justice system similarly reflects a punitive orientation.

The Lithuanian juvenile justice system encompasses a broad spectrum of criminal and other legal responses aimed at addressing children's delinquent conduct. Juveniles in Lithuania may be subject to: (1) criminal penalties and reformative measures applicable solely to criminal offences; (2) administrative penalties and sanction measures for administrative misdemeanours; (3) minimal and moderate supervision measures for offences where the child is under the age of criminal liability or for failing to comply with other legal obligations that do not constitute a criminal or administrative offense (e.g., failing to attend school) (see the Table 1).

In Lithuanian academic literature, this model is characterised as a system of wide intervention, whereby legal mechanisms are deployed to regulate virtually any form of socially undesirable behaviour exhibited by children of any age (see Nikartas et al. 2013; Nikartas et al. 2020). The system is structured in such a way that nearly all manifestations of problematic behaviour among children fall under the purview of state institutions, thereby facilitating institutionalised responses. Notably, intervention measures may be legally imposed on children of any age, not only for criminal conduct but also for school absenteeism or other behaviours deemed harmful or dangerous. This reflects an extraordinarily extensive degree of state control over children's behaviour—one that, in some respects, exceeds the accountability mechanisms applicable to adults for criminal offences (see Nikartas et al. 2013, 2020).

The following section provides a more detailed analysis of the penalties and legal measures applicable to juveniles under criminal liability, with a specific focus on community sanctions. Emphasis will be placed on community sanctions that operate as forms of criminal liability and are implemented by the probation service.

3.1 Penalties and Educational Measures for Juveniles in Lithuania

Juvenile criminal liability is governed by the Criminal Code of the Republic of Lithuania (Seimas of the Republic of Lithuania 2000) (hereinafter referred to as the CC).[3] In general, criminal liability applies only to individuals aged 16 and over. However, individuals aged 14 and above may be held criminally responsible for a limited number of serious offences specified in Article 13 of the Criminal Code.[4]

Lithuania also ranks high in the number of individuals under community sanctions. According to the SPACE II report (2022), as of 31 January 2022, there were 591.2 individuals under probation supervision per 100,000 inhabitants in Lithuania, compared to the European average of 211.

[3] There is no separate law specifically governing juvenile criminal liability. Nonetheless, a dedicated chapter addressing the criminal liability of minors is included within the Criminal Code.

[4] The offences for which minors aged 14 or older may be held criminally liable include: murder, infliction of serious bodily injury, rape, sexual harassment, theft, robbery, extortion, destruction or damage to property, unlawful seizure of firearms, ammunition, explosives or explosive materials,

Table 1 Juvenile justice system in Lithuania[a]

Legal grounds for the imposition of penalties or measures	Criminal offence	Criminal offence when a minor: is released from criminal liability; Probation is applied (suspension of sentence and conditional release from prison)	Administrative misdemeanour	1) Criminal offence/ administrative misdemeanour when the person is under the age of criminal or administrative responsibility 2) An administrative misdemeanour may occur without the imposition of either an administrative penalty or an administrative measure. 3) Failure to comply with the statutory requirement for minors under the age of 16 to attend school	1) Criminal or administrative misconduct committed by a child below the age of criminal or administrative liability may trigger state intervention where the child's behaviour poses a danger to their own life, health, or property, or that of others. 2) Intervention may also be applied in cases where no improvement in the child's behaviour is observed during the period of minimal supervision, with the exception of breaches involving school attendance obligations.
Types of penalties and measures	Criminal penalties	Reformative measures	Administrative penalties and administrative measures	Minimal supervision measures	Moderate supervision measures for children
Institutions Authorised to Impose Penalties or Measures	Court		Court	Municipal administrations and Child Welfare Commissions	Municipal administrations and Child Welfare Commissions, with the approval of a court

(continued)

illegal acquisition of narcotic or psychotropic substances, and intentional damage to vehicles or road infrastructure (Article 13 of CC). The age of administrative liability is 16 years (Article 6 of AMC).

Table 1 (continued)

Institutions Responsible for the Execution of Penalties and Measures	Juvenile correctional facilities (prisons designated for minors) Probation service (responsible for the enforcement of liberty restrictions, community service, and most reformative measures) Socialisation centre (for reformative measures involving placement in specialised facilities) Bailiffs (for the enforcement of fines) Other relevant bodies and organisations	Police Other competent public authorities	Educational institutions, children's and youth day care centres, health care institutions, and other service providers	Socialisation centre
Institutions Overseeing the Enforcement of Penalties and Measures	Prosecutor Prison Department	Police, municipal authorities, and other designated agencies	Municipal administrations and Child Welfare Commissions	
Coordinating Ministry	Ministry of Justice	Ministry of Justice Ministry of the Interior	Ministry of Education, Science and Sports	

The table was compiled by the author, although similar structures have been outlined in the work of other scholars (see Nikartas et al. 2013, 2020)

Juveniles who commit criminal offences may be subject to both criminal penalties and educational (reformative) measures. Children may receive the same types of penalties as adults, with the exception of life imprisonment, including custodial sentences, short-term detention, liberty restrictions, fines, and community service.

The Criminal Code provides for reduced and more lenient penalties for minors compared to those applicable to adults (see Table 2). For example, the maximum number of hours of community service for minors is capped at 240, in contrast to the 480-h limit applied to adults convicted of criminal offences, and the same 240-h ceiling for adults convicted of criminal misdemeanours A juvenile may be fined an amount ranging from 5 to 50 MSL,[5] whereas adults may be fined between 15 and 6000 MSL, depending on the nature of the offence. The CC further provides that a fine may only be imposed on a minor who is either employed or possesses property. A juvenile may be sentenced to a term of imprisonment ranging from 5 to 45 days;

[5] The MSL (Minimum Subsistence Level) is a statutory monetary unit formerly used in Lithuania for the calculation of fines and social benefits. As of 2025, the MSL has been replaced by the BSI (Basic Social Benefit), which has been fixed at 70 euro.

Table 2 Comparison of the duration of criminal penalties for minors and adults

Type of penalty	Length of the penalty for minors	Length of penalty for adults
Custodial sentence	From 1.5 months to 10 years	From 3 months to 20 years
Suspension of a custodial sentence (probation)	1–3 years	1–3 years
Partial suspension of a custodial sentence	Part of Sentence served in Prison: 6 months–1 year Part of Sentence served in Probation: 1–3 years	Part of Sentence served in Prison: 6 months–2 years Part of Sentence served in Probation: 1–3 years
Short-term custodial sentence	5–45 days	10–90 days From 15 to 90 days for crimes. From 10 to 45 days for misdemeanours
Liberty restriction	2 months–2 years	3 months–2 years
Community service	1–12 months Not more than 240 h of total time worked	1–12 months Not more than 480 h of total time worked for crimes and 240 h for misdemeanours
Fine	5–50 MSL	15–6000 MSL

for adults, the equivalent range is 15 to 90 days in the case of a crime, and 10 to 45 days for a misdemeanour.

The CC establishes specific provisions for the imposition of custodial sentences on minors. Firstly, the duration of imprisonment for a juvenile may not exceed 10 years. Secondly, a juvenile may be sentenced to imprisonment only where there is reason to believe that alternative sanctions are insufficient to modify the juvenile's criminal disposition, or if the juvenile has committed a serious or particularly serious offence. Thirdly, the CC provides for a reduction in the minimum term of imprisonment for minors: under Article 91 of the CC, the minimum sentence for a juvenile shall be half of the minimum sentence prescribed in the relevant provision of the CC, which would otherwise apply to an adult.

Compared to adults, minors benefit from more lenient conditions for suspending custodial sentences (i.e., probation). For a juvenile sentenced to imprisonment for one or more negligent offences, or for a term not exceeding 5 years for one or more intentional crimes, the court may suspend the execution of the sentence for a period ranging from 1 to 3 years. This provision indicates that the suspension of custodial sentences for juveniles is not solely contingent on the severity of the offence: a suspended sentence may also be applied for a serious or particularly serious crime, provided the maximum term of imprisonment does not exceed 5 years. Conversely, no such provision exists for the suspension of custodial sentences for adults convicted of serious or particularly serious crimes.

For a juvenile sentenced to more than 5 years of imprisonment for one or more intentional crimes, excluding serious crimes, very serious crimes, and those specified in the Criminal Code chapters dealing with crimes against humanity and war crimes, crimes against the state's independence and constitutional order, crimes against life, health, liberty, sexual self-determination, inviolability, crimes against children and families, crimes against public service and public interest, crimes against public safety, crimes related to the possession of narcotic or psychotropic substances, crimes against public administration, and crimes against morality, the court may partially suspend the execution of the sentence. In such cases, the court shall determine the portion of the sentence to be served immediately after the judgment becomes final (for a minimum of 6 months and a maximum of 1 year), while the suspension period for the remainder of the sentence shall range from 1 to 3 years. In contrast to juveniles, adults are subject to more stringent criteria for the partial suspension of sentence execution: for negligent crimes, the sentence must exceed 6 years; for minor and medium gravity intentional crimes, it must exceed 4 years; and for serious crimes, excluding the categories mentioned above, the sentence must not exceed 5 years. In comparison, juveniles are subject to a single general criterion: the imposed sentence must exceed 5 years for any intentional crime, excluding the aforementioned serious and particularly serious offences. Furthermore, the portion of the sentence that must be served immediately by juveniles ranges from 6 months to 1 year, whereas for adults, it may range from 6 months to 2 years.

In Lithuania, juveniles are most frequently subject to educational or reformative measures. Although the Criminal Code of the Republic of Lithuania does not explicitly articulate the specific aims of educational measures, these sanctions are intended to fulfil the general objectives of juvenile criminal liability, which are articulated as follows:

- To ensure that criminal responsibility is commensurate with the juvenile's age and social maturity;
- To minimise the application of custodial sentences and promote the imposition of educational measures;
- To support behavioural and lifestyle changes in juveniles by combining punishment for committed offences with personal development, education, and the resolution of the underlying causes of unlawful conduct;
- To deter juveniles from committing further criminal acts.

Educational measures may be imposed on a minor who has committed a criminal offence and has been released from criminal liability or punishment, as well as on a minor who has been conditionally released or placed under probation. A minor may be subjected to the following reformative sanctions:

A warning may be issued either as an autonomous educational sanction or in conjunction with other such measures. When imposing this sanction, the court must provide the juvenile with a written explanation of the legal consequences that may arise from committing subsequent criminal acts (Article 83). In judicial practice, warnings are typically imposed as supplementary measures in combination with other reformative sanctions.

Compensation for or elimination of property damage may be ordered only where the juvenile possesses resources over which they have autonomous control, or where they are capable of repairing the damage through their own labour.

Compensation or elimination of damage must be effected by the juvenile personally, within a time frame prescribed by the court (Article 84).

Unpaid educational work (community service) may be imposed for a duration ranging from 20 to 100 h. This work must be performed in institutions such as healthcare, curatorship, guardianship bodies, or other public or private organisations, where the tasks are deemed to have a reformative character. This measure requires the minor's informed consent (Article 85). Article 85 of the CC stipulates an exception: unpaid work may not be imposed if the minor is placed in a special reformative facility.

Placement for upbringing and care with parents or other natural or legal persons entrusted with child care may be ordered for a duration ranging from 6 months to 3 years, but not beyond the minor's eighteenth birthday. Pursuant to Article 86 of the CC, such a measure may be imposed if the following conditions are met:

- The parents or designated persons consent to care for the minor, are not deemed to exert a harmful influence, are capable of providing an environment conducive to the minor's development, and agree to cooperate with the institutions responsible for supervising the implementation of the sanction;
- The minor consents to being raised by the designated individuals and undertakes to obey and behave appropriately.

This measure may be imposed either as an independent sanction or in conjunction with other reformative sanctions. It may not be applied when the minor is placed in a special educational institution (Article 86).

Restriction on conduct encompasses court-imposed obligations and prohibitions, which may include: adhering to a curfew; enrolling in or resuming studies; entering into employment; acquiring specific knowledge or learning prohibitions (e.g. traffic safety regulations or school rules); or completing a full course of treatment for alcohol dependency, drug addiction, addiction to toxic substances, or sexually transmitted diseases. This mandatory injunction may be imposed at the request of the minor's parents or guardians, subject to the minor's consent. It may include obligations to participate in social education or rehabilitation programmes organised by state or non-state bodies; prohibitions on gambling; engagement in specified activities; operation of motor vehicles (including motorcycles and self-propelled vehicles); visiting locations deemed detrimental to the minor's conduct; associating with individuals who exert a negative influence; and changing one's place of residence without notifying the institutions responsible for supervising the enforcement of the sanction (Article 87 of CC). Restrictions on conduct may be imposed for a duration ranging from 30 days to 12 months. The term of such sanctions is calculated in days and months. Upon request by the minor, other participants in the criminal proceedings, or at its own discretion, the court may impose additional mandatory or prohibitive injunctions not expressly provided for in the criminal law, provided that such measures are considered likely to have a positive effect on the minor's conduct. A restriction on conduct may be imposed either as an independent reformative sanction or in combination with other educational measures. This sanction may not be applied where the minor is placed in a special reformative facility.

Placement in a special reformative facility refers to institutional socialisation centres, which are formally classified as educational establishments under the authority of the Ministry of Education, Science and Sports. In practice, however, these institutions bear significant resemblance to open correctional facilities: although minors are not physically deprived of liberty, they are required to remain within the facility for a specified period, and visits to parents or guardians are permitted only during designated holidays.

It is noteworthy that Lithuania does not provide for diversion measures for juveniles. Article 93 of the Criminal Code allows for the release of a minor from criminal liability. A minor who has committed a misdemeanour, a negligent criminal offence, or a minor or less serious intentional offence for the first time may be released from criminal liability by the court where one or more of the following conditions apply:

- The minor has offered an apology to the victim and has compensated for or repaired the property damage in full or in part, either through personal labour or monetary payment;
- The minor is found to be of diminished capacity;
- The minor has pleaded guilty and expressed remorse; or other circumstances provide a basis for concluding that the minor is likely to comply with the law and refrain from future offending. Where a minor is released from criminal liability, the court must impose reformative sanctions in their place.

3.2 *Juvenile Supervision Practices in the Probation Service: Key Trends and Challenges*

Juveniles serving community sanctions are supervised by the Probation Service. However, the number of juveniles under such supervision remains relatively low. For example, as of 31 December 2024, stock data indicated that 137 juveniles were under the supervision of the Probation Service, accounting for 2.4% of all individuals subject to probation (Probation Service 2025). By comparison, the number of juvenile suspects reached 677 in 2023 and 710 in 2024, respectively (Information Technology and Communications Department 2025). Only five juveniles served custodial sentences in 2023; however, around 20 juveniles served short-term imprisonment of up to 3 months (Prison Service 2024). These figures suggest that community sanctions constitute the predominant form of sentencing for juveniles in Lithuania.

An analysis of the structure of community sanctions in 2024 reveals that the majority of juveniles—88 individuals, or 64%—were serving educational measures imposed in conjunction with exemption from criminal liability. Additionally, 25 juveniles (18%) were placed on probation (i.e., received a suspended custodial sentence), 24 (17.5%) were subject to a restriction of liberty penalty, and none were assigned to community service (Probation Service 2025).

This distribution suggests that courts tend to favour more lenient measures for juveniles, such as exemption from criminal liability. However, the leniency of sanctions must also be assessed with reference to their substantive content—that is, the specific obligations and restrictions imposed within each sanction. A review of these measures shows that community sanctions applied to juveniles by the Probation Service mainly emphasise control and supervision, while interventions focused on education and resocialisation remain limited. For instance, in 2024, intensive supervision with electronic monitoring was applied to 38 juveniles (28%), and 95 juveniles (69%) were subjected to curfews requiring them to remain at home during designated hours. Meanwhile, 49 juveniles (52.5%) participated in behavioural correction or preventive social rehabilitation programmes (Probation Service 2025). The emphasis on punitive and supervisory measures is further evidenced by the fact that, in 2024, the courts received 40 submissions seeking the revocation of probation or the replacement of an existing sentence or educational measure with a stricter penalty or sanction (Probation Service 2025). In contrast, not a single submission was made for the early termination of probation based on good behaviour.[6]

Intensive supervision with electronic monitoring for juveniles was introduced in 2019 following amendments to the Criminal Code. The revised legal provisions authorised the application of electronic monitoring to individuals subject to probation and restriction of liberty sanctions, including juveniles, without establishing any criteria for individualised assessment. Lithuanian legal scholars have criticised these amendments, arguing that they impose excessive control on juveniles and contravene the principles of minimal intervention and the prioritisation of resocialisation (see Nikartas and Bikelis 2019).

The prevailing focus on control measures stands in marked contrast to the actual needs and challenges faced by minors under the supervision of the Probation Service. For example, the 2024 Report on the Resocialisation of Minors by the Lithuanian Probation Service indicates that most criminal acts committed by juveniles under supervision are not serious in nature. According to the report, minors are most frequently convicted of possession of small quantities of narcotic or psychotropic substances, violent offences, and theft. However, there is no effective system for identifying substance addiction among juveniles with drug-related problems. Addiction is recognised in only a small number of cases involving drug possession, and the report notes that "the problematic nature of use is latent – addiction may not

---

[6] Article 24 of the Republic of Lithuania Law on Probation provides that the court may terminate probation supervision prior to the expiration of the probation term, at the request of the Probation Service, if the probationer has completed at least three-quarters of the probation period—or two-thirds in the case of juvenile probationers. Such a decision may be taken if the probationer's level of risk and conduct during the probation period demonstrate that the aims of probation can be achieved without further supervision, provided that the probationer has not breached the conditions of probation, committed an administrative offence, or committed—or is not suspected or accused of committing—a new criminal offence.

be identified by other institutions, and treatment or other necessary support measures are not provided" (Probation Service 2024). This lack of identification hampers the capacity of probation officers to assess the risks associated with juvenile offending and to implement appropriately targeted interventions.

Moreover, a significant proportion of minors under probation supervision experience difficulties within the family or school environment and, in some cases, lack fundamental socialisation in their immediate surroundings (Probation Service 2024). In order to address these issues effectively, the involvement of child and family support institutions and organisations is of critical importance. However, interagency cooperation remains inconsistent across regions, and due to the insufficient infrastructure of services for children, probation officers are usually limited to offering correctional programs without broader support mechanisms.

4 Juvenile Justice in Romania: Legal Framework and Measures

The Romanian juvenile justice system underwent a substantial transformation following the adoption of the 2014 Penal Code. This reform reoriented the focus of juvenile justice from retribution to rehabilitation and education. This reform aligned with international child rights standards, notably the United Nations Convention on the Rights of the Child (CRC) and the Beijing Rules on Juvenile Justice. At the core of the reform is a recognition that juvenile delinquency constitutes a developmental and social issue, thereby necessitating a prioritisation of reintegration and rehabilitation over punitive isolation (Biriş and Feher 2020; Păroşanu 2016a, b).

The legal framework governing juvenile justice in Romania is founded upon two principal sources: the Criminal Code and child protection legislation. The Criminal Code sets out the sanctions and measures applicable to juveniles deemed criminally liable. In parallel, child protection legislation regulates interventions for children who are under the age of criminal responsibility or who commit offences but lack the requisite discernment. This dual framework enables a differentiated approach, ensuring that responses are proportionate to the child's age, developmental stage, and individual circumstances.

4.1 Criminal Liability Age and Legal Distinctions

Article 113 of the Romanian Penal Code defines clear criteria for the age of criminal responsibility, categorising minors into three groups based on age and cognitive maturity (Table 3). This classification plays a central role in determining whether a child falls within the remit of the penal or child protection systems.

Table 3 Criminal Liability Age in Romania

Age Group	Legal Status	Relevant Legislation	Description
Under 14 Years	Not Criminally Liable	Article 113, Romanian Penal Code	Children under 14 cannot be held criminally responsible, regardless of the nature or severity of the offence.
14–16 Years	Conditionally Criminally Liable	Article 113, Romanian Penal Code	Criminal liability applies only if discernment is established through psychological evaluation.
Over 16 Years	Fully Criminally Liable	Article 113, Romanian Penal Code	Juveniles over the age of 16 are presumed to possess full discernment, though they continue to benefit from specialised legal protections.

This graduated model of criminal responsibility reflects the principle of evolving capacities, as articulated in international instruments such as Article 40 of the CRC, which encourages the adoption of minimum age thresholds for criminal liability. Where criminal liability is inapplicable—either due to the child's age (under 14) or a lack of discernment—interventions fall under the scope of Law No. 272/2004 on the Protection and Promotion of Children's Rights. This legislation establishes a comprehensive and coordinated framework for ensuring the protection, development, and well-being of children in conflict with the law, with the best interests of the child serving as the guiding principle.

4.2 *Protection Measures under Child Protection Legislation*

For children below the age of criminal responsibility, or for those determined to lack discernment, the legal framework prioritises social and educational reintegration rather than punitive responses (Table 4). The National Authority for the Protection of Children's Rights and Adoption (NAPCRA) is responsible for overseeing the implementation of child protection measures as stipulated by Law No. 272/2004 on child protection.

The placement and supervision of juveniles under these measures prioritise the preservation of family ties and the reintegration of the child into the community, in alignment with the child's best interests (Article 3, CRC).

Table 4 Child Protection Measures in Romania

Protection Measure	Description	Legal Basis	Applicability
Placement in Residential Centres	Placement in specialised care facilities that provide education, psychological support, and care,	Article 62, Law No. 272/2004	Typically applied when a child lacks family support or poses a risk to themselves or others.
Emergency Placement	Temporary placement in urgent situations requiring immediate protection.	Article 68, Law No. 272/2004	Typically ordered in cases of severe neglect, abuse, or imminent risk to the child's safety.
Specialised Supervision	The child remains at home but under the supervision of child protection services,	Article 71, Law No. 272/2004	Applied for minor offences or when the family environment is stable and supportive.

4.3 *Educational Measures Under the Penal Code for Those Criminally Liable*

The 2014 Penal Code introduced a range of educational measures designed to rehabilitate juveniles who are criminally liable (Table 5). It should be noted that the new legislation makes no provision for imprisonment for juveniles, emphasising the exclusive application of educational measures. These educational measures are categorised into non-custodial and custodial options, reflecting the principle of proportionality in sentencing. Custodial educational measures are reserved for more serious offences and involve placement in educational or detention centres (Table 6).

Although custodial educational measures bear some resemblance to a prison sentence, they are, in both legal and practical terms, distinct in their objectives and implementation. Unlike conventional prison sentences, which are defined by punitive aims and reinforced security mechanisms, custodial educational measures are grounded in a rehabilitative approach, with particular emphasis on education and reintegration. The main objective of this measure is to promote personal development, provide juveniles with essential life skills and facilitate their successful reintegration into society. Much attention is paid to the empowerment and development support of juveniles, aiming to reduce the likelihood of recidivism and promote social inclusion. It also addresses the root causes of delinquency by applying the principles of restorative justice and prioritising the best interests of the child. The courts routinely review custodial measures to ensure that they remain aligned with the juvenile's progress and rehabilitation needs.

Table 5 Educational Measures for Juveniles in Romania

Educational Measure	Description	Legal Basis	Applicability
Civic Education Programmes	Programmes designed to instil respect for social norms and community values.	Article 117, Romanian Penal Code	Applied to juveniles who commit minor offences.
Supervision	The juvenile remains in the family environment under close monitoring.	Article 118, Romanian Penal Code	Recommended when the family environment is conducive to rehabilitation.
Weekend Restrictions	Restrictions on the juvenile's activities and movements during weekends.	Article 119, Romanian Penal Code	Applied to offences warranting limited punitive measures while maintaining community ties.
Daily Assistance	Continuous monitoring through regular contact with probation officers or social workers.	Article 120, Romanian Penal Code	Imposed when structured supervision is necessary to prevent recidivism.

Table 6 Custodial Educational Measures in Romania

Custodial Measure	Description	Legal Basis	Applicability
Placement in Educational Centres	Juveniles receive education, vocational training, and psychological support.	Article 124, Romanian Penal Code	Applied for serious offences or for repeat offenders.
Placement in Detention Centres	Juveniles placed in detention centres are confined but continue to engage in rehabilitative programmes.	Article 125, Romanian Penal Code	This measure is applied to juveniles involved in severe offences, particularly those with limited prospects for community-based rehabilitation.

4.4 Diversion and Alternative Measures in Romania's Juvenile Justice System

Diversion measures are a central component of the Romanian juvenile justice policy (Table 7). They implement a rehabilitative strategy aimed at preventing the negative consequences of the criminal process for minors by prioritising non-punitive measures, such as educational and social integration programs. Article 318 of the Romanian Penal Code authorises prosecutors to discontinue formal prosecution if the juvenile consents to participate in community service, counselling, or vocational training (Durnescu and Popa 2018). This legislative provision aligns with international standards, emphasising the child's best interests and the importance of avoiding unnecessary incarceration (United Nations 1989a, b).

Diversion measures may be applied when there is no public interest in prosecution, targeting minor or medium-severity offences committed by juveniles. The

Table 7 Key Diversion Programmes in Romania

Diversion Programme	Description	Legal Basis	Applicability
Community Service	Juveniles perform voluntary work for the benefit of the community under supervised conditions for a period ranging from 30 to 60 days.	Article 318, Romanian Penal Procedure Code	Typically applied to non-violent, first-time offenders.
Mediation and Reparation	Facilitated dialogue between the victim and the juvenile, promoting reconciliation and reparation.	Article 318, Romanian Penal Procedure Code	Imposed when the victim consents to participate, and reconciliation is deemed appropriate.
Public Apology to the Victim	A formal apology issued by the juvenile, as part of the mediation philosophy.	Article 318, Romanian Penal Procedure Code	Imposed when both the victim and the juvenile agree to participate, and reconciliation is deemed appropriate.
Counselling and Psychological Support	Therapeutic interventions aimed at addressing underlying behavioural issues and promoting mental health.	Article 318, Romanian Penal Procedure Code	Recommended for juveniles with emotional or psychological challenges contributing to delinquency.

main objective of these measures is to reduce the risk of recidivism and promote the development of socially responsible behaviour. They are applied at the pre-trial stage at the discretion of the prosecutor. The juvenile's willingness to cooperate and comply with the prescribed conditions is taken into account. An additional criterion is that the offence must not pose a serious threat to public safety.

4.5 *Trends and Statistical Overview*

According to the AWAY National Report on Romania's juvenile justice system (Durnescu and Popa 2018), approximately 4000 juveniles benefit from diversion programmes annually, representing nearly 50% of all juvenile cases processed through the legal system.

The high diversion rate underscores the significant emphasis placed on rehabilitative approaches over punitive measures. The data from the report further indicates that diversion is most commonly applied in cases of theft, vandalism, and minor assaults. The prominent focus on theft offences suggests that a substantial proportion of juvenile offenders are involved in non-violent crimes, often driven by economic motives. This trend aligns with broader criminological perspectives, which suggest that juvenile delinquency is more often a consequence of socio-economic vulnerabilities than a reflection of 'inherent criminal tendencies' (Biriş and Feher 2020).

The regional disparities in the application of diversion measures highlight significant challenges in ensuring equitable access to rehabilitative programmes across different areas. Empirical evidence indicates that urban centres, such as Bucharest, Cluj, and Timişoara, demonstrate higher rates of diversion compared to rural regions, where infrastructural limitations and a lack of social services may obstruct the effective implementation of such interventions (Durnescu and Popa 2018). This uneven distribution raises pressing concerns regarding access to diversionary measures, underscoring the need for policy interventions to address these disparities. To establish a comprehensive and equitable juvenile justice system, concerted efforts must be made to ensure that diversionary measures are consistently available across geographic regions.

A similar shift towards a less punitive approach within the Romanian juvenile justice system is reflected in the decreasing number of juveniles subjected to formal prosecution and sentencing. Statistical data (personal communication with the Statistical Office of the Superior Council of Magistracy) reveal a downward trend, with the number of juveniles prosecuted declining from 3527 in 2022 to 3208 in 2024. Similarly, the number of juveniles sentenced has reduced from 570 in 2022 to 415 in 2024.

These trends indicate an increasing focus on social and psychological interventions, avoiding traditional criminal law responses. This direction corresponds with contemporary theories that advocate rehabilitation rather than retribution in juvenile justice systems (Dünkel 2005). However, to sustain this trajectory, continued investment in alternative interventions is necessary. This is especially relevant in disadvantaged rural areas, where addressing inequalities is crucial to prevent the undermining of reform efforts.

4.6 Challenges in Implementation

Despite the overall success of diversion initiatives, the AWAY report identifies several obstacles to their comprehensive implementation. The main challenge is institutional fragmentation, which hinders effective communication and cooperation between probation services, child protection agencies and judicial authorities. In addition, there is a lack of training for law enforcement officers on the use of diversion, which results in inconsistent practices.

The scarcity of resources and inadequate infrastructure for diversion programmes, particularly in rural settings, exacerbate these challenges. The lack of qualified staff capable of addressing the specific needs of juvenile offenders further limits the ability of diversion programmes to provide comprehensive rehabilitative support (Durnescu and Popa 2018).

To improve the diversion system, the AWAY Report recommends the development of a national juvenile justice strategy, including formal training for all stakeholders involved in diversion measures. Although these recommendations were made in 2018, they remain relevant to the current context. Additionally, the report advocates for the establishment of dedicated juvenile units within probation services and police forces to ensure the consistent application of diversion practices nationwide.

In order to further strengthen diversion programs, it is important to promote and develop community-level partnerships and invest in vocational training and education initiatives tailored to the individual needs of youth in conflict with the law. Furthermore, raising awareness among families and communities about the benefits of diversion can foster effective support systems for juveniles through rehabilitation.

5 A Comparative Perspective on Juvenile Community Sanctions in Lithuania and Romania

A comprehensive comparison of practices in Romania and Lithuania is presented in Table 8. When reviewing the systems of measures applied to juvenile offenders in Lithuania and Romania, certain similarities emerge. First and foremost, both systems comply with the key provisions of international documents: they apply a wide range of alternative sanctions and measures for children, and prioritise community-based sanctions over imprisonment. Additionally, both systems impose more lenient punishments and measures than those applicable to adults, and provide special provisions for younger children (below the age of criminal responsibility). However, it can be argued that the extent of compliance with these standards differs between the two countries. In Lithuania, compliance is often more minimal and formal in nature. This formal approach to ensuring children's rights is also evident in previous studies examining various aspects of the juvenile justice system (see Nikartas et al. 2013; Vaičiūnienė 2020; Limantė et al. 2021).

As noted earlier, Lithuania's juvenile justice system is extensive in its scope: the state intervenes even in cases of minor legal violations or other forms of inappropriate behaviour (e.g., school absenteeism) through a variety of measures. The application of community sanctions is closely linked to the criminal liability system. For instance, educational measures are imposed as part of probation (such as the postponement of imprisonment) or as a condition for the suspension of criminal liability, meaning that children undergoing such measures continue to be involved in pre-trial investigations and court proceedings. Criminal sanctions and educational measures often mirror those applied to adults, albeit with some differences in their duration and content. Moreover, the absence of alternative diversion mechanisms reinforces the punitive and "labelling" nature of the system, as all children suspected of criminal conduct must undergo each stage of the criminal process.

Additionally, community sanctions in Lithuania often include restrictive control measures, such as the threat of imprisonment for probation violations, electronic monitoring, and curfews, without incorporating supportive measures aimed at addressing underlying issues like drug addiction or adverse social environments.

Table 8 Comparison of Lithuanian and Romanian Practices in Community Sanctions for Children

Aspect	Lithuania	Romania
Philosophical Approach	Neo-correctional model: The neo-correctional model focuses primarily on criminal behaviour and legal evaluation, with the needs of the child and justice playing a subordinate role.	In contrast, Romania's approach centres on the child and their needs, with criminal behaviour viewed as a social or developmental issue that requires resolution.
Child Involvement in the Criminal Process	All children suspected or accused of a crime participate in the criminal process until sanctions or measures are determined.	Children committing minor offences are diverted from the criminal process, while serious offenders are involved until the court decides on appropriate measures.
Intervention Level	Broad intervention: A wide array of measures is applied, addressing not only criminal behaviour but also administrative offences, school rule violations, and issues involving children of all ages, including those below the age of criminal responsibility. Diversion mechanisms are not used.	Minimal intervention: Numerous children are diverted from the criminal justice system into educational and social systems. Traditional penalties are not applied to children (for instance, juveniles cannot be sentenced to imprisonment).
Content of Measures	Measures focus on both control and the education/socialisation of the child, though control measures predominate. Probation services implement behavioural correction and prevention programmes for juveniles.	In Romania, the emphasis of measures is on resocialisation and control, with socialisation and educational measures taking precedence even within control measures.
Specialised Juvenile Institutions	No specialised juvenile courts or prosecutors.	Specialised juvenile courts or specialised judges handle cases.
Entities Responsible for Implementation	Probation service collaborates with other institutions and organisations. Some probation officers specialise in juvenile work.	Probation service and other entities involved in implementing measures.
Juvenile Control During Sentences	Children on probation or subject to restricted freedom may be monitored via electronic means in Lithuania. Probation officers in Lithuania are authorised to conduct home visits.	In Romania, juveniles are supervised by social services or probation services during the enforcement of community-based educational or protective measures.
Practical Issues	Lithuania faces limited inclusion of juveniles in behavioural correction programmes.	Additionally, diversion practices in provincial areas are hampered by staff shortages and inadequate financial resources.

Previous probation studies in Lithuania also highlight the control- and punishment-oriented nature of probation practices (see Nikartas and Paliauka 2024; Nikartas et al. 2021). This control-oriented approach raises questions about whether the principle of minimal intervention is being honoured, and whether education and resocialisation—key international norms in juvenile justice—are being adequately prioritised.

In contrast, the Romanian juvenile justice system aligns more closely with international standards, particularly those outlined in "soft law" instruments, such as the United Nations' and the Council of Europe's recommendations. Unlike in Lithuania, in Romania, the systems for responding to adult and juvenile criminal behaviour are clearly separated. In Romania, juveniles are not subject to traditional punishments and measures, with priority given to educational and resocialisation interventions. In addition, diversion programmes are applied to juveniles at an early stage of the criminal process. These programmes prevent the formal involvement of children who have committed minor offences in the criminal justice system. In this way, the principle of minimal intervention is ensured, and the risk of stigmatisation of children is reduced.

Different approaches to responses to juvenile delinquency are also reflected in institutional differences. Lithuania lacks a specialised juvenile justice system—neither structural court specialisation nor individual judicial specialisation has been established. All juvenile cases are heard in general criminal courts. In contrast, Romania has specialised juvenile justice courts, which ensure that cases involving children are handled by judges trained in child-sensitive legal principles.

From a theoretical standpoint, the Lithuanian justice system can be classified as neo-correctional (Cavadino and Dignan 2006), emphasising state intervention, control, and behavioural correction. An analysis of practices in Lithuania supports this classification: the system of criminal liability for juveniles is not separated from that of adults, either procedurally or institutionally. Children, even in cases of minor offences, are drawn into the formal criminal process. At the stage of sentence execution, numerous measures restricting freedom of movement are applied, while there is a lack of resocialisation initiatives and interventions addressing the root causes of juvenile offending. Such practices, although formally aligned with the main requirements of international instruments, nevertheless reflect a more formalistic rather than substantive adherence to international standards.

In contrast, the Romanian system is more closely aligned with a welfare-oriented model, which views juvenile delinquency as a social issue. This approach emphasises measures aimed at addressing the underlying problems faced by the child, rather than relying on punitive responses that are often ineffective and stigmatising. In line with the philosophy of the welfare model, Romania places significant emphasis on diversion, specialised juvenile justice institutions, and a clear separation between sanctions applied to adults and those applied to juveniles. Statistical data support this characterisation: diversion measures are widely implemented, and more than 50% of juvenile cases result in non-punitive outcomes (Durnescu and Popa 2018). Moreover, the declining number of formally convicted juveniles—from 570 in 2022 to 415 in 2024—indicates a systemic commitment to minimising the use of criminal justice intervention in favour of rehabilitation strategies.

6 Practical Challenges and Reform Trajectories

Despite these divergent approaches, both Lithuania and Romania face practical challenges in implementing community sanctions. Specialisation and training are critical to the success of juvenile justice systems. Romania, with its juvenile courts and probation services, is better positioned to apply child-friendly justice principles, whereas Lithuania's general criminal justice system restricts the application of rehabilitative measures. Expanding specialisation in Lithuania could facilitate the implementation of individualised interventions for young offenders.

A significant challenge for both systems is regional disparity in access to diversion and community sanctions, particularly in rural areas. In Romania, empirical data highlight a concentration of diversionary practices in urban centres such as Bucharest, Cluj, and Timişoara, while rural regions remain underserved due to limited infrastructure and social services (Durnescu and Popa 2018). Similarly, in Lithuania, probation officers report a lack of adequate social and psychological support services for juveniles, particularly in non-urban areas. In order to address regional disparities and ensure the nationwide availability of rehabilitative measures, it is important to allocate targeted investments to community-based programmes, inter-agency coordination, and the professional training of justice system personnel.

The insights derived from this comparative analysis point to several key policy recommendations for enhancing community sanctions for juveniles:

- **Developing diversion mechanisms:** It is recommended that Lithuanian policymakers assess the possibilities of introducing and implementing formal diversion programmes. Such programmes would help to better uphold the principles of minimal intervention and proportionality, while also reducing the negative impact of the criminal process and the harm caused by stigmatisation.
- **Strengthening institutional and individual specialisation:** It is recommended that Lithuanian policymakers consider the implementation of institutional specialisation for courts, individual specialisation of judges, and other law enforcement officials (e.g., prosecutors, police officers) working with minors. The specialisation would contribute to reinforcing child-friendly justice standards and promoting a criminal justice process that is responsive to the needs of the child.
- **Addressing regional disparities:** It is recommended that policymakers and practitioners in both countries implement strategies and measures to ensure that services provided under community sanctions and measures for children are equally accessible in both rural and urban areas. To achieve this goal, it is important to make continuous and targeted investments in community-based rehabilitation programmes, child-focused social services, and local resocialisation infrastructure adapted to the developmental needs of juveniles.
- **Shifting from Control to Support-Oriented Interventions:** Lithuanian policymakers should reconsider the role of electronic monitoring and probationary control measures within juvenile sanctioning frameworks. Greater emphasis

should be placed on educational, psychological, and social support interventions in order to align national practice with European standards of child-friendly justice.
- **Enhancing Training and Inter-Agency Cooperation:** Policymakers and practitioners in both countries' juvenile justice systems should develop and implement effective training programmes for judges and other professionals working with juveniles in law enforcement and correctional institutions. These training programmes should aim to equip professionals with the necessary competencies to address the needs of juveniles both during the legal process and at the stage of implementing community sanctions and measures. To support a holistic and sustainable approach to juvenile rehabilitation, it is essential to introduce strategies and measures that enhance cooperation and coordination among institutions and organisations in the justice, social services, and education sectors.

7 Concluding Remarks

This comparative overview of community sanctions systems for juveniles in Lithuania and Romania highlights the divergent paths and philosophical orientations adopted by these two Eastern European countries. Lithuania adheres to a neo-correctional, control-oriented model, whereas Romania reflects a welfare-based approach focused on reintegration. Empirical evidence suggests that Romania's system is more effective and more closely aligned with international, particularly child-friendly, justice standards. It limits the use of formal and traditional punitive measures for children, giving preference to rehabilitative interventions that avoid involving minors in the criminal justice system.

In contrast, Lithuania's current practice, where juveniles are subjected to a criminal process designed for adults and where community sanctions emphasise control mechanisms at the implementation stage, raises concerns regarding its compliance with child-friendly justice standards. Specifically, the principles of minimal intervention and the best interests and needs of the child are not only at risk of being implemented merely formally, but also lack substantive realisation in practice.

Looking to the future, both systems must continue to develop in line with international standards for child-friendly justice. In Romania, a key priority remains the consistent, nationwide application of diversion mechanisms. Lithuania, on the other hand, could make significant progress toward a rehabilitation-oriented model by implementing targeted legal reforms, developing diversion programmes, and establishing specialised institutional frameworks.

This analysis also indicates the need for a substantive, rather than merely formal, approach to child resocialisation and social integration. The Lithuanian case illustrates that compliance with international standards on paper is insufficient. Effectively addressing the problems underlying juvenile delinquent behaviour requires a child-centred perspective—one that moves beyond the application of traditional punitive responses and the prioritisation of control-based measures.

Legal Acts and Recommendations

Council of Europe (2010) *Guidelines of the Committee of Ministers of the Council of Europe on Child-Friendly Justice.* Available at: https://rm.coe.int/16804b2cf3.

Council of Europe (2017) *Recommendation CM/Rec(2017)3 of the Committee of Ministers to member States on the European Rules on community sanctions and measures.* Available at: https://rm.coe.int/168070c09b.

The Seimas of the Republic of Lithuania. (2000). *Criminal Code of the Republic of Lithuania.* Available at: https://e-seimas.lrs.lt/portal/legalAct/lt/TAD/TAIS.111555.

United Nations (1985) *United Nations Standard Minimum Rules for the Administration of Juvenile Justice (Beijing Rules).* Available at: https://www.ohchr.org/sites/default/files/Documents/ProfessionalInterest/beijingrules.pdf.

United Nations (1989) *Convention on the Rights of the Child.* Available at: https://www.ohchr.org/en/instruments-mechanisms/instruments/convention-rights-child.

United Nations. (1989). *Convention on the Rights of the Child.* New York: United Nations.

Statistics

Information Technology and Communications Department (2025) *Statistical report: Data on suspected (accused) and victimized juveniles in the Republic of Lithuania (Form_VSDN).* Available at: https://ird.lt/lt/reports/view_item_datasource?id=11393&datasource=102797.

Lithuanian Prison Service (2024) *Report on current statistics.* Available at: https://kalejimai.lrv.lt/public/canonical/1739357432/2076/Aktualioji%20statistika%202023%204%20ketv.pdf.

Lithuanian Probation Service (2025) *Statistical report on work with juveniles under the supervision of the Lithuanian Probation Service.* Available at: https://probacija.lrv.lt/public/canonical/1737355635/340/Darbo%20su%20nepilname%C4%8Diais%20esan%C4%8Diais%20LPT%20prie%C5%BEi%C5%ABroje%20statistin%C4%97%20ataskaita_2024%20m.%20met%C5%B3.pdf.

Lithuanian Probation Service, Resocialization and Supervision Division. (2024). *Report on targeted employment-promoting measures in the resocialization of juveniles and their risks and needs* [Unpublished report].

References

Books, Chapters, and Articles

Becker HS (1963) Outsiders. Studies in the Sociology of Deviance, p 1

Bernburg JG, Krohn MD, Rivera CJ (2006) Official labeling, criminal embeddedness, and subsequent delinquency: a longitudinal test of labeling theory. J Res Crime Delinq 43(1):67–88

Biriş I, Feher T (2020) Juvenile justice reform in Romania: a shift towards rehabilitation. Eur J Criminol 17(3):267–284
Cavadino M, Dignan J (2006) Penal systems. A comparative approach. Sage, London
Dünkel F (2005) Juvenile Justice in Germany – Between welfare and justice. Internet-publication European Society of Criminology, www.esc-eurocrim.org, working groups: thematic working group on juvenile justice
Dünkel F (2014) Juvenile Justice Systems in Europe–Reform developments between justice, welfare and 'new punitiveness'1. Kriminol Stud 1:31–76
Dünkel F (2024) Youth Justice-European and International Developments. Pravnik 79:285
Dünkel F, Pruin I (2009) Community sanctions and the sanctioning practice in juvenile justice systems in Europe. Reforming Juvenile Justice:183–204
Durnescu I, Popa C (2018) Juvenile diversion in Romania: working in isolation. Available at: https://eq-bg.org/wp-content/uploads/2021/09/Durnescu-Popa-2018-pdf-97.pdf
Henkes B (2000) The role of education in juvenile justice in Eastern Europe and former Soviet Union. CEU, Budapest College
Liberman AM, Kirk DS, Kim K (2014) Labeling effects of first juvenile arrests: Secondary deviance and secondary sanctioning. Criminology 52(3):345–370
Limantė A, Vaičiūnienė R, Apolevič J (2021) Child-friendly legal aid and individual assessment of children in conflict with the law: building the basis for effective participation. Int J Environ Res Public Health 19(1):17
Nikartas S, Bikelis S (2019) Dėl įstatymų projektų Nr. 18-12583-12589 suderinimo. Teisės e-aktualijos 16(1):21–32
Nikartas S, Paliauka J (2024) "I would work with a client, but I have to fill out papers": understanding professional roles and role conflicts experienced by Lithuanian probation officers. Probat J. Advanced online publication. https://doi.org/10.1177/02645505241267120
Nikartas S, Ūselė L, Zaksaitė S, Žukauskaitė J, Žėkas T (2013) Vaiko minimalios priežiūros priemonės Lietuvoje: prielaidos, situacija ir įgyvendinimo problemos. Lietuvos teisės institutas, Vilnius
Nikartas S, Vaičiūnienė R, Apolevič J (2020) Implementation of individual assessment in Lithuania. In: Vaičiūnienė R (ed) Individual assessment of suspected or accused children: insights into good practice in the light of Directive (EU) 2016/800. Žara, Vilnius, pp 85–114
Nikartas S, Vaičiūnienė R, Rinkevičiūtė G (2021) Probation officers' discretionary decisions in responding to probation violations: the case of Lithuania. Probat J 68(1):28–46
Păroşanu A (2016a) The evolution of juvenile justice in Romania: legislative changes and their implications. J Law Soc Policy 8(1):45–62
Păroşanu A (2016b) Juvenile justice in Romania – reform trends, legal aspects, sentencing practice and imprisonment trends. Revista de Estudios de la Justicia 25:1–20
Pruin I, Dünkel F, Grzywa J (2011) The implementation of alternative sanctions and measures into juvenile justice systems. Rom J Sociol 1(2):3–22
Robila M (2004) Families in Eastern Europe: context, trends and variations. In: Families in Eastern Europe. Emerald Group Publishing Limited, pp 1–14
Slade G, Light M (2015) Crime and criminal justice after communism: why study the post-Soviet region? Theor Criminol 19(2):147–158
Sakalauskas G (ed.), Jarutienė L, Kalpokas V, et al. (2020) Kalinimo sąlygos ir kalinių socialinės integracijos prielaidos. Vilnius: Žara, Lietuvos teisės institutas.
Vaičiūnienė R (ed) (2020) Individual assessment of suspected or accused children: Insights into good practice in the light of Directive (EU) 2016/800 (pp. XX–XX). Žara, Vilnius
World Prison Brief (2024) Lithuania, prison population rate (per 100,000 of national population). [online] Available at: https://www.prisonstudies.org/country/lithuania [Accessed 11 May 2025]

Simonas Nikartas is a chief researcher at the Law Institute of the Lithuanian Centre for Social Sciences and associate professor at the Department of Criminology at the Faculty of Philosophy of Vilnius University. His research covers different aspects of criminal justice and crime prevention. In recent years, he has focused his research on probation and community sanctions, child-friendly justice (focusing on legal aid and individual assessment in criminal proceedings), the discretion and professionalism of criminal justice officers, offenders' experiences of punishment, human rights in prisons and legal aid in criminal justice. He has taken part in a number of national and international research projects and authored more than 30 publications.

Dr. Nikartas is also a member of the Community Sanctions and Measures working group of the European Society of Criminology. He has work experience as head of the Probation Division in the Prison Department under the Ministry of Justice of the Republic of Lithuania. He carried out multiple criminological and legal expertise of law drafts and participated in different expert working groups for the preparation of laws or policy documents in the field of criminal justice.

Prof Dr Ioan Durnescu is a professor at the University of Bucharest, Faculty of Sociology and Social Work (Romania). His primary focus is on probation, prison, and deradicalization, where he teaches and conducts research. He has a special interest in comparative probation, reentry, and interventions for justice-involved individuals.

Prof Durnescu has had the privilege of conducting training sessions in various countries such as Jordan, Moldova, Spain, Kosovo, and others. He has also contributed as an editor to publications like "Probation in Europe" (WOLF) and "Understanding Penal Practice" (Routledge). Additionally, he has authored the book "Core Correctional Skills: The Training Kit". Furthermore, Prof Durnescu serves as a co-editor for the European Journal of Probation. His work reflects his dedication to the field of probation and criminal justice, as well as his commitment to sharing knowledge and promoting scholarly discussions.

Criminological Analysis of Juvenile Resocialisation Measures in the Lithuanian Probation Service

Rokas Uscila and Renata Mienkowska Norkienė

Abstract This chapter explores the current situation of juvenile offenders within the Lithuanian Probation Service. The study seeks to evaluate the existing resocialisation measures applied by the Service, focusing on their types, diversity, and the perceptions of probation officers regarding their effectiveness. Furthermore, it assesses programmes aimed at correcting adolescents' behaviour from the viewpoint of probation practitioners and identifies the limitations associated with the use of electronic monitoring for minors. The chapter employs both quantitative and qualitative research methods, presenting empirical findings alongside statistical data analysis.

1 Introduction

The Lithuanian probation system plays a crucial role in the national criminal justice framework, particularly in addressing juvenile delinquency, as probation officers bear primary responsibility for the rehabilitation and supervision of juvenile offenders. It is also essential to highlight that working with juveniles differs fundamentally from working with adult offenders. Probation staff must not only be equipped with effective resocialisation tools but also possess a comprehensive set of competencies that enable them to implement interventions successfully and achieve measurable outcomes.

On average, there are 10 to 12 minors serving custodial sentences in Lithuanian correctional institutions each year for serious or grave offences. The greatest responsibility for their supervision and resocialisation falls upon the Lithuanian Probation Service and its associated social partners. Numerous scholars have examined the efficacy of probation in preventing recidivism, reducing the financial burden of

R. Uscila (✉)
Law Institute, Lithuanian Centre for Social Sciences, Vilnius, Lithuania

R. Mienkowska Norkienė
Faculty of Political Science and International Studies, University of Warsaw, Warsaw, Poland

A. Limantė, R. Vaičiūnienė (eds.), *Children's Rights in Central and Eastern Europe*, European Union and its Neighbours in a Globalized World 29,
https://doi.org/10.1007/978-3-032-07092-0_15

institutionalising youth, and facilitating the reintegration of juvenile offenders into society. Most research findings indicate a positive impact of probation, particularly in reducing repeat offending. However, the effectiveness of probation largely depends on its specific form—for example, whether it is administered in a home environment—and whether the offender is a first-time juvenile delinquent (Ryan et al. 2014, pp. 7–19). A notable example from Cologne, Germany, demonstrated that enhanced support for juveniles on probation significantly reduces the likelihood of reoffending (Engel et al. 2023, pp. 468–475). A comprehensive and influential American research report (Robin et al. 2023), widely cited in the field of juvenile crime prevention, underscores the importance of gathering insights from probation practitioners concerning their knowledge of effective probation activities, their assessments of these interventions, and their practical needs to improve probation outcomes.

This chapter presents the findings of research conducted among probation practitioners in Lithuania. The results can inform future policy planning aimed at enhancing the probation system in the Republic of Lithuania and may also be applicable to countries with similar institutional structures and practices. Thus, examining the appropriateness of probation use, its specific forms, the perspectives of practitioners on its effectiveness, and the ongoing evaluation and refinement of such measures is essential for formulating informed and effective public policies within the justice sector. This imperative becomes even more apparent in light of research indicating that probation may not always constitute the optimal solution for juvenile offenders, a concern increasingly raised by Lithuanian scholars who question the suitability of existing probation approaches in addressing the real challenges of juvenile delinquency (Nikartas 2018, p. 383).

This chapter introduces an original methodological approach to the analysis of juvenile rehabilitation within Lithuania's probation system, examining it from the perspective of probation officers. It also offers an opportunity for foreign probation systems and offices to evaluate their own practices and draw comparisons. The analysis contributes to the relatively limited body of research on probation systems, as most existing studies focus on juvenile offenders in custodial institutions rather than those under community supervision.

The aim of this chapter is to assess probation officers' perceptions of the effectiveness of the resocialisation measures and services provided to adolescents by the Lithuanian Probation Service, and to formulate recommendations for improving the process of juvenile resocialisation and supervision.

2 Methodology

The chapter presents an analysis of statistical data provided by the Lithuanian Probation Service for the period from 2013 to 2023, as well as data from the databases of the State Data Agency. It also includes an analysis of empirical data collected through a survey conducted between 14 May 2024 and 14 June 2024. The questionnaire was distributed to 285 probation officers in Lithuania, of whom 120 responded. The survey instrument comprised 30 questions, including closed, semi-open, and open-ended formats. The questionnaire was disseminated electronically via email addresses of the Lithuanian Probation Service, containing links to the survey platform (www.apklausa.lt). The survey was conducted anonymously and aimed to gather probation officers' subjective opinions on existing resocialisation and control measures for juveniles, including those established under the Probation Law. The survey successfully reached probation officers with extensive practical experience, particularly in the area of juvenile supervision. Of the respondents, 46% had more than ten years of experience in probation, while 22% had between five and ten years. Therefore, the responses are grounded in considerable practical expertise and specific professional knowledge. Additionally, 57% of respondents held the position of chief or senior specialist, 8% were senior specialists, and 32% were specialists.

3 Measures for the Resocialisation of Juveniles in the Lithuanian Probation Service

Over the past decade, the number of minors under the supervision of the Lithuanian Probation Service has declined by a factor of 4.6 (see Fig. 1). In 2023, the number of minors under supervision stood at 113.62 per 100,000 minors, a sharp decrease from 408.77 per 100,000 minors ten years earlier. This encouraging trend continues and is attributed both to demographic shifts and to changes in the juvenile criminal justice system, in which criminal law is increasingly applied in accordance with the principle *of ultima ratio.*

According to statistics from the Lithuanian Probation Service, approximately 63% of supervised minors were sentenced to educational measures (Article 82 of

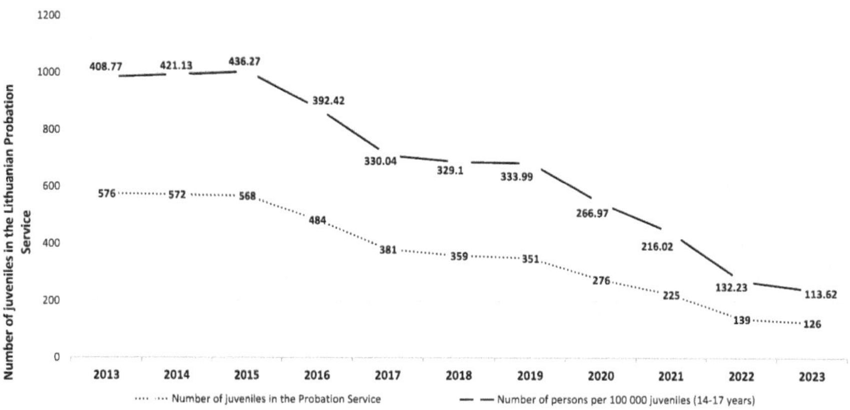

Fig. 1 Number of minors under the supervision of the Lithuanian Probation Service, 2013–2023

the Criminal Code), 18% received suspended sentences (Article 92), and 19% were sentenced to custodial penalties (Article 48).

The considerable fluctuations in the number of juveniles within Lithuanian correctional institutions are particularly noteworthy—over the past decade, this figure has decreased by a factor of 8.9. As of the reporting date in 2023, only 10 juveniles remained under the supervision of the Lithuanian Prison Service (refer to Fig. 2 for further details). These developments are significant not only for understanding changes in criminal and penal policy but also in the context of strategic goals such as reducing recidivism, limiting the proliferation of criminal subcultures, decreasing the overall prison population, and promoting alternatives to incarceration for minors. Accordingly, legal, strategic, and operational measures have been directed towards lowering the rate of juvenile imprisonment, preventing the onset of criminal careers, and fostering the full social integration of young offenders. In addition, one of the key priorities is the qualitative and effective resocialisation of juveniles, which must be systematically evaluated alongside a comprehensive analysis of the current practices employed by the Lithuanian Probation Service.

The necessity to assess resocialisation measures stems from the imperative to identify the most effective and appropriate methods for influencing behavioural change and shaping minors' attitudes towards their social environment. This study seeks to evaluate the current resocialisation measures employed by the Lithuanian Probation Service by analysing their types, diversity, and the perceived effectiveness of these measures as reported by probation officers. International practice suggests that the success of juvenile resocialisation programmes is determined by several factors:

- Accurate and timely risk assessment of re-offending, followed by the appropriate selection and implementation of corrective measures aimed at mitigating criminogenic factors;
- Application of motivational strategies in conjunction with ongoing resocialisation and supervision efforts;

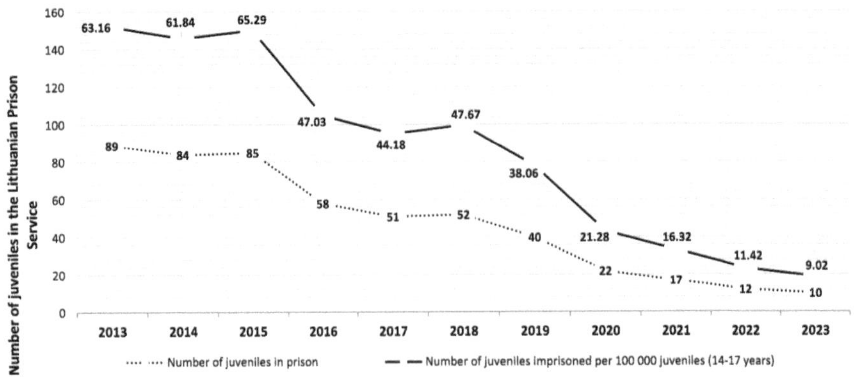

Fig. 2 Number of Juveniles under the Supervision of the Lithuanian Prison Service, 2013–2023

- Enrolment in approved programmes focusing on cognitive behavioural modification, development of social skills, and related areas;
- Tracking juvenile recidivism, including both repeated and new offences.

For instance, research conducted in Italy found that 86% of juveniles under probation supervision demonstrated positive behavioural change. Conversely, 14% did not benefit from the programme due to reasons such as non-compliance (56.1%), re-offending (34.1%), or other factors (9.8%) (di Gennaro 2020, pp. 1–19). Data from the Italian Department of Juvenile Justice indicate that only 10% of juvenile offenders placed on probation failed to achieve positive outcomes v Approximately one-third of juvenile offenders were charged with at least one further offence within a four-year period (Pieroni et al. 2013, pp. 1–14). A separate study in Spain concluded that juveniles who were subject to probation supervision without prior detention were less likely to re-offend compared to those who had been placed in closed institutions. The recidivism rate among juveniles on probation was 24%, whereas it stood at 39% for those in secure facilities (Villanueva and Cuervo 2018, pp. 4108–4123).

Findings from international research served as the impetus for an empirical study within the Lithuanian Probation Service, which aimed to collect staff perspectives on the implementation and effectiveness of legally sanctioned juvenile resocialisation measures.

The findings of the research indicate that, according to probation officers, the most effective resocialisation measures are those that are individualised in nature, with officers selecting both communication and supervisory strategies tailored to each juvenile. A total of 92.8% of probation officers identified individual counselling by a psychologist and addiction counselling services as the most effective interventions (Table 1). Furthermore, the survey data reveal that direct engagement with the juvenile and targeted interventions can foster the desired resocialisation outcomes by altering the juvenile's attitude towards the offence committed, addressing psychological issues, and enabling conditions conducive to social integration. Nonetheless, there remains a question regarding the extent to which individualised interventions are methodologically grounded and structured. Best practices in juvenile resocialisation should be informed by validated, evidence-based approaches. It is important to note that effectiveness studies are typically conducted when behaviour modification or other resocialisation programmes are implemented within a specific probation system. Therefore, to maximise resocialisation outcomes, it is recommended that scientifically validated programmes be employed—programmes that allow for both implementation assessment and evaluation of their impact on juveniles.

At the same time, the relatively low appraisal of mediation as an effective measure raises concerns, especially considering that, as a restorative justice model, mediation is highly regarded across Europe, particularly in juvenile justice contexts. For instance, studies conducted in Austria found that 81% of juvenile mediation cases were successfully concluded following the submission of a positive report by the mediator(s) to the public prosecutor. The recidivism rate in these cases was 14%

Table 1 Probation officers' perceptions of the effectiveness of resocialisation measures applied by the Lithuanian probation service to juveniles (percentage, N-120)

No.	Resocialisation measures for juveniles	Very effective	Effective	Neither effective nor ineffective	Ineffective	Very ineffective
1.	Individual work with the juvenile	30.9%	56.4%	11.8%	0.9%	0.0%
2.	Individual counselling on specific issues by the supervisory officer	27.8%	64.8%	7.4%	0.0%	0.0%
3.	Individual counselling by a psychologist	47.3%	45.5%	6.4%	0.9%	0.0%
4.	Group counselling by a psychologist	19.4%	51.9%	25.0%	3.7%	0.0%
5.	Risk assessment of the juvenile based on the START:AV methodology	12.1%	39.3%	38.3%	8.4%	1.9%
6.	Addiction counselling services for juveniles	27.5%	56.9%	12.8%	2.8%	0.0%
7.	Provision of mediation services for juveniles	17.4%	45.0%	29.4%	8.3%	0.0%
8.	Information interview with the juvenile, during which legal information concerning rights, obligations, and consequences is provided in accordance with the law	20.6%	54.2%	22.4%	2.8%	0.0%
9.	Information interview with the legal representatives of the juvenile, during which legal information on rights, obligations, and consequences is provided in accordance with the law	22.9%	56.0%	19.3%	1.8%	0.0%

over a period ranging from 2.5 to 3.5 years (Hofinger and Neumann 2018). Another study from Belgium revealed that 86% of victim–offender mediation cases resulted in full or partial reconciliation between the parties involved. In nearly half of these cases, the agreement included an apology by the juvenile; in over 60%, it involved financial compensation; and in 15%, it entailed other obligations, such as school attendance or participation in structured activities. Thus, mediation emerges as a particularly effective intervention for juveniles who have committed offences (Van Dijk 2004, pp. 8–23).

4 Behavioural Correction Programmes for Juveniles in the Probation Service

As previously mentioned, behavioural correction programmes represent one of the most effective means of resocialising juveniles. However, within probation service practice, questions persist as to whether general social skills programmes are sufficient, whether programmes designed for adults are appropriate for juveniles, and whether there is a need for specialised behavioural correction programmes—and, if so, which of these are most effective. Specialists employed by the Lithuanian Probation Service are trained to implement various behavioural correction programmes[1] that are specifically tailored for minors or young people. One such programme, widely regarded for its level of specialisation and implemented in educational institutions and the Probation Service, is the EQUIP programme.[2] This programme aims to teach minors to think and act responsibly, to foster mutual support among participants, and to promote personal and social responsibility. The programme emphasises the development and maintenance of positive relationships between juveniles and their immediate social environment through group activities focused on anger management, error reflection, social capital development, social skills acquisition, and responsible decision-making. Research conducted in Lithuania affirms the effectiveness of the EQUIP programme (Klimukienė and Kalpokienė 2018, pp. 115–132).

However, this programme is a group programme. However, despite its effectiveness, the EQUIP programme is not implemented in the Probation Service due to several objective constraints. These include an insufficient number of juveniles in specific regions to form viable groups, logistical difficulties in coordinating group work due to varying educational schedules and participation in extracurricular activities, the programme's complexity and unsuitability for remote delivery, and the frequent entry and exit of juveniles from the Probation Service, which results in group fragmentation. The study found that the most commonly implemented programme in practice is the Behaviour-Conversation-Change (BCC) model, which consists of structured, individual interviews with minors.[3] BCC is a motivational

[1] Lietuvos probacijos tarnybos direktoriaus 2022-10-17 d. įsakymas Nr. V-284 "Dėl elgesio pataisos programų vykdymo Lietuvos probacijos tarnyboje tvarkos aprašo patvirtinimo".

[2] Note: EQUIP is a group-based cognitive behavioural programme designed to foster responsible thinking and behaviour among young people using a self-help model. It is recommended for juveniles who have reoffended and for young persons up to the age of 24. The recommended delivery includes 4–5 sessions per week, with a minimum of three sessions weekly. The programme should be facilitated by two trained instructors. and is ideally attended by groups of 5–9 minors or young adults. Participants are expected to complete at least 55 sessions from the EQUIP manual, with a minimum attendance of 80% (i.e. at least 44 sessions) required to be considered as having successfully completed the EQUIP programme.

[3] Note: The BCC programme consists of six core sessions, each lasting between 45 and 60 min (comprising one introductory session and five motivational semi-structured interviews), with the possibility of an additional session by mutual agreement between the facilitator and the participant.

interviewing-based programme designed to activate and reinforce the juvenile's internal motivation for positive behavioural change, while also preparing the individual for participation in additional resocialisation programmes. On the one hand, probation officers report that juveniles are sufficiently well engaged in the programme, as it is short in duration, the work is conducted on an individual basis, the structure is straightforward and not time-consuming, and most staff are trained in its application and implement it regularly, thereby demonstrating proficiency in programme delivery. On the other hand, the programme's brevity is viewed as a limitation, with professionals noting that achieving meaningful behavioural change requires longer-term engagement. The programme primarily serves as a motivational tool that stimulates initial engagement; however, additional resources are necessary to support individualised work with juveniles, and such resources are currently lacking.

Probation officers also referenced the programme "Youth and Psychoactive Substances" (YSP) used less frequently. This is an individual educational programme designed to support juveniles in acquiring the knowledge, attitudes, and behavioural norms necessary for a healthy lifestyle. The programme is intensive, comprising 15 individual weekly sessions. It is preventive in nature and can be applied both in cases of primary prevention, where the juvenile has no experience with psychoactive substances, and in secondary prevention, where the juvenile has used such substances and the aim is to facilitate cessation. Experts highlight that the programme's effectiveness is enhanced by the involvement of specialised social partners who participate in the sessions and subsequently provide follow-up and support (e.g. youth centres, day centres, and non-governmental organisations).

Also noteworthy is the group-based behavioural correction programme "Early Intervention," which targets both minors and young people up to the age of 21. The programme is intended for juveniles who are experimenting with or sporadically using alcohol or other psychoactive substances but have not yet developed symptoms of dependence. It consists of four thematic group sessions designed to produce both motivational and behavioural change.

A survey of probation service staff indicated that 79% of probation officers believe that juveniles should participate in behavioural correction programmes tailored to their age, level of social maturity, and educational needs. However, in practice, there are instances in which programmes originally developed for adults—such as the Intervention Programme for Domestic Violence Offenders—are applied to juveniles. Although this programme is aimed at individuals who have committed domestic violence against a family member, its structure and the self-assessment tasks used in individual or group settings are not specifically adapted for minors. As a result, staff are compelled to modify certain elements of the programme, which, in

A participant is considered to have completed the BCC programme upon attending all six sessions. It is recommended that the sessions are conducted on a weekly basis. Following completion of the BCC programme, it is advised that the participant is assigned targeted behavioural correction measures.

principle, should be avoided, as such alterations may compromise the programme's structural integrity.

A more detailed analysis of the survey data revealed that only 32% of probation service staff reported that juveniles are assigned specialised behavioural correction programmes aligned with the specific nature of their offences (e.g. violent behaviour, substance-related offences, sexual offences, etc.).

Table 2 presents data on the resocialisation measures perceived by probation officers as the most effective, specifically those that are systematic in nature and require substantial time and human resources. 95% of respondents unambiguously indicated that referring juveniles to and involving them in behavioural correction programmes is effective.

In conclusion, the study demonstrates that the Lithuanian Probation Service has implemented evidence-based behavioural correction programmes, many of which are adapted from international models. Nevertheless, evolving patterns in juvenile socialisation and emerging challenges posed by information technologies necessitate a reassessment of the current programme offerings. The Lithuanian Probation Service is currently evaluating the need for additional resocialisation programmes for minors, particularly in the areas of anger management, social adaptability, and offences of a sexual nature. Accordingly, while individualised engagement with juveniles is crucial, it must be operationalised through structured behavioural correction programmes.

Table 2 Perceptions of probation officers regarding the effectiveness of juvenile resocialisation programmes (%) N-120

No.	Resocialisation programmes for juveniles	Very effective	Effective	Neither effective nor ineffective	Ineffective	Very ineffective
1.	Resocialisation measures encouraging juveniles to engage in leisure-time activities (e.g. educational trips, participation in military activities, etc.)	26.1%	51.4%	16.2%	5.4%	0.9%
2.	Referral of the juvenile to a motivational programme	25.9%	58.0%	14.3%	1.8%	0.0%
3.	Referral of the juvenile to an appropriate behavioural modification programme	26.8%	58.0%	13.4%	1.8%	0.0%
4.	Participation in initiatives organised by social partners aimed at developing social skills, and personal, interpersonal, and professional competences	26.8%	53.6%	18.8%	0.0%	0.9%

5 Evaluation of Control Measures Applied to Juveniles within the Probation Service

The following section provides an analysis of the control measures implemented by the Probation Service in relation to juvenile offenders. Here we are faced with the dilemmic situation that the Law on Probation and other regulations provide for a wide range of control measures for juveniles—which are extensively applied in practice—yet, probation officers themselves express critical views regarding the effectiveness of these measures. Specifically, 26.8% of probation officers consider that issuing warnings to juveniles for misconduct or failure to fulfil obligations is either ineffective or very ineffective. Some officers report that such warnings do not produce a positive behavioural response; instead, they tend to generate confrontation and heighten tension between the officer and the juvenile under supervision. In addition, 14.3% of the staff indicated that requiring juveniles to compensate for or repair property damage is ineffective. This ineffectiveness may be attributed to the fact that minors are primarily focused on participation in formal and non-formal education, while engagement in work-related activities is secondary. Consequently, a juvenile's capacity to make reparation independently is often limited, and the responsibility for compensation is frequently transferred to their legal guardians.

Further analysis of the data revealed that, according to probation officers, the most effective control measures include sobriety checks for suspected alcohol use and sobriety checks for suspected drug use, with 91% and 92% of staff respectively rating these measures as either very effective or effective (Table 3). This evaluation is consistent with the prevailing operational model of the Probation Service, which prioritises control and supervision functions.

6 Electronic Monitoring of Juveniles

Another important consideration is that, while electronic monitoring is classified as a resocialisation measure under the Lithuanian Law on Probation, if it is not combined with other resocialisation strategies, such as behavioural correction programmes, it may have unintended consequences. Specifically, electronic monitoring could further isolate juveniles from positive peer influences, potentially fostering the development of criminal personality traits. The application of information technology is not confined to the Lithuanian Probation Service; rather, each year, an increasing number of technological solutions, including electronic monitoring tools, are being implemented. However, the use of electronic monitoring for minors presents several challenges within the current probation system. The study revealed a lack of consensus on the effectiveness of this tool, with both positive and negative aspects identified.

Currently, electronic monitoring is employed for juveniles placed under intensive court supervision and for effectively monitoring compliance with other

Table 3 Probation officers' assessment of the effectiveness of control measures applied to juveniles (%) N-120

No.	Control measures in the probation service	Very effective	Effective	Neither effective nor ineffective	Ineffective	Very ineffective
1.	Monitoring the juvenile's location(s)	35.1%	49.5%	13.5%	1.8%	0.0%
2.	Conducting sobriety checks in cases of suspected alcohol intoxication	37.5%	53.6%	7.1%	1.8%	0.0%
3.	Conducting sobriety checks in cases of suspected drug intoxication	38.4%	53.6%	6.2%	1.8%	0.0%
4.	Supervising unpaid work assigned to the juvenile	18.8%	48.2%	25.0%	7.1%	0.9%
5.	Monitoring the juvenile's obligation to compensate for or repair property damage	19.6%	36.6%	29.5%	14.3%	0.0%
6.	Issuing warnings to the juvenile	14.3%	37.5%	21.4%	23.2%	3.6%

court-ordered obligations. An analysis of statistical data from the Lithuanian Probation Service reveals that, on average, 15 juveniles are placed under intensive supervision by the juvenile court each year. Additionally, approximately 20 juveniles are subjected to intensive supervision as an extra control measure in recent years, following decisions made by the Probation Service.[4]

The survey results indicated that probation officers themselves express a more critical view of using electronic monitoring for minors (Table 4). A total of 44% of probation officers involved in the research highlighted that electronic monitoring functions as a formal control measure, with limited impact on fostering sustained behavioural change in the juvenile.

The negative aspects of electronic monitoring stem from its inherently formal nature, designed primarily to control the juvenile's location and movement.

Furthermore, electronic monitoring does not contribute to building or strengthening the juvenile's internal self-control, but rather reinforces reliance on external oversight and intervention. In addition, electronic monitoring fails to act as an effective deterrent; instead, it may foster rebellious attitudes and a resistance to the law enforcement system. It has also been noted that electronic monitoring negatively affects the juvenile's intrinsic motivation to change. Excessive restrictions can also impede the juvenile's ability to develop social capital.

[4] For further details, the statistical reports from the Lithuanian Probation Service can be consulted. https://probacija.lrv.lt/lt/apie-lietuvos-probacijos-tarnyba/statistika/.

Table 4 Probation officers' perspectives on the use of electronic monitoring for minors (%) N-120

No.	Electronic monitoring tools used by the probation service	Per cent
1.	Serves as a formal control tool.	44%
2.	Serves and has a significant impact on behaviour.	27%
3.	Other	11%
4.	Serves as a deterrent.	9%
5.	Has no impact	7%
6.	Did not respond to the question	3%

Probation officers further observe a stigmatising effect associated with electronic monitoring. This stigma can manifest in two ways: first, by perpetuating stereotypes, and second, by leading to self-identification as part of an excluded subcultural group.

It is also important to note that the Probation Service's electronic monitoring specialists often lack the specific knowledge and competencies required to work effectively with juveniles, which further formalises the application of this measure.

Nevertheless, a significant proportion of probation officers (27% of the survey participants) reported that electronic monitoring has a meaningful impact on adolescent behaviour.

Those probation officers who are favourable towards electronic monitoring tools argue that they are particularly effective for juveniles who are challenging to discipline, lack any consistent daily routines, and have never demonstrated the ability to plan their time or maintain commitments. They also note that electronic monitoring integrates well with other obligations and restrictions (outlined in Table 5), such as visiting designated places and abstaining from psychoactive substances. This allows for the monitoring of the juvenile's whereabouts and the specific locations they have visited.

Probation staff further explain that electronic monitoring is effective in ensuring that the juvenile remains in the family home, prevents hunger, and helps maintain their relationship with guardians. This system also supports the development of family bonds and interpersonal relationships.

Probation officers highlight the specific advantages of electronic monitoring compared to imprisonment, particularly in terms of socialisation. Unlike incarceration, which severely limits social interaction, electronic monitoring allows juveniles to maintain contact with positive peers. Moreover, electronic monitoring facilitates access to education, both formal and non-formal, thus supporting the principle of normalisation enshrined in the law.

The survey data presented in Table 5 indicates that, according to probation officers, the most effective prohibitions are those that restrict juveniles from driving motor vehicles, visiting places that have a negative influence on their behaviour, and interacting with individuals who have a harmful impact. Additionally, staff

Table 5 Assessment of the prohibitions imposed by the probation service on juveniles (%) N-120

No.	Prohibitions imposed on juveniles by the probation service	Very effective	Effective	Neither effective nor ineffective	Ineffective	Very ineffective
1.	Participation in games of chance	23.2%	39.3%	31.2%	6.2%	0.0%
2.	Engagement in certain activities	22.3%	41.1%	29.5%	7.1%	0.0%
3.	Operation of a motor vehicle (motorcycle, car, etc.)	22.3%	49.1%	25.9%	2.7%	0.0%
4.	Visiting locations that adversely affect the juvenile's behaviour or having contact with individuals who negatively influence them	26.8%	41.1%	25.0%	6.2%	0.9%
5.	Changing residence without informing the authorities supervising the measure	14.4%	47.7%	27.0%	9.0%	1.8%

members note that the effectiveness of individual prohibitions is diminished when they are combined with other obligations or behavioural modification programmes.

7 Probation Service Staff and Work with Juveniles

The effectiveness of juvenile resocialisation is influenced not only by quality, evidence-based behavioural correction measures but also by the competence of the staff responsible for implementing them. Probation staff acknowledge that it has become increasingly challenging to understand the developmental and psychosocial needs of today's juveniles, emphasising the need for interventions that are targeted and tailored to the individual. Professionals note significant changes in the psychosocial needs of minors, particularly regarding the formation and maintenance of relationships, the development of autonomy—meaning the ability to function independently—and, most notably, the evolving need for self-expression.

The study also revealed that professionals prioritise communication skills with juveniles, which can only be effectively realised through an open and trusting relationship (Table 6). Effective cooperation is a crucial element in both the implementation of motivational and correctional programmes and in ensuring proper supervision and the fulfilment of court-ordered obligations. A total of 17% of probation staff indicated that the ability to establish a trustworthy relationship with the juvenile is paramount, while 15% highlighted the importance of effective communication with juveniles.

The survey revealed that 69% of probation staff rated their training in working with minors as either good or very good, while only 6% expressed a negative

Table 6 Assessment of the competencies of probation service staff working with minors (%) N-120

No.	Competences of a probation worker	Per cent
1.	Ability to establish a trustworthy relationship	17%
2.	Ability to communicate effectively with minors	15%
3.	Ability to assist in the development of social skills and to integrate minors into an active, meaningful, and fulfilling social life	13%
4.	Ability to motivate the minor	10%
5.	Ability to gain the minor's trust	10%
6.	Ability to understand the minor's position and perspective	8%
7.	Ability to work with aggressive juveniles or those with conflicting personality traits	7%
8.	Ability to refrain from blaming, moralising, making hasty generalisations, issuing warnings, lecturing, criticising, or interrogating	5%
9.	Ability to help minors resolve social problems	3%
10.	Other	12%

opinion. Those in the latter group noted that their training had not been updated for ten years or more and emphasised a lack of ongoing training opportunities. Staff members stressed the importance of a team-based approach, comprising a supervisor, a head of the correctional programme, and a psychologist, to work effectively with juveniles. This is particularly crucial, as many of the juveniles under their care face not only behavioural challenges but also mental health issues.

As previously mentioned, one of the most pressing concerns is the training and specialisation of probation staff working with minors. Currently, there is no distinct specialisation for working with minors under the supervision of the Probation Service, although such a specialisation existed ten years ago. This specialisation was discontinued due to a decline in the number of minors under the supervision of the Probation Service and an increase in the number of other individuals under supervision, such as those convicted of domestic violence.

The current situation within the Probation Service has created a dilemma: on the one hand, it has become inefficient to maintain a staff dedicated exclusively to a small number of juveniles, while, on the other hand, the need for specialisation in juvenile cases has not disappeared. As a result, a decision was made to assign probation officers to juvenile cases in major cities (Vilnius, Kaunas, Klaipėda, Šiauliai, and Panevėžys), while reducing the total number of cases under their supervision to 20.

87% of staff unequivocally state that probation officers should specialise in juvenile work. This refers not to officers working exclusively with juveniles, but to a workload that would allow them to dedicate more time to individual work with juveniles.

The analysis of the survey data showed that 36% of probation officers indicated that one officer may handle up to five juvenile cases at a time (Table 7). 30% reported that between six and ten juvenile cases could be assigned to a single staff member.

Table 7 Workload of probation officers working with minors (%)

No.	Number of juvenile cases assigned to one probation officer at a time	Per cent
1.	up to 5	36%
2.	between 6 and 10	30%
3.	between 11 and 15	19%
4.	16 and over	8%
5.	Did not respond to the question	7%

However, the workload associated with working with juveniles depends not only on the formal number of cases but also on the complexity of each case and the array of measures implemented in collaboration with probation's social partners (non-governmental organisations, public institutions, municipal agencies, etc.). While the current staffing model addresses some operational concerns, a more tailored approach, focusing on specialisation and considering the complexity of each case and the scope of implemented measures, is needed to enhance the effectiveness of juvenile supervision.

8 Concluding Remarks

In conclusion, the research reveals that probation officers regard individual resocialisation measures as the most effective approach for juveniles, highlighting the importance of tailored communication and control strategies. The majority (92.8%) of probation officers believe that individual counselling by psychologists and addiction counsellors produces the highest efficacy. However, there is a critical need to assess the methodological basis and structure of individual interventions to ensure that they are evidence-based and robust. To achieve a more significant resocialisation effect, it is essential to incorporate scientifically validated programmes that can be effectively assessed in terms of both their implementation and their impact on outcomes.

The findings indicate that juvenile control measures remain prevalent within the Lithuanian Probation Service. Therefore, it is recommended that the reliance on formal control measures be evaluated and reduced, with a shift towards behavioural correction and enhanced social and psychological services.

The use of electronic monitoring devices for juveniles raises concerns, particularly when implemented by probation officers rather than being mandated by the court for control purposes. There is an urgent need for clear methodological guidance and well-defined criteria regarding the appropriate circumstances for using electronic monitoring.

Furthermore, while the Law on Probation acknowledges the principle of restorative justice, its practical implementation is progressing slowly. Efforts must be made to enhance and expand the use of mediation in juvenile cases.

Finally, it is crucial for the Probation Service to ensure that qualified personnel are working with minors. The survey indicates that the current situation is satisfactory, but additional training is needed for individual professionals. Those with specialised knowledge and skills should have opportunities for ongoing training and supervision to maintain and enhance their competencies.

References

di Gennaro G (2020) Juvenile delinquency between probation and criminal careers. Criminology and post-mortem studies - analyzing criminal behaviour and making medical decisions. In: Palermo S, Dumache L (eds) Criminology and post-mortem studies - analyzing criminal behaviour and making medical decisions. IntechOpen, pp 1–19

Engel C, Goerg SJ, Traxler C (2023) Intensified support for juvenile offenders on probation: evidence from Germany. J Empir Leg Stud 19:447–490

Hofinger V, Neumann A (2018) Legal biographies of NEUSTART clients. Legal probation according to out-of-court offence resolution, Community Service and Probation Service – Project Report, CEP, Confederation of European Probation

Klimukienė V, Kalpokienė V (2018) Paauglių kognityvinių iškraipymų, socialinių įgūdžių ir probleminio elgesio pokyčiai taikant EQUIP programą Lietuvos vaikų socializacijos centruose. Kriminologijos studijos 5:115–132

Nikartas S (2018) Daugiau probacijos, mažiau kalinių? Ar pagrįstas kalinių skaičiaus mažinimo lūkestis? Jurisprudencija 25(2):380–401

Pieroni L, Bussini O, Lanari D (2013) Probation and recidivism in Italian juvenile crime: estimating the effect of intergenerational transmission of crime through a cohort of young criminals, IUSSP, Department of Economics, Finance and Statistics, University of Perugia, pp 1–14

Robin L, Jackson A, Henderson E (2023) Juvenile probation structure, policy, and practice in the United States: a full analysis of variation within and across states. Urban Institute Justice Policy Center

Ryan J, Abrams LS, Huang H (2014) First-time violent juvenile offenders: probation, placement, and recidivism. Soc Work Res 38(1):7–19

Van Dijk C (2004) Juvenile delinquency and juvenile justice in Belgium. Vrije Universiteit Brussel (Free University of Brussels), Faculty of Law, Department of Criminology, Brussels, 1–25. Retrieved on 16 April, 2025, from https://oijj.org/sites/default/files/documentos/documental_2141_en.pdf

Villanueva L, Cuervo K (2018) The impact of juvenile educational measures, confinement centers, and probation on adult recidivism. Int J Offender Ther Comp Criminol 62(13):4108–4123

Rokas Uscila is a senior researcher at the Law Institute of the Lithuanian Centre for Social Sciences and a professor at Mykolas Romeris University, Lithuania. Dr Uscila's scientific interests include penal law, criminology, restorative justice, probation and mediation. He has authored approximately 65 publications in national and international journals, along with several scientific handbooks and methodological manuals. Dr Uscila is a member of the Lithuanian Mediators Association. He has work experience as a senior adviser in the Prison Department under the Ministry of Justice of the Republic of Lithuania, also as a vice-minister to the Minister of Justice of the Republic of Lithuania.

Renata Mienkowska Norkienė is a lecturer and researcher at the Faculty of Political Science and International Studies, University of Warsaw. Earlier, from 2010 to 2019, she was a lecturer at Mykolas Romeris University in Vilnius. She is the author of more than 70 scientific publications (mainly on European integration, gender equality, democracy, and international politics) and a participant of many national and international research projects. She held fellowships at the University of Vilnius, EURAC-European Academy in Bolzano, Free University of Brussels, Liechtenstein-Institut in Liechtenstein, the London School of Economics and Political Science and SciencePo in Paris, University of Oslo. She was a Blue Book Trainee at the Directorate-General for Personnel and Administration of the European Commission in Brussels. Renata Mieńkowska-Norkiene is a member of the Evaluation Team of the Polish National Agency for Academic Exchange and an expert of the European Commission in the field of Erasmus+ projects; she is the chairwoman of the International Institute of Civil Society and a member of the Team Europe Direct Expert Network.

Emerging and Cross-Cutting Issues

Advancing Children's Privacy and Data Protection Rights: Emerging Data Protection Trends and Challenges in Selected CEE Countries

Ingrida Milkaitė and Milda Mačėnaitė

Abstract The digital environment has made the processing of childrens personal data a critical issue, particularly in settings where children spend substantial amounts of time, such as schools, homes, and leisure facilities. This chapter examines the implementation and enforcement of the European Union's General Data Protection Regulation (GDPR) in relation to childrens privacy and data protection rights, with a specific focus on Central and Eastern European (CEE) countries. Drawing on responses from national Data Protection Authorities (DPA) in six CEE countries, as well as recent enforcement actions, this analysis identifies trends, challenges, and potential gaps in current practices. The findings suggest that, while the GDPR provides a robust framework for the protection of children's personal data, notable disparities in enforcement and prioritisation remain across the region. Building upon the pioneering efforts of certain European countries to enhance childrens privacy and data protection rights, this chapter offers practical recommendations to improve enforcement, strengthen safeguards, and promote accountability among data controllers within the CEE region. It highlights the need for a more balanced approach combining education and awareness raising with effective regulatory oversight to ensure that childrens best interests remain at the centre of data protection efforts in an increasingly digitalised world.

I. Milkaitė (✉)
Vrije Universiteit Brussel (VUB), Brussels, Belgium
e-mail: Ingrida.Milkaite@UGent.be

M. Mačėnaitė
Law Institute, Lithuanian Centre for Social Sciences, Vilnius, Lithuania
e-mail: milda.macenaite@teise.org

A. Limantė, R. Vaičiūnienė (eds.), *Children's Rights in Central and Eastern Europe*, European Union and its Neighbours in a Globalized World 29,
https://doi.org/10.1007/978-3-032-07092-0_16

1 Introduction

In today's digital environment, safeguarding children's personal data is a growing concern, particularly in environments such as homes, schools, leisure and healthcare facilities, and administrative settings. These contexts increasingly involve complex data-driven systems (Montgomery et al. 2017), creating challenges for compliance with European Union (EU) privacy and data protection laws (van der Hof 2016). Children now grow up surrounded by digital devices and systems that collect their data in ways that are not always apparent (Milkaite et al. 2021; Stoilova et al. 2020, 2021). At home, smart devices, voice assistants, watches, connected toys, televisions, tablets, and parental control apps routinely track their interactions (Lupton and Williamson 2017; Mascheroni 2020; Milkaite and Lievens 2019c). In schools, learning platforms and administrative systems store pupils' personal information (Article 29 Data Protection Working Party 2008; Bradbury 2019; Day et al. 2022; Milkaite 2022). Healthcare facilities use electronic records and online portals to manage children's data, while public services increasingly digitise birth records, social benefits, and legal documentation (Lupton and Williamson 2017; UN General Assembly 2021). These everyday systems shape children's digital identities long before they can fully understand their rights, reinforcing the need for robust safeguards (CoE Committee of Ministers 2018; UN Committee on the Rights of the Child 2021).

This chapter examines recent EU legislative and policy developments aimed at strengthening children's privacy and data protection rights, with a particular focus on the enforcement of the General Data Protection Regulation (GDPR) (European Parliament and the Council 2016). While the GDPR provides a strong framework for the protection of children's personal data, its implementation raises unique challenges. Focusing on selected Central and Eastern European (CEE) countries, this chapter explores how these jurisdictions address the complexities of processing children's personal data. It also evaluates GDPR enforcement and highlights innovative child-centric regulations emerging outside the CEE region—such as national 'Children's Codes', also known as Age Appropriate Design Codes—to draw out best practices and inform recommendations for improving the protection of children's privacy across Europe.

The GDPR contains several provisions directly relevant to the processing of children's personal data. Notably, it recognises children as a vulnerable group requiring enhanced protection, owing to their limited awareness of the risks associated with the processing of their personal data (Recital 38). It specifically addresses risks related to marketing and profiling, mandating that controllers process children's data in line with the GDPR's key principles: lawfulness, fairness, transparency, purpose limitation, data minimisation, accuracy, storage limitation, integrity, confidentiality, and accountability (Article 5). While these principles apply universally, they assume heightened importance when children's personal data is involved (Lievens and Verdoodt 2017).

The GDPR also explicitly provides for child-specific safeguards that reflect their unique needs and vulnerabilities (Macenaite 2017; Milkaite 2021). These include the need for clear, accessible, and transparent information (Article 12, Recital 58); strict conditions for consent (Article 8) (Macenaite and Kosta 2017; Milkaite and Lievens 2019b); and limits on profiling and automated decision-making (Article 22, Recital 71). The right to erasure, or the 'right to be forgotten' (Article 17), is particularly important in the context of children, enabling the deletion of personal data when it is no longer necessary or consent is withdrawn. This aligns with the GDPR's recognition of children's evolving capacities and the need to protect their 'digital footprints'.

When the processing of children's data involves high risks, such as in the context of innovative technologies, controllers are required to conduct a data protection impact assessment (DPIA) under Article 35. They must also implement the principle of privacy by design and by default (Article 25), ensuring that services likely to be accessed by children adopt strong default privacy settings and minimize the collection of unnecessary data, especially in educational contexts (van der Hof et al. 2019). Furthermore, national Data Protection Authorities (DPAs) are tasked with promoting public awareness of data protection risks, with specific attention to children (Article 57).

These child-specific provisions reflect a broader commitment to aligning data protection with the best interests of the child and other children's rights (Milkaite 2021), as recognised in Recital 38 of the GDPR and rooted in international instruments such as the UN Convention on the Rights of the Child (UNCRC) (United Nations General Assembly 1989). While the GDPR provides a promising framework for balancing general principles with child-specific safeguards in the digital environment, its effective implementation demands a proactive approach (Milkaite and Lievens 2019a) by both data controllers and national DPAs responsible for ensuring compliance with the regulation.

In addition to the GDPR's foundational protections, several European States have introduced supplementary frameworks to enhance children's data protection. Notably, the United Kingdom, Ireland, Sweden, France, and the Netherlands have implemented 'Children's Codes' or equivalent guidance, establishing more defined and stricter standards for digital services affecting children. These frameworks prioritise the best interests of the child by emphasising transparency, data minimisation, and high privacy settings by default (Milkaite 2023). This chapter acknowledges these developments and explores how similar child-centric approaches could inform data protection practices in CEE countries.

2 Methodology

This chapter investigates the emerging trends and enforcement practices related to safeguarding children's privacy and data protection rights under the GDPR. To achieve this, a number of EU Member States from the CEE region were selected for analysis, reflecting their legal obligations to implement GDPR provisions within their national frameworks. These countries include Bulgaria, Croatia, Czech Republic, Estonia, Hungary, Latvia, Lithuania, Poland, Romania, Slovakia, and Slovenia.

The research began by contacting national DPAs directly, requesting information on past and ongoing cases concerning the processing of children's personal data in digital environments. The requests focused on cases and investigations under the GDPR and national data protection laws in various contexts. The scope of the enquiry was intentionally broad to capture emerging trends and areas of enforcement actions by DPAs. In our email enquiries, we provided the DPAs with illustrative examples to contextualise our research interests. These included the protection of children's personal data in the context of social media and gaming platforms, healthcare, schools or other educational institutions, leisure services or sports clubs. This chapter's findings are primarily derived from the responses provided by DPAs in six CEE countries (Estonia, Hungary, Latvia, Lithuania, Poland, and Slovenia). While some DPAs provided details on concrete investigations and court cases, others indicated that they do not systematically track statistics on cases specifically involving children's personal data. As such, quantifying the total number of relevant cases and trends remains a challenge. Nevertheless, all six DPAs shared a substantial amount of information on their awareness-raising initiatives and associated materials.

To supplement the analysis, a comprehensive search was conducted on the GDPR Hub, a publicly accessible database of GDPR-related decisions from DPAs and courts across Europe. The search was conducted using a predefined set of keywords: 'minor', 'children', 'child', 'student', 'pupil', and 'school'. This yielded a total of 15 relevant cases from the following CEE countries: Croatia (1), Poland (3), Hungary (4), Slovenia (5), and Romania (2). These sources, together with the DPA responses, offer some insight into current enforcement strategies, trends, and challenges in protecting children's rights to privacy and data protection across the CEE region.

3 DPA Decisions and Practices Related to the Processing of Children's Personal Data

This section presents the analysis, divided into thematic subsections that examine DPA cases and decisions across key domains where children's personal data is processed in the selected CEE countries. The most prominent areas include educational institutions (schools and kindergartens), digital service providers, commercial entities (e.g., banks and retail businesses), and public authorities outside the educational sector.

3.1 *Data Processing by Schools and Kindergartens*

Schools and kindergartens handle a vast amount of children's personal data, raising concerns regarding how such information is collected, used, and shared (Article 29 Data Protection Working Party 2008; CoE Convention 108 Committee 2020). While educational institutions must balance safety, administrative needs, and educational objectives, they must also ensure that data processing remains lawful, proportionate, and transparent under the GDPR. A recurring issue in this context is the use of intrusive technologies—such as video surveillance and biometric systems—often justified as security measures or tools for operational efficiency. However, as case law from CEE countries demonstrates, these practices frequently raise questions about proportionality, consent, and compliance with such GDPR principles as data minimisation and purpose limitation.

3.1.1 Video Surveillance and Photography at Schools

The use of video surveillance and photography in schools has become increasingly common for security, administrative purposes, and educational activities. However, such practices can have a significant impact on children's privacy and data protection rights and must comply with GDPR principles. A key challenge lies in avoiding excessive data processing by ensuring that surveillance and image collection remain necessary and proportionate. In an illustrative Lithuanian case, a school installed video cameras inside classrooms to address theft and vandalism. However, the Lithuanian DPA ruled that surveillance was disproportionate (Lithuanian DPA 2024), since the school failed to justify the necessity of such a broad measure and did not conduct a proper legitimate interest assessment under Article 6(1)(f) GDPR. The DPA found that the continuous recording of students went beyond what was needed for property protection, ultimately violating data minimisation and proportionality principles. As a result, the school was fined €2000. Therefore, while schools have a duty to provide a safe environment, they must also carefully balance operational needs with privacy rights by prioritising transparency, data minimisation, and security.[1]

Relying on student consent to mitigate these risks presents another particularly complex challenge in educational contexts, given the inherent imbalance of power between schools and pupils. This makes it essential to explore alternative legal bases for processing children's data (Article 29 Data Protection Working Party 2008; Article 29 Working Party 2018; CoE Convention 108 Committee 2020).

[1] Previously, the Austrian DPA ruled that video surveillance in a public middle school during school hours was impermissible under GDPR, as the school could not rely on legitimate interests as a legal basis while functioning as a public entity. However, limited surveillance was allowed outside school hours for property protection, highlighting the need for proportionate measures that balance privacy rights and security. Austrian Data Protection Authority, Decision on Video Surveillance in Schools, 2022-0.458.091, https://gdprhub.eu/index.php?title=DSB_(Austria)_-_2022-0.858.901.

When schools share images or videos, consent must be specific, informed, and revocable. In Slovenia, a gym teacher requested students to record themselves dancing and upload the videos to an online classroom platform. The Slovenian DPA found that relying on student consent in this scenario was problematic due to the power imbalance between teachers and students. Instead, the DPA recommended that such data processing be based on the school's legal obligation under Article 6(1)(c) GDPR and emphasised that educational objectives should be achieved using less intrusive methods—such as a live dance demonstration—wherever possible (Slovenian DPA 2020a).

With regard to the use of photography at schools, several CEE DPAs have reported complaints regarding teachers sharing daily activities of children on social media platforms, such as Facebook.[2] A common concern was that the provided parental consent was not fully specific and informed, often taking the form of a general consent given at the beginning of the academic year. In Hungary, the DPA addressed cases where teachers shared photos and videos of students on social media without obtaining specific and informed consent. The DPA clarified that consent must be specific, informed, and revocable, and that simply providing parents with an option to object after the fact is insufficient. These situations raise questions about the level of granularity required for consent, such as whether general consent for publishing a student's image on a school website or social media page is sufficient, or if consent should be obtained on a case-by-case basis for each specific school event. One DPA[3] has emphasised that, notwithstanding general consent, educational institutions must keep parents informed with detailed information of all events involving the processing of their child's personal data and enable active parental decision-making, particularly when recordings are shared publicly online.

3.1.2 Processing of Biometric Data by Schools

Biometric data[4]—such as fingerprints and facial features—carries unique privacy risks due to its sensitive nature and the challenges of obtaining valid consent from children. GDPR Article 9 treats biometric data as a special category, generally prohibiting its processing or requiring a very strong justification for its collection and use. Therefore, schools considering biometric systems must carefully assess whether they are truly necessary and ensure that neither parents nor students are pressured into providing consent.

In one Polish case, a primary school introduced a fingerprint-scanning system to verify and fast-track meal payments in the school canteen, granting priority meal

[2] Email responses by the Hungarian and Polish Data Protection Authorities.

[3] Email response by the Hungarian Data Protection Authority.

[4] The GDPR defines 'biometric data' as "personal data resulting from specific technical processing relating to the physical, physiological or behavioural characteristics of a natural person, which allow or confirm the unique identification of that natural person, such as facial images or dactyloscopic data" (article 4 (14) GDPR).

access to children whose parents had consented. Although 680 children were enrolled with parental consent, the Polish DPA found the consent invalid due to the power imbalance between the school and parents, further ruling that the processing was unnecessary and disproportionate as less intrusive alternatives (e.g., ID cards or PIN codes) were available. It also stressed that privileging children whose parents consented to the system created inequalities among students, raising questions relating to non-discrimination rights of children. As a result, the school was fined €4700 and ordered to delete the biometric data collected (Polish DPA 2018).

A separate case from Poland reached the Polish Supreme Administrative Court, which reviewed the same biometric meal-access practice in a school. The Polish DPA had initially fined the school for violating the GDPR's data minimisation principle and for processing biometric data without valid consent, as alternative verification methods for students not using the system were deemed discriminatory. However, the court overturned the DPA's decision, ruling that the biometric processing was proportionate, that consent was validly obtained under Article 9(2)(a) GDPR, and that no evidence of discrimination existed. The court further argued that valid consent inherently satisfies the principle of data minimisation if the scope of data processing is justified by its purpose (Polish Supreme Administrative Court 2024).

Notably, this ruling appears to diverge from the stricter approach adopted by other European DPAs –such as in Sweden, France, and the UK—where the processing of biometric data in schools is subject to more rigorous scrutiny (European Data Protection Board 2019; Pascu 2020; UK DPA (ICO) 2024a, b). These authorities emphasise the heightened sensitivity of biometric data under the GDPR, stressing that consent alone is not always a sufficient safeguard due to the inherent imbalance of power between schools and children. Instead, they prioritise necessity and proportionality assessments, often concluding that less intrusive alternatives should be considered before deploying biometric systems in educational settings. The Polish decision thus raises concerns regarding consistency in the interpretation and application of GDPR principles across Europe, particularly with respect to the handling of children's biometric data.

3.1.3 Data Processing Through Educational Technologies

The rise of educational technologies (EdTech) has transformed how schools manage student records, facilitate communication, and deliver online learning (Tuomi et al. 2023). Many of these platforms handle large amounts of children's personal data, including academic records and online interactions, making them particularly sensitive under the GDPR. A key compliance challenge is ensuring that schools and service providers implement robust security measures, maintain transparency, and comply with GDPR requirements—particularly regarding international data transfers. In the context of our research, two key cases from Hungary illustrate the risks posed by inadequate data security and accessibility.

In particular, the first case from Hungary highlights the risks of poor data management. The eKRÉTA system, which used to store student records and grades, faced two major issues. Firstly, in one case, a parent requested access to the modification records for a student's grades. However, due to system limitations, the school was unable to retrieve this information. The Hungarian DPA (NAIH) confirmed that grades constitute personal data under the GDPR, and that parents have a right to access them on behalf of minors. Nevertheless, as the system did not track grade changes, the school was not found in violation of the Regulation (Hungarian DPA 2022). The second issue with eKRÉTA revealed more serious failings: a major data breach exposed the personal data of millions of students, teachers, and staff due to an IT security fault. An investigation revealed weaknesses in the system's security, including inadequate logging practices and a lack of sufficient safeguards against unauthorised access. As a result, the NAIH fined the platform's service provider €300,000, citing a failure to implement appropriate security measures, in non-compliance with Article 32 GDPR (Hungarian DPA 2023b). The foregoing cases highlight the complexities of EdTech compliance, particularly in ensuring that platforms meet GDPR transparency, security, and accountability requirements.

Notably, similar concerns have arisen elsewhere. In Poland, a data breach at a private nursery and pre-school led to a loss of access to stored personal data. When the Polish DPA attempted to investigate, the controller failed to cooperate, violating Article 58(1)(e) GDPR, which requires entities to respond to supervisory authorities (Polish DPA 2020a). The DPA issued a fine of €1170, highlighting the crucial role of cooperation during data breach investigations and the heightened accountability educational institutions must uphold when handling children's personal data.

Beyond security failures, broader concerns have also emerged regarding how schools process personal data through digital platforms. During the COVID-19 pandemic, the Slovenian DPA issued a non-binding opinion addressing the use of personal communication tools, such as private phone numbers, to interact with students and parents. The opinion emphasised the need for data minimisation and robust security measures under Article 32 GDPR to protect both student and teacher data (Slovenian DPA 2020b). Additionally—and crucially—the case also raised important issues concerning international data transfers, particularly as many EdTech platforms rely on third-party technology providers that operate from outside the EU, often in the United States (Fernandes 2023; Livingstone et al. 2021). The DPA urged schools to ensure compliance with GDPR standards for cross-border data transfers and advised against relying on consent alone as a legal basis, recommending using Article 6(1)(c) GDPR, which permits data processing necessary to fulfil legal obligations. These developments highlight the urgent need for schools and authorities to prioritise data security, legal compliance, and accountability when adopting digital tools, ensuring children's personal data is safeguarded at all times.

3.1.4 Data Processing Beyond Classroom Activities: Surveys, Pre-Admission, and Attendance Records

Data protection concerns extend beyond digital learning environments. Schools and kindergartens also collect and process personal data for various administrative purposes, including surveys, pre-admission procedures, and attendance tracking. In this context, several cases from Poland, Slovenia, and Lithuania highlight the difficulties in ensuring that these practices align with GDPR principles.

Firstly, a case from Poland illustrates the risks associated with excessive data collection. A school conducted a survey titled "Diagnosis of Students' Home and School Situation" to identify students in need of psychological support. The survey gathered detailed personal data, including information on family structure, health conditions, and financial status. The Polish DPA ruled that this practice violated Article 5(1)(a) GDPR, as the school lacked a valid legal basis for collecting such sensitive data (Polish DPA 2020b). Furthermore, the scope of data collection was found to breach the data minimisation principle, as it exceeded what was necessary for the stated purpose. While the school's intention was to assist students, the ruling emphasised that even well-intentioned data collection must be lawful, fair, and proportionate.

Pre-admission processes can also raise concerns, particularly when schools and kindergartens request excessive personal data from applicants. In Slovenia, the DPA examined whether kindergartens could collect children's health, developmental, or immunisation data during the application stage. The DPA ruled that doing so violated the data minimisation principle under Article 5(1)(c) GDPR, as such information should only be collected after admission and only when strictly necessary (Slovenian DPA 2021), highlighting the critical importance of both timing and necessity in the processing of children's sensitive data. Similarly, in Lithuania, the Supreme Administrative Court held that a kindergarten had unlawfully disclosed a child's health status—stating that the child had not begun attending kindergarten due to "health conditions"—to the municipal Education Environment Department. The court ruled that this disclosure constituted an unlawful processing of special category data under Article 9 GDPR, as no valid legal basis had been established (Lithuanian Supreme Administrative Court 2024), reinforcing that institutions must ensure that sensitive data is only shared when legally justified.

Relatedly, further scrutiny of data processing in schools and kindergartens was conducted by the Lithuanian DPA, which carried out preventive inspections of 20 educational institutions in 2020. The inspections focused on how institutions justified absences and whether personal data collection practices complied with the GDPR. The findings revealed several violations (Lithuanian DPA 2021). Some schools processed absence-related data for students over 16 without a legal basis, as attendance tracking for this age group is not an educational obligation. Others kept attendance records but failed to define a lawful basis for processing. While no school actively collected medical certificates for absences, some had policies allowing it, which the DPA instructed them to remove to avoid GDPR violations. In kindergartens, similar issues arose. Since preschool is not mandatory under Lithuanian law, attendance data cannot be processed to ensure education. Any collection must be justified under other legal grounds, such as fee calculations or preventing misuse of placements. Some kindergartens also gathered excessive documentation, such as parental employment and health records, leading to unnecessary disclosures. The DPA instructed them to cease such practices and refine their internal policies to comply with the GDPR (Lithuanian DPA 2021).

These cases collectively demonstrate the broader data protection risks associated with administrative data collection in educational settings. Schools and kindergartens must ensure that their processing of children's personal data—whether for surveys, pre-admission, or attendance tracking—is clearly justified, limited to what is strictly necessary, and conducted with full transparency. Institutions must avoid collecting excessive data out of convenience and should be proactive in reviewing and refining their policies to prevent non-compliance with the GDPR.

3.2 Data Processing in the Digital Environment

Digital services, including social networks, gaming platforms, and mobile applications, provide children with valuable opportunities for learning, communication, and leisure activities. However, to ensure that children can fully benefit from these opportunities without compromising their privacy, digital service providers must demonstrate transparency in their data collection practices and implement robust, child-centered safeguards. A paramount concern associated with data-driven online services relates to commercial practices involving systematic and opaque data collection, such as the tracking of children's online activities for advertising purposes, which may be misleading or manipulative vis-à-vis children (Montgomery et al. 2017; FTC 2024). In recognition of such risks, the GDPR acknowledges that children's personal data requires specific protection, especially when used for marketing purposes or the creation of personality or user profiles (Recital 38, GDPR).

In response to similar ongoing concerns, child-specific privacy legislation began to emerge in the 1990s, notably with the introduction of the Children's Online Privacy Protection Act (COPPA) in the United States (Steeves and Mačėnaitė 2022). Globally, DPAs have called for stronger legislative measures to restrict the collection, use, and disclosure of children's personal data—particularly in the context of micro-targeting and behavioural advertising (ICDPPC 2008)—and to prohibit other potentially harmful practices (European Commission et al. 2022). Despite existing legislative safeguards, challenges remain in adapting digital marketing strategies and promotional activities to children as a distinct group of consumers and data subjects.

Another persistent concern in the digital environment is the unauthorized public disclosure of children's personal data online by third parties—including peers, teachers, or parents—without valid consent. Such disclosures can pose serious risks to children's privacy, safety, and reputation, and underline the importance of the right to be forgotten online. As case law from CEE countries demonstrates, data processing in the digital environment raises complex questions about transparency, age verification, consent mechanisms, and the adequacy of data security measures.

3.2.1 Data Processing by Online Service Providers

Several older EU states have issued guidelines (ICO 2020; Swedish Data Protection Authority 2021; CNIL 2021) and launched investigations into how digital service providers protect the privacy of children (ICO 2025; DPC 2020, 2022, 2023; CNIL 2024). However, our research indicates a lack of systematic GDPR investigation and enforcement by DPAs in the CEE region with regard to the collection and use of children's data by digital service providers, including social media, video-sharing platforms, and mobile applications.

Although no cases were found in which CEE DPAs were actively investigating or challenging the collection and use of children's data by digital service providers, several trends point to growing concern regarding emerging forms of data processing by some online actors, particularly influencers such as YouTubers and podcast hosts. These persons frequently collect data from their young audience, often under the pretext of sending them 'gifts' or promotional materials (e.g., magnets or T-shirts). The primary issue identified by DPAs in these instances is the lack of transparency and clear information regarding the processing of children's data, with such data often being collected without obtaining the necessary parental consent.

3.2.2 Disclosure of Children's Data Online

Despite the absence of a proactive and systematic GDPR enforcement in the CEE region, four cases involving unlawful disclosures of children's data online by companies, professionals, and parents illustrate that—in response to individual complaints—CEE DPAs are active in investigating data processing practices under the GDPR on a posteriori and ad hoc basis.

In one notable case, the Hungarian DPA investigated the unlawful public disclosure of a minor's data by a private healthcare provider (Hungarian DPA 2023c). The legal representative of a 15-year-old child requested a blood test appointment from a private healthcare provider and subsequently shared a negative Google Maps review, which included her full name and photo. In its response, the healthcare provider commented that minors could only be tested for sexually transmitted diseases with parental consent, implying that the legal representative sought such a test, which was not the case. The provider published misleading health-related information in its reply, despite being aware that the minor could be easily identified. As a result, the legal representative was compelled to remove her review to ensure the public disclosure of the data was retracted. This case underscores the need for extreme caution when disclosing health information, the potential negative impact on children's privacy and reputation, and the importance of the right to be forgotten online.

A second case, handled by the Lithuanian DPA, concerned a breach of the GDPR when a mother, attempting to register her child for a summer camp, was required to consent to a contract clause permitting the camp organiser to photograph and film her child for promotional purposes on social media (Lithuanian DPA 2022). The DPA found that the camp organiser failed to obtain specific, informed, voluntary, and revocable consent as required under the GDPR. Moreover, the DPA highlighted that photography, filming, and the publication of children's images was not necessary for the contract's performance, and that such public disclosures to broad and undefined audiences exposed children to increased risks of misuse, including unauthorised identification and manipulation. The case reinforces that children—due to their particular vulnerability—require enhanced safeguards and that controllers must carefully assess the lawfulness of publishing children's personal data online.

In Romania, an accidental data breach further illustrated the unintended risks of public data disclosure. A global retailer was fined by the Romanian DPA for a data breach that inadvertently exposed the personal data of 114 individuals, half of whom were children (Romanian DPA 2021). The breach occurred during a children's drawing contest, where legal guardians were required to upload drawings and consent forms containing personal data. The retailer inadvertently published the drawings along with the participation forms, exposing this personal data online for 40 hours. This breach violated Article 32(1)(b) and Article 32(2) of the GDPR, which mandate adequate measures to ensure the confidentiality and integrity of personal data. The DPA imposed a fine of RON 4948.8 (approximately €1000) and stressed the need for special protection of children's personal data, as articulated in Recital 38 of the GDPR.

Finally, in another Hungarian case, the DPA investigated the unlawful disclosure of sensitive data following a private conversation between a daycare employee and parents (Hungarian DPA 2021). A parent unlawfully recorded the conversation and subsequently shared it via email and a Facebook group. The Hungarian DPA found that the disclosure violated GDPR principles of purpose limitation and data minimisation, as well as provisions under Articles 6(1) and 9, which regulate the processing of sensitive data. While the DPA refrained from imposing a fine, it issued corrective orders, including a ban on further data processing and a requirement to request the deletion of shared data from recipients. The case demonstrates the limits of GDPR's household exemption, stressing that broader sharing of sensitive information subjects individuals to GDPR compliance.

Collectively, these cases illustrate the significant risks associated with both intentional and accidental disclosures of children's personal data. They underscore the importance of ensuring that any public dissemination of such data is strictly necessary, based on a valid legal ground, and accompanied by appropriate technical and organisational safeguards to prevent unauthorised access or misuse.

3.3 Data Processing by Commercial Companies

The collection, use, and disclosure of children's personal data by companies for commercial purposes outside the digital environment raise equally significant concerns under the GDPR. Recent cases from Hungary and Romania—spanning the banking and education sectors—highlight a broad range of compliance challenges that can emerge when processing children's data for service provision or direct marketing purposes. These examples expose both deliberate, profit-driven breaches and unintentional, negligent errors, underscoring the need for robust safeguards to protect children's personal data.

Following several complaints, the Hungarian DPA initiated an ex officio investigation into the lawfulness of a private company's processing of children's personal data for market research and direct marketing purposes (Hungarian DPA 2023a). The company, which offered preparation courses for secondary school entry exams, had accessed the official government register to obtain addresses under the pretext of conducting market research, but instead used the data for direct marketing activities, a purpose not permitted by law. The company sent targeted letters to students of various ages—likely those interested in taking entry exams—employing misleading language that suggested official communication or a legal obligation. Furthermore, the company failed to provide a clear, accessible, and transparent privacy statement. Its database contained personal data from diverse groups of individuals, including those who had explicitly withdrawn their consent. The investigation revealed that the company had violated multiple fundamental GDPR principles, including accountability, lawfulness, purpose limitation, fairness, transparency, and the rights of data subjects. In response, the DPA ordered the company to permanently delete all unlawfully processed personal data and imposed a fine of HUF 500,000 (approximately €1222). Aggravating factors included the large volume of data processed, the involvement of minors' personal data, and the profit-driven motivation.

A separate case investigated by the Hungarian DPA concerned a complaint filed by a minor's legal guardian regarding a 'baby loan' application with a bank. These loans are intended to cover expenses related to raising and supporting children. The bank had requested a copy of the minor's identification documents—including address, gender, birth date, and national identification number—citing Article 6(1)(b) of the GDPR as the legal basis for processing. However, the minor's legal guardian argued that the processing was disproportionate and unnecessary, as the minor was not a party to the contract. The DPA held that the processing was legitimate under Article 6(1)(c) as the bank was legally obliged to collect the minor's personal data pursuant to domestic banking regulations when granting baby loans (Hungarian DPA 2023d). The DPA concluded that the incorrect citation of the legal basis did not in itself render the processing unlawful.

These cases underscore the importance of data controllers ensuring transparency and fairness when processing children's data. They further highlight the necessity of identifying and articulating the correct legal basis, maintaining clear communication, and ensuring that purposes for data collection are explicitly stated.

In a Romanian case, the DPA imposed a fine on a bank for failing to implement adequate technical and organisational measures to ensure an adequate level of security for personal data (Romanian DPA 2020). An investigation revealed that the bank had collected and transmitted copies of identity documents of minors and their legal representatives via an employee's personal phone using the WhatsApp application. This practice contravened the bank's internal procedures and violated the GDPR, underscoring the critical need for robust technical and organisational measures to ensure a level of security commensurate with the risks involved in processing. It also highlights the need for companies to establish clear protocols and oversight mechanisms to prevent unauthorised processing of personal data by employees or agents acting on their behalf.

3.4 Data Processing for Child Protection Purposes

International human rights instruments, including the United Nations Convention on the Rights of the Child (UNCRC), affirm children's rights to protection, care, and participation in decisions that affect them (Article 12 UNCRC). While children's evolving maturity requires parents to provide appropriate direction and guidance in the exercise by the child of his or her rights (Article 5 UNCRC), parental authority is not absolute. In particular, the child's best interests may sometimes override the wishes of their parents or representatives (Article 29 Data Protection Working Party 2008).

Conflicts may arise in contexts where child welfare agencies or social services need to process personal data of children to fulfil their mandate and protect children from harm. This may involve collecting and analysing data on children and their families, as well as sharing data with other authorities or organisations—such as law enforcement or healthcare providers—without parental consent or notification. In some cases, parents may even be denied access to their child's personal data, particularly where access could compromise child protection investigations into risk of harm. Although parents may challenge such processing as an infringement of their rights, the principle of the child's best interests often prevails.

Cases from Hungary, Lithuania and Slovenia illustrate such tensions. In one Lithuanian court case, the legality of a transfer of the personal data of a child—which was part of an assessment of his special educational needs—from psychological services to the child protection authority was contested (Vilnius Regional Administrative Court 2023). The transfer was based on Article 9(2)(g) of the GDPR, which permits the processing of personal data for reasons of substantial public interest, on the basis of a law which is proportionate to the aim pursued, respects the essence of the right to data protection, and provides for suitable and specific measures to safeguard the fundamental rights and the interests of the data subject. The complainant argued that the data sharing was excessive, lacked consent, and that 'public interest' had been interpreted too broadly as a value to society. However, the court upheld the lawfulness of the processing, finding that is was carried out in accordance with the Law on the Protection of Children's Rights and Article 9(2)(g) of the GDPR. It noted that public interest includes the fundamental principles of state functioning and societal welfare, including the protection of children's rights, as stated in the Lithuanian Constitution (Article 39). The Court concluded that both Article 6(1)(c) and Article 9(2)(g) of the GDPR provided a lawful basis for the processing of special categories of personal data of a child, and reiterated that consent is not the sole basis for lawful processing.

In Slovenia, the DPA examined a case where a parent requested access to their child's data from a school (Slovenian DPA 2024). The school partially denied the request, redacting the names and addresses of individuals authorised to pick up the child, citing Article 15(4) of the GDPR and national legal provisions that prioritise the child's best interests. The redactions were based on a court-issued restraining order against the requesting parent. The DPA upheld the school's decision, affirming that the protection of the child's rights and safety justified the restriction. However, it found that the school had violated Article 12 GDPR by failing to respond to the access request within the prescribed timeframe.

These cases demonstrate that while children's right to privacy is fundamental, it may, in certain circumstances, be subordinated to the overarching principle of the child's best interests. In cases of suspected abuse or neglect, data protection rights may justifiably yield to ensure the child's physical and psychological safety.

4 DPA Awareness-Raising Activities

The majority of CEE DPAs place considerable emphasis on educational and awareness-raising activities in the realm of children's privacy and personal data protection. Many have launched various initiatives including conferences, educational campaigns and programs, and have issued specific recommendations and guidelines regarding children's rights in the digital environment. In Lithuania, for example, these include the "20 Steps for Children and Teens to Protect Their Personal Data Online" and the "Data Protection Guidelines for Youth" (Lithuanian DPA 2019, 2023). Estonia's DPA has adopted a broad approach, producing podcasts, publishing opinion articles, issuing circular letters to schools on data protection, and even offering personal data processing lessons for students. Notably, some DPAs have utilised innovative tools to engage young audiences, such as podcasts[5] and interactive educational materials.[6] These awareness efforts have addressed a wide range of issues from online safety and emerging technologies[7] to protection of personal data in educational institutions, including the use of video surveillance and IT solutions in education.[8]

However, the awareness-raising initiatives in CEE countries often appear to be confined to national contexts. In the scope of this research, only one example of cross-border cooperation was identified: the "*Introducing Data Protection and Privacy Issues in the European Union*" (ARCADES) project, co-funded by the European Union. This initiative involved the DPAs of Poland, Hungary, Slovenia, and the Free University of Brussels, and aimed to create new educational materials

[5] Email response from the Estonian Data Protection Authority.

[6] Email response from the Polish Data Protection Authority.

[7] Email responses by the Hungarian, Slovenian and Polish Data Protection Authorities.

[8] Email responses by the Lithuanian and Slovenian Data Protection Authorities.

to promote privacy and data protection awareness across EU Member States among school-aged children (ages 6-19). Although developing universally applicable resources can be challenging, collaborative efforts—such as adapting or co-producing materials within the region—may promote a more harmonised and effective approach.

Overall, these initiatives align with Article 57 of the GDPR, which requires DPAs to promote public awareness of data protection risks, particularly for children. Nevertheless, most current efforts focus primarily on informing children and schools as data subjects, with limited attention to other key actors involved in the processing of children's personal data, such as digital service providers and social services. In this regard, CEE DPAs could draw lessons from other European counterparts. For instance, the UK's DPA has been actively engaged in collaborative efforts with educational institutions, law enforcement agencies, and social service organisations to raise awareness about responsible data sharing to safeguard children from potential harm (ICO 2024b).

5 Discussion

Insights from CEE DPAs indicate increasing awareness of children's data protection challenges but also reveal some enforcement and regulatory gaps. A key area of focus has been the protection of children's personal data in educational settings. For example, inspections in Lithuanian schools uncovered excessive data collection (Lithuanian DPA 2021), while Hungary's DPA criticised the use of blanket parental consent for video recordings and photographs, highlighting ongoing tensions between operational needs with children's privacy rights. Although the best interests of the child principle—stemming from the UNCRC—is gaining traction in some CEE jurisdictions, it is not yet systematically referenced or applied across all DPA cases.

Indeed, enforcement across CEE countries remains somewhat fragmented. Some DPAs lack detailed data on child-specific cases, making it difficult to identify systemic issues. Others do not differentiate between cases involving minors and adults, limiting the visibility of child-specific data protection trends.[9] A more structured approach, including the creation of dedicated national DPA databases and the systematic tracking of cases involving children could help build a more coherent, child-focused regulatory framework. Such an approach could also inform the European Data Protection Board's forthcoming guidelines on the processing of children's personal data (EDPB 2019a, b).

Judicial decisions also reveal gaps in understanding children's unique vulnerabilities. For instance, the overturning of the Polish DPA decision on biometric data in schools points to the need for greater judicial understanding of, and sensitivity to, these vulnerabilities, as well as the heightened responsibilities under the GDPR and UNCRC when processing children's personal data in educational settings. Moreover,

[9] Email responses from Data Protection Authorities in CEE.

the commercial processing of children's personal data—particularly in influencer marketing and behavioral advertising—lacks sufficient focus and enforcement. In their response, one DPA raised concerns regarding YouTube influencers distributing gifts to children without appropriate safeguards, underscoring the need for DPAs to move beyond compliance checks toward proactive regulation and clear guidance for commercial data processing practices targeting minors. Cross-border data transfers, particularly via EdTech platforms established outside of the EU, also warrant stronger oversight. Many digital learning platforms used in CEE schools operate from outside the EU, particularly in the United States, raising concerns about GDPR compliance and the need for stricter enforcement of data minimisation and privacy-by-design principles.

CEE countries could strengthen their regulatory frameworks and policies by drawing on children's rights-based recommendations such as the UK's Age Appropriate Design Code and Ireland's Fundamentals for a Child-Oriented Approach to Data Processing (ICO 2020; DPC 2021). These frameworks, alongside similar initiatives in Sweden (Swedish Data Protection Authority 2021), France (CNIL 2021), and the Netherlands (Waag & Leiden University 2022), supplement GDPR with concrete, enforceable protections tailored to children's digital engagement (Milkaite 2023). They emphasise the importance of age-appropriate transparency, requiring services to provide clear, accessible information that enables children to understand and manage their data (Article 29 Data Protection Working Party 2018; Milkaite and Lievens 2020). They also prioritise high-privacy settings by default (OECD 2024), as well as requirements for data minimisation and purpose limitation, restricting data collection to what is necessary and preventing exploitative profiling and behavioral advertising (van der Hof et al. 2020). Furthermore, these so called 'Children's Codes' encourage balanced parental involvement, supporting parental guidance while respecting children's evolving autonomy and capacities by adjusting privacy controls as children mature (Lansdown 2005; Varadan 2019). By integrating these principles, CEE countries can ensure that children's well-being is prioritised over commercial and other interests, creating a safer and more transparent environment for children to grow and develop in.

Although the CEE DPAs actively engage in digital literacy initiatives and issue various guidelines to help children and young people protect their personal data online, an over-reliance on education and 'self-protection' campaigns risks shifting too much responsibility onto children and families (Milkaite and Lievens 2019c). In an increasingly complex and data-driven world, children and parents cannot be expected to navigate privacy risks alone. Educational and awareness-raising efforts are crucial but they must be complemented by strong accountability measures for organisations that process children's personal data. DPAs should issue sector-specific guidance for high-risk industries like EdTech and social media, continue conducting targeted inspections, and mandate risk assessments and DPIAs for processing children's data. Strengthening the accountability principle would ensure that responsibility lies with data controllers and processors, rather than children and their families (Milkaite 2021).

Integrating Children's Codes-style frameworks into national data protection laws and enforcement practices could help CEE countries close existing protection gaps across educational, commercial, and other sectors, and ensure that children's privacy is consistently prioritised. As artificial intelligence (AI) becomes more embedded in educational and online platforms, DPAs must proactively regulate AI-driven profiling and automated decision-making that could impact children's rights (Barassi 2018). By combining proactive enforcement with child-centric policies, CEE DPAs can more effectively safeguard children's data and create a safer, more equitable digital environment across the region.

6 Concluding Remarks

Our findings emphasise that while GDPR implementation is progressing, gaps in enforcement remain—particularly in enforcing rules around commercial data processing and regulating educational technologies. Cases from CEE countries highlight the importance of proportionality, transparency, and accountability when processing children's personal data, especially in vulnerable settings like schools and kindergartens.

The increasing monetisation of children's online experiences—through targeted advertising, influencer marketing, and conditional access to services in exchange for personal data—raises serious concerns (van der Hof et al. 2020). These practices expose children to commercial exploitation and privacy risks, mirroring issues identified decades ago in the United States, which led to the adoption of the Children's Online Privacy Protection Act (COPPA) in 1998 (Macenaite and Kosta 2017). Although the GDPR establishes a robust legal foundation, active enforcement actions have primarily occurred in jurisdictions where major tech firms are headquartered, such as Ireland. The experience of countries with dedicated Children's Codes—such as the UK, Ireland, and the Netherlands—demonstrates the potential for CEE countries to adopt similar child-centric frameworks. These initiatives emphasise transparency, data minimisation, and the best interests of the child. Embedding the principles of the UNCRC into data protection frameworks presents an opportunity to align enforcement strategies with the broader children's rights framework, spanning beyond privacy and data protection.

Looking ahead, the intersection of data protection and emerging technologies, particularly AI in education, calls for proactive risk assessments and privacy-by-design strategies (CoE Convention 108 Committee 2020; Council of Europe 2018; OECD 2021; UN Committee on the Rights of the Child 2021). To effectively protect children's rights in the digital age, DPAs must go beyond reactive enforcement and adopt forward-looking, systemic approaches.

References

Article 29 Data Protection Working Party (2008, February 11) Opinion 2/2009 on the protection of children's personal data (General Guidelines and the special case of schools) (WP 160). https://ec.europa.eu/justice/article-29/documentation/opinion-recommendation/files/2009/wp160_en.pdf

Article 29 Data Protection Working Party (2018, April 11) Guidelines on Transparency under Regulation 2016/679 (WP260 rev.01). http://ec.europa.eu/newsroom/article29/item-detail.cfm?item_id=622227

Article 29 Working Party (2018, April 10) Guidelines on Consent under Regulation 2016/679 (wp259rev.01). https://ec.europa.eu/newsroom/article29/item-detail.cfm?item_id=623051

Barassi V (2018) The child as datafied citizen: critical questions on data justice in family life. In: Mascheroni G, Jorge A, Ponte C (eds) Digital parenting: the challenges for families in the digital age. NORDICOM, pp 169–177. https://www.nordicom.gu.se/sv/publikationer/digital-parenting

Bradbury A (2019) Datafied at four: The role of data in the 'schoolification' of early childhood education in England. Learn Media Technol 44(1):7–21. https://doi.org/10.1080/17439884.2018.1511577

CNIL (2021) 8 recommendations to enhance the protection of children online. https://www.cnil.fr/en/cnil-publishes-8-recommendations-enhance-protection-children-online

CNIL (2024) CNIL investigations in 2024: minors data, Olympic Games, right of access and digital receipts. https://www.cnil.fr/en/cnil-investigations-2024-minors-data-olympic-games-right-access-and-digital-receipts

CoE Committee of Ministers (2018) Guidelines to respect, protect and fulfil the rights of the child in the digital environment. Recommendation CM/Rec(2018)7. https://edoc.coe.int/en/children-and-the-internet/7921-guidelines-to-respect-protect-and-fulfil-the-rights-of-the-child-in-the-digital-environment-recommendation-cmrec20187-of-the-committee-of-ministers.html

CoE Convention 108 Committee (2020, November 20) Guidelines on Children's Data Protection in an Education setting. https://rm.coe.int/t-pd-2019-6bisrev5-eng-guidelines-education-setting-plenary-clean-2790/1680a07f2b

Council of Europe (2018, July 4) New Recommendation adopted on children's rights in the digital environment. Children's Rights. https://www.coe.int/en/web/children/newsroom/-/asset_publisher/6ZtVCaG3cc7i/content/new-recommendation-adopted-on-children-s-rights-in-the-digital-environment

Day, E., Pothong, K., Atabey, A., & Livingstone, S. (2022). Who controls children's education data? A socio-legal analysis of the UK governance regimes for schools and EdTech. Learn Media Technol, 0(0), 1–15. https://doi.org/10.1080/17439884.2022.2152838

DPC (2020) Data Protection Commission's two statutory inquiries into Facebook's processing of children's data on Instagram. https://www.dataprotection.ie/en/news-media/press-releases/data-protection-commissions-two-statutory-inquiries-facebooks-processing-childrens-data-instagram#children%E2%80%99s

DPC (2021) The Fundamentals for a Child-Oriented Approach to Data Processing. https://www.dataprotection.ie/en/dpcguidance/fundamentals-child-oriented-approach-data-processing

DPC (2022) Data Protection Commission announces decision in Instagram Inquiry. https://www.dataprotection.ie/en/news-media/press-releases/data-protection-commission-announces-decision-instagram-inquiry#Instagram

DPC (2023) Data Protection Commission announces conclusion of two inquiries into Meta Ireland. https://www.dataprotection.ie/en/news-media/data-protection-commission-announces-conclusion-two-inquiries-meta-ireland#Instagram

EDPB (2019a, February 12) Work Programme 2019-2020. https://edpb.europa.eu/our-work-tools/our-documents/work-program/edpb-work-program-20192020_en

EDPB (2019b) Facial recognition in school renders Sweden's first GDPR fine. https://www.edpb.europa.eu/news/national-news/2019/facial-recognition-school-renders-swedens-first-gdpr-fine_sv

European Commission, EDPB and CPC (2022) 5 key principles of fair advertising to children. https://commission.europa.eu/live-work-travel-eu/consumer-rights-and-complaints/enforcement-consumer-protection/cooperation-between-consumer-and-data-protection-authorities_en

European Parliament and of the Council (2016) Regulation (EU) 2016/679 of the of 27 April 2016 on the protection of natural persons with regard to the processing of personal data and on the free movement of such data, and repealing Directive 95/46/EC (General Data Protection Regulation). https://eur-lex.europa.eu/eli/reg/2016/679/oj/eng

Fernandes E (2023) Edtech companies need to learn: Children's data must be processed in their best interest. https://www.law.kuleuven.be/citip/blog/edtech-companies-need-to-learn/

FTC (2024) A look behind the screens examining the data practices of social media and video streaming services. https://www.ftc.gov/system/files/ftc_gov/pdf/Social-Media-6b-Report-9-11-2024.pdf

Hungarian DPA (2021) NAIH-1743/2021. https://gdprhub.eu/index.php?title=NAIH_(Hungary)_-_NAIH-1743/2021

Hungarian DPA (2022) NAIH-4667-10/2022 case on access to a child's grade history. https://gdprhub.eu/index.php?title=NAIH_(Hungary)_-_NAIH-4667-10/2022

Hungarian DPA (2023a) NAIH-373-31/2023 case on several infringements in handling the data of minors and parents. https://gdprhub.eu/index.php?title=NAIH_(Hungary)_-_NAIH-373-31/2023

Hungarian DPA (2023b) NAIH-1245/2023 on data breach within the eKRÉTA system

Hungarian DPA (2023c) NAIH-3888/2023 illegal disclosure of minor's sensitive data online

Hungarian DPA (2023d) NAIH-5377-12/2023 case on the processing of a minor's personal data by a bank, for the purpose of a of a 'baby loan'. https://gdprhub.eu/index.php?title=NAIH_(Hungary)_-_NAIH-5377-12/2023

ICDPPC (International Conference of Data Protection and Privacy Commissioners) (30th, 2008). 'Resolution on Children's Online Privacy' (Strasbourg, 17 October 2008)

Lansdown G (2005) The evolving capacities of the child. UNICEF. http://unicef-irc.org/publications/pdf/evolving-eng.pdf

Lievens E, Verdoodt V (2017) Looking for needles in a haystack: key issues affecting children's rights in the General Data Protection Regulation. Comput Law Secur Rev 34(2):269–278. https://doi.org/10.1016/j.clsr.2017.09.007

Lithuanian DPA (2019) Data protection guidelines for youth. https://vdai.lrv.lt/uploads/vdai/documents/files/02_%20SolPriPa%20Asmens%20duomenu%20apsaugos%20gaires%20JAUNIMUI%202019-11-06.pdf

Lithuanian DPA (2021) Schools and kindergartens inspected for processing personal data to justify reasons for absence from an educational institution. https://vdai.lrv.lt/lt/naujienos/mokyklos-ir-darzeliai-patikrinti-del-asmens-duomenu-tvarkymo-ugdymo-istaigos-nelankymo-priezastims-pagristi/

Lithuanian DPA (2022) Decision on the processing of children's image data. https://vdai.lrv.lt/uploads/vdai/documents/files/Sprendimas%20sutikimas%20tvarkant%20vaiku%20atvaizdo%20duomenis%202022-09-30.pdf

Lithuanian DPA (2023) 20 steps for children and teens to protect their personal data online. https://vdai.lrv.lt/lt/naujienos/vaikams-ir-paaugliams-valstybine-duomenu-apsaugos-inspekcija-parenge-su-asmens-duomenu-apsauga-susijusias-saugaus-elgesio-internete-gaires/

Lithuanian DPA (2024) Decision No. 3R-741 on monitoring classrooms during school hours via video surveillance. https://gdprhub.eu/index.php?title=VDAI_(Lithuania)_-_3R-741&mtc=today

Lithuanian Supreme Administrative Court (2024) Case No. eA-442-629/2024 on disclosure of a child's personal data. https://www.e-tar.lt/portal/lt/legalAct/c0cdf814776911efabdbb4a1fc8b0b63

Livingstone S, Atabey A, Pothong K (2021) Addressing the problems and realising the benefits of processing children's education data: Report on an expert roundtable. Digital Futures

Commission, 5Rights Foundation. https://digitalfuturescommission.org.uk/wp-content/uploads/2021/11/Roundtable-report-25112-final.pdf
Lupton D, Williamson B (2017) The datafied child: the dataveillance of children and implications for their rights. New Media Soc 19(5):780–794. https://doi.org/10.1177/1461444816686328
Macenaite M (2017) From universal towards child-specific protection of the right to privacy online: dilemmas in the EU General Data Protection Regulation. New Media Soc 19(5):765–779. https://doi.org/10.1177/1461444816686327
Macenaite M, Kosta E (2017) Consent for processing children's personal data in the EU: following in US footsteps? Inf Commun Technol Law 26(2):146–197. https://doi.org/10.1080/13600834.2017.1321096
Mascheroni G (2020) Datafied childhoods: contextualising datafication in everyday life. Curr Sociol 68(6):798–813. https://doi.org/10.1177/0011392118807534
Milkaite I (2021) A children's rights perspective on privacy and data protection in the digital age: a critical and forward-looking analysis of the EU General Data Protection Regulation and its implementation with respect to children and youth [PhD Dissertation, Ghent University]. http://hdl.handle.net/1854/LU-8714018
Milkaite I (2022) An international perspective on data protection for children's education data. In: Livingstone S, Pothong K (eds) Education data futures: critical, regulatory and practical reflections. Digital Futures Commission, 5Rights Foundation, pp 174–187. https://educationdatafutures.5rightsfoundation.com/essays/the-value-of-better-regulation/international-perspective-data-protection-children
Milkaite I (2023) Strengthening children's rights to privacy and data protection in the digital environment: walking the tightrope in the EU. In: European yearbook on human rights 2023. Intersentia, pp 391–436. http://hdl.handle.net/1854/LU-01HREWR3595KK2K8ZS22NQSEK6
Milkaite I, Lievens E (2019a) Children's rights to privacy and data protection around the world: challenges in the digital realm. Eur J Law Technol 10(1). http://ejlt.org/article/view/674
Milkaite I, Lievens E (2019b) The changing patchwork of the child's age of consent for data processing across the EU. Better Internet for Kids. http://hdl.handle.net/1854/LU-8601665
Milkaite I, Lievens E (2019c) The internet of toys: playing games with children's data? In: Mascheroni G, Holloway D (eds) The internet of toys: practices, affordances and the political economy of children's smart play. Springer International Publishing, pp 285–305. https://doi.org/10.1007/978-3-030-10898-4_14
Milkaite I, Lievens E (2020) Child-friendly transparency of data processing in the EU: from legal requirements to platform policies. J Children Media 14(1):5–21. https://doi.org/10.1080/17482798.2019.1701055
Milkaite I, De Wolf R, Lievens E, Leyn TD, Martens M (2021) Children's reflections on privacy and the protection of their personal data: a child-centric approach to data protection information formats. Children Youth Serv Rev 129:106170. https://doi.org/10.1016/j.childyouth.2021.106170
Montgomery KC, Chester J, Milosevic T (2017) Children's privacy in the big data era: research opportunities. Pediatrics 140(Supplement 2):S117–S121. https://doi.org/10.1542/peds.2016-1758O
OECD (2021, May 31) Recommendation of the Council on Children in the Digital Environment. https://legalinstruments.oecd.org/en/instruments/OECD-LEGAL-0389
OECD (2024) Towards digital safety by design for children. OECD Publishing, Paris. https://doi.org/10.1787/c167b650-en
Pascu L (2020, February 28) French high court rules against biometric facial recognition use in high schools | Biometric Update. https://www.biometricupdate.com/202002/french-high-court-rules-against-biometric-facial-recognition-use-in-high-schools
Polish DPA (2018) Decision No. ZSZZS.440.768.2018 on fingerprint-based biometric system for verifying meal payments in the school canteen. https://www.uodo.gov.pl/decyzje/ZSZZS.440.768.2018

Polish DPA (2020a) DKE.561.2.2020 case on failure to provide the DPA with access to personal data and other information necessary for the performance of its tasks. https://gdprhub.eu/index.php?title=UODO_(Poland)_-_DKE.561.2.2020

Polish DPA (2020b) DKN.5112.7.2020 case on the processing of students' personal data without legal basis in connection with a survey. https://gdprhub.eu/index.php?title=UODO_(Poland)_-_DKN.5112.7.2020

Polish Supreme Administrative Court (2024) NSA – III OSK 4804/21. The Supreme Administrative Court found that a school obtained valid consent under Article 9(2)(a) GDPR for the usage of a fingerprint scanner for its canteen. https://gdprhub.eu/index.php?title=NSA_-_III_OSK_4804/21&mtc=today

Romanian DPA (2020). https://gdprhub.eu/index.php?title=ANSPDCP_(Romania)_-_Banca_Comercial%C4%83_Rom%C3%A2n%C4%83_S.A

Romanian DPA (2021). https://gdprhub.eu/index.php?title=ANSPDCP_(Romania)_-_Fine_against_IKEA_ROM%C3%82NIA_SA

Slovenian DPA (2020a) Decision No. 07121-1/2020/2263 on whether a gym teacher's decision to ask children to record their dance videos and submit them to an online classroom was in accordance with Article 6 GDPR. https://gdprhub.eu/index.php?title=IP_-_07121-1_/_2020/2263

Slovenian DPA (2020b) IP - 07121-1/2020/638 case on the processing of personal data of teachers and pupils when new technologies are used. https://gdprhub.eu/index.php?title=IP_-_07121-1/2020/638

Slovenian DPA (2021) IP - 07121-1/2021/540 case on kindergarten preadmission data. https://gdprhub.eu/index.php?title=IP_-_07121-1/2021/540#Facts

Slovenian DPA (2024) 07101-37/2023/30 case on a refusal to act on an access request filed by the parent of a data subject, if the disclosure of certain data can impair the best interest of the minor. https://gdprhub.eu/index.php?title=IP_(Slovenia)_-_07101-37/2023/30

Steeves V, Mačėnaitė M (2022) Chapter 17: Data protection and children's online privacy. https://www.elgaronline.com/edcollchap/edcoll/9781786438508/9781786438508.00025.xml

Stoilova M, Livingstone S, Nandagiri R (2020) Digital by default: children's capacity to understand and manage online data and privacy. Media Commun 8(4)., Article 4. https://doi.org/10.17645/mac.v8i4.3407

Stoilova M, Nandagiri R, Livingstone S (2021) Children's understanding of personal data and privacy online – a systematic evidence mapping. Inf Commun Soc 24(4):557–575. https://doi.org/10.1080/1369118X.2019.1657164

Swedish Data Protection Authority (2021) The rights of children and young people on digital platforms. https://www.imy.se/en/publications/the-rights-of-children-and-young-people-on-digital-platforms/

Tuomi I, Cachia R, Villar-Onrubia D (2023) On the futures of technology in education: emerging trends and policy implications. Publications Office of the European Union. https://publications.jrc.ec.europa.eu/repository/bitstream/JRC134308/JRC134308_01.pdf

UK DPA (ICO) (2020) Age appropriate design: A code of practice for online services (the final version). ICO. https://ico.org.uk/for-organisations/guide-to-data-protection/key-data-protection-themes/age-appropriate-design-a-code-of-practice-for-online-services/

UK DPA (ICO) (2024a) Essex school reprimanded after using facial recognition technology for canteen payments. ICO. https://ico.org.uk/about-the-ico/media-centre/news-and-blogs/2024/07/essex-school-reprimanded-after-using-facial-recognition-technology-for-canteen-payments/

UK DPA (ICO) (2024b) New ICO campaign promotes sharing data to safeguard children. https://ico.org.uk/about-the-ico/media-centre/news-and-blogs/2024/01/new-ico-campaign-promotes-sharing-data-to-safeguard-children

UN Committee on the Rights of the Child (2021, March 2). General comment No. 25 (2021) on children's rights in relation to the digital environment. https://tbinternet.ohchr.org/_layouts/15/treatybodyexternal/Download.aspx?symbolno=CRC%2fC%2fGC%2f25&Lang=en

UN General Assembly (2021, January 25). Artificial intelligence and privacy, and children's privacy. Report of the Special Rapporteur on the right to privacy, Joseph A. Cannataci. https://undocs.org/A/HRC/46/37

United Nations General Assembly (1989) Convention on the Rights of the Child. Treaty Series vol. 1577. https://www.ohchr.org/en/instruments-mechanisms/instruments/convention-rights-child
van der Hof S (2016) I Agree, or Do I: a rights-based analysis of the law on children's consent in the digital world. Wisconsin Int Law J 34:409–445. https://heinonline.org/HOL/P?h=hein.journals/wisint34&i=421
van der Hof S, Lievens E, Milkaite I (2019) The protection of children's personal data in a data-driven world: a closer look at the GDPR from a children's rights perspective. In: Monitoring children's rights in the Netherlands: 30 years of the UN convention on the rights of the child. Leiden University Press, pp 77–123. http://hdl.handle.net/1854/LU-8642862
van der Hof S, Lievens E, Milkaite I, Verdoodt V, Hannema T, Liefaard T (2020) The child's right to protection against economic exploitation in the digital world. Int J Childrens Rights 28(4)., Article 4. https://doi.org/10.1163/15718182-28040003
Varadan S (2019) The principle of evolving capacities under the UN Convention on the Rights of the Child. https://doi.org/10.1163/15718182-02702006
Vilnius Regional Administrative Court (2023) Case No. I2-577-816/2023
Waag & Leiden University (2022) Dutch Code for Children's Rights. https://codevoorkinderrechten.nl/wp-content/uploads/2021/07/Code-voor-Kinderrechten-Wordversie_EN.pdf

Ingrida Milkaitė is a postdoctoral researcher at Vrije Universiteit Brussel (VUB), where she works on the Horizon Europe SALVUS project and a voluntary postdoctoral researcher at the Law & Technology research group and the Human Rights Centre at the Faculty of Law and Criminology, Ghent University, Belgium. Her work focuses on the intersections of human rights law, privacy, data protection, freedom of expression, and emerging technologies, with a particular emphasis on childrens rights in the digital environment. Ingrida obtained her PhD in 2021 with a thesis examining privacy and data protection from a childrens rights perspective in the digital age. For this research, conducted with Professor Eva Lievens, they were awarded the inaugural Stefano Rodotà Award by the Council of Europe. Ingrida's research, advisory, and consultancy work promote evidence based, rights respecting approaches to digital governance. She collaborates regularly with international organisations and interdisciplinary research groups on regulatory and policy initiatives at the intersection of technology and human rights. Ingrida regularly contributes to international and European policymaking, including as a member of the Working Group on Gaming and Regulation, embedded within the NYU Stern Center for Business and Human Rights, the Special Group on the EU Code of Conduct on Age Appropriate Design, the Legal Affairs Committee of the European Centre for Press and Media Freedom and the Strasbourg Observers Blog.

Milda Mačėnaitė received her PhD from Tilburg Institute for Law, Technology and Society (TILT), the Netherlands. Her PhD research focused on the protection of childrens privacy and personal data in the digital environment. She was a Senior Fellow at the UNICEF Office of Research Innocenti, Italy and a visiting researcher at the University of Ottawa, Canada.

Parenting in the Digital Age: Addressing the Sharenting Phenomenon in Central and Eastern Europe

Gergely Ferenc Lendvai and Kristina Ambrazevičiūtė

Abstract Sharenting, though widely practiced, is both commonplace and deeply controversial due to its potential for harm in the online landscape. This paper explores the concept of sharenting and its diverse international trends, with a particular focus on the Central and Eastern European (CEE) region, including the Visegrad 4 and Baltic States. First, by synthesising over thirty academic definitions, the paper aims to offer a conceptual foundation for understanding sharenting, enabling a clearer interpretation of legislative and regulatory trends. Second, with a special emphasis on the CEE region, this chapter delves into regulatory philosophies, legislative frameworks, and platform-based self-regulation initiatives. It is to be noted that except for France, European countries have not developed any sharenting-related legislation. This results in jurisdictional conflicts, enforcement hurdles, and potential legal loopholes exploited by parents seeking less restrictive regulatory environments. The third section of the paper provides a comparative examination of current policies, proposals, and challenges specific to the Visegrad 4 and Baltic regions, identifying potential pathways for more cohesive frameworks. Our findings underline the need for nuanced, adaptable regulatory approaches that account for cultural, legal, and ethical variations, particularly within the cross-border digital context. Ultimately, this paper advocates for collaborative efforts to establish unified frameworks, fostering legal coherence across the region.

G. F. Lendvai
Luvodika University of Public Service, Budapest, Hungary

University of Richmond, School of Arts and Sciences, Richmond, VA, USA
e-mail: lendvai.gergely.ferenc@stud.uni-nke.hu

K. Ambrazevičiūtė (✉)
Law Institute, Lithuanian Centre for Social Sciences, Vinius, Lithuania
e-mail: kristina.ambrazeviciute@teise.org

A. Limantė, R. Vaičiūnienė (eds.), *Children's Rights in Central and Eastern Europe*, European Union and its Neighbours in a Globalized World 29,
https://doi.org/10.1007/978-3-032-07092-0_17

1 Introduction

Imagine a photograph on Facebook or a video on TikTok of a young boy on his first day of school, wearing an oversized backpack and a shy smile. His father posts it on social media with a heartfelt caption, celebrating this important milestone. Within hours, friends, relatives, and colleagues have liked, shared, and commented on the post. And so did hundreds, if not thousands, of strangers. For the father, it's a cherished memory, he is proud to share this moment with his network; for the boy, however, it's a digital footprint created without his consent—a permanent mark in the digital world that he had no word or choice in. This scene, familiar to countless families across the globe, captures the essence of 'sharenting', a term used to describe the widespread sharing of children's lives online by their parents.

As common as it has become, sharenting raises complex questions about children's rights, privacy, and safety online. One may rightly argue that the now 'cliché' of the 'digital age' has transformed parenting, providing unprecedented access to tools that document, share, and celebrate family life (Clark 2012; Gee et al. 2017). One may also claim that the sharing of audiovisual content is not a new phenomenon—rightly so, as baby books have been around for centuries (Atkinson 2021), and the sharing of pictures of children has been noted to help new mothers understand the novel challenges of being a parent since decades (McDaniel et al. 2011; Blum-Ross and Livingstone 2017). Nonetheless, sharenting is substantially different in one significant criterion: the sharer does not control the audience with whom they share the content. To put it more bluntly, the picture of the schoolboy in the above example may appear on a colleague's feed; however, it is likely to appear on an unbeknownst person's, too, who may or may not use that picture for illegal and detrimental purposes.

In this regard, an interesting dilemma emerged; the widespread practice of sharing personal information about children online—often from infancy, which is a 'niche' form of sharenting (Nottingham 2019; Peng 2023)—has become both normalised and controversial, inciting a plethora of dualistic debates about children's autonomy and parents' rights, freedom of expression and data vulnerability, as well as potential parenting benefits and polemics about the usage of children's face in pornographic content (Walrave et al. 2023; Briazu et al. 2021; Aydoğdu et al. 2023; Lendvai 2024). The present chapter aims to investigate sharenting from a legal, more specifically, regulatory perspective, with particular emphasis on the Central and Eastern Europe (CEE), examining the challenges faced by nations within this area, notably the Visegrad 4 and the Baltic States, in implementing comprehensive and cohesive frameworks for managing sharenting.

It is critical to outline the two focal points: the legal aspects of sharenting and the regional assessment of the phenomenon. Firstly, from a legal standpoint, sharenting is a key dilemma for policymakers as it touches upon various domains of law, including privacy, data protection, and family law (Lendvai 2024). As Lendvai (2024) outlines, most countries' legal systems are fragmented in addressing sharenting, and there are considerable regional differences, making the assessment of this global phenomenon incredibly difficult. Though, for instance, France has started to implement explicit legislative measures addressing sharenting, reflecting a growing recognition of the phenomenon's potential impact on children's rights, the grand majority of countries still rely on already existing regulatory frameworks, which are often not sufficient in interpreting the nuances of sharenting (Lendvai 2024). Secondly, the CEE region is particularly important as there is a glaring research gap in this regard in the scholarship of sharenting. If the most prestigious journals' outputs are taken into account, most papers on sharenting regulation either concern the United States (Steinberg 2017; Yates 2023), the supranational legislation of the European Union (Lendvai 2024), or highly populated countries like Brazil (Von Teschenhausen Eberlin 2018; da Silva 2022), Indonesia (Sihabudin 2023), or Malaysia (Salleh et al. 2024). However, literature on sharenting, not only from a regulatory standpoint, is extremely scarce. To fill this scholarly gap, the Visegrad countries (namely, Hungary, Poland, the Czech Republic, and Slovakia) and the Baltic States (Lithuania, Latvia, and Estonia) are examined. For instance, countries like Hungary and Poland have conservative cultural attitudes that might influence the acceptance and framing of regulatory measures on digital parenting. Representing about 70 million people, or in a more comprehensive interpretation, around 16% of the European Union's population, the studying of these two regions' regulatory framework provides insights into sharenting practices on peripheral regions of the Global North.

The chapter is structured into three key segments. First, the Baltics are investigated, then the Visegrad Four, followed by a comparative doctrinal analysis of the similarities and differences between the regulations. As the GDPR and other pertaining regulations, such as the Digital Services Act, are well-researched fields of the scholarship of sharenting regulation, the chapter primarily focuses on principles in children's data protection in the two regions. This consideration stems from two key considerations. On the one hand, while overarching frameworks like the GDPR provide baseline protections, local interpretations and applications often vary significantly, influenced by cultural, social, and political factors unique to each region. On the other hand, despite the legal framework's universality within the EU, each country's regulatory authorities exercise varying degrees of rigour in enforcing these laws, especially concerning children's data rights. Hence, this chapter aims to assess not only the existing legislative measures but also the societal and cultural forces shaping sharenting practices and regulatory responses within the CEE region, offering a comprehensive understanding of how these nations navigate the balance between children's rights and parental responsibilities.

2 An Interlude on the Conceptualization of Sharenting and the Lack of Legal Attention to the Issue

Conceptualising sharenting is rather complex. Scholars have continuously tried to provide a comprehensive definition of the phenomenon; however, even the most renowned dictionaries failed to propose a uniform description of what sharenting is. Sharenting is a term made up of the English words 'share' or 'sharing' and 'parenting' referencing the practice of parents, guardians, or family members publicly sharing information, images, or videos of children on social media or other online platforms (Steinberg 2017; Brosch 2018). A key component of sharenting is the interpersonal relation between the actor (or 'sharenter') and the subject of sharenting, namely, the sharenter's child.

One of the key problems with the legal assessment of sharenting is the very ambiguous nature of defining sharenting. Though the General Data Protection Regulation (GDPR) and the Digital Services Act in the European Union, or the COPPA in the United States may be applicable—in a general sense—to cases involving sharenting, there seems to be a legislative gap in addressing sharenting with more attention to its details. As of November 2024, there is only one individual piece of legislation that addresses sharenting directly. Promulgated in February 2024, Act no. 2024–120 as an amendment to the French Civil Code, or as some refers to it the "Children's Image Rights Law", mandates that both parents are jointly responsible for decisions related to sharing their child's images online and must consider the child's age-appropriate opinion (Le Clerc and Leportois 2024). The new segment, Article 372–1, also underlines that in cases of disagreement between parents, a judge can intervene, even prohibiting one parent from publishing content without the other's consent and if sharing a child's image significantly harms their dignity or moral integrity, the court may impose a forced delegation of parental authority concerning the child's image rights. Additionally, the legislation includes educational measures to inform parents about the potential risks of sharenting, fostering more cautious and informed online behaviours. In the other countries, including the countries in the scope of this paper's investigation, however, there are no specific laws addressing sharenting. For this reason, this study proposes the aforementioned understanding of sharenting to contextualise it in the respective regional legislative framework.

3 The Baltics and Sharenting Rules

Estonia, Latvia, and Lithuania exemplify a global trend by lacking specific regulations that address sharenting within their legal frameworks. Moreover, in the Baltic States, the phenomenon of sharenting still needs to be better understood and recognised. For instance, offices responsible for protecting children's rights in Lithuania do not track or possess statistics regarding sharenting cases despite acknowledging encountering such cases in practice. The low awareness of sharenting is also reflected in the lack of research conducted by legal scholars in this area. There are only two notable studies: one is an Estonian article that discusses a child's right to privacy in sharenting, focusing on legal regulations and their interpretations at international, EU, and national levels (Isküll and Joamets 2022). The other is a study by Lithuanian students that explores the use of a child's image for advertising on social networks, primarily through the analysis of national regulations (Jasinskaitė and Ubavičiūtė 2021). More research and awareness in this field are crucial to understanding and addressing the challenges of sharenting. The following section will present the legal norms in Estonia, Latvia, and Lithuania that regulate children's right to privacy in the context of sharenting.

When considering the adaptation of Estonian legal norms to address the issue of sharenting, two key factors must be taken into account: the child's right to privacy and parental responsibilities. Both of these rights have a constitutional basis in Estonian law. Section 26 of the Constitution (The Constitution of the Republic of Estonia 1992) establishes the right to protection and respect for private life, while Section 27 grants parents the right and duty to raise and provide for their children.

Estonian law does not explicitly refer to the child's right to privacy, but such rights can be inferred from general laws. Section 8 of the Estonian Personal Data Protection Act (2018) regulates the processing of children's data in the context of information society services, stating that children aged 13 and older can independently consent to process their data. For children under 13, processing their data requires the consent of a legal representative (parents or guardians). Regarding sharenting, this means that if parents share information about a child on public social media platforms, they must obtain the child's consent if they are over 13. This relatively low age threshold reflects Estonian culture's emphasis on promoting children's independence. However, for children under 13, publishing their data rests entirely with the parents. Legal scholars note that parental authority over children's data often leads to decisions that may not always be in the child's best interests (Isküll and Joamets 2022). Therefore, the child participation principle is especially significant (Section 5 of the Estonian Child Protection Act 2014). This principle affirms that every child has the right to have an independent viewpoint on issues concerning them and express their opinions. While the child's opinion about sharing personal information is not binding on parents, these opinions must be respected and considered in the decision-making process. However, young children may not have the capacity to fully understand the situation and its long-term consequences, which limits the practical application of the child participation principle.

The Estonian Family Law Act (2010) and the Child Protection Act govern parental responsibility in Estonia. According to these laws, parents are the legal representatives of their children and hold both the obligation and the right to care for their underage children. It is essential to reference Section 21 of the Child Protection Act, which states that the child's best interests must be considered in all decisions that affect them. The law specifies that such decisions should be based on assessing the child's situation. This assessment includes clarifying proposed solutions to the child, listening to their opinion, and considering their age and developmental level.

If a child's opinion differs from the parent's decision, the parents are required to explain why their viewpoint was not taken into account. While the law provides a framework for making child-friendly decisions, it also grants parents broad discretion, which can lead to subjective decision-making concerning young children. This subjective decision-making can lead to parental decisions not serving the child's best interests. Therefore, although Estonian legal norms regarding child privacy and parental responsibility can be beneficial in addressing the challenges associated with sharenting, they may be inadequate in situations where parental decisions do not serve the child's best interests. Even though the principle of child participation encourages consideration of the child's opinion, it does not protect against the long-term consequences of potential abuses of parental authority or violations of privacy.

When discussing sharenting in the context of Latvian laws, it is essential to consider norms related to a child's right to privacy and parental responsibility. Section 96 of the Constitution (The Constitution of the Republic of Latvia 1922) guarantees everyone's right to the inviolability of their private life, which serves as the legal foundation for protecting children's privacy. This principle is further articulated in Section 9 of the Law on the Protection of Children's Rights (1998), which explicitly establishes a child's right to privacy. The Latvian Personal Data Processing Law (2018) governs the child's right to privacy, which is similar to Estonian rules. Under this law, if a child is under 13, a parent or legal guardian must consent to process the child's data. In contrast, children who are 13 years old or older can give consent on their own (Section 33).

In Latvia, parental responsibility encompasses the obligation of parents to care for their child until the child reaches adulthood, as well as to represent the child in personal and property matters (Section 177 of the Latvian Civil Law 1937). Section 6 of the Law on the Protection of Children's Rights outlines that parents' authority is determined by prioritising the child's best interests. It is important to note that this law goes beyond merely declaring the principle of the child's best interests; it also outlines criteria for evaluating decisions that uphold these interests. With regard to sharenting, such criteria established by law include ensuring that parental behaviour aligns with the child's needs and development, providing a safe environment, involving the child in decision-making processes, and considering and respecting the child's opinions based on age and maturity level. While Latvian laws are similar to those in Estonia, they offer more comprehensive regulation. These laws clearly define a child's right to privacy and establish parents' obligations to prioritise the child's rights and interests, reflecting a blending of traditional family values with modern principles of privacy and children's rights. However, there remains a risk that parents may make subjective decisions that do not align with the child's best interests.

To examine the regulations regarding sharenting in Lithuania, two issues can be considered: the child's right to privacy and parental responsibilities. Like other Baltic States, the Constitution of Lithuania (1992) emphasises the inviolability of private life (Article 22). This principle is elaborated in Article 2.23 of the Civil Code (2000), which states that information about a person's private life may be published only with their consent. Additionally, a child's right to privacy is affirmed in Article

10 of the Law on Fundamentals of Protection of the Rights of the Child of the Republic of Lithuania (LFPRC, 1996).

In Lithuania, the age at which children can independently consent to use information society services is slightly higher than in Estonia and Latvia, set at 14 years old according to Article 6 of the Law on Legal Protection of Personal Data (1996). Additionally, Lithuania distinguishes itself from the other Baltic states in regulating an individual's right to their image. According to the Civil Code, the image of a person can only be used with their consent (Article 2.22(1)). Parents, as the legal representatives of minor children, have the authority to consent to the use of their child's image (Article 3.157(1)). However, the child's opinion is important; it must be considered in decisions affecting them as long as it does not conflict with the child's best interests (Article 3.164(1)). Article 13(1.5) of the Law on the Provision of Information to the Public (2006) outlines a more detailed provision, which states that filming, photographing, or recording a child can only take place with the consent of both the parents and the child. This distinctive emphasis on privacy regulation could be linked to the cultural value of individual autonomy. However, case law indicates that parents remain the primary decision-makers (Case No. e2A-800-886/2022 of the Kaunas County Court).

In Lithuanian law, the responsibility of parents is grounded in the principles of prioritising the protection and defence of children's rights and interests (Article 3.3 of the Civil Code) and ensuring the best interests of the child (Article 4(1) of the LFPRC). Therefore, parents must create conditions that support their children's comprehensive and harmonious development (Articles 3.155, 3.165 of the Civil Code). The Supreme Court of Lithuania has stated that parents should not abuse their authority over their children in ways that violate the child's honour and dignity. Any such conduct or negligence in protecting the child's rights contravenes the child's interests (Review No. A2-35 of the Supreme Court of Lithuania). Thus, the principle of best interests of the child is significant in the Lithuanian legal system; however, its ambiguity may allow parental decisions to overshadow the child's autonomy.

4 Sharenting in the Context of Privacy Laws in the Visegrad Four Region

Despite the lack of legislative measures in the Visegrad countries concerning sharenting, the phenomenon resulted in a growing scholarship among Czech, Polish, and Hungarian researchers. Outside of legal literature, this region has been home to notable figures, such as Kamil Kopecky from the Czech Republic, whose work has influenced the empirical research on information sharing and the interpersonal relations related thereto and who was among the authors who introduced the Sharenting Evaluation Scale (SES), a groundbreaking model in assessing the rate and types of sharenting among adults (cf. Kopecky et al. 2020, 2023; Romero-Rodríguez et al.

2022), and Anna Brosch from Poland who was among the first scholars to ever conceptualise sharenting (Brosch 2016) and whose prevalent conceptual framework has been instrumental in the study of sharenting in social sciences (Brosch 2018). However, the legal scholarship on sharenting with particular attention to the V4 countries is rather rudimentary. In the present section, therefore, the pertaining laws will be analysed that can be applied regarding children's privacy with the use of existing literature in the field.

In the Czech Republic, the phenomenon of sharenting is limited to biological or adoptive parents, as only they have legal parental responsibility over a child (Sehnálek 2023, p. 115). Therefore, per Czech law, the broad understanding of the act of sharenting where perhaps siblings acting as *de facto* parents or grandparents share information about the child, falls out of the question of sharenting. Per Sehnálek (2023), in Czech law, two key points are to be taken into account when examining privacy rights in the context of sharenting: the privacy provisions that are enshrined under Section 81 and subsequent paragraphs, and Section 858 on parental responsibilities in the Czech Civil Code (the latter read together with Section 875 on the child's best interest). The former stipulates that the personality and natural rights of individuals are protected, requiring respect for their freedom to live as they choose. Sections 84–87, in this regard, are of particular interest. The Code mandates consent for capturing an individual's image, yet children, as minors, cannot provide valid consent, placing the responsibility on parents (Sehnálek 2023). Furthermore, though Section 86 prohibits unauthorized intrusion into privacy, including recording or distributing private content, unless a lawful reason exists, underscoring the risk of violating children's rights through sharenting, Section 85 presumes implied consent for distribution when circumstances indicate reasonable expectation, but this presumption is problematic for children who lack the capacity to foresee such implications. As with all privacy rights, the Czech Civil Code also allows for withdrawal of consent (Section 87), however, one may rightly ask the question: are children even able to exercise this right effectively, particularly for content shared long before they can comprehend its impact?

Parental responsibilities shall also be analysed. Alas, whether sharenting falls under or out of parental responsibilities is seemingly an unsolvable dilemma (Lendvai 2024), Section 858 and related stipulations reflect a framework that is both comprehensive and challenging in its implications for child-rearing. While the law emphasises the child's best interests (Section 875), it is lamentable that such an ideal often rests heavily on parents' interpretations, which may lack the more nuanced understanding necessary to fully respect the child's rights, particularly regarding privacy. As with other legal instruments, such as the French sharenting law, the requirement for parents to inform children of decisions affecting them and consider their opinions (Section 875(2)) is seemingly progressive, but it can also be argued that is impractical for young children, who may lack the maturity to meaningfully engage in such discussions. Similarly to other pertaining regulations, such as Article 3 of the United Nations Convention on the Rights of the Child, the Czech Civil Code also accentuate that the parents should act in the child's well-disputed 'best interest'. This provision, however, is overly abstract. Following Kravchuk's

(2021) line of thought on privacy and the best interest doctrine, the term 'best interest' is not only not defined in Czech law, but if Section 879 is considered too, this principle is accompanied by the presumption that relies on the good faith and knowledge of parents, a standard that may falter when one parent's intentions conflict with the other's or with the child's interests. In this regard, the Czech law *presumes* parents will inherently act with altruism and wisdom yet provides insufficient mechanisms and conceptualisation for addressing situations where parental responsibility is exercised recklessly or selfishly, especially in an era of digital 'oversharing' (Ranzini et al. 2020). To conclude, while these provisions aim to balance parental authority with the child's rights, the Czech law imposes an idealised vision of parenting that often fails to account for the complexities and conflicts of real-world family dynamics, leaving children, particularly in the context of sharenting, insufficiently protected against privacy violations and exploitation.

Though studies have examined sharenting dangers in Poland (cf. Tofil and Jagielska 2024), the legal reception of sharenting in Poland is a relatively developing area in Polish scholarship. These two aspects are enshrined in the Polish Constitution (Article 47–48) too, laying down the foundation of privacy being a universal constitutional right and that parents shall have the right to raise their children according to their beliefs, respecting the child's maturity, conscience, and convictions, while parental rights may only be limited or revoked by statute through a final court judgment. The Polish Civil Code offers general stipulations regarding these two rights. Article 23 enumerates personal interests, including privacy, which are protected under civil law, and Article 24 allows individuals to seek legal remedies if these personal interests are violated. Also, Article 81 of the Copyright Act states that any dissemination of a child's image requires parental or legal guardian consent, with the obligation to prioritize the child's best interest (Borkowska and Witkowska 2020). These provisions imply that children, as individuals, possess personal rights, including the right to privacy.

For parental rights, the Polish Family and Guardianship Code ("FGC") guides the issues pertaining to sharenting. Article 95 of the FGC provides a framework for parental authority, emphasising that it must be exercised with respect for the child's dignity and rights. Considering sharenting, this means parents are legally obligated to ensure that sharing their child's personal information, images, or videos does not undermine the child's privacy or subject them to ridicule or harm, which is close to equivalent to the doctrines in Czech law. This is further assured by the fact that the law further requires parents to act in the child's best interests and in alignment with social values; underscoring the need for thoughtful consideration of the long-term consequences of publicly sharing private details about a child's life. Importantly, the FGC specifies that parents must listen to the child's opinions on significant matters if the child's maturity allows. This provision suggests that children, particularly older ones, should be consulted before their information is shared online, fostering a sense of autonomy and mutual respect. A critically important stipulation is enshrined in Section 2 of Article 95. This provision grants children under the parental authority the duty of obedience, however, it also recognises their capacity to make independent decisions in appropriate situations, emphasising that parental authority is not absolute—a crucial perspective considering the overwhelmingly negative attitudes toward sharenting among more mature children and adolescents (Siibak and Traks 2019). Though, from a privacy standpoint, the Polish stipulations fall short of the Czech regulation, it shall also be underlined that from the view of parental responsibilities, the Polish laws make a better case for a progressive sharenting approach. The principle of safeguarding a child's dignity, explicitly stated in Section 1 of Article 95, implies that actions like oversharing or exposing sensitive details for parental gratification could constitute a violation of this duty. Furthermore, as parental authority is exercised until the child reaches maturity, parents must be vigilant in ensuring their actions do not compromise the child's future reputation or personal rights.

In Slovakia, the two examined aspects, children's privacy and parental responsibilities are protected under multiple legal instruments. The Slovakian Family Act (Act No. 36/2005, Coll.), particularly Section 28, establishes that parents share equal rights and responsibilities toward their child, emphasising the child's best interests in all decisions, a general principle existing in both Czech and Polish law. Though the Slovakian law exemplifies 'best interests' via mentioning consistent and comprehensive care for the child's upbringing, health, nutrition, and overall development (Section 28(1)(a)), privacy remains an *implicit* element of 'best interests'. Privacy is more articulated in the Slovakian Civil Code (Act No. 40/1964, Coll.), in particular, under Sections 11 to 16. The provisions explicitly safeguard individual personality rights, including the right to privacy, applying these protections equally to minors. Article 12(1) specifically mentions that "documents of personal nature, portraits, pictures and image and sound records concerning an individual or expressions of his personal nature may be taken or used only with his or her consent." Additionally, the Slovakian Personal Data Protection Act (Act No. 18/2018 Coll.), in line with the GDPR, requires that any processing of children's personal data must have explicit consent from legal guardians and adhere to strict data protection principles. Criticised for their imperfections (Bezáková et al. 2021), the Slovakian laws seem to establish a similar framework to the Czech Republic and Poland obliging parents to act responsibly when managing their child's personal information, whether online or offline, however, once again, it fails to accentuate the interpersonal relation of the conflict underlying in the act of sharenting and assumes that the parent(s) sharent in good faith.

Lastly, Hungarian law uses a comparable approach to that of other V4 countries. Literature, again, on the Hungarian regulation is rather scarce. Kriston and Tóth (2023), as well as Lendvai (2024) refer to the Hungarian Civil Code as the primary legal instrument concerning sharenting activities. Book 2, Articles 42–43 of the Hungarian Civil Code state that everyone has the right, within the limits of the law and the rights of others, to freely exercise their personality rights, including the right to respect for private and family life, home, communication by any means, and reputation, without interference. The Hungarian approach, in this regard, is more focused on the personality rights of the children. As in the previous cases, personality rights may be interfered with if consent is given. It is a dilemma, however, whether a child is legally capable of giving consent. In this context, it is important to revisit the age of consent-giving in the Hungarian Civil Code. Hungarian law classifies children under 14 as legally incompetent, meaning their legal declarations are null, and their legal representatives (typically parents) act on their behalf (Articles 2:11–12). Children aged 14 or older are considered partially competent, and while their legal declarations are valid, they require the consent of their legal representative to be enforceable (Article 2:14). In disputes regarding personality rights, two conditions must be met to establish a violation: the parent exercising parental authority must have consented to the sharenting content, and it must be proven that the parent consulted the child's opinion (Kriston and Tóth 2023). This dual consideration, however, in practice leads to the child having no means of proving consent. Moreover, the debate over whether the consultation occurred and its efficiency and comprehensiveness are highly contentious.

5 Similarities and Differences: A Comparative Table

To add to the goal of our paper, namely, the presentation of the sharenting-related laws in seven different countries, it is important to summarise the key points in brief. For this, a comparative and comprehensive framework table is introduced (Table 1).

Table 1 Comprehensive comparative table of the Baltic and Visegrad countries' sharenting-related laws and principles

<table>
<tr><th></th><th colspan="3">Baltics</th><th colspan="4">Visegrad Four</th></tr>
<tr><th></th><th>Estonia</th><th>Latvia</th><th>Lithuania</th><th>Czech R.</th><th>Poland</th><th>Slovakia</th><th>Hungary</th></tr>
<tr><td>Guiding principles</td><td colspan="3">• The principle of the "best interests of the child"
• Constitutional law, civil law, and data protection instruments
• Child's participation, albeit limited</td><td colspan="4">• The principle of the "best interests of the child"
• Civil law and data protection instruments, lesser accent on constitutional law
• Assumption of good faith in parental actions, rather limited participation rights for the child</td></tr>
<tr><td>Key takeaways</td><td>The child's right to privacy is based on general principles</td><td>Criteria for evaluating decisions that best support the interests of the child</td><td>Detailed regulation of child privacy, particularly in establishing the right to one's image</td><td>The right to withdraw consent</td><td>Focus on personal dignity Copyright rights are liaised to parental rights.</td><td>Clearer definition of 'the best interests of the child' which may be applicable to privacy cases</td><td>A strong 'privacy-dilemma' for children under the age of 14, limited privacy rights and strong parental control</td></tr>
</table>

Source: Prepared by the authors

On a doctrinal level, the key difference may be highlighted in terms of the child's participation. As seen above, though the difference in practice may be considered minuscule, one can note that the Baltic states propose a more forward-thinking set of stipulations in the context of the participation of the child or children in decision-making. The core similarity and the unequivocal guiding principle, however, is still the extremely abstract and difficult-to-interpret "child's best interests" doctrine, which, as seen above, in all case is hard to contextualise in a non-case-to-case manner.

Estonia stands out in regards to data protection, presenting a detailed regulation that most certainly can be an example to follow for both the Baltic and Visegrad countries in the future. What is evident, nonetheless, is the lack of particular definitions even in the more progressive laws such as the ones in Estonia or the Czech Republic. This issue is one to be addressed in all countries, and it is suggested to progress with this task at a fast-moving pace.

6 Concluding Remarks

The present analysis of sharenting regulation across the Visegrad and Baltic regions aimed to come to a critical conclusion: while existing frameworks in privacy and parental responsibility offer some protection in these two regions, they remain extremely general and 'parent-leaning' to adequately address the complexities of sharenting. Privacy provisions, in general, rely on broad interpretations of children's rights, such as dignity and personal autonomy, yet fail to provide clear and actionable mechanisms that are more tailored to sharenting. Similarly, parental responsibilities are rooted in the omnipresent principle of the best interests of the child, however, this concept remains undefined or overly abstract in all jurisdictions analysed, leaving significant room for subjective interpretation by parents and legal authorities. This issue can also be rooted in the fact that current laws *presuppose* good faith and rational decision-making by parents, resulting in the overlooking of situations where sharenting is without regard for the child's future privacy and dignity.

Addressing these challenges calls for action in policy-making, and one may confidently claim that the present fragmented framework fails to protect children in an overly vulnerable position in the virtual sphere. The authors consider that there is a pressing need for more detailed and harmonised sharenting laws across the Central and Eastern European region. Future laws on children's privacy and parental rights must go beyond general provisions, introducing explicit safeguards, education for parents on digital risks, and mechanisms to ensure children's voices are considered in age-appropriate ways. Nonetheless, it is to be accentuated that policy-making solely is and will not be sufficient in addressing the problems of sharenting. There is a burning need for the involvement of child protection agencies and authorities in both legislation and—even more importantly—in raising awareness through visibility campaigns on the issue of sharenting (Borkowska and Witkowska 2020). This is critical, as following Conti et al.'s (2024) results 93% of those who "sharent" have little to no understanding of the dangers or the legal concerns related thereto. Without these advancements, the current frameworks risk perpetuating a regulatory gap that leaves children vulnerable in the online space.

References

Atkinson VS (2021) Every picture tells a story: parenting advice books provide a window on the past. Soc Sci 11(1):11. https://doi.org/10.3390/socsci11010011

Aydoğdu F, Güngör BŞ, Öz TA (2023) Does sharing bring happiness? Understanding the sharenting phenomenon. Children Youth Serv Rev 154:107122. https://doi.org/10.1016/j.childyouth.2023.107122

Bezáková Z, Madleňák A, Švec M (2021) Security risks of sharing content based on minors by their family members on social media in times of technology interference. Media Lit Acad Res 4(1):53–69

Blum-Ross A, Livingstone S (2017) "Sharenting," parent blogging, and the boundaries of the digital self. Pop Commun 15(2):110–125. https://doi.org/10.1080/15405702.2016.1223300

Borkowska A, Witkowska M (2020) Sharenting i wizerunek dziecka w sieci. NASK Academy, Warsaw

Briazu RA, Floccia C, Hanoch Y (2021) Facebook sharenting in mothers of young children: the risks are worth it but only for some. Technol Mind Behav 2(4). https://doi.org/10.1037/tmb0000051

Brosch A (2016) When the child is born into the internet: sharenting as a growing trend among parents on facebook. New Educ Rev 43(1):225–235. https://doi.org/10.15804/tner.2016.43.1.19

Brosch A (2018) Sharenting – why do parents violate their children's privacy? New Educ Rev 54(4):75–85. https://doi.org/10.15804/tner.2018.54.4.06

Clark LS (2012) The Parent App. https://doi.org/10.1093/acprof:oso/9780199899616.001.0001

Conti MG, Del Parco F, Pulcinelli FM, Mancino E, Petrarca L, Nenna R, Di Mattia G, Matera L, La Regina DP, Bonci E, Caruso C, Midulla F (2024) Sharenting: characteristics and awareness of parents publishing sensitive content of their children on online platforms. Ital J Pediatr 50(1). https://doi.org/10.1186/s13052-024-01704-y

Da Silva JSL (2022) Sharenting Com Ercial E A Viol Ação Aos Direitos Da Personalidade Das Crianças: A Respo Nsabilização Diante Do Uso Indevido De Dados Pessoais E Da Publ Icidade Abusiva Explor Ador A De Consumidor Es, Por Equiparação, Hipervulnerabilizados. Revista de Direito Civil Contemporaneo 33(9):123–157

Estonian Child Protection Act, Official Gazette RT I, 06.12.2014, 1 (2014). https://www.riigiteataja.ee/en/eli/ee/510042023004/consolide/current

Estonian Family Law Act, Official Gazette RT I, 60, 395 (2009). https://www.riigiteataja.ee/en/eli/ee/515092023004/consolide/current

Estonian Personal Data Protection Act, Official Gazette RT I, 04.01.2019, 11 (2018). https://www.riigiteataja.ee/akt/111032023011?leiaKehtiv

Gee E, Takeuchi LM, Wartella E (2017) Children and families in the digital age. In: Routledge eBooks. https://doi.org/10.4324/9781315297170

Isküll A-M, Joamets K (2022) Child right to privacy and social media – personal information oversharing parents. Baltic J Law Polit 14(2):101–122. https://doi.org/10.2478/bjlp-2021-0012

Jasinskaitė B, Ubavičiūtė M (2021) Use of a child's image for advertising on social networks. Vilnius University Open Series, 162–181. https://doi.org/10.15388/TMP.2021.9

Kopecky K, Szotkowski R, Aznar-Díaz I, Romero-Rodríguez J (2020) The phenomenon of sharenting and its risks in the online environment. Experiences from Czech Republic and Spain. Children Youth Serv Rev 110:104812. https://doi.org/10.1016/j.childyouth.2020.104812

Kopecky K, Szotkowski R, Mičková H, Krejčí V (2023) Sharenting among Czech parents and its risks. Pediatrie Pro Praxi 24(1):8–12. https://doi.org/10.36290/ped.2023.011
Kravchuk N (2021) Privacy as a new component of "the best interests of the child" in the new digital environment. Int J Children Rights 29(1):99–121. https://doi.org/10.1163/15718182-29010006
Kriston E, Tóth DA (2023) A képmáshoz és hangfelvételhez való jog aktualitásai, különös tekintettel a gyermekeket érintő "sharenting" jelenségére. Publicationes Universitatis Miskolcinensis Sectio Juridica et Politica 41(2):85–97
Latvian Civil Law, Official Gazette, 41 (1937). https://likumi.lv/doc.php?id=90223
Latvian Law on the Protection of the Children's Rights, Official Gazette, 199/200 (1998). https://likumi.lv/doc.php?id=49096
Latvian Personal Data Processing Law, Official Gazette, 132 (2018). https://likumi.lv/doc.php?id=300099
Le Clerc MD, Leportois J (2024) France introduces new law to enhance the protection of children's rights in France - Connect On Tech. Connect on Tech. https://www.connectontech.com/france-introduces-new-law-to-enhance-the-protection-of-childrens-rights-in-france/
Lendvai GF (2024) Sharenting as a regulatory paradox – a comprehensive overview of the conceptualization and regulation of sharenting. Int J Law Policy Family 38(1). https://doi.org/10.1093/lawfam/ebae013
McDaniel BT, Coyne SM, Holmes EK (2011) New mothers and media use: associations between blogging, social networking, and maternal well-being. Maternal Child Health J 16(7):1509–1517. https://doi.org/10.1007/s10995-011-0918-2
Nottingham E (2019) 'Dad! Cut that Part Out!' Children's rights to privacy in the age of 'generation tagged': sharenting, digital kidnapping and the child micro-celebrity'. In: Jane Murray, Beth Blue Swadener, Kylie Smith (eds) The Routledge international handbook of young children's rights, pp 1–14.
Peng Z (2023) Your growth is my growth: Examining sharenting behaviours from a multiparty privacy perspective. Commun Res Pract 9(3):271–289. https://doi.org/10.1080/22041451.2023.2216584
Ranzini G, Newlands G, Lutz C (2020) Sharenting, peer influence, and privacy concerns: a study on the Instagram-sharing behaviors of parents in the United Kingdom. Soc Media + Soc 6(4). https://doi.org/10.1177/2056305120978376
Republic of Lithuania Civil Code, Official Gazette, Nr. 74-2262 (2000). https://www.e-tar.lt/portal/lt/legalAct/TAR.8A39C83848CB/asr
Republic of Lithuania Law on Fundamentals of Protection of the Rights of the Child, Official Gazette, Nr. 33-807 (1996). https://e-seimas.lrs.lt/portal/legalAct/lt/TAD/TAIS.26397/asr
Republic of Lithuania Law on Legal Protection of Personal Data, Official Gazette, Nr. 63-1479 (1996). https://www.e-tar.lt/portal/lt/legalAct/TAR.5368B592234C/asr
Republic of Lithuania Law on Provision of Information to the Public, Official Gazette, Nr. 82-3254 (2006). https://e-seimas.lrs.lt/portal/legalAct/lt/TAD/TAIS.286382?jfwid=oikisy64s
Romero-Rodríguez J, Kopecký K, García-González A, Gómez-García G (2022) Sharing images or videos of minors online: validation of the Sharenting Evaluation Scale (SES). Children Youth Serv Rev 136:106396. https://doi.org/10.1016/j.childyouth.2022.106396
Salleh ASM, Azhar ANM, Noor NAM, Isa YM, Bahadin SA (2024) Mengekang impak negatif sharenting: satu kajian tentang keterlibatan agensi kerajaan dan badan bukan kerajaan ketika pandemik Covid-19 (Curbing the negative impact of sharenting: a study on the involvement of government agencies and non-governmental organizations during the Covid-19 Pandemic). UUM J Leg Stud 15(1):303–327. https://doi.org/10.32890/uumjls2024.15.1.13
Sehnálek D (2023) Sharenting and children's privacy protection in international, EU, and Czech Law. Central Eur J Comp Law 4(1):111–132. https://doi.org/10.47078/2023.1.111-132
Sihabudin S (2023) Expanding the limitations of the protection and processing of children's personal data: an overview of current regulations, challenges, and recommendations. Brawijaya Law J 10(1):59–71. https://doi.org/10.21776/ub.blj.2023.010.01.04
Siibak A, Traks K (2019) The dark sides of sharenting. Catalan J Commun Cult Stud 11(1):115–121. https://doi.org/10.1386/cjcs.11.1.115_1

Steinberg SB (2017) Sharenting: children's privacy in the age of social media. Emory Law J 66(4):839–884

The Constitution of the Republic of Estonia, Official Gazette RT 26, 349 (1992). https://www.riigiteataja.ee/en/eli/530102013003/consolide

The Constitution of the Republic of Latvia, Official Gazette, 43 (1922). https://likumi.lv/doc.php?id=57980

The Constitution of the Republic of Lithuania, Official Gazette, No. 220-0 (1992). https://www.e-tar.lt/portal/lt/legalAct/TAR.47BB952431DA/asr

Tofil G, Jagielska D (2024) Children of Polish Parents Online - dimensions and sharenting risks. Studia Z Teorii Wychowania XV(1(46)):85–99. https://doi.org/10.5604/01.3001.0054.4424

Von Teschenhausen Eberlin FB (2018) Sharenting, liberdade de expressão e privacidade de crianças no ambiente digital: o papel dos provedores de aplicação no cenário jurídico brasileiro. Revista Brasileira De Políticas Públicas 7(3). https://doi.org/10.5102/rbpp.v7i3.4821

Walrave M, Robbé S, Staes L, Hallam L (2023) Mindful sharenting: how millennial parents balance between sharing and protecting. Front Psychol 14. https://doi.org/10.3389/fpsyg.2023.1171611

Yates C (2023) Influencing "kidfluencing": protecting children by limiting the influencing "kidfluencing": protecting children by limiting the right to profit from "sharenting" right to profit from "sharenting". Vanderbilt J Entertain Technol Law 25(4):854–870

Gergely Ferenc Lendvai is a PhD candidate at Pázmány Péter Catholic University and Ludovika University of Public Service and a research fellow at the Information Society Law Center (University of Milan, 23/25), Rosztoczy Grant Holder fellow at the University of Richmond (VA, USA) and research fellow at CAIS, Bochum (2025). He is also a research fellow at the Digital Authoritarianism Research Lab (DARL, Budapest, Hungary). He graduated from Eötvös Loránd University (ELTE) and Panthéon-Assas University (Paris II). Mr Lendvai focuses his research on new media phenomena, sharenting, deepfake regulation, platform regulation, AI and law, and scientometrics. He has written over 60 peer-reviewed publications in prestigious journals and publishes his works in English, Hungarian, German and Spanish.

Kristina Ambrazevičiūtė is a research fellow and Head of the Legal System Research Department at the Law Institute of the Lithuanian Centre for Social Sciences. She holds academic degrees in both philosophy and law. Her work focuses on private and labour law, with particular attention to the legal protection of socially vulnerable groups. Dr Ambrazevičiūtė has published extensively on issues such as the effects of demographic change on the labour market, age discrimination, gender inequality in employment, women's rights in the workplace, and the position of older individuals in the labour market. She has also explored the concept of family, as well as legal challenges related to minors' right to privacy.

Dr Ambrazevičiūtė was a lecturer at Mykolas Romeris University (2010–2017). She has also carried out numerous legal reviews and expert evaluations of legislation and draft laws. She has authored over 20 scientific publications and book chapters in both national and international outlets, regularly presents at academic conferences, and participates in national and international research projects.

Towards Inclusive Education for Children with Disabilities: Developments and Challenges in Lithuania and Poland

Lina Beliūnienė and Katarzyna Roszewska

Abstract Lithuania and Poland have embraced the principles of inclusive education as outlined in the UN Convention on the Rights of Persons with Disabilities, implementing legislative amendments and policy reforms to enhance educational access for children with disabilities. Both countries have also made progress in fostering inclusion within mainstream schools. However, significant barriers persist and current situation still requires futher reconsideration and improvement. First and foremost, in practice, discrimination based on disabilities remains a concern, with dozens children excluded from primary and secondary education or placed in segregated settings, particularly those with severe disabilities. Secondly, reasonable accommodation tailored to individual needs is often unavailable. Thirdly, students with disabilities frequently lack the necessary individualised support within general education frameworks.

This chapter critically examines the primary and secondary education systems in Lithuania and Poland, identifying key regulatory and systemic challenges to the implementation of inclusive education.The findings underscore the need for more robust mechanisms to ensure equitable access to education and compliance with international standards as it is ensured by the UN Convention. The chapter draws on comparative analysis of legal frameworks, national and international reports, non-governmental organisation findings, and academic literature to assess both achievements and gaps.

L. Beliūnienė (✉)
Law Institute, Lithuanian Centre for Social Sciences, Vilnius, Lithuania
e-mail: lina.beliuniene@teise.org

K. Roszewska
Institute of Law and Administration, Cardinal Stefan Wyszyński University, Warsaw, Poland
e-mail: k.roszewska@uksw.edu.pl

A. Limantė, R. Vaičiūnienė (eds.), *Children's Rights in Central and Eastern Europe*, European Union and its Neighbours in a Globalized World 29,
https://doi.org/10.1007/978-3-032-07092-0_18

1 Introduction

Issues related to the implementation of the right to education have garnered significant attention, given its essential role in fostering the integral development of children and advancing societal progress in the face of modern challenges. For children with disabilities, this right has evolved from mere access to education, to their inclusion within the broader framework of human rights. However, the right to education continues to provoke debate, both in terms of its normative foundations and its substantive content (Beco 2022, p. 1330). This right is so multi-faceted that it cannot be captured by the simple term of the right to 'education'. Scholars argue that the term 'education rights' better encapsulates the multifaceted nature of this entitlement, reflecting a comprehensive package of rights (Lundy and O'Lynn 2019, pp. 259, 261). Without addressing these disputes, this chapter examines the transition towards inclusive education (IE) in Lithuania and Poland, focusing on its legal and practical dimensions. It explores the shift from segregated education systems to inclusive frameworks, as shaped by international and national legal obligations.

Recognising that this process remains ongoing in Lithuania and Poland, as in the other states (UNESCO Global education monitoring report, 2020) and could be treated as a complex and long-term challenge, the research aims to analyse the path from segregated education to IE. It also seeks to overview the most important recent developments in primary and secondary education, while identifying legal shortcommings and systemic barriers to the implementation of IE. Specifically, the chapter investigates constitutional standards and international obligations relevant in case of IE in both countries. It highlights persistent challenges, including the segregation of students with disabilities, inadequate accessibility measures, insufficient reasonable accomodation and the lack of individualised support for these children. Drawing on national experiences, the chapter proposes legal and policy interventions to enhance the realisation of inclusive education. The research employs a comparative analysis of legal documents, national and international reports, non-governmental organisation findings, academic literature and other available sources.

As a conceptual foundation, it adopts the definition of IE embedded in the 2006 UN Convention on the Rights of Persons with Disabilities (CRPD). The CRPD, as the first legally binding international instrument to address quality IE (General comment No. 4, 2016), obligates Lithuania and Poland to ensure full participation, accessibility, attendance and achievement of all students, including those with disabilities. This comparative approach aims to illuminate shared challenges and effective strategies, contributing to the broader discourse on advancing inclusive education.

2 Constitutional, International and Regional Obligations for the Right to IE in Lithuania and Poland

The right to education is included in the constitutions of Lithuania and Poland, serving as a foundational guarantee for IE of children with disabilities within mainstream schooling systems.

The right to education in both constitutions is embedded in their chapters addressing social, cultural and economic rights, emphasising the availability of education and its guarantees. While the age for compulsory education differs—16 years in Lithuania and 18 years in Poland—both constitutions ensure free education in public schools (Articles 41 and 70, respectively). The Polish Constitution explicitly grants parents the right to choose non-public schools, permits the establishment of private educational institutions, and obligates public authorities to provide universal and equal access to education for Polish citizens, including certain guarantees for the implementation of this right (Article 70). In contrast, the Lithuanian Constitution mandates state oversight of educational institutions to ensure compliance with established standards (Article 41).

The Lithuanian Constitution obligates the state to safeguard the rights and legitimate interests of all minors (Article 38), recognising childhood as a constitutional value that must be fostered and nurtured.[1] Similarly, the Polish Constitution ensures institutional protection of children's rights (Article 72), mandates special protection of children's health (Article 68(3)) and emphasises family protection (Article 71).

Human dignity, a cornerstone of constitutional law in both countries, further strengthens the framework for IE. Enshrined in Articles of 21 and 30 of the Lithuanian and Polish constitutions, respectively, human dignity is regarded as a fundamental value,[2] requiring comprehensive protection and defence.[3]

The principles of equality and non-discrimination, central to both constitutions, are crucial to the realisation of IE. Articles 29 and 32 of the Lithuanian and Polish constitutions, respectively, establish the universality of equality rights and prohibit discrimination. While neither constitution explicitly mentions disability-based discrimination, judicial interpretations, such as the decision of Lithuanian Constitutional Court of 14 March 2024, and rulings of the Polish Constitutional Tribunal, affirm that equality and non-discrimination principles apply universally and without restriction to specific criteria. Article 32 explicitly prohibits discrimination 'on any grounds'.[4] Also the strong right to information in Articles 25 and 61 of the Lithuanian and Polish Constitutions is essential for the realisation of IE.

The constitutions of Poland and Lithuania incorporate elements of the international standard for the right to education, as established by the International Covenant on Economic, Social and Cultural Rights (1966) and the Convention on the Rights of the Child (CRC) (1989). However, the historical roots of these constitutional guarantees reveals limitations in their application to the rights of students with disabilities. The constitutional frameworks in both countries were developed during a period when the rights of persons with disabilities were predominantly viewed through a welfarist lens, rooted in the medical model of disability. This perspective is evident in provisions such as Articles 68(3), 69 of the Polish Constitution

[1] Ruling of the Lithuanian Constitutional Court (CC) of 19-09-2019.

[2] CC conclusion of 14-03-2024.

[3] CC conclusion of 19-12-2017.

[4] Ruling of Polish Constitutional Tribunal (CT) of 16-12-1997.

and Article 52 of the Lithuanian Constitution, which place a greater emphasis on state care rather than individual empowerment.

Although neither constitution explicitly refers to 'inclusive education', the constitutional right to education implies state obligations to ensure its realisation. The extensive content of the subjective right to education with the obligations of public authorities strengthens the position of entities using science and narrows the possibility to intervention of public authorities, to impose restrictions (Garlicki and Derlatka 2016).

The concept of education, as articulated by CC, encompasses a multifaceted process aimed at achieving purposefulness, quality and diversity.[5] As education is recognised as a constitutional value, the state bears the responsibility to allocate adequate resources to finance education[6] and to ensure that all individuals under the age of 16 have real opportunities to access free education in public general education schools where learning is equally accessible to everyone.[7] The legislature is tasked with establishing and maintaining standards of education quality, ensuring that uniform learning criteria are upheld across the system.[8]

In Poland, the constitutional right to education also establishes a legal basis for demanding free access to education from the state (Zięba-Załucka 2009; Bała 2009) and financial assistance from public authorities to universal and equal access (Banaszak 2012[9]). Scholars argue that the right to education encompasses the guarantees necessary for its implementation, including financial and structural support (Grzejdziak-Przybyłowicz 2017; Jarosz-Żukowska & Żukowski 2014; Mikosz 1991; Oniszczuk 2006; Zawadzka 1996). Universal and equal access to education is treated as a necessary element of the 'right to education', reinforcing its enforceability through mechanisms such as constitutional complaints to the CT (Garlicki and Derlatka 2016). At the same time, Article 70 directs the legislature to issue a specific act.[10]

The analysis of the constitutional provisions in both countries reveals shared foundational values, including equality, non-discrimination, respect for human dignity, and positive obligations to uphold these principles. The constitutional right to education in Lithuania and Poland encompasses broad responsibilities, including the provision of free and accessible education for all, without discrimination based on disability. This responsibility extends to the obligation of allocating adequate to ensure high quality education. These duties must be understood within the context of human rights obligations that both countries have assumed under international law, specifically recognising the right to IE for children with disabilities.

---

[5] CC conclusion of 14-03-2024.

[6] CC ruling of 26-04-2023.

[7] CC conclusion of 14-03-2024.

[8] CC ruling of 19-09-2019.

[9] CT ruling of 26-04-2004.

[10] CT rulings of 02-07-2002 and 13-11-2007.

From the perspective of children with disabilities, Lithuania and Poland are bound by fundamental standards of the CRC (ratified in 1995 and 1991, respectively). The CRC is the first human rights treaty to explicitly reference disability, notably in Article 2 on non-discrimination and Article 23, which addresses the rights and needs of children with disabilities (UN Committee on the Rights of the Child, General Comment No. 9, 2006) including the right of children with mental or physical disabilities, recognising their special needs and providing necessary assistance to ensure their effective access to education. Subsequently, Lithuania and Poland ratified the CRPD (in 2010 and 2012, respectively). The CRPD underscores IE as a fundamental right for children with disabilities, articulated in Article 24, which promotes quality IE (UN Committee on the Rights of Persons with Disabilities (Commitee), General Comment No. 4, 2016). The CRPD further establishes that persons with disabilities must not be excluded from the general education system on the basis of disability. This reflects the human-rights model of disability, which prioritises the inherent dignity of the human being, emphasising societal barriers rather than personal limitations as the source of challenges faced by persons with disabilities (Degener 2016). The realisation of the right to education under the CRPD is supported by related provisions, such as Article 2 on reasonable accommodation, Article 3 on full social inclusion, Article 5 on equality and non-discrimination, and Article 9 on accessibility.

However, there are significant differences in the extent to which Lithuania and Poland have adopted optional protocols and complementary legal instruments. Poland has not signed the Optional Protocol to the CRPD and the Optional Protocol to the CRC on a communications procedure (2011). Lithuania has ratified both instruments in 2010 and 2022, respectively. Poland ratified the UNESCO Convention against Discrimination in Education in 1964, while Lithuania has yet to do so. Both countries could strengthen their commitments to non-discrimination by ratifying Protocol No 12 to the 1950 European Convention on Human Rights (ECHR), which prohibits discrimination.

The European Social Charter (ESC) presents another area of divergence. Poland ratified the original 1961 ESC in 1997 and signed the revised version in 2005, but has not yet ratified the latter. Lithuania, by contrast, has been bound by the revised ESC since 2001. The ESC offers broader protection of children with disabilities, including provisions related to education, compared to the ECHR. Through the European Court of Human Rights, the ECHR also plays a critical role in safeguarding the rights of students with disabilities, particularly with respect to reasonable accommodation and equal access to education.[11]

Lithuania and Poland also engage in broader initiatives under the Council of Europe. Both countries participate in strategies such as the Disability Strategy 2017–2023 and the Strategy for the Rights of the Child 2022–2027, which address a wide range of of issues, including the right to IE, social inclusion, access to

[11] European Court of Human Rights judgements in cases *G. L. v. Italy*, no 59751/1; *Cam v. Turkey*, no 51500/08; *Stoian v. Romania*, no 289/14 and *Enver Sahin v. Turkey*, no 23065/12.

infrastructure and cultural activities, universal design, and the use of new technologies. These strategies underscore the ongoing commitment of both states to advancing the rights of children with disabilities within a broader European framework.

The accession of Lithuania and Poland to the European Union (EU) membership placed both countries within a shared framework of policies and legal obligations regarding the rights of persons with disabilities. Among these obligations, equal treatment and non-discrimination in access to education have been central. In 2021, the European Commission adopted the Strategy for the Rights of Persons with Disabilities 2021–2030, a comprehensive framework guiding the implementation of the CRPD at the EU level. This strategy emphasises the diversity of disabilities and seeks to achieve full inclusion and equal rights for persons with disabilities, including equal access to education and non-discrimination. At the national level, the strategy encourages member states to enhance their educational systems by fostering inclusivity and removing barriers to participation.

Complementing this, the EU Strategy for the Rights of the Child (2021) and the new Strategy for a Better Internet for Children (2022) address additional dimensions of inclusion. These initiatives aim to to ensure that the digital environment diverse, inclusive and free from stereotypes, enabling children, including those with disabilities, to play, learn and interact online in a safe and equitable manner.

The Charter of Fundamental Rights of the EU further reinforces the rights of children and the persons with disabilities. Article 24 affirms the rights of children to protection, care, and participation in decisions affecting their lives, guided by the principle of the child's best interests. Article 26 acknowledges the EU's commitment to ensuring independence, social and occupational integration, and community participation for persons with disabilities. These provisions are bolstered by the EU's ratification of the CRPD in 2011, which has influenced the jurisprudence of the EU Court of Justice takes into account the CRPD particularly in cases addressing emplyment[12]).

To sum up, the obligations of Lithuania and Poland under constitutional, international and regional frameworks collectively reflect the foundational principles of IE: ensuring access to quality, free primary and secondary education on an equal basis with others in local communities; providing accessible information and physical environments; prohibiting exclusion from general education systems or compulsory primary and secondary education on the basis of disability; promoting full and equal participation in education and community life; encouraging regular school attendance; offering individualised support measures, such as reasonable accommodation; and allocating adequate funding to sustain inclusive educational practices.

[12] EU Court of Justice judgements C-485-20, C-518/22, and C-631/22.

3 Review of National Approaches to Inclusion and the Transition to IE for Children with Disabilities

Until the 1990s, the educational systems in Lithuania and Poland operated predominantly within a segregated model where children with disabilities were educated separately from their peers (Ruškus 2020, p. 37; Ališauskienė and Miltenienė 2018, p. 13; Marcinkowska 2015, p. 211). In both countries, mandatory school attendance was not absolute; children could be directed to home-based education, not only due to health conditions but also due to limited capacity in special education facilities.

The shift towards inclusive education in Lithuania began with the Law on Special Education (1998), which introduced the principle of integration. This principle emphasised the inclusion of individuals with special needs together in local community life and their equal participation in educational settings. Although special home-based and education options persisted, this Law marked a significant shift by focusing on addressing the individuals rather than their impairments (Ališauskienė and Miltenienė 2018, pp. 13, 27).

Subsequent legislative developments broadened this foundation. The Law on Education (2011) introduced the concept of 'educational assistance', encompassing support for children, parents and teachers. By 2017, the Law on Equal Treatment mandated that educational establishments provide equal conditions for all individuals, ensuring non-discrimination in admission, teaching and programme implementation.

In Poland, the transition to inclusion began with the Education System Act (1991), which allowed children with disabilities to attend various types of schools—special, integrated, and mainstream—based on their individual developmental and educational needs. The implementing regulations reduced education in mainstream schools to the possibility of organizing integrated classes in them. Over time, the emergence of integrated schools and classes in mainstream schools sparked a broader dialogue on the rightful place of children with disabilities within mainstream education. The extension of compulsory education to include children with profound intellectual disabilities represented another milestone. The Education Act (2016) reinforced these provisions and introduced updated terminology, replacing outdated and stigmatising language with more respectful formulations such as 'student with physical or intellectual disability'.

Both Lithuania and Poland have implemented measures to support children with disabilities in diverse educational settings. In Poland, these include the requirement for individual educational, as well as therapeutic plans and multi-specialist assessments, initially introduced in special education settings and expanded to all types of schools by 2010. Lithuania later adopted similar practices, allowing for extended educational stages to accommodate students' developmental and psychosocial needs. Key organisational solutions in both countries include the the provision of smaller class sizes, and the availability of additional personal support, individual assistance where necessary. In turn, the possibility of postponing compulsory schooling and extending educational stages enables the adjustment of the learning pace to align with the developmental age, psychosocial capabilities, and health of the child. This flexibility has been adopted in Lithuania as well.

The National Education Strategy 2013–2022 adopted by the Lithuanian Parliament (2013), includes an Action Plan for Inclusion of Children in Learning and Diverse Education (2017), which seeks to strengthen support for children with special needs. Key measures outlined in the government's programme (2020) include reducing class sizes, increasing the number of special educators and assistant teachers, and integrating universal design principles into building legislation. Additionally, the programme emphasises adaptation of physical and informational environments to ensure accessibility.

In Poland, the Strategy for People with Disabilities 2021–2030 (2021) acknowledges the crucial role of education in shaping the quality of life for individuals. However, it falls short in its implementation, offering either overly optimistic targets, such as aiming for 85% of children to be included in universal education by 2030, or overly cautious approaches, with fewer than 10% of schools being deemed accessible by 2030. While these indicators may be unrealistic or timid, the government has taken steps to enhance accessibility and inclusion. Initiatives include programs such as the 'Digital School', 'Active Desktop', 'Pilot implementation of modular e-textbooks', and 'School kit', aimed at improving access to teaching materials (including financing of these materials and aids), technological innovations, and raising awareness of inclusive education.

The CRPD has significantly shaped the national understanding of IE in Lithuania, aligning with a human rights-based approach to disability. This influence is evident in both the Law on Education and the Law on Fundamentals of Protection of the Rights of Persons with Disabilities (FPRPD) (effective from January 2024). The 2020 amendments to the Law on Education, which came into force on 1 September 2024, establish the principle of inclusion: 'Inclusion means that the education system enables every person to develop their education, capacities, and abilities, provides the necessary support for success in educational, social, cultural and/or other activities, and prohibits discrimination based on the diversity of learning needs and/or the requirement for educational support'. These amendments also guarantee equal access for pupils with disabilities, ensuring that mainstream schools in their area cannot refuse admission. Following the CRPD, the FPRPD further reinforces the right of persons with disabilities to access an inclusive and accessible educational environment.

In 2021, Lithuania adopted an action plan for 2021–2024, aimed at preparing for the full implementation of inclusion. This plan focuses on adapting school environments, providing special teaching aids and educational support, improving teachers' competences, and fostering positive attitudes towards inclusion. The action plan aimed to increase the percentage of pupils with disabilities in mainstream schools: 65% in 2024, 85% in 2025 and 90% by 2030. Notably, progress has been achieved beyond expectations. By 2024, around 90% of all pupils with special educational needs, including those with disabilities, had been successfully enrolled in mainstream education (in the words of the representative of the Ministry of Education, Science and Sports; News portal 15min.lt, 17-07-2024).

Despite these indications, Lithuania and Poland face significant obstacles in ensuring access to and effectiveness of learning measures for children with disabilities in primary and secondary education.

In Lithuania, schools vary widely in their experiences with the enrolment of children with disabilities. Schools that have adopted IE have done so by creating groups and classrooms that embrace pupils‘ diversity. One successful pilot project, which aimed to help 100 educational institutions prepare for the inclusion of children with diverse learning needs, has introduced several models of IE. Among these, full inclusion is the most widely implemented (2023). In this model, pupils with special educational needs, supported by a second teacher and/or a pupil's assistant, participate in regular classroom activities. Tasks or formats are adapted as necessary, teaching/learning resources are carefully selected, and additional learning support is provided to ensure that all pupils can engage effectively (15min.lt, 17-07-2024). These inclusion models have the potential to be extended to other schools across the country. However, not all schools are adequately prepared to deliver quality IE. The Law on Education, supplemented in 2020, established a four-year preparatory period to help schools transition toward IE. Despite this legislative foundation, many schools still struggle to implement effective IE. Furthermore, the provisions within this regulation have not been sufficiently tested in the courts, leaving some ambiguity about their practical application.

In Poland, the concept of IE is recognised in public policy and professional discourse but lacks a clear statutory definition, despite the fact that education standards include understanding of IE, its genesis, theoretical and legal foundations, and the organization of IE. This regulatory gap has resulted in limited legal and institutional support for IE. Polish courts rarely invoke the principles of equal treatment and non-discrimination in cases involving children with disabilities. Administrative courts tend to prioritise explicit statutory obligations over broader principles, further limiting the development of jurisprudence supporting IE. As a result, efforts to advance IE remain fragmented and overly reliant on localised initiatives rather than systemic reforms.

A positive aspect of the education system in Poland is the integration of provisions that address the needs of children with disabilities within common statutory educational regulations. However, it is only during implementation of provisions that separate regulations specifically targeting students with special educational needs are applied. Placing the education of students with disabilities within mainstream settings reflects a commitment to the legal recognition of their rights, while also fostering awareness of their unique needs among educators, policymakers, and other stakeholders in the education system.

Despite these efforts, statutory provisions concerning the education of children with disabilities in Poland are extensive and scattered. Determinations of disability and educational needs, along with various benefits, are handled through separate administrative processes administered by different entities. Efforts to coordinate these provisions have yet to yield substantial results.

3.1 Segregation of Pupils Based on Disability

Despite legal provisions aimed at eliminating discrimination, segregation of pupils based on disability remains a significant concern in Lithuania. The Law on Education, as amended in 2020, did not entirely eliminate the practice of placing children with disabilities in separate schools. The 2016 Recommendation by the Committee highlighted the lack of reasonable accommodation and accessibility in mainstream schools, emphasising the need for transformation (2016 Recommendation, paragraph 47). However, according to the Lithuanian Disability Organisations Forum (DOF) Shadow Report (2024), the number of special education establishments and the enrolment of children with disabilities in them has remained largely unchanged since 2020. In 2022, there were still 47 special schools in the Lithuania and despite incremental increases in mainstream school enrolment—8592 pupils in 2020–2021, 8772 in 2021–2022, and 9262 in 2022–2023 (data from the Education Management Information System)—many of these special schools have not transitioned into effective support systems for mainstream integration.

The challenges faced in practice, including the regulation outlined in the Lithuania's Law on Education of 2020, highlight significant obstacles to the inclusion of children with severe or very severe special educational needs. The adoption of new provisions (2024) only allows for exceptional circumstances under which families may transfer their children to a different school (other than that in his/her teritory of residence), further demonstrating the limited readiness of educational institutions to fully implement inclusive practices.

Prior to 2024, schools in Lithuania were requested that parents bring their children in to assess their needs before agreeing to admit them. This practice led to instances where families of children with disabilities were denied enrolment or adequate learning conditions. The Office of Equal Opportunities Ombudsperson (OEOO) in Lithuania received reports regarding these refusals, emphasising the ongoing barriers to inclusive education (Report 2024, 27). Furthermore, some families opt to enrol their children with disabilities in private institutions, which often offer smaller class sizes and tailored learning environments. However, these private schools may require additional fees, including the cost of hiring specialists to support students with disabilities.

Mass media reports confirm that many mainstream schools in Lithuania are not adequately prepared to accommodate children with behavioural impairments. In some cases, class sizes reach up to 30 students, which, combined with even a single child with behavioural challenges, leads to disruption and confusion in the educational process.

However, according to amendments to the Lithuanian Law on Education (2024) the composition of classes in mainstream schools should not exceed one-fitth of pupils with severe and very severe special educational needs, unless all pupils with such educational needs reside within the school's designated area. Parents, in consultation with specialists, decide on the most suitable school for their child, with municipalities and educational psychological services working together to develop appropriate solutions.

In 2022, the OEOO investigated complaints related to children with psychosocial disabilities and fortunately, these issues were resolved amicably (Report 2023, 25). The DOF has expressed its concern over a growing trend where pupils with disabilities are being directed toward home-based education with partial integration into mainstream schools (Shadow report 2024, 36). The DOF also reported instances where parents are pressured to accept this form of education, under the threat of schools terminating agreements (Ibid).

According to the Commission for Monitoring the Rights of Persons with Disabilities (MCRPD) (Report 2023, 35) (which monitors the implementation of the CRPD from 2018), public understanding and recognition of IE as a human rights issue remain insufficient. A survey of the Lithuanian population conducted in 2022 revealed that less than half (43%) of respondents agreed with the statement 'Children with disabilities should be educated in the same classes as those without disabilities'. Similarly, less than half (45%) of respondents indicated they supported their own children receiving general education in mixed classes with disabled children. A subsequent representative survey of the Lithuanians (2023) confirmed negative attitudes towards people with psychosocial disabilities, with 65% of respondents indicating they would not want to live with such individuals. The Parliamentary Ombudsman (PO) highlights this resistance, noting that 'society still harbours resistance to the creation of an IE system, which requires changing stereotypical attitudes and fostering respect for all individuals' (Report 2024, 10).

Currently, only 38% of students with disabilities in Poland are educated in special schools, which make up 9.7% of all schools within the education system. The remaining 62% of students with disabilities are enrolled in mainstream and integrated schools. While integrated schools represent a small segment of educational institutions (7.3%), they account for a significant proportion of students with disabilities (22%) (Substantive report 2021, 18, 21). The report confirms that this segregation in education is largely driven by the level of intellectual ability (85% of students with moderate intellectual disabilities and as many as 94% of students with severe intellectual disabilities). A notable portion of those outside mainstream education includes deaf students and blind students (52% and 72%), the latter often choosing schools closer to Deaf and Blind cultures. Another important factor is that the Polish Sign Language does not have the status of a formal subject within the curriculum (Report of the Expert Commission on Deaf People 2020, 33). An alarming issue in Polish schools is the prevalence of peer violence directed at students with disabilities. As many as 20.3% of students with disabilities are exposed to peer violence (Makaruk 2022, p. 269). Cases of this violence are mainly reported by the media related to the topic of disability (Niepełnosprawni.pl, 06-10-2020).

The Committee expressed concern over the segregation of students with disabilities, particularly those with moderate and severe disabilities, into separate educational settings in Poland. The Committee has drawn attention to the lack of awareness among school principals and parents of able-bodied children about IE, the lack of appropriate training of teachers in this area, and, most importantly, the lack of specific provisions to support the implementation of IE, as well as the confusion between the concepts of 'integration' and 'inclusion' (2018, paragraph 41).

The continued existence of special schools in both Lithuania and Poland hinders the full realisation of IE, which is embedded in Article 24 of the CRPD. The segregated educational environment prevents students with disabilities from receiving the necessary support in mainstream settings, which is essential to fostering their full participation in society.

3.2 Denial of Accessibility, Reasonable Accomodation and Individual Support in Mainstream Schools

The accessibility of the build environment, public transportation, as well as information and communication technologies—including computers, network hardware and software (Comment of Committee 2014, 2)—remains incomplete for students with disabilities in both Lithuania and Poland.

It is positive that both Lithuania and Poland are gradually adopting legal regulations necessary to comply with the Directive of 2019/882 of the European Parliament and of the Council of 17 April 2019, which focuses on the accessibility requirements for products and services, including aspects relevant to IE (such as accessibility features for children's books (the content protected by copyright and related rights; e-books and e-readers). The Directive emphasises the need for the systematic removal and prevention of barriers with only legitimate reasons—excluding time constraints or lack of time or knowledge—permissible as exceptions in assessments regarding the feasibility of meeting accessibility requirements without imposing disproportionate burdens.

In Lithuania, the Law on Requirements for Accessibility of Products and Services (2022) which will take effect in June 2025, is a significant step forward, particularly concerning the accessibility of computers. This Directive has also been incorporated into the Lithuanian Law on Equal Opportunities.

In Poland, significant progress in ensuring accessibility is expected due to the Act on Ensuring Accessibility for Persons with Specific Needs (2019). It obliges every public school to adhere to accessibility standards as outlined in the Act. Ultimately, however, under the CRPD, this obligation should extend to non-public schools as well. The Polish legislator, however, chose to limit this requirement initially, citing concerns about legal complications related to the future implementation of the EU Directive of 2019/882. Instead, the Directive was implemented through the Act of 26 April 2024, which focuses primarily on ensuring compliance with accessibility requirements for certain products and services by economic entities. This Act does not introduce a broad obligation for private entities to ensure accessibility in services offered to the public.

Persons with disabilities in Lithuania face only gradual progress in modifying physical environments within primary and secondary schools, particularly those built before the amendments of the Law on Education of 2020. The implementation of accessibility requirements remains insufficient due to various obstacles, including the presence of cultural heritage restrictions or limited available space. In schools without elevators or ramps, classes for children with physical or mobility disabilities are typically planned on the ground floor, while some schools have portable ramps for temporary use (15min.lt 21-06-2024).

In 2023, the OEOO received a complaint from the Lithuanian Autism Association regarding the procedure for transporting students to and from school. The Vilnius City Municipality's current transport system discriminates against some pupils with special needs, particularly those with multiple developmental disabilities, who face challenges traveling safely on the street. The Ombudsperson suggested that the transportation arrangements be revised to ensure that all children with disabilities are included and can access these services (Report 2024, 27).

In Poland, a significant number of cases have involved disputes over the obligation to provide free transportation and care during the transport of children to commute, or reimbursement of transport costs incurred by parents. The provisions governing these issues are stipulated in education law but have led to ambiguities. Administrative courts have interpreted the obligation to provide transport to the 'nearest school' as the school best equipped, in terms of method and organisation (specialists, available vacancies, etc.), to meet the educational needs outlined in the decision regarding special education needs or disability (or the child's Individual Education Plan).[13] The 'nearest school' does not necessarily refer to the school geographically closest, but the one that can most effectively implement the educational recommendations suited to the child's psychophysical abilities. A school closer in actual distance, but less equipped to meet those recommendations, does not fulfil this requirement under education law.[14]

Furthermore, doubts have been raised regarding the financial aspect of transportation to school (reimbursement of costs to parents) in cases where parents decide to provide transport for their child themselves. The Supreme Court has ruled that if transportation and care are organised by parents, the local government is still obligated to reimburse the costs of travel incurred by both the student and the guardian. These responsibilities cannot be waived merely because the commune has provided transportation and care to another centre or school of the same type (Resolution of 17-02-2011).

The Polish case law has led to some clarification of interpretational doubts. Yet, numerous cases still reveal significant deficiencies in the implementation of the obligation to provide transportation for children with disabilities to and from school. Similarly, the recruitment process often violates regulations, as children with disabilities or health conditions that limit their educational options are frequently given priority in admission procedures.

[13] Judgment of the Polish Supreme Administrative Court (SAC) of 23-01-2024.

[14] Judgments of the SAC of 08-10-2021 and 09-02-2024.

Currently, Polish schools face considerable challenges in architectural accessibility. Many schools lack the necessary architectural features to accommodate students with disabilities. Moreover, there are significant gaps in communication accessibility, particularly for deaf children and those with complex communication needs. Even special schools for deaf children are not obliged to provide bilingual education, and regulations for children with complex communication needs are limited. Textbooks and teaching materials adapted to the diverse needs of students, such as e-textbooks, remain insufficient. This issue has been raised repeatedly, and in 2020, the Supreme Audit Office drew attention to this problem (Information on the results of the inspection 2020, 24).

These problems are being addressed gradually. As part of the government project, Cross-sectoral Support Model – Strategy and Challenges (April 2022–May 2024), aims to implement the Accessible School Model, which involves adopting successive, increasingly advanced solutions to ensure full accessibility and inclusion for students with disabilities. Additionally, the project funded by European Funds for Social Development, 'Supporting the accessibility of education for children and youth' (October 2023–April 2029), focuses on developing methodological and organisational strategies to support children in education and enhance staff competences.

All non-implemented aspects of accessibility should be addressed with a focus on raising awareness, as many accessibility barriers result from a lack of information or insufficient awareness and technical know-how (Comment of the Committee 2014, 10, 6).

Until mainstream schools across both states become fully accessible for students with disabilities, reasonable accommodations should be employed to provide access. For instance, individuals with rare impairments might require accommodations that fall outside the scope of accessibility standard (Comment of the Commitee 2014, 8). In Lithuanian schools, sensory, calming or leisure rooms have been established based on availability and demand, particularly under the Millennium Schools programme, which aims to ensure high-quality education and IE in municipalities. However, the Committee's recommendation that the lack of reasonable accommodation should be recognised as a form of disability-based discrimination has not yet been implemented in Lithuanian legislation (Shadow report 2024, 36).

In both Lithuania and Poland, there is a persistent shortage of teachers, which affects the ability of schools to provide adequate support to students with special needs. The law allows for other specialists, in addition to classroom teachers, to assist children with disabilities in the educational setting. However, a related challenge is the insufficient availability of education specialists. In 2024, the UN Committee on the Rights of the Child recommended that Lithuania increase the number of education support specialists and provide comprehensive training for all teachers on IE and special education needs. DOF further emphasised the lack of appropriate teaching materials and resources tailored to the diverse needs for children with disabilities, as well as the issue of excessively large educational groups (Report 2024, 34–35).

Both countries also face significant limitations in material resources necessary for the effective implementation of accessibility, reasonable accomodation and individualised support for children with disabilities, hindering their ability to fully exercise their right to IE In Lithuania, schools are primarily owned by municipalities, which are responsible for ensuring the implementation of the principle of inclusion. These municipalities must ensure that schools are physically accessible and equipped to provide adequate educational support. This responsibility is largely carried out with financial assistance from the state budget. However, municipalities are strongly encouraged to supplement the state subsidy with their own funds, rather than relying solely on the state budget, to ensure sustainable support. Currently, only 20% of educational support is funded by municipalities, while the rest comes from state subsidies.

This analysis highlights the numerous barriers that remain to achieving full implementation of IE for children with disabilities in Lithuania and Poland.

4 Concluding Remarks

In Poland and Lithuania, the national understanding of the key elements of inclusion, such as accessibility, non-discrimination, and other essential positive obligations related to primary and secondary education, demonstrates significant alignment. This alignment is primarily driven by shared constitutional values and adherence to international commitments, particularly the CRPD.

Both countries have made gradual improvements in implementing the principles of inclusive education through various legislative, institutional and policy measures aimed at fostering a comprehensive understanding of the right to inclusive education and its effective support. While both states have individually structured their legislative frameworks, a more systematic approach is required to organise regulations concerning inclusive education. This approach would help ensure the stability of legal provisions introduced in Lithuania in 2020, and address the issue of extensive statutory provisions regarding the education of children with disabilities in Poland. A key foundation for this systematic approach is recognising that the lack of reasonable accommodation constitutes a form of discrimination on grounds of disability in national legislation.

The challenge of ensuring the right to inclusive education remains a complex and long-term, as societal attitudes continue to display discriminatory tendencies despite ongoing awareness-raising efforts. Both Lithuania and Poland face similar difficulties in ensuring accessibility, reasonable accommodation and individualised support for children with disabilities, leading to their exclusion from primary and secondary education. A central issue is the extent to which both states allocate sufficient resources to meet the needs of children with disabilities and how they prioritise these resources in public spending (Lundy and O'Lynn 2019, p. 273). These barries must be systematically and continuously addressed to achieve full inclusion and prevent the emergence of new obstacles, as the right to inclusive education is inherently linked to other rights of children with disabilities.

Both countries, building on their successful practices and sharing accumulated knowledge in educating children with disabilities, must continue advancing toward the full implementation of inclusive education. This includes ensuring access to inclusive education for children with disabilities and sustaining their education journey to the greatest extent possible. By doing so, they will create the necessary foundations for future opportunities and an improved quality of life for these children.

Legal Acts and Their Travaux Préparatoires

Action Plan for Inclusion of Children in Learning and Diverse Education 2017–2022 of Republic of Lithuania (2017). Register of legal acts TAR, 2017 2017-06-28, No. 10872

Action Plan for 2021–2024 on Preparing to Implement Law on Education of the Republic of Lithuania Amending Articles 5, 14, 21, 29, 30, 34 and 36 of the Law on Education of the Republic of Lithuania and Supplementing the Law with Article 45-1 (2021). Register of legal acts TAR, 2021-10-14, No. 21515

Act of 7 September 1991 on System of Education, Journal of Laws 2024, item 750

Act of 14 December 2016 – Education Law, Journal of Laws 2024, item 737

Act of 19 July 2019 on Ensuring Accessibility for Persons with Specific Needs, Journal of Laws 2019, item 1696

Act of 26 April 2024 on Ensuring Compliance with Accessibility Requirements for Certain Products and Services by Economic Entities, Journal of Laws 2024, item 731

Constitution of the Republic of Lithuania (1992). Official gazette Valstybės Žinios, 1992, No. 33-1014

Constitution of the Republic of Poland (1997). Journal of Laws 1997, No. 78, item 483

Description of Establishment of Groups and Classes Open to Pupils' Diversity and Organisation of Education in Them, and of Conditions for Financing Them. Register of legal acts (2023). Register of legal acts TAR, 2023-05-02, No. 8308.

Law Amending Articles 1, 16 and 17 of the Law of Republic of Lithuania on Equal Opportunities No. IX-1826 and Supplementing the Law with Article 15-1 (2018). Register of legal acts TAR, 2018-12-18, No. 20741

Law Amending Articles 5, 14, 21, 29, 30, 34 and 36 of the Law on Education of the Republic of Lithuania No. I-1489 and Supplementing the Law with Article 45-1 (2020). Register of legal acts TAR, 2020-07-10, No. 15543

Law Amending Articles 5, 14, 21, 29, 30, 34 and 36 of the Law on Education of the Republic of Lithuania No I-1489 and Supplementing the Law with Article 45-1 of the Law on Education of the Republic of Lithuania No XIII-3268 Amending Articles 2 and 9 (2024). Register of legal acts TAR, 2024-07-25, No. 13617

Law Amending Articles 28 and 29 of Law on Education of the Republic of Lithuania No I-1489 (2024). Register of legal acts TAR, 2024-06-30, No. 12156

Law on Fundamentals of Protection of Rights of Persons with Disabilities of Lithuania (2022). Register of legal acts TAR, 2023-01-04, No. 135

Law on Education of Republic of Lithuania (1991). Official gazette Valstybės žinios, 1991, No. 23-593

Law on Education of Republic of Lithuania (2011). Official gazette Valstybės žinios, 2011, No. 38-1804
Law on Equal Treatment of Lithuania (2016). Register of legal acts TAR, 2016-11-17, No. 26967.
Law on Requirements for Accessibility of Products and Services of Republic of Lithuania (2022). Register of legal acts TAR, 2022-12-22, No. 26360
National Education Strategy 2013-2022 of Republic of Lithuania (2013). Official gazette Valstybės žinios, 2013, No. 140-7095
Programme of Eighteenth Goverment of Republic of Lithuania (2020). Register of legal acts TAR, 2020-12-11, No. 27121
Regulation of the Council Of Ministers of 23 October 2020 on Detailed Conditions, Forms and Procedures for the Implementation of the Government Program for the Development of School Infrastructure and Competences of Students and Teachers in the Field of Information and Communication Technologies for the Years 2020-2024 - 'Active Board', Journal of Laws 2024, item 158
Regulation of the Council of Ministers of 19 May 2023 on Detailed Conditions for Providing Assistance to Disabled Students in the Form of Co-financing the Purchase of Textbooks, Educational Materials and Exercise Materials in the Years 2023-2025 ('School kit'), Journal of Laws 2023, item 1046
Resolution (2012) No. 40 of the Council of Ministers of 3 April 2012 on the Government Programme for the Development of Competences of Students and Teachers in the Application of Information and Communication Technologies - 'Digital School'
Resolution (2021) No. 27 Council of Ministers of 16 February 2021 on the adoption of the document Strategy for People with Disabilities 2021-2030, Polish Monitor 2021, item 218
Special Education Law of Republic of Lithuania (1998). Official gazette Valstybės žinios, 1998, No. 115-3228
UN Convention on the Rights of Persons with Disabilities of 2006. Retrieved October 26, 2024, from https://www.ohchr.org/en/instruments-mechanisms/instruments/convention-rights-persons-disabilities

Case Law

Constitutional Court of the Republic of Lithuania (2004). Ruling of 29 December 2004. Official gazette Valstybės Žinios, 2005, No. 1-7
Constitutional Court of the Republic of Lithuania (2017). Conclusion of 19 December 2017, No. KT20-I1/2017. Register of legal acts TAR 2017 2017-12-19, No. 20413
Constitutional Court of the Republic of Lithuania (2019). Ruling of 19 September 2019, No. KT25-N11/2019. Register of legal acts TAR, 2019 2019-09-19, No. 14836

Constitutional Court of the Republic of Lithuania (2023). Ruling of 26 April 2023, No. KT40-N4/2023. Register of legal acts TAR 2024 2024-01-02, No. 1

Constitutional Court of the Republic of Lithuania (2024). Conclusion of 14 March 2024, No. KT24-I1/2024. Register of legal acts TAR 2024 2024-03-14, No. 4688

Constitutional Tribunal of the Republic of Poland (1997). Ruling of 16 December 1997, K 8/97. Case Law of the Constitutional Tribunal, Official Collection 1997, No. 5-6, item 70

Constitutional Tribunal of the Republic of Poland (2002). Ruling of 2 July 2002, U 7/01 Case Law of the Constitutional Tribunal, Official Collection, Series A, 2002, No. 4, item 48

Constitutional Tribunal of the Republic of Poland (2004). Ruling of 26 April 2004, K 50/02 Case Law of the Constitutional Tribunal, Official Collection, Series A, 2004, No. 4, item 32

Constitutional Tribunal of the Republic of Poland (2007). Ruling of 13 November 2007, P 42/06 Case Law of the Constitutional Tribunal, Official Collection, Series A, 2007, No. 10, item 123

Supreme Administrative Court of Poland (2021). Judgement of 28 October 2021, III OSK 4012/21. Retrieved October 26, 2024, from https://orzeczenia.nsa.gov.pl/doc/74F36FA4A3

Supreme Administrative Court of Poland (2024). Judgment of 23 January 2024, III OSK 428/23. Retrieved October 26, 2024, from https://orzeczenia.nsa.gov.pl/doc/24D8B5600E

Supreme Administrative Court of Poland (2024). Judgment of 9 February 2024, III OSK 2510/23. Retrieved October 26, 2024, from https://orzeczenia.nsa.gov.pl/doc/BDEE134AB7

Supreme Court of Poland (2011). Resolution of 17 February 2011. III CZP 133/10. Supreme Court Case Law, Civil Chamber, Official Collection 2011, No. 10, item 111

Reports

Annual Report of 2023 of Office of Equal Opportunities Ombudsperson of Republic of Lithuania (2024). Retrieved October 26, 2024, from https://lygybe.lt/wp-content/uploads/2024/06/2023-annual-report-of-the-equal-opportunities-ombudsperson-in-lithuania.pdf

Deaf People in Poland 2020 – challenges and recommendations. Report of the Expert Commission on Deaf People (2020). Office of the Commissioner for Human Rights. Retrieved October 26, 2024, from https://bip.brpo.gov.pl/sites/default/files/Osoby_Gluche_w_Polsce_2020_Wyzwania_i_Rekomendacje.pdf

Report on Monitoring of the Implementation of the Provisions of the UN Convention on the Rights of Persons with Disabilities (2023). Monitoring Commission on the Rights of Persons with Disabilities in the Office of Equal Opportunities Ombudsperson of Republic of Lithuania. Retrieved October 26, 2024, from https://lygybe.lt/wp-content/uploads/2023/08/Zmoniu-su-negalia-teisiu-stebesenos-komisijos-stebesenos-ataskaita-2023-m.pdf

Shadow Report on the Implementation of Rights of People with Disabilities in Lithuania. *Position of the Lithuanian Disability Organisations Forum on the implementation of the EU Convention on the Rights of Persons with Disabilities in Lithuania* (2024). Retrieved October 26, 2024, from https://www.lnf.lt/wp-content/uploads/2024/02/seseline-ataskaita-apie-zmoniu-su-negalia-teisiu-igyvendinima-Lietuvoje.pdf

Substantive report. *Inclusive education – opening balance 2020* (2021), ed. D. Podgórska-Jachnik. Centre for Education Development. Retrieved October 26, 2024, from https://ore.edu.pl/2021/10/raport-edukacja-wlaczajaca-w-polsce/

Supreme Audit Office. (2020). Information on the results of the inspection. Education in special schools, Warsaw. Retrieved October 26, 2024, from https://www.nik.gov.pl/plik/id,23409,vp,26129.pdf

UN Committee on the Rights of Persons with Disabilities. (2016). *Concluding observations on the initial report of Lithuania*. CRPD/C/LTU/CO/1. Retrieved October 26, 2024, from https://digitallibrary.un.org/record/830769?ln=en&v=pdf

UN Committee on the Rights of Persons with Disabilities. (2018). *Concluding observations on the initial report of Poland.* CRPD/C/POL/CO/1. Retrieved October 26, 2024, from https://digitallibrary.un.org/record/1656309?v=pdf

UNESCO. (2020). Global Education Monitoring Report. *Inclusion and education: All means all.* Retrieved October 26, 2024, from https://unesdoc.unesco.org/ark:/48223/pf0000373718

Other

Enrolment of children with disabilities in mainstream schools. Data from the Education Management Information. In *Replies of Lithuania to the List of Issues in Relation to the Combined Second and Third Periodic Reports of Lithuania to the Committee on the Rights of Persons with Disabilities* (2023). Retrieved October 26, 2024, from https://socmin.lrv.lt/uploads/socmin/documents/files/veiklos-sritys/tarptautinis/ebpo/CRPD%20replies.pdf

Grigaliūnaitė, V. (2024, June 16). 'Different' children in schools of bug cities – is there enough space and support for them? Retrieved October 26, 2024, from https://www.15min.lt/naujiena/aktualu/lietuva/kitokie-vaikai-didziuju-miestu-mokyklose-ar-jiems-uzteks-vietos-ir-pagalbos-56-2260752

Pilot implementation of modular e-textbooks (2023-2028), EFSD, Measure 01.04 Development of the education system. Retrieved October 26, 2024 from https://ore.edu.pl/2023/07/o-projekcie-pilotazowe-wdrozenie-modulowych-e-podrecznikow-oraz-opracowanie-zalozen-do-zaawansowanych-technologicznie-e-materialow-wspierajacych-nowoczesne-metody-nauczania-i-uczenia-sie/

Public survey of the Lithuanian population 'Societal attitudes towards ethnic, religious, migrant and other social groups in Lithuania' (2023). Ethnic Studies Department of the Sociology Institute of the Lithuanian Social Sciences Centre and the Diversity Development Group. Retrieved October 26, 2024, from https://www.diversitygroup.lt/wp-content/uploads/2024/03/Visuomene%CC%87s-nuostatos-2023.pdf

Różański, M. (2020, October 6). Violence and Discrimination: What Do Students with Special Needs Experience? Retrieved October 26, 2024 from http://www.niepelnosprawni.pl/ledge/x/1178966

Special project. (2024, July 17). Open classrooms for all: successful examples of inclusion for special children – what's the recipe? Retrieved October 26, 2024, from https://www.15min.lt/naujiena/aktualu/svietimas/atviros-klases-visiems-sekmingi-ypatingu-vaiku-itraukties-pavyzdziai-koks-receptas-233-2274648?utm_medium=copied

UN Committee on the Rights of Persons with Disabilities. (2014). *General comment on Article 9: Accessibility*. Retrieved October 26, 2024, from https://www.ohchr.org/en/documents/general-comments-and-recommendations/general-comment-no-2-article-9-accessibility-0

UN Committee on the Rights of Child. (2007). *General Comment No. 9. The rights of children with disabilities*. Retrieved October 26, 2024, from https://docstore.ohchr.org/SelfServices/FilesHandler.ashx?enc=6QkG1d%2FPPRiCAqhKb7-yhsqIkirKQZLK2M58RF%2F5F0vHrn2YtDgO4ZjHSiu4mMCNKxeV7PxOOmQZL5v2IpgSJyXYy3ETTtUI65KMAgOvcRYyPXQKoIa4QlaT-vSVKFUBC0

UN Committee on the Rights of Persons with Disabilities. (2016). *General Comment No. 4 on the right to inclusive education*. Retrieved October 26, 2024, from https://tbinternet.ohchr.org/_layouts/15/TreatyBodyExternal/Download.aspx?symbolno=CRPD/C/GC/4&Lang=en

References

Books, Book Chapters, Journal Articles

Death Ališauskienė S, Miltenienė L (2018) Inclusive or engaging ('absorbing') education: interpretations of social constructs in the context of change in education. Special Educ 1(38):11–32. https://doi.org/10.21277/se.v1i38.430

Bała P (2009) The constitutional right to education and the Polish education system. von Borowiecky Publishing House, Warsaw

Banaszak B (2012) Constitution of the Republic of Poland. Commentary. Warsaw

Beco G (2022) The right to 'inclusive' education. Mod Law Rev 85(6):1329–1356. https://doi.org/10.1111/1468-2230.12742

Degener T (2016) Disability in a human rights context. Laws 5(3):35, 1–24. https://doi.org/10.3390/laws5030035

Garlicki L, Derlatka M (2016) Comment to Article 70. In: Zubik M (ed) Constitution of the Republic of Poland. Commentary. Warsaw, Legalis

Grzejdziak-Przybyłowicz A (2017) The right to education. The rights of the child-student. Stud Public Law 4(20):95–127. https://doi.org/10.14746/spp.2017.4.20.4

Jarosz-Żukowska S, Żukowski Ł (2014) The right to education and its guarantees. In: Bisztyga A, Jabłoński M (eds) Implementation and protection of constitutional freedoms and individual rights in the Polish legal system. E-Publishing. Legal and Economic Digital Library, Warsaw, pp 631–658
Lundy L, O'Lynn P (2019) The education rights of children. In: Kilkelly U, Liefaard T (eds) International human rights of children. Springer, Singapore, pp 259–276
Makaruk K (2022) Peer violence. In Children Count. Report on Threats to Children's Safety and Development in Poland. Empowering Children Foundation, 2022, pp 256–273
Marcinkowska B (2015) Education of students with disabilities in Poland – past, present, future. Educ Psychol 7:205–219. https://doi.org/10.5604/00332860.1161613
Mikosz J (1991) The right to education. In: Wieruszewski R (ed) Human rights. Legal model. Ossolineum Publishing House, Warsaw -Cracow-Warsaw, pp 879–1015
Oniszczuk J (2006) Problems with the implementation of freedoms and social rights guaranteed by the Constitution of the Republic of Poland. In: Wiśniewski L (ed) Individual freedoms and rights and their guarantees in practice. Parliamentary Publishing House, Warsaw, pp 195–237
Ruškus J (2020) Right to inclusive education for children with disabilities at stake in Lithuania. Special Educ 1(41):11–52. https://doi.org/10.21277/se.v1i41.526
Zawadzka B (1996) Economic, social and cultural rights. Parliamentary Publishing House, Warsaw, pp 5–15
Zięba-Załucka H (2009) The right to education. In: Skrzydło W, Grabowska S, Grabowski R (eds) The Constitution of the Republic of Poland. Encyclopaedic commentary, Warsaw, entry 'The right to education', pp 390–391

Lina Beliūnienė is a researcher at the Law Institute of the Lithuanian Centre for Social Sciences. She has received PhD degree in human rights and constitutional law (title of the thesis: "Protection of Human Rights as the Constitutional Values in the Jurisprudence of the Constitutional Court of the Republic of Lithuania") from Mykolas Romeris University, Lithuania. Overall, after defending her PhD thesis, Lina Beliūnienė has published over 17 scientific papers, and her scientific activities continue to be particularly related to human rights protection.

Dr Beliūnienė has extensive experience working in projects covering the system of human rights in Lithuania, as well as projects which are of special importance to people with disabilities, i. e. the right to health care and the specific aspects of their accessibility ("Human rights in Lithuania" (2005); "The Most Relevant Problems of Ensuring of Human Rights in Lithuania 2008–2013: Legal Research" (2012–2014); "The Problems of Ensuring of Reasonable Accommodation Requirement in Education According to UN Convention on the Rights of Persons with Disabilities" (2015)). In 2022, her chapter "Protecting Persons with Disabilities in the Baltic States: Empowering by Law" was published in the Springer book "Legal Protection of Vulnerable Groups in Lithuania, Latvia, Estonia and Poland. Trends and Perspectives".

Katarzyna Roszewska is an associate professor of law at the Institute of Law and Administration of the Cardinal Stefan Wyszyński University in Warsaw. She has published several dozen scientific articles and monographs. Her areas of interest include social law, human rights of persons and children with disabilities, accessibility law.

She participated in several international projects regarding the rights of persons and children with disabilities. The most important: "Legal protection of children with disabilities" as part of the "Polish-Hungarian Research Platform" (2023); "Active persons with disabilities - tools supporting the independence of persons with disabilities" (2020–2023); "AAC Guide - local government office friendly to people with communication difficulties" (cooperation with Austria, 2019–2022); Direction: Inclusive education in Europe, ERASMUS+, Action 2 - Strategic partnerships for the school education sector (2016–2019); Implementation of the Convention on the Rights of Persons with Disabilities in Georgia as a condition for professional and social activation, Helsinki Foundation for Human Rights, Tbilisi, Georgia (June 2015); LLP Leonardo da Vinci Partnership: Recommendations for inclusive vocational and higher education for people with disabilities (2013–2015); US State Department scholarship: Equal Right for Persons with Disabilities (2015).

Katarzyna Roszewska regularly participates in various teams working on the implementation of the CRPD: member of the National Development Council of the President of the Republic of Poland (since 2021), member of the Social Working Group for Deinstitutionalization at the Minister of Family, Labour and Social Policy (2020), expert of the Government Working Team for Disability and Inability to Work Assessment according to ICF (2017–2018), member of the Team for Special Educational Needs at the Minister of Education (2016); member of the Social Consultative Council at the State Fund for Rehabilitation of Persons with Disabilities (2013–2015), member of the Team for Systemic Solutions for Persons with Disabilities at the Minister of Labour and Social Policy (2013–2015).

Education Rights of Children Belonging to National Minorities in the Baltic States

Jolanta Apolewicz and Elżbieta Kuzborska-Pacha

Abstract This chapter provides an analysis of the education rights of children belonging to national minorities in the Baltic States, exploring the historical context, current policies, and future challenges in this area. It explores the legislative frameworks and institutional practices that govern minority education rights, highlighting the existing international norms and judicial practice (especially under the Council of Europe, OSCE frameworks and recent ECHR judgments).

By examining case studies from Lithuania, Latvia and Estonia, the chapter analyses how national legislative changes reflect a broader trend in the Baltic States towards strengthening education in state language while balancing the cultural and linguistic rights of minorities. It also critically evaluates the effectiveness of existing educational programs, integration strategies and identifies common challenges such as lack of consultative mechanism with minority communities while reforming educational systems, inadequate funding, limited access to quality education, and the prevalence of socio-economic disparities. In the end, recommendations for policy reforms to enhance the educational rights and outcomes of national minorities in the region are suggested.

Through its comprehensive approach, this chapter contributes to the broader discourse on minority rights, emphasising the importance of context-specific strategies and international collaboration to ensure the fulfilment of education rights for all.

J. Apolewicz (✉)
Law Institute, Lithuanian Centre for Social Sciences, Vilnius, Lithuania
e-mail: jolanta.apolevic@teise.org

E. Kuzborska-Pacha
Faculty of Law and Administration, University of Lodz, Lodz, Poland

A. Limantė, R. Vaičiūnienė (eds.), *Children's Rights in Central and Eastern Europe*, European Union and its Neighbours in a Globalized World 29,
https://doi.org/10.1007/978-3-032-07092-0_19

1 Introduction

Commonly referred to as the 'Baltic States', Lithuania, Latvia, and Estonia have faced significant challenges throughout the twentieth century. Having reinstated independence in 1918, these nations were thrust into the Soviet sphere of influence as a result of the secret protocol of the Ribbentrop-Molotov Pact in 1939, which led to their annexation by the USSR in 1940. During the interwar period, the demographic makeup of these countries was diverse: in Lithuania, the titular nation comprised 83.9% of the population, with a 2.5% Russian minority, a 50% Polish minority concentrated around the capital Vilnius, and a significant Jewish minority comprising 43.5% of Vilnius' population. Latvia's titular population stood at 75.5%, with Russians making up 10.6%, Poles 2.5%, and Jews 4.8%. In Estonia, Estonians constituted 88.1% of the population, with Russians making up 8.2%, while the Polish and Jewish minorities each comprised 0.1%. Additionally, the German minority across the three states numbered around 100,000, accounting for approximately 1.4% of Lithuania's population, 3.2% in Latvia, and 1.5% in Estonia (Kuzborska-Pacha 2019, p. 5).

World War II and the subsequent Soviet occupation brought dramatic changes to the ethnic composition of these states. *En mass* immigration from the USSR and the implementation of Russification policies[1] led to the 'minoritization' of the titular nations of the Baltic States within their own territories. By 1989, the demographic landscape had shifted significantly: in Latvia, Latvians made up 52% of the population, with Russians accounting for 34%; and in Estonia, the titular nation made up 61.5%, while the Russian minority had grown to 30%. The smaller influx of Russian-speaking populations in Lithuania, with Russians comprising 9.4% and Poles 7%, was mainly due to Lithuania's larger native population, which could meet the domestic labour market's needs.

The Soviet occupation era was marked by policies that favoured the Russian language and culture, often at the expense of local languages and traditions. Russian became the dominant language in public life, education, and administration, resulting in a form of asymmetric bilingualism where many residents, including those from the titular nations, communicated in Russian. By 1989, only 13.7% of Russians in Estonia, 21.2% in Latvia, and 33.5% in Lithuania reported knowledge of the Estonian, Latvian or Lithuanian respectively (Kuzborska-Pacha 2019, p. 6). These policies of Russification had long-lasting effects on the Baltic States, deeply influencing their post-independence policies toward language and minority rights (Muižnieks et al. 2013, p. 290 and subseq.).

After gaining independence in 1990, Lithuania, Latvia, and Estonia worked to rebuild their national identities and integrate their large Russian-speaking

[1] The Russification policy had two dimensions—the construction of the civic identity of the Soviet nation and the widespread use of the Russian language in the public sphere as a 'means of international communication.'

minorities,[2] including through educational policies regarding children. They passed language laws making Lithuanian, Latvian, and Estonian the sole official languages, replacing the previous bilingualism and restoring cultural and political dominance (Dudzińska 2012). Integrating Russian-speaking minorities into the Baltic States has been a complex process influenced by the Soviet legacy and concerns over national security and cultural preservation.

The ongoing aggression of Russia against Ukraine and its spillover effects have heightened concerns in the Baltic States about national security and the loyalty of Russian-speaking minorities. This has intensified efforts to further strengthen state language policies and reduce the influence of Russian, particularly in children education, while balancing the need to protect minority rights. The conflict has reinforced the Baltic States' focus on cultural preservation and integration, making the management of minority relations more sensitive and strategic in light of regional geopolitical tensions.

This chapter examines education rights for minority children in the Baltic States. At the outset it presents an overview of legal frameworks and international norms governing minority education, followed by detailed case studies of Lithuania, Latvia, and Estonia's approaches to minority education reform and concludes with recommendations for balancing state language acquisition with minority rights protection.

2 Legal Frameworks and International Norms Governing Education Rights of Children

International education standards emphasize the right *to* education and the rights *in* education regarding children belonging to national minorities. These standards recognize this as fundamental to preserving and developing their cultural identity. Although no single international instrument explicitly mandates the child's right to education in his/her mother tongue, several key documents, such as the Universal Declaration of Human Rights and the International Covenant on Economic, Social and Cultural Rights, the European Convention on Human Rights (ECHR), affirm the right to education without discrimination and encourage states to accommodate minority languages within their educational systems. Only Framework Convention for the Protection of National Minorities (FCNM), the first legally binding

[2] The term 'Russian-speaking minorities' refers to members of minorities for whom Russian is their native language (i.e., native Russian speakers), such as Russians, and to some extent Ukrainians, Belarusians, and others. On the other hand, the terms 'minority' or 'minorities' refer to national minorities. It should be noted that in the European context, the term 'national minorities' is commonly used (for example, in OSCE and Council of Europe documents—the Framework Convention for the Protection of National Minorities and the European Charter for Regional or Minority Languages). Meanwhile, on the universal level, the term 'minorities' (without an adjective) is widely used, encompassing national, linguistic, ethnic, and religious minorities.

multilateral instrument devoted to the protection of national minorities and the most comprehensive international standard in the field of minority rights, which all three Baltic States are parties to,[3] obliges states to "endeavour to ensure, as far as possible and within the framework of their education systems, that persons belonging to those minorities have adequate opportunities for being taught the minority language or for receiving instruction in this language", while maintaining the learning of the official state language.[4,5] It should be noted that the child's right to education is a right in itself but it is also instrumental as a precondition for the full enjoyment of many other rights, such as the right to participation, expression, association, etc.

The same document in Article 12 advocates for educational measures that enhance understanding of minority cultures and history, including teacher training and access to educational resources. Moreover, the FCNM recognizes the right of minorities to establish private educational institutions, though without financial obligations for the state (Art. 13). These provisions collectively aim to protect the rights of children belonging to minorities to preserve their cultural and linguistic identity while ensuring equal access to education and non-discriminatory treatment in all aspects of life. However, the extent of these provisions highly depends on national legislation and the state's willingness to implement them.

Other European instruments, such as the European Charter for Regional or Minority Languages and the OSCE HCNM Hague Recommendations, provide more specific guidance. These documents advocate for the use of minority languages in education, highlighting the importance of both preserving these languages and ensuring that minority children also learn the state language to integrate effectively into broader society.

Educational rights of children belonging to minorities are closely tied to preserving cultural identity, particularly through mother-tongue education.[6] Research

---

[3] Lithuania ratified the FCNM without reservations. When Latvia ratified the document on June 6, 2005, it made three reservations. One reservation specified that 'national minority' refers only to Latvian citizens who differ from Latvians in culture, religion, or language, have lived in Latvia for generations, and wish to preserve their cultural identity. This is the de facto legal definition in Latvia, as there is no national definition. Latvia also reserved the right to limit certain rights for stateless persons and clarified that the use of minority languages in official contexts must comply with Latvia's Constitution and laws governing the state language.When Estonia ratified the Council of Europe's Framework Convention, it made a reservation similar to Latvia's, concerning the definition of 'national minority.' Estonia specified that this term applies to citizens who have long-standing and permanent ties to Estonia, differ from Estonians in ethnic, cultural, religious, and linguistic characteristics, and intend to preserve their cultural traditions, religion, or language, which form the basis of their collective identity. See: Declaration of the Republic of Latvia contained in the instrument of ratification of the Framework Convention for the Protection of National Minorities deposited on 6 June 2005, Council of Europe; Declaration of the Estonia contained in the instrument of ratification of the Framework Convention, deposited on 6 January 1997, Council of Europe.

[4] Art. 14 par 2 of FCNM.

[5] Art 14 par 3 of FCNM.

[6] The term 'mother tongue' refers to the first language a child learns, often referred to in specialized terminology as the 'first language' or L1. In many cases, children from minority backgrounds grow

shows that children achieve better academic outcomes when taught in their native language, helping retain cultural heritage.[7] International law supports this connection, emphasizing language's role in education and cultural continuity, especially in the context of multilingual education.[8] Studies highlight that early education in a child's first language leads to better performance and lower dropout rates.[9] While governments may cite costs as a barrier to bilingual education, research from organizations like UNESCO and UNICEF suggests it leads to long-term benefits, including reduced dropout rates and improved academic success (Muižnieks et al. 2013, pp. 288–308; UNESCO 2003, p. 16 and subseq).[10]

A key challenge for states is balancing minority (and their children) integration with the preservation of their linguistic and cultural identity. Effective educational policies should support bilingual education, allowing minority languages to thrive while ensuring children learn the state language for full societal participation. This approach respects minority rights and enriches national cultural diversity, promoting cohesion and inclusivity, but also serves as a conflict prevention strategy.[11]

---

up in bilingual or multilingual households, where multiple languages are used concurrently, leading to what is known as simultaneous L1 acquisition or early bilingualism.

[7] For more information see: Parliamentary Assembly of the Council of Europe, *Report on the place of mother tongue in school education*, Doc 10837, Committee on Culture, Science and Education, 7 February 2006.

[8] See, for example, point 74 of the Explanatory Report to the FCNM: "The obligation to recognise the right of every person belonging to a national minority to learn his or her minority language concerns one of the principal means by which such individuals can assert and preserve their identity. There can be no exceptions to this." Explanatory Report to the Framework Convention for the Protection of National Minorities, Strasbourg, 1.II.1995, European Treaty Series, No. 157.

[9] The OSCE HCNM recommendations provide a clear indication for minority education at primary and secondary levels:"11) The first years of education are of pivotal importance in a child's development. Educational research suggests that the medium of teaching at pre-school and kindergarten levels should ideally be the child's language. Wherever possible, States should create conditions enabling parents to avail themselves of this option.

12) <…> in primary school, the curriculum should ideally be taught in the minority language. <…> Towards the end of this period, a few practical or non-theoretical subjects should be taught through the medium of the State language. Wherever possible, States should create conditions enabling parents to avail themselves of this option.

13) In secondary school, a substantial part of the curriculum should be taught through the medium of the minority language. <…>Throughout this period, the number of subjects taught in the State language, should gradually be increased. Research findings suggest that the more gradual the increase, the better for the child.

14) The maintenance of the primary and secondary levels of minority language education depends a great deal on the availability of teachers trained in all disciplines in the mother tongue. Therefore, ensuing from their obligation to provide adequate opportunities for minority language education, States should provide adequate facilities for the appropriate training of teachers and should facilitate access to such training." OSCE/HCNM Hague Recommendations regarding the Education Rights of National Minorities, 1 October 1996."

[10] More on the research see: Skutnabb-Kangas (2004), p. 2 and subseq.

[11] See the OSCE/HCNM Hague Recommendations regarding the Education Rights of National Minorities, 1 October 1996.

The implementation of this approach within national legal frameworks remains a contentious issue, particularly regarding the use of minority languages in education and public life. Recent rulings by the European Court of Human Rights (ECtHR) in cases such as *Džibuti and Others v. Latvia* and *Valiullina and Others v. Latvia* have highlighted the ongoing challenges in interpreting and enforcing these rights, particularly in the context of language laws and education policies. Namely, the ECtHR in its judgments[12] found that Latvia's 2018 educational reforms, which reduced the use of Russian as a language of instruction in private schools, did not violate the rights of Russian-speaking pupils. It found no violation of Article 14 combined with Article 2 of Protocol No. 1, as the reforms were deemed legitimate in promoting the Latvian language and ensuring educational unity.

It is crucial to highlight the main points of the judgments, as they will significantly impact the educational framework in the Baltic States and beyond. The ruling sets a precedent for how international standards can be integrated into national systems, particularly in balancing state discretion in educational matters with minority rights protection. This decision emphasises the state's authority to regulate children's education, including language use, while ensuring that these measures align with broader democratic principles and respect for minority cultures within a unified educational framework. Already in 2024, in its report to the Advisory Committee of the FCNM, the Estonian government opposed to the opinion of the ACFNM and referred extensively to the judgements of ECtHR, pointing out that the transition to official-language-only education in minority schools is in accordance with international law, including the FCNM.[13]

It should be expected that other countries in the region will follow the same pattern. Firstly, the ECtHR recognized that Latvia's goals of strengthening the Latvian language and unifying the educational system were legitimate. These aims were seen as essential in eliminating the remnants of Soviet-era segregation and fostering social cohesion. At the same time, the Court determined that the educational reforms were proportionate. They did not entirely remove the use of Russian as a language of instruction, particularly in primary children's education, where significant portions of the curriculum could still be taught in Russian.

Secondly, the ECtHR found that the differences in treatment between Russian-speaking pupils and Latvian-speaking pupils were justified. Given the context of Latvia's historical and social background, the reforms were not seen as discriminatory but as necessary for promoting the use of the state language. Also, the Court upheld that private schools in Latvia, which receive state funding, are part of the state education system. Therefore, the state has the right to regulate them, including setting language requirements.

And thirdly, while the judgment allows for reduced use of minority languages in children education, it accentuated the state's responsibility to provide education in

[12] *Valiullina and Others v. Latvia* 56928/19, 7306/20, 11937/20, 14.09.2023; *Džibuti and Others v. Latvia*, applications nos. 225/20 and 2 others, ECtHR judgement of 16 November 2023.

[13] Sixth Report submitted by Estonia, pursuant to Article 25, paragraph 2 of the Framework Convention for the Protection of National Minorities, 5 June 2024, Par. 167.

a manner that respects national cohesion, without completely disregarding minority rights. In other words, it reinforced Latvia's approach to language and education policy, confirming the state's authority to regulate the language of instruction even in private schools, while highlighting the balance between minority rights and state sovereignty in educational matters.

3 Case Studies: Lithuania, Latvia, and Estonia

3.1 Lithuania

According to the results of the 2021 census, Lithuania has a population of 2.810 thousand inhabitants, of which 432,000 (14.5%) are representatives of national minorities.[14] Poles constitute 6.5% of the population, Russians 5%, Byelorussians 1% (more than 28.000), Jews 0.08% (2.256 individuals). Roma 0.08% (2251 individuals), also Latvians, Armenians, Moldovans and other. Until recently, the Ukrainian population in the country was around 14,000. However, due to the war in Ukraine and the subsequent influx of refugees, the number has now risen to 76,300.

Schools with minority language instruction operated in Lithuania starting from the inter-war period – Polish, Russian, Jewish, German, Latvian and Belorussian. Currently, there are about 90 schools and around 80 kindergartens offering education in minority language - Polish, Russian, and Belarusian, reflecting the diverse ethnic makeup of the country.[15]

An important achievement for Polish community in Lithuania is the establishment of a higher education institution where the language of instruction is Polish - the Branch of the University of Białystok in Vilnius.[16]

Before the 2011 reforms, the teaching of the Lithuanian language in minority schools followed the 'state language' curriculum, whereas in Lithuanian-language schools, it was taught as the 'mother tongue'. Before 2011, minority schools taught all subjects in the minority language, though they could opt to teach some subjects in Lithuanian. The Lithuanian language was taught as a 'state language' with 800 fewer hours than in Lithuanian schools where it was taught as a 'mother tongue'- a distinction that lacked pedagogical justification since Lithuanian was not the native language of minority students.

In March 2011, Lithuania introduced the first significant reform of minority education since the country regained independence in 1990. The reform aimed to strengthen the role of the Lithuanian language in minority schools. However, it was

---

[14] The Department of National Minorities to the Government of the Republic of Lithuania. https://tmde.lrv.lt/lt/tautiniu-mazumu-kulturos-centrai-ir-tautines-bendrijos/statistika/.

[15] LRytas news portal. https://www.lrytas.lt/lietuvosdiena/svietimas/2022/12/26/news/isanalizavo-pastaruju-ketveriu-metu-tautiniu-mazumu-mokyklu-rezultatus-25610229.

[16] Branch of the University of Bialystok in Vilnius website. https://wilno.uwb.edu.pl/en/.

met with strong opposition from the affected communities, particularly from the Polish minority, and faced criticism from international observers.[17] Minority representatives argued that the reform was being imposed top-down without effective consultation with minority communities, including school communities. Minority representatives acknowledged the importance of a good command of Lithuanian but emphasized that the reform did not include a proper transitional period, leaving school communities unprepared for the changes.

The 2011 reforms included several key changes: modifications to the curriculum in minority schools, the introduction of Lithuanian as the language of instruction for subjects related to Lithuanian history, geography, and civic education (previously, the decision on teaching certain subjects in Lithuanian rested with the parents/students in minority schools), and the implementation of a unified Lithuanian language matriculation exam starting in 2013, without prior unification of the Lithuanian language teaching programs in Lithuanian and minority schools. It is important to note that those changes were implemented against the recommendations of Lithuanian educational experts, who as early as 2006 emphasized that any unification of the Lithuanian language matriculation exam should occur only after unifying the 12-year curriculum for minority and Lithuanian schools (Merkys et al. 2006).[18]

The results of the unified Lithuanian language matriculation exam revealed a significant decline in performance among minority students, affecting their ability to enter universities. According to data from minority organizations, in 2012, only 6% of minority school students failed the state language (Lithuanian) exam, but this percentage rose to 11.8% in 2013 (after the exam was unified) and to 16.3% in 2014. In 2011, 47% of minority school graduates scored between 50–99% on the exam,

[17] E.g. see Resolution CM/ResCMN(2016)9, on the implementation of the Framework Convention for the Protection of National Minorities by Lithuania, adopted by the Committee of Ministers on 6 July 2016 at the 1262nd meeting of the Ministers' Deputies: "A too hasty implementation [of education reform] could negatively affect the quality of teaching in minority language schools. Teachers and school administrations require continued and targeted support and training to ensure that the focus on promoting the State language in the education system does not disadvantage students of minority language schools in their general access to and participation in education. There should have been more flexibility in the implementation of the reform with a view to ensuring that the quality of education at minority language schools generally did not suffer as a result of a disproportionate focus on the promotion of the State language". See also: Advisory Committee on the Framework Convention for the Protection of National Minorities, Third Opinion on Lithuania adopted on 28 November 2013, p. 7 and subseq.

[18] In a 2006 study, experts noted: "Applying the same examination standards to individuals of Lithuanian descent in families where Lithuanian is spoken, and in schools where all subjects are taught in Lithuanian, as well as to representatives of national minorities who do not speak Lithuanian at home and attend schools where subjects are not taught in Lithuanian, would be inappropriate and partly discriminatory. (...) Standardization would make sense and be correct only if the standards and curricula for the state language were unified beforehand (it is necessary to standardize not only the formal program requirements but also all conditions of the teaching process – primarily the number of lessons, etc.). Until this is done, unifying examination requirements is inappropriate. (...) Ideally, a unified Lithuanian exam for national minorities could only be applied when a generation of graduates who have been taught according to standardized standards and programs throughout the entire 12-year education cycle has emerged."

but this percentage dropped to 18% in 2013. This trend is progressing,[19] as in 2018, 23.5% and in 2024, 21% of minority students failed the state language exam, significantly higher than the national average of 7.8% in 2018 and 8.7% in 2024.[20]

The reform sparked tensions in bilateral relations with Poland, leading to the establishment of the Polish-Lithuanian Educational Experts Group in September 2011, aimed at discussing minority education in both countries and assessing and mitigating an impact of the reform. However, no agreement was reached. Although, Lithuanian authorities responded to the call for involving minority representatives in the decision-making process by establishing a permanent working group on minority education in November 2011, which included representatives of the Lithuanian Ministry of Education and Science and national minorities, its work did not lead to any changes in the assumptions and course of the minority education reform.

Also, in 2011/2012, the OSCE High Commissioner on National Minorities, Knut Vollebaek, undertook mediation efforts between the two countries. However, Lithuanian side restricted his recommendations on minority education reform.

In 2019, the Committee of Minister of CoE called Lithuanian government to "ensure that education reform does not result in discrimination against students from minority language schools through pursuing an evidence-based rather than deadline-driven policy as regards transition measures, and through involving minority language teachers in a strong advisory role; develop and implement a conceptual approach towards bi- and multilingual teaching in schools and pre-schools and support the exposure of children from national minorities to a Lithuanian-language environment and vice versa; consider the possibility of reflecting exam results in minority languages in the final grade relevant for entrance into university".[21]

[19] In first years after the reform, Lithuanian authorities temporarily introduced exam accommodations for minority school students, including extended time, the use of dictionaries, and more lenient grading. However, in 2013, a group of MPs challenged these measures, arguing they violated the constitutional principle of equality. The Lithuanian Supreme Administrative Court ruled that the accommodations were unconstitutional and unjustified. The Court, however, did not address the significant curriculum differences between Lithuanian and minority schools, including a gap of 800 hours in Lithuanian language instruction. In October 2013, the education minister repealed the accommodations, fully standardizing exam conditions, though differentiated grading criteria for minority students remained in place. See: LT Supreme Administrative Court of Lithuania, ruling of 18 June 2013, No.I261-16/2013. See more: Kuzborska (2014).

[20] EFHR: Ujednolicony egzamin z języka litewskiego sprawia trudności uczniom szkół mniejszości – Wiadomości. Znad Wilii news portal. https://www.lrt.lt/pl/wiadomosci/1261/2320499/dlaczego-21-proc-maturzystow-szkol-mniejszosci-narodowych-nie-zdalo-jezyka-litewskiego.

[21] Resolution CM/ResCMN(2019) 4 on the implementation of the Framework Convention for the Protection of National Minorities by Lithuania, adopted by the Committee of Ministers on 27 March 2019 at the 1342nd meeting of the Ministers' Deputies.

3.2 *Latvia*

Latvia has a significant history of minority education, dating back to the interwar period, when the state established a broad network of public primary and secondary schools offering instruction in various minority languages, including German, Russian, Yiddish, Polish, Belarusian, Estonian, and Lithuanian. In these schools, only subjects such as Latvian history and geography were taught in the state language. Notably, the Herder Institute conducted its studies in German, while the Russian Institute of University-type Education offered courses in Russian. However, during the authoritarian rule of Kārlis Ulmanis (1934–1940), minority institutions were closed, and the number of public minority schools was reduced. During the Soviet occupation, education from preschool to university was conducted either in Latvian or Russian. The period of Perestroika allowed the revival of smaller minority schools, including Jewish, Polish, Belarusian, Lithuanian, and Estonian institutions, and for the first time in history, a Ukrainian school was established (Cilevičs 2015; Kuzborska 2019, p. 178 and subseq.).

Since the 1990s, the network of secondary schools in Latvia, including those for minorities, has gradually diminished. For example, in the 1998/1999 school year, Latvia had 728 schools with Latvian as the language of instruction, 145 bilingual Latvian-Russian schools, 195 bilingual schools with partial Russian instruction, and five bilingual schools with partial Polish instruction. By the 2015/2016 school year, there were 620 Latvian schools, 60 bilingual schools, 94 Russian schools, and four Polish schools.[22] In 2020, Latvia had 643 pre-primary and 678 general education institutions. Of these, 10.2% of pre-schools and 16.8% of general education schools offered programs in both Latvian and minority languages. Russian was the most common minority language used in education, with several schools offering bilingual programs in Latvian and Russian. Other minority languages included Polish, Jewish, Belarusian, Ukrainian, Lithuanian, and Estonian.[23]

In 1998, the Education Law was passed, which abolished the use of languages other than Latvian in university education, with certain exceptions for official EU languages. The law also mandated the transition to teaching in the state language in grades 10–12 of general education schools by 2004. Due to widespread opposition from the Russian minority, amendments to the Education Law were passed in 2004, introducing bilingual education in minority primary schools (grades 1–9) and requiring that at least 60% of subjects in grades 10–12 be taught in the state language.

The reforms of minority education in Latvia have been primarily focused on increasing proficiency in the state language, especially by increasing the number of

[22] It is important to note that the decline in the number of Latvian schools, due to demographic changes, has been slower than the decline in the number of minority schools.

[23] Fourth Report submitted by Latvia Pursuant to Article 25, paragraph 2 of the Framework Convention for the Protection of National Minorities – received on 27 October 2021, ACFC/SR/IV(2021)002, par. 76.

subjects taught in Latvian and standardizing the state language exam. The ultimate goal of these reforms has been to transition to teaching exclusively in Latvian.

The implementation of these changes, particularly the requirement for 60% of instruction in Latvian, sparked significant opposition, particularly from the Russian minority. The lack of consultation with minority communities regarding the number of students in classes and the introduction of teaching certain subjects in Latvian was a major point of contention - the reforms were perceived by minority representatives as a threat to their culture and language. A survey conducted in 2013 revealed that only a quarter of respondents—students from minority schools—expressed a desire to receive education solely in Latvian.

Latvian authorities view bilingual education as a success story of the Latvian education system, highlighting the improved academic performance of students in these schools (primarily referring to Russian schools). However, a comparison of exam results before and after the 2004 reforms suggests otherwise—the average exam results in subjects taught in Latvian declined.

The standardized program for teaching the state language and Latvian literature in minority schools at the primary school level (grade 10) was introduced in the 2008/2009 school year. The first standardized exam in the Latvian language in public and private schools was conducted in 2012. Until then, minority school students took the Latvian language exam as a state language exam, but from that year onward, it was administered as a native language exam. Since then, separate exam results for Latvian and minority schools have not been made public. A comparison of achievements from individual schools showed significantly lower exam results among minority school students. Since the results of the state language exam are considered when applying for higher education, the standardization of the exam without an adequate transition period significantly impacted the ability of minority school graduates to gain admission to state universities, especially for tuition-free spots. The Latvian Ombudsman criticized the insufficient transition period for implementing the standardized Latvian language exam for minority schools, citing expert opinions from the Advisory Committee of the Council of Europe. The Ombudsman pointed out that unifying the curriculum in minority secondary schools in the 2009/2010 school year and conducting the first standardized exam in the 2011/2012 school year did not allow teachers and students to properly prepare for the changes. He also highlighted several problems related to the reform that introduced bilingual education in minority schools and called for improvements and adherence to the principle of proportionality in this area.

In 2022, Latvia adopted a reform that will phase out teaching in minority languages in most public and private preschools, schools, and universities by 2025. While exceptions exist for schools teaching in Polish and Ukrainian, the elimination of Belarusian and Russian will impact around 20% of school-aged children. Plans to discontinue Russian as a foreign language are also in place, limiting it to extracurricular courses. According to the Advisory Committee of the FCNM, if fully implemented, these changes will likely conflict with the FCNM's provisions on equal access to education and the right to minority language instruction. The reduction in Russian-language education will also affect other minorities who speak Russian as their first language.[24]

3.3 Estonia

In Estonia, during the Soviet period, education was conducted in both Estonian and Russian across all levels, from preschool to university. However, starting in the 1990s, the number of students in Russian-language schools began to decline, largely due to a decrease in the minority population from emigration and low birth rates, as well as a shift by some non-Estonian speakers towards education in the state language. In the autumn of 1990, 40.6% of first-grade students attended Russian-language schools, but by 1999, this percentage had fallen to 20%. By the 2011/2012 academic year, 19.1% of students were still receiving education in Russian, with 3.4% of minority students attending classes where most subjects were taught in Estonian (Kuzborska 2019, p. 331).

According to the 2021 census, 25% of Estonia's population (322,700 people) identify as having a Russian background, with 20% of these also being Estonian citizens. The number of Russian speakers is actually higher, as Russian is also the mother tongue of other minorities, such as Ukrainians and Belarusians. Estonia is one of the few European countries with an official definition of national minorities. When ratifying the Council of Europe Framework Convention for the Protection of National Minorities, the Estonian Parliament established this definition, later included in the National Minorities Cultural Autonomy Act.[25] The Act defines a national minority as Estonian citizens who reside in Estonia, have long-term and permanent ties to the country, differ from Estonians by ethnicity, culture, religion, or language, and are committed to preserving their collective cultural customs, religion, or language, which form the basis of their common identity.[26]

Between 2007 and 2011, Estonia implemented educational reforms that mandated that at least 60% of subjects in minority secondary schools be taught in Estonian. Despite opposition from the Russian-speaking minority, these reforms went ahead, with only 31% of the Russian-speaking minority expressing full or partial support for the changes in 2007.

Until recently, Estonia's Basic and Secondary School Act allowed municipal primary schools (grades 1–9) to choose their language of instruction based on the school council's request and local municipal council's approval. In state primary schools, the Ministry of Education and Research determined the language of instruction. While Estonian law permitted exceptions for municipal schools or specific

[24] Fourth Opinion on Latvia, Advisory Committee on the FCNM, 9 October 2023, ACFC/OP/IV(2023)1, p. 4.

[25] National Minorities Cultural Autonomy Act (1993) of the Republic of Estonia adopted on 26 October 1993, available at: https://www.riigiteataja.ee/akt/182796.

[26] Ibidem, art. 1.

classes, the government had to approve these, often allowing for bilingual education models. Controversy arose when the Estonian government granted an exception to the 60% rule for the Tallinn German Upper Secondary School but refused similar exceptions for Russian-language schools.

Education in primary schools could be conducted in Estonian, Russian, English, or Finnish. Approximately 81% of general education schools in Estonia used Estonian as the language of instruction, 14% used Russian, 1% used English or Finnish, and 4% offered bilingual education in Estonian and Russian, known as 'language immersion.'[27] In secondary schools (grades 10–12), Estonian was typically the language of instruction. However, municipal schools or individual classes could teach in another language with government approval. In private schools, the language of instruction was determined by the school's founder.

On 12 December 2022, the Riigikogu adopted "The Amendment Law to the Basic School and Gymnasium Law and Other Laws (Transition to Estonian-Language Education)",[28] which establishes that the full transition to Estonian-language education will start in 2024 and would be finalised by 2030.[29] It is estimated that transition to Estonian-medium education directly affects 31,571 pupils and 2245 teachers who do not meet the language requirements.[30] The justification for the transition to Estonian-language-only education presented by the Government stressed the need to ensure quality education in Estonian for all children, regardless of their mother tongue, as this fosters national identity, promotes social integration, reduces segregation, and enhances opportunities for further education, employment,

[27] Estonia's 'language immersion' program, which began in 2000, includes both 'early immersion' and 'late immersion.' In 'early immersion,' first-grade students receive all instruction in Estonian, with Russian introduced in the second year and a foreign language in the third year, after which education becomes bilingual. In 'late immersion,' starting from the sixth grade, four subjects are taught in Estonian, increasing to almost all subjects by the ninth grade, with a balance of 50% in Estonian and 50% in Russian by the final year of primary school.

[28] Act on Amendments to the Basic School and Gymnasium Act and Other Acts (Transition to Estonian-Language Education) of Republic of Estonia, No. 722 SE (2022), available at: https://www.riigikogu.ee/tegevus/eelnoud/eelnou/1e58a907-7cd0-41b9-b898-aa8eee5e94bf/Põhikoo%20li-+ja+gümnaasiumiseaduse+ning+teiste+seaduste+muutmise+seadus+%28eestikeelsele+õppele+üleminek/.

[29] "Ministry of Education and Research of the Republic of Estonia. Transition to Estonian-language education, https://www.hm.ee/en/node/234.

Minister Tõnis Lukas. Transition to Estonian-language education will definitely happen. https://www.hm.ee/en/news/minister-tonis-lukas-transition-estonian-language-education-will-definitely-happen.

[30] Starting from September 1, 2025, Estonian language proficiency requirements will be integrated into the qualification criteria for teachers, head teachers, school heads, and support specialists. Depending on the position, proficiency levels must be B2 or C1. Employees must meet these requirements by this date, or they will not be eligible for indefinite work contracts. See: European Commission. National reforms in general school education. https://eurydice.eacea.ec.europa.eu/national-education-systems/estonia/national-reforms-general-school-education.

and shared values in Estonia.[31] On a number occasions, the Estonian government highlighted unequal learning outcomes for Russian-speaking students compared to the majority.[32]

Already in June 2022, the Council of Europe experts urged Estonian authorities to ensure access to Russian as a language of instruction at all levels of the public education system and intensify the dialogue with representatives of the Russian minority, assess and improve the quality of education with Russian as the language of instruction and look into the causes of any educational disparities in academic performance from students in Estonian-language and Russian-language schools.[33] They underlined that according to the international standards, the ongoing educational reform, and any future reform, should be accompanied by a dialogue between the authorities and minority representatives as well as measures which guarantee the continued use of minority languages as languages of instruction for a substantial part of the curriculum while ensuring quality education at all levels.[34] Moreover, in their opinion, the promotion of bilingual and multilingual education would ensure conditions for the proficient learning of both Estonian and minority languages.

The Advisory Committee recognized the legitimacy of promoting the state language for societal integration but stressed the need for effective consultations with national minorities when decisions impact minority language education. It emphasized that increasing state language instruction should not compromise the quality of education in minority language schools. The Committee also expressed concern over the unequal learning outcomes for Russian-speaking students compared to the majority and called for independent research to address these disparities. Previous concerns raised during Estonia's transition to Estonian as the language of instruction highlighted the lack of analysis on education quality, questioning its compatibility with the right to education.[35]

Also, according to the UN experts (OHCHR Press release 2023), by eliminating minority language instruction in pre-schools and schools, the new law severely restricts minority language education in Estonia, in contravention of international human rights instruments.

The implementation of this reform was intended to improve proficiency in the state language among minority students but also sparked significant dissatisfaction among the Russian-speaking minority. The reform, seen as limiting the right to

[31] Ministry of Education and Research of the Republic of Estonia. Transition to Estonian-language education, https://www.hm.ee/en/node/234.

[32] The Advisory Committee, and the Committee of Ministers, have previously raised these concerns with the Estonian authorities when the transition to Estonian as a language of instruction began. It warned then that the lack of analysis of the quality of education raised questions about the compatibility of the transition with the right to education for students studying at Russian language schools. See: ACFC Fifth Opinion on Estonia, ACFC/OP/V(2021)5, 9 June 2022, par. 184 https://rm.coe.int/5th-op-estonia-en/1680a6cc9e.

[33] Ibidem, par. 186.

[34] Ibidem, par. 185.

[35] Ibidem, par. 183, 184.

education in their native language, led to protests, petitions, and legal challenges. At the same time, it is indicative that each year, Russian-speaking parents are increasingly interested in enrolling their kids in Estonian-language schools.[36]

4 Concluding Remarks

The educational reforms in Lithuania, Latvia, and Estonia demonstrate a shared focus on integrating children belonging to national minority through increased emphasis on state language education. In Estonia and Latvia, children's bilingual education is seen as a transitional step towards full state language instruction, often implemented rapidly without adequate consultation or transitional periods. In all three countries, minority education reforms have been often implemented without sufficient support for teachers, educational materials, or phased transitions. This has resulted in dissatisfaction among minority communities, a decline in educational outcomes, and reduced opportunities for higher education and employment. The reforms' impact on children's fundamental rights deserves particular attention. Research demonstrates that children achieve better academic outcomes and have lower dropout rates when taught in their native language. Moreover, the right to education is not only fundamental in itself but serves as a gateway to other essential rights such as participation, expression, and association. Therefore, educational reforms that limit instruction in minority languages may have far-reaching consequences for children's overall development and their ability to fully exercise their rights.

Despite legitimate goals of improving state language proficiency, these reforms often undermine the principle of children's equality in education and fail to respect the proportionality of changes in long-established minority language schools. The Advisory Committee of the FCNM and the Committee of Ministers of Council of Europe have repeatedly emphasized the need for effective consultations with minority communities when planning, implementing education reforms, and balancing state sovereignty with minority rights in education sphere. The ECtHR judgments in cases *Džibuti and Others v. Latvia* and *Valiullina and Others v. Latvia* highlighted these challenges and presented a guidance that will be followed by many European countries.

In addition, the current geopolitical context, particularly the ongoing war in Ukraine, further complicates the minority protection systems in all three countries. On one hand, it has led to the securitization of children education reforms, while on the other, it requires a delicate balance in upholding international obligations to protect minority rights and foster long-term social cohesion. It is important to note that Russian is also the mother tongue for some Ukrainian and Belarusian children

---

[36] Salum, M.: Tallinn's Estonian-language schools seeing more and more Russian-speaking kids, ERR, https://news.err.ee/1609431352/tallinn-s-estonian-language-schools-seeing-more-and-more-russian-speaking-kids.

migrants and refugees who have joined the Lithuanian, Latvian and Estonian education systems.

When considering children belonging to national minority education reforms, governments could benefit from establishing more comprehensive consultative mechanisms that include minority communities in the decision-making process. This would help ensure that policies are inclusive and reflect the diverse needs of all groups, while striving for a balanced approach between state language acquisition and the preservation of minority identities.

Increased investment in the transitional phases of education reforms would be advantageous, particularly in areas like teacher training, curriculum development, and language instruction that supports both state language proficiency and the continued use of minority languages. This approach would help smooth the transition and mitigate potential challenges.

Implementing gradual transitional periods for new language and education policies is also important to give children and educators sufficient time to adjust. This could help minimize disruptions and ensure that no pupil is disadvantaged by the reforms.

Linking children education reforms with broader integration strategies, particularly those addressing socio-economic disparities, would improve employment opportunities for minority communities and ensure that education serves as a bridge to greater socio-economic inclusion. A balanced educational system, backed by inclusive consultation and carefully managed transitions, would not only support integration but also respect the cultural and linguistic rights of national minorities and their children. This approach would enhance social cohesion and long-term stability in Lithuania, Latvia, and Estonia.

International Organizations Documents

Parliamentary Assembly of the Council of Europe, *Report on the place of mother tongue in school education*, Doc 10837, Committee on Culture, Science and Education, 7 February 2006

OSCE High Commissioner on National Minorities, *The Hague Recommendations Regarding the Education Rights of National Minorities* and Explanatory Report (1996)

Committee of Ministers, *Resolution on the implementation of the Framework Convention for the Protection of National Minorities by Lithuania* (2016) CM/ResCMN(2016)9

Committee of Ministers, *Resolution on the implementation of the Framework Convention for the Protection of National Minorities by Lithuania* (2019) CM/ResCMN(2019)4

Advisory Committee on the Framework Convention for the Protection of National Minorities, *Fifth Opinion on Estonia* (9 June 2022) ACFC/OP/V(2021)5

Advisory Committee on the Framework Convention for the Protection of National Minorities, *Fourth Opinion on Latvia* (9 October 2023) ACFC/OP/IV(2023)001
Advisory Committee on the Framework Convention for the Protection of National Minorities, *Third Opinion on Lithuania* (28 November 2013) ACFC/OP/III(2013)005
Advisory Committee on the Framework Convention for the Protection of National Minorities, *Sixth Report Submitted by Estonia* (2024) ACFC/SR/VI(2024)007
Advisory Committee on the Framework Convention for the Protection of National Minorities, *Fourth Report Submitted by Latvia* (27 October 2021) ACFC/SR/IV(2021)002

Opinions

ACFC Fifth Opinion on Estonia, ACFC/OP/V(2021)5, 9 June 2022, par. 186 https://rm.coe.int/5th-op-estonia-en/1680a6cc9e
Council of Europe: Advisory Committee on the Framework Convention for the Protection of National Minorities. Fourth Opinion on Latvia adopted on 9 October 2023, ACFC/OP/IV(2023)001
Council of Europe: Advisory Committee on the Framework Convention for the Protection of National Minorities. Third Opinion on Lithuania adopted on 28 November 2013, ACFC/OP/III(2013)005

Reports and Comments

Council of Europe: Sixth Report Submitted by Estonia pursuant to article 25, paragraph 2 of the Framework Convention for the Protection of National Minorities, 2024, ACFC/SR/VI(2024)007
Fourth report submitted by Latvia pursuant to article 25, paragraph 2 of the Framework Convention for the Protection of National Minorities - received on 27 October 2021, ACFC/SR/IV(2021)002
Resolution on the implementation of the Framework Convention for the Protection of National Minorities by Lithuania (2016) CM/ResCMN(2016)9
Resolution on the implementation of the Framework Convention for the Protection of National Minorities by Lithuania (2019) CM/ResCMN(2019)4

Legal Acts

International Legal Acts and Court Rulings

Council of Europe: Framework Convention for the Protection of National Minorities and Explanatory Peport, H(95)010, adopted on February 1995, Strasbourg

European Convention for the Protection of Human Rights and Fundamental Freedoms (ECHR) (1950), adopted by the Council of Europe on 4 November 1950. https://www.echr.coe.int/Documents/Convention_ENG.pdf

European Charter for Regional or Minority Languages (1992), ETS No. 148, 5 November 1992

International Covenant on Economic, Social and Cultural Rights (1996), adopted and opened for signature, ratification and accession by General Assembly resolution 2200A (XXI) of 16 December 1966. https://www.ohchr.org/en/professionalinterest/pages/cescr.aspx

Preamble of the United Nations Universal Declaration of Human Rights, 10 December 1948.

UN Convention on the Rights of the Child (1989), adopted by the United Nations General Assembly on 20 November 1989. https://www.ohchr.org/Documents/ProfessionalInterest/crc.pdf

UNESCO Convention Against Discrimination in Education (1960) http://portal.unesco.org/en/ev.php-URL_ID=12949&URL_DO=DO_TOPIC&URL_SECTION=201.html

Valiullina and Others v Latvia (Application Nos 56928/19, 7306/20, 11937/20) [2023] ECtHR 14 September 2023;

Džibuti and Others v Latvia (Applications Nos 225/20 and 2 others) [2023] ECtHR 16 November 2023.

National Laws and Court Rulings

Law on the State Language (1995) of the Republic of Lithuania, No. I-779, 31 January 1995, Vilnius, available at: https://e-seimas.lrs.lt/portal/legalAct/lt/TAD/TAIS.21941?jfwid=32wf6lrn

Official Language Law (1999) of the Republic of Latvia, adopted by Saeima on 9 January 1999

National Minorities Cultural Autonomy Act (1993) of the Republic of Estonia adopted on 26 October 1993, available at: https://www.riigiteataja.ee/akt/182796

Act on Amendments to the Basic School and Gymnasium Act and Other Acts (Transition to Estonian-Language Education) of Republic of Estonia, No. 722 SE (2022), available at: https://www.riigikogu.ee/tegevus/eelnoud/eelnou/1e58a907-7cd0-41b9-b898-aa8eee5e94bf/Põhikoo%20li-+ja+gümnaasiumiseaduse+ning+teiste+seadu ste+muutmise+seadus+%28eestikeelsele+õppele+üleminek/

Supreme Administrative Court of Lithuania (2013). Ruling of 18 June 2013, No. I261-16/2013.

Other Sources

The Department of National Minorities to the Government of the Republic of Lithuania. https://tmde.lrv.lt/lt/tautiniu-mazumu-kulturos-centrai-ir-tautines-bendrijos/statistika/.

LRytas news portal. https://www.lrytas.lt/lietuvosdiena/svietimas/2022/12/26/news/isanalizavo-pastaruju-ketveriu-metu-tautiniu-mazumu-mokyklu-rezultatus-25610229.

Branch of the University of Bialystok in Vilnius website. https://wilno.uwb.edu.pl/en/.

EFHR: Ujednolicony egzamin z języka litewskiego sprawia trudności uczniom szkół mniejszości – Wiadomości. Znad Wilii news portal. https://www.lrt.lt/pl/wiadomosci/1261/2320499/dlaczego-21-proc-maturzystow-szkol-mniejszosci-narodowych-nie-zdalo-jezyka-litewskiego.

Ministry of Education and Research of the Republic of Estonia. Transition to Estonian-language education, https://www.hm.ee/en/node/234.

Minister Tõnis Lukas. Transition to Estonian-language education will definitely happen.https://www.hm.ee/en/news/minister-tonis-lukas-transition-estonian-language-education-will-definitely-happen.

European Commission. National reforms in general school education. https://eurydice.eacea.ec.europa.eu/national-education-systems/estonia/national-reforms-general-school-education.

Salum, M.: Tallinn's Estonian-language schools seeing more and more Russian-speaking kids, ERR, https://news.err.ee/1609431352/tallinn-s-estonian-language-schools-seeing-more-and-more-russian-speaking-kids.

OHCHR Press release. The experts: Mr. Fernand de Varennes, Special Rapporteur on minority issues; Ms. Alexandra Xanthaki, Special Rapporteur in the field of cultural rights, and Ms. Farida Shaheed, Special Rapporteur on education. Estonia: New law banning mother-tongue education for minorities may violate human rights, warn UN experts. https://www.ohchr.org/en/press-releases/2023/08/estonia-new-law-banning-mother-tongue-education-minorities-may-violate-human.

References

Books and Articles

Cilevičs B (2015) Language policies in Latvia: lessons for minority protection. In: Kuzborska E (ed) Integration and exclusion. Language. Rights of National Minorities in Europe. Artprint

Dudzińska K (2012) (Nie)rozwiązany problem mniejszości narodowych w państwach bałtyckich. Biuletyn PISM, No 30(895)

Kuzborska E (2014) Reforma oświaty mniejszości narodowych na Litwie w 2011 r. w świetle międzynarodowych standardów ochrony. Rocznik Stowarzyszenia Naukowców Polaków Litwy 13(14):68–81

Kuzborska-Pacha E (2019) Ochrona prawna mniejszości narodowych w państwach bałtyckich. Wydawnictwo Sejmowe
Merkys G, Balčiūnas S, Balžekienė A, Lapienienė A, Pauliukaitė Z, Telešienė A (2006) Ministry of Education of the Republic of Lithuania. Research report
Muižnieks N, Rozenvalds J, Birka I (2013) Ethnicity and social cohesion in the post-Soviet Baltic states. Patterns Prejudice 47(3):288–308. https://doi.org/10.1080/0031322X.2013.812349
Skutnabb-Kangas T (2004) The right to mother tongue medium education – the hot potato in human rights instruments. II Mercator International Symposium: Europe 2004: A new framework for all languages?
UNESCO (2003) Education in a Multilingual World. ED.2003/WS/2

Jolanta Apolewicz is a researcher at the Law Institute of the Lithuanian Centre for Social Sciences. She has received PhD degree from Vilnius University, Lithuania. Her research interests include public international, environmental and human rights law. Dr Apolewicz has extensive experience working in international teams and conducting comparative research (which results were published by Routledge, Springer and Brill). Also, she taught international law at Vilnius University for a number of years and is now a vice-dean of the School of Law of Mykolas Romeris University.

Elżbieta Kuzborska-Pacha is an international expert on human rights. She has experience working as a Senior Minorities Fellow at the OHCHR. Dr Elżbieta Kuzborska-Pacha has cooperated with different NGOs where she provided legal training. Currently, Dr Kuzborska-Pacha is a professor of law at Gdansk University.

Challenges to the Protection of the Child's Right to Health

Edita Žiobienė

Health is not everything; but without health, everything is nothing.—Arthur Schopenhauer

Abstract This chapter examines the challenges involved in realising the child's right to health, with a particular focus on Central and Eastern European (CEE) countries, and Lithuania. The realisation of the right to health entails not only effective access to high-quality health services guaranteed by law, but also the assurance that the child receives healthcare that is in his or her best interests. According to national constitutions and the United Nations Convention on the Rights of the Child, parents bear the primary responsibility for the upbringing of their child and are expected to fulfil this responsibility in good faith. This chapter explores the limits of parental rights, the tensions, and the necessity of striking a fair balance between the interests of parents and children, as well as the balance between the right to privacy, autonomy and the right to information, through an analysis of academic commentary and the jurisprudence of the European Court of Human Rights. It also examines the legal requirements for informed consent in relation to medical examination, treatment, vaccination, and biomedical research, with particular emphasis on the importance of involving the child in the decision-making process, thereby enhancing the child's competencies and medical literacy.

E. Žiobienė (✉)
Law School, Mykolas Romeris University, Ombudsperson for Child's Rights of Lithuania, Vilnius, Lithuania
e-mail: ziobiene@mruni.eu

A. Limantė, R. Vaičiūnienė (eds.), *Children's Rights in Central and Eastern Europe*, European Union and its Neighbours in a Globalized World 29,
https://doi.org/10.1007/978-3-032-07092-0_20

1 Introduction

The fundamental right to health is recognised in several international human rights instruments (such as the Universal Declaration of Human Rights and the International Covenant on Economic, Social and Cultural Rights[1]), regional instruments (including the European Social Charter and the European Convention on Human Rights[2]), as well as national constitutions and other domestic laws. Every human being is entitled to the enjoyment of the highest attainable standard of health, enabling them to live a life of dignity.[3] The United Nations Convention on the Rights of the Child (CRC), the most widely ratified human rights treaty in the world, enshrines the child's right to health under Article 24. Furthermore, under Article 3 of the CRC, the principle of the best interests of the child constitutes a fundamental element and a primary consideration in all matters affecting the child, including those concerning the child's health.

Children and young people represent approximately 25 per cent of the European population. According to Eurostat, more than 95% of children in the European Union are reported to be in good or very good health, whilst 3.6% of children are identified as having unmet medical needs.[4] The comprehensive care of children's health requires specific and specialised expertise. Children deserve medical care of the highest professional standard, based on thorough and robust training combined with comprehensive continuing education (Dornbusch et al. 2024).

The right to health may be understood in a broad sense, encompassing all factors that can influence a healthy childhood. Significant adverse childhood experiences—such as parental divorce, illness or death of a close relative, violence, neglect, or bullying—have detrimental and long-lasting effects on a child's development, as well as on their physical and mental well-being. Both external and internal factors, including air quality, neighbourhood noise, sedentary lifestyles, sleeping and eating habits, and screen time, can negatively affect children's health. Estimated rates of overweight or obese children in Europe vary from approximately 20 to 25% in Estonia, Latvia, and Lithuania, to around 40% in Cyprus and Greece, with predictions indicating a continued rise (UNICEF 2024). Childhood obesity gives rise to significant health issues, including high blood pressure, diabetes, asthma, and is also linked to poor emotional well-being. Researchers assert that children are often targeted by commercial entities promoting unhealthy or low-nutritional-value foods, as well as alcohol, tobacco, and nicotine-containing products—all of which

[1] The Universal Declaration of Human Rights and the International Covenant on Economic, Social and Cultural Rights. Adopted and opened for signature, ratification and accession by General Assembly resolution 2200A (XXI) of 16 December 1966, entry into force 3 January 1976, in accordance with article 27.

[2] The European Social Charter and the European Convention on Human Rights, adopted 18 October 1961, and the Revised Charter, adopted in 1996.

[3] General Comment No. 14 (2000), the right to the highest attainable standard of health (Article 12 of the International Covenant on Economic, Social and Cultural Rights). E/C.12/2000/4.

[4] European Commission. Eurostat. See: https://ec.europa.eu/eurostat/web/products-eurostat-news.

are major contributors to non-communicable diseases that lead to childhood obesity and overweight, with long-lasting effects across the lifespan (Clark et al. 2020, pp. 605–658). In light of these concerns, a new Optional Protocol to the UN Convention on the Rights of the Child has been proposed (De Dominicis and Kluge 2025, pp. 377–378).

This chapter focuses on the narrow interpretation of the right to health, as enshrined in Article 24 of the Convention on the Rights of the Child (CRC): specifically, how a child's right to the highest attainable standard of health, and access to facilities for the treatment of illness and the rehabilitation of health, is guaranteed. However, it is important to acknowledge that all provisions and principles of the CRC are interrelated, and the content of the child's right to health cannot be fully understood without considering the principle of ensuring the best interests of the child, equal opportunities, and the meaningful participation of the child in decision-making processes, among other factors. Effective access to healthcare fundamentally impacts the quality of life, not only for individuals but also for society as a whole. Yet, healthcare services are typically designed with adults in mind, often adhering strictly to the requirement that services for children be provided only with the informed consent of their parents. This emphasis on rapid, high-quality treatment, vaccinations, or health screenings sometimes results in a lack of attention to whether the child's voice is heard. Can a medical service truly be considered high-quality if the patient is not given the opportunity to discuss their well-being or voice concerns?

This chapter examines the limitations of parental consent and the child's participation in decisions regarding their health, alongside the adolescent's trust, respect for their privacy or autonomy, and the parental right to be involved in sensitive decisions, such as those concerning physical or mental health. It further analyses the provision of essential child health services when the child's parents are unavailable, unable, or unwilling to provide consent. It also addresses situations where a parent refuses to consent to a specific treatment, exploring whether such a decision can be overridden by a court if the treatment is deemed to be in the child's best interests. The impact of misinformation regarding the negative effects of treatment and vaccination, particularly on social media, will also be explored.

2 The Child-Centred Care and the Role of Parents

An increasing understanding and respect for children's rights has led to notable changes in the healthcare sector. Approaches such as patient-centred and family-centred care have evolved, and their principles have now been adapted into the concept of child-centred care. This concept places the child's interests at the core of healthcare practices (Ford et al. 2018a, pp. 845–851) providing a holistic view of the child that transcends merely their illness or condition (Ford et al. 2018b, pp. e39–e43). It also requires that the child be included as an active participant in their own healthcare process and decision-making.

There are significant variations across European countries in how doctors, who provide care for children, specialise and approach child health. The healthcare system is characterised by three primary models: paediatric care, a mixed model combining paediatricians and family physicians, and family physician care alone (Burokiene et al. 2022, pp. 435–442). Hoey argues that the most effective approach in paediatric healthcare is one that harmonises primary, secondary, and tertiary care, thereby ensuring the provision of comprehensive health services for children and adolescents. However, many European countries have either reduced or eliminated primary care paediatrics, prioritising budgetary constraints over the provision of quality healthcare for children, which should be supported by appropriately trained professionals (Hoey et al. 2021, pp. 732–733). The number of primary care paediatricians in Europe is steadily declining, and in one-third of European countries, children and adolescents receive care exclusively from general practitioners, whose level of training and experience with this age group can vary significantly (Dornbusch et al. 2024). The Lithuanian healthcare model is mixed: the number of primary care paediatricians in clinical practice is declining, while health policy increasingly favours family physicians. This model allows parents the right to choose their healthcare provider, yet research indicates that parents tend to place greater trust in paediatricians (Burokiene et al. 2022, pp. 435–442). Researchers state that paediatrics continues to be something of a "Cinderella" speciality, while incomparably larger research resources are devoted to adult diseases, debilitating but less remarkable disorders such as obesity, constipation in children receive less research funding (Stephenson 2024).

The European Court of Human Rights (ECtHR) has asserted that healthcare policy falls within the margin of appreciation of domestic authorities, who are best positioned to assess national priorities, resource allocation, and social needs (ECtHR, *Hristozov and Others v. Bulgaria*, § 119[5]). However, a child's health is influenced not only by the doctor's specialisation and competence but also by economic factors, family traditions, culture, beliefs, and parental responsibility.

In Lithuania,[6] as well as in other European countries such as Ireland, Bulgaria, the Netherlands, Poland, and Croatia, the healthcare system operates on the principle that parents must consent to the health examination and treatment of their child until the child reaches the age of 16. The age at which consent becomes the child's responsibility varies across European countries, ranging from 12 to 18 years. Medical professionals have both a moral and legal obligation to first inform parents about proposed medical procedures, treatments, or interventions, disclose any potential diagnoses, risks, or complications, and obtain informed consent. Thus, appropriate decisional capacity and legal empowerment are key determinants of authority in medical decision-making (Katz et al. 2016). As legal representatives of their children, parents are the primary decision-makers, which is logical given their

[5] *Hristozov and Others v. Bulgaria*, Nos. 47039/11 and 358/12, 29 April 2013.

[6] LR Pacientų teisių ir žalos sveikatai atlyginimo įstatymas [Law on the Rights of Patients and Compensation of the Damage to their Health]. 2009-11-19, No. XI-499. Art. 14.

deep concern for their child's welfare and their specific knowledge of the child's unique needs. The ECtHR found a violation of the child's right to physical integrity under Article 8 when doctors provided medical services, such as blood tests, without parental consent (*M.A.K. and R.K. v. the United Kingdom*, 2010). In most cases, parents are deeply concerned about their child's health, seeking the best available medical care and adhering to routine medical advice.

However, in more serious medical situations, parents may face challenges in making informed decisions, due to a lack of knowledge or fear when confronted with the doctor's proposed treatment plan for their child. This raises an important moral question: What does informed consent truly entail? While some parents may place their trust in the doctor and accept the recommended treatment, others may seek second opinions or turn to social media for alternative advice. Many parents may prefer to share—or even transfer—the responsibility for decision-making to the doctor. Nevertheless, parents are expected to exercise their parental responsibility and make decisions that prioritise the best interests of the child.

In many countries, constitutional provisions grant parents the right to raise their children in accordance with their values, including their religious and moral beliefs. However, this right, while fundamental, is not absolute. National courts in various European countries, as well as the European Court of Human Rights (ECtHR),[7] have examined cases in which children's rights were potentially violated due to parental refusal of medical treatment on religious grounds, such as the refusal of blood transfusions or surgery. In all of these cases, the jurisprudence has sought to strike a fair balance between protecting the child's best interests and upholding parental rights, including other fundamental rights such as autonomy, privacy, and freedom of religion. Children's interests do not always align with those of their parents, and there may be inherent contradictions between parental interests and the child's best interests.

In cases where parents are unwilling to trust the treatment plan or method proposed by the doctor, they may seek alternative or additional information. The Internet and social media have become powerful forces in society, where parents may find information from groups that reject evidence-based medicine, promote unconventional treatments, or endorse anti-vaccine movements, among other things (Kollataj et al. 2020, pp. 553–561). Therefore, it is crucial to establish trust between the doctor and the parents, as a lack of trust could result in harm to the child.

In Lithuania, a doctor has several options when assessing whether a parent's refusal to provide medical treatment to a child poses a risk to the child's health or life. The mildest course of action would be to contact the State Child Rights Protection and Adoption Service under the Ministry of Social Security and Labour, requesting their mediation to persuade the parents of the necessity of the treatment. Another option is to consult a medical consilium to determine whether the child requires treatment and subsequently bring the case before the court. According to

[7] *Jehovah's Witnesses of Moscow and Others V. Russia*, No. 302/02, 22 November 2010; *Hoffmann v. Austria*, No. 12875/87, 16 January 1992.

the Civil Code[8] (Art. 3.163 (3)), if a conflict of interests arises between the child's parents, between the parents and the child, or between the healthcare institution and the parents, the court may, either ex officio or at the request of either parent or the state authority responsible for the protection of the rights of the child, appoint an ad hoc guardian to represent the child in resolving the specific dispute. In such cases, only the parents' right to make decisions regarding the child's health is limited, while all other parental rights and obligations remain intact. Although this provision of the Civil Code has been in force since 2016, it has not yet been applied by Lithuanian courts in the domain of child health.

National courts and the ECtHR typically examine whether all procedural requirements have been met, including obtaining informed consent (a process that applies to both the acceptance and refusal of treatment). (*Glass v. the United Kingdom, 2004*). The European Court of Human Rights (ECtHR) has on numerous occasions, examined the manner in which domestic authorities intervene in situations where families are in conflict, often in cases concerning care and custody arrangements. In such instances, the Court has consistently emphasised that the decisive issue is whether a fair balance has been struck between the competing interests at stake—those of the child, the two parents, and public order—within the margin of appreciation afforded to States in such matters, while underscoring that the best interests of the child must always be the primary consideration.[9] The assessment of a child's best interests involves a thorough evaluation and balancing of all the relevant factors necessary to make an informed decision in a particular case, in accordance with formal processes that are governed by strict procedural safeguards designed to ensure the child's best interests are determined (CRC, GC, No.14, 2013, § 47). One of the most critical elements of the principle of the best interests of the child is the opportunity for the child to participate in the decision-making process.

3 Participation of Children in the Decision-Making Process and Their Autonomous Decision

In discussions concerning children's opportunities to exercise their rights, it must first be acknowledged that every child should be treated as an active participant. Although it is often easier for a doctor to briefly inform a parent about a necessary procedure—such as a blood test, vaccination, or treatment—paediatricians should also be proficient in explaining such interventions to the child in a manner that is age-appropriate and easily understandable. For children (and adolescents) to be able

[8] LR Civilinis kodeksas [Civil Code], *Official Gazette,* 2000, No. 74 as amended.

[9] See: *X v. Latvia* [GC], No. 27853/09, § 95, 2013; *Paradiso and Campanelli v. Italy* [GC], no. 25358/12, § 208, 2017; *Dubská and Krejzová v. the Czech Republic* [GC], Nos. 28859/11 and 28473/12, § 74, 2016; *Mandet v. France*, No. 30955/12, §§ 53-55, 2016; *Korneykova and Korneykov v. Ukraine*, No. 56660/12, § 129-130, 2016; *N.Ts. and Others v. Georgia*, No. 71776/12, §§ 81-83, 2016.

to safely and effectively exercise their rights, it is essential that parents, as well as other adults involved in their care, establish an environment grounded in trust, information-sharing, attentive listening, and sound guidance, which facilitates adolescents' full participation, including in decision-making processes (CRC, GC, No. 4, 2003, § 4). Typically, children appreciate the opportunity to build relationships with different professionals. Positive experiences foster trust and confidence, thereby laying the groundwork for more complex and meaningful conversations. Adolescents value care providers who demonstrate technical competence, trustworthiness, attentiveness to their needs, and the ability to communicate in an age-appropriate manner (Koller et al. 2024, pp. 1–12).

Article 12 of the UN Convention on the Rights of the Child (CRC) redefines the role of the child: every child who is capable of forming their own views must be given the opportunity to express those views freely on all matters affecting them. The possibility for children to participate in decision-making processes concerning their lives is considered one of the most significant achievements of the CRC. However, some critics argue that Article 12 inadvertently grants adults the power to determine whether, and to what extent, a child's voice should be considered, enabling adults to label children as immature and, consequently, to silence them (Peleg 2023, pp. 7–12). This criticism highlights the need for adults who are committed to creating structures that facilitate children's participation in the first place (Lundy 2007, pp. 927–942).

The child's active participation in dialogue with health professionals and in the decision-making process has a profoundly positive impact on the parent-child relationship: understanding and strengthening relationships, particularly during adolescence, is essential for fostering trust and communication. Given that children are in a constant state of growth and development, it is crucial to recognise that today's investment in building their relationship with health professionals, alongside enhancing their health literacy, will yield long-term benefits for future patients. The UN Committee on the Rights of the Child asserts that parents should provide guidance and direction to their adolescent children in the exercise of their rights; parents are obliged to consider their adolescents' views, in accordance with their age and maturity, and to create a safe and supportive environment conducive to the adolescent's development (CRC, GC, No. 4, 2003, § 7).

In Lithuania, the child's right to participate in decision-making is explicitly outlined in the Constitution of Lithuania, the CRC, the Civil Code, the Framework Law on the Protection of the Rights of the Child,[10] and the Law on the Rights of Patients and Compensation of the Damage to their Health.[11] However, the key area of contention lies in determining when children are capable of providing sole consent. Article 5 of the CRC introduces the principle of evolving capacities, which allows children the space to exercise their autonomy and rights in accordance with their

[10] LR Vaiko teisių apsaugos pagrindų įstatymas [the Framework law on the protection of the rights of the child], Nr. XIII-643, 2017-09-28, TAR 2017-16087.

[11] LR Pacientų teisių ir žalos sveikatai atlyginimo įstatymas [Law on the Rights of Patients and Compensation of the Damage to their Health], 2009-11-19, No. XI-499.

evolving capacities, as assessed by adults. As previously noted, the majority of European countries have set legal limits on the age of consent, with variations ranging from 12 to 18 years across different nations. In Latvia, however, the lowest minimum age for children's autonomous consent to medical treatment has been established within the EU.[12] Research indicates that a child's decision-making capacity is influenced not only by their age but also by their maturity, cognitive ability, and the duration of any illness. Children with long-term conditions, for instance, often demonstrate greater maturity (Alderson et al. 2006).

In Lithuania, the law stipulates that healthcare services for patients aged 16 and over are provided only with their consent. However, the law includes an exception for minors under the age of 16, who, in the doctor's professional opinion, are capable of making their own decisions regarding their health. Such minors have the right to seek and independently decide on the healthcare services they require, except in cases specifically outlined by law. Thus, the law not only sets age limits but also allows for the assessment of a minor's maturity.

Conflicts arise when a child and their parent hold differing views, with the adolescent exercising the right to access healthcare services independently, or conversely, when an adolescent seeks to override parental consent. The adolescent period is characterised by rapid physical, cognitive, and social changes, alongside the acquisition of new responsibilities. However, the lack of social maturity and life experience can make adolescents more vulnerable and susceptible to persuasion. As a result, adolescents may make impulsive and spontaneous decisions with potentially long-lasting negative consequences, particularly when these decisions relate to mental health (such as eating disorders, anxiety, or depression), reproductive health (such as abortion or contraceptive use), or the treatment of complex diseases.

Various movements—including anti-vaccine campaigns, pro-anorexia (pro-ana) groups, pro-suicide websites, and forums promoting dangerous eating practices—as well as communities rejecting evidence-based medicine in favour of new or traditional unconventional treatments (Kollataj et al. 2020, pp. 553–561)), found online, can exert a detrimental influence on adolescents' health-related decision-making. In such cases, where legal conflicts arise between an adolescent and their parent, the resolution must be a well-considered decision that prioritises the best interests of the child or adolescent. As previously mentioned, in these instances, an *ad hoc* guardian may be appointed, or 'soft' interventions, such as psychological services or mediation, may be employed.

---

[12] FRA Consenting to medical treatment without parental consent (2017). Available online: http://fra.europa.eu/en/publication/2017/mapping-minimum-age-requirements-concerning-rights-child-eu/consenting-medical-treatment-without-parental-consent.

4 Protection of Children's Health Through Routine Immunisation

The introduction of routine childhood immunisation represents one of the most significant public health achievements, both in terms of saving lives and promoting overall health. Immunisation is not only highly effective during childhood but continues to offer protection throughout an individual's life. It is estimated that vaccines have saved 154 million lives globally since 1974, which equates to approximately six lives saved every minute; of these lives, 95% were children under the age of five (Shattock et al. 2024, pp. 2307–2316). Research substantiates the direct benefits of childhood vaccination in reducing the spread of vaccine-preventable diseases, minimising the costs of treating these diseases and their potential complications. Furthermore, vaccines are associated with indirect benefits, such as enhanced cognitive development and academic performance, ultimately contributing to long-term economic productivity (Nandi and Shet 2020, pp. 1900–1904). Many vaccines provide dual protection: they reduce the risk to the vaccinated individual and lower the transmission and exposure to infectious diseases within the wider community. As the European Court of Human Rights (ECtHR) has noted in its jurisprudence, vaccination is one of the most successful and cost-effective public health interventions. The Court further emphasises that each state should aim to achieve the highest possible level of vaccination coverage among its population, while recognising that healthcare policy matters fall within the margin of appreciation of national authorities (ECtHR, *Vavricka and other v. the Czech Republic,* 2021). According to the WHO,[13] achieving 95% vaccination coverage is necessary to establish herd immunity and prevent the community transmission of highly contagious and life-threatening diseases.

International instruments, such as the CRC, the International Covenant on Economic, Social and Cultural Rights, and the European Social Charter, impose a positive obligation on states. This obligation not only prohibits interference with private and family life but also requires states to implement a legal framework that ensures a substantial proportion of the population is vaccinated, thereby safeguarding the life and well-being of society at large from health risks. In principle, legislators are presented with three primary options: recommendation, requirement, and coercion. Thus, legislators must carefully consider which of these options would have the most significant and effective impact within the specific context of their society.

[13] https://www.who.int/europe/teams/vaccine-preventable-diseases-immunization/vaccine-preventable-disease-surveillance-data.

4.1 *The Right to Choose Vaccination*

Vaccine uptake has declined in European countries, including those in Central and Eastern Europe (CEE), partly due to growing criticism of vaccination, with arguments against vaccination contributing to widespread distrust in scientific evidence. Research on vaccine confidence indicates that trust in vaccines remains relatively low across Europe when compared to other continents, with populations in Eastern European countries expressing heightened concerns regarding the safety and efficacy of vaccines (De Figueiredo et al. 2020, pp. 898–908).

The legal framework for vaccination in Lithuania can be viewed as a relatively liberal model of regulation. There was initially an expectation that, with adequate information provided directly by healthcare professionals, voluntary vaccination schemes would be sufficient to ensure widespread vaccination and achieve herd immunity. The Minister of Health has adopted the Calendar of Prophylactic Vaccinations for Children,[14] which outlines the organisation of preventive vaccinations and ensures that all 10 childhood vaccines are administered free of charge. Historically, Lithuania has maintained high childhood vaccination coverage; however, recent trends show a decline: vaccination coverage for tuberculosis has fallen from 97.3% in 2017 to 93.2% in 2023, and vaccination rates for measles, rubella, whooping cough, and other diseases have dropped from 93.5% in 2017 to 87.1% in 2023.[15]

In contrast, Poland has maintained a mandatory vaccination scheme since the 1960s, and under Polish law,[16] failure to comply with the vaccine mandate incurs administrative penalties (Reczulska et al. 2022, p. 811). Between 2006 and 2010, approximately 4000 individuals annually refused vaccinations in Poland; this number increased from around 5000 to over 16,000 between 2011 and 2015, reaching nearly 24,000 in 2016. Researchers note that the decline in vaccination rates can be attributed to the influence of the anti-vaccine movement, which advocates for the abolition of mandatory vaccination in Poland (Żuk et al. 2019, pp. 1491–1494).

In Lithuania, according to the law,[17] healthcare services, including vaccination, for minors under the age of 16 are provided only with the consent of their representatives (one of the parents or caregivers). For patients aged 16 and over, healthcare services are provided only with their explicit consent. Parental decision-making regarding vaccination is a complex issue, and the quality of informed consent is often influenced by the information provided, the trust between the doctor and the parent, and other contextual factors. Typically, parents are informed primarily about

---

[14] LR Sveikatos apsaugos ministro įsakymas. Dėl Lietuvos Respublikos vaikų profilaktinių skiepijimų kalendoriaus patvirtinimo. 2018, No. V-955.

[15] Official Statistics Portal. Children immunization coverage. https://osp.stat.gov.lt/statistiniu-rodikliu-analize?hash=d76ac373-3dd0-43c8-8459-686266ad54eb#/.

[16] Law on enforcement proceedings in administration. 17 June 1966. Article 119 (1).

[17] Law on the Rights of Patients and Compensation of the Damage to their Health. 2009-11-19, No. XI-499.

the benefits of vaccination. However, to foster trust and transparency, and to avoid any potential fears or misconceptions, doctors should ensure that both the benefits and potential risks of vaccination are clearly explained. This should include outlining the advantages for both the child and public health, as well as providing accurate information regarding the likelihood of adverse effects and potential complications. Explanations should be based on empirical data, such as statistical figures, and should emphasise that the risks associated with vaccination are exceedingly small in comparison to the benefits (Roush et al. 2007, pp. 2155–2163). Parents should be encouraged to voice any concerns or misconceptions they may have and to ask questions freely. The knowledge, attitudes, and beliefs of medical professionals regarding vaccination are shaped by broader organisational, political, cultural, and historical factors. Many of the concerns raised by parents are rooted in misinformation and disinformation circulating on the internet or through social media, which often discredit vaccines by propagating debunked medical claims and conspiracies (Čaplinskas 2016, pp. 536–548).

4.2 *Mandatory Vaccination and the Restriction of Rights*

In an effort to achieve target immunisation coverage rates, several European countries, such as France,[18] Italy[19] have adopted mandatory vaccination policies and introduced penalty-based measures. The constitutionality of these restrictions on human rights has been scrutinised by the respective Constitutional Courts in these jurisdictions.[20] These courts also examined whether the legal measures introduced met the proportionality test. In all cases, it is essential to recognise that, should the legislator opt to implement mandatory vaccination for children, this would restrict parental autonomy in decisions regarding their child's health. This raises the pertinent question of how the best interests of the child should be evaluated. Who holds the authority to determine how a child's rights are protected—the authorities or the parents? Furthermore, it is the responsibility of the authorities to ensure that, in the case of mandatory vaccination, the best interests of the child are safeguarded by ensuring access to the highest attainable standard of health. To assess whether such interference is legitimate, it is necessary to determine whether it is in accordance with the law, whether it pursues one or more legitimate aims set forth by the law, and whether it is deemed necessary in a democratic society. The European Court of

[18] Legifrance Décret No. 2018-42 du 25 Janvier 2018 Relatif à la Vaccination Obligatoire. 2018 Available online: https://www.legifrance.gouv.fr/jorf/id/JORFTEXT000036543886.

[19] Luglio 2017, n. 119. Conversione in Legge, con Modificazioni, del Decreto-Legge 7 Giugno 2017, n. 73, Recante Disposizioni Urgenti in Materia di Prevenzione Vaccinale. (17G00132). GU Serie Generale n. 182 del 05-08-2017. Available online: http://www.gazzettaufficiale.it/eli/id/2017/08/5/17G00132.

[20] Conseil Constitutionnel, Decision No. 2015-458 QPC, Epoux L. (Mar. 20, 2015); Corte Constituzionale, No. 5/2018, 24 January 2018.

Human Rights (ECtHR) has established through its case law that compulsory vaccination, as an involuntary medical intervention, constitutes an interference with the right to respect for private life under Article 8 of the European Convention on Human Rights (ECHR).[21]

In 2021, the ECtHR made a landmark ruling on the mandatory vaccination[22] in the case of *Vavricka and others v. the Czech Republic*.[23] This ruling is of great significance, not only for the Czech Republic, but also for other European countries contemplating the introduction of mandatory vaccination, as it provides guidance on how to achieve a fair balance between values and the proportionality of restrictions or penalties. Within certain margins, this judgment condones mandatory vaccination policies and paves the way for the adoption of similar policies (Toebes 2022, pp. 856–924). The judgment stresses that, in all decisions concerning children, their best interests must take precedence. It further stipulated that, in the context of necessary childhood vaccination, the interests of the child supersede the parental right to refuse vaccination. The ECtHR also assessed the strict proportionality and legitimate aim of the state's measures, which were deemed necessary in a democratic society due to the "compelling social need" for such interventions. The ECtHR also examined the proportionality of fines imposed on parents who refuse to allow their children to be vaccinated and the legal prohibition on the admission of unvaccinated children to preschool. The Court emphasised that these measures were preventive rather than punitive and noted that they were time-limited. Additionally, it observed that the child's vaccination status did not affect their right to attend primary school once they reached the age of mandatory school attendance.

The Constitutional Courts of various European countries are likely to follow this ECtHR jurisprudence when evaluating the proportionality of national mandatory vaccination measures, should such cases arise. In addition to the Czech authorities, several other European countries have implemented restrictions on the admission of unvaccinated children to educational institutions, recognising that such settings are particularly conducive to the spread of infectious diseases among children and educators. In Italy since 2017,[24] as well as in Latvia since 2000,[25] mandatory vaccination for school-age children was introduced for 10 vaccines. In Ukraine, as of 2019, the law stipulates that children who have not been vaccinated according to the national immunisation schedule are prohibited from attending educational

[21] See: Solomakhin v. Ukraine, No. 24429/03, § 33, 2012; Boffa and others v. San Marino, § 35.

[22] https://strasbourgobservers.com/2021/06/02/anti-vaxxers-before-the-strasbourg-court-vavricka-and-others-v-the-czech-republic/.

[23] *Vavricka and others v. the Czech Republic,* No. 47621/13, 8 April 2021.

[24] Luglio 2017, n. 119. Conversione in Legge, con Modificazioni, del Decreto-Legge 7 Giugno 2017, No. 73, Recante Disposizioni Urgenti in Materia di Prevenzione Vaccinale. (17G00132). GU Serie Generale n. 182 del 05-08-2017. Available online: http://www.gazzettaufficiale.it/eli/id/2017/08/5/17G00132.

[25] Vaccination Regulations, No. 330, adopted 26 September 2000. Available online: https://likumi.lv/wwwraksti/VVC_TULKOJUMI/LRTA/MK_...

institutions.[26] Since 2020, Germany has enacted federal law requiring all children from the age of one to provide proof of measles vaccination prior to enrolling in kindergarten.[27]

In Lithuania, the authorities attempted to prevent unvaccinated children from attending pre-school and pre-primary education institutions; however, this regulation was annulled by the Supreme Administrative Court.[28] The regulation in question, issued by the Minister of Health, stipulated that a child whose health certificate indicated non-compliance with the national vaccination schedule—specifically regarding measles, rubella, and poliomyelitis—would not be admitted to pre-school or pre-primary education, provided there were no medical contraindications to vaccination. Upon reviewing the regulation, the Supreme Administrative Court emphasised that the scope of an individual's right to physical integrity, as a component of their right to private life, cannot be restricted by subordinate legislative acts. Any limitation of this right must be founded on statutory grounds and procedures and must pursue a legitimate and necessary aim in a democratic society. In this case, the Court reiterated that sub-legislative acts cannot substitute for law nor impose new restrictions on personal rights.

As the analysis reveals, the justification for mandatory vaccination policies must be grounded in the necessity of such measures within a democratic society, as prescribed by law, and must be scrutinised to determine whether mandatory vaccination is the most effective means of achieving higher vaccination coverage. The authorities must undertake measures to restore public confidence and enhance vaccination rates, thereby safeguarding herd immunity and ensuring the individual protection of every child. In addition, comprehensive compensation systems should be established, alongside real-time surveillance platforms to monitor vaccine side effects and ensure vaccine safety (Savulescu et al. 2021, pp. 10–16), Moreover, the trustworthiness of the information source is a critical factor in strengthening the efficacy of vaccination policies.

5 Children's Participation in Biomedical Research

A fundamental aspect of modern medicine is the ongoing advancement of treatment methods and diagnostic tools. Biomedical research, epidemiological studies, and healthcare research have all played pivotal roles in the progression of healthcare, benefiting children in diverse ways and enabling those with rare diseases, chronic conditions, and disabilities to live longer, healthier lives (Zillén 2023, pp. 108–120).

[26] Law of Ukraine on Protecting the Population from Infectious Diseases. No. 1645-III, 6 April 2000.

[27] Gesetz für den Schutz vor Masern und zur Stärkung der Impfprävention vom 20.02.2020, BGBl. I 2020, 148.

[28] The Supreme Administrative Court. Administrative Case No. I-6-662/2016, 5 July 2016.

However, the divergent objectives of treatment and research create a significant moral and legal distinction between the two. The enrolment of children in health research must be approached with utmost caution, adhering to international instruments such as the United Nations Educational, Scientific and Cultural Organization's Universal Declaration on Bioethics and Human Rights,[29] the Declaration of Helsinki,[30] the Convention on Human Rights and Biomedicine (Oviedo Convention),[31] European Union law,[32] and domestic legal frameworks.

One of the core ethical principles in biomedical research is informed consent. It is the duty of the investigator to ensure that both the parents and the child are fully informed of all relevant details, including an explanation that the risks associated with the experimental nature of the research procedures may be heightened, and that the outcomes may be unknown or untested. The parents and the child must clearly understand that they are being asked to participate and must provide explicit consent for the research.

In Lithuania, the Law on Biomedical Research Ethics[33] is particularly stringent in safeguarding the interests of children in research. It stipulates that information must be conveyed to the child in a manner appropriate to their age and capacity for understanding. Should a child express a desire not to participate in biomedical research or wish to withdraw, their participation in the study must not be initiated or continued, unless such a decision would conflict with the child's best interests. In cases where a conflict of interest arises between the child and their parents, the decision regarding the child's participation in biomedical research must be made in accordance with the procedure outlined in Article 3.163 of the Civil Code, which permits the appointment of an ad hoc guardian by the court.

For several years, a debate has persisted among politicians, scientists, and children's rights experts regarding the lowering of the requirements for informed

[29] Universal Declaration on Bioethics and Human Rights, adopted by the United Nations Educational, Scientific and Cultural Organization 20 October 2005.

[30] The Declaration of Helsinki is the World Medical Association's (WMA) best-known policy statement. The first version was adopted in 1964 and has been amended seven times since, most recently at the General Assembly in October 2024.

[31] Convention on Human Rights and Biomedicine (ETS No 164) was opened for signature on 4 April 1997 in Oviedo (Spain), entered into force 1 December 1999. It sets out fundamental principles applicable to daily medical practice and is regarded as such at the European treaty on patient's rights. It also deals specifically with biomedical research, genetics and transplantation of organ and tissues.

[32] In the European Union, Regulation (EU) No 536/2014 of the European Parliament and of the Council, which governs clinical trials on medicinal products for human use and repealing Directive 2001/20/EC, mandates that investigators must respect the explicit wishes of a minor who may express their opinion and assessment of relevant information, particularly regarding participation in clinical trials. This includes the right to refuse participation or withdraw from a clinical trial at any time.

[33] LR biomedicininių tyrimų etikos įstatymas [the Law on Biomedical Research Ethics], Nr. XII-1938, TAR 2015-09-25, i. k. 2015-14272.

consent in research.[34] The Law on Biomedical Research stipulates that consent must be obtained from both parents of the child, whereas for medical treatment, the consent of only one parent is required. However, after extensive deliberation, it was decided to uphold the higher level of protection for the child's rights, meaning that consent from both parents is necessary for participation in research. This ensures that both parents fully understand and evaluate the risks involved in the research and, in the case of clinical trials, comprehend the distinction between treatment and research.

6 Concluding Remarks

The right to the highest attainable standard of health is enshrined in both international and national legal instruments; however, the practical implementation of this right remains a subject of ongoing legal disputes. Parents (or guardians), as the child's legal representatives, bear primary responsibility for making decisions on all matters concerning the child, including healthcare. Nevertheless, the parental right and responsibility to consent to healthcare services for their child are not absolute. In Lithuania, as in other European countries, the government, in accordance with its international obligations and guided by the judgments of the European Court of Human Rights (ECtHR), seeks to ensure that the principle of the best interests of the child is upheld in all matters concerning the child's health. The flexible nature of the concept of the child's best interests enables decision-makers—doctors, parents, and, to a certain extent, the child—to determine the most appropriate course of action, whether it pertains to treatment, vaccination, or participation in biomedical research or clinical trials.

The importance of involving children in the decision-making process should be acknowledged, as it is crucial not only for the child's individual development (e.g., fostering their capacity and acquiring new competencies) but also for the broader society (e.g., promoting investment in health literacy). Professionals should ensure that all necessary information is conveyed to the child in a manner appropriate to their age and maturity, taking the time to engage in meaningful conversation and provide clear explanations. As public scepticism regarding medical treatment plans persists and individuals often seek alternative sources of information that may not be scientifically grounded, the importance of health literacy has never been greater.

[34] Conclusions of the Health Committee of the Parliament of Lithuania. This document presents the different positions of state institutions, scientists, and experts. Available online: https://e-seimas.lrs.lt/rs/legalact/TAK/c3c067501afe11e585eaba374ef4b409/; Ombudsperson's suggestions available online: http://vtaki.lt/uploads/documents/files/teisine-informacija/vaiko-teisiu-padeties-vertinimas/siulymai/27.pdf; article in media: https://www.bernardinai.lt/2015-09-28-k-zamaryte-sakaviciene-biomedicinos-tyrimu-etikos-istatymas-turi-etikai-priestaraujanciu-kabliuku/.

References

Alderson, P., Sutcliffe, K., & Curtis, K. (2006). Children as partners with adults in their medical care. Arch Dis Child 91(4):300–303.

Burokiene S, Sutkus V, Vaideliene L, Urbonas V, Kevalas R, Labanauskas L et al (2022) Primary child health care services in Lithuania: does it meet the needs of the children? Child: Care Health Dev 48(3):435–442

Čaplinskas S (2016) Imunoprofilaktikos svarba siekiant suvaldyti skiepais valdomas užkrečiamąsias ligas. Lietuvos bendrosios praktikos gydytojas 20(8):536–548

Clark H, Coll-Seck AM, Banerjee A, Peterson S, Dalglish SL, Ameratunga S et al (2020) A future for the world's children? A WHO–UNICEF–Lancet Commission. Lancet 395(10224):605–658

De Dominicis R, Kluge HHP (2025) Future-proofing Europe and Central Asia: a renewed focus on child and adolescent health. Lancet 405(10476):377–378

De Figueiredo A, Simas C, Karafillakis E, Paterson P, Larson HJ (2020) Mapping global trends in vaccine confidence and investigating barriers to vaccine uptake: a large-scale retrospective temporal modelling study. Lancet 396(10255):898–908

Dornbusch HJ, Kurz R, Del Torso S, Hadjipanayis A, Tenore A (2024) Is there a "European Paediatrics"? Front Pediatr 12. https://doi.org/10.3389/fped.2024.1326157

Ford K, Campbell S, Carter B, Earwaker L (2018a) The concept of child-centered care in healthcare: a scoping review protocol. JBI Evid Synth 16(4):845–851

Ford K, Dickinson A, Water T, Campbell S, Bray L, Carter B (2018b) Child centred care: challenging assumptions and repositioning children and young people. J Pediatr Nurs 43:e39–e43

General Comment No. 14 (2000) The right to the highest attainable standard of health (article 12 of the International Covenant on Economic, Social and Cultural Rights). E/C.12/2000/4

General Comment No. 14 (2013) On the right of the child to have his or her best interests taken as a primary consideration. CRC/C/GC/14

General comment No. 4 (2003) Adolescent health and development in the context of the Convention on the Rights of the Child. CRC/GC/2003/4

Hoey H, Pettoello-Mantovani M, Vural M (2021) Diversity of child health care in Europe. Arch Dis Childhood 106(8):732–733

Katz AL, Webb SA, Committee on Bioethics (2016) Informed consent in decision-making in pediatric practice. Pediatrics 138(2):e20161485

Kollataj BM, Kollataj WP, Karwat ID, Sobieszczanski J, Panasiuk L (2020) Anti-vaccine movements-health care, ignorance or a diversion aimed at destabilizing the health situation? Part 2. Contemporary conditions for the functioning and development of anti-vaccination movements. Ann Agric Environ Med 27(4):553–561

Koller D, Espin S, Indar A, Oulton A, LeGrow K (2024) Children's participation rights and the role of pediatric healthcare teams: a critical review. J Pediatr Nurs 77:1–12

Lundy L (2007) 'Voice' is not enough: conceptualising Article 12 of the United Nations Convention on the Rights of the Child. Br Educ Res J 33(6):927–942

Nandi A, Shet A (2020) Why vaccines matter: understanding the broader health, economic, and child development benefits of routine vaccination. Hum Vaccines Immunother 16(8):1900–1904

Peleg N (2023) A children's rights dilemma–Paternalism versus autonomy. The rights of the child: legal, political and ethical challenges, pp 7–12

Reczulska A, Tomaszewska A, Raciborski F (2022) Level of acceptance of mandatory vaccination and legal sanctions for refusing mandatory vaccination of children. Vaccines 10(5):811

Roush SW, Murphy TV, Vaccine-Preventable Disease Table Working Group (2007) Historical comparisons of morbidity and mortality for vaccine-preventable diseases in the United States. JAMA 298(18):2155–2163

Savulescu J, Giubilini A, Danchin M (2021) Global ethical considerations regarding mandatory vaccination in children. J Pediatr 231:10–16

Shattock AJ, Johnson HC, Sim SY, Carter A, Lambach P, Hutubessy RC et al (2024) Contribution of vaccination to improved survival and health: modelling 50 years of the Expanded Programme on Immunization. Lancet 403(10441):2307–2316

Stephenson T (2024) Importance and benefits of investing in child health and research. Global Pediatr 9:100217

The State of Children in the European Union. UNICEF, 2024

Toebes B (2022) Vavřička v. Czech (Eur. Ct. HR). Int Leg Mater 61(6):856–924

Zillén K (2023) Children's right to health (care)–in light of medical advancements and developments in paediatric care. In: The rights of the child. Brill Nijhoff, pp 108–120

Żuk P, Żuk P, Lisiewicz-Jakubaszko J (2019) The anti-vaccine movement in Poland: the socio-cultural conditions of the opposition to vaccination and threats to public health. Vaccine 37(11):1491–1494

Edita Žiobienė is the Ombudsperson for Child's Rights in Lithuania (since 2010) and Professor at the Institute of Public Law, Mykolas Romeris University (since 2003). She has many years of experience in the protection of human rights in various capacities as the head of the Centre for Human Rights (2004–2010), chair of the Ethics Commission for Journalists and Publishers (2005–2010), member of the Central Electoral Commission (2008–2010), member and vice-chair of the Advisory Committee on the Framework Convention for the Protection of National Minorities (2010–2020), and member of various expert groups of the European Union and the Council of Europe. Her main scientific interests and research areas are constitutional law, human rights, children's rights.

Correction to: Peculiarities of Criminal Liability of Children in Lithuania

Mindaugas Girdauskas and Darius Pranka

Correction to:
Chapter 11 in: A. Limantė, R. Vaičiūnienė (eds.), *Children's Rights in Central and Eastern Europe*, European Union and its Neighbours in a Globalized World 29, https://doi.org/10.1007/978-3-032-07092-0_11

The original version of the chapter 'Peculiarities of Criminal Liability of Children in Lithuania' was inadvertently published before incorporation of the final corrections to the publication year and last accessed dates of the references listed under the titles, 'Statistics' and 'Available Translations of References' of the chapter back matter. The chapter has been updated with the following important changes to the references listed under the titles, 'Statistics' and 'Available Translations of References':

Statistics

Information Technology and Communications Department under the Ministry of the Interior of the Republic of Lithuania [ITCD] (2025a) Nusikalstamos veikos, kurias padarė nepilnamečiai. Available via https://www.ird.lt/lt/tvarkomu-valdomu-registru-ir-informaciniu-sistemu-paslaugos-3/nusikalstamu-veiku-zinybinio-registro-nvzr-atviri-duomenys-paslaugos-2/nusikalstamos-veikos-lietuvoje-2006-2024-metais-2/oid.1040. Accessed 7 Dec 2025

ITCD (2025b) Duomenys apie įtariamus (kaltinamus) ir nukentėjusius nepilnamečius Lietuvos Respublikoje (Forma_VSDN). Available via https://www.ird.lt/lt/reports/view_item_datasource?id=11781&datasource=110353. Accessed 7 Dec 2025

The updated version of this chapter can be found at
https://doi.org/10.1007/978-3-032-07092-0_11

A. Limantė, R. Vaičiūnienė (eds.), *Children's Rights in Central and Eastern Europe*, European Union and its Neighbours in a Globalized World 29,
https://doi.org/10.1007/978-3-032-07092-0_21

ITCD (2025c) Nusikalstamos veikos Lietuvoje 2006-2024 metais. Available via https://www.ird.lt/lt/tvarkomu-valdomu-registru-ir-informaciniu-sistemu-paslaugos-3/nusikalstamu-veiku-zinybinio-registro-nvzr-atviri-duomenys-paslaugos-2/nusikalstamos-veikos-lietuvoje-2006-2024-metais-2. Accessed 7 Dec 2025

ITCD (2025d) Bausmių vykdymo statistika. Available via https://www.ird.lt/lt/tvarkomu-valdomu-registru-ir-informaciniu-sistemu-paslaugos-3/nusikalstamu-veiku-zinybinio-registro-nvzr-atviri-duomenys-paslaugos-2/ataskaitos-3/bausmiu-vykdymo-statistika-2. Accessed 7 Dec 2025

Lithuanian probation service (2025) Metų ataskaitos. Available via https://probacija.lrv.lt/lt/apie-lietuvos-probacijos-tarnyba/statistika/metines-ataskaitos/. Accessed 7 Dec 2025

State Data Agency (2025a) Teismų nuteistų nepilnamečių skaičius. Available via https://osp.stat.gov.lt/lt/statistiniu-rodikliu-analize?hash=af4ee30e-9571-4a7c-a813-f1645b80aed8. Accessed 7 Dec 2025

State Data Agency (2025b) Nepilnamečiai, kuriems paskirtos auklėjimo poveikio priemonės. Available via https://osp.stat.gov.lt/lt/statistiniu-rodikliu-analize?hash=19032429-48ed-45c2-83ed-c671281460aa. Accessed 7 Dec 2025

State Data Agency (2025c) Nuteistų nepilnamečių laisvės atėmimo įstaigose skaičius metų pabaigoje. Available via https://osp.stat.gov.lt/lt/statistiniu-rodikliu-analize?hash=4ee9467a-4b49-4f46-8837-19c086788831. Accessed 7 Dec 2025

State Data Agency (2025d) Nepilnamečiai, kuriems atidėtas bausmės vykdymas. Available via https://osp.stat.gov.lt/lt/statistiniu-rodikliu-analize?hash=179f390a-94f5-413a-accb-6426af5ed87b. Accessed 7 Dec 2025

Available Translations of References

Constitution of the Republic of Lithuania. Consolidated version in force. Available via https://e-seimas.lrs.lt/portal/legalAct/lt/TAD/079fcad0cf8711ecb69ea7b9ba9d787b?jfwid=b454lz9dz. Accessed 7 Dec 2025

German Code of Criminal Procedure (StPO). The translation includes the amendment(s) to the Act by Article 2 of the Act of 17 July 2025. Available via https://www.gesetze-im-internet.de/englisch_stpo/englisch_stpo.pdf. Accessed 7 Dec 2025

German Youth Court Act (JGG). The translation includes the amendment(s) to the Act by Article 21 of the Act of 25 June 2021. Available via https://www.gesetze-im-internet.de/englisch_jgg/englisch_jgg.pdf. Accessed 7 Dec 2025

Lithuanian Criminal Code. Consolidated version valid until 30 September 2018. Available via https://e-seimas.lrs.lt/portal/legalAct/lt/TAD/28b18041843311e89188e16a6495e98c?jfwid=9pfnh2ul8. Accessed 7 Dec 2025

MIX
Papier aus verantwortungsvollen Quellen
Paper from responsible sources
FSC® C105338

If you have any concerns about our products,
you can contact us on
ProductSafety@springernature.com

In case Publisher is established outside the EU,
the EU authorized representative is:
Springer Nature Customer Service Center GmbH
Europaplatz 3, 69115 Heidelberg, Germany

Printed by Libri Plureos GmbH
in Hamburg, Germany